Routledge International Handbook of Poverty

The first of the UN Millennium Goals was to reduce extreme poverty and in 2014 it was halved compared to 1990, and now the goal is to eradicate poverty and hunger by 2030. The reduction in poverty is, to a high degree, the consequence of the rapid economic development in a few countries, especially China, but in many countries around the globe poverty is still at a high level and is influencing societies' overall development. It is against this background that this Handbook provides an up-to-date analysis and overview of the topic from a large variety of theoretical and methodological angles.

Organised into four parts, the Handbook provides knowledge on what poverty is, how it has developed, and what type of policies might be able to succeed in reducing poverty. Part I investigates conceptual issues and relates concepts to people's relative position in society and the understanding of justice. Part II shows how poverty has developed. It combines existing empirical knowledge with regional/national understandings of the issue of poverty. Part III analyses policies and interventions with the aim of reducing or alleviating poverty within a national as well as global context. It includes a variety of countries and examples. Finally, Part IV tells us what can be done about poverty; what instruments are available to end poverty as we know it today.

This volume will be an invaluable reference book for students and scholars throughout the social sciences, particularly in sociology, social policy, public policy, development studies, international relations and politics.

Bent Greve is Professor of Welfare State Analysis in the Department of Society and Business at Roskilde University, Denmark. He has published widely on different topics surrounding the welfare state, including technology and the labour market, happiness and social policy, labour market policy, and most recently on populism and the welfare state. He is editor of *Social Policy and Administration.*

Routledge International Handbooks

The Routledge International Handbook of Language Education Policy in Asia
Edited by Andy Kirkpatrick and Anthony J. Liddicoat

Routledge International Handbook of Migration Studies 2e
Edited by Steven J. Gold and Stephanie J. Nawyn

Routledge Handbook of Contemporary Feminism
Edited by Tasha Oren and Andrea Press

Routledge Handbook of the Belt and Road
Edited by Cai Fang and Peter Nolan

Routledge Handbook of Language Acquisition
Edited by Jessica S. Horst and Janne von Koss Torkildsen

Routledge Handbook of Identity Studies, 2e
Edited by Anthony Elliott

Routledge International Handbook of Poverty
Edited by Bent Greve

Routledge International Handbook of New Digital Practices in Galleries, Libraries, Archives, Museums and Heritage Sites
Edited by Hannah Lewi, Wally Smith, Dirk vom Lehn and Steven Cooke

Routledge International Handbook of Human Trafficking
A Multi-Disciplinary and Applied Approach
Edited by Rochelle L. Dalla and Donna Sabella

For more information about this series, please visit: www.routledge.com/Routledge-International-Handbooks/book-series/RIHAND

Routledge International Handbook of Poverty

Edited by Bent Greve

Routledge
Taylor & Francis Group
LONDON AND NEW YORK

First published 2020
by Routledge
2 Park Square, Milton Park, Abingdon, Oxon OX14 4RN

and by Routledge
605 Third Avenue, New York, NY 10017

First issued in paperback 2020

Routledge is an imprint of the Taylor & Francis Group, an informa business

British Library Cataloguing-in-Publication Data
A catalogue record for this book is available from the British Library

Library of Congress Cataloging-in-Publication Data
Names: Greve, Bent, editor.
Title: Routledge international handbook of poverty / edited by Bent Greve.
Description: 1. Edition. | New York : Routledge, 2019. | Includes bibliographical references and index. |
Identifiers: LCCN 2019025331 (print) | LCCN 2019025332 (ebook) | ISBN 9780367178666 (hardback) | ISBN 9780429058103 (ebook)
Subjects: LCSH: Poverty. | Poor. | Economic development—Social aspects.
| Social policy.
Classification: LCC HC79.P6 R68 2019 (print) | LCC HC79.P6 (ebook) | DDC 339.4/6—dc23
LC record available at https://lccn.loc.gov/2019025331
LC ebook record available at https://lccn.loc.gov/2019025332

ISBN 13: 978-0-367-72670-6 (pbk)
ISBN 13: 978-0-367-17866-6 (hbk)

Typeset in Bembo
by Swales & Willis Ltd, Exeter, Devon, UK

Contents

Tables

Figures

Contributors

Camila Arza is a member of the National Scientific and Technical Research Council (Argentina) and principal researcher at the Interdisciplinary Centre for the Study of Public Policies. She holds a PhD and a Master of Sciences from the London School of Economics and Political Sciences (LSE, United Kingdom) and a first degree in Sociology from the University of Buenos Aires (Argentina). Over the past 15 years, she has collaborated with several international organisations, including ECLAC, UNRISD, UN-WOMEN and UNU-WIDER, and taught graduate and post-graduate courses on social policy at several national and international universities. Her research focuses on comparative social policy in Latin America, social security, old age and childhood, and socio-economic and gender inequalities. Her work has been published extensively in academic books and journals, including *Social Policy and Administration, World Development, Journal of International and Comparative Social Policy, Journal of Latin American Studies, International Social Security Review, International Journal of Social Welfare*, and *Social Policy and Society*.

Thomas Bailleul is completing his study of Economics and Political Science at Whittier College (USA).

Mel Bartley is Emeritus Professor of Medical Sociology at University College London. She studied Sociology and Philosophy at Reading University, followed by an MSc in Medical Sociology at the Bedford College, London where she was inspired by the idea that social and employment conditions could influence health and even the length of life. Her PhD studied the social construction of public health debates (in particular unemployment and health) in The Department of Social Policy & Administration in Edinburgh. After working at London and Oxford Universities she joined the Department of Epidemiology and Public Health, UCL in 1996 and built up a small research group with a succession of grants, culminating in an ESRC Research Centre (ICLS). She was granted a personal Chair in 2001 and retired in 2012.

Felicitas Becker is Professor of African History at Ghent University (Belgium) and has previously held positions at SOAS University of London, Simon Fraser University, Vancouver, and the University of Cambridge. Her PhD thesis from the University of Cambridge won the Ellen MacArthur Prize in economic history, and her first book, *Becoming Muslim in Mainland Tanzania, 1890–2000* (2008), obtained a British Academy postdoctoral fellowship publication award. She is currently working on the interaction between notions of progress used in development discourse and those deployed by religious reformers in East Africa. She is principal investigator for a European Research Council-funded research project on the aftermath of slavery in East Africa.

Katrien Boone holds a PhD in social work. Her field of expertise is the relationship between poverty, participation and social work. Between 2013 and 2018 she worked at the Department of Social Work and Social Pedagogy at Ghent University (Belgium). In this period, she engaged in a research project on 'Associations where People in Poverty Raise their Voice', in which practitioners collaborate with people in poverty in order to stimulate societal change. Since 2019, she is a lecturer at the department of social work at Howest (University College West-Flanders).

Fabrizio Bresciani is Lead Economist at Asia and the Pacific Division of the International Fund for Agricultural Development.

Koen Caminada is Professor of Empirical Analysis of Tax and Social Policy at Leiden University (the Netherlands). He is Academic Director of the Leiden Institute of Tax Law and Economics and board member of the Faculty of Governance and Global Affairs. His research interests include empirical analysis of tax law and social policy, social security, fiscal and tax policy, income distribution and poverty (EU and OECD). He has been Visiting Professor at the Institute for Research on Poverty, University of Wisconsin – Madison.

Katherine Curchin is an applied political philosopher with research interests in social policy and public administration. She is a Lecturer in Social Policy at the Australian National University Centre for Social Research and Methods and an Honorary Lecturer in the School of Philosophy at the Australian National University. She has published in the *Journal of Political Philosophy*, the *Journal of Social Policy* and *International Political Science Review*.

Jennifer Dagg holds a PhD in Sociology from the National University of Ireland, Galway. As a postdoctoral researcher she has worked on national and European funded projects. Respectively, these projects have explored immigrant integration in Ireland, and the resilience of low-income households in Europe because of the 2008 financial crisis. More broadly, her research interests revolve around the dynamics of power, inequality, exclusion and marginalisation, and migration.

Mary Daly is Professor of Sociology and Social Policy at the University of Oxford. Among the fields on which she has published are poverty and social exclusion, welfare state, gender, family and labour market, and EU social policy. Much of her work is comparative, in a European and international context. She is a member of a number of networks and boards on topics related to the welfare state, employment, family and gender and is a former editor of the journal *Social Politics*. Her latest book is *Families and Poverty: Everyday Life on a Low Income* (co-authored with Grace Kelly, Policy Press, 2015). Mary Daly's research has been supported by the Economic and Social Research Council (UK), the EU, Council of Europe, ILO, UN and UNICEF.

David Denney is Professor of Social and Public Policy in the School of Law, Royal Holloway University of London. He has researched extensively in the areas of risk within the criminal justice system. His most recent research has been related to cybersecurity in different types of organisations.

Caroline Dewilde is Associate Professor at the Department of Sociology, Tilburg University (the Netherlands). Her main research interests concern the dynamics of inequality and poverty at different levels of analysis, from the individual life course to the welfare state, from a cross-national perspective. She has published in a range of (inter)national journals and books across the social sciences. In 2011, Caroline received an ERC Starting Grant. In the

HOWCOME-project, the interplay during recent decades between trends in economic and social inequalities and changing housing regimes (housing markets, housing policies, housing wealth) was analysed.

Bernhard Ebbinghaus is Professor of Social Policy, Head of the Department of Social Policy and Intervention and Senior Research Fellow of Green Templeton College at the University of Oxford. He is also visiting Mercator Fellow (2018–21) at the Collaborative Research Centre (SFB 884) Political Economy of Reform and MZES External Fellow, University of Mannheim. His most recent publication is *Welfare State Reforms Seen from Below: Comparing Public Attitudes and Organized Interests in Britain and Germany* (co-edited with Elias Naumann, Palgrave Macmillan, 2018).

Anders Ejrnæs is an Associate Professor in the Department of Social Sciences and Business, Roskilde University (Denmark). His most recent publications have focused on comparative analysis of political engagement, inequality, wellbeing and happiness and work–life balance across European states. He is currently working on explaining populism and Euroscepticism across the EU.

Guy Feldman is an Assistant Professor in the Bob Shapell School of Social Work at Tel Aviv University (Israel). His research explores the interplay of poverty, social welfare policy, and macro practice in social work. He is particularly interested in how the problem of poverty is managed and governed in the face of a changing economic, political and institutional environment. His research also investigates the opportunities and challenges for achieving social change in this transformed environment.

Ewout Frankema is Professor and Chair of Rural and Environmental History at Wageningen University (the Netherlands), editor-in-chief of the *Journal of Global History* and research fellow of the UK Centre for Economic Policy Research. His research agenda focuses on a deeper understanding of the long-term comparative economic development of developing regions (Africa, Latin America, Asia) and the historical origins and nature of present-day global inequality. Frankema has studied History, Economics and Philosophy at the University of Groningen, where he obtained his PhD in Economics in 2008. He has taught a broad range of courses in history, economics and development studies at the University of Groningen, Utrecht University, Wageningen University, and offered guest lectures at universities in Benin, Uruguay, Uganda, Spain, Sweden and the UK.

Raghav Gaiha is Honorary Professorial Research Fellow at the Global Development Institute, University of Manchester, and Visiting Scholar at the Population Studies Center, University of Pennsylvania (USA).

Kees Goudswaard is Professor of Economics at the Law School, Leiden University and Professor of Social Security at the Gak Institute, Leiden University (the Netherlands). He is Head of the Department of Economics at Leiden University. His research areas are social policy, pensions and public finance. Goudswaard is also a member of the Supervisory Board of the Dutch Central Bank.

Jane Gray is Professor of Sociology and a Research Associate in the Social Sciences Institute at Maynooth University. Her scholarship centres on questions relating to families, households and social change. Her most recent book is a co-authored textbook (with Ruth Geraghty and David Ralph), *Family Rhythms: Changing Textures of Family Life in Ireland*, published by Manchester University Press. She was national coordinator for Ireland on the FP7 project RESCuE: Citizens' Resilience in Times of Crisis (http://rescueproject.net/)

Bent Greve is Professor in Social Science with an emphasis on welfare state analysis at the University of Roskilde (Denmark). His research interest focuses on the welfare state, and social and labour market policy, often from a comparative perspective. He has published extensively on social and labour market policy, social security, tax expenditures, public sector expenditures and financing of the welfare state. He is editor of *Social Policy & Administration*. Recent books include *Long-Term Care for the Elderly in Europe. Development and Prospects* (ed., Routledge, 2016), *Handbook of Social Policy Evaluation* (ed., Edward Elgar, 2017), *Technology and the Future of Work: The Impact on Labour Markets and Welfare States* (Edward Elgar, 2017), *The Routledge Handbook of the Welfare State*, 2nd edition (Routledge, 2018), *Welfare, Populism and Welfare Chauvinism* (Bristol University Press, 2019).

M. Azhar Hussain has a PhD in Economics and is an Associate Professor in Economics and Quantitative Methods at Roskilde University (Denmark). His research areas include empirical analyses of the distribution of welfare, inequality, poverty, deprivation, polarisation, and robust multidimensional rankings. The focus of his analyses is primarily Denmark, the EU and developing countries. He publishes both nationally and internationally in journals, books and newspaper articles.

Katsushi Imai is Associate Professor in Economics at the Department of Economics, the University of Manchester.

Philip N. Jefferson is the Centennial Professor of Economics at Swarthmore College, and a Faculty Affiliate of the Institute for Research on Poverty at the University of Wisconsin-Madison (USA). He serves on the Board of Advisors of the Opportunity and Inclusive Growth Institute at the Federal Reserve Bank of Minneapolis. He is the author of *Poverty: A Very Short Introduction* (Oxford, 2018) and is the editor of the *Oxford Handbook of the Economics of Poverty* (2012).

Emily W. Kane is Professor of Sociology, and a member of the Program in Gender and Sexuality Studies, at Bates College in Lewiston, Maine (USA). Her research focuses on poverty and policy, particularly family policy. Other areas of her work include gender and parenting, community-based research, publicly engaged pedagogy, and beliefs/narratives about poverty and economic inequality.

Christian Christrup Kjeldsen is an Associate Professor in Educational Sociology and Deputy Head of the Danish School of Education at Aarhus University (Denmark). For a number of years, his research has been conducted within the area of vulnerable children and young people in a social justice perspective with particular emphasis on the Capability Approach, such as in the transition from secondary education to the labour market. He is a member of the European network of experts researching the social dimension of education, with a particular focus on inclusion and equal opportunities. Other research areas include large scale assessments and advanced quantitative methods.

Wim Van Lancker is an Assistant Professor in Social Work and Social Policy affiliated with the Centre for Sociological Research (CESO) at the University of Leuven (Belgium). His research is focused on the design and effectiveness of social policy measures in reducing poverty and inequality, with a particular focus on childhood inequality. He has published widely on these issues in high-standing journals such as *Journal of European Public Policy, Journal of Social Policy, Journal of European Social Policy* and *Social Science Research*. With Rense Nieuwenhuis he is co-editor of the *Handbook of Family Policy*, forthcoming with Palgrave.

Lutz Leisering is Professor Emeritus of Social Policy in the Faculty of Sociology, Bielefeld University (Germany), and founding member of the Institute for World Society Studies. He has a PhD in Economics from the London School of Economics. He has authored publications on social policy in Europe and the Global South, especially on old-age security, social assistance, international organisations, and the global diffusion of ideas. His most recent book is *The Global Rise of Social Cash Transfers* (Oxford University Press, 2019).

Ira Malmberg-Heimonen works at the Oslo Metropolitan University (Norway). Her expertise is in conducting randomised trials within social and educational fields. Currently she is leading three RCTs. The ongoing studies are: the evaluation of an early warning system to reduce school dropout; the evaluation of the comprehensive follow-up model for low-income families; and the evaluation of an intervention with the aim of improving inter-professional collaboration in primary schools. In addition to the evaluations, she has also studied poverty, unemployment and the effects of activation programmes for long-term social assistance recipients.

Ive Marx is a Professor at the University of Antwerp (Belgium). He is a Research Fellow at the Institute for the Study of Labour IZA in Bonn (Germany). He directs research on minimum income protection and poverty, especially in relation to labour market change and migration at the Herman Deleeck Centre for Social Policy. His main research interest is labour market and welfare state change in relation to the distribution of income, with a particular focus on poverty. He has published extensively on the issue of in-work poverty and minimum income protection policies.

Roxana Maurizio is Associate Researcher and Professor at the Instituto Interdisciplinario de Economía Política (University of Buenos Aires, Argentina) and at Argentina's National Scientific and Technical Research Council (CONICET). She also works as a consultant for national and international organisations (ILO, ECLAC, World Bank, UNDP). Her areas of interest are labour economics, income distribution, poverty and social policies in Latin America. She has published articles (in journals such as *Journal of Development and Change, International Review of Applied Economics, Journal of Income Distribution, Journal of Development Studies, Journal of Economic Inequality, International Social Security Review, International Labour Review*) and books about labour informality, labour institutions, international migration, income mobility, inequality and poverty, and labour and social programmes. She holds an undergraduate degree in Economics, a Master's degree in Economics and a PhD in Economics.

Kenneth Nelson is Professor of Sociology and Head of the Social Policy Unit at the Swedish Institute for Social Research, Stockholm University (Sweden). His research focuses on the causes and consequences of welfare states and social policy. Nelson's research is often comparative in character, analysing the role of social protection for wellbeing and living conditions in Sweden and other countries. His latest book is *The Generational Welfare Contract*, published by Edward Elgar.

Rense Nieuwenhuis, Associate Professor in Sociology at the Swedish Institute for Social Research (SOFI) at Stockholm University, examines how family diversity and social policy affect poverty and economic inequality. Typically, his research is country-comparative and has a gender perspective. His recent focus was on single-parent families, how women's earnings affect inequality between households, and family policy outcomes. He has published in journals such as *Journal of Marriage and Family*, *European Sociological Review*, *Acta Sociologica*, and *Review of Income and Wealth*. He co-edited (with Laurie C. Maldonado) *The Triple Bind of Single-parent Families* (Policy Press, 2018) and he is currently co-editing (with Wim van Lancker) the *Palgrave Handbook of Family Policy*.

Griet Roets is Associate Professor of Social Work, affiliated to the Department of Social Work and Social Pedagogy at Ghent University (Belgium). Her research interests include conceptualisations of citizenship and social rights, and intersections of social inequalities of poverty, gender, disability and age. Her research is mainly informed by interpretative and biographical research methodologies.

Clíona Rooney holds a PhD in Architecture from Queen's University, Belfast. She has conducted research as part of an Irish Research Council funded project exploring the resilience practices of low-income Irish families. Her research interests include housing policy, universal design, children in care and qualitative research methods. She has also worked as a Part II Architect in both urban and rural practices.

Rudi Roose is Associate Professor of Social Work in the Department of Social Work and Social Pedagogy at Ghent University (Belgium). His main research area is the development of critical social work in managerial times. His research focuses on a broad field of practices (poverty work, child protection, sport social work, health social work, outreach work) with a focus on the development of socially just practices. He is Editor-in-Chief of the *European Journal of Social Work*, member of the editorial board of *Child and Family Social Work* and Chair of The International Social Work and Society Academy. He is also Head of the Social Work Programme at Ghent University.

Therese Saltkjel holds a PhD in Social Work and Social Policy and is currently a Postdoctoral Fellow at OsloMet – Oslo Metropolitan University (Norway), Faculty of Social Sciences, Department of Social Work, Child Welfare and Social Policy.

Meltem Yilmaz Sener has a PhD from the University of Illinois, Urbana-Champaign (USA) and she is currently a Visiting Scholar at the Norwegian Centre for Human Rights, University of Oslo.

Adrian Sinfield, Professor Emeritus of Social Policy, University of Edinburgh, has worked on social security, poverty, unemployment and the social division of welfare. Publications include *What Unemployment Means and the Workless State* (Martin Robertson, 1981). Chair and President of the Social Policy Association, he received its first lifetime achievement award. Co-founder of the Unemployment Unit and Chair for its first ten years, he was Vice-chair of the Child Poverty Action Group for eight years.

Kate Summers is an LSE Fellow in Qualitative Methodology and an Associate of the Centre for Analysis of Social Exclusion at the London School of Economics and Political Science.

Caroline Vandekinderen is a postdoctoral researcher based at the Department of Social Work and Social Pedagogy of Ghent University (Belgium) and at the Department of Social Work of University College, Ghent. Her research interests include citizenship, social exclusion, disability (including mental health issues), gender and interpretative and biographical research approaches.

Julie Vinck holds a Master's Degree in Social and Economic Sciences (University of Antwerp, 2012) and in Social Policy Analysis (KU Leuven, 2013). Currently she is affiliated to the Herman Deleeck Centre for Social Policy at the University of Antwerp (Belgium) and works as a PhD Fellow of the Research Foundation Flanders (FWO). The topic of her research concerns 'The poverty-care nexus in the social investment state: an empirical investigation of childhood disability, child poverty and parental employment in Belgium'.

Olaf van Vliet is Professor of Comparative Welfare State Analysis at the Department of Economics and at the Institute of Public Administration, Leiden University (the Netherlands). His research and teaching interests include political economy, welfare state reform, income inequality, globalisation, European integration and labour economics. He has been Visiting Researcher at Harvard University and Marquette University (Wisconsin).

Udaya R. Wagle is a Professor and Director of the School of Public Affairs and Administration, Western Michigan University (USA). He holds a PhD in public policy, a Master's degree in nonprofit management, and Bachelor's and Master's degrees in business administration. He has authored two books and over three dozen other academic and professional publications focusing on social policies, underdevelopment and comparative studies. He currently serves on the editorial boards of *Global Social Policy*, *Poverty & Public Policy*, and *Social Indicators Research*.

Robert Walker is Professor in the School of Social Development and Public Policy, Beijing Normal University under China's 'High Level Foreign Talents' programme. He is Professor Emeritus at the University of Oxford where he is also Emeritus Fellow of Green Templeton College. He was formerly Professor of Social Policy at the University of Nottingham and, before that, Professor of Social Policy Research, Loughborough University where he was Director of the Centre for Research in Social Policy.

Jinxian Wang is an Assistant Professor at the Central South University, Changsha (China) and a Research Fellow at the Department of Economics, Leiden University (the Netherlands). Her research interests include minimum income protection, income polarisation, income inequality and poverty. Some of her recent work has been published in *Cambridge Journal of Economics*, *Eastern European Economics*, *Health & Place*, *European Journal of Social Security* and *China Journal of Social Work*.

Mark Wang is Professor in the School of Geography at the University of Melbourne (Australia). He is a development geographer who for the past 20 years has been studying China's transition. This work has been published in such books as *Mega Urban Regions in China* and co-authored books *Water Supply in a Mega-City: A Political Ecology of Shanghai* (Edward Elgar, 2017), *China's Urban Space: Development under Market Socialism* (Routledge, 2007) and *China's Transition to a Global Economy* (Palgrave Macmillan, 2002).

John Welshman was educated at the Universities of York and Oxford, and is Senior Lecturer in the History Department, Lancaster University, UK. His research interests are in the history of public policy in twentieth-century Britain, on which he has published widely. Articles have been published in *Children & Society* (2008 and 2010); *Contemporary British History* (2009); *Economic History Review* (2006); the *Journal of Epidemiology and Community Health* (2006 and 2007); the *Journal of Social Policy* (2004); the *Political Quarterly* (2006); *Social History of Medicine* (2006 and 2012); *Social Policy & Society* (2016); and *Twentieth Century British History* (2005 and 2008). His books include *From Transmitted Deprivation to Social Exclusion: Policy, Poverty, and Parenting* (Policy Press, 2007, PB edition, 2012). His most recent book is *Underclass: A History of the Excluded Since 1880* (Continuum, 2006, second edition Bloomsbury, 2013).

Roger White is a Professor of Economics and the Douglas W. Ferguson Chair in International Economics at Whittier College (California, USA). Roger received his PhD in International Economics from the University of California, Santa Cruz (2004), has authored/ edited seven books and has authored more than 40 book chapters and peer-reviewed articles. His current research is largely focused on multidimensional poverty, the immigrant-trade link, and cross-societal cultural differences/distance.

Tao Xue is a Research Assistant in the School of Geography at the University of Melbourne (Australia). Tao's research focuses on rural China development, including rural land policies, spatial analysis of rural development, land acquisition and resettlement projects, gender and equity, and sustainable livelihood. Tao has published several refereed journal articles on development and change, and global environmental change.

Preface

Poverty has been a central issue in social science for centuries. It has also, historically, been a condition implying living conditions that we today, in most cases, do not find acceptable. We have further seen, at least partly due to economic growth, that a reduction in the overall level of absolute poverty has taken place in many countries. There are, though, still places on the globe where the level of poverty is very high. This is the background for this book which discusses poverty from a number of perspectives, ideas and understanding. Contributions come from a number of theoretical approaches, varied geographical areas and different types of instruments to do with poverty. There are arguments on conceptual and measurement issues.

Thanks to all who have contributed and helped in ensuring the broad and varied perspectives that can be found throughout the book.

I do hope that the book will increase the understanding of causes of poverty, but also that, in fact, there are instruments available which might make it possible to reach the UN goal of eradicating poverty.

Bent Greve
Roskilde, April 2019

1

Poverty

Still an important issue

Bent Greve

Introduction

Throughout the history of humanity there have been people living under harsh conditions – and many in dire poverty. Poverty has thus been a central part of society's development. Economic development has caused life conditions to improve in many ways. However, we do still see poverty around the globe, naturally with variations, but it is still an important issue in many countries and for many persons.

The first of the UN Millennium Goals was to reduce extreme poverty. In fact, in 2014, poverty was halved compared to 1990, and now the goal is to eradicate poverty and hunger by 2030.[1] The new UN 2030 plan has as its first goal, to "end poverty in all its forms everywhere".[2] In the preamble, it argues: "We are determined to end poverty and hunger, in all their forms and dimensions, and to ensure that all human beings can fulfil their potential in dignity and equality and in a healthy environment."

Poverty is thus still high on the international agenda, although one could argue that it has been on the agenda around the world for many decades without being able to be fully eradicated. This in the context of the first social policy laws in many countries being poor laws focusing on the most destitute, albeit often with harsh conditions and punishment of the poor in need of support.

The reduction in poverty is, to a high degree, the consequence of the rapid economic development in a few countries, especially China, but in many countries around the globe poverty is still at a high level and influencing societies' overall development. Still, close to one billion people live in extreme poverty.

It is against this background that this book provides an analysis and overview of the topic from a wide variety of theoretical and methodological angles. The range of topics covered by the authors enable them to show what poverty is, how it has developed, and what type of policies might be able to cope with the issue. This is because the possible policies and understanding of the importance thereof might depend on individual countries' ability to handle poverty, and the different national and historical understanding of, and size of, the problem. At the same time, the interaction between poverty and global development is an important part of the discussion as, for example, poverty has been and can be part of the reason for migration around the globe.

Poverty has many different understandings and faces which partly reflect national and regional contexts of living standards, but also ideological and political issues. The implication of this is that poverty, on the one hand, is context dependent, while on the other there are general issues one needs to consider, including how it can be measured, and how a variety of measurements might influence our understanding of the size and type of problems poverty causes for different kinds of societies. Furthermore, there can be a need to understand those causes, and what the short- and long-term consequences of living in poverty are. The many and often interrelated issues imply the need for different concepts in order to understand the subject. There is thus poverty in relation to the day-to-day ability to pay for food and shelter – and there is also poverty in relation to being at risk of social exclusion. There are discussions on the impact of poverty, including the link between inequality and societal development (see, for example, Wilkinson and Pickett 2009, 2018; Case and Deaton 2003).

This chapter sets the scene for the book by first presenting some important aspects related to the issue of poverty. It then gives an overview of the book, why the book is structured as it is, and ends with some reflections on why poverty is still a strong and important policy issue.

Important aspect

First of all, a core question to ask is: What is poverty? There is no international agreement on the definition of what poverty is, although some common understanding of what to include can be found. This is because the understanding of the size and implication of poverty might influence decision makers' willingness to do something. For example, if the data used point towards the fact that there is no poverty, then the implication of this is that there is no need for policy intervention.

Rowntree's poverty study in the UK at the beginning of the last century (Rowntree 1901), looking at what, today, we call absolute poverty, was one of the first studies to point out that there was a need for a basket of goods (including food and shelter) in order not to live in poverty. Thus, for example, not including what we today, at least in part of the world, consider as necessary in order to be socially included in society. There has always been discussion about how much and what kind of food is necessary in order to be in a position to ensure a decent life with a necessary set of capabilities, as understood by Sen (2005). This points to the fact that it is not sufficient to analyse poverty in isolation, but that one also needs to include and touch upon issues such as equality, justice and social rights. This is because poverty can also be a feeling of not being able to do what one sees others are able to do.

There are many and varied explanations and arguments for the size and development of poverty. One is related to structural factors, for example, that some people are born poor and/or born to be poor. This reflects elements such as difficulties in social mobility, lack of education and lack of options in the labour market. Industrial explanations relate to how change, especially in the labour market, influences the risk of poverty, and explains why some people end up living in poverty. This might especially be the case for children growing up in jobless households who will have a long-term risk of ending up living in poverty (Macmillan et al. 2018). Overall, there are many and varied possible causes of poverty, which are also shown throughout the book. These include elements and consequences of issues such as: social inclusion, discrimination, lack of redistributive policies, labour market changes (technology, business cycle), globalization and migration.

The debate on poverty further has a strong normative dimension related to issues of deserving/non-deserving as a classical social policy issue (Greve 2015; van Oorschot 2006; Will 1993). There is no simple way to deduce who is deserving and who is not deserving, although those reaching the age of retirement who have been working in the labour market are often, in general, seen as deserving in most countries. People with disabilities – i.e. the reason that they are living in poverty is not due to their own fault – are often also seen as deserving, whereas migrants are less often seen as deserving, as well as those who – at least in some people's eyes – could have participated in the labour market. The perception and understanding of the reasons for poverty also influence policies towards poverty both within countries and in discussion on transfers from richer countries to less economically well-developed countries. Naturally, there is variation that is also framed by national historical traditions and influenced by different ideas over time, such as whether it is an individual problem or a collective issue. Still, the book will, hopefully, enable the reader to get some ideas about the most important aspects in relation to how to understand and to deal with poverty, including what we know about policies that might reduce the overall size and impact of poverty.

Ensuring that people have the necessary capabilities as a way to cope with poverty, after the important work of Sen (Nussbaum 2005; Sen 2005, 2006), has for some time been seen as important, although not always pointing towards specific interventions.

In recent years, there has also been a debate about how to ensure that what is spent on poverty issues is efficient and has an effective impact in relation to the money spent. This also includes whether and how focus could be on prevention (Fisher and Buckner 2018; Berghman, Debels and Van Hoyweghen 2019). (For a short introduction to poverty, see Saunders 2019.)

Content of the book

The book is divided into four different Parts:

I Conceptual issues
II Poverty around the world and development in poverty
III Policies towards poverty
IV The way forward – what will influence poverty in the years to come?

Part I investigates conceptual issues in order to be clearer about what and how one can actually understand the concept, including relating it to people's relative position in society and the understanding of justice. Understanding what a just society is might influence decisions and attitudes towards poverty, and thereby also indicate that the ideas and national development can influence how it is perceived. The first Part further includes debates on how to measure poverty in different ways, as counting the number of people in poverty might have an impact on whether or not there is a societal need for interventions in order to be able to reduce poverty.

The chapters in Part II paint a picture of how poverty has developed and what it looks like around the globe. They thus combine existing empirical knowledge with regional/national understandings of the issue of poverty. By doing so it should be possible to grasp the variety and difference in, and the consequences of, poverty in different parts of the world. This also includes specific topics related, for example, to whether we can find working poor, poverty in old age and the consequence of poverty, for example in relation to migration and crime. This given that, again, referring to the issues of deserving/non-deserving and which groups live in poverty or at risk of poverty can have an impact on what types of intervention, if any, are decided.

Part III moves towards what we know about policies and interventions with the aim of reducing or alleviating poverty within a national as well as a global context. It includes a variety of countries and examples, ranging from aspects of social benefits towards labour market policies, to how to redistribute from the rich to the poor. For more detail, see below in the overview of the individual chapters.

Part IV includes only one chapter, with the aim of synthesizing the knowledge arising from the presentations and analysis in the book, and as a consequence pointing to what can be important policies, or aspects thereof, in order to deal with poverty around the globe and how to reach the goal set for 2030 as presented at the beginning of this chapter.

Given the intention that it should be possible to read each chapter as an individual, there might be a few overlaps between some of the chapters in the book.

After this first chapter, the book starts with a number of chapters having a more conceptual focus in Part I.

Chapter 2 has an emphasis on the concept of absolute poverty, how it has evolved over time, including the recent estimate of the size of the problem. This includes information on the variation of regional poverty rates. The chapter also presents an example from Mozambique on the calculation of what should be in a basket of goods and services in order to avoid living in poverty in a developing country. This will have an impact on the size of the absolute poverty line in different countries.

Chapter 3 looks into how the absolute or relative understanding of poverty is defined, but more importantly the implication of using the different types of definitions when related to the understanding of the development in poverty. This also means that one type of measurement might be more useful for some societies than in other countries, and also depending on their economic development.

Recent years have seen a stronger emphasis on how to understand poverty as a multidimensional issue. Chapter 4 presents aspects and elements related to this. These also include a reference to the UN's Multidimensional Poverty Index (MPI). The chapter also points to Sen's capability theory as a reason why it is important to have a number of indicators available if one wants to present and discuss poverty over time.

Poverty is not only an economic issue and related to the impact during one year, but there are also other related aspects, discussed as multidimensional poverty across the life-cycle, which is the focus in Chapter 5. The chapter provides new information using the US as an empirical example for the years 2008–2017. The analysis shows that jobs are important, as are health insurance and social security benefits if the aim is to reduce the number living in poverty using a multidimensional framework. This is no doubt also the case in other countries.

Prevention is better than cure – this is the focus of Chapter 6. As the quote by Franklin in the chapter argues, "an ounce of prevention is worth a pound of cure". This is still valid, the question being why there is still so little focus on prevention as an ambition in many countries, given that a combination of management of the economy, and welfare state and labour market policies could help in reducing poverty.

Poverty is also related to the subjective position in a given society, as analysed in Chapter 7. Thus, deprivation as a consequence of poverty is not only due to economic hardship, but also the understanding of position and place in a given society.

A specific and important topic is the consequence for children growing up in poverty, as presented in Chapter 8. This is done by showing the impact in both rich and poor countries, and also how living in poverty can have far reaching consequences for children over the life-cycle as well as interacting with other socioeconomic conditions, such as disability, gender, migration and class.

How we understand what is just can also have an impact on poverty, as argued in Chapter 9. This is due to the fact that what is understood as just sets a framework for intervention and policies, and this can have practical, ethical and analytical impacts on welfare state policies. It can further be argued to influence who is seen as deserving, and also the criteria for who is eligible for different kinds of benefits.

After these chapters, Part II contains a number of chapters focusing on poverty around the world and the development in poverty.

There are many recent phenomena, however poverty is not one of them. It has been in existence for many centuries. Chapter 10 takes a historical perspective of its development over the last 200 years – from a time with growing absolute levels of poverty as a consequence of rapid demographic development, to recent times where, especially due to the development in Asia, we have seen a reduction in the absolute numbers. Relatively, the historical trend has been fewer people living in poverty.

History is also the central focus of Chapter 11, albeit here more about how it has been understood in theoretical approaches, including from both a structural and a behavioural approach. This also includes going back to issues of understanding in different case studies, such as Rowntree and Townsend. Further, it moves on to an understanding of poverty being mainly due to people's own fault and as a consequence of their own behaviour, including Murray's depiction of the underclass.

One question is whether there is a difference in the poverty level dependent on economic development. In Chapter 12, the focus is on poverty development in affluent countries. The chapter shows that welfare policies differ in their ability to reduce poverty, with the highest ability in the Nordic welfare states, and the lowest in the southern part of Europe. Thus, the chapter also informs about the impact of different welfare regimes on the level of poverty.

Chapter 13 delves into poverty in developing countries. The conclusion is clear – even when using different poverty lines, the degree of poverty is highest in sub-Saharan Africa and second highest in East-Asia and the Pacific. This points to strong international differences in the level of poverty, and is thereby one of the issues that one needs to be aware of as to how it influences life conditions at different places around the globe.

For a long time, the movement from the countryside to cities has been part of the development in many countries, and often results in many people living in poverty afterwards. Chapter 14 presents a resettlement programme in China indicating that voluntary resettlement, in fact, might have a positive impact on the degree of poverty, especially if flexibility is included in the use of the instrument and the involvement of those citizens expected to move.

Chapter 15 focuses on how changes in production, including diversification in rural societies in Asia and the Pacific, can help in reducing poverty – not only in rural areas, but also with regard to the level in the cities – thus, also confirming that better and more efficient ways of ensuring different kinds of production can have a stronger and broader impact on poverty than often foreseen.

Africa has, for a long time, been seen as a continent with the highest level of poverty, as also touched upon in Chapter 13. Chapter 16 argues that in the coming years, due to demographic circumstances, we might see a decline in relative poverty in Africa, but an increase in absolute poverty. The chapter further argues that there are also success stories in Africa, and the growing middle class is a sign of improvement. Still, however, there are strong challenges emerging from the large number of people living in extreme poverty.

Latin America is a continent with a relatively high level of poverty, as depicted in Chapter 17. In most countries on the continent, around one in every five live in poverty – and in some countries the figure is even higher. There are also many working poor, and the lack of a strong social safety net is part of the reason. The chapter also presents cases of intervention having a positive impact on the poverty level, including how to ensure that children receive an education.

Chapter 18 looks into poverty in North America, and shows that there are variations in the ways this is measured in the countries. There is further variation in national discourse on the reasons and explanations for poverty, and also a varied approach from the Personal Responsibility and Work Opportunity Reconciliation Act in the US, to poverty reduction strategies such as Ontario Works in Canada and Opportunidades in Mexico. The latter point is also a recurrent theme in many other countries with the aim of trying to ensure education for many groups.

After this follow a number of chapters, in Part III, with a focus on policies toward poverty.

It is often argued that if people get a job they will not be living in poverty. As presented in Chapter 19, this is not at all the case as there are people who are working poor. This might reflect not working full time, but it can also be due to a very low wage level for some groups in different countries. Some of those working part time might not even be able to get a full-time job. So, it is not always the case that getting a job will be a sufficient condition to escape poverty, and there can also be a poverty trap by the combined impact of the need to pay taxes and the reduction in social benefits when having a wage income.

Old age has been considered to be a specific risk of poverty. Chapter 20 shows that despite austerity measures in relation to pensions, the risk of poverty has been reduced in old age. This is based upon data from the Luxembourg Income Study covering the period from 1985 to 2015 in the more mature welfare states. However, this does not imply that there are no groups at risk of not attaining a sufficiently high level of benefits in old age – such as women, migrants and those with lower levels of education – who are therefore at risk of living in poverty.

Access to benefits is important not only for the elderly population. As shown in Chapter 21, benefits are a central element in reducing poverty. Linked hereto is the understanding of what kind of social investment policies can have an impact on the level of poverty. Parts of these developments are, in different welfare regimes, influenced by the historical power struggle. It also reflects the fact that benefits have a strong role for many persons in developed welfare states if they are to be enabled to avoid living in poverty.

Coping with poverty can be difficult, which is the focus of Chapter 22. Life styles and changes therein can be necessary, but also shame and stigma can be attached to living in poverty and this can be related to the social, personal and institutional levels. Qualitative studies are referred to as a way of both analysing and understanding what it is like to live in poverty. The analysis is linked to theoretical understanding within the sociology of culture.

Crime and poverty can be linked, as discussed in Chapter 23. The chapter presents different theoretical understanding of the link between poverty and crime, although also arguing that it is difficult to find a clear causal link. Those who have grown up in care, based upon UK data, have a higher risk of ending up in prison than other people; a clear indication that living conditions for children can influence crime.

Chapter 24 deals with taxation and poverty, showing that the use of a well-designed tax and duty system is an important element in dealing with poverty in different countries, both as a way of redistributing resources and, at the same time, being able to finance public policy initiatives that can help in alleviating and/or minimizing the degree of poverty.

Poverty policies are very different. In Chapter 25, the focus is on the variations in different kinds of social cash transfer programmes in the Global South. They can have different conditions and can be related to a variety of situations, including work, pension, disability, children or specific circumstances. National traditions and historical reasons can explain part of this, but different understandings of who is deserving and who is not also influence this.

Poverty is often seen as reason for "voluntary" migration as this can be a way of improving living standards both for those migrating and those staying back when receiving remittance. Chapter 26 looks into this issue and discusses the conditions for, and elements in relation to, migration that can contribute to poverty alleviation.

Neoliberalism with its emphasis on the individual's responsibility and the relation to poverty is the central tenet of Chapter 27, also raising the question whether this is an unavoidable relation.

At the same time, the chapter points to the reason why a neoliberal approach has certain implications for the policies pursued with regard to, and the understanding of, the course of policy, including changes in welfare states' approaches.

It has for a long time been known that inequality in income also reflects inequality in health. In Chapter 28, the focus is on the link between poverty and health (and health inequality). Surprisingly, it seems that nations (in Europe) with lower levels of poverty have a higher rate of health inequality. Still, this does not change the fact that reducing inequality could have a positive impact on overall health.

Part of the risk of poverty is the variation in the different pension systems. Chapter 29 presents a new comparative analysis, based upon data from the Luxembourg Income Study covering the period from 1985 to 2013. The analysis shows a strong decline in poverty due to the impact of the pension system, while in the same period it increased for those of working age. Nevertheless, there is still a higher poverty rate for the elderly, which also implies that pension policies in the years to come will still be an important aspect related to the possible reduction of the overall level of poverty, at least in the more affluent countries.

Recent years have seen an upsurge in public policy using insights from behavioural research. Chapter 30 presents the central aspects of behavioural economics and how this is related to poverty. This includes the knowledge that living in poverty might have an impact on the cognitive ability to make decisions, and thus reducing the pressure from living in poverty can help. Support for saving and searching for a job can also be improved by using different kinds of nudges.

Poverty is often measured as a situation for persons or households, but as pointed out in Chapter 31, the family has a role with regard to whether or not people actually live in poverty. There are cultural, relational and structural aspects influencing the situation in families. For families living within one household there is a question on distribution of resources, and across families living in different households there is also the question of variation in support – in-cash as well as in-kind.

This leads to the last Part, Part IV, and the last chapter. Chapter 32 thus sums up the knowledge gathered, including central elements that might be used if one wants to reduce the level of poverty in a given country.

Some reflections

As always when editing a book, several issues arise. These include what specific topics should be included, what would be nice to include and how to ensure a variety of theoretical and methodological approaches. Having different viewpoints implies, as I see it, a better ability to grasp the possible variation and understanding of a concept, how poverty has developed and what the possible consequence thereof is. Therefore also, if one is, in principle, in favour of reducing the number of people living in poverty, how can this then be put into practice using a variety and number of options in different sets of contextual conditions and in a variety of societal structures and development? It will also include how one can prescribe policies that will have an impact on the number of people living in poverty and, if at all possible, the number of people who will be influenced thereby. Furthermore, for those readers interested in children, the elderly, those working and/or those in developing countries (including transfers from rich to poor countries), the book will give information and ideas about what the central aspects are that need to be understood and how, given the available resources, one can, as best as possible, do something. Lastly, the book should enable the reader more generally to know what the impact is of a variety of welfare state polices that might have certain intended outcomes, but also might have unintended ones. This, as there is seldom just one way of doing things, and we are often left with the fact that the best choice might not necessarily be possible.

Hopefully, the book and the individual chapters mean that readers – whether just reading a few of the chapters or the book as a whole – get a clear knowledge about what poverty is, what can be done about it, how it has developed, and what policies will cause a decrease in the number of people living in poverty.

Notes

1 See www.un.org/millenniumgoals/poverty.shtml
2 From https://undocs.org/A/RES/70/1, accessed 7 September 2018.

References

Berghman, J., Debels, A. and Van Hoyweghen, I. 2019. "Prevention: The Cases of Social Security and Healthcare." In *Routledge Handbook of the Welfare State*, edited by B. Greve, Second Edition, 46–57. Oxon: Routledge.

Case, A. and Deaton, A. 2003. "Consumption, Health, Gender, and Poverty." World Bank Working Paper: 3020.

Fisher, Pamela and Buckner, Lisa. 2018. "Time for 'Resilience'." *International Journal of Sociology & Social Policy* 38 (9/8): 794–808. http://10.0.4.84/IJSSP-12-2017-0167.

Greve, B. 2015. *Welfare and the Welfare State: Present and Future*. London: Routledge. https://doi.org/10.4324/9781315761022.

Macmillan, L., Gregg, P., Jerrim, J. and Shure, N. 2018. "Children in Jobless Households across Europe: Evidence on the Association with Medium- and Long-Term Outcomes." *Journal of Poverty and Social Justice* 26 (3): 335–58.

Nussbaum, Martha C. 2005. "Capabilities as Fundamental Entitlements: Sen and Social Justice." In *Capabilities Equality: Basic Issues and Problems*, edited by A. Kaufman. London: Routledge, 44–70. https://doi.org/10.4324/9780203799444.

Rowntree, B.S. 1901. *Poverty: A Study of Town Life*. London: Macmillan.

Saunders, P. 2019. "Poverty." In *Routledge Handbook of the Welfare State*, edited by B. Greve, Second Edition, 58–70. Oxon: Routledge.

Sen, Amartya. 2005. "Human Rights and Capabilities." *Journal of Human Development* 6 (2): 151–66. https://doi.org/10.1080/14649880500120491.

——. 2006. "The Capability Approach in Development." *The Journal of Political Philosophy* 14 (3): 351–76. https://doi.org/10.1111/j.1467-9760.2006.00263.x.

van Oorschot, Wim. 2006. "Making the Difference in Social Europe: Deservingness Perceptions among Citizens of European Welfare States." *Journal of European Social Policy* 16 (1): 23–42. https://doi.org/10.1177/0958928706059829.

Wilkinson, R. and Pickett, K. 2009. *The Spirit Level: Why Equality Is Better for Everyone*. London: Allen Lane.

——. 2018. *The Inner Level: How More Equal Societies Reduce Stress, Restore Sanity and Improve Everyone's Well-Being*. St. Ives: Allen Lane.

Will, Jeffry A. 1993. "The Dimensions of Poverty: Public Perceptions of the Deserving Poor." *Social Science Research* 22 (3): 312–32. https://doi.org/10.1006/ssre.1993.1016.

Part I
Conceptual issues

2
Absolute poverty

M. Azhar Hussain

Introduction

There is no agreement about the definition of the absolute poverty concept, but it surely defines a very low consumption level. Different authors and different organizations have different assessments and operationalizations of the concept. In this chapter the minimum needs approach to poverty will be in focus. The approach is widely applied in academia as well as by international organizations that have focused on absolute poverty for decades. It is a monetary approach. But one could also mention other absolute poverty related measures, such as deprivation of specific goods, services, and activities. This chapter will not go through the numerous (standard) problems involved in obtaining required data or the discussion about applying the purchasing power parity concept in international comparisons. The chapter presents a historical overview over the development of the absolute poverty concept starting with Rowntree's seminal work using a minimum necessaries approach applied within a narrowly defined smaller geographical area. Next the latest conceptual developments are considered by exploring the cost of basic needs methodology applied to the national level. Then the focus turns to the analysis of absolute poverty on a global scale. Finally, there is an empirical presentation and analysis of the spatial structure of, and temporal change in, absolute poverty in the world as a whole, regions, and individual countries.

The absolute poverty concept

Absolute poverty exists when fundamental necessities of life, such as food, clothing and shelter, are lacking to various degrees. It is an absolute measure in the sense that the poverty threshold does not per se depend on the general welfare level in society. Instead the absolute poverty line is fixed over time and only adjusted for inflation, e.g. a fixed consumption bundle is used. Absolute poverty could also, or rather should be interpreted as a fixed utility level over time, where adjustment is made not to obtain a fixed consumption bundle, but a fixed utility level. In rich societies there will be very little absolute poverty since practically everyone has enough disposable income to finance expenditure on necessities.

Cost of minimum necessaries approach

It is difficult to exactly identify who coined the "absolute poverty" concept, but among the very early researchers in the field we find Rowntree (1902). Veit-Wilson (1986) considers this as a misunderstanding and argues that Rowntree promoted a relative poverty concept. Rowntree was occupied with identifying the expenditure level required to function well physiologically. He has a monetary approach to consumption poverty. His chapter four has the title "The Poverty Line" which is still a crucial concept in poverty research to this day. The applied poverty definition is (Rowntree 1902, p. 86): "Families whose total earnings are insufficient to obtain the minimum necessaries for the maintenance of merely physical efficiency."

This is very much the same definition applied in modern analyses of poverty in developing countries under the heading "cost of basic needs approach" (CBN, see next section). The necessities first of all included food. Next, also the non-food items housing rent and household sundries were included. The latter are divided into boots, clothes and fuel, and "all other sundries".

Rowntree and his helpers held interviews with each and every wage-earning family in York (UK). This meant visiting 338 streets, where the 11,560 families (46,754 individuals) were living. In other words, this was not a survey, but something as rare as a whole population been interviewed.

Food expenditure was based on physiological requirements, which means the necessary level for men at moderate work was 3,500 calories and 2,800 calories for women. Twenty types of food products were included in the food basket (Table 2.1).

The average weekly minimum required food expenditure was 3 shillings for an adult and 2.25 shillings for a child.

Many of the working people respondents "knew what poverty meant, and had learnt by hard experience what could be 'done without,' and how to obtain most cheaply that which was absolutely necessary" (ibid., p. 107). The non-food measure was thus what was an absolute minimum to get along, although there was a slight relaxation in the sense that the clothing "should not be so shabby" that it reduced job chances.

Based on separate estimates of the minimum expenditure on food, clothing, and rent, the poverty line for a family with two adults and three children was estimated to be 21.67 shillings (per week). This is the sum of 12.75 shillings for food (the food poverty line), 4 shillings for rent and 4.92 shillings for household sundries, which implies food expenditure's fraction of total expenditure was 0.59.

Based on the achieved poverty lines, 27.84% of the York inhabitants were in poverty, while this was the case for 43.40% of the wage-earning class of people living in York.

Cost of basic needs approach

The cost of basic needs approach essentially has the same kind of starting point as Rowntree's approach to analysis of absolute poverty but needs numerous extensions in order to analyse more complex

Table 2.1 Food product prices in Rowntree (1902). Pence per lb*

Flour	16	Bacon	6	Butter	12	Treacle	1.663
New milk	1.5	Cheese	6.5	Biscuits	4	Onions	0.5
Skim milk	0.75	Sugar	1.75	Cocoa	11.4	Yeast	8
Oatmeal	1.9	Potatoes	0.5	Tea	17	Currants	3.5
Dried peas	2.138	Margarine	7.6	Coffee	11.4	Suet	8

* Except for flour and milk, which are, respectively, per stone and per pint.

Source: Own calculations based on Rowntree (1902).

settings than when analysing a much more homogenous small area such as York. On a more general level, there are still a number of similarities between both approaches: monetary poverty is analysed; poverty line is estimated; distinction is made between food and non-food items in the consumption basket; nutritional calorie requirement, quantities and prices of food items are considered. In contrast to Rowntree, present-day consumption poverty analysis never relies on population-level interviews, but instead relies on a sufficiently large representative consumption survey of households.

After obtaining the data, there are a number of steps in the cost of basic needs approach that have acquired widespread recognition and are followed in standard poverty line construction, and thus also followed here (Ravallion and Sen 1996; Deaton and Zaidi 1999; Deaton and Grosh 2000; Deaton and Zaidi 2002; Ravallion and Lokshin 2006; Arndt and Simler 2010).

In many countries the food consumption composition varies considerably across different areas depending on agricultural, market, and climatic conditions. Thus regional consumption baskets must be specified for the persons experiencing poverty. That is done by finding the expenditure share of each main food item out of total expenditure for the people in poverty.

The calorie content of each food item is taken from external sources such as agricultural or health agencies of a country or from an international organization or data from other countries (West et al. 1987; USDA 1998). Calorie needs vary across demographic groups such as gender and age. On average, calorie needs end up at around 2,000 calories a day. This is much lower than the above levels suggested by Rowntree since the 2,000 calorie requirement is an average including children.

Regional (median) prices of consumed products among the people in poverty are calculated. Using the information on consumption composition, calorie content, and prices, we are then able to calculate the quantities of each product to enter the food basket such that it fulfils the calorie requirement and also reflects the consumption pattern of the persons experiencing poverty. This will produce an initial candidate for the food basket. Initial only, since we have from the outset pretended that we were focusing on the persons in poverty by assuming that a certain fraction of the lowest part of the expenditure distribution is persons in poverty. That initial fraction could be, for instance, the poverty rate estimated at the last survey. But in fact we do not know who are the persons in poverty as of yet. Therefore, an iterative procedure is implemented where the estimated poverty rate is the assumed new fraction, and then we run the whole above procedure of getting prices, quantities and calories, and finally a resulting poverty rate. When the assumed fraction and the estimated poverty rate are the same (or close enough), the iteration stops. For illustrative purposes an example of an actual food basket for the capital of Mozambique, Maputo City, is shown in Table 2.2.

In principle we could stop here, since we now have a candidate for the consumption basket giving an adequate number of calories and, at the same time, representing the consumption composition of the poverty-affected part of the population. A potential problem is that the procedure does not assure regionally consistent poverty lines, meaning spatially arriving at the same levels of utility. Arndt and Simler (2010) thus suggest an adjustment of the consumption basket based on so-called revealed preference tests which are well known from microeconomic theory. The idea is that each region's bundle is optimal, e.g. the budget line is tangential to the indifference curve, which can be translated into the fact that utility has been maximized. This then also implies that using prices from any other region together with a region's own consumption bundle will increase utility. If that is not the case, then we can conclude utilities were not initially the same. The adjustment of consumption bundles happens in such a way that required calories are maintained, but quantities are adjusted such that the revealed preference tests are passed. This consistency of consumption bundles across regions also must be true across years, e.g. revealed preference tests must also be passed temporally. This then highlights why a fixed

Table 2.2 Food basket content in Maputo City, Capital of Mozambique, 2008/2009

	Daily consumption (grams per person)	*Price (Meticais per gram)*	*Calories per gram*	*Expenditure share, % of food poverty line*
Current grain rice	152.43	0.02	3.63	16.06
Normal wheat bread	105.72	0.03	2.53	12.73
Peanut (peel and kernels)	44.47	0.04	4.07	8.39
Horse mackerel (fresh, chilled or frozen)	30.91	0.05	0.51	6.87
Coconuts	258.48	0.01	1.95	6.16
Corn flour	42.92	0.02	3.54	4.43
Tomato	50.82	0.02	0.18	4.40
Sunflower oil	14.62	0.06	9.00	4.40
Granulated yellow sugar	30.65	0.02	3.89	3.17
Butter bean	16.14	0.04	3.35	2.82
Onion	18.63	0.03	0.40	2.37
Portuguese cabbage	47.28	0.01	0.22	2.36
Broths	4.11	0.12	3.25	2.30
Pumpkin leaves	22.37	0.01	0.22	1.37
Saw (fresh, chilled or frozen)	6.97	0.04	0.51	1.37
Lettuce	16.72	0.01	0.12	1.12
Cacana	10.21	0.02	0.58	1.04
Beans, dried	8.53	0.03	3.39	1.04
Spaghetti	5.20	0.04	3.30	0.98
Live birds and other live animals	1.66	0.11	0.83	0.91
Nhemba bean leaf	29.76	0.01	0.11	0.91
Cabbage	14.16	0.01	0.19	0.75
Chicken meat in pieces (fresh, chilled or frozen)	2.45	0.06	0.83	0.73
Fresh cassava	12.08	0.01	1.30	0.68
Simple black tea	0.39	0.36	2.93	0.67
Sheets of mandioqueiraira	10.86	0.01	0.27	0.60
Fresh potato (reno)	5.88	0.02	0.65	0.54
Garlic	1.02	0.08	1.21	0.41
Whole chicken meat with or without offal	1.10	0.08	0.83	0.41
Total cost, calorie requirement and exp. share	20.87		2227	90

Source: Own translation based on NDSPA (2010).

bundle over time is such a bad idea, since changes in relative prices necessarily lead to changes in the consumption bundle, which is not "allowed" with a (traditional) absolute poverty line, which is only adjusted (upwards) by the inflation rate (to reflect increasing costs over time). A fixed consumption bundle is problematic because changes in relative prices will alter the optimal consumption bundle (substitution), which does not happen in the case of a fixed bundle, which then overstates the required adjustment of the consumption expenditure (inflation).

The costs of the adjusted food basket represent the food poverty line. What remains is then the non-food part of the poverty line. Non-food expenditure typically includes money spent on clothing, shelter, education, fuel, communication, health, and transportation. Durable goods expenditure is also included but not in the form of the purchase value; instead an estimated use value is used

(Deaton and Zaidi 2002). That is constructed as a weighted average of non-food expenditure for people around the poverty line, where the weights for people near the food poverty line are higher, e.g., ceteris paribus, these individuals have a higher influence on the final non-food expenditure level of the persons experiencing poverty (Ravallion 1998). The sum of the food poverty line and the non-food expenditure of the persons experiencing poverty is the final poverty line for a region in a country. From this, regional as well as national poverty rates can be estimated.

A technical introduction to poverty line construction applying the absolute poverty line estimation analytical software (PLEASe) can be found in Arndt et al. (2016). It is based on the statistical package STATA and on the optimization package GAMS (General Algebraic Modelling System).

The US$k a day approach

Independent researchers and the World Bank, a United Nations organization, developed a seemingly simple poverty line consisting of a given dollar amount per day (k). The US$k a day poverty line can be used to monitor poverty rates over time and to compare poverty rates between countries and regions of the world.

The United Nations Administrative Committee on Coordination has the following definition of poverty (Economic and Social Council 1998):

> Poverty is a denial of choices and opportunities, it is a violation of human dignity. It means lack of basic capacity to participate effectively in society. It means not having enough to feed and clothe a family, not having a school or a clinic to go to, not having the land on which to grow one's food or a job to earn one's living, nor having access to credit. It means insecurity, powerlessness and exclusion of individuals, households and communities. It means susceptibility to violence and it often implies living on marginal and fragile environments, not having access to clean water and sanitation.

Just like Rowntree, the definition includes the basic needs, but it is much broader and includes aspects of dignity, education and health, and also social exclusion and the capacity to effectively participate in society. The latter reflects the capability approach (Sen 1985).

Whereas the cost of basic needs approach produces poverty lines specific for a given national context, the US$k a day approach is aimed at measuring extreme poverty at a global level. Nevertheless, we still need a measure of expenditure (or income) in order to implement the global poverty line.

The logic behind the global poverty line is that persons across the world should be subject to the same poverty line after adjusting for purchasing power differences. A given US$ denominated international poverty line must therefore first be converted into a national currency, but not using the exchange rates which often do not represent purchasing power differences. Instead, PPP (purchasing power parity) is used (World Bank 2011; Feenstra et al. 2015). The PPP conversion factor is the number of units of a country's currency required to buy the same amounts of goods and services in the domestic market as a US dollar would buy in the USA. It must be noted that this conversion factor is for GDP, e.g. all sectors of the economy, and not only for consumption, which is the focus in poverty studies, and particularly it is not targeting the people in poverty.

The first international poverty line stood at US$1 a day in the 1980s and was based on six national poverty lines for some of the poorest developing countries (Ravallion et al. 1991). Until 2005, the US$1.25 poverty line is the average of 15 of the poorest countries (Ravallion et al. 2009). The present US$1.90 poverty line is, again, an average of the same 15 countries (Ferreira et al. 2016).

Not all countries have information on poverty in each year, since survey information is either missing or inadequate. When publishing country-level data this is not a problem as such, because the poverty rate will just be missing that year. But it poses a serious problem when regional, continent or world poverty rates are published by aggregating survey information for several countries. In principle, missing information for even one country in a region will disable the construction of the regional poverty rate, but then the whole idea behind the US$k a day will be unsuccessful. Therefore, missing information for countries is imputed by interpolation or extrapolation of survey data and assumptions regarding income distribution-neutral growth, as well as by assuming that surveyed real per capita consumption growth is reflected by real consumption growth in national accounts. No one, including the World Bank, disagrees on the uncertainty introduced by this imputation and restrictive assumptions, but this is so far the best that can be inferred from the data, and thus the best internationally comparable poverty estimates based on an international poverty line.

The structure and development in absolute poverty rates

The overview over monetary absolute poverty around the world will here apply the US$k a day approach which is also followed by the World Bank. This approach was originally developed within academia. The presented data stems from the World Bank's various databases (World Bank 2018a, 2018b) and uses the US$1.90 a day as the poverty line for all countries.

World poverty over time

Based on the US$1.90 international poverty line, we clearly see that poverty globally has dropped continuously from 42.2% in 1981 to 10% in 2015, except for 1990, where there was a slight increase of 0.5%-points (Figure 2.1).

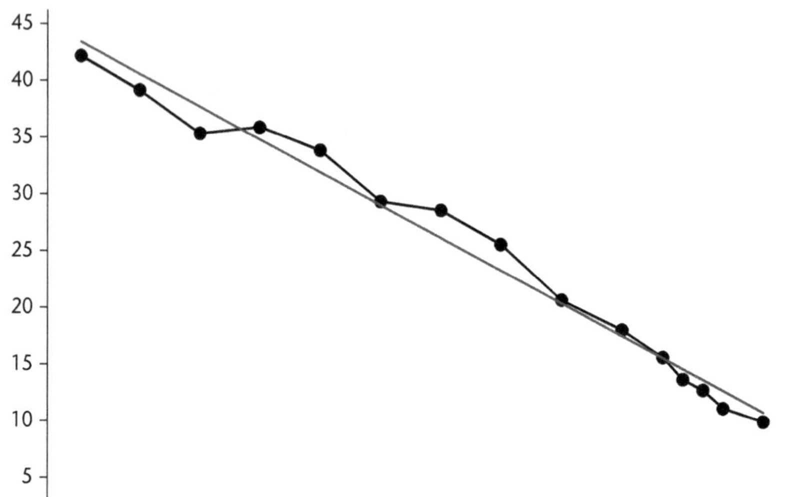

Figure 2.1 World poverty rates based on US$1.90 a day poverty line, 1981–2015.

Source: Own calculations based on World Development Indicators, World Bank.

The reduction of 32.2%-points over the 34-year period implies that on average the annual reduction was 0.95%-points, equivalent to a 4.1% average reduction annually. This means that in 1981 around 1.9 billion people were experiencing poverty using the international poverty line, while the same count was 736 million people in 2015. This can be considered one success story which gets very little attention in the public domain, where conflict and other problems are at the centre of the debate when world problems are discussed. Although, this is a success in relative terms, one must not forget that the world population increased by 2.8 billion individuals over the period from 1981 to 2015, which implies an average increase of 1.4% per year. Therefore, the reduction in the number of poverty stricken people globally was at 2.8% per year on average. Also, while poverty decreased heavily globally, the nearly ¾ billion people in poverty is in itself a huge number, which still needs attention and effort.

Poverty in regions of the world

Regional poverty rates are developed by the World Bank, but with various degrees of certainty as indicated by the "survey coverage", which was as low as 51% (range 0–86%) in 1981 and much better with 68% (range 21–98%) in 2015 (World Bank 2018b). This reflects why the above mentioned imputations are required to arrive at a complete world poverty picture.

As is often true for any average, it hides a lot more than it reveals. This is also true, both for the world averages as well as changes in those averages (Figure 2.1). The 42% world poverty rate in 1981 is made up of regional differences ranging from 0.6% in "other high income countries" to 81% in East Asia and Pacific (Table 2.3). Sub-Saharan Africa is nearly in the middle with 49% poverty in 1981. This picture has changed dramatically over time as sub-Saharan Africa has taken over as the region with the highest poverty rate (41%) since this region experienced the clearly lowest poverty reduction among the non-high-income countries (16% reduction over 34 years). The largest poverty reduction was for East Asia and Pacific with 97%, equivalent to an annual reduction close to 10%. The other regions also had large poverty reductions (52–78%) such that regional poverty is everywhere below or at 5% in 2015 except for sub-Saharan Africa (41%) and South Asia (12%).

A, or rather probably the, prime reason behind the reduction in absolute poverty around the world is due to the increases in the purchasing power of the average citizen of the world.

Table 2.3 Regional poverty rates using US$1.90 a day poverty line, 1981 and 2015

	1981	*2015*	*Change, %-points*		*Change, %-points*	
			All	*Per year*	*All*	*Per year*
East Asia and Pacific	80.8	2.3	–79	–2.31	–97	–9.9
Europe and Central Asia	3.1	1.5	–2	–0.05	–52	–2.2
Latin America and the Caribbean	13.0	4.1	–9	–0.26	–68	–3.3
Middle East and North Africa	11.4	5.0	–6	–0.19	–56	–2.4
Other high income	0.6	0.7	0	0.00	11	0.3
South Asia	55.6	12.4	–43	–1.27	–78	–4.3
Sub-Saharan Africa	49.0	41.1	–8	–0.23	–16	–0.5
World total	42.2	10.0	–32	–0.95	–76	–4.1

Source: PovcalNet, World Bank (2018b).

While the average monthly household per capita income/consumption expenditure was US$295 (2011 PPP) it was US$458 in 2015 (World Bank 2018b), which represent an annual average real growth rate of 1.3%. The regional increase in real income very much reflects the changes in poverty rates in Table 2.3 since East Asia and Pacific saw a staggering 5.6% average annual increase in real income in 1981–2015, while this increase was only 0.1% in sub-Saharan Africa. The correlation coefficient between the percentage poverty reduction in Table 2.3 and the percentage change in real income is 0.91, meaning poverty reductions are highly (positively) correlated with real income increases.

Polarization in poverty has clearly been the result of this uneven poverty reduction across the globe. The number of persons in absolute poverty in sub-Saharan Africa is now higher than the rest of the world combined (413 million compared to 323 million in 2015).

Globally the poverty challenge has clearly been reduced over time. This is because fewer persons are experiencing poverty in 2015 compared to 1981, which means it costs less to lift these people above the poverty line in 2015 compared to 1981. At the same time, world real income has continued to increase over the period. Both factors reduce the "burden" on people of the world above the poverty line in terms of how much of their income is theoretically needed to eradicate poverty globally. Nevertheless, it is hard to see if this linearly negative trend in poverty in Figure 2.1 can be continued, since one might expect that further poverty reduction is now very much dependent on what happens in sub-Saharan Africa, where poverty reduction has historically been low (Table 2.3). A clear risk is that the curve might see a kink at some point in the future because enough efforts are not in place to manage poverty development, particularly in sub-Saharan African and, to some extent, in South Asia.

This section has primarily focused on regions with high poverty. But other regions also experience poverty, as evidenced by Edin and Shaefer (2015) for the USA, and Gaisbauer et al. (2019) for Europe.

Country poverty rates

In the World Bank databank (2018a), 218 countries (territories are also classified as countries in the following) were identified for 2015. In World Bank (2018b) there is published data on poverty rates for 163 countries, which means we have data on 75% of the countries of the world. The missing data do not pose a major problem since the included population represent 95% of the world's total population.

A first glimpse of the countrywise poverty rates is found in Figure 2.2 (see also the complete list of poverty rates in Appendix 2.1). Not surprisingly, the difference among countries is even larger than among regions. The poverty rates thus vary from 0% experiencing poverty in countries such as Switzerland, Finland or Malta, to 77.7% experiencing poverty in the Central African Republic and with Burundi and the Democratic Republic of Congo with nearly the same very high poverty rate. Also, we see that 57 countries have poverty rates above the world weighted average of 10%. While the increase in poverty rates is small for low poverty rates when moving up on the ranks in Figure 2.2, the poverty increase becomes bigger for countries from just above the average, and ends up with big poverty increases when poverty is above 50%.

While the world poverty rate of 10% should be manageable when taking a world view on matters, it is clear that many countries are really struggling with poverty rates two, three or even seven times higher than the world average. Combined with the fact that these countries are also among the poorest, the challenge facing governments and civil society in those countries becomes evident.

Some caution needs to be shown when interpreting the poverty rates for individual countries at the lower end of the distribution (see Appendix 2.1). For instance, we have countries such as

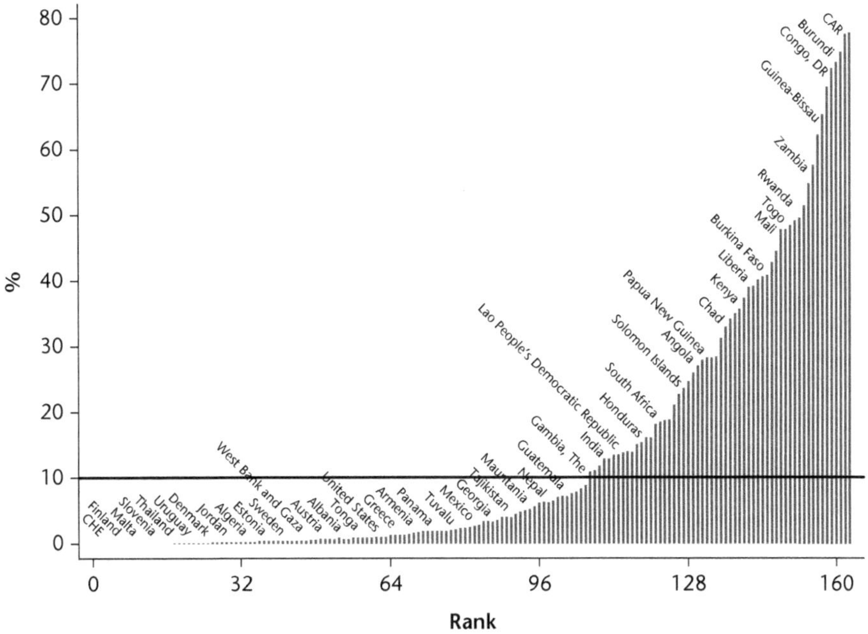

Figure 2.2 Ranked country poverty rates based on US$1.90 a day poverty line, 2015.

Note: Only sample countries are shown. CHE is Switzerland and CAR is Central African Republic. The horizontal line is the world poverty rate. 163 countries and territories are depicted.

Source: Own calculations based on World Bank (2018a, 2018b).

Azerbaijan, Kazakhstan, and Lebanon with recorded poverty rates of 0%, while countries including Luxembourg, Denmark, and Japan are recorded as having positive, albeit very low, poverty rates (0.2%). This is, by any means, against expectations, unless somehow the former three countries have lower inequality or are particularly targeting the persons experiencing poverty and better at that than the latter three countries. Thus, the positive poverty rates could probably without much error be interpreted as 0% poverty rates. Another reason for caution is statistical uncertainty. Take Mozambique as an example where the standard error for the national poverty rate was 1.8%-points in 2008/09 (Arndt et al. 2012) when taking survey design into account, and this despite a large survey sample size as big as 10,832 households (more than 40,000 persons). A standard error of 1.8%-points implies that poverty rates below roughly 3.5% are within the margin of (statistical) error and are therefore not significantly different from 0%, e.g. could actually be (very close to) 0%.

The huge differences between countries both in terms of poverty levels as well as poverty reductions are, again, to a large degree explained by differences in economic growth rates across countries (Figure 2.3). The correlation coefficient is 0.65, but when weighted with country population size, the correlation is 0.83. Regressing the two series and also including the relative increase in the Gini coefficient as a regressor shows a clearly significant effect from economic growth and change in inequality (though sample size is reduced as bigger countries such as China, India and the USA are excluded from the regression since the World Bank does not supply national inequality rates for those countries, but there is no reason to believe they should be behaving differently regarding the analysed relationships). A 1%-point increase in real income growth is associated with a 1.84%-point increase in the poverty rate reduction rate, which is

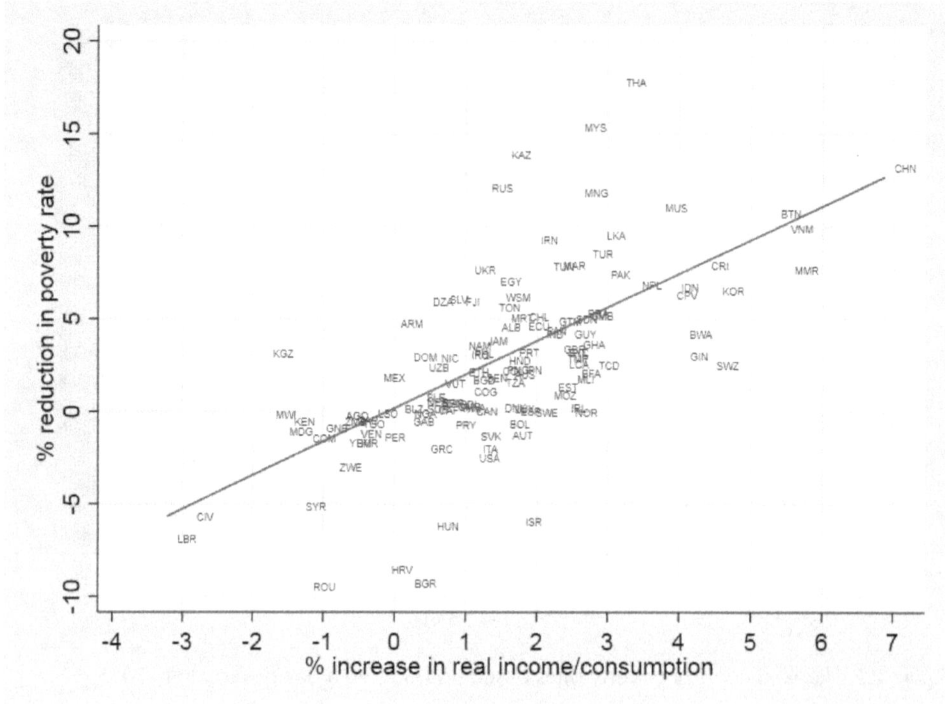

Figure 2.3 Reduction in poverty rate and increase in PPP adjusted income/consumption based on US$1.90 a day poverty line. Annual average percentage change, 1981–2015.

Source: Own calculations based on World Bank (2018a, 2018b).

close to the slope in Figure 2.3. A 1%-point increase in the Gini coefficient increase is adversely associated with a 6.13%-point decrease in the poverty reduction rate. The dividend from economic growth can thus be drastically reduced if inequality is not properly controlled. This is an empirical illustration of the iron "Poverty-Growth-Inequality Triangle" (Bourguignon 2004).

An example is South Africa, which saw a reduction in poverty of 14% from 1981 to 2015, which is 0.44% per year. During the same period inequality increased 0.18% per year. According to the regression (counter factual), had there been no increase in inequality, the poverty reduction would have been 1.08%-points (= 0.18 × 6.13) higher, meaning 1.53% per year instead of the actual 0.44%. This would have given a poverty reduction over the period from 1981 to 2015 of 41% instead of the actually observed 14%, meaning a further reduction of 27% which is equivalent to 3.3 million fewer South Africans under the international poverty line in 2015 – a substantial number in a country with 55 million inhabitants. This just underscores that economic growth might not be enough; inequality must also be managed if there is a goal of eradicating absolute poverty.

Conclusion

Rowntree's innovative approach to measuring absolute poverty in UK's York more than a century ago has later, and particularly in the last few decades, been followed by numerous surveys and analysis of the topic, especially in a developing country context.

The state of the art methodology to measure absolute poverty is the cost of basic needs approach. It involves creating a consumption poverty line consisting of expenditure on food and expenditure on non-food. The food expenditure reflects the food composition and prices paid by people in poverty while assuring the required number of calories for individuals. The non-food expenditure reflects the level for persons experiencing poverty around the food poverty line. Using this approach almost certainly requires different poverty lines to be applied within the same country. In the end poverty lines across time and space must reflect the same level of welfare (utility), which is assured by adjusting the food-baskets (slightly) such that revealed preferences tests are passed while at the same time meeting the calorie requirements.

While this approach works in a national setting, there is the argument that international or global comparisons of poverty require a harmonized measure which is implemented by the international poverty line of US$1.90 a day converted to national currencies using PPP, reflecting differences in the purchasing power of one US dollar across the world. In order to produce internationally comparable or even regional or global poverty rates, we would need information for all countries included in the aggregate poverty rate. Since many or most countries do not have annual consumption surveys, imputations of poverty rates are carried out, which involves some sometimes restrictive assumptions. With a US$1.90 poverty line, world poverty has hugely decreased from 42% to 10% over the available 34-year period from 1981 to 2015. But it is also seen that poverty reduction has been very uneven, and thus has seen huge decreases in initially high-poverty countries, except for sub-Saharan Africa where poverty only fell a little and is still above 40% in 2015 (it was 49% in 1981). The observed reduction in poverty and the differences in poverty reductions among nations and regions are closely linked to economic growth. But it also seems to be linked to economic inequality such that increased inequality, on average, adversely affects poverty reduction.

Appendix 2.1 Poverty rates in 163 countries and territories representing 95% of the world's population, based on the $1.90 a day international poverty line, 2015.

Azerbaijan	0	Hungary	0.5	Nicaragua	2.9	South Africa	18.9
Belgium	0	Portugal	0.5	Mexico	3.3	Syrian Arab Rep.	21.2
Belarus	0	Sweden	0.5	Brazil	3.4	Cameroon	22.8
Switzerland	0	Canada	0.5	Ecuador	3.4	Haiti	23.7
Cyprus	0	Australia	0.5	Peru	3.6	Solomon Islands	24.7
Czech Rep.	0	Trinidad & Tob.	0.6	Georgia	4.0	Sao Tome and Prin.	25.9
Germany	0	West Bank & Ga.	0.6	Gabon	4.1	Ethiopia	27.0
Finland	0	China	0.7	Maldives	4.1	Angola	27.9
France	0	Slovak Rep.	0.7	Colombia	4.5	Cote d'Ivoire	28.2
Iceland	0	Latvia	0.7	Tajikistan	4.8	St. Lucia	28.3
Lebanon	0	Austria	0.7	Macedonia, former Y. Rep. of	5.0	Papua New Guinea	28.4
Malta	0	Lithuania	0.7	Pakistan	5.2	Timor-Leste	31.2
Montenegro	0	Croatia	0.7	Romania	5.7	Guinea	33.0
Netherlands	0	Sri Lanka	0.8	Mauritania	6.2	Chad	34.1
Poland	0	Albania	0.8	Bolivia	6.4	Congo, Rep. of	34.9
Slovenia	0	Morocco	0.9	Myanmar	6.4	Senegal	35.7
Malaysia	0.0	Tunisia	0.9	Guyana	6.5	Kenya	37.3
Kazakhstan	0.0	Fiji	1.0	Nepal	7.0	Eswatini	39.0
Russian Fed.	0.0	Tonga	1.0	Indonesia	7.2	Uganda	39.2

(continued)

Appendix 2.1 (continued)

Thailand	0.0	Spain	1.0	Cabo Verde	7.2	Liberia	40.2
Moldova	0.0	Seychelles	1.0	Sudan	7.7	Tanzania	40.7
Serbia	0.1	Samoa	1.1	Guatemala	7.9	Yemen, Rep. of	40.8
Ukraine	0.1	United States	1.2	Philippines	8.3	Burkina Faso	42.8
Uruguay	0.1	Bulgaria	1.2	Venezuela, Rep. Bol. de	8.9	Niger	44.5
Mongolia	0.2	Chile	1.3	Ghana	10.9	Nigeria	47.8
Luxembourg	0.2	Egypt	1.3	Gambia, The	11.1	Mali	47.8
Bosnia and Herz.	0.2	Greece	1.5	Kiribati	11.8	Sierra Leone	48.4
Denmark	0.2	Costa Rica	1.5	Botswana	12.8	Togo	49.2
Japan	0.2	Bhutan	1.7	Vanuatu	12.8	Benin	49.6
United Kingdom	0.2	Jamaica	1.8	India	13.4	Rwanda	51.5
Ireland	0.2	Armenia	1.9	Namibia	13.4	Lesotho	54.8
Jordan	0.2	Paraguay	1.9	Belize	13.8	Zambia	57.5
Norway	0.2	Dominican Rep.	1.9	Uzbekistan	14.0	Mozambique	62.1
Korea, Rep. of	0.2	El Salvador	1.9	Lao People's Dem. Rep.	14.0	Guinea-Bissau	65.3
Turkey	0.3	Panama	2.0	Bangladesh	15.2	Malawi	69.6
Algeria	0.3	Italy	2.0	Micronesia, Fed. States of	15.4	Congo, Dem. Rep. of	72.3
Kosovo	0.4	Iraq	2.2	Zimbabwe	16.0	South Sudan	73.3
Iran, Isl. Rep. of	0.4	Vietnam	2.3	Honduras	16.2	Burundi	74.7
Mauritius	0.4	Tuvalu	2.3	Comoros	18.2	Madagascar	77.5
Estonia	0.5	Kyrgyz Rep.	2.5	Djibouti	18.6	Central African Rep.	77.7
Israel	0.5	Turkmenistan	2.8	Suriname	18.8		

Source: World Bank (2018a, 2018b).

References

Arndt, C., and K. Simler (2010). Estimating Utility Consistent Poverty Lines. *Economic Development and Cultural Change*, 58, 449–474.

Arndt, C., U.R. Beck, M.A. Hussain, K. Mahrt, K. Simler, and F. Tarp (2016). *User Guide to Poverty Line Estimation Analytical Software – PLEASe*. In C. Arndt and F. Tarp (eds.) *Measuring Poverty and Wellbeing in Developing Countries*, Appendix 1. London: Oxford University Press.

Arndt, C., M.A. Hussain, E.S. Jones, V. Nhate, F. Tarp, and J. Thurlow (2012). Explaining Poverty Evolution: The Case of Mozambique. *American Journal of Agricultural Economics*, 94(4), 854–872.

Bourguignon, F. (2004). *The Poverty-Growth-Inequality Triangle*. Paper presented at the Indian Council for Research on International Economic Relations, New Delhi, February 4.

Deaton, A., and M. Grosh (2000). Consumption. In M. Grosh and P. Glewwe (eds.) *Designing Household Survey Questionnaires for Developing Countries: Lessons from Ten Years of LSMS Experience* (pp. 91–133). Washington, DC: World Bank.

Deaton, A., and S. Zaidi (1999). *Guidelines for Constructing Consumption Aggregates for Welfare Analysis*. Working Paper No. 217. Princeton University, Woodrow Wilson School of Public and International Affairs, Research Program in Development Studies.

Deaton, A., and S. Zaidi (2002). *Guidelines for Constructing Consumption Aggregates for Welfare Analysis, Living Standards Measurement Study*. Working Paper No. 135. World Bank, Washington, DC.

Economic and Social Council (1998). Statement of Commitment for Action to Eradicate Poverty. Adopted by Administrative Committee on Coordination (ACC). Press Release. ECOSOC/5759. 20 May 1998. www.un.org/press/en/1998/19980520.eco5759.html. Accessed 23 November 2018.

Edin, K., and H.L. Shaefer (2015). *$2.00 a Day: Living on Almost Nothing in America*. Boston, MA: Houghton Mifflin Harcourt.

Feenstra, R.C., R. Inklaar, and M.P. Timmer (2015). The Next Generation of the Penn World Table. *American Economic Review*, 105(10), 3150–3182.

Ferreira, F.H.G., S. Chen, A. Dabalen, Y. Dikhanov, N. Hamadeh, D. Jolliffe, et al. (2016). A Global Count of the Extreme Poor in 2012: Data Issues, Methodology and Initial Results. *The Journal of Economic Inequality*, 14(2), 141–172.

Gaisbauer, H.P., G. Schweiger, and C. Sedmak (2019). *Absolute Poverty in Europe: Interdisciplinary Perspectives on a Hidden Phenomenon*. Bristol: Policy Press.

NDSPA (2010). *Poverty and Well-being in Mozambique: The Third National Assessment*. National Directorate of Studies and Policy Analysis, Ministry of Planning and Development, Maputo, Mozambique.

Ravallion, M. (1998). *Poverty Lines in Theory and Practice*. Living Standards Measurement Study Working Paper No. 133. Washington, DC: World Bank.

Ravallion, M., and M. Lokshin (2006). Testing Poverty Lines. *Review of Income and Wealth*, 52(3), 399–421.

Ravallion, M., and B. Sen (1996). When Method Matters: Monitoring Poverty in Bangladesh. *Economic Development and Cultural Change*, 44, 761–792.

Ravallion, M., S. Chen, and P. Sangraula (2009). Dollar a Day Revisited. *World Bank Economic Review*, 23(2), 163–184.

Ravallion, M., G. Datt, and D. van de Walle (1991). Quantifying Absolute Poverty in the Developing World. *Review of Income and Wealth*, 37, 345–361.

Rowntree, B.S. (1902). *Poverty, A Study of Town Life*. Second edition. London: Macmillan and Co. Ltd.

Sen, A. (1985). *Commodities and Capabilities*. Amsterdam: North-Holland.

USDA (1998). *Composition of Foods Commonly Eaten*. Data files. Washington, DC: USDA.

Veit-Wilson, J.H. (1986). Paradigms of Poverty: A Rehabilitation of B.S. Rowntree. *Journal of Social Policy*, 15(1), 69–99.

West, C.E., F. Pepping, I. Scholte, W. Jansen, and H.F.F. Albers (1987). *Food Composition Table for Energy and Eight Important Nutrients in Foods Commonly Eaten in East Africa*. Technical Center for Agriculture and Rural Cooperation of the ACP/ECP Convention of Lomé, and the Food and Nutrition Cooperation Department of Human Nutrition. Wageningen: Wageningen Agricultural University.

World Bank (2011). *Purchasing Power Parities and the Real Size of World Economies*. A Comprehensive Report of the 2011 International Comparison Program (ICP).

World Bank (2018a). *http://databank.worldbank.org/data/reports.aspx?source=2&Topic=11*. Accessed 12 November 2018.

World Bank (2018b). *http://iresearch.worldbank.org/PovcalNet/povDuplicateWB.aspx*. Accessed 24 November 2018.

3

Absolute or relative?

Definitions and the different understandings of poverty

Therese Saltkjel and Ira Malmberg-Heimonen

Introduction

Various definitions of poverty lead to different perceptions of who is poor and who is not, and imply different understandings of human needs, welfare and wellbeing. Depending on our definition, socio-political solutions to poverty can be either residual (i.e. based on the residual model) and target the neediest, aiming to secure their basic needs, or redistributive and focus on enhancing living standards and welfare. An important question is whether only the most deprived people in the world should be defined as poor. Alternatively, do we simultaneously need to recognise that even in a wealthy nation with high living standards and a comprehensive welfare state some people experience intolerable material and economic hardships?

The aim of this chapter is to discuss the merits and shortcomings of absolute and relative definitions of poverty, and their implications for socio-political interventions. First, we will discuss wider frameworks of welfare and wellbeing for a more in-depth understanding of poverty. Second, we will elaborate on absolute and relative approaches and their assumptions and opposing arguments. We will end the chapter by summarising the implications of the various understandings of poverty.

Poverty as an aspect of welfare

One major debate in defining poverty is whether we should concentrate on physical survival only, or include a broader understanding of people's wellbeing and welfare. Behind varying perspectives lie competing visions of human agency, needs and welfare. These perspectives should be recognised and discussed, also with regard to their contribution to policies that address poverty.

In Scandinavia, the level of living research has a strong tradition and has been influenced by British socio-political research. Drawing on Richard Titmuss (1907–1973), resources in terms of money, possessions, knowledge, social relations and security are highlighted as central elements of welfare. Understanding level of living as "command over resources" implies that individuals are active human beings, a perspective that has roots in classical sociological theory (e.g. Marx, Weber) (Johansson 1970, 25; Erikson and Uusitalo 1987, 184–186).

Resources can be individual, collective or acquired (Official Norwegian Reports (NOU) 2009:10, 10). In the possession of resources, individuals can actively control and direct their living conditions, as opposed to being viewed as passive human beings who are provided for. Having command over resources also increases individuals' life chances and opportunities to maximise welfare. The value of the resources an individual has command over depends, however, on the circumstances in which she lives and whether there is a possibility to use the resources.

In contrast to the resource perspective, the basic needs perspective gives prominence to day-to-day survival (Esping-Andersen 2000, 6; Erikson and Uusitalo 1987, 189). Within the Scandinavian welfare approach, welfare problems are seen as interrelated. In other words, they do not affect individuals and families as isolated problems, but tend to correlate and accumulate over time (Esping-Andersen 2000, 5; Fritzell and Lundberg 2007, 6).

Social policies involve normative standards and value judgements, and should therefore be subject to dispute and discussion. Nevertheless, the more general a welfare problem is, the more difficult it is to arrive at a single, unambiguous answer (Weber 1949, 56). Johansson (1970, 29) argues that, while it is difficult to agree on what characterises a good life, it is easier to agree on the opposite, i.e. what characterises poor life conditions. The aim of the level of living approach, as described by Johansson (1970, 30), is to give priority to problems or conditions that can be addressed through political decisions and relieved by means of institutional arrangements such as national health services, educational institutions or labour market institutions.

The resources approach is closely related to Amartya Sen's concept of capabilities (Esping-Andersen 2000, 5) as part of a more subjective wellbeing approach to welfare. Sen distinguishes between functionings and capabilities. Functionings are the many things a person may value to be or to do. Examples of such functionings are being able to work and being in good health. Capabilities are a person's actual freedom to choose from combinations of functionings, irrespective of whether that person chooses to exercise this freedom or not (Sen 1999, 75). Emphasis is placed on the level of freedom that people can achieve and resources are instrumental to increased wellbeing (Robeyns 2005, 95). People are seen as active and able to make changes. Moreover, individual achievements are assessed in terms of people's own values, objectives and choices (Sen 1999, 19).

According to Sen, poverty should be seen as deprivation of basic capabilities, rather than low income (Sen 1999, 87). There are aspects of human needs that are universal, meaning capabilities that apply at all times and in all places. For instance, the capability of avoiding shame (Sen 1983, 161). However, the resources we need to meet a capability, say, to buy adequate clothing for our children, require varying commodities, which are relative to the society we live in. In such cases an "absolute approach in the space of capabilities translates into a relative approach in the space of commodities" (Sen 1983, 167–168).

The capability and wellbeing approaches are oriented more toward individual agency and less toward the influence of institutions and processes (Daly 2011, 45). Theoretically, the command over resources approach stresses the importance of individual agency and the commitment of the welfare state to enabling citizens to uphold agency.

Absolute poverty: minimum necessities and basic needs

Picture an unemployed single mother living in an urban slum in Southern Asia. The mother and her children are deprived of basic human needs in terms of money to buy nutritious food, and access to safe shelter, clean water and proper sanitation. There are no available collective benefits. The mother, lacking command over minimum resources to provide for the livelihood and security of her children, is forced to live from hand to mouth to survive. The choices and opportunities open to her and her children are severely restricted by lack of resources. This fictitious, but realistic example suggests that absolute definitions of poverty shed light on the severity of deprivation of those who are worst off globally.

Absolute poverty is often associated with objective and definable basic needs, irrespective of time and place. Examples of basic needs are food, clothing, shelter, which are all essential to the physical survival of humans (Roll 1992, 14). An absolute standard measuring poverty can also serve as a fixed benchmark that is used to measure progress, or lack of progress, over time (Townsend 2010).

Absolute approaches based on basic *needs* tend to treat individuals as passive human beings. Seen from the perspective of the poor there is, however, and this applies to all of us, a fundamental desire to have freedom of choice and action, to be able to make choices, to do basic things without constraints, and to have some form of control over what happens in the future (Narayan et al. 2000, 29).

Poverty definitions based on basic needs have been criticized, as judgements of what constitutes minimum necessities cannot be objective. Instead, they represent normative standards and value judgements usually established through expert opinions (Langan 1998, 1; Roll 1992, 15).

Needs comprise both elements that arise from nature, such as physical survival, and elements that are socially determined (Langan 1998, 4). The World Bank report, *Crying Out for Change: Voices of the Poor* (Narayan et al. 2000, 29), shows variation in needs by individual characteristics, such as livelihood, age and gender, and across contexts including region and rural and urban areas. Townsend argues that we cannot separate people's "physical efficiency" from their wellbeing and without reference to the way their society is organised and structured and the available societal resources. Hence, poverty is a dynamic concept as needs change over time and across different contexts (Townsend 2010, 93–94).

When living patterns and activities change, the definitions of basic needs also change (Ruggles 1990). In the United States, the official poverty measure, developed in the 1960s, is based on an absolute standard, at a fixed level of income (adjusted to family size, number of children, and inflation rate) (Royce 2015, 10). The measure has not been revised to take account of new patterns of consumption. As a result, the poor in the first decades of the 21st century can afford fewer basic needs for an ordinary way of life compared with the poor in the decade the poverty measure was developed. Shaefer and Edin (2013, 259, 266) showed that, between 1996 and 2011, the number of US households that lived on US$2 or less per person per day had increased from 636,000 to 1.65 million.[1] Explanations for this change were the welfare reform leading to reductions in the cash safety net for non-workers, and the slow economic growth and job losses of the 2000s.

Ruggles (1990, 20) points out that when the poverty line is far below the norms of consumption within a society, the absolute poor are more likely to suffer severe and multiple disadvantages. Policy makers may interpret increases in multiple disadvantages among the poor as a sign that policies aimed to reduce poverty are, in fact, creating a more socially disadvantaged poor population over time. Ultimately, such interpretations may prompt politicians to advocate less generous social policies. Looking back historically, this latter point is illustrated by Charles Murray (1984). In the context of the US, he argues that benefits did not alleviate poverty; rather, they created it through changing incentives and, consequently, changing behaviour of the poor (King and Ross 2010, 50). In *Losing Ground: American Social Policy 1950–1980*, Murray (1984, 154) holds that it was the changes in financial incentives that explained increasing unemployment among the young. Within a rational decision-making framework, the argument is that when poor people got more money from welfare than from low-paying jobs, "maximizing short-term gains" led to lower labour force participation. According to Murray (1984, 204), welfare transfers should be treated in the same way as a doctor applies a dangerous drug: "not at all if possible and no more than necessary".

Relative poverty: socially determined needs

A long-term social assistance recipient with a history of mental ill health and sparse work experience, who is living in a rich and generous welfare state, is likely to have access to minimum resources. He probably has a roof over his head with help from housing support and he can buy food and other necessities with his monthly social assistance payments. If we compare his situation with the severe situation of the poor mother in the urban slum in Southern Asia, we do not think of him as poor. However, multiple interacting disadvantages, sparse and depleted resources, and difficulties to convert resources into a good life will reduce his ability to control and direct his living conditions and take part in ordinary life. Relative to most people in affluent societies, we would still view the situation of the long-term social assistance recipient as one of living in poverty. Hence, relative definitions remind us that even within a wealthy nation with high living standards and access to collective welfare resources, some people experience degrees of material and economic hardship that most of us would deem intolerable (Roll 1992, 18).

According to Gordon (2007, 32), poverty can be defined as an "insufficient command of resources over time", which leads to deprivation. The idea of the relative poverty approach is that we should not "discount the flesh and blood, and the problems, of ordinary life" (Townsend 2010, 94). Hence, relative approaches to poverty emphasise that needs are socially determined. That is, the resources needed to acquire food, clothes and consumption goods, and to take part in social activities vary based on where in the world and at what time we live. In Norway, the Red Cross offers summer holiday trips to children from economically deprived families.[2] The example illustrates that going on a summer holiday, at least occasionally, is a part of ordinary living patterns and activities in a wealthy country such as Norway.

Critics argue that relative poverty is more an assessment of inequality, than of poverty (Sen 1983). Relative definitions take the "moral imperative that something should be done" out of the definition when the situation of the relative poor is compared to a situation of extreme deprivation were almost everyone lacks basic necessities (Roll 1992, 17; Piachaud 1987, 161). In the example mentioned above, the Red Cross offers economically deprived children in Norway summer holiday trips. By contrast, the single mother in the urban slum of Southern Asia cannot provide her children with safe housing, clean water or sanitation. Relative definitions are further based on constantly changing criteria, as they relate to contemporary standards of what is a decent life (Sen 1983, 156).

An example from the global financial crisis of 2008, the "Great Recession", illustrates this latter point. Duiella and Turrini (2014, 10) report that increases in poverty during the crisis were mainly increases in material deprivation, not relative income poverty. The result is surprising in light of high unemployment rates, combined with austerity measures as the default policy response within many European Union (EU) countries (Blyth 2013; Martin 2015; OECD 2014, 2015). However, the measures of relative income poverty are difficult to interpret in times of economic change, because the poverty line changes. Those at the bottom may suffer income loss; however, when the income of all households falls, the relative poverty will decline if the income of those in the middle falls by more than that of those at the bottom (OECD 2014, 112). Therefore, a more absolute measure of relative income poverty is sometimes used, referred to as "anchored" poverty, in which a certain year is used as a benchmark for the poverty line

(OECD 2014, 23). Results from the OECD (2014, 112) showed that, when assessed by this method, relative poverty rates increased by as much as two percentage points in several of the countries during the first years of the crisis.

However, Sen (1983, 159) argues that there is an "irreducible absolutist core in the idea of poverty", which implies that a relative approach to poverty cannot entirely capture the severity of the situation in which the most deprived people in the world live. In 2016, about 815 million people in different parts of the world were undernourished, and the UN reports that hunger and malnutrition are rising globally (United Nations 2018, 3–4). The humanitarian crisis in Yemen is currently the worst in the world, where three-quarters of the population are in need of aid and protection.[3] People who do not know how to get their next meal and whose children die because of malnourishment are poor by any standard.

Estimates from the UN indicate that in 2013, 783 million people lived below the World Bank's international poverty line (IPL), which is below US$1.90 per person per day (United Nations 2018, 3). The IPL is intended to capture poverty based on the standards of the poorest countries (Ravallion, Chen and Sangraula 2009, 164). Although the measure serves to reflect low economic resources, the US$1.90-a-day[4] poverty line does not necessarily reflect a standard adequate to meet basic human needs (Allen 2013, 6).

In 1995 after the World Summit, the UN defined absolute poverty as a condition "characterized by severe deprivation of basic human needs" distinguished from "overall poverty". The merits of this definition of absolute poverty are that it sheds light on the more "absolute" aspects of relative deprivation without treating poverty as a fixed standard and taking into account the situation of the globally worst off (United Nations 1995, 57; Gordon 2007, 35).

Equality of opportunity or results?

When poverty is seen as inability to participate in society, it involves both a low income and a low standard of living (Gordon 2007, 39; Townsend 1979). According to Ringen (1988, 355), definitions of financial poverty emphasise the equality of opportunities, while definitions of material deprivation emphasise the equality of results. Material deprivation includes achieved living standards, as opposed to the money people have at their disposal. Hence, the measure of material deprivation aims to capture key aspects of customary living conditions across the EU, aspects that people do not possess when they lack resources (Guio et al. 2016, 221).

A given income level can mean different standards of living across contexts due, for instance, to varying price levels, living requirements and availability of welfare services (Blackwood and Lynch 1994, 568). The availability of benefits in cash and in kind may influence people's income and consumption differently (Nelson 2012, 150–151). Kenworthy, Epstein and Duerr (2011, 37) suggest that social policies are related to reduced material deprivation since they provide services to meet individuals' needs. Services may indirectly enhance the earning capacity of a household through, for instance, active labour market policies and caring services for the elderly or for children (Nelson 2012, 151), while cash upholds purchasing power, enabling individuals and households to buy material necessities.

Sen is critical of perspectives that take account of the opportunities people have through the economic means they possess, but neglect the different opportunities they have to convert means into good living or capabilities (Sen 2009, 65–66). A person with a chronic disease will, for instance, need more resources to achieve the same living standard, compared with a healthy person. The above example of the long-term social assistance recipient with ill mental health serves to illustrate the notion of "coupling" of disadvantages (Sen 1999, 88). Mental health problems may first restrict the opportunities to earn an adequate living by working. Second, they restrict the ability to convert low earnings into material necessities due to the extra expenses related to medicines and medical treatments.

Another criticism of the concept of material deprivation is that lack of material necessities is not always equal to poverty; instead, it may reflect taste, preferences and diversity in living styles (Piachaud 1981, 420). The material deprivation indicator adopted by the EU assesses whether lack of consumption goods is related to an "enforced lack", meaning that people would like to possess them, but cannot afford them (Fusco, Guio and Marlier 2013, 45). Hick (2012, 296) argues that lack of material items due to other impediments, such as disability and discrimination, is still unaccounted for. A key challenge in measuring material deprivation in the EU is to find suitable, valid and reliable indicators across countries with heterogeneous living standards, that can be aggregated into a material deprivation indicator (cf. discussion by Fusco, Guio and Marlier 2013, 44–46; Guio et al. 2016, 221–222).

The measures of at-risk-of-income-poverty and material deprivation, adopted by Eurostat, use a national and cross-national framing for social comparisons (Fahey 2010, 16). Therefore, the rate of material deprivation across countries varies much more than does the rate of income poverty. In this sense, material deprivation has an absolute characteristic assessing differences in living standards across countries while the at-risk-of-income-poverty measure assesses relative deprivation within countries (Nolan et al. 2010, 310–311). Analyses show that there is only moderate overlap between income poverty and material deprivation, meaning that people who are income poor are not always materially deprived, and vice versa (Nolan et al. 2010).

Discussion and concluding remarks

The aim of this chapter was to discuss the merits and shortcomings of absolute and relative definitions of poverty, and their implications for socio-political interventions. We view poverty as an aspect of welfare and draw on the command over resources approach where resources are seen as the most central element of welfare. Depending on the resources an individual has, she can actively control and direct her living conditions, rather than being viewed as a passive human being who needs to be provided for. We also draw on Sen's subjective wellbeing approach in which the concept of capabilities is a central element. Both approaches emphasise the freedom people can achieve through resources.

Through discussions of various definitions, critical debates and understandings of poverty, we have shown that, in order to understand poverty, we need definitions that account for absolute and relative perspectives in combination. Absolute definitions help shed light on the unacceptable situation of the global poor, and show that some forms of poverty are worse than others. If we adopt narrow definitions based on basic needs, we nonetheless risk losing sight of people's need to have a variety of resources in order to be able to make choices and to take control and direct their lives.

An absolute approach to relative deprivation therefore helps shed light on the severe situation of those who are worst off, without treating poverty as a fixed state. Relative approaches to poverty ultimately consider people's broader welfare and wellbeing, relative to the society in which they live, and view poverty as a dynamic concept (Townsend 2010, 93–94). Hence, relative definitions remind us that, even within a wealthy nation with high living standards and access to comprehensive welfare resources, some people experience degrees of material and economic hardship that most of us would deem intolerable (Roll 1992, 18). Absolute perspectives imply that some needs may be universal. However, the resources needed to satisfy needs are conditional to time and place as well as to the individual's characteristics and opportunities.

Poverty seen as the inability to participate in society involves both low income and low standards of living (Townsend 1979). Economic and material definitions of poverty emphasise opportunities and achievements differently. Measures of material deprivation shed light on achieved living standards, as opposed to the financial means at people's disposal.

There are numerous unresolved issues involved in how to measure relative poverty and most of the measurements have drawbacks. When they help shed light on one aspect, for instance the number of income poor, they leave out other aspects, such as the extent of economic impoverishment or the distribution of income among the poor (Blackwood and Lynch 1994, 569).

Whether poverty is defined narrowly in absolute terms or more broadly in relative terms may result in different socio-political solutions (Lister 2004, 35). Sen (2009) contends that lack of financial resources is not the sole cause of poverty. This is due to, among other things, individual characteristics and conversion problems. We agree, in line with Lister (2004, 19), that if we downplay the importance of money we risk policies that do not sufficiently acknowledge the need to raise the incomes of people who experience poverty. Services alone, and opportunities for children from economically deprived families to occasionally go on a summer holiday, will not suffice to lift economically deprived people and families out of poverty. In the context of post-industrial societies new needs arise and so do new policies to address these needs (Taylor-Gooby 1997, 171). Similar welfare challenges are, however, addressed differently in different welfare contexts (Esping-Andersen 2002, 5; Lister 2003). One important challenge is, as we see it, not to replace "passive" income maintenance policies with "active" (human capital investment) policies. Rather, the two policy approaches should be combined to prevent people from falling into poverty, and assist people (back) into working life.

There is, however, no guarantee that more comprehensive social policies introduced in countries with a limited welfare state would succeed in reducing poverty. There are other important factors to account for, such as the absence of institutions and social partners (e.g. unions) (Barth and Moene 2008), armed conflicts, natural disasters, and corruption within society. In order to be able to eradicate poverty we need to understand the complex societal dynamics involved (Sieger 2011, 887). In the literature, there are competing claims for who should bear the responsibility to ameliorate global poverty: is it the state or those who have power and resources to act (Sieger 2011, 887)? Although this is an important question, it is beyond the scope of this chapter.

Notes

1 The authors adopted one of the World Bank's key indicators of global poverty (Shaefer and Edin 2013, 254).
2 www.rodekors.no/tilbudene/ferie-for-alle/ (accessed 2 November 2018).
3 https://unocha.exposure.co/eleven-facts-about-the-yemen-crisis (accessed 27 October 2018).
4 The IPL was adjusted from \$1.25 to \$1.90 in 2015, www.worldbank.org/en/topic/poverty/brief/global-poverty-line-faq (accessed 16 October 2018).

References

Allen, Robert. 2013. *Poverty Lines in History: Theory, and Current International Practice*. University of Oxford, Department of Economics.

Barth, Espen, and Kalle Moene. 2008. "Likhet og åpenhet [Equality and openess]." *Norwegian Journal of Welfare Research* 11 (1): 5–16.

Blackwood, D. L., and R. G. Lynch. 1994. "The measurement of inequality and poverty: A policy maker's guide to the literature." *World Development* 22 (4): 567–578. https://doi.org/10.1016/0305-750X(94)90112-0.

Blyth, Mark. 2013. "The austerity delusion: Why a bad idea won over the West." *Foreign Affairs* 92 (3): 41–56.

Daly, Mary. 2011. *Welfare: Key Concepts*. Cambridge: Polity Press.
Duiella, Matteo, and Alessandro Turrini. 2014. "Poverty developments in the EU after the crisis: A look at main drivers." *ECFIN Economic Brief* (31). https://doi.org/10.2765/72447.
Erikson, Robert, and Hannu Uusitalo. 1987. "The Scandinavian approach to welfare research." In *The Scandinavian Model: Welfare States and Welfare Research*, edited by Robert Erikson, Jørgen Hansen Erik, Stein Ringen and Hannu Uusitalo, 177–193. New York: Sharpe.
Esping-Andersen, Gøsta. 2000. "Social indicators and welfare monitoring." *Social Policy and Development programme paper*, 2. Geneva: United Nations Research Institute for Social Development.
——. 2002. "Towards the good society, once again?" In *Why We Need a New Welfare State*, edited by Gøsta Esping-Andersen, Duncan Gallie, Anton Hemerijck and John Myles, 1–25. New York: Oxford University Press.
Fahey, Tony. 2010. "Poverty and the two concepts of relative deprivation." Working Paper. University College Dublin, School of Applied Social Science (Belfield, Dublin). Available at: www.ucd.ie/t4cms/wp15%20fahey.pdf (accessed 2 October 2015).
Fritzell, Johan, and Olle Lundberg. 2007. "Health, inequalities, welfare and resources." In *Health Inequalities and Welfare Resources: Continuity and Change in Sweden*, edited by Johan Johan Fritzell and Olle Lundberg, 1–18. Bristol: The Policy Press.
Fusco, Alessi, Anne-Catherine Guio, and Eric Marlier. 2013. "Building a material deprivation index in a multinational context: Lessons from the EU experience." In *Poverty and Social Exclusion around the Mediterranean Sea: Economic Studies in Inequality, Social Exclusion and Well-Being*, edited by Valerie Bérenger and Florent Bresson, 43–71. New York: Springer Science and Business.
Gordon, David. 2007. "The concept and measurement of poverty." In *Poverty and Social Exclusion in Britain*, edited by Christina Pantazis, David Gordon and Ruth Levitas, 22–69. Bristol: The Policy Press.
Guio, Anne-Catherine, Eric Marlier, David Gordon, Eldin Fahmy, Shailen Nandy, and Marco Pomati. 2016. "Improving the measurement of material deprivation at the European Union level." *Journal of European Social Policy* 26 (3): 219–333. https://doi.org/10.1177/0958928716642947.
Hick, Rod. 2012. "The capability approach: insights for a new poverty focus." *Journal of Social Policy* 41 (2): 291–308. https://doi.org/10.1017/S0047279411000845.
Johansson, Sten. 1970. "Om levnadsnivåundersökningen: utkast till kapitel 1 och 2 i betänkande att avgivas av Låginkomstutredningen [Draft for Chapters 1 and 2 on the Report on the Swedish People's Living Conditions]." In *Låginkomstutredningen [The Low Income Inquiry]*. Stockholm: Allmänna förlaget.
Kenworthy, Lane, Jessica Epstein, and Daniel Duerr. 2011. "Generous social policy reduces material deprivation." In *Progress for the Poor*, edited by Lane Kenworthy, 33–38. New York: Oxford University Press.
King, Desmond, and Fiona Ross. 2010. "Critics and beyond." In *The Oxford Handbook of the Welfare State*, edited by Francis G. Castles, Stephan Leibfrid, Jane Lewis, Herber Obinge and Christopher Pierson, 45–57. Oxford: Oxford University Press.
Langan, Mary. 1998. *Welfare: Needs, Rights, and Risks*. London: Routledge in association with the Open University.
Lister, Ruth. 2003. "Investing in the citizen-workers of the future: transformations in citizenship and the state under New Labour." *Social Policy & Administration* 37 (5): 427–443. https://doi.org/10.1111/1467-9515.00350.
——. 2004. *Poverty: Key Concepts*. Cambridge: Polity.
Martin, Andrew. 2015. "Eurozone economic governance: 'a currency without a country'." In *European Social Models from Crisis to Crisis: Employment and Inequality in the Era of Monetary Integration*, edited by Andrew Martin and Jon Erik Dølvik, 20–48. Oxford: Oxford University Press.
Murray, Charles A. 1984. *Losing Ground: American Social Policy, 1950–1980*. New York: Basic Books.
Narayan, Deepa, Robert Chambers, Meera K. Shah, and Patti Petesch. 2000. *Crying Out for Change: Voices of the Poor*. Oxford University Press for the World Bank. ProQuest Ebook Central.
Nelson, Kenneth. 2012. "Counteracting material deprivation: the role of social assistance in Europe." *Journal of European Social Policy* 22 (2): 148–163. https://doi.org/10.1177/0958928711433658.
Nolan, Brian, Christopher T. Whelan, Kenneth Couch, and Maureen A. Pirog. 2010. "Using non-monetary deprivation indicators to analyze poverty and social exclusion: lessons from Europe?" *Journal of Policy Analysis and Management* 29 (2): 305–325. https://doi.org/10.1002/pam.20493.
OECD. 2014. *Society at a Glance 2014: OECD Social Indicators*. Paris, France: OECD Publishing. http://dx.doi.org/10.1787/soc_glance-2014-en.
——. 2015. *In it Together: Why Less Inequality Benefits All*. Paris, France: OECD Publishing. http://dx.doi.org/10.1787/9789264235120-en.

Official Norwegian Reports (NOU) 2009:10. *Fordelingsutvalget [The Comission on Distribution]*. Ministry of Finance (Oslo).

Piachaud, David. 1981. "Peter Townsend and the Holy Grail." *New Society* 10 (September): 419–421.

——. 1987. "Problems in the definition and measurement of poverty." *Journal of Social Policy* 16 (2): 147–164. https://doi.org/10.1017/S0047279400020353.

Ravallion, Martin, Shaohua Chen, and Prem Sangraula. 2009. "Dollar a day revisited." *World Bank Economic Review* 23 (2): 163–184. https://doi.org/10.1093/wber/lhp007.

Ringen, Stein. 1988. "Direct and indirect measures of poverty." *Journal of Social Policy* 17 (3): 351–365. https://doi.org/10.1017/S0047279400016858.

Robeyns, Ingrid. 2005. "The capability approach: a theoretical survey." *Journal of Human Development* 6 (1): 93–117. https://doi.org/10.1080/146498805200034266.

Roll, Jo. 1992. *Understanding poverty: a guide to concepts and measures*. Vol. 15. Occasional paper/Family Policy Studies Centre. London: FPSC.

Royce, Edward Cary. 2015. *Poverty and Power: The Problem of Structural Inequality*. Second edition. Maryland: Rowman & Littlefield.

Ruggles, Patricia. 1990. *Drawing the Line: Alternative Poverty Measures and their Implications for Public Policy*. Washington, DC: Urban Institute Press.

Sen, Amartya. 1983. "Poor, relatively speaking." *Oxford Economic Papers* 35 (2): 153–169. https://doi.org/10.1093/oxfordjournals.oep.a041587.

——. 1999. *Development as Freedom*. Oxford: Oxford University Press.

——. 2009. *The Idea of Justice*. London: Allen Lane.

Shaefer, H. Luke, and Kathryn Edin. 2013. "Rising extreme poverty in the United States and the response of federal means-tested transfer programs." *Social Service Review* 87 (2): 250–268. https://doi.org/10.1086/671012.

Sieger, Lynette E. 2011. "Poverty." In *Encyclopedia of Global Justice*, edited by D. K. Chatterjee, 886–888. Dordrecht: Springer.

Taylor-Gooby, Peter. 1997. "In defence of second-best theory: state, class and capital in social policy." *Journal of Social Policy* 26: 171–192.

Townsend, Peter. 1979. *Poverty in the United Kingdom: A Survey of Household Resources and Standards of Living*. Harmondsworth: Penguin.

——. 2010. "The meaning of poverty." *British Journal of Sociology* 61 (Supp. 1): 85–102. https://doi.org/10.1111/j.1468-4446.2009.01241.x.

United Nations. 1995. *Report of the World Summit for Social Development* (Copenhagen, Denmark). Available at: www.un.org/documents/ga/confl66/aconfl66-9.htm (accessed 1 November 2018).

——. 2018. *Progress Towards the Sustainable Development Goals*. United Nations, Economic and Social Council. Available at: https://sustainabledevelopment.un.org/content/documents/18541SG_SDG_Progress_Report_2018_ECOSOC.pdf.

Weber, Max. 1949. *The Methodology of the Social Sciences*, edited by Edward Shils and Henry A. Finch. New York: Free Press.

4

Multidimensional poverty

Whose poverty is it?

Robert Walker

Poverty is multidimensional. This is not a new realisation. It has long been recognised as such. Even Seebohm Rowntree, famed as one of the inventors of income-based poverty measurement, was aware of the complex nature of poverty. He explained that his investigators:

> in the course of their house-to-house visitation, noted those families who were obviously living in a state of poverty, i.e. in obvious want and squalor. Sometimes they obtained definite information that the bulk of earnings was spent in drink or otherwise squandered, sometimes the external evidence of poverty in the home was so clear as to make verbal evidence superfluous.
>
> *(Rowntree, 1908, pp. 297–298)*

If poverty is inherently multidimensional, why does multidimensional poverty require a chapter of its own in a handbook on poverty? Surely all chapters will be about multidimensional poverty. Not so. The *concept* of poverty is most often equated (or confused) with the *measure* of poverty: income falling below a poverty line. This is most evident in the measures used by the World Bank: income of less than $1/day (in 1990); $1.25 (2008) and $1.90 (2015). Income is straightforward to measure and, as a variable, it is generally well behaved with a right-skewed distribution that can readily be transformed into a statistically useful 'normal' curve. It is also easy to express income poverty in both absolute and relative forms. That said, in certain settings, defining and measuring income can sometimes be very difficult. For example, home production is very important in rural areas reliant on subsistence farming and would not be captured by a measure of income based on money. Likewise, income measures typically omit the value of publicly provided services, making cross-national comparisons suspect given the large variation in the extent of welfare provision. Estimates of income based on household surveys are also typically most unreliable at both extremes of the income distribution, which clearly affects estimates of poverty and measures of median, and particularly mean, incomes used to establish relative poverty.

Nevertheless, multidimensional poverty is, by definition, even more complex to measure than income poverty, with more demanding data requirements. These are certainly reasons why multidimensional poverty has only comparatively recently migrated from academic writings to policy prescriptions. Other reasons for this migration are various. The European Union's measure of being at risk of poverty and social exclusion, which combines income poverty, material deprivation and low work intensity, was launched in 2010 as part of the Europe 2020 Strategy. It was the product of political wrangling rather than conceptual clarity. At the time, the Commission needed a policy response to the Great Recession and inclusion of low work intensity reflected fears of a stagnating labour market and the policy fashion for activation policies to encourage flexible job-search (EC, 2010). It also obviated the need for governments to admit that poverty, rather than the risk of poverty, exists anywhere in the European Union. The inclusion of 'poverty in all its dimensions' to United Nation's Sustainable Development Goals (SDGs) reflected dissatisfaction with the World Bank's income measure of extreme poverty, especially among civil society organisations, although this was sometimes simply because the threshold was thought to be too low. However, its inclusion was also a consequence of technical advance with the development of the Multidimensional Poverty Index (MPI) by Alkire and Foster (2011), adopted by the United Nations Development Programme (UNDP). The MPI currently combines just the three dimensions of poor health, lack of education, inadequate living standard and therefore has modest data demands, while the methodology allows the measure to be disaggregated to provide sub-national and sub-group estimates of poverty.

However, while poverty may be intrinsically multidimensional, and the concept of multidimensional poverty is now widely accepted in policy circles, there is still considerable doubt as to how multidimensionality should be conceptualised and measured. There is little consensus as to whether dimensions are cumulative or merely manifestations of some underlying social phenomenon. Likewise, and related, there is debate as to whether dimensions should correlate and/or be differentially weighted. There is also no consensus as to what the dimensions of poverty should be; this Bedük (2018a) attributes to inadequate theorising of the concept of poverty, a deficiency which this Handbook should alleviate. These issues will be elucidated with reference to four approaches to exploring the dimensionality of poverty: pragmatic; data driven; theoretically informed and experiential.

Pragmatic dimensionality

Few studies of multidimensional poverty have had the luxury of collecting new data (Townsend [1979] and Bramley and Bailey [2017] are important exceptions). Instead, most have had to rely on existing data. The UNDP's Human Development Index (HDI), introduced in 1990, is a case in point that effectively marks the beginning of multidimensional measurement on a global scale. Not a measure of poverty, it has been described as an achievement index averaging national 'achievement' with respect to three dimensions of development or functioning: income expressed as per capita GDP; health – life expectancy at birth; and educational attainment measured by literacy and rates of enrolment (Chakravarty and Majumder, 2005).

The HDI highlights several generic issues with respect to multidimensionality. First, it is not comprehensive in terms of the set of dimensions. It reflects Sen's idea that what a person can do rather than what they can purchase is the 'ultimate metric of well-being' (Sen, 1985; 1987); but does not include all capabilities alluded to by Sen and elaborated by Nussbaum (2000) (Anand and Sen, 1994). Second, by averaging scores across three dimensions it assumes perfect substitutability between dimensions such that a low score on one dimension can be fully offset by a high score on another. It also assumes that each dimension has the same weight or is equally important. This, in turn, raises the question: important for what? In the context of the HDI, this issue has been discussed mainly in relation to the differential policy goals of nation states but, in a broader sense, weighting has to do with the dimensions that contribute most to the characterisation of poverty.

If the HDI is an index of a national achievement, the UNDP's Human Poverty Indicator (HPI), employed between 1997 and 2010, was an index of a national failing. Like the HDI, it was a national level indicator and calculated as the unweighted sum of three indicators but negative ones: mortality rate (by age 40), illiteracy and economic deprivation (measured by access to health care and safe water and the incidence of child malnourishment). Conceptually, it is simply the inverse of the HDI which was, as noted, an attempt to operationalise Sen's concept of well-being. The HPI, therefore, was a measure of low well-being, or 'ill-being', rather than poverty per se. Moreover, lack of data meant that, like the HDI, the HPI relied on macro rather than individual-level data and therefore described the attributes of countries rather than the characteristics of people living in poverty in those countries.

This last deficiency was rectified by the 2010 introduction of the MPI which is also a descendant of Sen's capability thinking but is based on individual-level data. Ten indices relate to what are essentially the same three dimensions as the HPI: education, health and living standard and deprivation cut-offs, or thresholds established normatively for each indicator prior to aggregation (Table 4.1). Each dimension is arbitrarily accorded equal weight with the individual indices weighted proportionately. The cross-dimensional poverty threshold is set at weighted deprivations summing to one – above which people are considered to be in multidimensional poverty.

Table 4.1 The dimensions, indicators, deprivation cut-offs and weights of the 2018 MPI

Dimension of poverty	*Indicator*	*Deprived if . . .*	*Weight*
Health	Nutrition	Any adult under 70 years of age or any child for whom there is nutritional information is undernourished	$\frac{1}{6}$
	Child mortality	Any child has died in the family in the five-year period preceding the survey	$\frac{1}{6}$
Education	Years of schooling	No household member aged 10 years or older has completed six years of schooling	$\frac{1}{6}$
	School attendance	Any school-aged child is not attending school up to the age at which he/she would complete class 8	$\frac{1}{6}$
Living standards	Cooking fuel	The household cooks with dung, wood, charcoal or coal	$\frac{1}{18}$
	Sanitation	The household's sanitation facility is not improved (according to SDG guidelines) or it is improved but shared with other households	$\frac{1}{18}$
	Drinking water	The household does not have access to improved drinking water (according to SDG guidelines) or safe drinking water is at least a 30-minute walk from home, round trip	$\frac{1}{18}$
	Electricity	The household has no electricity	$\frac{1}{18}$
	Housing	At least one of the three housing materials for roof, walls and floor is inadequate: the floor is of natural materials and/or the roof and/or walls are of natural or rudimentary materials	$\frac{1}{18}$
	Assets	The household does not own more than one of these assets: radio, TV, telephone, computer, animal cart, bicycle, motorbike or refrigerator, and does not own a car or truck	$\frac{1}{18}$

Source: Alkire and Jahan (2018).

The headcount ratio is then adjusted by poverty intensity which is taken to be who are multidimensionally poor multiplied by the average share of deprivations among the people counted as being in poverty (Alkire and Foster 2011).

By 2018, estimates of poverty based on the MPI were available for 105 countries covering 77 per cent of the global population (UNDP, 2018). According to the MPI measure, 1.3 billion people are estimated to be in poverty – about 560 million more than indicated by the $1.90/day standard – of whom 83 per cent live in sub-Saharan Africa and South Asia. Even so, the statistical correlation coefficient between the MPI and the $1.90/day standard is quite high (0.81) meaning that some 65 per cent of the between-country variation in the MPI can be explained in terms of differences in income poverty.

The MPI is an advance in that it permits sub-group and sub-national analyses. Eighty-five per cent of people live in rural areas, but with marked within-country variations; in South Africa, for example, poverty rates in rural areas average 12 per cent compared to 2.3 per cent in urban ones; in Bolivia the risk of poverty is 11 times greater in rural areas (44.1) than in urban ones (4.1 per cent) (OPHI, 2018). In Indonesia, poverty is as low as 2% in the metropolitan city of Jakarta but rises to 45 per cent in the eastern province of Papua. Lack of nutrition contributes most to the MPI in sub-Saharan Africa, South Asia, East Asia and the Pacific while education is more important in the Arab states. Half of the people identified as being in poverty multidimensionally are aged under 17, with one-third of all children being counted as poor. In 35 countries located in sub-Saharan Africa, more than half of all children are MPI poor.

At the national level, there are a few dramatic differences between the MPI and the $1.90/day index. The headcount multidimensional poverty rate in Niger is 91 per cent compared with 26 per cent, in Mali it is 78 per cent compared to 28 per cent and in Guinea, 62 per cent compared to 27 per cent; in each case educational disadvantage contributes disproportionately to the overall MPI. In Mexico, where the income poverty rate is quite low at 3.9 per cent, the somewhat higher MPI (6.3 per cent) is associated with a low health status, but in South Africa the dimension of health appears to contribute to the MPI poverty rate being lower than the income rate (8 per cent compared to 19 per cent). South Africa is not the only country recording an MPI that is significantly lower than the $1.90/day income threshold but, with the exception of Malawi, they all have small populations: Lesotho, the Kingdom of Eswatini and the island Republic of Sao Tome and Principe.

While the MPI is a marked improvement over the HPI in that it is measured at household level, it has a number of serious deficiencies. First, each dimension is accorded equal weight; this is not a result of the Alkire-Foster algorithm for devising the index but simply the absence of any justifiable reason for differential weighting. Second, with equal weighting, setting the threshold for poverty at a weighted deprivation of a third means that a person who is deprived on just one dimension could count as poor. This solution has been criticised by some because it means that the MPI includes people who are unidimensionally poor rather than multidimensionally poor (Bedük, 2018a). Be this as it may, the experience of poverty of three people, each poor on a separate dimension, is likely to be very different, arguably different in kind. Moreover, the MPI has two further categories, both pragmatic or, indeed, arbitrary: severe poverty (people deprived on at least half of the weighted indicators) and vulnerability (people deprived on 20 to 33 per cent of weighted indicators). It is not altogether clear which is the best indicator of poverty.

Third, the three dimensions health, education and living standards have ambiguous causal relationships with each other and with low income; they are in fact inherited from the HDI as dimensions of well-being rather than poverty. This can be seen when Alkire and Jahan (2018, 8) write of deprivation 'depending upon the joint *achievements* of household members' (italics added); poverty – the 736 million people living on less than $1.90/day – is to a large degree structural, not the result of individual actions.

Ironically, given Sen's influence on the MPI, it has been criticised as being 'inconsistent with the Universal Declaration of Human Rights principles of indivisibility, inalienability, and equality' (Arndt et al., 2018). The indicators (taken as rights) are not indivisible because, if weighted (which in most formulations they are not), they are explicitly ranked; they are not inalienable in that it is possible to be better-off because increases in deprivation can be offset by gains on others; and they are unequal in 'that welfare losses among worse-off subgroups can be outweighed by gains among better-off' ones. While technically true, these criticisms apply to all known methods that seek to establish the number of people who are multiply deprived and by how much. (First-order dominance techniques which escape these criticisms have only been used to establish rankings between countries, not spot estimates of poverty rates [Permanyer and Hussain, 2018].)

Finally, the dimensionality of MPI is severely constrained by available data. The architects of the MPI had initially considered including the additional dimensions of empowerment, work, environment, safety from violence, social relationships and culture among others (Alkire and Santos, 2014). And when the index was being revised for 2018, they tried but failed to locate adequate data to add dimensions covering environmental issues, work and employment, and security (Alkire and Jahan, 2018). That said, it remains an open question why these dimensions should have been added rather than the others and, indeed, whether they are attributes that are intrinsic to poverty rather than causes or consequences.

Data-driven dimensionality

The challenge of determining what dimensions are intrinsic to poverty is arguably circumvented by methods that derive dimensionality from analysis of data. Several different approaches have been used (Kakwani and Silber, 2008; Asselin, 2009; Alkire et al., 2015). One set, including the application of discriminant analysis, latent class analysis and factor mixture modelling, premises the existence of social categories comprising people who are poor and those who are not and seeks a set of dimensions that characterise their difference (Barnes et al., 2017; Catalan, 2017; Lee and Joung, 2014; Nolan and Whelan, 2007). A second set of approaches, using principal components analysis, factor analysis and structural equation modelling, explores the patterning of personal attributes to identify clusters or dimensions of attributes and the relationships between them (Ferragina et al., 2017; Ningaye et al., 2013; Wagle, 2008). A third approach treats poverty as a fuzzy concept (Lemmi and Betti, 2006; Neff, 2013).

The first approach requires an a priori definition of poverty to be established before determining the full set of indicators. Nolan and Whelan (2007) chose to use an income definition, dividing a sample of the population in Ireland into four groups defined in terms of income thresholds: below 50 per cent of median equivalised income, between 50 per cent and 60 per cent, between 60 per cent and 70 per cent, or over 70 per cent. They found that the lowest income group was more likely to experience 'economic strain' (measured as an 11-item scale recording lack of food, clothing, holidays, etc.) and to report it being difficult to make ends meet. But, in addition to these variables that were included in the analysis, people in poverty experienced consumption deprivation, poor housing conditions and neighbourhood degradation; all dimensions of poverty previously identified using factor analysis (Whelan et al., 2001).

This coincidence of deprivations raises the question as to whether a person who is multiply deprived is experiencing more severe poverty than someone with fewer deprivations. This might not be true if some dimensions were weighted as being more severe than others. Moreover, different scores on different dimensions might define different types of poverty. In terms of measurement, Atkinson (2003) distinguished the union approach, in which a person is counted as being poor if they are deprived on just one dimension, from the intersection approach that requires them to be deprived on every dimension. This distinction has major consequences which can be illustrated with reference to the countries of Europe (Whelan et al., 2014). Computing the adjusted headcount ratio as proposed by Alkire and Foster (2011) but with the dimensions of economic strain, consumption deprivation, poor housing facilities, housing deterioration and neighbourhood degradation, as suggested by Whelan et al., (2001), poverty rates vary from 3 per cent in Iceland to 31 per cent in Romania. Taking the union criteria of being poor on any dimension significantly increases recorded rates: those for Iceland and Romania increasing to 31 per cent and 82 per cent, respectively, although the correlation with the adjusted headcount rate is very high (0.96). In contrast, the intersection definition cuts poverty rates to close to zero, 0.6 per cent in Romania with the highest value of 1.6 per cent in Latvia. This points to the existence of many kinds of poverty experience but also suggests that, with many dimensions in play, the intersection approach to measuring multidimensional poverty is not particularly helpful.

Working in Scotland, Barnes et al. (2017) used latent class analysis to characterise different forms of poverty using 20 indices covering resources, participation and quality of life together with 12 socioeconomic variables. They recognised 13 forms of poverty, four each affecting families with children, five affecting elders and four affecting people of working age without children. Among the last group, to illustrate, 'insecure singles' are mostly men, typically aged between 25 and 44, who

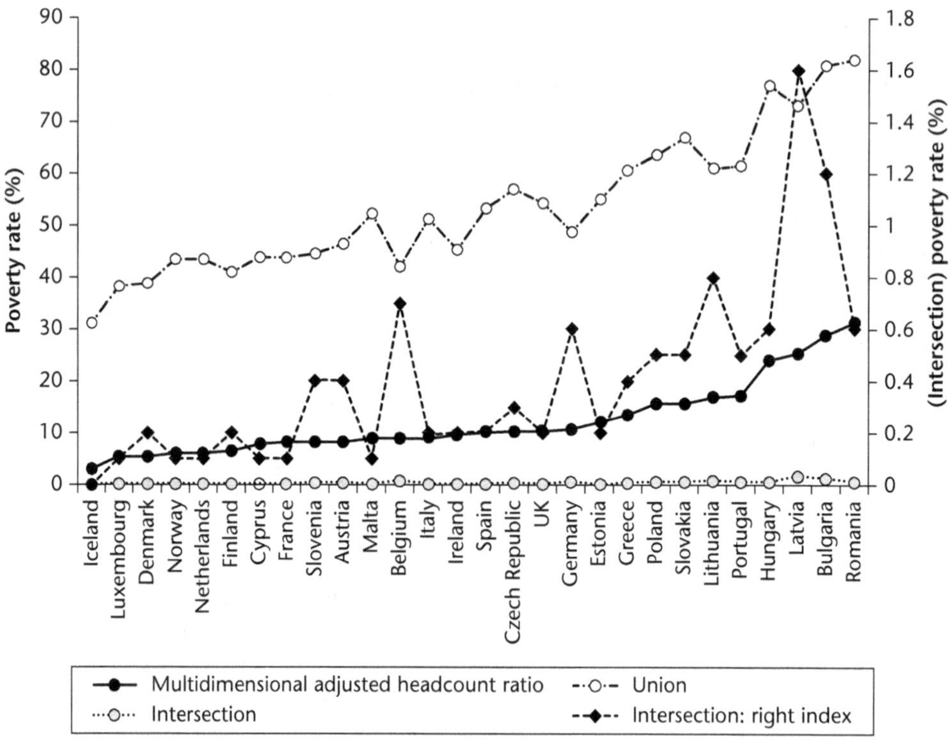

Figure 4.1 Impact of union and intersection approaches to multidimensionality.

Source: Adapted from Whelan et al. (2014).

suffer multiple disadvantages with respect to health, education, housing and employment. They differ markedly from a group categorised as the 'new poor' who are typically older, and although they have low incomes mostly own their own homes and have some savings, suggesting that many of them may be new to poverty and either in a transitional phase or only temporarily poor.

Factor analysis techniques peruse the pattern of correlations between variables such as poverty indicators to identify a reduced set of meta-variables; dimensions that adequately account for the variation between the original variables. Some techniques are purely descriptive, others assume the existence of latent dimensions and yet others test a hypothesised set of relationships. They relax the assumption of non-correlation between dimensions inherent in the simple additive formulation of the MPI (Alkire and Foster, 2011).

Tomlinson et al.'s (2008; Tomlinson and Walker, 2009) analysis of UK data is both typical of this approach, using structural equation modelling to establish the existence of underlying dimensions, but unique in plotting the change in dimensions over time and suggesting how they might differentially influence child outcomes. The five dimensions portray poverty as a deeply stressful experience dominated by financial pressure that is comprised of two sub-dimensions: financial strain – the difficulty of making ends meet on a day-to-day basis; and material deprivation, the product of long-term financial hardship (Figure 4.2). This is compounded by psychological stress (anxiety, depression, lack of confidence and social dysfunction), social isolation and a lack of civil participation (measured in the model as active engagement which explains the negative coefficient). The negative experience of poverty is further exacerbated by environmental factors: bad housing conditions and a deprived neighbourhood.

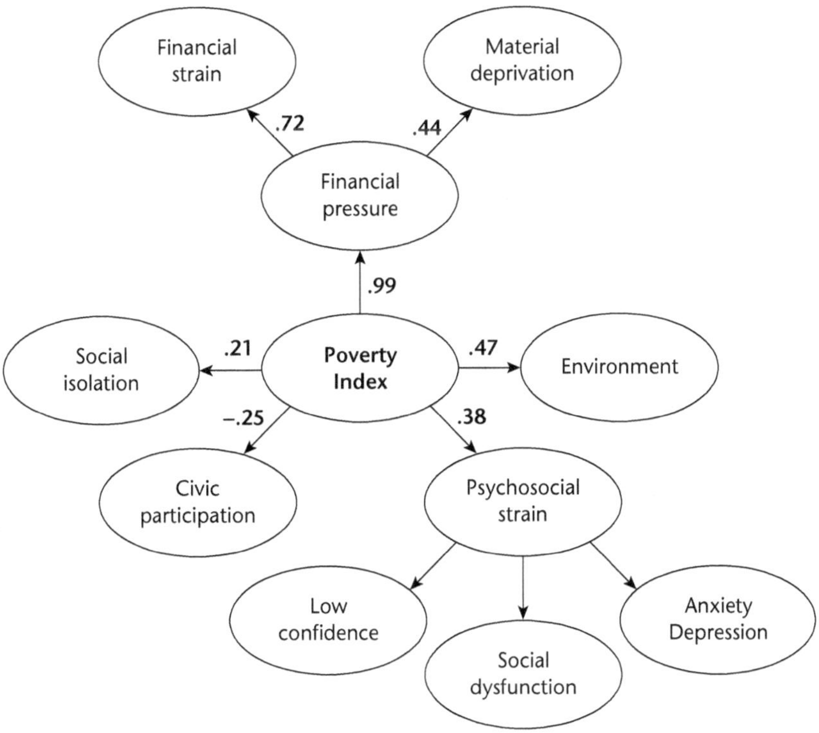

Figure 4.2 The structure of multidimensional poverty, United Kingdom, 2000s.

Source: Adapted from Tomlinson and Walker (2009).

Tomlinson et al. (2008) report trends in poverty in the United Kingdom between 1991 and 2003, a period bifurcated by the 1997 election of a Labour government committed to economic growth and enhanced social welfare. Income poverty measured in absolute terms fell throughout the period whereas relative income poverty declined only after the arrival of the Labour government. The multidimensional measure revealed a more complex story because it included both absolute and relative components. The income components were measured in real terms, thereby reducing the extent to which people could be lifted out of poverty by economic growth alone. The measures of material deprivation were socially salient but not weighted to take account of their social significance, while indices of strain are measured in absolute terms. Multidimensional poverty fell throughout the period, driven more by reductions in financial strain and material deprivation than by increases in income per se. People found it easier to manage and gained more by way of increased material living standards than increases in income would imply. Noting that the reduction in financial strain occurred before the increased government investment in welfare, it is at least possible that living standards rose due to increased borrowing, a precursor to the credit crunch and the Great Recession which was to follow. Although remaining a salient component of multidimensional poverty, psychological strain, civic participation and social isolation were largely stable throughout the period.

Poverty is known to reduce children's life chances in the long term, but the various dimensions of poverty also appear to be associated with current well-being, conceptualised as comprising four dimensions: home life; educational orientation; self-worth; and behavioural traits (Tomlinson and Walker, 2009). Financial strain experienced by adults seems to affect all four dimensions of child well-being while material deprivation is associated with just two: increasing risky behaviour and negatively affecting home life. Environmental poverty, comprising poor housing conditions and a deprived neighbourhood, is associated with reduced quality of home life, low self-worth and risky behaviour. However, the social isolation of the head of household, sometimes interpreted as a measure of social capital, has no bearing on any of the four indicators of child well-being.

The literature is remarkably silent as to whether there is any causal ordering among the dimensions of poverty. This may reflect the point-in-time estimations of poverty or the unstated presumption that the dimensions of poverty are simply intrinsic. Reflecting the tradition that prioritises income, Tomlinson et al. (2008) and Ferragina et al., 2013) forced the inclusion of income even though this added little to the fit of the model since its effect was largely captured by the dimensions of financial stress and/or deprivation. Wagle (2005, 2007) interprets as causal the loadings between dimensions in a five-dimensional structural equation model comprising capability, economic well-being and economic, civic and political inclusion. Fitted to data from both Nepal and the USA, capability, measured as educational underachievement was taken to be causal, directly and indirectly, with respect to all other dimensions. However, economic well-being did not appear to influence any of the other dimensions in Nepal and directly only civic inclusion in the USA. This, Wagle (2005) acknowledges, is surprising given the centrality of economic resources and income in most discussions of poverty. However, Wagle approached measurement through the lens of capability, with the result that she may have measured well-being rather than poverty per se.

Point-in-time measures of multidimensional poverty obviate the need to reflect on causality; they simply describe the multiple dimensions that are simultaneously experienced by people in poverty. However, the longer the window of observation, the more likely some dimensions will appear as causes or consequences of others (Tomlinson and Walker, 2010). For some scholars, especially followers of Amartya Sen, distinguishing the order of causality is unimportant (Alkire, 2018; cited in Godinot and Walker, 2019); yet for others it is critical in distinguishing poverty, the product of a lack of resources, from other kinds of well-being (Bennett, 2018). Indeed, while there is considerable similarity in the dimensions of poverty that emerge from primarily data-driven studies (itself possibly a product of the limited range of variables available for inclusion in analysis), there is still disagreement as to the dimensions that are intrinsic to poverty, both necessary and sufficient as delimiters of poverty. Bedük (2018a) blames this on weak theorising.

Theoretically informed dimensionality

Bedük's response to the undertheorising of multidimensionality is to develop a measure derived as closely as possible to Townsend's (1979) concept of poverty as relative deprivation; the dimensions of poverty 'are considered as different needs required for being able to perform social roles, while relevant deprivation items represent the conditions of life required to satisfy these needs' (Bedük 2018b, p. 15). The needs identified are psycho-social as well as physiological, and each one, if unmet for reasons other than free choice, becomes evidence of poverty. This is a strong version of the union approach to multidimensionality and Bedük goes further by arguing that if an individual item or component of need is missing then a person is in poverty according to that dimension and hence is in poverty overall. The needs are also universal and absolute while, analogous to Sen's (1983) distinction between capabilities and functionings, the conditions of life required for them to be met are relative to societal norms and vary by individual circumstances.

Bedük's theoretical proposition specified four dimensions. The first was lack of basic needs covering food deprivation, shortage of clothing, 'habitancy' (precarious housing circumstances), fuel poverty and poor housing conditions. Inability to afford healthcare services, health promoting goods, a healthy diet and life style and to avoid harmful environments constituted the second dimension, with education being the third, comprising the impossibility of affording facilities, goods and services to support educational achievement. The final dimension identified by Bedük related to social relationships and leisure, namely the lack of resources to participate in the relevant activities.

Using data from EU-SILC, a survey with comparable data for 29 European countries, the four dimensions of 'basic goods', 'health', 'education' and 'leisure and social relationships' were, respectively, captured by 11, eight, six and five binary indicators. Each indicator marked the presence or absence of necessities, mostly conditioned on a respondent's admission that they could not afford them. Poverty was defined as any person unable to afford one or more items, but a correction was applied to reduce measurement error by including persons with income lower than 60 per cent of median earnings who reported financial strain and excluding those with higher incomes who did not report financial stress.

The multidimensional measure resulted in a headcount rate of 25 per cent, one percentage point higher than the EU's risk of poverty and social exclusion measure. It typically returned a lower figure in more affluent countries and similar or higher rates in less affluent countries (except Bulgaria and Romania) (Figure 4.3). As well as identifying more people in low-income countries, the new measure was more likely to capture those disadvantaged risk groups with lower resources and needs: for example, persons unemployed, with health problems or caring for children. The four dimensions were, as anticipated, highly correlated, but the associations were far from perfect, suggesting that poverty is indeed cumulative and, therefore, possibly not a latent phenomenon. Moreover, income poverty, less than 60 per cent of median income, accounted for only about 6 per cent of the cross-national variation in the multidimensional measure. The two most closely related dimensions were 'basic needs' and 'leisure and social relationships' (correlation [R] = 0.77), while 'education and health needs' were the least closely associated (R = 0.43), no doubt a product of life-cycle

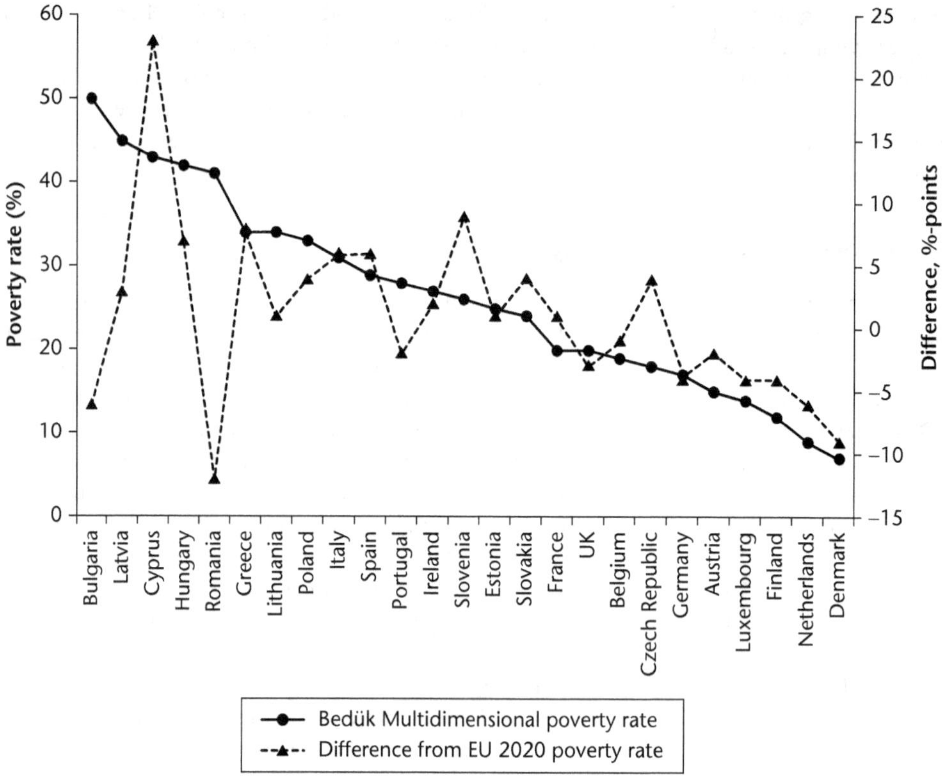

Figure 4.3 A theoretically informed measure of multidimensional poverty, 2009.

Source: Adapted from Bedük (2018b).

differences. Taking account of people poor on just one dimension increased the headcount rate by an unweighted average of 21.8 percentage points, ranging from 10 per cent in Bulgaria to 30 per cent in Slovakia.

At face value, Bedük's theoretically derived measure is remarkably like the MPI with three common dimensions: basic needs, health and education. However, Bedük's index is more clearly related to poverty rather than well-being for it measures resource constraints on achievement rather than achievements per se. Moreover, the fourth dimension is important in capturing Townsend's focus on exclusion from social participation as being central to understanding of poverty. Townsend, though, hypothesised a relationship between income and participation, with the latter falling proportionately with decreasing income until a point when participation falls markedly; it was this 'breakpoint' that Townsend sought and used as his poverty threshold. Ferragina et al. (2013) have sought to identify such a breakpoint, testing a multidimensional measure designed to simulate Townsend's thesis, comprising deprivation, participation and trust. They fitted a structural equation model to UK data derived from interviews conducted in 2009 and 2010 for the Understanding Society project. They found participation fell with income, but rather than participation collapsing at a particular level, they found that it stabilised because social norms demanded, and institutions required, a basic level of participation. Below the threshold, empirically established at the 30th percentile, people had to choose between basic necessities and participation in social activities and, unlike those above the floor, extra income did not translate into greater participation, to measurably increased living standards or to higher levels of trust.

Bedük's work is important is demonstrating the contribution individual dimensions make to the distribution of poverty, bringing into sight some groups and excluding others, affecting the types and numbers of people counted as poor and pointing potentially to different anti-poverty programmes. Poverty construed in this way is heterogeneous with scores on individual dimensions potentially defining different kinds of poverty. Moreover, the sensitivity of poverty counts to the dimensions which are included, emphasises the need to choose the correct dimensions.

Experiential dimensions

Bedük selected dimensions based on Townsend's theorising but he was nevertheless frustrated by lack of available data, bemoaning his inability to include needs related to caring, and personal and political security. The data that are collected, especially by governmental and inter-governmental agencies, reflect political and administrative logic rather than the reality of poverty. While perhaps inevitable, this runs counter to the aspirations under-pinning the SDGs and the target of reducing 'poverty in all its dimensions' since the UN's *Guiding Principles on Extreme Poverty and Human Rights* affirm the need to: 'ensure the active, free, informed and meaningful participation of persons living in poverty at all stages of the design, implementation, monitoring and evaluation of decisions and policies affecting them' (CHR, 2012, 10).

Two recent studies have sought to make real these aspirations. Both challenge the 'top-down' measures of poverty that 'reflect the values and priorities of experts rather than those of women and men who have experienced poverty' (Wisor et al., 2015), both use participatory methods working with people experiencing poverty, and both involve research in multiple countries (Bray et al. 2019). However, whereas one ('the ATD4W study' [Godinot and Walker, 2019]) involves people in poverty in all stages of the research including design, data collection, analysis and report writing, the other (Wisor et al., 2015) limits their participation to the formative stages of discussing possible dimensions of poverty.

The Wisor et al. (2015; Bessell 2015) study was conducted in Angola, Fiji, Indonesia, Malawi, Mozambique and the Philippines and, after interviews with key informants, involved group discussions with men and women experiencing poverty who, among other activities, were asked about the 'sorts of things' they took into consideration when thinking whether 'someone was poor or not'. From these deliberations, some 27 dimensions were identified, eight of which were commonly mentioned. These dimensions were subsequently mapped onto pre-existing survey questions and included in an interview survey to be ranked by respondents. Analysis led the research team to propose an additive measure of poverty based on 15 dimensions with each dimension transformed into a five-point interval scale.

The ATD4W study was conducted by research teams in Bangladesh, Bolivia, France, Tanzania, Britain and the USA, each comprising a majority of people in poverty together with practitioners and academics. The project was funded by the French and sponsored by ATD Fourth World, a France-based NGO that developed the core methodology, merging of knowledge. This postulates that different forms of knowledge are held by people with direct experience of poverty, by academics and by practitioners and that it is only by merging this knowledge that a full appreciation of the dimensions is possible. Hence, representatives of the three groups were recruited in each country, assigned to work in peer groups to identify and detail the dimensions of poverty with representatives coming together in mixed peer groups to exchange views and to seek a possible consensus. Groups often met multiple times with people in poverty frequently spending over 20 hours in discussion and in preparation for the merging of knowledge events. National representatives in the three peer groups subsequently met together in a week-long meeting in France in which 72 separate dimensions were considered, evaluated and reduced to nine that were manifest in all six countries.

The outcomes of the ATD4W and Wisor studies are compared in Table 4.2, prioritising the former on the grounds that it more closely reflects the UN *Guiding Principles*. While there is considerable overlap, there is notably more agreement between the ATD4W study and the initial groupwork with people in poverty reported in the Wisor study, than between the former and the final Wisor measure which was influenced by existing survey questions, and perhaps by the academic 'peer-group' perspective of the research team. The ATD4W study suggests that while poverty is about lack of resources, the implications of this lack are more important, and these are often felt directly through emotions such as shame, worry, fear, guilt, depression and anger. Hence, the dimension of 'suffering in body, mind and heart' and its proactive counterpart 'struggle and resistance' emerge as dominant, shaping the core experience of poverty along with the feeling of powerlessness. Similarly, discussion about the content of the dimension 'insufficient and insecure income' focused on the inability to meet basic needs and social obligations, to keep harmony within the family, the denial of choice, the risk of indebtedness and temptation to engage in risky behaviour in order to survive. Many of the key material dimensions of the Wisor study – food, shelter, clothing, sanitation, healthcare and education – are embraced in the ATD4W study within the single dimension: 'material and social deprivation'.

Three dimensions from the ATD4W study, each referring to relational aspects of poverty, were also present in the early discussions with people in poverty in the Wisor study. 'Disempowerment' refers to the extent to which people in poverty feel that they have no control over their lives, feel exploited and oppressed. As already noted, disempowerment was viewed as a core component in the experience of poverty and is intimately connected with the dimensions of 'institutional and social maltreatment'. The former reflects the stigmatising and discriminatory behaviour of state and other institutions, lack of access to justice and being the victims of corruption and violence, while social maltreatment speaks directly to inter-personal relationships and to being excluded, isolated, humiliated and discriminated against by others in the community. A further relational dimension not highlighted in the Wisor study is the social contribution made by people living in poverty that often goes unrecognised. Survival requires knowledge, skills and resourcefulness and most people in poverty are successful in many roles if not in the economic sphere.

To conclude, poverty is inherently multidimensional, experienced as the simultaneous, multiple, immediate consequences of inadequate resources that may have long-term effects and which undoubtedly make the future more uncertain and riskier. However, as explained above, it remains unclear how best to conceptualise and measure this complex and dynamic phenomenon. Indeed, it may be necessary to conceptualise multiple phenomena if combinations of scores on the various dimensions serve to describe different kinds of poverty. However, debates about how to operationalise, aggregate and weight dimensions may be immaterial if the dimensions are poorly specified. To date, the dimensions used have been constructed from pre-existing data and fail to capture the emotional and relational dimensions of poverty identified by people living in poverty. The challenge, of course, is to find measures of these new dimensions and ATD4W, with support from OECD, is currently attempting to do this with the help of people living in poverty. In so doing, they may shift the focus away from poverty conceptualised as the absence of material things to a recognition of the suffering of people, and to resistance: the skills necessarily honed to ensure physical and social survival in a hostile world. It is, after all, the experience of people in poverty that we are seeking to characterise with dimensions.

Table 4.2 Comparison of dimensions from IDM and ATD4W studies

*ATD4W study**		*Individual Deprivation Measure (IDM) (Wisor study)*		
Type	*Dimensions*	*Proposed for poverty index*	*Dimensions most commonly mentioned in focus groups*	*Dimensions less frequently mentioned in focus groups*
Privations	• Lack of decent work • Insufficient and insecure income • Material and social deprivation	• Respect and freedom from risk at work • Time use • Food • Water • Shelter • Sanitation • Health care • Education • Energy/cooking fuel • Clothing/personal care	Lack of employment and income-earning opportunities • Insufficient or low-quality food • Inadequate and low-quality shelter with low-quality household assets • Inadequate clothing especially by the standards of the community • Inadequate sanitation • Lack of adequate, clean or easily accessible water • Lack of quality education, for oneself and one's children • Lack of adequate health care for oneself and household or frequently falling ill	• Begging and degrading or dangerous work • Being subject to economic exploitation • Being subject to sexual exploitation • A lack of ownership of assets and secure property rights to those assets • Lack of electricity
Relational dynamics	• Institutional maltreatment	• Family planning		• Inadequate transport and roads • Lack of access to social services or other basic services • Inability to access financial services and productive capital or being heavily in debt

(continued)

Table 4.2 (continued)

ATD4W study[*]		*Individual Deprivation Measure (IDM) (Wisor study)*		
Type	*Dimensions*	*Proposed for poverty index*	*Dimensions most commonly mentioned in focus groups*	*Dimensions less frequently mentioned in focus groups*
				• Being displaced • Lacking official identification and citizenship • Not having secure access to contraception and/or sanitary pads • Being subject to violence
	• Social maltreatment	• Family relationships • Violence		• A lack of support from friends and family
	• Disempowerment	• Voice in the community		• Inability to contribute to others or to participate in community functions
Core experience	• Suffering in body, mind and heart • Struggle and resistance			
		• The environment		

Note: * The ATD4W study suggests that each dimension can be modified according to a person's identity, location, the timing and duration of poverty, cultural beliefs and by the environment and environmental policies.

References

Alkire, S. (2018) Personal Communication, 5 March.

Alkire, S. and Foster, J. (2011) Counting and multidimensional poverty measurement. *Journal of Public Economics, 95*(7), 476–487.

Alkire, S. and Jahan, S. (2018) 'The New Global MPI 2018: aligning with the Sustainable Development Goals'. New York: HDRO Occasional Paper, United Nations Development Programme (UNDP).

Alkire, S. and Santos, M. (2014) Measuring acute poverty in the developing world: robustness and scope of the Multidimensional Poverty Index. *World Development, 59*: 251–274.

Alkire, S., Roche, J., Ballon, P., Foster, J., Santos, M. and Seth, S. (2015) *Multidimensional Poverty Measurement and Analysis*. Oxford: Oxford University Press.

Anand, S. and Sen, A. (1994) 'Human Development Index: methodology and measurement'. Human Development Report Office Occasional Paper 12, United Nations Development Programme, New York.

Arndt, C., Mahrt, K., Hussain, M. and Tarp, F. (2018) A human rights-consistent approach to multidimensional welfare measurement applied to sub-Saharan Africa. *World Development, 108*: 181–196.

Asselin, L.-M. (2009) *Analysis of Multidimensional Poverty: Theory and Case Studies*. Dordrecht: Springer.

Atkinson, A. (2003) Multidimensional deprivation: contrasting social welfare and counting approaches. *Journal of Economic Inequality*, 1: 51–65.

Barnes, M., Stares, S., Wood, C., Vibert, S. and Lord, C. (2017). *Poverty in Perspective: A Typology of Poverty in Scotland*. Edinburgh: The Scottish Government.

Bedük, S. (2018a) Missing the unhealthy? Examining empirical validity of Material Deprivation Indices (MDIs) using a partial criterion variable. *Social Indicators Research*, 135(1): 91–115

Bedük, S. (2018b) 'Identifying people in poverty: a multidimensional deprivation measure for the EU'. Barnett Papers in Social Research, 18–03, Oxford.

Bennett, F. (2018) *Submission from Fran Bennett to UN Special Rapporteur*. Available at www.ohchr.org/Documents/Issues/. . ./IndividualSubmissions/FranBennett.docx (accessed 15 July 2019)

Bessell, S. (2015) The Individual Deprivation Measure: measuring poverty as if gender and inequality matter. *Gender & Development*, 23(2): 223–240.

Bramley, G. and Bailey, N. (eds) (2017) *Poverty and Social Exclusion in the UK, Volume 2: The Dimensions of Disadvantage*. Bristol: Policy Press.

Bray R., De Laat, M., Godinot, X., Ugarte, A., and Walker, R. (2019) *The Hidden Dimensions of Poverty*. Pierrelaye: International Movement ATD Fourth World.

Catalan, H. (2017) Multiple deprivation, severity and latent sub-groups: advantages of factor mixture modelling for analysing material deprivation. *Social Indicators Research*, 131: 681–700.

Chakravarty, S. and Majumder, A. (2005) Measuring human poverty: a generalized index and an application using basic dimensions of life and some anthropometric indicators. *Journal of Human Development*, 6(3): 275–299.

CHR (2012) *Guiding Principles on Extreme Poverty and Human Rights*. Geneva: Office of the High Commissioner for Human Rights. Available at www.ohchr.org/Documents/Publications/OHCHR_ExtremePovertyandHumanRights_EN.pdf (accessed 5 July 2019).

EC (2010) *Europe 2020: A Strategy for Smart, Sustainable and Inclusive Growth*. Brussels: Communication from the Commission, COM(2010) 2020 final, 3.3.2020.

Ferragina, E., Tomlinson, M. and Walker, R. (2013) *Poverty, Participation and Choice: The Legacy of Peter Townsend*. York: Joseph Rowntree Foundation.

Ferragina, E., Tomlinson, M. and Walker, R. (2017) Poverty and participation in twenty-first century multicultural Britain. *Social Policy and Society*, 16(4): 535–559.

Godinot, X. and Walker, R. (2019, in press) Poverty in all its forms: determining the dimensions of poverty through merging knowledge. In H. Henning and R. Lepenies (eds) *Dimensions of Poverty*. Heidelberg: Springer.

Kakwani, N. and Silber, J. (eds) (2008) *Quantitative Approaches to Multidimensional Poverty Measurement*. London: Palgrave-Macmillan.

Lee, H.-J. and Joung, E. (2014) Multidimensional poverty in Korea: utilizing a Latent Class Analysis. *Social Welfare Policy*, 41(2): 1–25 (in Korean).

Lemmi, A. and Betti, G. (eds) (2006) *Fuzzy Set Approach to Multidimensional Poverty Measurement*. New York: Springer.

Neff, D. (2013) Fuzzy set theoretic applications in poverty research. *Policy and Society*, 32(4): 319–331.

Ningaye, P., Alexi, T. Y. and Virginie, T. F. (2013) Multi-poverty in Cameroon: a structural equation modeling approach. *Social Indicators Research*, 113(1): 159–181.

Nolan, B. and Whelan, C. T. (2007). On the multidimensionality of poverty and social exclusion. In S. P. Jenkins and J. Micklewright (eds), *Inequality and Poverty Re-examined* (pp. 146–165). Oxford: Oxford University Press.

Nussbaum, M. (2000) *Women and Human Development: The Capabilities Approach*. New York: Cambridge University Press.

OPHI (2018) *Global MPI 2018*. Oxford: Oxford Poverty and Human Development Initiative. Available at https://ophi.org.uk/multidimensional-poverty-index/global-mpi-2018/ (accessed 5 July 2019).

Permanyer, I. and Hussain, M. (2018) First order dominance techniques and multidimensional poverty indices: an empirical comparison of different approaches. *Social Indicators Research*, 137(3): 867–893.

Rowntree, B. S. (1908) *Poverty: A Study of Town Life*. London: Macmillan and Co. New and cheaper 4th edition (1908 reprint).

Sen, A. (1983) Poor, relatively speaking. *Oxford Economic Papers*, 35: 153–169.

Sen, A. (1985) *Commodities and Capabilities*. Amsterdam: North–Holland.

Sen, A. (1987) *Standard of Living*. Cambridge: Cambridge University Press.

Tomlinson, M. and Walker, R. (2009) *Coping with Complexity: Child and Adult Poverty*. London: CPAG.

Tomlinson, M. and Walker, R. (2010) *Recurrent Poverty: The Impact of Family and Labour Market Changes*. York: Joseph Rowntree Foundation.

Tomlinson, M., Walker, R. and Williams, G. (2008) Measuring poverty in Britain as a multi-dimensional concept, 1991 to 2003. *Journal of Social Policy*, 37(4): 597–620.

Townsend, P. (1979) *Poverty in the United Kingdom: A Survey of Household Resources and Standards of Living*. London: Allen Lane and Penguin Books.

UNDP (2018) *The 2018 Global Multidimensional Poverty Index (MPI)*. Available at http://hdr.undp.org/en/2018-MPI (accessed 5 July 2019).

Wagle, U. (2005) Multidimensional poverty measurement with economic well-being, capability, and social inclusion: a case from Kathmandu, Nepal. *Journal of Human Development*, 6(3): 301–328.

Wagle, U. (2007) Poverty in Kathmandu: what do subjective and objective economic welfare concepts suggest? *Journal of Economic Inequality*, 5(1): 73–95.

Wagle, U. (2008) *Multidimensional Poverty Measurement: Concepts and Applications*. New York: Springer.

Walker, R. (2019) Measuring absolute poverty: shame is all you need. In H. Gaisbauer, G. Schweiger and C. Sedmak (eds) *Absolute Poverty in Europe: Interdisciplinary Perspectives on a Hidden Phenomenon* (pp. 97–118). Bristol: The Policy Press.

Whelan, C., Layte, R., Maître, B. and Nolan, B. (2001) Income, deprivation and economic strain: an analysis of the European Community Household Panel. *European Sociological Review*, 17: 357–372.

Whelan, C., Nolan, B. and Maître, B. (2014) Multidimensional poverty measurement in Europe: an application of the adjusted headcount approach. *Journal of European Social Policy*, 24(2): 183–197.

Wisor, S., Bessel, S., Castillo, F., Crawford, J., Donaghue, K., Hunt, J. et al. (2015) *The Individual Deprivation Measure: A Gender-Sensitive Approach to Poverty Measurement*. Melbourne: International Womens' Development Agency.

5

Multidimensional poverty across the life cycle

The United States as an empirical example

Roger White[1] *and Thomas Bailleul*

Introduction

The first Sustainable Development Goal (SDG) is to "End poverty in all its forms everywhere" by 2030 (UN DESA, 2016). A portion of this goal, identified as Target 1.2, reads: "By 2030, reduce at least by half the proportion of men, women and children of all ages living in poverty in all its dimensions according to national definitions." Addressing this target and, thus, working to achieve the corresponding SDG requires identification of both the incidence of impoverishment *and* the specific types of deprivation that are suffered. Effectively, this necessitates a multidimensional summation of the breadth and depth of poverty within a society. Consequently, detailed information on poverty incidence and intensity is essential for the design and implementation of public policies that seek to reduce or eliminate deprivation-related suffering.

Traditional poverty measures typically represent the proportion of the population that falls below a predetermined minimum level of income or consumption (i.e., a poverty line). The popularity of these measures may follow from ease of calculation and interpretation and/or because the data necessary for calculation are often readily available. Unfortunately, these traditional measures indirectly represent poverty incidence. As such, they fail to indicate the ways in which an individual is poor (i.e., deprived) beyond that of insufficient income and/or consumption.[2] Alkire and Santos (2014) note several shortcomings of indirect poverty measures. For example, consumption is unlikely to be uniform across individuals and it is possible that deprivation involves limited access to non-market products (e.g., clean water, sanitation, electricity, etc.). Likewise, consumers may face different product prices or may vary in terms of how well a given level of income equates to the alleviation of deprivation. These shortcomings suggest that public policies seeking to raise incomes, even if successful, may fail to address all forms of deprivation. Additionally, because many materially deprived individuals do not also experience income- or consumption-based poverty, traditional poverty measures often undercount deprivation. In a few words, the emphasis on income and/or consumption, coupled with a lack of detail regarding non-monetary forms of deprivation, hinders the usefulness of traditional poverty measures for the formulation of public policies that seek to reduce deprivation/poverty.

As a direct measure of deprivation, the Multidimensional Poverty Index (MPI) addresses the deficiencies of traditional measures and serves as a useful complement to indirect poverty measures. Alkire and Foster (2011), for example, consider three dimensions (i.e., health, education, and standard of living) that are each comprised of related indicators that represent whether an individual is deprived in terms of the corresponding dimension. For instance, the health dimension often identifies individuals who are disabled and those who do not receive proper nutrition as being deprived. Similarly, individuals are considered deprived in terms of education if they lack a basic education or have a limited ability to speak the common language of the society in which they live. Note that while these dimensions and indicators are not directly related to income or consumption, their incidence would render an individual significantly deprived (i.e., poor). An example of this would be a person who earns a salary above a predetermined poverty line but does not speak English well and has no access to healthcare. A traditional income-based approach would not consider this individual to be poor or deprived despite their apparent shortcomings. A contrary example would be an individual whose income is slightly below the poverty line but who has access to most other social amenities. This individual would be considered poor and could even become the recipient of social welfare benefits such as food stamps and educational waivers. Ultimately, a unidimensional approach to poverty analysis relies entirely on one factor – typically, income – to infer deprivation across all other dimensions of life. Such reliance risks an inefficient allocation of assistance to the poor.

While the MPI explicitly acknowledges that poverty is often multidimensional, it also allows for presentation of deprivation at an aggregate level. For example, we find the 2017 MPI value for the U.S. was equal to 0.0295, with 7.1 percent of the population identified as being multidimensionally poor and an average intensity of deprivation (i.e., deprivation score) among this cohort equal to 0.4157.[3] Further, considerable variation is identified across age groups; 6.0 percent of residents below the age of 18 years were multidimensionally poor as compared to 5.8 percent and 5.0 percent of those aged 18–64 years and 65 or more years, respectively. Average deprivation scores varied to a much lesser extent, ranging from 0.4089 for those aged 65 or more years and 0.4115 for those 18 to 64 years of age to 0.4193 for those below the age of 18 years. By contrast, the official income-based U.S. poverty rate in 2017 was 12.3 percent (Fontenot et al., 2018). Considering differences across age categories, the poverty rate for residents below the age of 18 years was 17.5 percent while the rates for those aged 18–64 years and 65 or more years were 11.2 percent and 9.2 percent, respectively (Fontenot et al., 2018).

Decomposition of the MPI into four component dimensions and 11 associated indicators allows for an even more detailed depiction of deprivation.[4] For example, nearly one-third of the U.S. population in 2017 (31.3%) experienced health-related deprivation. More specifically, in that year, 9 percent of the population lacked health insurance coverage, 14.4 percent of the population received benefits from a public nutrition assistance program, and 13.1 percent were disabled.[5] The information regarding the health dimension, coupled with similar information for the other three dimensions, permits individuals to be classified according to the extent of their multidimensional deprivation and, thus, allows measurement of the incidence and intensity of deprivation at the national level.

The ability to identify and target the specific forms of deprivation that contribute to poverty is of immense value in the formulation of related public policies. To further illustrate this point and to demonstrate the usefulness and applicability of the MPI to policy formulation, we present an empirical example of multidimensional poverty in the U.S. across the life cycle (i.e., for each age (0–95 years)).[6] Using annual, individual-level data from the American Community Survey Public Use Microdata Sample (ACS-PUMS) for the period from 2008 through 2017, we identify deprivation incidence across the 11 indicators for each observation (i.e., individual) in our data. We then weight and aggregate the resulting indicator values to produce corresponding values for each of the four dimensions. These dimension values are then used to quantify the incidence and intensity of multidimensional poverty and to calculate the MPI.

Crucial to a multidimensional analysis of poverty is the choice of the dimensions and indicators considered. The capability approach (Sen, 1980; Alkire, 2009) is often referred to when discussing the selection of these components. The capability approach considers what individuals are able to achieve which, of course, is a relative determination since what can be achieved, and the resources necessary to achieve, vary across individuals.[7] A simple example is that of a disabled individual perhaps requiring equipment to allow them to be as mobile as an otherwise comparable able-bodied person. A similar example would be a worker who requires a higher daily caloric intake as compared to someone who is not in the labor force (Clark, 2005). This level of relativity can become significantly more complicated when we consider dimensions of culture and/or societal freedoms that may hinder access to resources. It is because of this relativity that assessing an individual's ability to achieve, and thus, well-being at a societal level is most comprehensively determined through a multidimensional analysis of well-selected dimensions and indicators.

To further illustrate the relativity of multidimensional poverty analysis, Table 5.1 lists the dimensions and indicators (i.e., questions/criteria) used in three prior studies. We see considerable differences both across studies of developing economies and between studies of developing and developed economies. For example, Alkire and Seth (2009) use access to electricity, clean drinking water, and improved sanitation to represent standard of living among residents of India. Rippin (2016), to the contrary, uses mobility and household characteristics when examining deprivation in Germany. Somewhat similarly, perhaps because democracy and civil rights are generally more prominent in developed societies, empowerment is frequently included in studies of poverty in developing countries but is less commonly included in studies of developed countries. Last, studies involving developing countries often use body mass index (BMI) values as poverty cutoffs in the health dimensions but do not use access to health care or health insurance as indicators (Batana, 2008; Alkire and Seth, 2009). This may be due to a lack of comprehensive micro-level data on health care access in developing countries. In sum, dimensions and indicators are not absolute. Much to the contrary, assessing poverty accurately requires consideration of individuals' capabilities when selecting the indicators and dimensions for which individuals may suffer deprivation.

Considering the dire circumstances of the poor in developing countries (as reflected by the indicators listed in Table 5.1), it may seem counterintuitive to examine poverty in a developed economy. However, we note that extreme poverty persists even in these settings. For example, Azpitarte (2012) finds incidences of multidimensional poverty in both the U.S. and Spain and particularly among younger individuals, minorities, and those with lower levels of education. Whelan et al. (2014) examine 20 non-monetary indicators of deprivation in 28 European countries and document poverty in each country despite there being fluctuation consistent with national income levels. Variation in the incidence and intensity of multidimensional poverty in the U.S. is also identified by Mitra and Brucker (2015) who report differences in poverty across demographic cohorts with Hispanics, blacks, single-parent households, immigrants, disabled persons, and persons in metropolitan areas being most likely to experience multiple deprivations. Similarly, White and Yamasaki (2017) report that foreign-born individuals in the U.S. are significantly more likely to experience multidimensional poverty as compared to the native-born.

In the next section, we discuss the calculation of the MPI. This is followed in by our empirical example, while the final section summarizes and discusses public policy implications.

Table 5.1 Multidimensional poverty dimensions and indicators from select studies

Author(s)	*Dimensions*	*Indicators (i.e., Deprived if . . .)*
Alkire and Seth (2009), India	Air quality	household does not have a separate room for a kitchen and uses coal, lignite, charcoal, wood, straw/shrubs/grass, agricultural crop, animal dung, and other* for fuel.
	Assets	individual does not own a refrigerator, motorcycle, car, phone, mattress, table, color television, computer, thresher, or tractor.
	Child status	the main reason child does not go to school is: school is too far away, transport not available, further education not considered, child is required for household work, child is required for work on farm, child is required for outside work, school costs too much, no proper school facilities, not safe to send girls to school, no female teacher, child is required for care of sibling, child is not interested in studies, repeated failures in school, child was married, child did not get admission, or other*.
	Education	maximum years of education completed by any household member is less than five years.
	Empowerment	any woman in the household does not have right to go alone in the market, health facility, or somewhere outside of village.
	Health	the lowest BMI among the women in the household is less than 18.5 kg/m^2.
	Livelihood	individual and her partner both fall into the following occupation categories: unemployed, agricultural laborer, plantation laborers, simple laborers, and new workers seeking jobs.
	Living standard	individual lives in a kachha house.
		individual has no access to electricity.
	Water and sanitation	sources of water are an unprotected well and/or spring, river, dam, lake, pond, stream, tanker truck, cart with small tank, bottled water, or other*.
		household uses one of the following: pit latrine without slab, no facility/uses bush/field, composting toilet, dry toilet, or other*.
Batana (2008), sub-Saharan Africa	Assets	individual has no access to electricity.
		individual does not have at least a radio.
		individual does not possess a refrigerator.
		individual does not have a motorcycle or a car.
		floor of individual's household is natural or rudimentary.
		individual does not own a phone.
		Individual's domicile does not have at least piped water.
		Individual's domicile does not have at least a flush toilet.

	Empowerment	individual has no say on visits to family and relatives.
	Health	Individual's BMI is less than 18.5 kg/m^2.
	Schooling	individual has completed less than six years of education.
Rippin (2016), Germany	Education	individual has completed fewer than nine years of schooling.
		individual has completed at least nine years of schooling but neither graduated nor earned a training qualification.
	Employment	individual is unemployed, earns poor wage (below minimum), or is time poor (excessive labor hours).
	Health	subjective health condition is either poor or bad.
		individual answers "yes" to one of the following: Have trouble climbing stairs? Health limits activities? Achieved less due to health? Achieved less due to mental health? Reduced social contacts due to health?
	Housing	condition of house needs improvement or is critical.
		household lacks bath/shower, warm water, heating, or toilet.
		living space is below minimum (defined as 45 m^2 for the first individual and 15 m^2 for every additional person). (Infants below 2 years of age are excluded.)
	Income	disposable income is below the "breadline" (defined as 356 euros for the first adult plus 322 euros for each additional adult in household).
	Mobility	public transport is more than 20 minutes away and no car is available.
		neighborhood is either insecure or dangerous.

Note: * "Other" is provided as an alternative option that represents an equal level of deprivation.

Calculating the Multidimensional Poverty Index

The Alkire and Foster (2011) (AF) method permits identification of whether individuals suffered deprivation in terms of the indicators and corresponding dimensions.[8,9] We employ ACS-PUMS data that span the period from 2008 through 2017. Our data set includes 31,077,061 individual-level observations, effectively providing a one percent sample, annually, of the U.S. population.[10] Figure 5.1 identifies the specific indicators and dimensions that we consider while providing a schematic representation of MPI calculation. From the indicator and dimension series, we construct individual-specific deprivation scores which are employed in conjunction with population weights to identify the incidence and the intensity of multidimensional poverty in the U.S. as well as MPI values.[11]

The MPI is calculated as the product of multidimensional poverty incidence (*H*) and the average intensity of deprivation that is experienced by those who are considered to be multidimensionally poor (*A*). Whether an individual is categorized as multidimensionally poor is based on the value of their deprivation score (DS). The DS is a weighted sum of deprivations experienced. Equal weighting is applied to the dimensions of education, health, housing costs, and standard of living. As there are four dimensions, each is weighted as 25 percent of the DS. Similarly, equal weights are applied to the indicators within each dimension so that they sum to 25 percent. For example, the education dimension is comprised of two indicators, each of which is weighted by 12.5 percent, while the standard of living dimension consists of four indicators that are equally weighted at 6.25 percent. Individuals for whom the DS value is equal to or greater than one-third are identified as multidimensionally poor.

Alkire (2009) notes that explanations and justifications for selected indicators and dimensions are often missing from studies of multidimensional poverty. With this in mind, we now discuss the indicators and dimensions presented in Figure 5.1. Looking to the four dimensions, we see the two indicators that comprise the education dimension are whether the individual has failed to attain a high school diploma or lives in a limited English-speaking household. Such indicators are logical since Americans who do not complete high school commonly experience limited employment opportunities and those who have a limited ability to speak English suffer the detrimental impacts of linguistic isolation. The health dimension assesses whether an individual is disabled, receives benefits from the Supplemental Nutrition Assistance Program (SNAP), or lacks health insurance.[12] These indicators allow us to interpret whether an individual experiences disadvantages in everyday life through physical, mental, or other disability, is experiencing a shortage of food, or has limited or no access to medical care. The housing costs dimension includes whether an individual is living in a crowded house (i.e., a house with more residents than rooms) and if their housing costs are equal to or greater than 50 percent of their monthly household income. These indicators address the impact of living in crowded homes and the economic hardship of high housing costs. Last, the standard of living dimension indicates whether an individual's income level is such that they are experiencing income poverty, if the individual lacks complete kitchen/plumbing facilities, if they lack a private vehicle, and if they are unemployed.

To illustrate the calculation of the MPI, consider an individual living in a house that lacks complete plumbing facilities but who answers "no" to all other questions that correspond to the indicators presented in Figure 5.1. The DS for this person is 0.0625; thus, they are classified as "not deprived". Consider a second individual who lacks a high school diploma, is unemployed, lives in a crowded house, and lacks health insurance. This person's DS is 0.3958 (i.e., 0.125 + 0.0625 + 0.125 + 0.0833). Because the DS is greater than 0.33, this individual is identified

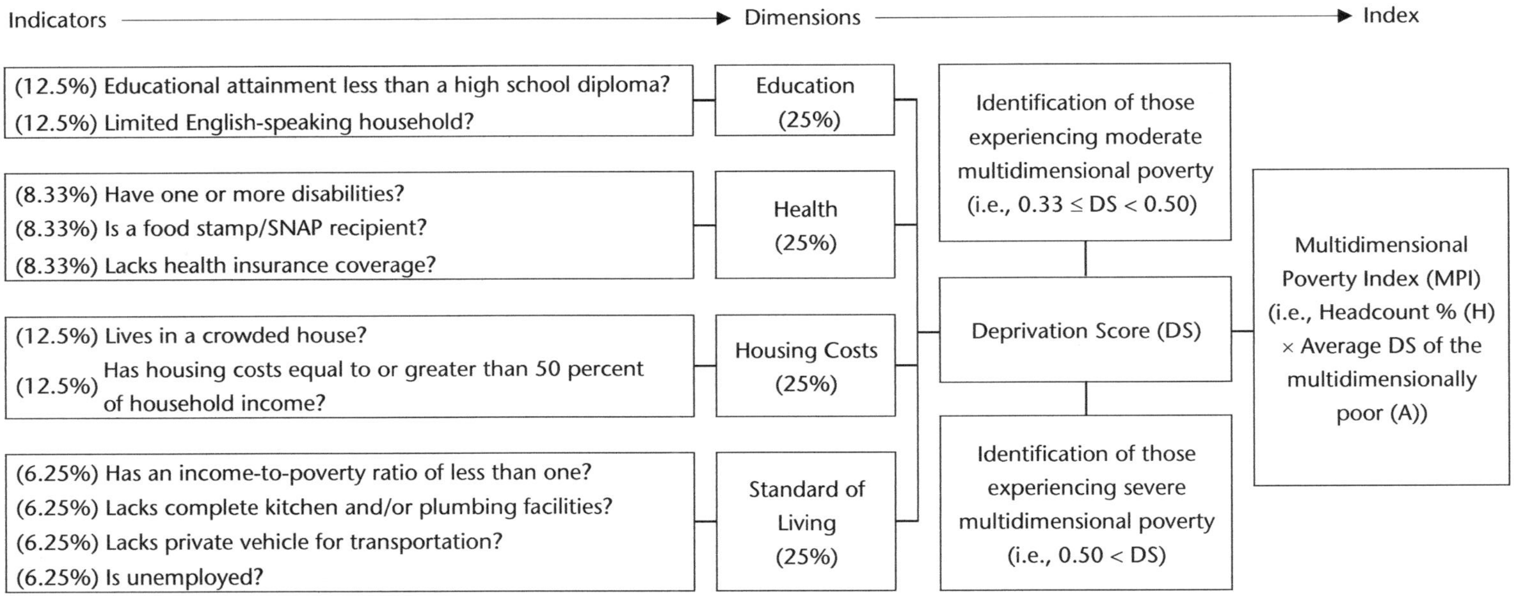

Figure 5.1 Indicators, dimensions, and construction of the Multidimensional Poverty Index for empirical example of the U.S.

as multidimensionally poor. Now consider a third individual who is disabled, lacks a private vehicle for transportation, and lives in a limited English-speaking household that is crowded and for which monthly costs exceed 50 percent of household income. The DS for this individual is 0.5208 (i.e., 0.0833 + 0.0625 + 0.125 + 0.125 + 0.125). This individual is also classified as multidimensionally poor. If these individuals constituted a society, then 66.67 percent (*H*) of all individuals are multidimensionally poor and the average DS (*A*) for these individuals is 0.4583. Thus, the MPI would equal 0.3055 (i.e., $H \times A$).

Turning attention to our data set, Table 5.2 presents frequency values for each of the dimensions and indicators that we use to construct our MPI series. During our reference period, about 6.8 percent of all observations in our data set are identified as experiencing multidimensional poverty. The most common forms of deprivation are health-related, but considerable shares of the population experienced deprivation in one or more of the remaining dimensions. All three indicators within the health dimension have frequency values of 12.8 percent or higher. Similarly, the values for the indicators that identify deprivation in terms of educational attainment, housing costs relative to monthly income, and income relative to the poverty line are all greater than 10 percent. For all other indicators, however, the frequency values are 6.5 percent or lower. Finally, as may be anticipated, we see stark differences in average frequency values between individuals categorized as being multidimensionally poor and those who are not. This is observed regardless of whether we consider the mean values of the dimension series or the indicator series.

In our empirical example, we produce MPI values and measures of multidimensional poverty incidence and intensity for each age (i.e., 0 years of age through 95 years or more). Also, for each dimension and indicator we document the incidence of multidimensional poverty

Table 5.2 Frequency values for dimensions and corresponding indicators (2008–2017)

		All obs.	*Multidimensionally poor?*	
			Yes	*No*
Dimension/indicator (indented)	*Weight/*	31,077,061	2,115,860	28,961,201
Education	*N* =25%	0.1331	0.7104	0.0830
• Educational attainment < a high school diploma	12.50%	0.1006	0.4424	0.0719
• Lives in a limited English-speaking household	12.50%	0.0483	0.4277	0.0141
Health	25%	0.3455	0.9030	0.2953
• Has one or more disabilities	8.33%	0.1288	0.2671	0.1164
• Lacks health insurance coverage	8.33%	0.1306	0.4233	0.1043
• Is a food stamp/SNAP recipient	8.33%	0.1519	0.5679	0.1144
Housing Costs	25%	0.1754	0.7279	0.1257
• Lives in a crowded house	12.50%	0.0649	0.3263	0.0414
• Has housing costs ≥ 50% of household income	12.50%	0.1234	0.5338	0.0864
Standard of Living	25%	0.1998	0.7074	0.1541
• Lacks complete kitchen and/or plumbing facilities	6.25%	0.0080	0.0335	0.0057
• Has an income-to-poverty ratio less than one	6.25%	0.1288	0.5861	0.0876
• Lacks private vehicle for transportation	6.25%	0.0646	0.3015	0.0433
• Is unemployed	6.25%	0.0400	0.1203	0.0328

Note: Authors' calculations based on ACS data (US Census, 2018). Values have been constructed using ACS-PUMS population weights.

across all ages. This permits examination of heterogeneity in multidimensional poverty across the life cycle. We also are able to identify the dimensions and specific indicators that primarily contribute to multidimensional poverty. Collectively, calculation of these values at each age allows the construction of a detailed portrait of multidimensional poverty in the U.S. Accordingly, our empirical example illustrates the usefulness of the MPI in the identification of deprivation, its intensity, and the forms of deprivation experienced by those who are multidimensionally poor.

The United States as an empirical example

Observed variation in deprivation across the life cycle

We begin our example with the illustration, in Figure 5.2, of age-specific MPI values and multidimensional poverty frequencies (i.e., headcount ratios, or incidences) and intensities. We see that MPI values range from as low as 0.021 at age 15 to as high as 0.05 at age 95 and above. Given the construction of the MPI (i.e., as the product of *H* and *A*), we can gain a better understanding of observed variation in the series by considering variation in the frequency (*H*) and intensity (*A*) series. Looking first to the intensity series, as compared to the MPI and frequency series, we see that values are relatively constant across the life cycle, ranging only between 0.39 and 0.43. This indicates that variation in the frequency of multidimensional poverty – which ranges from 0.051 to as much as 0.122 – largely accounts for the observed variation in the MPI series. While it is useful to know the extent to which these three series vary across ages and that variation in MPI values is primarily due to variation in multidimensional poverty frequency, more detailed information can be obtained by looking at the frequency values for each of the four dimensions.

Figure 5.3 depicts the frequency of multidimensional poverty over the life cycle for each of the four dimensions we consider. There are several items to note. First, at all ages, the frequency values for the health dimension are higher than those for any of the remaining

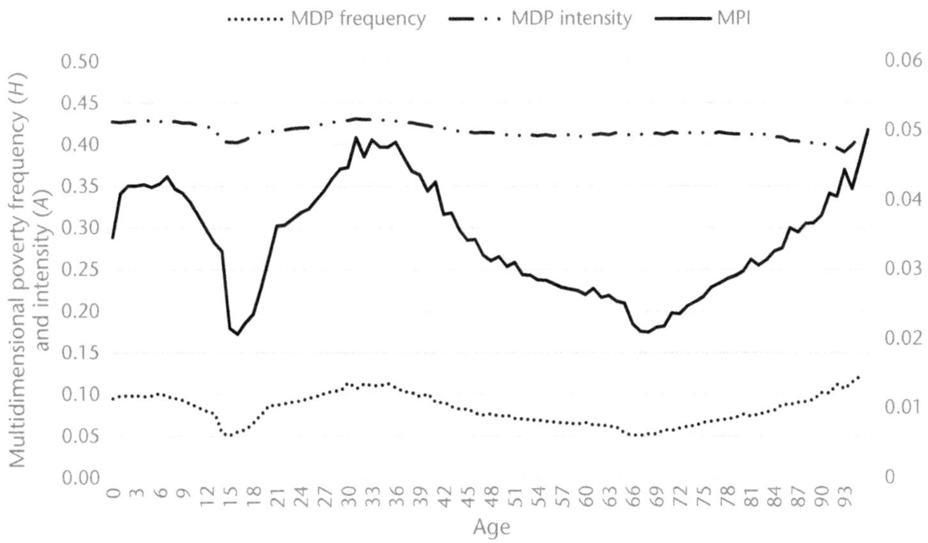

Figure 5.2 Multidimensional Poverty Index (MPI), frequency, and intensity, by age (2008–2017).

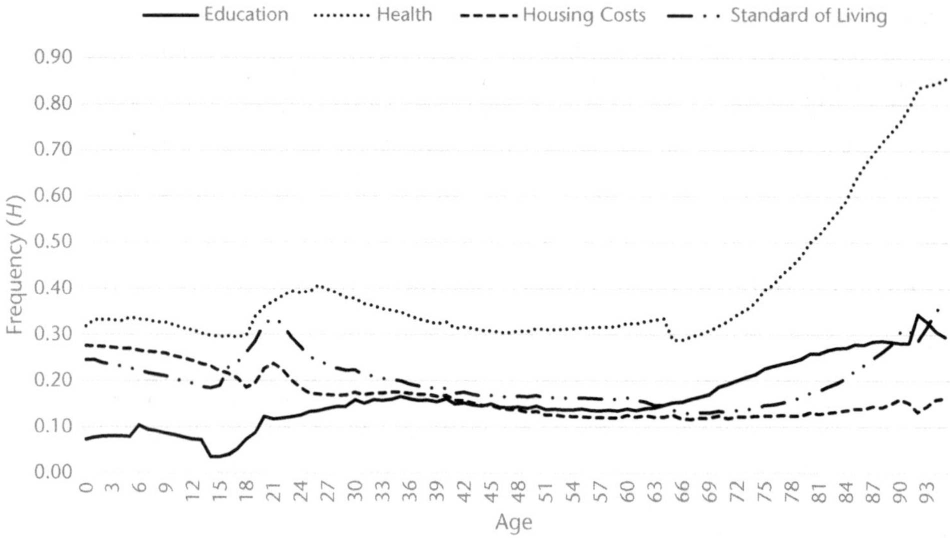

Figure 5.3 Multidimensional poverty frequencies by dimension and age (2008–2017).

three dimensions. Additionally, the health series follows a very interesting path. From birth until age 18, the values remain close to 0.3, indicating that about 30 percent of individuals suffer one or more disabilities, receive SNAP benefits, and/or lack health insurance coverage. However, beginning at age 19 the series sharply increases, reaching 0.41 by age 26. This is followed by a gradual decline, again reaching just about 0.3 by the late 40s before increasing slightly to 0.34 by age 64, after which we see sustained increases, finally reaching a value of 0.86 at age 95 and above. Since the marked increase in the series begins with adulthood, it coincides with the age at which individuals lose eligibility for state-level children's health insurance (i.e., SCHIP). When coupled with the significant decrease observed in the early to mid-60s when more individuals gain access to public health insurance (i.e., Medicare), the higher frequency values for the health dimension during the range of 18–64 years of age appears attributable, and perhaps to a large degree, to a continued reliance on employer-sponsored health insurance coverage in the U.S.[13]

Similar to the sharp increase that is observed in the health dimension series between the ages of 18 and 26 years and the subsequent period during which values generally decline, in Figure 5.3 we see marked increases in the values of the standard of living and housing costs series during the late-teen years before sustained declines begin in the early 20s. Intuitively, this may be attributable to relatively low early-career earnings. These latter two series follow similar, declining paths until about the age of 70 after which the standard of living series increases while the housing costs series remains largely flat. Exhibiting a somewhat different path, the education series dips during the teenage years and then steadily increases until the mid-30s. It then remains relatively constant until about age 60 when it again increases through age 95 and above. The education dimension is comprised of indicators that may largely remain fixed over time for the typical individual, while the indicator values and, thus, the dimension values for the health, housing costs, and standard of living dimensions may vary significantly more over the life cycle.

As with the values presented in Figure 5.2 for the MPI series and its frequency and intensity, the values depicted in Figure 5.3 provide interesting but incomplete information since each dimension is comprised of multiple indicators. To better understand the observed variation in multidimensional poverty frequency across dimensions and, thus, in the MPI across the life cycle, we look to the series that identify deprivation in specific indicators. Simultaneously, this also permits identification of the indicators for which individuals most frequently suffer deprivation which, as noted, is valuable information for policy makers. Panels (a) through (d) of Figure 5.4 illustrate the indicator frequencies for the education, health, housing costs, and standard of living dimensions, respectively.

a) Education dimension

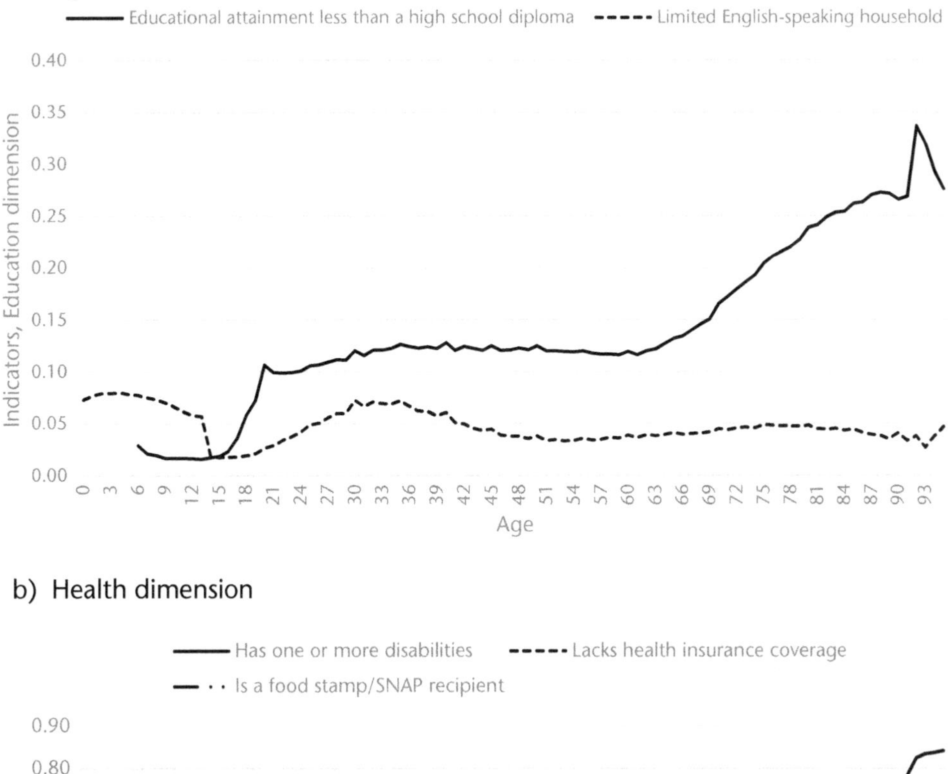

b) Health dimension

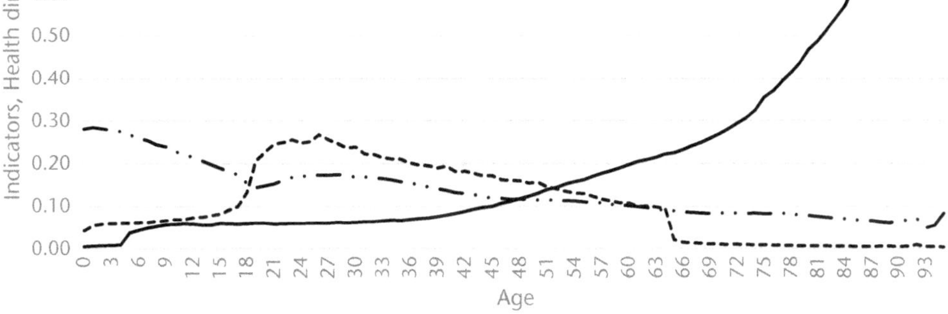

Figure 5.4 (continued)

(continued)

c) Housing Costs dimension

d) Standard of Living dimension

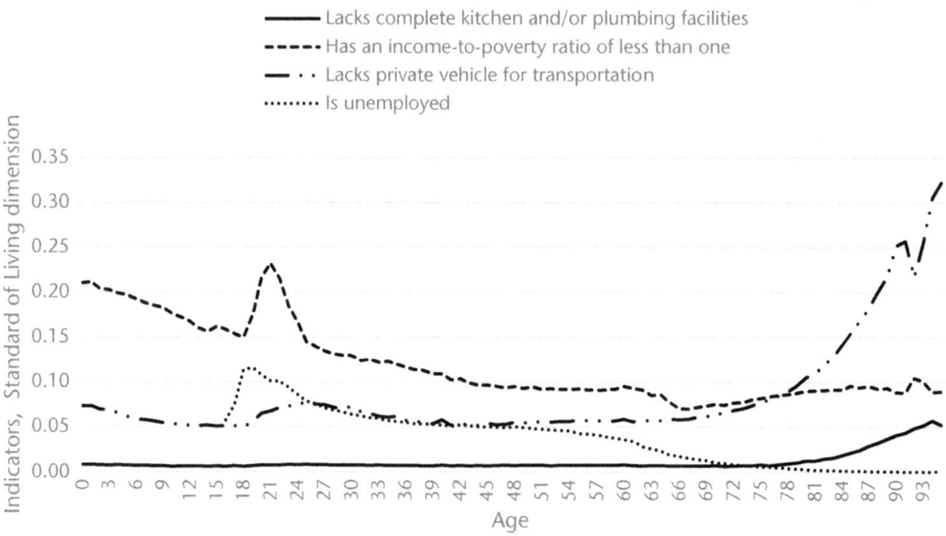

Figure 5.4 Multidimensional poverty frequencies by indicator and age (2008–2017): (a) education; (b) health; (c) housing costs; (d) standard of living.

Beginning with the indicators for the education dimension (panel a) and looking to the frequency of individuals living in limited English-speaking households, there is a significant decrease in the series at age 14. More than likely, this is an artifact of how the indicator is constructed. The corresponding variable in the ACS-PUMS data identifies a household as being limited in terms of English-speaking abilities if no one aged 14 years or older speaks English well. Since children younger than 14 years of age may speak English quite well but are not captured by the variable, the higher series values at ages below 14 years likely overestimate the extent to which English abilities are limited. The increase in the series values after age 18 are consistent with children who have English-speaking abilities leaving their limited English-speaking parents' homes. That the series peaks at age 30 at a value quite similar to those observed at ages below 10 years before generally declining until the late 40s and then remaining largely constant is consistent with this notion.

We note that the series that identifies the frequency at which individuals lack a high school diploma remains at a very low level until age 16 when it increases sharply until age 20 then rises slightly through the mid-30s before remaining stable until after age 60 when it again rises significantly. Educational attainment is not something that comes and goes. Once an individual earns a high school diploma that achievement remains with them. Thus, the higher values for this series after the age of 60 reflect not a change in educational attainment over the life cycle but instead a lower high school (or General Educational Development (GED) credential) completion rate during the period prior to about 1980 as compared to more recent years. Returning to the education dimension series in Figure 5.3, we can now see that the decline observed in the early teen years seems principally due to English-speaking abilities properly being accounted for. The subsequent increase in the series appears attributable to the occurrence of high school dropouts while the further rise that begins after age 60 is most likely representative of lower high school completion rates several decades prior.

Turning attention to panel (b), we see that the frequencies of the three indicators that comprise the health dimension follow very different paths. The SNAP recipient frequency series varies the least and decreases almost continuously with age. The health insurance coverage series follows a path quite similar to that of the overall health dimension until age 66. The disability series generally increases with age beginning in the mid–late 30s. Since the three indicator series are equally weighted in the health dimension series, it appears that the observed variation in the health dimension series is largely attributable to variation in the health insurance coverage indicator until about age 65 after which the increase in the health dimension series is due to individuals being more likely to suffer one or more disabilities.

Last, simultaneously considering the indicator frequency values presented in panels (c) and (d), we see three commonalities that correspond with individual income. First, in panel (c) there is a stark rise (and equally stark subsequent decrease) across the ages of 19 to 25 years in the frequency of individuals facing housing costs in excess of one-half of their monthly incomes. Likewise, in panel (d) we see sharp increases at the ages of 16 and 19, respectively, in the frequencies of unemployment and in whether an individual has an income that falls below the poverty level. In both instances, the series begins to decrease only a few years later. Where we do see more variation over the life cycle is in the series which represents lack of a private vehicle for transportation. This indicator is generally constant until about age 70 when it begins to increase rather consistently through age 95 and above.

Select counterfactuals

Our examination of variation in deprivation across the life cycle contributes to an enhanced understanding of poverty in the U.S.; however, to highlight the usefulness of multidimensional analysis, we also consider a number of counterfactuals from observed outcomes for the year 2017. During 2017, an estimated 23,081,748 individuals in the U.S. experienced multidimensional poverty. This equated to 7.09 percent of the population. Given the observed intensity of multidimensional poverty (0.4157), the U.S. MPI value for 2017 was 0.0295. In our first counterfactual, holding all else constant, we assume that no one in the U.S. lacked health insurance in 2017. The corresponding effect of this change on the intensity of multidimensional poverty is rather small, a decrease to 0.4139 (i.e., a decline in value of only 0.43%). The frequency of multidimensional poverty, however, declines by a much greater extent – a 17.21 percent decrease in the value, leading to an estimated frequency value of 5.87 percent. Thus, the corresponding MPI value falls to 0.0243 (i.e., a decrease equal to 17.63%). The implication is that universal health insurance coverage would have resulted in the DSs of an estimated 3,953,656 individuals falling below 0.33. This would have reduced the number of individuals who were categorized as being multidimensionally poor by 17.13 percent.

Table 5.3 illustrates the counterfactual scenario in which it is assumed that no one lacks health insurance as well as three other scenarios. Each of these three additional counterfactuals involves an assumed change in an income-related indicator.[14] Specifically, a scenario in which there is no income poverty, all else equal, corresponds with a 19.43 percent decrease in the number of individuals who suffer multidimensional poverty. An alternative scenario in which no one faces housing costs equal to or greater than 50 percent of their monthly income would reduce the number of individuals who experience multidimensional poverty by more than one-third (i.e., 33.95%). Lastly, if no individual requires SNAP benefits, the number of individuals who live in multidimensional poverty would be 42.24 percent lower than the observed level. The reductions posited under these three counterfactual scenarios represent decreases of at least 4.5 million to as many as 9.8 million in the number of people categorized as living in multidimensional poverty.

Assuming one additional scenario in which, again, all else is held constant, no one lacks health insurance *and* no one requires SNAP benefits, the frequency of multidimensional poverty would be only 2.93 percent (i.e., 58.7% lower than the observed level), and the estimated number of U.S. residents who experience multidimensional poverty would decrease from 23,081,748 individuals to only 9,535,173. The estimated effects of these simultaneous changes is a 58.7 percent decrease in the number of individuals who experience multidimensional poverty and, due to the SNAP program's income-to-poverty ratio eligibility requirement, a 100 percent

Table 5.3 Select counterfactuals

	Individuals experiencing MDP (estimated)	*MPI* (H × A)	*Frequency* (H)	*Intensity* (A)
Observed values, 2017:	23,081,748	0.0295	0.0709	0.4157
Counterfactual . . .				
No one lacks health insurance	19,128,092	0.0243	0.0587	0.4139
% change from observed levels:	−17.13%	−17.63%	−17.21%	−0.43%
No one has an income-to-poverty ratio < 1	18,596,692	0.0229	0.0571	0.4019
% change:	−19.43%	−22.37%	−19.46%	−3.32%
No one has housing costs > 50% of monthly income	15,245,866	0.0187	0.0468	0.399
% change:	−33.95%	−36.61%	−33.99%	−4.02%
No one requires SNAP benefits	13,330,869	0.0161	0.0409	0.3925
% change:	−42.24%	−45.42%	−42.31%	−5.58%
No one lacks health insurance or requires SNAP benefits	9,535,173	0.0115	0.0293	0.3945
% change:	−58.69%	−61.02%	−58.67%	−5.10%

decrease in the number of individuals who suffer income poverty.[15] While this does not achieve the first SDG (i.e., "End poverty in all its forms everywhere"), it would contribute significantly to the accomplishment of the related Target 1.2: "By 2030, *reduce at least by half* the proportion of men, women and children of all ages living in *poverty in all its dimensions* [emphases added] according to national definitions."

Some implications for public policy

While our empirical example serves to illustrate a multidimensional approach to the identification and measurement of poverty/deprivation, it simultaneously provides important information that can be used to craft public policies that seek to enhance societal well-being through the reduction or elimination of deprivation. Looking to the information presented earlier, it is noteworthy that six of the 11 indicators (i.e., receipt of SNAP benefits, living in a crowded house, having an income below the poverty level, lacking complete kitchen and/ or plumbing facilities, and being unemployed) are more closely related to income than are the remaining five indicators. This is important as public policies that aim to increase incomes and/or create jobs, if effective, may simultaneously reduce income- and consumption-based poverty levels and, in turn, address these income-related deprivations. In fact, given the observed variation across ages in the frequency values for these indicators, programs that seek to increase the incomes of young adults and seniors would be most impactful in terms of reducing deprivation that is related to the housing costs, income-to-poverty ratio, and unemployment indicators.

Deprivation related to the remaining five indicators (i.e., lacking a high school diploma, living in a limited English-speaking household, having one or more disabilities, lacking health insurance, and lacking a private vehicle for transportation) would less likely be remedied by public programs focused on income and/or employment. In these instances, alternative policy efforts are likely required. For instance, incentives to complete high school (e.g., free community college or undergraduate education for all high school graduates), improved funding for secondary schools across the system, provision of universal access to health insurance, and increased funding for and expansion of adult English language programs would all be expected to reduce corresponding deprivations. The remaining two indicators – lacking a private vehicle for transportation and having one or more disabilities – are found to affect seniors to a greater extent than younger individuals. Thus, implementing new (or expanding existing) programs that address/provide for senior transportation and that ease the burden related to living with disabilities would serve to ameliorate the impact of related deprivations.[16]

At the outset, we touted the multidimensional approach as a complement to more traditional poverty measures. To illustrate, we examine multidimensional poverty in the United States using annual data from the ACS-PUMS for the period from 2008 through 2017. Applying the Alkire-Foster method to our sample of 31,077,061 individual-level observations, we have detailed variation in MPI values, the frequency and intensity of multidimensional poverty, and the frequencies at which individuals suffer deprivation at both the dimension and indicator levels across the life cycle. Our findings provide a detailed portrait of multidimensional poverty in the United States. Considerable variation is found across the dimensions and indicators that comprise the MPI as well as across the life cycle. Additionally, a counterfactual analysis reveals that universal health insurance would have decreased the number of U.S. residents who lived in multidimensional poverty in 2017 by as many as 3.95 million individuals (i.e., a 17.1% reduction in incidence). Further, in a scenario where all U.S. residents have health insurance and have household income levels at/above 130 percent of the poverty level, the number of individuals suffering multidimensional deprivation would be decreased by up to 13.55 million individuals (i.e., a 58.7% decrease in multidimensional poverty incidence).

Our empirical example, while focused on the United States, is applicable for any country. Multidimensional poverty analysis carries the potential to provide detailed information on deprivation and, accordingly, to offer a starting point for the formulation and implementation of public policies that may reduce such deprivation. This opportunity is available both to developed and developing societies alike. An example is provided in Table 5.1, where the indicators and dimensions employed by Batana (2008) in the analysis of 14 African countries are presented. Knowing the extent of deprivation in each of the four dimensions (i.e., assets, empowerment, health, and schooling) provides information that may allow for targeted policy prescriptions. The ability to look deeper at indicators that comprise the dimensions provides even greater detail. Further, indicator- and dimension-level measurement that identifies deprivation also allows for follow-up measurement to assess the effectiveness of implemented policies and, thus, allows for more refined targeting of subsequent policy efforts.

Notes

1 Corresponding author. Email: rwhite1@whittier.edu. 13406 E. Philadelphia Street, Whittier, CA 90602 USA. Ph: (562) 907-4908. Fax: (562) 907-4956.
2 See Laderchi et al. (2003), Whelan et al. (2004, 2014), Alkire and Seth (2009), and Alkire and Santos (2014) for discussions of dissimilarities between various types of poverty measurement and limitations of unidimensional analysis.
3 While discussed in detail later in this chapter, we note here that MPI values range from 0 to 1 with higher values representing higher deprivation frequency and/or deprivation intensity. Likewise, deprivation scores range from 0 to 1. Individuals with scores equal to or greater than one-third are viewed as experiencing multidimensional poverty (UNDP, 2015). The range of MPI values across countries is considerable. Although calculated using different criteria (i.e., dimensions and associated indicators) and not directly comparable to the MPI value for the U.S., some examples of MPI values include Niger (2012): 0.591, South Sudan (2010): 0.581; Chad (2014/2015): 0.535; Cambodia (2014): 0.158; Guatemala (2014/2015): 0.134; The Philippines (2013): 0.038; Mexico (2016): 0.025; China (2014): 0.017; and Ukraine (2012): 0.001 (UNDP, 2018).
4 A listing of the dimensions and indicators used in our empirical example is provided in Figure 5.1 and in Table 5.2.
5 Since an individual may experience multiple forms of deprivation, the sum of the three listed population shares (i.e., 36.5%) is greater than the share of the population that experienced health-related deprivation (i.e., 31.3%).
6 Due to relatively small numbers of observations for each age beyond 94 years (as compared to younger ages), we aggregate all ages greater than 94 years to form a "95 years and above" cohort.
7 The capability approach views the needs of individuals and their ability to achieve those needs as relative. This is valuable, as it prevents the common mistake of interpreting poverty as a baseline statistic that a person fails to meet. The reality is that forms of deprivation (e.g., economic, social, health, etc.) may be interconnected and interdependent.
8 An alternative approach was employed by Wagle (2014) who applied both the AF method and a dimensional approach to data from the 2004 U.S. General Social Survey.
9 In fact, the AF method has proven so useful that it was adopted by the United National Development Programme in 2010 for use in the creation of the global MPI (UNDP, 2015). The method is based on a double-cutoff approach that includes vectors of deprivation cutoffs for each dimension and a poverty cutoff to identify a person as sufficiently deprived to be considered poor. Alkire et al. (2018) provide a detailed overview of the 2018 Global Multidimensional Poverty Index, including its construction (i.e., dimensions, indicator, and weights) and country coverage.
10 During our reference period, our annual samples vary in size from 3,000,657 observations (2008) to 3,190,040 observations (2017) with the average number of observations per year equal to 3,107,706. Effectively, each year represents a one percent sample of the U.S. population. We assume no repeat participation in the ACS during our reference period.

11 Calculation of deprivation scores allows for identification of individuals as "not deprived" or as experiencing multidimensional poverty. Although we do not delve so deeply into the data here, the deprivation scores can also be used to identify observations as "vulnerable to multidimensional poverty", "experiencing moderate multidimensional poverty", or "experiencing severe multidimensional poverty".
12 The SNAP was previously named the Food Stamp Program. SNAP provides food-purchasing assistance to individuals with incomes below 130 percent of the poverty level.
13 Even with implementation of the Affordable Care Act (i.e., Obamacare) and its individual mandate in January 2014, either due to an inability to afford an insurance plan or because they have opted to forgo insurance coverage and instead pay the associated financial penalty, an estimated 12.2 percent of U.S. adults lacked health insurance as of December 2017 (Auter, 2018).
14 We focus on these indicators to stress complementarity of the MPI measure with income-based measures of poverty.
15 While the obvious caveat that changes in these indicator values would be unlikely to occur without changes in additional indicator values, a look to the remaining indicators suggests that universal health insurance and income levels that are sufficiently high to render all ineligible for SNAP benefits would most likely result in positive effects (i.e., changes that correspond with reduced deprivation) for the remaining indicators.
16 Note that the MPI and its dimensions and indicators can inform policy only to the extent that data are available to represent deprivation. A relevant example is that our data do not represent access to child care provision. Further, even when data are available, the choice of indicators and dimensions is, to an unknown degree which may be situation-specific, influenced by political considerations. We contend that these shortcomings underscore the complementarity of multidimensional poverty analysis and traditional unidimensional poverty measurement.

References

Alkire, Sabina (2009) "The Human Development and Capability Approach", in Séverine Deneulin and Lila Shahani (eds.), *An Introduction to the Human Development and Capability Approach: Freedom and Agency* (pp. 22–48). Earthscan: London, UK and Sterling, Virginia.

Alkire, Sabina, and James Foster (2011) "Counting and Multidimensional Poverty Measurement", *Journal of Public Economics* 95(7): 476–487.

Alkire, Sabina, and Maria Emma Santos (2014) "Measuring Acute Poverty in the Developing World: Robustness and Scope of the Multidimensional Poverty Index", *World Development* 59: 251–274.

Alkire, Sabina, and Suman Seth (2009) "Measuring Multidimensional Poverty in India: A New Proposal", OPHI Working Paper No. 15, Oxford Poverty and Human Development Initiative, University of Oxford.

Alkire, Sabina, Usha Kanagaratnam, and Nicolai Suppa (2018) "The Global Multidimensional Poverty Index (MPI): 2018 Revision", OPHI MPI Methodological Notes 46, Oxford Poverty and Human Development Initiative, University of Oxford.

Auter, Zac (2018) "U.S. Uninsured Rate Steady at 12.2% in Fourth Quarter of 2017", *Gallup-Sharecare Well-being Index*. Online. Available: https://news.gallup.com/poll/225383/uninsured-rate-steady-fourth-quarter-2017.aspx. Accessed November 24, 2018.

Azpitarte, Francisco (2012) "Measuring Poverty Using Both Income and Wealth: A Cross-Country Comparison between the US and Spain", *Review of Income and Wealth* 58(1): 24–50.

Batana, Yele (2008) "Multidimensional Measurement of Poverty in Sub-Saharan Africa", OPHI MPI Working Papers No. 13, Oxford Poverty and Human Development Initiative, University of Oxford.

Clark, David A. (2005) "The Capability Approach: Its Development, Critiques and Recent Advances", GPRG Working Paper 32. Universities of Manchester and Oxford.

Fontenot, Kayla R., Jessica L. Semega, and Melissa A. Kollar (2018) "Income and Poverty in the United States: 2017", U.S. Census Bureau, Current Population Reports, P60–263. U.S. Washington, DC: Government Printing Office.

Laderchi, Caterina Ruggeri, Ruhi Saith, and Frances Stewart (2003) "Everyone Agrees We Need Poverty Reduction, But Not What This Means: Does This Matter?", WIDER Conference on Inequality, Poverty and Human Well-being. Online. Available: www.eldis.org/document/A13727. Accessed September 30, 2018.

Mitra, Sophie, and Debra Brucker (2015) "Income Poverty and Multiple Deprivations in a High-Income Country: The Case of the United States", Fordham University Department of Economics, Discussion Paper Series No. 2014–05, August.

Rippin, Nicole (2016) "Multidimensional Poverty in Germany: A Capability Approach", *Forum for Social Economics* 45(2–3): 230–255.

Sen, Amartya K. (1980) "Equality of What?", in Sterling M. McMurrin (ed.), *The Tanner Lectures on Human Value* (pp. 195–220). Salt Lake City: University of Utah Press.

United Nations Department of Economic and Social Affairs (UN DESA) (2016) *The Sustainable Development Goals Report 2016*. Online. Available: https://doi.org/10.18356/3405d09f-en. Accessed November 24, 2018.

United Nations Development Programme (UNDP) (2015) *2015 Human Development Report*. Online. Available: http://hdr.undp.org/sites/default/files/2015_human_development_report.pdf. Accessed September 20, 2018.

United Nations Development Programme (UNDP) (2018) *Human Development Indices and Indicators, 2018 Statistical Update*. New York: United Nations Development Programme.

United States Census Bureau/American FactFinder (US Census) (2018) *American Community Survey (Annual data, 2008–2017)*. U.S. Census Bureau's American Community Survey Office, 2018. Online. Available http://factfinder.census.gov. Accessed August 1, 2018.

Wagle, Udaya R. (2014) "The Counting-Based Measurement of Multidimensional Poverty: The Focus on Economic Resources, Inner Capabilities, and Relational Resources in the United States", *Social Indicators Research* 115(1): 223–240.

Whelan, Christopher T., Richard Layte, and Bertrand Maître (2004) "Understanding the Mismatch between Income Poverty and Deprivation: A Dynamic Comparative Analysis", *European Sociological Review* 20(4): 287–302.

Whelan, Christopher T., Brian Nolan, and Bertrand Maître (2014) "Multidimensional Poverty Measurement in Europe: An Application of the Adjusted Headcount Approach", *Journal of European Social Policy* 24(2): 183–197.

White, Roger, and Stacy Yamasaki (2017) "Multidimensional Poverty among the Native- and Foreign-born in the United States: Evidence from the 2010–2014 American Community Surveys", in Roger White (ed.), *Measuring Multidimensional Poverty and Deprivation: Incidence and Determinants in Developed Countries* (pp. 183–222). New York, NY: Palgrave Macmillan.

6
Preventing poverty

Adrian Sinfield

Introduction

'An ounce of prevention is worth a pound of cure' (Benjamin Franklin, 1735) is much quoted but the general failure to put more effort into prevention continues. 'Everyone says that prevention is better than cure, and hardly anyone acts as if he believes it' (Mackintosh on ill-health, 1953, p. 5). This is particularly true in tackling poverty. Lifting people out of poverty is also regarded as 'more tangible, more exciting, and more immediately rewarding' (ibid.) than preventing it.

Preventing poverty is an obvious part of the basic strategy for a civilised society. How far can a society be described as satisfactory, let alone democratic, if its members are unable to participate fully because they do not have enough income and other resources to do so? T. H. Marshall regarded 'the elimination of poverty' as the most modest of the goals of social policy in a modern society (Rees, 1985, p. 241). Yet preventing poverty receives remarkably little attention in most national and international strategies to tackle poverty. Sometimes included in opening or concluding statements of new policy initiatives, it tends to receive little mention, if any, in the body of virtually every strategy examined. Similarly, analytical studies tend to overlook prevention.

Engagement with issues of prevention requires a focus 'upstream' to prevent poverty occurring, as opposed to the more common 'downstream' work to help repair, alleviate or compensate. This chapter sets out the urgent need to improve the balance between preventing poverty compared to lifting people out of it, and the potential value of doing so. The lessons to be learnt from letting prevention slide off the agenda and the challenges that have to be tackled to push it back up policy priorities are set out and examined. It establishes the need for structural changes in the economy, particularly in the labour market, and the value of an effective welfare state with a social security system that works to prevent poverty by tackling social and economic insecurity (Sinfield, 2012).

The lack of developed core concepts

The case for preventing poverty has long been made. For example, the 1942 Beveridge Report declared the failure to abolish poverty in the UK 'was a needless scandal due to not taking the trouble to prevent it' (Beveridge, 1942, para. 445). But there is still no significant body of literature on poverty-preventive policies and analyses of them (Hoelscher, 2006; Sinfield, 2007). Ambitious programmes, such as Europe 2020 which has set a target of reducing poverty by 20 million people, that is by 25 per cent, give little, if any, space to prevention even in the most relevant component of the plan, the European Platform Against Poverty.

In analysing the concept of prevention in terms of human damage, Jos Berghman and colleagues distinguish it from repair and compensation (Berghman et al., 2018), although they also draw on a tripartite categorisation used by some analysts of prevention in public health and medical areas. A primary form would prevent disease by tackling causes and reducing risks; a secondary by curing or reducing the severity with early diagnosis and quick treatment; a tertiary by preventing complications, reducing disabilities and minimising pain (Beaglehole et al., 1993, pp. 88, 91 and 93). The term 'primordial' has also been used to indicate higher strategies preventing those societal conditions that give rise to the causes of disease. In relation to poverty it is not clear how far preventing at secondary or tertiary level differs from lifting out or alleviating as opposed to preventing. In practice, analyses tend to lapse back into these approaches and lose the force of prevention.

The concept of poverty, its definition and measurement receive more detailed consideration in Chapters 2–5. In developing and evaluating preventive policies, the need is not for a measure that can be accepted as indicating a person or household is living in poverty, but one that demonstrates that they are not. Assessing the prevention of poverty requires a measure of a minimum standard of living that keeps people out of poverty. It 'includes, but is more than just food, clothes, and shelter'. It is about having what you need in order to have the opportunities and choices necessary to participate in society (MIS, 2018, p. 4; see also Veit-Wilson, 1998). However, very few empirical studies, let alone any series of statistics, adopt such a definition of freedom from poverty in their analyses: the reader needs to bear in mind that poverty data cited below are virtually all based on more limited measures used to enable comparison.

Having enough to be able to participate in society is costlier when people have special needs such as disability or when scarce or cut social services and other community facilities require more expenditure in the market. Equally their greater cost in some areas, such as rural, sparsely populated districts, can push up the income needed to meet higher costs for essential items such as travel, energy and shopping.

The costs of poverty

The case for the better prevention of poverty is greatly strengthened by the gains to the individual, family and society from avoiding the very substantial costs of poverty. Those who grow up in poverty are likely to have lower earnings than they would have had otherwise. The loss to them also means lower tax receipts and social security contributions. They are also more likely to have periods out of work, resulting in more spending on benefits as well as losses in taxes. For example, deliberately 'cautious' estimates for the UK have suggested that predicted increases in child poverty by 2020 could bring total costs to some 3 per cent of GDP (Hirsch, 2013). A similar analysis concluded that one-fifth of UK public spending on services was only 'making up for the way that poverty damages people's lives' (Bramley et al., 2016).

Such calculations do not take many important effects into account. Poverty lies at the root of many risk factors for infant mortality and the general health of children and young people. In England and Wales recent rises in infant mortality have been most striking among more deprived families. Among the most deprived groups in England mortality is twice that of the most affluent, where the rate is comparable to the best in Europe (RCPCH,

2018, p. 8). 'Nearly a third (32.9%) of the disease burden in Scotland could be avoided if the whole population had the same rate of burden as those in the least deprived areas of Scotland' (ScotPHO, 2016, p. 2). Evidence on the greater risk of disease in more deprived areas reveals, for example, both a higher risk of cancer and of its being detected later: so it is also harder to cure.

Less measurable costs that need to be avoided result from the damage to children and their families with, for example, a higher risk of mental health problems (Davie, 2016). Children can carry the impact of poverty throughout lives reduced in many ways, as research has shown over some 100 years (Titmuss, 1943). Poverty can negatively affect the warmth of the relationship between lone mothers and their children with long-term implications (Kiernan and Huerta, 2008). The consequences of problems such as these usually require extra spending on services quite apart from the personal costs for the individuals and families. Remarkably only within the last decade has there been systematic research across many countries that has revealed the global prevalence of the shame of being poor and the harmful impact that this has on individuals and families (Walker, 2014). Taking this work into account adds considerably to the argument for better and more sustained prevention of poverty.

The importance of prevention is underlined by the many commitments to realise human rights that are being adopted by an increasing number of countries. The successful prevention of poverty is integral, for example, to meeting the objectives of the International Covenant on Economic, Social and Cultural Rights (ICESCR). Adopted by the United Nations General Assembly in 1966 and coming into force a decade later, it is part of the International Bill of Rights and has been ratified by 169 countries. It specifically sets out the duty of any government to 'take steps . . . to the maximum of its available resources, with a view to achieving progressively the full' enjoyment of economic, social and cultural rights 'without discrimination of any kind' (ICESCR, article 2 (1); see also the Convention on the Rights of the Child, CRC 2016, para. 31, article 4). The recent European Pillar of Social Rights, for example, has more limited objectives: 'in-work poverty shall be prevented', 'children have the right to protection from poverty' and other groups should have the right to 'adequate' social or income protection. How such strategies can be strengthened to include the full force of rights set out in the statements above depends on the ways they are established in law and how these laws are then implemented with remedies and compensation (Veit-Wilson, 2006 and 2007). Achieving a consensus for routine enforcement may involve a challenge to those with considerably more power than those at risk of poverty.

The processes that prevent poverty

Strategies to prevent poverty require careful attention to the processes that succeed or fail in preventing it. The main way that most households escape poverty in industrial and post-industrial societies is by obtaining an adequate income from employment. This applies to most people in retirement too as the pensions built up through working lives provide the most effective and common protection against loss of earnings: 'work history matters' (Bardasi and Jenkins, subtitle, 2002).

This underlines the value of a labour market where full employment means, as William Beveridge argued over 70 years ago, jobs 'at fair wages, of such a kind, and so located that the unemployed can reasonably be expected to take them' (Beveridge, 1944, p. 18). The growth in insecure, precarious employment in many countries has weakened the labour market's traditional role in preventing poverty. Workers become locked into a 'low-pay no-pay' poverty cycle that further impoverishes them and their families over time, cutting them off from a more secure labour market and making it even more difficult to escape poverty (Shildrick et al., 2012a and b). In the UK, for example, more than half the households with children in poverty have someone in work, many in fulltime jobs that do not pay enough to support them and their families out of poverty; and these are more likely to be vulnerable to discrimination, single parents, in minority ethnic or religious groups, or with disabilities (Marsh, 2017).

Underemployment has continued higher in many countries since the end of the Great Recession (Bell and Blanchflower, 2018). Developments such as the 'gig economy' and 'zero-hours' contracts can mean that the 'work-first' strategy increasingly adopted by many governments is even less likely to succeed in keeping workers and any dependants out of poverty. Failing to prevent problems and having to tackle them later brings extra social and economic costs (Andersen and Keuschnigg, 2017).

In some countries the concern to reduce public spending has dominated other goals and led to an increase in working conditions and sanctions that reduce the chances of preventing poverty. A comparison between Denmark and Sweden of support for young adults with health problems that limit their ability to work, shows how preventive goals are undermined in 'social inclusion' programmes that only mean employment. The focus of 'front-line workers' became shifted 'from focusing on individual-centred goals such as preventing economic poverty and enhancing quality of life by addressing social problems, to focusing on state-centred goals such as reducing benefits expenditure and promoting work' (Hultqvist and Nørup, 2017, p. 152). 'Some Swedish front-line workers remain focused on goals related to the individual, while Danish front-line workers have now adopted state-centred goals to a larger extent' (Hultqvist and Nørup, 2017, p. 158). One Danish reform in 2013 was given the title 'Being Part of Society', and this rhetoric of social inclusion enhanced its counter-productive impact because the workfare emphasis in reality reinforced the practices excluding these young people. However,

> the logic expressed by politicians in Denmark and in Sweden is identical and might be summarised in two statements: if you do not participate in wage labour for health reasons as a young adult, you are not part of society; consequently, the key to be included in society is to participate in wage labour.
>
> *(Hultqvist and Nørup, 2017, p. 155)*

In ways like this many work and benefit policy adjustments have facilitated the normalisation of precarious work and undermined the standard employment relationship and the prevention of poverty. A review of labour markets in six European countries found that these policies have not been 'sustainable financially, both because the whole burden falls on the state and because employers are left free to continue creating precarious and fragmented work'. They have played 'into the hands of those keen simply to deregulate the employment system'. 'The policy framework needs to disincentivise employers from offering fragmented and precarious work . . . and instead find ways to tax employers that discourage the use of precarious work' (Rubery et al., 2018, pp. 523 and 524). Otherwise poverty may be at best ameliorated but not prevented.

By contrast, encouraging 'good jobs, organizational learning cultures, and company-level innovation, as witnessed in various Finnish working life development programs' can result in a general improvement of working conditions, rates of pay and general career prospects (Findlay, 2017, p. 6). Within this environment, workers are better protected against poverty, and initiatives such as the Scottish Fair Work Action Plan attempt to build on this, encouraging businesses to recognise the benefits of a wider social interest (Scottish Government, 2019).

> The reasons for paying the Living Wage usually go beyond any narrow weighing of financial cost against financial return. Sometimes this is because the benefits to the business, though direct, are intangible. But it can also be because the business sees a wider social interest as being its interest too. Altruism without a measure of self-interest is rare.
>
> *(Hughes et al., 2016, p. 28)*

The need for 'upstream' policies

Engagement with issues of prevention involves a focus 'upstream' to prevent risks occurring as opposed to the more common 'downstream' work to help repair or compensate. The prevention of poverty requires significant reductions in broader inequalities that may well challenge the power of dominant groups and institutions (Titmuss, 1965). 'Where poverty is widespread . . . there has been a failure to institutionalize equality' (Brady, 2009, p. 6). Higher rates of poverty and poor pay tend to go together, and low pay is 'much more common in nations where the labour sector is weak, government does little to manage the economy in the service of all, and public participation is less than the case in other countries' (Raphael, 2014, drawing on UNICEF research). This point is reinforced by the findings of a major study of the severe impact on child poverty of the financial crisis of 2008 and its consequences in industrial economies with in-depth studies of 11 OECD countries. 'Much responsibility' is placed on 'economic mismanagement, which created the conditions in which the financial crisis could occur and could have such serious consequences' (Cantillon et al., 2017, p. 325). As an important part of this the study emphasises 'the lack of progress in protecting children in the pre-crisis years'. This 'highlights the existence of structural constraints, against which many of the rich welfare states have proved powerless' (Cantillon et al., 2017, p. 1). The success of Belgium's strong trade union and collective arrangements in keeping in-work poverty very low throughout the financial crisis is a major exception (Marx and Van Cant, 2017).

A broad equality agenda can provide the framework within which specific goals of reducing and preventing poverty among the more vulnerable can be achieved (McKnight et al., 2017). It improves the chances of a successful attack on 'the major drivers of poverty, such as high levels of wage and wealth inequality' that have not only long undermined preventive policies but in recent years have been allowed to grow in many countries (Harker, 2006, p. 9). 'Income inequality at the same age has increased from one generation to the next in most countries' (OECD, 2017, chapter 4).

Structural measures to promote greater equality across all groups help to decrease the greater risk of poverty, and long-term poverty, for particular groups and areas. 'Child well-being' including protection from poverty 'is better in more equal societies' (Wilkinson and Pickett, 2009, pp. 23–24). Measures to tackle discrimination by gender, ethnicity, religion, disability and other factors can help to reduce the barriers affecting those who are more vulnerable to poverty. For example, women are at greater risk of poverty in most countries. Their concentration in low-paid part-time jobs through occupational segregation and the lack of affordable childcare 'make them more vulnerable to poverty and also make it more difficult for them to establish themselves in secure, well-paid employment that protects them from falling back into poverty even when in work' (Breitenbach and Wasoff, 2007). Reducing the gender gap in pay helps to reduce the inequality and the poverty. Lone parents are predominantly women and they are particularly vulnerable to losing their jobs. More family-friendly working conditions all the way down the earnings hierarchy help those at greater risk.

A poverty-prevention strategy working upstream also requires attention to policies that may undermine preventive strategies against poverty by reducing the resources available. One common example is taxation that is generally and uncritically assumed to reduce inequalities. It is little recognised that the substantial number of tax and related reliefs in very many countries, both rich and poor, work in an upside-down and regressive reinforcement, if not promotion, of inequality. This is particularly so where reliefs are given at the marginal rate of tax, thus benefiting those on higher incomes – a form of means-enhancing instead of the means-testing in much public spending. In the UK for instance, the top tenth of income taxpayers receive half of the £25 billion net income tax reliefs on private pensions but the bottom half receive only a tenth (Treasury Committee, 2018, pp. 35–36). Another £16 billion results from exemptions of National Insurance (NI, social security) contributions on the amount paid into these private pensions. The total net relief is six times the amount spent on pension credit, the means-tested support for those older people with the least resources. These NI reliefs effectively subsidise the private pensions market while the public austerity regime has frozen the rates of NI working-age benefits.

The significant scale of such reliefs has received increasing criticism from international agencies. Tax expenditure 'violates' both vertical and horizontal equity in both rich and poor economies (World Bank, 2003, p. 2).

> Scaling back tax expenditures that are not well-targeted at redistributive objectives may help achieve both greater efficiency and a narrower distribution of disposable income. Tax bases should be broadened first by removing or reducing tax expenditures that disproportionately benefit high income groups.
>
> *(OECD, 2016, p. 51)*

These changes could release more funds for preventive measures to protect lower-income groups (see Chapter 24).

All economies, however 'developed', need broad, structural strategies that connect economic, industrial, environmental and social policies giving specific attention to preventing poverty. '*What* is produced, *how* it is produced and *where* it is produced have important effects on the production or elimination of poverty. [We need] to move toward economic development paths that are more poverty preventive' (Miller 1999, p. 1, emphasis in the original).

This is a particular challenge given the need to work with and support the necessary transition to a sustainable economy achieving a fairer 'prosperity without growth' (Jackson, 2016, book title). While there is increasing acknowledgement of climate change and other environmental problems and their urgency, little sustained attention in countries at any level of development has been given to how strategies to tackle them and poverty might be most effectively combined. There have been some small-scale but successful examples: for example, in Scotland young people were helped to get established in the labour market by being trained to install effective insulation in the homes of older people. With young people better qualified to get work, older people warmer at less expense and a reduction in energy use, these schemes brought multiple gains (Heatwise Glasgow, 1994). But initiatives such as this have rarely been maintained and integrated into broader policies.

The preventive powers of a good social security system and a robust welfare state

The preventive achievements of a labour market providing fair work at decent wages with long-term prospects are not enough. Earnings do not adjust to family responsibilities or to high housing costs. Many cannot find work and others are unable to work. Both short-term and long-term needs require services and support (Treanor et al., 2017). Decent housing and access to good social services, including health, play an important role in preventing poverty (Schorr, 1964).

An effective welfare state, with a good benefits system, is an essential complement to an efficient labour market. Two major comparative studies of 'developed' societies have brought this out clearly. Analysing the experience of 18 countries over more than 30 years, David Brady found that a generous welfare state was a 'dominant' factor in preventing poverty (Brady, 2009, p. 166). The same point was emphasised by Bea Cantillon: in the European Union 'rich, high employment countries where social spending is low end up with high poverty. This leads to the conclusion that, if it is possible to attain a low risk of poverty without substantial spending, it has not yet been demonstrated' (Cantillon, 2009, p. 240).

The importance of social protection for children in poorer countries 'is essential for reducing and preventing child poverty and achieving the SDGs [social development goals] of ending extreme child poverty and halving child poverty according to national definitions by 2030' (ILO-UNICEF, 2019, p. 9). Yet globally only

> 35 per cent of children receive social protection benefits, with significant regional disparities: while 87 per cent of children in Europe and Central Asia and 66 per cent in the Americas receive benefits, this is the case for only 28 per cent of children in Asia and the Pacific and 16 per cent in Africa.
>
> *(ILO-UNICEF, 2019, p. 2)*

They 'need to be part of a broader social policy that ensures access to the high-quality services and social care that children and families require' (ILO-UNICEF, 2019, p. 29). 'Recognition of social insurance as one of the best means of building an inclusive society and preventing the slide into poverty as well as contributing to social and economic stability would represent one major step forward' (Policy Press, 2010, p. 321).

The preventive value of a good social security system can be considerable (Sinfield, 2012). It results in an effective automatic stabiliser, not only economic but political and social, that helps to maintain consumer spending and so support demand and employment. Communities particularly hit by loss of jobs are better protected as local shops remain open and services are maintained. Neglecting the importance of this and cutting and freezing benefits also undermines other strategies to boost the economy as well as adding to poverty and insecurity.

'Automatic stabilizers work, always and everywhere' was the subtitle to an IMF analysis of data from 49 industrial and developing economies over 40 years (Debrun and Kapoor, 2010). Already built in, the automatic stabilising elements come into effect instantly to prevent further problems: they do not have to wait for generally slow political and policy reactions to crises (Callan et al., 2018). Their value has been all the greater given the widespread governmental and 'expert' failure to anticipate financial and other crises amid general euphoria over the workings of markets. 'One of the sad facts of the so-called reforms in recent decades is that we have been weakening these important automatic stabilizers' (Stiglitz, 2009, p. 4; Dolls et al., 2012). It is a sign of the dominance of privatising interests that the collective, solidaristic strengths of social security became overlooked. In consequence, they were less effective in protecting against the harshness of the financial crisis in many countries (Cantillon et al., 2017).

The imposition of austerity policies in Greece, Italy, Spain and even Portugal have had such a destabilising effect that 'rising inequality and social exclusion now threaten to become lasting features of the social landscape' (Perez and Matsaganis, 2018, Conclusion). While many governments have accepted a view of benefits as 'passive' in contrast to 'active' policies that help or push people into work, there has been insufficient recognition of the demoralising effects of inadequate benefits that leave recipients in poverty, especially when myths about the generous 'culture of dependency' lead their neighbours – and often those in poverty themselves – to see them as undeserving (Shildrick et al., 2012a and b). The resulting poverty is made worse by cuts and reductions in a wide range of community services that are of special value in helping to prevent poverty for those on low incomes (Treanor et al., 2017). To enable children to take part in school activities, parents may be forced to reduce spending on essential items including their own food, and this can lead to longer-term problems.

Political choices behind policy decisions can lead to great differences in preventing the poverty of different groups. Older people have often been explicitly exempted from the tougher austerity regimes introduced in many countries, resulting in much greater success in reducing and preventing their poverty in most of the EU since the financial crisis of 2008 (Eurostat, 2018). In the UK, for example, poverty rates among older people have fallen below the average for the first time with pensions being protected against inflation while most working-age benefits have been frozen (Marsh, 2017).

However, the greater risk of poverty among older women continues (EC, 2018). Their working lives are more likely to have been in lower-paid jobs, not only with periods out of work but also without private pensions. This leaves them more dependent on minimum income schemes often inadequate to keep them out of poverty. The gender gap in pensions is now wider than that in pay in many countries, and this requires changes in access to, and the arrangements of, both state and private pensions.

The preventive effectiveness of established social security policies has been undermined in many countries by inadequate uprating policies that fail to sufficiently maintain the value of benefits against rising prices: the impact is even worse when benefit levels are frozen (Sutherland et al., 2008). Disregards (where certain income is not taken into account fully or partially when calculating benefit entitlements) protect certain vulnerable groups such as those with disabilities, but they can be left unchanged for many years, making these people even more liable to poverty.

Preventive protection is also reduced when social security benefits are uprated less than income tax thresholds. In the UK, for example, uprating for most social security benefits for working-age people was first limited and then frozen altogether for the four years until 2020. In the last six years this has meant total increases of only 3 per cent, well below inflation: not surprisingly, poverty is being predicted to rise significantly (Hood and Waters, 2017, p. 6). By contrast, the basic income tax threshold has been lifted by 46 per cent over the same period. Many social security beneficiaries gain nothing from these tax changes because they are not in work, and many others in low-paid or part-time jobs do not earn enough to get much benefit from them.

Preventing and reducing the worst effects of poverty are helped by public and voluntary efforts to promote universal, or at least high, take-up of the full range of benefits available. Across the EU in 2009 'non-take-up' was 'a very widespread phenomenon that needs to be addressed much more systematically' (Frazer and Marlier, 2009, p. 11). In the UK in 2008 the poverty of one in seven of the children living in poverty could have been prevented if they had received all the benefits and tax credits to which they were entitled (CPU, 2009, p. 1).

Research has shown that 'the largest part of the responsibility' lies with administration and not lack of knowledge (Oorschot, 2002, pp. 185–186). Staff rewards for identifying fraud and abuse but not for improving take-up, combined with inadequate checks on discrimination, undermine preventive effectiveness. An independent and nationwide welfare rights service can help to ensure that all members of society are able to obtain the full range of benefits which are available to protect them against poverty (Treanor et al., 2017).

Conclusion

Preventing poverty brings double benefits to societies and their members. It saves individuals, families and the wider community and its institutions from having to bear the social and economic costs of poverty, the costs of measures needed to treat these and the costs of recovery over time. In addition, the improved quality of life for all those not caught in poverty brings social and economic benefits in many ways including a fuller participation in society and a greater contribution from the increased productivity of those avoiding poverty.

Benjamin Franklin's quotation was cited in the introduction: 'an ounce of prevention is worth a pound of cure' (Benjamin Franklin, 1735). In tackling poverty the failure to implement it continues. The urgent need to help those already in poverty absorbs virtually all the action. The dominant individualist discourse adds to the problem, deflecting attention from its structural causes. That helps to explain why those seen as deserving in their old age are more likely to be protected from poverty than those of working age and their dependants, despite the long-term costs, individual, social and economic, that are being built up.

Successful prevention of poverty requires changes at all levels of policy, including the better direction and management of the economy, the labour market and the welfare state, especially social security. At lower levels more attention to prevention can still bring considerable gains, and it deserves to be given higher priority at local, national and international levels than it is currently receiving.

A major problem in developing analyses and strategies focused on preventing poverty is the dominance in many, if not most, countries of an individualist narrative that presents poverty as a matter of personal responsibility that ignores the structural factors. In addition, it reinforces the debilitating sense of shame that research has revealed across all types of society (Walker, 2014). The global issue of obesity faces similar problems of individualising and shaming. Those involved in research into it have recently put forward a strong case for developing a new rights-based narrative 'using words and images . . . framed around an inter-related set of approaches rather than single, siloed solutions . . . to shift blame away from individuals and towards upstream drivers' (Ralston et al., 2018, pp. 1385–1386). Preventing poverty, too, requires a fresh and more developed narrative that focuses on dominant, structural causes and upstream policies that take account of the existing patterns of power and resources that preserve high levels of poverty.

Acknowledgements

I would particularly like to thank Professor Morag Treanor at Heriot-Watt University who allowed me to draw on her forthcoming study, *Child Poverty: Aspiring to Survive*, to be published by Policy Press, and Dorothy Sinfield who once again helpfully commented on successive drafts.

References

Andersen, T. M. and Keuschnigg, C. (2017). *Labour-Market Reforms in Europe: Repairing Problems or Investing to Prevent?* sim Europe, www.wpz-fgn.com/wp-content/uploads/BSt_SIM_Labour_Markets_web.pdf (accessed 2 July 2019).

Bardasi, E. and Jenkins, S. (2002). *Income in Later Life: Work History Matters*. Bristol: Policy Press.

Beaglehole, R., Bonita, R. and Kjellström, T. (1993). *Basic Epidemiology*. Geneva: WHO.

Bell, D. N. F. and Blanchflower, D. G. (2018). The lack of wage growth and the falling NAIRU. *National Institute Economic Review*, 245(1): R40–R55.

Berghman, J., Debels, A. and Van Hoyweghen, I. (2018). Prevention: the cases of social security and healthcare. In B. Greve (Ed.), *Routledge Handbook of the Welfare State*. London: Routledge, 2nd ed., 46–57.

Beveridge, W. H. (chair) (1942). *Report on Social Insurance and Allied Services*. London: HMSO.

Beveridge, W. H. (1944). *Full Employment in a Free Society*. London: Allen and Unwin.

Brady, D. (2009). *Rich Democracies Poor Societies: How Politics Explain Poverty*. Oxford: Oxford University Press.

Bramley, G., Hirsch, D., Littlewood, M. and Watkins, D. (2016). *Counting the Cost of UK Poverty*. York: Rowntree Foundation.

Breitenbach, E. and Wasoff, F. (2007). *A Gender Audit of Statistics: Comparing the Position of Women and Men in Scotland*. Edinburgh: Scottish Government.

Callan, T., Doorley, K. and Savage, M. (2018). *Inequality in EU crisis countries: how effective were automatic stabilisers?* Euromod Working Papers EM 10/18, April.

Cantillon, B. (2009). The poverty effects of social protection in Europe: EU enlargement and its lessons for developing countries. In P. Townsend (Ed.), *Building Decent Societies: Rethinking the Role of Social Security in Development*. Basingstoke: ILO & Palgrave Macmillan, 220–241.

Cantillon, B., Chzhen, Y., Handa, S. and Nolan, B. (2017). *Children of Austerity: Impact of the Great Recession on Child Poverty in Rich Countries*. Oxford: UNICEF and Oxford University Press.

Child Poverty Unit (2009). *Take Up – The Challenge: the role of local services in increasing take up of benefits and tax credits to reduce child poverty*. A report by the Take Up Taskforce. London: Child Poverty Unit.

CRC – Committee on the Rights of the Child (2016). *General comment No. 19 (2016) on public budgeting for the realization of children's rights (art. 4)*. 20 July.

Davie, M. (2016). Children's mental health, poverty and life chances. In J. Tucker (Ed.), *Improving Children's Life Chances*. London: Child Poverty Action Group, 58–68.

Debrun, X. and Kapoor, R. (2010). *Fiscal policy and macroeconomic stability: Automatic stabilizers work, always and everywhere*. IMF working paper 10/111. Washington, DC: International Monetary Fund.

Dolls, M., Fuest, C. and Peichl, A. (2012). Automatic stabilizers and economic crisis: US vs Europe. *Journal of Public Economics* 96: 279–294.

EC (2018). *The 2018 Pension Adequacy Report: current and future income adequacy in old age in the EU*. Brussels: EC, volume 1.

Eurostat (2018). *Income poverty statistics*. Statistics Explained, Eurostat Online. https://ec.europa.eu/eurostat/statistics-explained/index.php/Income_poverty_statistics (accessed 2 July 2019).

Findlay, P. (2017). Opportunity knocks? The possibilities and levers for improving job quality. *Work and Occupations*, 44(1): 3–22.

Franklin, B. (1735) *The Electric Ben Franklin*. www.ushistory.org/franklin/philadelphia/fire.htm (accessed 2 July 2019).

Frazer, H. and Marlier, E. (2009). *Minimum income schemes across EU member states*. Synthesis report. Brussels: EU Network of Independent Experts on Social Inclusion.

Harker, L. (2006). *Delivering on Child Poverty: What Would it Take?* London: Department for Work and Pensions.

Heatwise Glasgow (1994). *Going beyond Draughtproofing: A report on the activities of Heatwise, Glasgow's Jobs and Energy Project, November 1987–November 1994*. Glasgow: Heatwise.

Hirsch, D. (2013). *An estimate of the costs of child poverty in 2013*. Loughborough: Centre for Research in Social Policy.

Hoelscher, P. (2006). What works? Preventing and reducing child poverty in Europe. *European Journal of Social Security*, 8(3): 257–277.

Hood, A. and Waters, T. (2017). *Living standards, poverty and inequality in the UK: 2017–19 to 2021–22*. London: Institute of Fiscal Studies.

Hughes, C., Kenway, P., Kelly, P. and Barry-Born, T. (2016). *Enlightened Self-interest: The Role of Private Sector Employers in Reducing Poverty*. London: New Policy Institute.

Hultqvist, S. and Nørup, I. (2017). Consequences of activation policy targeting young adults with health-related problems in Sweden and Denmark. *Journal of Poverty and Social Justice*, 25(2): 147–161.

ICESCR (no date). *International Covenant on Economic, Social and Cultural Rights*. New York: UN. www.ohchr.org/en/professionalinterest/pages/cescr.aspx (accessed 2 July 2019).

ILO – UNICEF (2019). *Towards universal social protection for children: Achieving SDG 1.3*. Joint Report on Social Protection for Children. www.ilo.org/secsoc/information-resources/publications-and-tools/books-and-reports/WCMS_669336/lang--en/index.htm (accessed 2 July 2019).

Jackson, T. (2016). *Prosperity without Growth: Foundations for the Economy of Tomorrow*. London: Routledge, 2nd ed.

Kiernan, K. E. and Huerta, M. C. (2008). Economic deprivation, maternal depression, parenting and children's cognitive and emotional development in early childhood. *British Journal of Sociology*, 59: 783–806.

Mackintosh, J. M. (1953). *Trends of Opinion about the Public Health, 1901–51*. London: Oxford University Press.

Marsh, A. (2017). *Poverty: The Facts*. London: Child Poverty Action Group, 6th ed.

Marx, I. and Van Cant, L. (2017). Belgium: is robust social concertation providing a buffer against growing inequality? In D. Vaughan-Whitehead (Ed.), *Reducing Inequalities in Europe: How Industrial Relations and Labour Policies Can Close the Gap*. Cheltenham: Edward Elgar, chapter 3.

McKnight, A., Duque, M. and Rucci, M. (2017). *Double trouble: A review of the relationship between UK poverty and economic inequality*. London: LSE, Centre for Economic Analysis.

Miller, S. M. (1999). Prevention of Poverty. *CROP Newsletter*. Comparative Research Programme on Poverty, 6(2): 1–2.

MIS (2018). *A Minimum Income Standard for the UK 2008–2018*. York: Joseph Rowntree Foundation.

OECD (2016). *Tax Design for Inclusive Economic Growth*. OECD Taxation Working Papers 26. Paris: OECD.

OECD (2017). *Preventing Ageing Unequally*. Paris: OECD.

Oorschot, W. van. (2002). Targeting welfare: on the functions and dysfunctions of means-testing in social policy. In P. Townsend and D. Gordon (Eds.), *World Poverty: New Policies to Defeat an Old Enemy*. Bristol: Policy Press, 171–193.

Perez, S. A. and Matsaganis, M. (2018). The political economy of austerity in Southern Europe. *New Political Economy*, 23(2): 192–207.

Policy Press (Ed.) (2010). *The Peter Townsend Reader*. Bristol: Policy Press.

Ralston, J. et al. (2018). Time for a new obesity narrative. *The Lancet*, 392(10156): 1384–1386. http://dx.doi.org/10.1016/S0140-6736(18)32537-6

Raphael, D. (2014). The issue is not poor children but family poverty. www.thespec.com/opinion-story/4299112-the-issue-is-not-poor-children-but-family-poverty/ (accessed 2 July 2019).

RCPCH – Royal College for Pediatrics and Child Health (2018). *Child health in England in 2030: comparisons with other wealthy countries*. London: RCPCH.

Rees, A. M. (Ed.) (1985) *T. H. Marshall's Social Policy*. London: Hutchinson, 5th ed.

Rubery, J., Grimshaw, D., Keizer, A. and Johnson, M. (2018). Challenges and contradictions in the 'normalising' of precarious work. *Work, Employment and Society*, 32(3): 509–527.

Schorr, A. (1964). *Slums and Social Insecurity*. Edinburgh: Nelson.

Scottish Government (2019). *Fair Work Action Plan*. Edinburgh: Scottish Government.

ScotPHO (2016). *The Scottish Burden of Disease Study, 2016: Deprivation Report*. Edinburgh: NHS Scotland.

Shildrick, T., Furlong, A., MacDonald, R., Roden, J. and Crow, R. (2012a). *Are 'Cultures of Worklessness' passed down the Generations?* York: Joseph Rowntree Foundation. www.jrf.org.uk/report/are-cultures-worklessness-passed-down-generations (accessed 2 July 2019).

Shildrick, T., MacDonald, R., Webster, C. and Garthwaite, K. (2012b). *Poverty and Insecurity: Life in Low-Pay, No-Pay Britain*. Bristol: Policy Press.

Sinfield, A. (2007). Preventing poverty in the European Union. *European Journal of Social Security*, 9(1): 11–28.

Sinfield, A. (2012). Strengthening the prevention of social insecurity. *International Social Security Review*, 65(4): 89–106.

Stiglitz, J. (2009). Global crisis, social protection and jobs. *International Labour Review*, 148(1/2): 1–13.

Sutherland, H., Evans, M., Hancock, R., Hills, J. and Zantomio, F. (2008). *The Impact of Benefit and Tax Uprating on Incomes and Poverty*. York: Joseph Rowntree Foundation.

Titmuss, R. M. (1943). *Birth, Poverty and Wealth*. London: Hamish Hamilton.

Titmuss, R. M. (1965). Poverty vs. inequality: diagnosis. *Nation*, February, pp. 130–133.

Treanor, M. et al. (2017). *Tackling child poverty: actions to prevent and mitigate child poverty at the local level*. Edinburgh: What Works Scotland Evidence Review. September.

Treasury Committee (2018). *Household finances: income, saving and debt*. House of Commons 565, 26 July.

Veit-Wilson, J. (1998). *Setting Adequacy Standards: How Governments Define Minimum Incomes*. Bristol: Policy Press.

Veit-Wilson, J. (2006). No rights without remedies: necessary conditions for abolishing child poverty. *European Journal of Social Security*, 8(3): 317–337.

Veit-Wilson, J. (2007). Some social policy implications of a right to social security. In J. Van Langendonck (Ed.), *The Right to Social Security*. Antwerp: Intersentia, 57–84.

Walker, R. (2014). *The Shame of Poverty: Global Perspectives*. Oxford: Oxford University Press.

Wilkinson, R. and Pickett, K. (2009). *The Spirit Level: Why More Equal Societies Almost Always Do Better*. London: Allen Lane.

World Bank (2003). Why worry about tax expenditures? *PREMnotes* Economic Policy, no. 77, January.

7

Relative deprivation and subjective social position

Anders Ejrnæs

This chapter introduces the concept of relative deprivation and social comparison theory in order to discuss the perceived or subjective experience of poverty. The aim is to analyse the association between objective poverty, perceived poverty, frustration, reaction and collective action. The theory of relative deprivation can be divided into two approaches: simple and more complex (Fahey, 2010). The simple approach focuses on analysis of poverty as socially relative but objectively measurable. Relative poverty, according to the simple perspective, occurs when people have a living standard which is far below the living standard needed to have a sufficient level of consumption to participate in society. Within this approach, the most common way to define poverty is to say that people are living in poverty if they earn less than 50 or 60 per cent of the median income. Poverty, in this approach, compares income with half of the median income level in the country, and the frame of reference is fixed. The more complex perspective on relative deprivation has originated from social psychology and aims at analysing the role of multiple social comparisons (Fahey, 2010). This approach recognises that people use multiple frames of reference when they make comparisons. These comparisons go beyond a national frame of reference. This perspective focuses on the subjective feeling of poverty and deprivation. This chapter introduces the issue of the relative position in society and the perceptions of the position as key concepts to study individuals' perception of their own objective situation, and tries to investigate how this distinction contributes to the enlightenment of poverty.

Scholars of sociology, economics and psychology have discovered that subjective comparisons – rather than objective circumstances – shape people's wellbeing, anger and collective action (Smith & Pettigrew, 2014). The subjective feeling of relative deprivation emerges when a person experiences dissatisfaction when being deprived of something that she or he believes they deserve. According to social comparison theory and relative deprivation theory, people perceive their situation in comparison with a certain reference point (Merton, 1957). This reference point could be: (1) one's past outcomes, (2) perception of the situation of others, and (3) expected future outcomes (Levine & Moreland, 1987). In this approach, another significant distinction is between collective relative deprivation and individual relative deprivation. Individual relative deprivation is produced by a disadvantaged individual's comparison between his or her own situation and the situation of other in-group members. Group relative deprivation is produced by in-group members' comparisons between the situation of the in-group and an out-group (Runciman, 1966).

First, the chapter will analyse the link between the subjective measure of poverty and position in society and the objective measure of poverty and income inequality. Second, using empirical examples, the chapter will show how different forms of comparisons produce different kinds of reactions.

Associations between subjective and objective poverty: empirical illustration

In order to measure the level of subjective poverty, the following question is used: 'Which of the descriptions on this card comes closest to how you feel about your household's income nowadays?'

The four response categories are: (1) living comfortably on present income, (2) coping on present income, (3) finding it difficult on present income, and (4) finding it very difficult on present income. In this chapter, subjective poverty is defined as finding it difficult or very difficult on present economy.

Figure 7.1 shows the trend in subjective poverty from 2002 to 2016. For most of the countries, the level of subjective poverty increases from 2002 to 2012, while it decreases from 2012 to 2016. In Germany and Poland, the subjective poverty level decreases over the entire period from 2002 to 2016. In Hungary, Portugal, Spain and Ireland, there are some dramatic changes

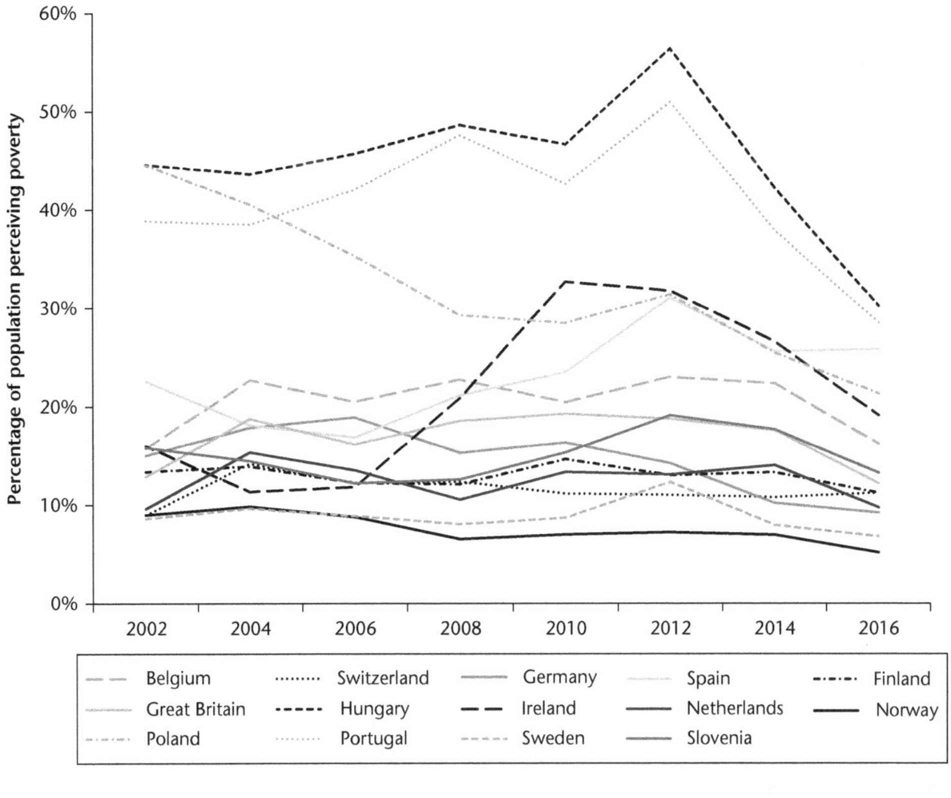

Figure 7.1 Trends in subjective poverty.

Source: European Social Survey Cumulative File, ESS 1–8 (2018).

in the levels of subjective poverty. In these countries, the subjective poverty peaks in 2012 and then declines. Figure 7.1 shows that the level of poverty varies considerably among countries and fluctuates over time. This could indicate that the frame of reference in which people compare their income is more complex than countries' median income. People compare their income level with their past income or their future income prospects and the income of people in other countries. The rise of subjective poverty in Ireland could be explained by the financial crisis, which comes after a long period of economic growth. Norway and Sweden have the lowest levels of subjective poverty in the whole period.

In order to compare trends in the subjective level of poverty with the at-risk-of-poverty rate (cut-off point: 60% of median equivalised income after social transfers), Germany and Ireland were selected, in which economic development was very different during the crisis. In Germany the unemployment rate was reduced during the crisis, while there was a rapid increase in unemployment in Ireland after the financial crisis. Figure 7.2 shows that in Germany, the risk of poverty increases slightly, while there is a significant decline in subjective poverty. This indicates that when people judge whether they have difficulties on present income, they do not just compare themselves with people in their own country, but also compare their income level with their past income. The rising overall level of wealth in Germany compared to other countries seems to reduce the level of subjective poverty.

Ireland shows the opposite trend. Subjective poverty rises rapidly after the financial crisis, while the indicator of poverty risk falls. Figure 7.2 indicates that the measure of monetary poverty is too simple if one wants to measure whether people actually feel deprived.

The result could indicate that social comparison is multiple, shifting and varied. Figure 7.3 shows that at the individual level, the subjective poverty rate is linked to the relative position within the society measured by income deciles. People in the lowest income group are most likely to perceive poverty. In Sweden and Norway the lowest income group perceives less poverty than in the other countries. When it comes to the top of the income scale, it is only a

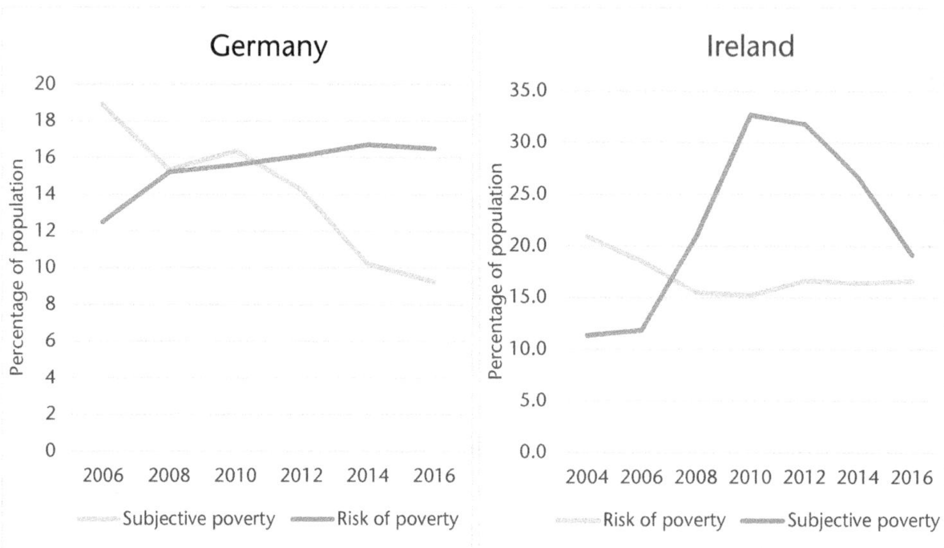

Figure 7.2 Trends in risk of poverty and subjective poverty in percentage terms. At-risk-of-poverty rate (cut-off point: 60% of median equivalised income after social transfers).

Source: Eurostat extracted 21.02.19 and European Social Survey Cumulative File, ESS 1–8 (2018).

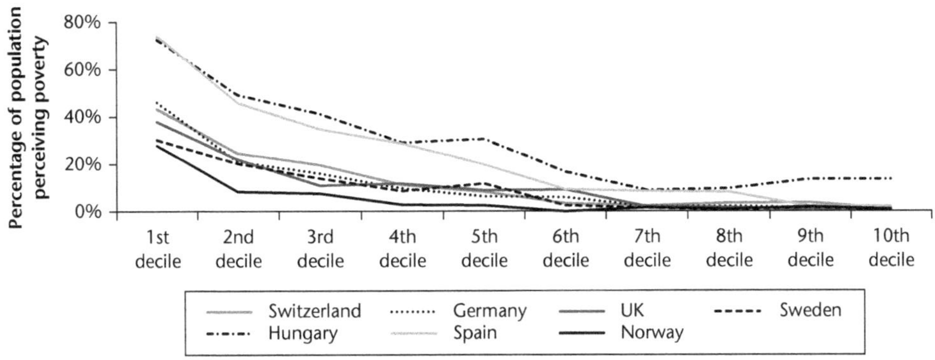

Figure 7.3 Decile location and subjective poverty (as percentages).

Source: ESS Round 8: European Social Survey Round 8 Data (2016).

tiny minority who perceive poverty, except for Hungary. Figure 7.3 indicates that subjective poverty is influenced by objective position both within and among countries.

The origin of relative deprivation theory and social comparison theory

There are also several sociological theories on relative position that emphasise how subjective comparison with other people affects wellbeing independently of a person's objective situation.

The term 'relative deprivation' was first used in several studies of American armed forces published in 1949 (Stouffer et al., 1949). It was used to explain that dissatisfaction among US soldiers does not primarily stem from objective hardship they suffered, but from their perception of their own situation compared to others in their group. Reference group theory assumes that people evaluate their own situation by comparing it with that of other individuals or groups. According to Festinger's (1954) social comparison hypothesis, people prefer to compare themselves with individuals who are similar to them. People have, then, a tendency to perceive the world in the context of the people around them. Since family friends, colleagues and neighbours often have a similar income, occupation and education, people tend to see themselves in the middle of the social hierarchy (Festinger, 1954). People in positions of high objective status in terms of income, educational level or class position compare themselves with other people of high objective social status, perceiving their social status as unexceptional and average because they know both people who are above them and people who are below them (Evans & Kelley, 2004; Savage, 2015; Lindemann & Saar, 2014). Those of low objective status will compare themselves with other people of low objective status. The paradoxical consequence of social comparison among people who are similar is that most people perceive that their own position is in the middle of the social hierarchy. If one compares people's perception of their position in four different countries, one finds that in all countries people see themselves as located near the centre of the social hierarchy. Very few locate themselves in the top strata or in the bottom strata.

The subjective perception of position in society was measured by the following question in ISSP:

> In our society, one sometimes talks about how some groups are perceived as higher-ranked in society and other groups are perceived as lower-ranked. Below there is a scale which runs from top to bottom. If you were to place yourself on this scale, where 1 is the bottom of society and 10 is the top of society, where would you be?

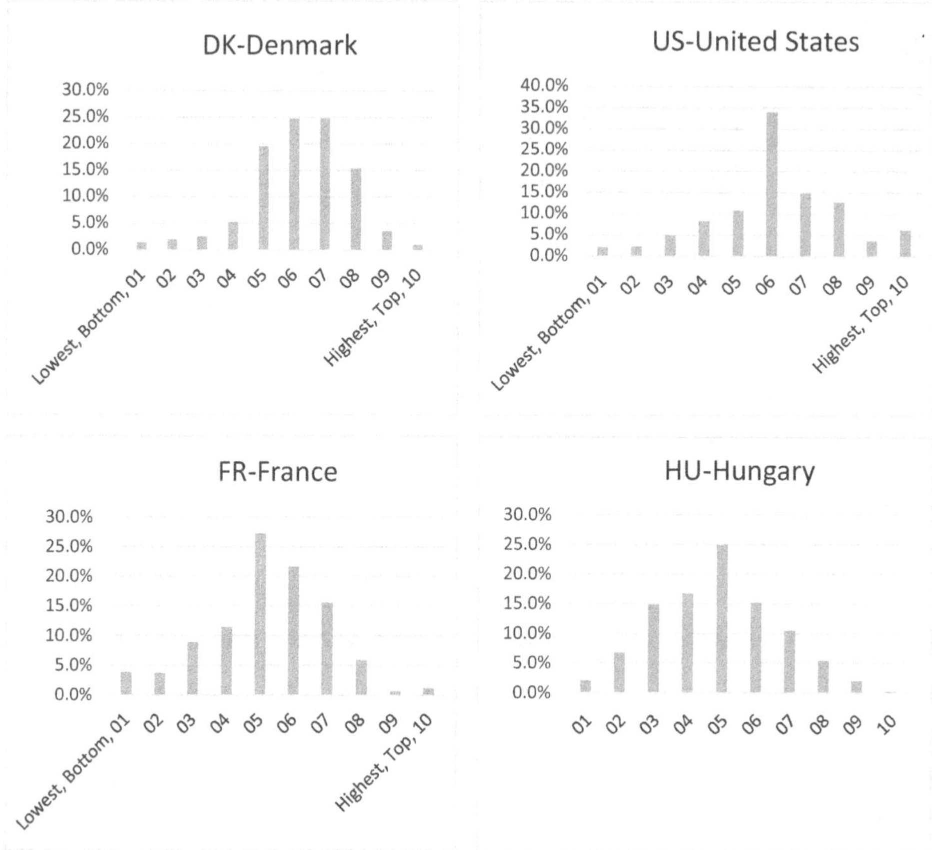

Figure 7.4 Subjective social position: percentage in each stratum.

Source: ISSP 2009.

In Denmark, the average subjective position is higher than in other countries and people tend to concentrate on strata 5, 6, 7 and 8. In the US, the average subjective position is also high, but the standard deviation is much higher than in Denmark. In Hungary, France and Spain, the average is considerably lower than in Denmark and the UK. The modal stratum in these three countries is 5.

Stratification within society

The reference group argument suggests that income has a minor effect on subjective social standing because people compare themselves with people who are similar to themselves. Table 7.1 shows the average subjective position for different income groups. The table shows that the variation in the average subjective position between the lowest and the highest income group is approximately 2 points. This emphasises that it is not only the objective social position that has an impact on how people perceive themselves in the social hierarchy. The lowest income group has an average subjective position on 4.6, while the highest income group has an average subjective position

Table 7.1 Average subjective position in different income groups

Household's total net income, all sources	*Mean*	*95% confidence interval*	
		Lower bound	*Upper bound*
1st decile	4.6	4.3	4.9
2nd decile	4.9	4.6	5.1
3rd decile	5.2	4.9	5.5
4th decile	5.3	5.1	5.6
5th decile	5.5	5.2	5.8
6th decile	5.7	5.4	6.0
7th decile	5.8	5.6	6.1
8th decile	6.0	5.7	6.3
9th decile	6.2	5.9	6.5
10th decile	6.6	6.3	6.9

Source: ESS 2012. All European countries covered by ESS. The table is controlled for country variance. Data are only available for 2012.

on 6.6. Table 7.1 shows that the poorest group within each country does not consider itself to be at the bottom of society (if so, the average would have been between 1 and 2) and the richest group does not consider itself to be at the top of society (if so, the average would have been between 9 and 10). Although income has some influence on the average subjective position, the result confirms the reference theory that people primarily tend to place themselves in the middle of the social hierarchy.

Expanded reference theory

With increasing internationalisation and globalisation and the growth of social media, some authors claim that people's horizons have expanded and the reference group for comparison is no longer restricted to the local area or even to the country (Fahey, 2010). Following an expanded reference group argument, one can then assume that Europeans have a larger frame of reference group than their immediate surroundings. This means that somebody who lives in a poor European country compared to other countries will have a lower subjective social position than people who live in a wealthy European country.

Figure 7.5 shows a relatively high correlation between countries' gross domestic product (GDP) per capita and average subjective social location. This means that people from Bulgaria have a lower subjective social position than people from Denmark, because they not only compare their living standard to people within their country, but also to the living standards and opportunities of other European citizens. This feeling of collective relative deprivation could also explain why the average subjective position is lower in less prosperous countries such as Bulgaria. If people feel that the economy is stagnating in their country compared to other countries, the average subjective position will decline.

According to Wilkinson and Pickett (2010), problems associated with relative deprivation are more prevalent in unequal societies. Wilkinson and Pickett argue that status differentiation is related to the scale of income distribution. In a more unequal society, more people suffer from relative deprivation and status frustration, which could depress the level of subjective position in society. Wilkinson argues that the feeling of inferiority will increase in more unequal societies (Wilkinson, 2000). Figure 7.6 shows that average subjective position also tends to be lower in countries with a high level of income inequality. However, the correlation is much weaker than with GDP.

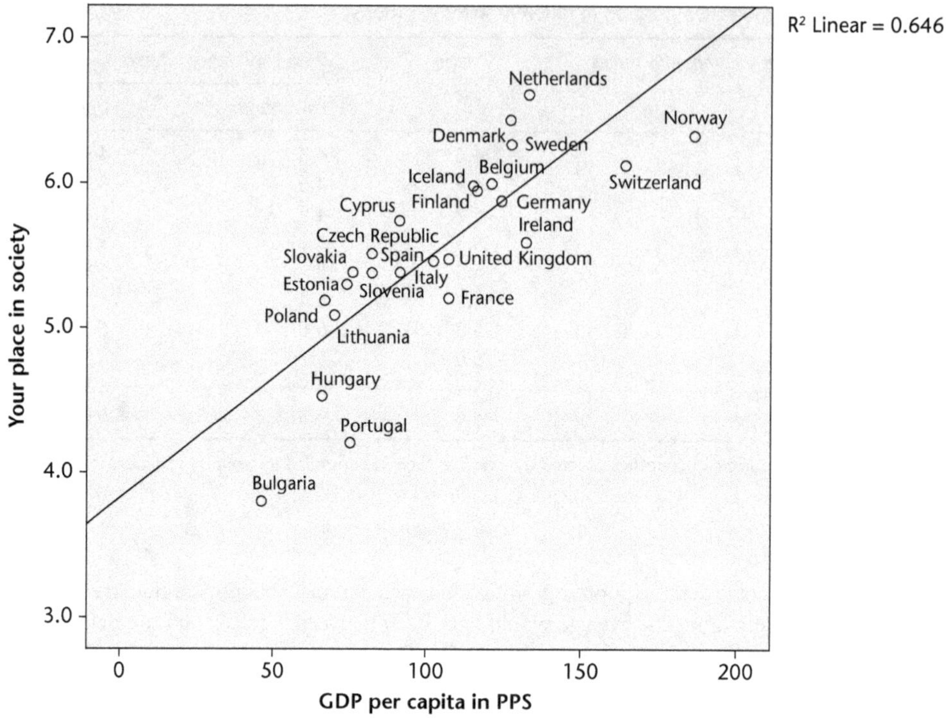

Figure 7.5 GDP and subjective position in society.

Source: Eurostat and ESS Round 6: European Social Survey Round 6 Data (2018).

The figure indicates that despite the fact that most people tend to see themselves in the middle of the hierarchy, the middle varies among different countries. Economic prosperity has a positive effect on people's subjective positions, while income inequality has a negative effect. These finding are in line with other studies that show there are socioeconomic forces that influence the level of subjective social position (Lindemann & Saar, 2014).

It seems that subjective position not only reflects the way people perceive their position in comparison within the country, but also how they imagine their position will be in the future (Lindemann, 2007; Ejrnæs & Greve, 2017). It seems that in the Nordic welfare states that offer more social security and economic opportunities, the average level of subjective social position is higher. This might suggest that the welfare state plays a mediating role. Welfare states, which provide universal social protection, could then decrease the social distance between people. People in the lower strata might feel more stigmatised in an unequal society and in less developed welfare states due to the large social distance from others and the lack of social mobility. According to that perspective, perception of inequality and social justice could be an important predictor of perceived subjective position.

Perceived inequality and subjective social position

In the next section, how people perceive inequality in society is analysed. Respondents were asked to choose which of five diagrams best describes the stratification of their country's society.

Type A indicates a society with a small elite at the top, very few people in the middle and a great mass of people at the bottom. Table 7.2 shows that the majority of people in many

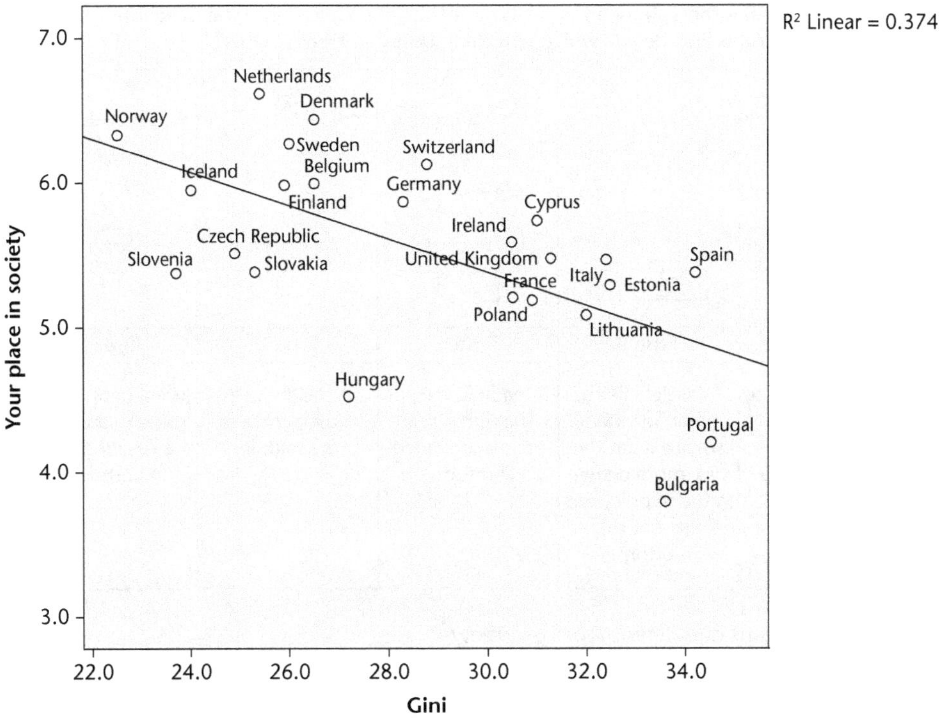

Figure 7.6 Gini coefficient and subjective social position.

Source: Eurostat and ESS Round 6: European Social Survey Round 6 Data (2018).

of the post-communist countries, such as Ukraine, Bulgaria, Hungary, Croatia and Latvia perceive their society as Type A. Type B indicates a society like a pyramid with a small elite at the top, more people in the middle, and most at the bottom. Countries where people describe their society as Type B include continental, South European and Anglo-Saxon countries, as well some of the Asian countries. Type C is a society like a pyramid except that just a few people are at the bottom. In Cyprus and Austria, Type C is the most frequent answer. Type D indicates a society with most people in the middle. In the Nordic countries, Switzerland and Australia, the most frequent description of the society is Type D. It is not possible to find a country where the most frequent answer is Type E. The central question is whether perceived inequality has an impact on the subjective position in society. One can expect that in countries where people describe their society as Type A, people will have a lower average subjective position because society is expected to provide few opportunities for upward mobility and is perceived as very unjust. On the other hand, one can expect that in countries where the majority describe their society as Type D, the average subjective position will be higher because society is perceived as more just and offering more opportunities for upward mobility.

Figures 7.8 and 7.9 show that, on the one hand, in countries where inhabitants mainly describe their society as Type A, the average subjective position is much lower. On the other hand, in countries in which the majority describe their society as Type D, the level of subjective position is higher.

Q15. These five diagrams show different types of society. Please read the descriptions and look at the diagrams and decide which you think best describes [COUNTRY] . . .

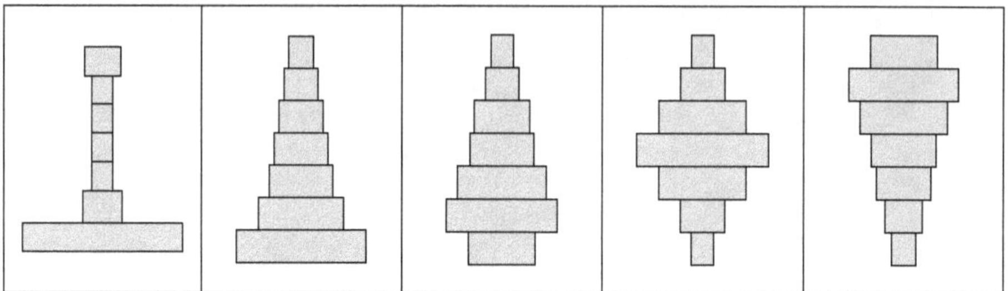

Type A	Type B	Type C	Type D	Type E
A small elite at the top, very few people in the middle and the great mass of people at the bottom.	A society like a pyramid with a small elite at the top, more people in the middle, and most at the bottom.	A pyramid except that just a few people are at the bottom.	A society with most people in the middle.	Many people near the top, and only a few near the bottom.

Figure 7.7 Diagrams of different types of society.

Source: ISSP 2009.

Table 7.2 How people describe their society

	Type A (%)	*Type B (%)*	*Type C (%)*	*Type D (%)*	*Type E (%)*	*Q10a Groups tending toward top+bottom. Where would you put yourself on this scale?*
Type A: the majority describe their society as Type A						
UA	69.1	22.1	4.8	2.4	1.6	3.54
LV	68.3	20.2	5.4	2.4	3.7	4.47
BG	63.5	27.2	5.5	3.3	0.5	3.97
HR	57.4	28.8	6.4	5.5	1.9	4.62
HU	56.6	32.3	6.0	3.7	1.4	4.04
ZA	50.8	31.8	8.7	6.6	2.2	4.90
LT	48.8	36.2	7.4	5.9	1.7	4.25
AR	45.6	36.1	9.4	7.0	1.9	4.96
SK	43.6	39.1	8.5	7.4	1.4	4.86
PT	40.8	36.2	12.5	6.5	4.0	4.42
RU	40.7	35.0	12.5	8.4	3.4	4.66
TR	40.0	35.9	12.0	8.9	3.2	4.02
PL	37.1	33.0	13.6	12.6	3.7	5.27
Average						4.46
Type B The majority describe their society as Type B						
IL	18.6	55.8	15.3	9.3	1.1	5.38
FR	16.4	53.6	16.3	12.1	1.6	4.89
CN	21.9	51.4	12.2	12.2	2.2	4.60
CL	24.3	48.0	13.1	11.7	2.9	4.03
EE	32.6	46.6	9.6	9.8	1.5	4.94
GB-GBN	14.9	41.9	18.8	20.9	3.5	5.24
ES	16.8	41.2	21.5	17.0	3.5	4.98

IT	32.4	41.0	12.8	11.7	2.1	4.61
PH	31.5	40.4	11.2	10.0	6.8	4.49
US	17.1	38.9	15.0	26.0	2.9	5.79
JP	11.1	38.5	26.4	20.0	4.0	4.65
TW	18.3	36.9	26.3	16.0	2.4	4.26
VE	31.4	36.0	17.1	10.2	5.3	5.43
DE	18.8	35.4	23.0	18.6	4.2	5.70
CZ	30.9	35.1	18.5	13.5	2.1	4.87
KR	19.1	35.0	25.8	15.1	5.0	4.51
BE-FLA	6.8	34.5	23.5	32.1	3.0	5.86
NZ	6.5	33.0	25.5	33.3	1.7	5.94
SI	26.4	31.5	27.2	12.3	2.7	4.93
Average						5.00
Type C: The majority describe their society as Type C						
CY	4.5	24.0	57.4	13.0	1.1	5.84
AT	17.4	26.5	31.0	22.6	2.5	5.71
Average						5.77
Type D: The majority describe their society as Type D						
DK	1.6	10.7	25.5	58.7	3.5	6.48
NO	1.9	10.9	22.3	58.7	6.2	5.86
IS	9.7	18.6	19.5	47.6	4.5	5.77
AU	6.1	29.5	21.7	40.7	2.1	6.12
CH	6.7	24.8	25.0	39.8	3.7	5.89
SE	7.1	23.3	29.8	37.9	1.9	5.50
FI	6.9	23.7	32.6	35.6	1.2	6.01
Average						5.95

Source: ISSP Research Group (2017): International Social Survey Programme: Social Inequality IV – ISSP 2009.

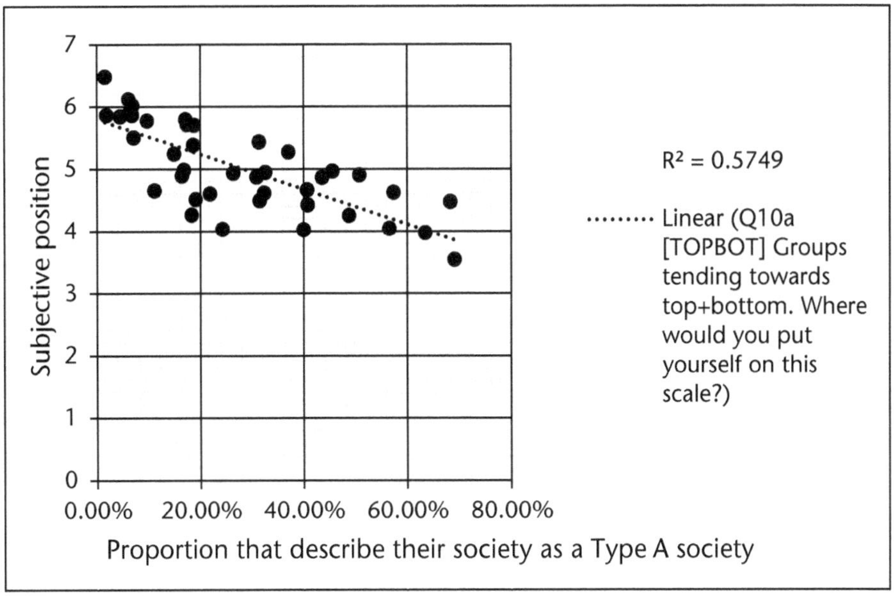

Figure 7.8 Proportion that describe their society as Type A (small elite, most people at the bottom) and subjective position.

Source: ISSP Research Group (2017): International Social Survey Programme: Social Inequality IV – ISSP 2009.

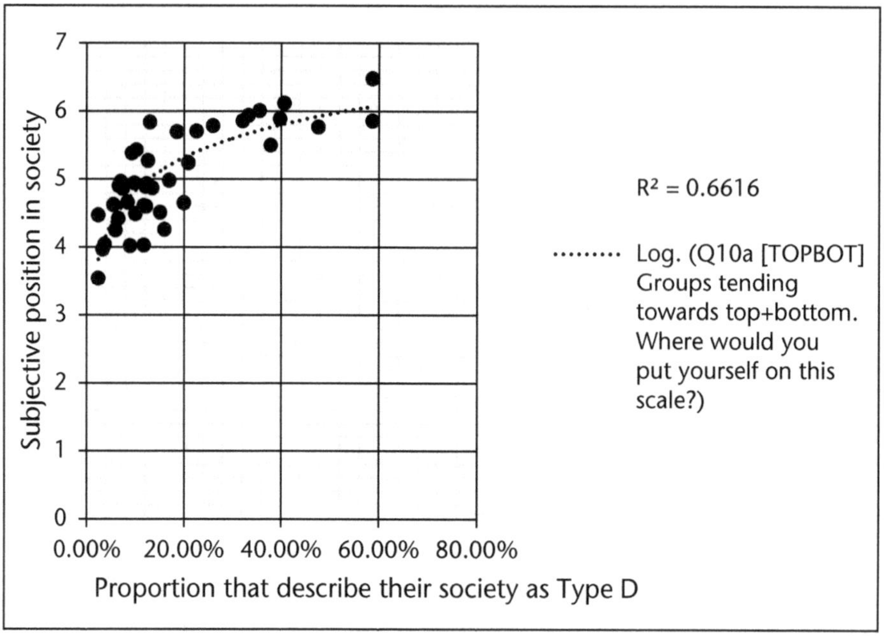

Figure 7.9 Proportion that describe their society as Type D (most people in the middle) and subjective position.

Source: ISSP Research Group (2017): International Social Survey Programme: Social Inequality IV – ISSP 2009.

Subjective position and happiness

There are several sociological, psychological and epidemiological studies that show how subjective comparisons with others affect wellbeing independently of a person's objective situation (Ejrnæs & Greve, 2017; Präg, Mills, & Wittek, 2016; Callan, Kim, & Matthews, 2015; Mishra & Carleton, 2015). People's level of satisfaction and wellbeing is expected to be influenced by how they perceive their situation in comparison with a given reference point, such as: (1) one's past outcomes, (2) perceptions of others' situations, and (3) expected future outcomes (Levine & Moreland, 1987). People's experiences of relative social position are expected to have a negative impact if they perceive their situation to be below that of those with whom they normally compare and identify themselves. The perception of having a lower status than one's peers, and the feeling of being assigned an unjust position, may lead to lower wellbeing and mental health. That is the reason why subjective perceptions of social position could have an impact on individuals' wellbeing independently of their objective economic situation. Wilkinson and Pickett (2010) have shown that inequality is highly correlated with social problems and bad health. The underlying mechanism behind the relationship is that inequality accelerates the feeling of relative deprivation where individuals or groups feel deprived compared to others. Socioeconomic comparison in a more unequal society will undermine social cohesion and wellbeing because the distance between the higher and the lower social strata will be greater.

Looking at the relationship between mean level of happiness and subjective perceptions of position in society as in Figure 7.10, then this shows that in countries where people have a high-level perception of their subjective position in society, they also enjoy high levels of happiness.

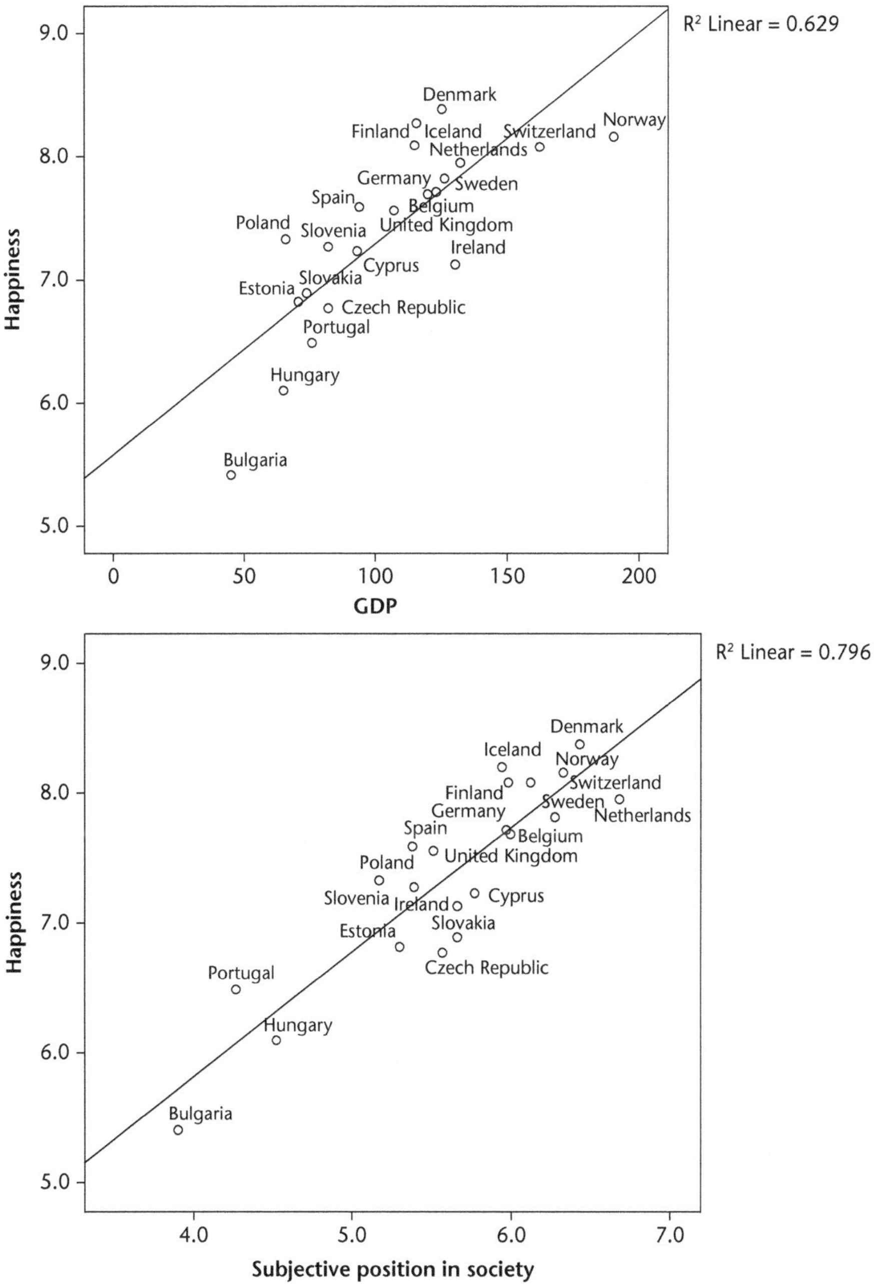

Figure 7.10 Relation between GDP and happiness and relation between subjective position and happiness.

Source: Ejrnæs & Greve, 2017: 212.

On the macro level, the feeling of happiness is strongly positively correlated on the aggregate level with subjective perceptions of individuals' position in society (Ejrnæs & Greve, 2017). The r square shows that the correlation between average subjective social position and average happiness is stronger than the correlation between GDP and average happiness. On the micro level, the study by Ejrnæs and Greve (2017) also shows that people's perceived position in society is a stronger predictor of their happiness than an objective measure of their position in society based on income deciles. However, the same study also shows that welfare state regimes shape the connection between subjective position in society and happiness. In the Nordic welfare states, people's subjective position in society has less influence on happiness than in other welfare regimes. It seems that the Nordic welfare states are more likely to generate greater social and economic equality and mobility, which in turn could raise happiness levels at the bottom of society (Ejrnæs & Greve, 2017).

Relative deprivation, reaction and protest

In this section, if, when, where and why people who perceive relative deprivation act politically is analysed. Our vantage point is still social comparison theory.

In contrast to much of the psychological literature on relative deprivation, sociological and political science research uses social comparison theory to explain when and why people engage in political activism. Classical theory on social movements suggests that people engage in collective action as a response to grievances stemming from relative deprivation and perceived injustice. Relative deprivation theories are among the most prominent theories in explaining how grievances motivate collective action. Ted Gurr defines relative deprivation as the 'perceived discrepancy between value expectations and value capabilities' (Gurr, 1970, p. 37). In this context, values are defined as material needs or opportunities. For example, relative deprivation emerges in situations where people's expectations of what they should be entitled to exceed what they can actually get.

As mentioned previously, the literature on relative deprivation distinguishes between personal (egoistic) relative deprivation and collective (fraternal) relative deprivation (Runciman, 1966; Klandermans, Van der Toorn, & Van Stekelenburg, 2008; Dion & Kawakami, 1996). Individual relative deprivation refers to a single individual's feeling of deprivation compared to other individuals. Collective or group relative deprivation stems from the discontent felt by an entire group compared to a reference group. Collective relative deprivation is an important concept in understanding perceptions of discrimination. Collective relative deprivation occurs if an individual feels that their own group has fewer opportunities compared to the majority group. Most studies show that people who feel collective relative deprivation are more likely to protest than people who experience individual relative deprivation (Smith & Pettigrew, 2014). Feelings of discrimination and unfair treatment will foster collective interests, identity and group consciousness. Collective relative deprivation occurs when one's in-group, e.g. an ethnic or religious group, is perceived to be disadvantaged compared to one or more out-groups (Dion & Kawakami, 1996).

Studies on group mobilisation have documented that perceptions of discrimination can increase the level of various forms of political activity (Schildkraut, 2005). Research shows that relative deprivation or discrimination based on group comparison is more important for political mobilisation than individual comparison (Major, 1994; Dion & Kawakami, 1996). According to this perspective, protest and political mobilisation are linked to the degree of perceived discrimination which a minority group experiences (Salamon & Van Evera, 1973).

Relative deprivation and protest in different institutional settings

According to James C. Davies' (1962) theory about revolution, protest and political revolt, these phenomena occur when a prolonged period of objective economic prosperity and social development is followed by a sharp reversal. In a period with economic improvements, people have growing expectations as to their future standard of living. When an economic recession or crisis occurs, people's standard of living normally declines and the gap between what people expect to have and what they get will increase. In this situation, people become dissatisfied and frustrated with their economic situation, which could lead to protest action and collective mobilisation (Davies, 1962). However, the empirical evidence that feelings of relative deprivation have an impact on protest action and collective mobilisation is relatively weak. A central question is when feelings of relative deprivation will be transformed into political action or angry resentment. Smith and Pettigrew (2014) present four situational appraisals that could influence people's reactions to relative deprivation.

The first and more obvious situational appraisals are that people only react if people care about the domain where they feel they have an undeserved disadvantage. If people feel disadvantaged in terms of their pay, it will often create an emotional reaction which could be translated into collective protest because people often care about their pay.

The second situational appraisal is whether people believe that the process that has produced the undeserved disadvantage is legitimate. If people believe that the process is fair, they will be less willing to engage in protest, while people will be more willing to voice their anger if they believe the process is unfair.

The third situational appraisal is whether people believe that they could be blamed for the disadvantageous situation. If people believe that they are responsible for being poor or unemployed, they are less likely to voice their anger through protest. If people believe that the government or capitalist system is responsible for the unemployment, they will be more willing to express their anger through protest.

The last situational appraisal is whether people believe that the situation could be changed through collective action. If people believe that there is no chance that the situation will improve, they will tend to react with resignation. If people believe that the situation will improve regardless of what they do themselves, they will feel hopeful and not voice their criticisms. Protest and angry resentment are most likely when improvement can be imagined but not guaranteed.

A central question is whether relative deprivation will be translated into political activism, and how political institutions influence protest action and to what extent relative deprivation motivates the latter. In order to measure the level of relative deprivation, an index based on the following statements was constructed (Ejrnæs, 2017):

- I have had to manage on a lower household income.
- I have had to draw on my savings or get into debt to cover ordinary living expenses.
- I have had to cut back[1] on holidays or new household equipment.[2]

The measure of non-institutional political participation is constructed as a simple summation of the four individual policy-oriented activities, consisting of: participating in a demonstration, signing a petition, boycotting a product, and wearing badges or stickers (Ejrnæs, 2017). Figure 7.11 shows that, on the macro level, there is no evidence that perceived economic deprivation motivates protest action. It is more likely that relative deprivation has a negative influence on people's capability to participate (Ejrnæs, 2017). A possible explanation could be that a decrease in economic resources among citizens might lead to political disengagement. However, there is a risk of ecological fallacy, which means making assumptions about the actions of individuals based on aggregate statistics collected for the countries to which those individuals belong (Ejrnæs, 2017).

In what follows, how factors at the country level interact with factors at the individual level is analysed.

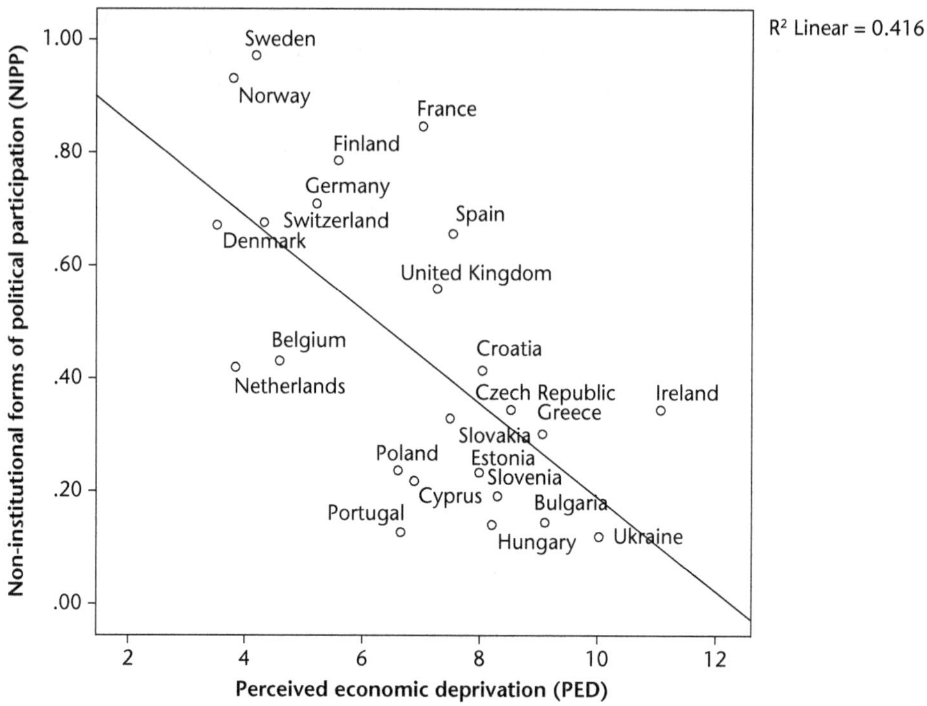

Figure 7.11 Cross-country comparison between mean level of perceived economic deprivation and mean level of non-institutional forms of political participation.

Source: Ejrnæs, 2017: 438.

If looking at the correlation between perceived economic deprivation and political protest, at the individual level within the different countries there is a significant negative correlation in most countries. This means that at the individual level, perceived economic deprivation seems to motivate political action. The analysis shows a classic example of ecological fallacy (Robinson, 1950) where one can find a negative correlation between perceived economic deprivation at the aggregate level, while there is a positive correlation at the individual level.

However, the strength of the correlation varies among European countries. The highest positive correlation is in Scandinavian countries and the Netherlands, while East European countries have either zero correlation or a negative correlation.

The central question is why perceived economic deprivation in some countries motivates lawful protest, while people in other countries seem to be more disengaged when they perceive economic deprivation. One explanation could be that people only protest if they believe that they actually have a possibility of improving their situation through political protest. In Scandinavian countries, with their high level of trust in political institutions, people are more willing to voice their criticism through peaceful protests because they believe that they can actually improve their situation. In more corrupt and authoritarian regimes, such as post-communist countries, the unresponsiveness of government institutions could alienate citizens from the state, creating a society where citizens are not able or willing to voice their criticism through democratic means (Mieriņa, 2014).

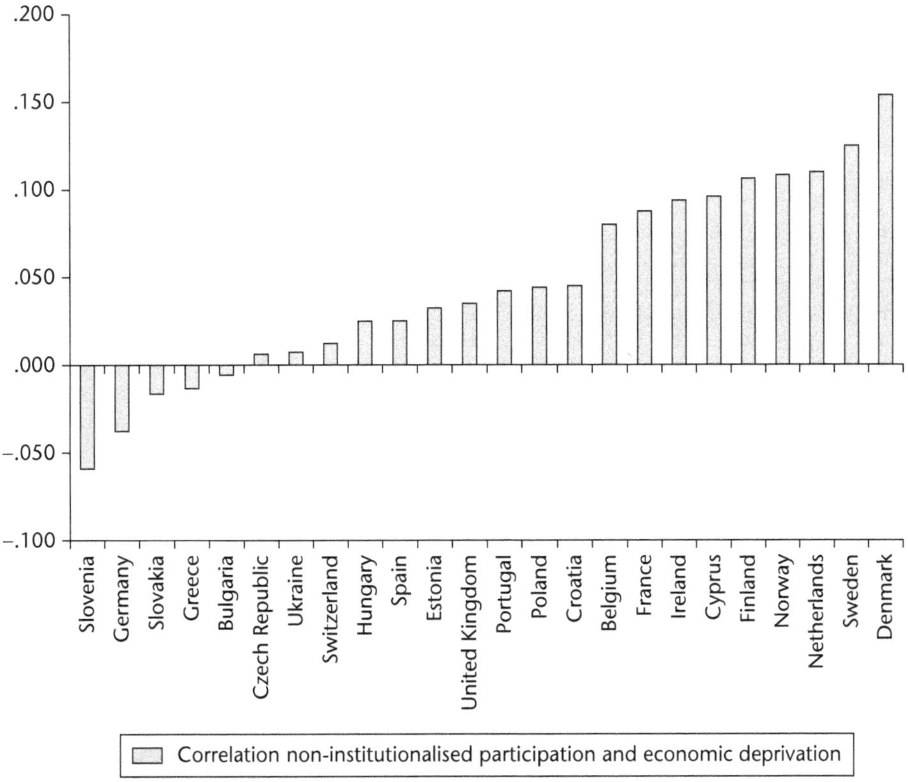

Figure 7.12 Correlation between non-institutionalised participation and economic deprivation in different countries.

Source: Ejrnæs, 2017: 439.

Conclusion

This chapter shows that, in line with reference group theory, people tend to see themselves as occupying a middle position in society. However, this is not the whole story. Different societal contexts have an impact on people's location in the social hierarchy. In more prosperous and equal societies, average subjective position is higher than in poorer, more unequal societies. When it comes to the emotional and behavioural reaction to relative deprivation and perceived subjective position, societal context also has a huge influence. First, subjective social position seems to have more influence on happiness than does income. Second, subjective position has a different impact on happiness in different welfare states. In Nordic welfare states, the subjective position in society has a smaller impact on the level of happiness than in other welfare regimes. The behavioural response to feelings of relative deprivation differs also in different societal contexts. In countries with a high level of trust in political institutions, relative deprivation seems to motivate political engagement, while in countries with a low level of trust in the institutions, relative deprivation seems to depress political engagement.

Notes

1 'Cut back' in the sense of reducing the number of (quantity) or the amount spent on (quality).
2 'Household equipment' includes things like irons, vacuum cleaners or washing machines. Translations should not specifically include these examples but should use words or phrases that allude to such things.

References

Callan, M. J., Kim, H., & Matthews, W. J. (2015). Predicting self-rated mental and physical health: The contributions of subjective socioeconomic status and personal relative deprivation. *Frontiers in Psychology*, *6*, 1415.

Davies, J. C. (1962). Toward a theory of revolution. *American Sociological Review*, *27*(1).

Dion, K. L., & Kawakami, K. (1996). Ethnicity and perceived discrimination in Toronto: Another look at the personal/group discrimination discrepancy. *Canadian Journal of Behavioural Science/Revue canadienne des sciences du comportement*, *28*(3), 203.

Duncan, G. J., & Brooks-Gunn, J. (Eds.). (1999). *Consequences of Growing up Poor*. New York, NY: Russell Sage Foundation.

Ejrnæs, A. (2017). Deprivation and non-institutional political participation: Analysing the relationship between deprivation, institutional trust and political activism in Europe. *European Politics and Society*, *18*(4), 428–445.

Ejrnæs, A., & Greve, B. (2017). Your position in society matters for how happy you are. *International Journal of Social Welfare*, *26*(3), 206–217.

ESS Round 6: European Social Survey (2018): ESS-6 2012 Documentation Report. Edition 2.4. Bergen, European Social Survey Data Archive, NSD – Norwegian Centre for Research Data for ESS ERIC. doi:10.21338/NSD-ESS6-2012.

ESS Round 8: European Social Survey Round 8 Data (2016). Data file edition 2.1. NSD – Norwegian Centre for Research Data, Norway – Data Archive and distributor of ESS data for ESS ERIC. doi:10.21338/NSD-ESS8-2016.

European Social Survey Cumulative File, ESS 1–8 (2018). Data file edition 1.0. NSD – Norwegian Centre for Research Data, Norway – Data Archive and distributor of ESS data for ESS ERIC. doi:10.21338/NSD-ESS-CUMULATIVE.

Evans, M. D., & Kelley, J. (2004). Subjective social location: Data from 21 nations. *International Journal of Public Opinion Research*, *16*(1), 3–38.

Fahey, T. (2010). Poverty and the two concepts of relative deprivation. *UCD School of Applied Social Science Working Paper Series WP10/1*.

Festinger, L. (1954). A theory of social comparison processes. *Human Relations*, 7(2), 117–140.

Gurr, T. (1970). *Why Men Rebel*. Princeton, NJ: Princeton University Press.

ISSP Research Group (2017). International Social Survey Programme: Social Inequality IV – ISSP 2009. GESIS Data Archive, Cologne. ZA5400 Data file Version 4.0.0, doi:10.4232/1.12777

Klandermans, B., Van der Toorn, J., & Van Stekelenburg, J. (2008). Embeddedness and identity: How immigrants turn grievances into action. *American Sociological Review*, *73*(6), 992–1012.

Levine, J. M., & Moreland, R. L. (1987). Social comparison and outcome evaluation in group contexts. In J. C. Masters & W. P. Smith (Eds.), *Social Comparison, Social Justice, and Relative Deprivation: Theoretical, Empirical, and Policy Perspectives* (pp. 105–127). Hillsdale, NJ: Lawrence Erlbaum Associates, Inc.

Merton, R. K. (1957). *Social Theory and Social Structure*. Glencoe, IL: Free Press.

Lindemann, K. (2007). The impact of objective characteristics on subjective social position. *Trames*, *11*(1), 54–68.

Lindemann, K., & Saar, E. (2014). Contextual effects on subjective social position: Evidence from European countries. *International Journal of Comparative Sociology*, *55*(1), 3–23.

Major, B. (1994). From social inequality to personal entitlement: The role of social comparisons, legitimacy appraisals, and group membership. In M. P. Zanna (Ed.), *Advances in Experimental Social Psychology* (Vol. *26*, pp. 293–355). San Diego, CA: Academic Press.

Mieriņa, Inta. (2014). The vicious circle: Does disappointment with political authorities contribute to political passivity in Latvia? *European Societies*, *16*(4), 615–637.

Mishra, S., & Carleton, R. N. (2015). Subjective relative deprivation is associated with poorer physical and mental health. *Social Science & Medicine*, *147*, 144–149.

Präg, P., Mills, M. C., & Wittek, R. (2016). Subjective socioeconomic status and health in cross-national comparison. *Social Science & Medicine*, *149*, 84–92.
Robinson, W. S. (1950). Ecological correlations and the behavior of individuals. *American Sociological Review*, *15*(3), 351–357. doi:10.2307/2087176
Runciman, W. G. (1966). *Relative Deprivation and Social Justice: A Study of Attitudes to Social Inequality in Twentieth-century England*. London: Routledge & Kegan Paul.
Salamon, L. M., & Van Evera, S. (1973). Fear, apathy, and discrimination: A test of three explanations of political participation. *American Political Science Review*, *67*(4), 1288–1306.
Savage, M. (2015). *Social Class in the 21st Century*. London: Penguin UK.
Schildkraut, Deborah J. (2005). The rise and fall of political engagement among Latinos: The role of identity and perceptions of discrimination. *Political Behavior*, *27*(3), 285–312.
Smith, H. J., & Pettigrew, T. F. (2014). The subjective interpretation of inequality: A model of the relative deprivation experience. *Social and Personality Psychology Compass*, *8*(12), 755–765.
Stouffer, S. A., Lumsdaine, A. A., Lumsdaine, M. H., Williams, R. M., Jr., Smith, M. B., Janis, I. L., & Cottrell, L. S., Jr. (1949). *The American Soldier: Combat and its Aftermath. (Studies in Social Psychology in World War II)*. Princeton, NJ: Princeton University Press.
Wilkinson, R. G. (2000). Social relations, hierarchy, and health. *The Society and Population Health Reader: A State and Community Perspective*, *2*, 211–235.
Wilkinson, R., & Pickett, K. (2010). *The Spirit Level: Why Equality is Better for Everyone*. London: Penguin UK.

8

The consequences of growing up poor

Wim Van Lancker and Julie Vinck

Introduction

Poor children often become poor parents. Such often-heard truism succinctly summarizes the main reason why poverty is considered a problem in the first place: growing up poor has important, detrimental consequences for one's individual life chances. In addition, this disadvantage is reproduced at the societal level, incurring costs for society as a whole.

In fact, child poverty is a persistent multi-dimensional and intergenerational problem in developed welfare states (UNICEF 2007). Over the past decade, the number of children in relative poverty has been increasing in the majority of OECD countries (OECD 2014), a trend that was reinforced by the *Great Recession* in some of them (Cantillon et al. 2017; Jenkins et al. 2012). Accordingly, combating child poverty is a key policy priority in European welfare states (European Commission 2013). Unlike regular redistributive policies (see Part III in this book), combating child poverty enjoys broad based popular support since children are not responsible for them growing up in poverty; it is beyond their control and they are seen as deserving (van Oorschot 2006). Children are regarded a key target for policy interventions not only in European welfare states but all across the globe. In a recent joint World Bank and Unicef report (Unicef & World Bank Group 2016), for instance, it is argued that children living in extreme poverty deserve specific attention because they are 'affected by poverty in different ways than adults and are almost certain to miss out on a good start in life' (2016: 2).

In this chapter we review the consequences of growing up poor at the individual level and at the level of society across different countries and contexts. We start this chapter with an overview of child poverty concepts and measures. It is of utmost importance to have a good grasp of the myriad ways poverty can be defined and measured. The aforementioned references to extreme poverty across the globe and relative poverty in European welfare states demonstrates that definitions matter; the consequences of child poverty differ for different concepts and measures. Subsequently, the empirical evidence of the impact of growing up poor on children's (later) life chances, opportunities for social mobility, health, status, and income is reviewed, followed by a section in which we focus on how child poverty intersects with multiple categories of disadvantage, such as disability, gender, immigration status, and social class. Finally, the consequences for society in terms of budgetary cost, employment, and productivity are discussed.

The measurement of child poverty

How poverty can be approached from several theoretical frameworks and defined and operationalized in many different ways is the subject of Chapters 2, 3 and 4 in this book. Here we focus briefly on the peculiarities of measuring child poverty (see Lichter (1997) for an overview of child poverty measurement).

Child poverty, akin to poverty among other age groups, is usually conceptualized as a lack of resources, and this can be measured drawing on a monetary or a non-monetary approach (Minujin et al. 2006; Roelen & Gassmann 2008). First, with a monetary approach child poverty is operationalized as the share of children living in households with low income. As such it is an *indirect* approach to child poverty since it does not directly measure the living conditions of children but of the household, which is directly related to parental income (see also Chapter 32). Second, drawing on the non-monetary approach, child poverty is operationalized as a lack of goods and services considered necessary for child development and indispensable for the realization of their basic human rights and capabilities (e.g. Biggeri & Mehrotra 2011; also Chapter 9). This is a more *direct* approach to child poverty since it aims to capture what is necessary from the point of view of the children themselves.

Child poverty is predominantly measured using a monetary approach (Cantillon et al. 2017; Minujin et al. 2006). A poverty line is set to distinguish between the poor and non-poor child population. This poverty line can be defined in an absolute or a relative way (Ravallion 1994). An absolute monetary approach regards children as poor when their household's income is insufficient to provide for their basic needs such as food, housing, and clothing, and the standard against which children are compared is the same across countries and over time. Contrarily, a relative monetary approach assesses the household's income against the living standard of the society the child grows up in and the child is considered poor when its household does not have enough resources to live a minimally acceptable way of life (Unicef 2005). In this case, the applied threshold is time and place dependent.

In low-income countries an absolute child poverty measure is typically applied. The 'international poverty line' is set at \$1.90 a day and measures the number and share of children growing up in extreme poverty. In middle-income countries, extreme poverty is nearly eradicated and hence, higher, still absolute, poverty lines fixed at \$3.20 and \$5.50 a day are employed to identify poor children. Recently, a measure combining both absolute and relative logics, coined the 'societal poverty line', has been proposed by the World Bank (2017) to assess the poverty situation in countries where extreme poverty declined strongly. This measure applies the logic of the absolute international poverty line with a standard that is relative to the country's median income. Specifically, its threshold is set either at \$1.90 a day, corresponding to the international poverty line, or at \$1.00 increased with 50% of median consumption on a daily basis in the country, whichever value is the higher. In high-income countries, relative rather than absolute measures are often used to measure child poverty. Children are considered to live in relative income poverty in richer countries when the household's income is below a certain percentage of the country's median (be that 40%, 50% or 60%).

Child poverty has been measured in a non-monetary way as well. Conceptualized in the deprivation framework (Townsend 1979), the European Union has included a material deprivation index into its leading social indicators, complementary to the relative, monetary poverty definition. With this indicator, poverty is regarded as a lack of access to a set of goods and services at the household level due to non-affordability. Recently, Guio et al. (2012, 2016) proposed a *child-specific* material deprivation index. This includes various child-level and household-level deprivation items including, for example, being able to provide some new clothes, the possession of books suitable to the child's age, the ability to go on regular leisure activities and to invite friends of the child around to play and eat from time to time. The list of items included in the index as well as the threshold to be considered deprived is the same across countries in Europe, yet it is not an absolute child poverty measure in the true meaning of the word. The items included in the index are deemed necessary for a child *currently* growing up in a *high-income* country, hence this measure is both time and place dependent (Unicef, 2012). It is of course important to realize that even such a direct, 'non-monetary' approach is related to money, in this case the lack of means to afford basic goods and services.

Individual consequences of growing up poor

In 1992, the Great Smokey Mountains Study was initiated in a sparsely populated rural area in the Appalachian mountain region of North Carolina (Copeland et al. 2014). The purpose of the study was to assess the well-being of children and youth in the area and to estimate the need for mental health services. The longitudinal study in which 1,420 participants were assessed up to 11 times between the age of 9 and 26 years old included several questions on anxiety disorders and the development of psychiatric problems, personality traits, and well-being. Over time, the study expanded its scope to assess the family environment and family relations, physical development, stress, and poverty. The longitudinal nature of the study made it possible to study changes in several of these outcomes over time and their predictors up until adulthood (Costello et al. 2016). At this point over 100 papers have been published based on this data, and it continues to be studied.

The interesting thing for our purpose here is that the area under study comprises the Eastern Band of Cherokee Indians. Since the opening of a casino on the reservation grounds in 1996 a proportion of the profits (roughly the amount of an average child benefit in Western Europe) were distributed equally among the Cherokee families. Hence these children saw an unexpected increase in family income while the other children and youth living in the same area did not receive such supplement. Since this was a longitudinal study, a natural experiment emerged in which the causal effects of boosting family incomes could be identified by comparing outcomes in treatment (the Cherokee children and youth) and control (the other children and youth) groups. The results show that children growing up in families who received the additional money did substantially better on several domains of life in the subsequent years, and that these beneficial effects of increasing family income lasted into adulthood. Cherokee families were more likely to exit poverty, and this was followed by a significant decline in substance abuse, lower rates of psychiatric disorders, and even changes in two personality traits (agreeability and neuroticism) that are considered important for later-life success (Costello et al. 2003). Moreover, the extra money led to a longer-term reduction in criminal behavior and an improvement in educational attainment, in particular for the household who started off poorest (Akee et al. 2010, 2018).

Since the start of the Great Smokey Mountains Study, the direct, causal impact of family income on later-life outcomes of children in terms of well-being, educational attainment achievement, health, behavior, and earnings has been demonstrated many times (Brooks-Gunn & Duncan 1997; Duncan et al. 2010; 2011; Milligan & Stabile 2011; Evans 2016). In a recent meta-review, Cooper and Stewart (2013; update in 2017) identified 34 studies in which causal claims of family income on child outcomes could be examined. They conclude that 'poorer children have worse cognitive, social-behavioural and health outcomes in part because they are poorer, and not just because poverty is correlated with other household and parental characteristics' (2013: 5). Importantly, the authors emphasize that longer spells of poverty have stronger effects on long-term outcomes than shorter poverty spells. Recent analyses based on the UK Millennium Cohort Study, for instance, show that *any* exposure to poverty in childhood is associated with adverse health outcomes but that for children who were persistently poor throughout childhood the effects were larger (Lai et al. 2019). Added to that, a large body of qualitative research indicates that poverty is associated with lower levels of well-being (Main 2014), and affects children's friendships and social relations as well, which in turn generates anxiety and unhappiness (Sutton 2008; Ridge 2002). Importantly, evidence gathered from the Great Smokey Mountains Study suggests the positive impact of income supplements on children's outcomes is mediated by parental quality (Akee et al. 2018). Indeed, according to the Family Stress Model, the outcomes of children are not only directly influenced by low family income or low socioeconomic status but also indirectly through parental behavior and relationships (Yeung et al. 2002; Davis-Kean 2005; Ponnet 2014).

In sum, the literature shows that growing up poor affects children's outcomes through two channels (OECD 2018). First, poverty means that parents are not able to financially invest properly in goods and services considered necessary for healthy child development, including quality housing, healthy food, proper care, quality education, a safe environment at home to learn and play, and goods that promote the social and cognitive capabilities of children, such as summer camps, books, computers, or musical instruments (Duncan & Murnane 2011; Bradbury et al. 2015). Second, poverty induces financial stress which has a negative effect on parental quality and family relationships. Parents living under financial strain argue more and adopt a more authoritarian parenting style which is less responsive to children's needs and well-being (McLeod & Shanahan 1993). Briefly stated: parents who are living hand to mouth are usually less able to read bedtime stories every night because they have fewer books at hand and they live under stress. These two channels reinforce one another. For example, deteriorating family relationship can lead to divorce which in turn puts an even higher strain on monetary resources (Uunk 2004; De Vaus et al. 2017). So, growing up poor affects children in a negative, profound way, and limits their opportunities in later life. These effects are long-lasting, making it difficult to escape poverty. Research showed that poor children are indeed likely to become poor parents themselves (Wagmiller & Adelman 2009; Bellani & Bia 2019).

Although most evidence is from the US, research in European settings with often more developed welfare states generally points to similar mechanisms (Bellani & Bia 2019). Lesner (2018) exploits variation among siblings to causally estimate the long-term consequences of childhood poverty in Denmark. The findings show that adults who have experienced relative poverty during childhood have lower levels of education which translates in lower earnings and poorer job conditions. Moreover, growing up poor has a negative impact on the probability to marry or cohabit. Yet, there are some findings that seem to be almost exclusively linked to the situation in the US, such as the link between growing up poor and later-life criminal behavior and incarceration, and the outcomes of growing up poor in terms of health (Cooper & Stewart 2013). The difference in healthcare system between the US and almost any European welfare state seems to be the main culprit here. Context indeed matters. Research for instance indicates that more generous and more equal welfare states do better in mitigating the intergenerational transmission of poverty and to promote the education and labor market opportunities of children growing up in low-income families (Corak 2013). There also differences between growing up poor in developed or developing countries. Research examining the outcomes of poor children by means of measures of extreme poverty (such as the World Bank's $1.90/day) not only identify lower future earnings, lower skills, and poorer health as longer-term consequences of growing up poor, but also stunted development due to malnutrition and undernourishment (Newhouse et al. 2016). Stunted development as an extreme form of poor health is a consequence of growing up in extreme poverty in poor countries but not necessarily a consequence of growing up relatively poor in rich welfare states. Still, that growing up poor has important consequences for long-term health and employment outcomes, skills attainment, and income is a robust finding across developed and developing countries.

Finally, it is important to keep in mind that the consequences of poverty will be dependent on the way poverty is measured. In a recent article, Mood and Jonsson (2016) draw on longitudinal data to assess the outcomes in terms of social relations and social support of being poor according to absolute, relative, and deprivation ways of measuring poverty. The results show that the poor have worse social relations and are more socially isolated. Importantly, however, the strength of the association varies between different poverty definitions. Deprivation, here measured as the inability to pay unexpected expenses, is a much better predictor of poor social relations than relative or absolute approaches

Intersection of child poverty with social risks groups

The risk of growing up poor is not evenly distributed but is more likely to occur among families belonging to specific social risk groups, such as parents with low educational qualifications, parents with poor health, single parents, or parents with an immigration background (Galloway et al. 2015; Gornick & Jäntti 2011; Vandenbroucke & Vinck 2013). Moreover, the consequences of childhood poverty may be different at the *intersection* of these sources of disadvantage. Rooted in labor market studies on race and gender, an intersectionality approach asserts that multiple sources of disadvantage not only have an additive impact on future outcomes but might also reinforce each other (e.g. McCall 2001, 2005). Two issues are of particular relevance here.

First, the consequences of growing up poor differ across risk groups. It is well known that children living in a single-parent household run an increased poverty risk (Gornick & Jäntti 2011; OECD 2018). The majority of single parents are mothers and the elevated poverty risk is related to the absence of a second earner and its associated difficulties in balancing work and care responsibilities (Nieuwenhuis & Maldonado 2018). Here, poverty intersects with gender. Some US research has shown that single motherhood affects children's outcomes, such as the child's school success, future employment changes and well-being, through the two aforementioned channels: lower incomes on the one hand, lower parenting quality and the experience of stressful life events on the other (Amato 2005; Lee & McLanahan 2015; McLanahan & Sandefur 1994; Waldfogel et al. 2010). For instance, single mothers are more likely to work nonstandard hours, decreasing the time they are able to spend with their children. This, in turn, is related to worse socioemotional and school outcomes for their offspring (Presser et al. 2008). As such, the consequences of growing up poor in single-parent families will be different compared with growing up poor in couple families. Similarly, in his causal study on the long-term consequences of childhood poverty in Denmark, Lesner (2018) finds that growing up poor with low-educated parents has stronger negative effects than growing up poor with high-educated parents. It is hypothesized this is because high-skilled parents can more easily compensate for their lack of monetary resources through borrowing or relying on their social network.

Second, taking due account of the intersection of multiple disadvantages also helps understanding the direction of causality in the longer-term outcomes associated with child poverty. It has already been mentioned that growing up poor has a detrimental effect on the child's health, an effect that accumulates as the child gets older (Case et al. 2002; Currie & Stabile 2003). This is true for a variety of health indicators such as the child's health status as assessed by their parents or a physician, for more quantifiable indicators like the number of times the child was hospitalized or experienced activity limitations in the recent past (Case et al. 2002), as well as for chronic conditions and disabilities (Boat & Wu 2015; Stein & Silver 2002). Yet, the causality of the co-occurrence of child poverty and poor health might run in both directions. Take the association between childhood disability and child poverty as an example (Lustig & Strauser 2007; Mont 2014; Porterfield & Tracey 2003). Childhood disability can be a cause of child poverty because it entails higher costs. These costs include direct costs, such as increased expenditure on healthcare and medical needs, as well as indirect costs stemming from parents' reduced labor market supply to deal with the higher care needs of disabled children. Higher expenditures and lower incomes might push families below the poverty threshold. Alternatively, growing up in poverty can also cause disability since low-income families have poor nutrition, reside in bad or dangerous living conditions, and have less access to affordable, good quality health care while they exhibit poorer health behavior (see Lustig & Strauser 2007, for an overview). Although it is empirically difficult to properly distinguish cause from effect, a vicious circle between childhood disability and child poverty might have long-lasting, mutually reinforcing, adverse effects on a child's future opportunities in life (Mont 2014).

Societal consequences

It is generally acknowledged that an important societal cost is attached to child poverty. The adverse effects for individuals growing up poor translate into an aggregated total cost for society. Given the strong association between growing up poor and early and later-life outcomes (*supra*), increasing child poverty means that in the future more people will rely on benefits and will be in poor health, and fewer people will be working and earning wages, which in turn will increase social and health spending and decrease consumption and fiscal revenues. The societal cost, then, is the aggregated total of these different effects. Beyond the economic cost, child poverty can also affect innovation and productivity due to lower aggregated skill levels, school drop outs, etc. Such indirect costs of child poverty are, however, extremely difficult to measure and reliable estimates of these costs are still lacking. In this section we therefore focus on the economic cost of child poverty.

It is important to acknowledge that the total cost of child poverty is context-specific. It obviously depends on the level of child poverty and the exit rates out of poverty. The total cost of child poverty will be lower if fewer children are growing up poor, while higher initial poverty levels do not necessarily translate into higher societal costs if poverty spells are shorter in duration. That in turn depends on the institutional context, such as the generosity of the welfare state and the quality and accessibility of social services (Fouarge & Layte 2005; Vandecasteele 2010). Such social institutions come with a price tag attached as well, which means it is difficult, if not impossible, to calculate the net, aggregate gains of reducing child poverty. The budgetary gains might be offset by increased expenditures on social programs. In countries with high incarceration rates, such as the US, the association between poverty and crime is stronger and the cost of poverty in terms of incarceration costs will be higher compared with countries in which fewer people are at risk of being incarcerated (Beckett & Western 2001). Yet usually in these countries, such as Sweden, social work interventions will be more extensive, hence more expensive. The ultimate question, then, is how the interaction between these different policy measures and their effects play out. This all means that it matters a great deal what kind of costs are measurable in a reliable way. For example, measuring a total cost of poverty is not necessarily the same thing as estimating budgetary revenues forgone. Many measures that prevent poverty in the first place come with a cost as well, and the question is how these costs can be reliably taken into account. Finally, as mentioned before, how poverty is operationalized matters. Depending on the poverty indicator used, the number of poor children can be lower or higher, while the cost for reducing poverty will differ according to different indicators as well. Basically, one should always bear in mind that estimating the societal consequences of child poverty is prone to a serious margin of error.

Perhaps for that reason, few studies have attempted to quantify the societal cost of child poverty. A recent study estimated the annual societal cost of child poverty in the US (McLaughlin & Rank 2018). The cost-measurement analysis takes due account of costs associated with the loss of economic productivity, increased health costs (including direct health costs, costs for special education, and the cost associated with reduced number of quality years in life), increased costs associated with crime (including the cost associated with street crime, correction costs, incarceration, and private spending on crime deterrence), and costs associated with homelessness and maltreatment (including child welfare and social services costs). These costs are calculated over the life span of poor children in the year 2015. The estimate total annual cost of child poverty amounts to $1.0298 trillion or 5.4 percent of gross domestic product (GDP). Recently, the American Congress commissioned the National Academies of Sciences, Engineering and Medicine to write a so-called Consensus Report *Roadmap to Reducing Child Poverty* (2019). Next to concrete policy proposals to cut child poverty in half in the US, the report also includes an update of these estimates. In terms of 2018 GDP, the total annual cost of child poverty amounts to $1.1 trillion.

Earlier studies took a more narrow approach to the calculation of the cost of child poverty. Holzer et al. (2008) calculate the average cost per poor child in the US on the basis of their future lost earnings, propensity to commit crime, and poorer health. They estimate the aggregated cost of child poverty in the year 2006 to be 3.8 percent of GDP. Finally, one early study estimated the cost of child poverty in terms of future loss of economic production alone (Sherman & Edelman 1994). They arrived at an estimate of the cost of one year of child poverty between $36 billion and $177 billion for the year 1992. This is between about 0.6 and 2.8 percent of GDP.

For the UK, the Joseph Rowntree Foundation recently published a report in which the cost of poverty in general and child poverty in particular is estimated (Bramley et al. 2016). In the report, first the total cost of poverty on public service cost is estimated. This includes spending on services and policies to mitigate the effects of living in poverty and to cater for the specific needs of poor people. This includes directly identifiable spending on health care but also the cost for, among other things, school meals targeted toward poor children. The analyses also include estimates based on differences in spending between rich and poor neighborhoods and regions. Finally, like in the US studies, the report estimates the costs associated with lower future earnings, fiscal revenues and higher social spending. In the report, the public service cost of poverty is estimated to be about £69.2 billion with an additional knock-on effect of child poverty of £6 billion and a knock-on effect of adult poverty of £2.7 billion in the year 2015. This in total amounts to £77 billion or 4.1 percent of GDP.

Two older studies for the UK looked specifically at the cost of child poverty. First, Hirsch (2008) included costs stemming from additional social service costs to remedy poor health and learning difficulties among poor children, as well as long-term costs in terms of earnings and fiscal revenues forgone. His conservative estimation of the annual, aggregated cost of child poverty amounted to 2 percent of GDP. Second, Blanden et al. (2010) focused on the costs associated with healthcare costs, crime, future loss in employment, fiscal revenues and earnings, and reduced levels of well-being. They find an economic cost of child poverty amounting to at least 1 percent of GDP.

Finally, researchers have estimated the cost of poverty in three Canadian provinces: British Columbia (BC), Ontario and Québec. Since these studies are not specifically focused on child poverty we will only briefly mention them here. Akin to the aforementioned US studies, the three studies include costs for healthcare, crime, and lost future earnings. Their estimate for the total economic cost of poverty in 2008 amounts to between 4.1 and 4.7 percent of BC's GDP (Ivanova 2011). For Ontario, Laurie (2008) took due account of costs incurred by policies to remedy the consequences of poverty (including healthcare, criminal justice, and social assistance costs), the costs associated with future losses in earnings and future low skill levels. Laurie estimates these costs to amount to 5.5 to 6.6 percent of Ontario's GDP. Finally, drawing on the same methodology, Barayandema and Fréchet (2012) estimate the total economic cost of poverty for Québec in 2008 to be between 5.8 and 6.3 percent of Québec's GDP.

The differences in the estimates of all of these studies clearly show that the methodology used and the costs included have an important impact on the outcomes. At the same time all studies show that the societal cost of child poverty is significant and poses a burden to the public purse.

Conclusion

The consequences of growing up poor are negative and long-lasting, for individuals and for society as a whole. Poor children exhibit lower levels of well-being, lower educational achievement, and poorer health which translates into lower levels of employment, lower earnings, poorer health, and more benefit dependency in adult life. This persistent chain of disadvantage over the lives of poor children is caused directly by a lack of financial resources as well as indirectly by parental quality. For the public purse, an increase in child poverty is associated with an increase in social and health spending and a decrease in consumption and fiscal revenues.

Yet, how poverty is conceptualized and measured is important, since different measurement methods do not necessarily identify similar situations of disadvantage and this determines the extent to which the consequences of child poverty are generalizable. A perspective on monetary resources might obscure important facets of children's living conditions. The same holds for the institutional context of the countries in which poor children live. Generous welfare states with affordable services do better in mitigating the level of child poverty as well as improving the exit rates out of poverty. Finally, to fully understand the causes and consequences of child poverty it is important to acknowledge that the risk of child poverty intersects with other sources of disadvantage in terms of gender, class, ethnicity, and health.

References

Akee, R. K., Copeland, W. E., Keeler, G., Angold, A., & Costello, E. J. (2010). Parents' incomes and children's outcomes: a quasi-experiment using transfer payments from casino profits. *American Economic Journal: Applied Economics*, *2*(1), 86–115.

Akee, R., Copeland, W., Costello, E. J., & Simeonova, E. (2018). How does household income affect child personality traits and behaviors? *American Economic Review*, *108*(3), 775–827.

Amato, P. R. (2005). The impact of family formation change on the cognitive, social and emotional well-being of the next generation. *The Future of Children*, *15*(2), 75–96.

Barayandema, A., & Fréchet, G. (2012). The costs of poverty in Québec according to the model proposed by Nathan Laurie. Québec: Centre d'étude sur la pauvreté et l'exclusion.

Beckett, K., & Western, B. (2001). Governing social marginality: welfare, incarceration, and the transformation of state policy. *Punishment & Society*, *3*(1), 43–59.

Bellani, L., & Bia, M. (2019). The long-run effect of childhood poverty and the mediating role of education. *Journal of the Royal Statistical Society: Series A (Statistics in Society)*, *182*(1), 37–68.

Biggeri, M., & Mehrotra, R. (2011). Child poverty as capability deprivation: how to choose dimensions of child wellbeing and poverty? In M. Biggeri, J. Ballet, F. Comim (Eds.), *Children and the Capability Approach* (Chap. 3). New York: Palgrave/Macmillan.

Blanden, J., Hansen, K., & Machin, S. (2010). The economic cost of growing up poor: estimating the GDP loss associated with child poverty. *Fiscal Studies, 31*(3), 289–311.

Boat, T. F., & Wu, J. T. (Eds.). (2015). *Mental Disorders and Disabilities among Low-income Children*. Washington, DC, USA: The National Academies Press.

Bradbury, B., Corak, M., Waldfogel, J., & Washbrook, E. (2015). *Too Many Children Left Behind: The US Achievement Gap in Comparative Perspective*. New York: Russell Sage Foundation.

Bramley, G., Hirsch, D., Littlewood, M., & Watkins, D. (2016). *Counting the Cost of UK Poverty*. York: Joseph Rowntree Foundation.

Brooks-Gunn, J., & Duncan, G. J. (1997). The effects of poverty on children. *The Future of Children*, 7(2), 55–71.

Cantillon, B., Chzhen, Y., Handa, S., & Nolan, B. (Eds.). (2017). *Children of Austerity: Impact of the Great Recession on Child Poverty in Rich Countries*. Oxford: Oxford University Press.

Case, A., Lubotsky, D., & Paxson, C. (2002). Economic status and health in childhood: the origins of the gradient. *American Economic Review, 92*(5), 1308–1334.

Cooper, K., & Stewart, K. (2013). *Does money affect children's outcomes? A systematic review*. York: Joseph Rowntree Foundation.

Cooper, K., & Stewart, K. (2017). *Does money affect children's outcomes? An update*. Centre for Analysis of Social Exclusion Paper 203. London: Centre for Analysis of Social Exclusion, London School of Economics.

Copeland, W. E., Angold, A., Shanahan, L., & Costello, E. J. (2014). Longitudinal patterns of anxiety from childhood to adulthood: the Great Smoky Mountains Study. *Journal of the American Academy of Child & Adolescent Psychiatry, 53*(1), 21–33.

Corak, M. (2013). Income inequality, equality of opportunity, and intergenerational mobility. *Journal of Economic Perspectives, 27*(3), 79–102.

Costello, E. J., et al. (2003) Relationships between poverty and psychopathology: a natural experiment. *JAMA, 290*(15), 2023–2029.

Costello, E. J., Copeland, W., & Angold, A. (2016). The Great Smoky Mountains study: developmental epidemiology in the southeastern United States. *Social Psychiatry and Psychiatric Epidemiology, 51*(5), 639–646.

Currie, J., & Stabile, M. (2003). Socioeconomic status and child health: why is the relationship stronger for older children? *American Economic Review, 93*(5), 1813–1823.

Davis-Kean, P. E. (2005). The influence of parent education and family income on child achievement: the indirect role of parental expectations and the home environment. *Journal of Family Psychology, 19*(2), 294–304.

De Vaus, D., Gray, M., Qu, L., & Stanton, D. (2017). The economic consequences of divorce in six OECD countries. *Australian Journal of Social Issues, 52*(2), 180–199.

Duncan, G. J., & Murnane, R. J. (eds.) (2011). *Whither Opportunity? Rising Inequality, Schools, and Children's Life Chances*. New York: Russell Sage Foundation and Spencer Foundation.

Duncan, G. J., Ziol-Guest, K. M., & Kalil, A. (2010). Early-childhood poverty and adult attainment, behavior, and health. *Child Development, 81*(1), 306–325.

Duncan, G. J., Morris, P. A., & Rodrigues, C. (2011). Does money really matter? Estimating impacts of family income on young children's achievement with data from random-assignment experiments. *Developmental Psychology, 47*(5), 1263–1279.

European Commission. (2013). *Investing in children: breaking the cycle of disadvantage*. Commission Recommendation (p. 21). Brussels, Belgium: European Commission.

Evans, G. W. (2016). Childhood poverty and adult psychological well-being. *Proceedings of the National Academy of Sciences, 113*(52), 14949–14952.

Fouarge, D., & Layte, R. (2005). Welfare regimes and poverty dynamics: the duration and recurrence of poverty spells in Europe. *Journal of Social Policy, 34*(3), 407–426.

Galloway, T. A., Gustafsson, B., Pedersen, P. J., & Österberg, T. (2015). Immigrant child poverty: the Achilles heel of the Scandinavian welfare state. *Measurement of Poverty, Deprivation, and Economic Mobility. Research on Economic Inequality, 23*, 185–219.

Gornick, J. C., & Jäntti, M. (2011). *Child poverty in comparative perspective: assessing the role of family structure and parental education and employment*. LIS Working Paper Series No. 570. Luxembourg: Luxembourg Income Study.

Guio, A.-C., Gordon, D., & Marlier, E. (2012). *Measuring material deprivation in the EU: indicators for the whole population and child-specific indicators*. Eurostat Methodologies and Working Papers. Luxembourg: Office for Official Publications of the European Communities.

Guio, A.-C., Gordon, D., Najera, H., & Pomati, M. (2016). *Measuring child material deprivation in the EU.* Report prepared for Eurostat: Analysis of the 2014 EU-SILC thematic module.
Hirsch, D. (2008). *Estimating the Cost of Child Poverty.* York: Joseph Rowntree Foundation.
Holzer, H. J., Whitmore Schanzenbach, D., Duncan, G. J., & Ludwig, J. (2008). The economic costs of childhood poverty in the United States. *Journal of Children and Poverty, 14*(1), 41–61.
Ivanova, I. (2011). *The cost of poverty in BC.* Canadian Centre for Policy Alternatives BC Office.
Jenkins, S. P., Brandolini, A., Micklewright, J., & Nolan, B. (Eds.). (2012). *The Great Recession and the Distribution of Household Income.* Oxford: Oxford University Press.
Laurie, N. (2008). *The cost of poverty: an analysis of the economic cost of poverty in Ontario.* Ontario Association of Food Banks.
Lee, D., & McLanahan, S. (2015). Family structure transitions and child development: instability, selection, and population heterogeneity. *American Sociological Review, 80*(4), 738–763.
Lesner, R. V. (2018). The long-term effect of childhood poverty. *Journal of Population Economics, 31*(3), 969–1004.
Lichter, D. T. (1997). Poverty and inequality among children. *Annual Review of Sociology, 23*(1), 121–145.
Lustig, D. C., & Strauser, D. R. (2007). Causal relationships between poverty and disability. *Rehabilitation Counseling Bulletin, 50*(4), 194–202.
Main, G. (2014). Child poverty and children's subjective well-being. *Child Indicators Research,* 7(3), 451–472.
McCall, L. (2001). *Complex Inequality: Gender, Class and Race in the New Economy.* New York: Routledge.
McCall, L. (2005). The complexity of intersectionality. *Signs, 30*(3), 1771–1800.
McLanahan, S., & Sandefur, G. (1994). *Growing Up with a Single Parent: What Hurts, What Helps.* Cambridge, MA: Harvard University Press.
McLaughlin, M., & Rank, M. R. (2018). Estimating the economic cost of childhood poverty in the United States. *Social Work Research, 42*(2), 73–83.
McLeod, J. D., & Shanahan, M. J. (1993). Poverty, parenting, and children's mental health. *American Sociological Review, 58*(3), 351–366.
Minujin, A., Delamonica, E., Davidziuk, A., & Gonzalez, E. D. (2006). The definition of child poverty: a discussion of concepts and measurements. *Environment & Urbanization, 18*(2), 481–500.
Mont, D. (2014). *Childhood disability and poverty.* Working Paper 25. London: Leonard Cheshire Disability and Inclusive Development Centre, University College London.
Mood, C., & Jonsson, J. O. (2016). The social consequences of poverty: an empirical test on longitudinal data. *Social Indicators Research, 127*(2), 633–652.
National Academies of Sciences, Engineering, and Medicine. (2019). *A Roadmap to Reducing Child Poverty.* Consensus Study Report. Washington, DC: National Academies Press.
Newhouse, D., Suarez-Becerra, P., Evans, M. C., & Data for Goals Group. (2016). *New estimates of extreme poverty for children.* Policy Research Working Paper 7845. Washington, DC: World Bank.
Nieuwenhuis, R., & Maldonado, L. C. (Eds.). (2018). *The Triple Bind of Single-parent Families: Resources, Employment and Policies to Improve Well-being.* Bristol: Policy Press.
OECD. (2014). *Rising inequality: youth and poor fall further behind.* Income Inequality Update: OECD.
OECD. (2018). *Poor children in rich countries: why we need policy action.* Policy Brief on Child Well-Being. Paris: OECD Publishing.
Ponnet, K. (2014). Financial stress, parent functioning and adolescent problem behavior: an actor–partner interdependence approach to family stress processes in low-, middle-, and high-income families. *Journal of Youth and Adolescence, 43*(10), 1752–1769.
Porterfield, S. L., & Tracey, C. (2003). *Disentangling the dynamics of family poverty and child disability: does disability come first?* Working Paper No. 03–01. Saint Louis: Centre for Social Development, Washington University.
Presser, H. B., Gornick, J. C., & Parashar, S. (2008). Gender and nonstandard work hours in 12 European countries. *Monthly Labor Review, 131*(2), 83–103.
Ravallion, M. (1994). *Poverty Comparisons.* Chur, Switzerland: Harwood.
Ridge, T. (2002). *Childhood Poverty and Social Exclusion: From a Child's Perspective.* Bristol: Policy Press.
Roelen, K., & Gassmann, F. (2008). *Measuring child poverty and well-being: a literature review* Maastricht Graduate School of Governance Working Paper Series No. 2008/WP001. Maastricht: Maastricht Graduate School of Governance.
Sherman, A., & Edelman, M. W. (1994). *Wasting America's Future: The Children's Defense Fund report on the costs of child poverty.* Boston, MA: Beacon Press.

Stein, R. E. K., Silver, E. J. (2002). Comparing different definitions of chronic conditions in national data set. *Ambulatory Pediatrics, 2*(1), 63–70.
Sutton, L. (2008). The state of play: disadvantage, play and children's wellbeing. *Social Policy & Society*, 7(4), 537–549.
Townsend, P. (1979). *Poverty in the UK*. London: Penguin.
Unicef. (2005). *The state of the world of the children 2005: childhood under threat*. New York: Unicef.
Unicef. (2007). *Child poverty in perspective: an overview of child well-being in rich countries*. Innocenti Report Card 7 (p. 48). Florence: Unicef Innocenti Research Centre.
Unicef. (2012). *Measuring child poverty: new league tables of child poverty in the world's rich countries*. Innocenti Report Card 10. Florence: Unicef Innocenti Research Centre.
Unicef & World Bank Group (2016). *Ending extreme poverty: a focus on children*. Briefing Note. New York.
Uunk, W. (2004). The economic consequences of divorce for women in the European Union: the impact of welfare state arrangements. *European Journal of Population, 20*(3), 251–285.
Vandecasteele, L. (2010). Poverty trajectories after risky life course events in different European welfare regimes. *European Societies, 12*(2), 257–278.
Vandenbroucke, F., & Vinck, J. (2013). Child poverty risks in Belgium, Wallonia and Flanders: accounting for a worrying performance. In P. Maystadt, E. Cantillon, L. Denayer, P. Pestieau, B. Van der Linden, & M. Cattelain (Eds.), *Le modèle social belge: quel avenir?* (pp. 85–144). Charleroi, Belgium: Presses Interuniversitaires de Charleroi.
van Oorschot, W. (2006). Making the difference in social Europe: deservingness perceptions among citizens of European welfare states. *Journal of European Social Policy, 16*(1), 23–42.
Wagmiller, R. L., & Adelman, R. M. (2009). *Childhood and Intergenerational Poverty: The Long-Term Consequences of Growing Up Poor*. New York, NY: National Center for Children in Poverty, Columbia University, Mailman School of Public Health.
Waldfogel, J., Craigie, T.-A., & Brooks-Gunn, J. (2010). Fragile families and child wellbeing. *The Future of Children, 20*(2), 87–112.
World Bank. (2017). Societal poverty: a relative and relevant measure. *Policy Research Working Paper 8073*.
Yeung, W. J., Linver, M. R., & Brooks-Gunn, J. (2002). How money matters for young children's development: parental investment and family processes. *Child Development, 73*(6), 1861–1879.

9

Social justice as parity of participation

Katrien Boone, Rudi Roose, Christian Christrup Kjeldsen, Caroline Vandekinderen and Griet Roets

Introduction

In recent decades, the number of people living in poverty or at risk of ending in situations of poverty has increased in many European welfare states (Eurostat, 2013). Even in the Nordic welfare state Denmark, known to be one of the most egalitarian countries in the world, child poverty rates have been rising during recent years and in some Danish municipalities one out of ten children live in poverty (Caspersen, 2018). Many of these states are currently facing existing as well as new social and economic crises and risks (Taylor-Gooby, 2011). It is argued that "the question of poverty is still the most central issue of the social dimension of Europe" (Fritzell & Ritakallio, 2010, S25). Therefore, an urgent political concern is to achieve tangible results in European anti-poverty policies, which for instance is reflected in the ambitious target of the Lisbon strategy (2000–2010) and the EU 2020 strategy (2010–2020) of lifting at least 20 million people out of poverty and social exclusion (Copeland & Daly, 2012).

Notwithstanding the agreement of many states that poverty should be a high priority on the political agenda, this does not imply that poverty can be conceived as a fixed and neutral concept. Poverty is a 'normative construct', varying according to the ways in which it is defined by different actors in different societies (Lister, 2004; Mestrum, 2011). As such, our understanding of poverty and the resulting policies become influenced by prevailing welfare state regimes (Dean, 2010). In relation to this, it is being argued that in European welfare states we see a new type of welfare architecture taking shape, what has been called the Welfare Service State (Bonvin et al., 2018). In the Welfare Service State we see a growth in the expenses for social welfare services, aimed at direct support of people in poverty through diverse forms of relational work, such as parental support, debt counselling, child protection, etc. Although redistribution remains present (there is, for instance, in many countries still a huge investment in pension funds and child allowances), social investment rather than a focus on redistributive cash transfers becomes pivotal in anti-poverty policies. We see "a notable decline in the ratio of 'old' transfers to overall social expenditures: statistics show an increase of the relative importance of 'new social spending' on childcare and other work-related aspects compared with traditional transfer payments" (Cantillon, 2011, p. 440). This evolution entails great challenges for social welfare services in dealing with poverty, as these welfare services become the main terrain for combating poverty, while at the same time they are urged to make themselves redundant and run the risk of becoming merely a residual answer to structural problems of poverty. As such, thinking about social justice in relation to social welfare services becomes of vital importance.

Hence, the important question that we discuss in this chapter is the way social welfare services construct the relation between anti-poverty strategies and social justice. Social welfare services, such as diverse forms of Social Work, often refer to their overall mission (IFSW, 2014) as being to pursue social justice while describing poverty as a violation of human rights (O'Brien, 2011). However, also the notion of social justice can be constructed in various manners, leading to various approaches to combating poverty. In this chapter, we give depth to the analysis of the notion of social justice in the context of delivering social services toward people in poverty. More specifically, we discuss the Capability Approach as a relevant social justice framework that can offer inspiration for social welfare services in developing socially just practices. The Capability Approach is an *approach* rather than a theoretical framework and therefore needs to be related to other social theory in order to reach its full potential. To do so, we use Nancy Fraser's idea of *parity of participation*, as she states that her theory can be seen as a capability approach framework (see Gupta, 2017), bringing important issues on the concept of poverty in relation to welfare services to the fore.

A focus on capabilities

Amartya Sen, who was the founding father of the Capability Approach, argued that he found the existing understandings of poverty and inequality insufficient and raised his main question in the end of the 1970s: "Equality of what?" (Sen, 1979). This was a reaction to a resource-based approach of measurement of inequalities in the metric of primary goods, as John Rawls proposes (Nussbaum, 2011). Even though the Capability Approach acknowledges Rawls' ideas of justice as fairness, Sen departs from this idea of primary goods (Nussbaum, 2006, 2011; Sen, 2009). The Capability Approach may be seen as a conceptual framework that challenges social inequalities and enables us to theorise the pursuit of social justice and equality. The Capability Approach is conceived as an innovative, flexible and multi-purpose framework providing a process-oriented instead of an outcome-based approach of social welfare (Gupta, Featherstone, & White, 2014).

Rawls' idea of justice as fairness is to a great extent founded on two principles. First, everyone should have an equal right to "extensive basic liberty compatible with similar liberty for others" (Rawls, 2005 [1971], p. 60) and, second in case of inequalities these "social and economic inequalities are to be arranged so that they are both (a) reasonable respected to be to everyone's advantage, and (b) attached to positions and offices open to all" (Rawls, 2005 [1971], p. 60). For Rawls the absence of justice therefore becomes the inequalities that are not to some degree for the benefit of all and open for competition. In this way, inequalities in the perspective of Rawls become "arbitrary unless it is reasonable to expect that they will work out for everyone's advantage" (Rawls, 1958, s. 165). The ideas of inequality and justice are tightly linked together in both Rawls' and Sen's approaches, still Sen argues that the connection between equality and justice is not an easy matter (Kjeldsen, 2014). The main objection against Rawls' idea of justice is that primary goods or other resources may not represent what the individuals actually are capable of doing or being holding these bundles of goods. It does not to a sufficient degree represent the substantial freedom one person enjoys in comparison to another (Sen, 1992, 2009). The main argument for this is that individuals convert commodities (primary goods) differently due to personal conversion factors. In order to prove the point, Sen gives the following example:

"a person who has a disability can have more primary goods (in the form of income, wealth, liberties, and so on) but less capability (due to the handicap)". (Sen, 1992, p. 82).

Early proponents of the human capital theory, such as Schultz (1960, 1961) and Becker (1962, 1975), claimed that the development of human capital – marketable skills, knowledge and social attitudes – will equip people to find and retain suitable jobs and, as such, has a positive correlation with economic growth (Regmi, 2015). When welfare policies and practices informed by the metaphor of 'human capital' call for addressing the problem of inequality, the concern is often narrowly construed in terms of economic loss (Gale & Molla, 2015), while Sen (1999) introduces a more holistic view of welfare interventions within a social justice framework (Regmi, 2015). The Capability Approach may offer another perspective on the relationship between human development and welfare and poverty. In the human capital paradigm the societal economic growth comes first and is achieved by the means of human investments that likewise benefit the individual in different domains of wellbeing and poverty, but the overall aim is capital growth, whereas in the human development paradigm influenced by a capability perspective the individual's substantial freedom to live a life he or she has reason to value comes first (Sen, 1989).

Within the Capability Approach, capabilities are conceived as the real alternatives (substantial freedoms or effective opportunities) available to an individual to undertake the actions and activities s/he wants to engage in and whom s/he wants to be (functionings) (Sen, 2004). The notion of capability relates to freedom in terms of the ability of human beings to lead lives they have reason to value and to enhance the substantive choices they have (Sen, 1997). However, we want to highlight that choice in Sen's conceptualisation is not to be confused with neo-liberal advocates of individual choice. As Walker (2005, p. 106) explains, "the crucial difference is that the Capability Approach is ethically individualistic; neo-liberalism by contrast is ontologically individualist". While in the latter, the focus on individual autonomy individualises success, failure and the social consequences that flow from personal choices, in Sen's formulation, individual freedom and agency, strengthen social life rather than fragmenting it since he works with the 'basic heterogeneity' of persons (Walker, 2005). Furthermore, the choices we make "makes us accountable for what we do. Freedom to choose gives us opportunity to decide what we should do, but with that opportunity comes the responsibility for what we do – to the extent that they are chosen actions" (Sen, 2009, p. 19). We want to point out that choice is a complex concept and that we do not refer to a humanist conception of 'choice' (Gowlett, 2012), since freedoms to choose are intrinsically linked to and constrained by their sociocultural, economic, political and historical positioning (Hammad & Singal 2015). In the same vein, the concept of aspirations, referring to 'a desirable life project' that is intrinsically linked to the idea of realising a life one has reason to value, is socially constrained although it draws upon an individual's preferences (Baillergeau & Duyvendak, 2016). Aspirations strongly depend on the available resources and opportunities, the future that can be imagined and desired in relation to these resources and opportunities and, as such, on the choices that can be made in certain (socially unequal) situations. Aspirations may be understood both as a functioning – the doing of creative reflective thinking, etc. but likewise as a capability (substantial freedom) to imagine a life the individual favours (Hart, 2018) and we would furthermore argue that this should also be taken into account in policy making. Therefore, focusing on capabilities unavoidably requires us to consider the social processes through which young people's aspirations develop and crystallise (Baillergeau & Duyvendak, 2016). Capabilities are therefore not confined to psychological aspects of human 'functionings' but are dynamically and significantly shaped by their environmental and social circumstances, both in the past and in the present (Gupta, Featherstone & White, 2014). As such, capabilities refer to an arrangement of living conditions of a material, symbolic, legal and normative kind that is necessary to allow for the 'flourishing' of individual capabilities (Dean, 2015). Bringing together these conditions (barriers and opportunities) and connecting them to the individual situations and aspirations of people requires a careful and comprehensive examination of the perspectives of these people, that are interpreted as situated within their social, cultural and political contexts (Lorenz, 2013).

A thorough understanding of the capabilities of people therefore requires an in-depth exploration of the resources and conversion factors, referring to the social factors that affect (positively or negatively) the ability of people to transform resources into capabilities (Gupta, Featherstone & White, 2014). The capability perspective suggests that the availability of resources and opportunities is not enough for ensuring social justice, because one's ability to effectively make use of resources and opportunities depends on a range of conversion factors, i.e. variables, circumstances or persons, influencing an individual's ability to convert resources and opportunities into the functionings s/he values (Gale & Molla, 2015). Therefore, we need to examine the processes in which welfare services and social welfare actors – understood as both resources and possible conversion factors – can support people in realising their capabilities (Lumby & Morrison, 2009).

As Walker (2005) highlights, Sen leaves his framework deliberately open. Hence, we explicitly insist on a critical awareness of the diversity of possible meanings about what counts as valuable and on the responsibility to understand these meanings through addressing the "lived capacities at the level of everyday life" (Walker, 2005, p. 104). For this the notion of the 'Informational Basis of the Judgements in Justice' (IBJJ) (Sen, 1990, p. 111) is important. An important element in the debate about poverty and anti-poverty policies is the way in which social justice is defined. In addition, the informational basis for the judgement of justice is, in this regard, a political question and decision, as it questions which figures, data and levels of poverty are regarded important and taken into account. The selection of the IBJJ involves a decision on which perspectives and information are seen as valid and relevant, and which information should be dismissed and seen as irrelevant (Otto, 2012).

Social justice: the problem of participation

The IBJJ refers to the importance of the knowledge base in the debate on poverty and the question of participation: who has a voice in this knowledge base? In relation to this issue, we already addressed that the conceptualisation of poverty is a construction as it is dependent on the political, social and economic conditions and concerns in prevailing welfare states and is also constructed differently by a variety of groups within societies. In Amartya Sen's work on poverty he often draws on the liberal thinker Adam Smith and the idea that a decent society will secure their citizens the ability to appear in public without shame. Therefore, Sen argues that the "commodity requirements of established patterns of behaviour may vary between communities, depending on conventions and customs" (Sen, 1999, p. 71). This is poverty in the relative sense, in relation to culture etc. of a given society at a particular time and personal resources needed for the fulfilment of self-respect should be secured. On the other side, poverty in the space of capabilities becomes absolute: "poverty is an absolute notion in the space of capabilities but very often it will take a relative form in the space of commodities or characteristics" (Sen, 1983, p. 161).

As such, Lister (2004) very rightly argues that poverty is "a political concept", as it is highly contested and "the policies developed to tackle poverty reflect dominant conceptualizations" (p. 3). Consequently, this illuminates how the notion of social justice in relation to poverty and anti-poverty strategies closely relates to questions of power and participation, as it deals with questions of who has the power to define poverty and formulate anti-poverty strategies.

Bouverne-De Bie (2003) defines poverty as "an interplay of a lack of sufficient resources, being excluded from society and multiple deprivation" (p. 4, own translation). While a lack of sufficient resources, first of all, connects poverty to a lack of income, it also refers to a lack of opportunities to acquire social and cultural capital and to effectuate political and social rights. Moreover, societal exclusion on different levels of society – micro, meso and macro – is at the core of the poverty problem.

Next to the given that poverty has got to do with material deprivation, the focus on societal exclusion also reveals that people in poverty are marginalised, in the sense that their power to actively define and shape their own situation is taken away, possibly leading to acquiescence in this situation (cf. Freire, 1970). In other words, people in poverty have little power to participate in the definition of what poverty is and in considering what measures should be set up to combat it (Roets et al., 2012a). Poverty can therefore be regarded as a 'structural participation problem', since people in poverty are granted a marginal and passive position in society and they experience a lack of resources, due recognition and institutional power to influence their subordinated position (Doom, 2003; see also Fraser, 1995, 2005; Krumer-Nevo, 2005, 2009, 2016; Lister, 2004, 2013).

With regard to this issue, it is essential to stress that the emphasis on the direct participation of people in poverty in research, policy and social welfare practices has gained tremendous weight since the 1990s (Beresford, 2002; Krumer-Nevo, 2016; Lister, 2004). Many international scholars have described how in the last decades of the 20th century, a growing focus on relational, symbolic and social aspects of poverty arose (Fraser, 1997, 2000, 2005, 2008; Garrett, 2010; Gupta, Blumhardt, & ATD Fourth World, 2017; Houston, 2016; Krumer-Nevo, 2016; Lister, 2004, 2013; Thompson, 2006, 2009; Webb, 2010, 2014), leading to social policies paying greater attention to recognition of the inherent worth and need for participation of people in poverty. Such developments derived partly from the political macro level of the welfare state with its own rationalities, as, for instance, the social investment perspective gave rise to participatory initiatives. However, these rationalities were also complemented and supported by social movements, which grabbed opportunities to stipulate publicly the importance of giving recognition and voice to people in poverty (Roets et al., 2012b) and as such, get beyond their *"second-class citizenship"* (Lister, 2004, p. 165). Here, the main argument was that while people in poverty had the same political status and equality as citizens, their welfare rights were on many occasions not realised in practice, as they experienced that they were denied the right to participate in social interactions (Lister, 2003, 2004; Roets et al., 2012b; Boone, Roets, & Roose, 2018).

This focus on participatory opportunities can indicate that attempts are being made to address power-related issues and the marginalisation of people in poverty, as a diversity of participatory approaches in policy and practice have germinated. This is, for instance, clear in the attention given to the use of testimonials from people in poverty to inspire social welfare practices and social policy makers, to the employment of people with poverty experience in governmental services, to the focus on the participation of people in poverty in the planning of activities and to the formal participation of people in poverty in internal board meetings and local consultation groups.

Nevertheless, it is also argued that the complexity of such projects should not be taken lightly and it is necessary to keep the mechanisms and purpose of such participatory practices under continuous review as participation within the relation to the social welfare service providers may become instrumental instead of socially just. This may result in focusing only on recognition of people instead of also looking at the structural problems of redistribution within society. As such, empowerment for instance becomes an individual rather than collective responsibility.

Let us therefore follow up on this problem and sharpen our understanding with Nancy Fraser's concept of parity of participation.

Fraser and parity of participation

From the conceptualisation of poverty as, in its essence, a structural participation problem, inspiration can be found in the work of Nancy Fraser (1995, 1997, 2000, 2005, 2008, 2010). There are many synergies between the work of Fraser and the Capability Approach, as both capture the economic inequalities as well as structural injustices (Gupta, 2017) and as such offer social welfare services a framework to look beyond recognition and individual empowerment. Gupta (2017) even notices that Fraser describes her own theory as "belonging to the family of the capability approaches" and that the Capability Approach in combination with the idea of parity of participation can provide a framework for social justice that can be a practical, ethical and analytical tool for the evaluation and promotion of socially just policies and welfare practices. Fraser argues that the central notion in the fight for social justice is 'parity of participation' since "justice requires social arrangements that permit all to participate as peers in social life" (Fraser, 2005, p. 73). She provides a theoretical frame of reference that sheds light on the complexity to work for and with people in poverty, since their lives and opportunities are determined by numerous related fields of subordination on the economic, cultural and political levels (Garrett, 2010). Overcoming injustice therefore implies dismantling institutionalised obstacles on those three domains "that prevent some people from participating on a par with others, as full partners in social interaction" (p. 73). It coincides with the Capability Approach in the notion that you cannot judge policies as being socially just on a disruption of formal entitlements given to the individual alone. You will have to move into the institutions and empirically look for the real opportunities possessed by the individual. An 'epistemological break' – in the understanding of Althusser – where science breaks with its own ideologies (that formed the same science) and becomes able to formulate new theoretical developments (see Kjeldsen, 2014), is needed and the Capability Approach will have to be combined with social theory such as Fraser's. The interconnection of those three domains implies that parity of participation is not only impeded by a lack of resources or by the misrecognition of the voices of people, but also by the misframing of the issues of social justice that are affecting them (Fraser, 2010). Therefore, anti-poverty strategies should not only invest in a 'politics of recognition' and a 'politics of redistribution', but also be connected with a radical 'politics of representation'. By establishing participatory parity as a normative social justice orientation, societal efforts should be made to create opportunities through which oppressed and subordinated groups can represent their concerns, questions and experiences of injustice in public debate. As such, "the political" can be conceived as the forums or "the stage on which struggles" in the different (in-)justice domains can occur (Fraser, 2005, p. 75).

In relation to such a politics of representation, Fraser furthermore stresses the need to explore three types of questions on the substantive level of social justice. She argues that – although vitally important – questions should not only fixate on 'what' a just society is, but also meta-level questions on the 'who' and 'how' of social justice are vital. Reflecting on questions such as "what constitutes a just distribution of wealth and resources? What counts as reciprocal recognition or equal respect?" (Fraser, 2008, p. 396) intrinsically requires a reflection on "who counts as a subject of justice in a given matter? Whose interests and needs deserve consideration? Who belongs to the circle of those entitled to equal concern?" (Fraser, 2008, p. 399). Moreover, in contemporary times, it becomes increasingly important to not only critically reflect on the 'what' and the 'who' of justice, but also on 'how': how are voices being brought into the arena, by whom, and how are they respected or disrespected? (Fraser, 2008). Therefore, a politics of representation crucially addresses interrelated questions about 'who', the 'how', and the 'what' of social justice.

Conclusion: the social justice orientation of social welfare services

Notwithstanding the rather philosophical nature of her work, Fraser has recently inspired numerous scholars in the field of social welfare services, often concerned with the issue of poverty (Boone, Roets, & Roose, 2018; Davies, Gray, & Webb, 2014; Dean, 2013; Garrett, 2010; Marston & McDonald, 2012; Webb, 2010). In line with the work of Fraser, Lister (2002) not only emphasises the need to think about representative democratic means but advocates for "the provision of public space in which voices of different groups can be heard", and a participatory and deliberative democratic praxis can occur (p. 40). Social welfare services could occupy a privileged position in striving for parity of participation and social justice through a politics of representation in which a so-called cultural forum can be created as a space where the private concerns of people who experience injustice in overlapping cultural, economic and political realms are translated into public issues. It is argued that for welfare services concerned with poverty issues it is vital that they are aware of how poverty relates to dimensions of structural inequality and "to accept that what Nancy Fraser terms 'struggles for recognition' also need to be 'integrated with struggles for redistribution, rather than displacing and undermining them'" (Garrett, 2002, p. 200, quoting Fraser, 2000, p. 187). This may furthermore be strengthened by the Capability Approach, which is only a normative approach that needs a strong social theory in order to fulfil its potential as an instrument of interpreting poverty in practice. Such a politics of representation might engender transformative potential, since social welfare services can reframe, project and (re-)politicise the lifeworlds, experienced injustices and concerns of people in poverty "from the private sphere of commodities and market relations, on the one hand, and family and personal relations, on the other, into the public forum of political debate" (Dean, 2013, p. 42). Of course, welfare services may experience major tensions, bottlenecks and complexities in their commitment to supporting and shaping such participatory ventures. In some situations, social services' or professionals' strivings for social justice can be curtailed by governmental or societal rules, depending on their position in the relation between government and the people in poverty. The who, the how and the what of participation might get a totally different shape in a public or a private service, a liberal or a conservative policy context, a professional organisation or working with volunteers, etc. Nevertheless, a pertinent challenge in the development of anti-poverty strategies is to pose questions concerning which situations are defined as poverty, and on what grounds and with what arguments are they defined as such, and also consider what the contributions are of diverse actors in this process (Bouverne-De Bie et al., 2014). As Marston and McDonald (2012) accordingly argue, the depoliticisation of social issues such as poverty requires us to focus attention on how welfare services act when the 'how', the 'who', and the 'what' of social justice are all in dispute.

References

Baillergeau, E., & Duyvendak, W. J. (2016). Social Inequality and Young People in Europe: Their Capacity to Aspire. In Amsterdam Institute for Social Science Research (Eds.), *World Social Science Report 2016: Challenging Inequalities: Pathways to a Just World* (pp. 155–156). Paris: Unesco.

Becker, G. S. (1962). Investment in human capital: a theoretical analysis. *Journal of Political Economy*, 70(5), 9–49.

Becker, G. S. (1975). *Human Capital: A Theoretical and Empirical Analysis with Special Reference to Education*. Chicago, IL: University of Chicago Press.

Beresford, P. (2002). User involvement in research and evaluation: liberation or regulation? *Social Policy and Society*, 1(2), 95–105.

Bonvin, J. M., Otto, H. U., Wohlfarth, A., & Ziegler, H. (2018). Introduction. ambivalences of the rising welfare service state: hopes and hazards of fundamentally realigning the architecture of welfare modernity. *Social Work and Society*, 16(2), 1–5.

Boone, K., Roets, G., & Roose, R. (2018). Social work, poverty and anti-poverty strategies: creating cultural forums. *British Journal of Social Work*, 48(8), 2381–2399.

Bouverne-De Bie, M. (2003). Een rechtenbenadering als referentiekader. In M. Bouverne-De Bie, A. Claeys, A. De Cock & J. Vanhee (Eds.), *Armoede en participatie* (pp. 1–20). Gent: Academia Press.

Bouverne-De Bie, M., Roose, R., Coussée, F., & Bradt, L. (2014). Learning democracy in social work. In G. Biesta, M. De Bie & D. Wildemeersch (Eds.), *Civic Learning, Democratic Citizenship and the Public Sphere* (pp. 43–54). London: Springer.

Cantillon, B. (2011). The paradox of the social investment state: growth, employment and poverty in the Lisbon era. *Journal of European Social Policy*, 21(5), 432–449.

Caspersen, 2018. I nogle kommuner er hvert 10. barn under fattigdomsgrænsen. Copenhagen: AE Retrieved 15 December 2018 from: www.ae.dk/sites/www.ae.dk/files/dokumenter/analyse/ae_i-nogle-kommuner-er-hvert-10-barn-under-fattigdomsgraensen.pdf

Copeland, P., & Daly, M. (2012). Varieties of poverty reduction: inserting the poverty and social exclusion target into Europe 2020. *Journal of European Social Policy*, 22(3), 273–287.

Davies, K., Gray, M., & Webb, S. (2014). Putting the parity into service-user participation: an integrated model of social justice. *International Journal of Social Welfare*, 23(2), 119–127.

Dean, H. (2010). *Understanding Human Need. Social Issues, Policy and Practice*. University of Bristol: The Policy Press.

Dean, H. (2013). The translation of needs into rights: reconceptualising social citizenship as a global phenomenon. *International Journal of Social Welfare*, 22(S1), 32–49.

Dean, H. (2015). *Social Rights and Human Welfare*. London: Routledge.

Doom, R. (2003). Armoede: een essay van de open deur. In M. Bouverne-De Bie, A. Claeys, A. De Cock & J. Vanhee (Eds.), *Armoede en participatie* (pp. 245–277). Gent: Academia Press.

Eurostat (2013). *Key figures on Europe: 2013 digest of the online Eurostat yearbook*. Luxembourg: Publications Office of the European Union. Retrieved 7 July 2019 from https://ec.europa.eu/eurostat/documents/3930297/5969538/KS-EI-13-001-EN.PDF/98fe7e02-d76a-45b9-9c72-7af791c672c2

Fraser, N. (1995). From redistribution to recognition: dilemmas of justice in a post-socialist age. *New Left Review*, 212, 68–93.

Fraser, N. (1997). *Justice Interruptus*. New York and London: Routledge.

Fraser, N. (2000). Rethinking recognition. *New Left Review*, 3, 107–120.

Fraser, N. (2005). Reframing justice in a globalizing world. *New Left Review*, 36, 69–88.

Fraser, N. (2008). Abnormal justice. *Critical Inquiry*, 34(3), 393–422.

Fraser, N. (2010). Injustice at intersecting scales: on 'social exclusion' and the "global poor". *European Journal of Social Theory*, 13(3), 363–371.

Freire, P. (1970). *Pedagogy of the Oppressed*. New York: Continuum.

Fritzell, J., & Ritakallio, V. M. (2010). Societal shifts and changed patterns of poverty. *International Journal of Social Welfare*, 19, S25–S41.

Gale, T., & Molla, T. (2015). Social justice intents in policy: an analysis of capability for and through education. *Journal of Education Policy*, 30(6), 810–830. doi: 10.1080/02680939.2014.987828

Garrett, P. M. (2002). Social work and the just society: diversity, difference and the sequestration of poverty. *Journal of Social Work*, 2(2), 187–210.

Garrett, P.M. (2010). Recognizing the limitations of the political theory of recognition: Axel Honneth, Nancy Fraser and social work. *British Journal of Social Work*, 40(5), 1517–1533.

Gowlett, C. (2012). Injurious assumptions: Butler, subjectification and gen(d)erational poverty. *International Journal of Inclusive Education*, 16(9), 885–900.

Gupta, A. (2017). Learning from others: an autoethnographic exploration of children and families social work, poverty and the capability approach. *Qualitative Social Work*, 16(4), 449–464.

Gupta, A., Blumhardt, H., & ATD Fourth World (2017). Poverty, exclusion and child protection practice: the contribution of 'the politics of recognition and respect'. *European Journal of Social Work*. Advance Access published 17 February 2017.

Gupta, A., Featherstone, B., & White, S. (2014). Reclaiming humanity: from capacities to capabilities in understanding parenting in adversity. *British Journal of Social Work*, 46, 339–354.
Hammad, T., & Singal, N. (2015). Education of women with disabilities in Pakistan: enhanced agency, unfulfilled aspirations. *International Journal of Inclusive Education*, 19(12), 1244–1264.
Hart, C. S. (2018). *Aspirations, Education and Social Justice: Applying Sen and Bourdieu*. London: Bloomsbury.
Houston, S. (2016). Empowering the 'shamed' self: recognition and critical social work. *Journal of Social Work*, 16(1), 3–21.
IFSW (International Federation of Social Workers) (2014). Global definition of social work. Retrieved 7 July 2019 from http://ifsw.org/get-involved/global-definition-of-socialwork/
Kjeldsen, C. (2014). *Capabilities and Special Needs: An Educational Foundation*. Hamburg: Verlag Dr. Kovac.
Krumer-Nevo, M. (2005). Listening to 'life knowledge': a new research direction in poverty studies. *International Journal of Social Welfare*, 14(2), 99–106.
Krumer-Nevo, M. (2009). From voice to knowledge: participatory action research, inclusive debate and feminism. *International Journal of Qualitative Studies in Education*, 22(3), 279–295.
Krumer-Nevo, M. (2016). Poverty aware social work: a paradigm for social workpractice with people in poverty. *British Journal of Social Work*, 46(6), 1793–1808.
Lister, R. (2002). A politics of recognition and respect: involving people with experience of poverty in decision making that affects their lives. *Social Policy & Society*, 1(1), 37–46.
Lister, R. (2004). *Poverty*. Cambridge: Polity Press.
Lister, R. (2013). 'Power, not pity': poverty and human rights. *Ethics and Social Welfare*, 7(2), 109–123.
Lorenz, W. (2013). Social Pedagogy and Social Work. Retrieved April 12, 2014 from: www.ioe.ac.uk/Research_Home/Walter_Lorenz_Handout.pdf.
Lumby, J., & Morrison, M. (2009). Youth perspectives: schooling, capabilities frameworks and human rights. *International Journal of Inclusive Education*, 13(6), 581–596.
Marston, G., & McDonald, C. (2012). Getting beyond heroic agency in conceptualizing social workers as policy actors in the twenty-first century. *British Journal of Social Work*, 42(6), 1–17.
Mestrum, F. (2011). Child poverty: a critical perspective. *Social Work & Society*, 9(1), 161–168.
Nussbaum, M. (2006). *Frontiers of Justice: Disability, Nationality, Species Membership*. Cambridge, MA: Harvard University Press.
Nussbaum, M. (2011). *Creating Capabilities: The Human Development Approach*. London: The Belknap Press of Harvard University Press.
O'Brien, M. (2011). Equality and fairness: linking social justice and social work practice. *Journal of Social Work*, 1(1), 143–158.
Otto, H. U. & Ziegler, H. (in press). Ambivalences of the rising welfare service state: hopes and hazards of fundamentally realigning the architecture of welfare modernity. *Social Work & Society*.
Rawls, J. (1958). Justice as fairness. *The Philosophical Review*, 67(2), 164–194.
Rawls, J. (2005 [1971]). *A Theory of Justice [Reprint, Original]*. Cambridge, MA: Harvard University Press.
Regmi, K. D. (2015). lifelong learning: foundational models, underlying assumptions and critiques. *International Review of Education – Journal of Lifelong Learning*, 61(2): 133–151.
Roets, G., Roose, R., Claes, L., Vandekinderen, C., Van Hove, G., & Vanderplasschen, W. (2012a). Reinventing the employable citizen: a perspective for social work. *British Journal of Social Work*, 42(1), 94–110.
Roets, G., Roose, R., De Bie, M., Claes, L., & Van Hove, G. (2012b). Pawns or pioneers? The logic of user participation in anti-poverty policy-making in public policy units in Belgium. *Social Policy and Administration*, 46, 807–822.
Schultz, T. W. (1960). Capital formation by education. *Journal of Political Economy*, 68(6), 571–583.
Schultz, T. W. (1961). Investment in human capital. *The American Economic Review*, 51(1), 1–17.
Sen, A. (1983). Poor, relatively speaking. *Oxford Economic Papers*, 35(2), 153–169.
Sen, A. (1989). Development as capability expansion. *Journal of Development Planning*, 19, 41–58.
Sen, A. (1990). Justice: means versus freedoms. *Philosophy & Public Affairs*, 19(2), 111–121.
Sen, A. (1992). *Inequality Re-examined*. Oxford: Oxford University Press.
Sen, A. (1997). Editorial: human capital and human capability. *World Development*, 25(12), 1956–1961.
Sen, A. (1999). *Development as Freedom*. New York: Knopf.
Sen, A. (2004). Capabilities, lists, and public reason: continuing the conversation. *Feminist Economics*, 10(3), 77–80.
Sen, A. (2009). *The Idea of Justice*. London: Allen Lane, Penguin Group.

Taylor-Gooby, P. (2011). Politics of risk-taking: welfare state reform in advanced democracies. *Journal of Social Policy*, 40, 194–196.

Thompson, S. (2006). *The Political Theory of Recognition*. Cambridge: Polity.

Thompson, S. (2009). On the circularity of democratic justice. *Philosophy and Social Criticism*, 35(9), 1079–1098.

Walker, M. (2005). Amartya Sen's capability approach and education. *Educational Action Research*, 13(1), 103–110.

Webb, S. A. (2010). (Re)assembling the left: the politics of redistribution and recognition in social work. *British Journal of Social Work*, 40(8), 2364–2379.

Webb, S. A. (2014). *Social work and the politics of recognition*. Retrieved 23 November 2018 from: www.academia.edu/4489946/Social_Work_and_the_Politics_of_Recognition

Part II

Poverty around the world and development in poverty

10
Global poverty
Trends, measures, and antidotes

Philip N. Jefferson

Introduction

Few issues reverberate on a global scale like poverty. We witness civil and international wars in Syria and Yemen. We witness political unrest in Jordan and Venezuela. We witness outbreaks of ebola in West Africa, polio in Pakistan and Afghanistan, and tuberculosis in India, Indonesia, China, and the Philippines. Not to mention the ongoing difficulty of ending the spread of HIV/AIDS in sub-Saharan Africa. Today, global poverty is in some cases the cause and in other cases the consequence of these and other immiserating scenes. These scenes have their precursors in history and their likely legacies in the future.

Building on Jefferson (2018), this chapter considers the long view of global poverty trends while providing highlights of the scenery that contextualizes changes in the trends. We do this by addressing four questions: (1) What are the historical trends in global poverty? (2) What are alternative ways of measuring historical trends in global poverty? (3) What explains historical trends in global poverty? (4) What are likely future trends in global poverty?

These questions are relevant because their answers help us to make sense of aspects of our modern world. We witness social imbalances because of inequitable market outcomes. We witness the compromise of human dignity because of our societies' incomplete provision of opportunity. We wonder about accountability for the poverty we witness, if not experience ourselves. Our realization is that poverty anywhere affects us, wherever we happen to live.

We organize the remainder of this chapter as follows. The next section provides an overview of the long-run behavior of the global poverty rate. The third section considers why the poverty rate was so high historically. Then we cover primary issues pertaining to measurement of poverty on a global scale, followed by a section that conveys our understanding of factors driving the long-term decline in the global poverty rate. We then consider obstacles to poverty reduction, and forecasts of global poverty in 2030.

Historical trends in global poverty and well-being

The fraction of the global population living in extreme poverty has declined steadily over the past two hundred years. Using historical data compiled by Bourguignon and Morrisson (2002) and

Figure 10.1 Global poverty.

Note: Data in all figures in this chapter come from Bourguignon and Morrisson (2002).

the World Bank (2018a), Figure 10.1 shows the fraction of people living at less than $2/day and $1/day from 1820 to 2015. The Bourguignon and Morrisson data are in 1985 purchasing power parity dollars. The World Bank data are in 2011 purchasing power parity dollars. The World Data Lab's (2018) forecast of the poverty rate in 2030 is also included in Figure 10.1. We will discuss that forecast later in the chapter. In 1820, ninety-four out of every one hundred people lived in poverty worldwide according to the $2/day threshold. Almost one hundred years later, the global poverty rate was still extraordinarily high at 82 percent. We see a downward bend in the curves starting in the post-World War II period, circa 1950. After 1980, the decline in the global poverty rate is rapid.

Figure 10.2 shows the global population and absolute number of people living in poverty worldwide corresponding to the poverty rates in Figure 10.1. The World Data Lab's forecast of the number of people living in poverty and global population in 2030 is included in Figure 10.2. We will also discuss these forecasts below. We see the global population growing slowly before accelerating around 1910. The number of people living in poverty rose with population as the poverty rate was falling. Therefore, until around 1990, population growth outpaced the reduction in the poverty rate. Post 1990, we see for the first time in recorded history a steady decline in the number of people living in poverty.

We cannot assess the quality of a human life using monetary measures alone. Money is instrumental to well-being but it is not well-being itself. There are dimensions of well-being such as bonds of love, affection, and belongingness that money cannot buy. Therefore, in order to evaluate historical trends in well-being, we must examine non-monetary measures. Bourguignon and Morrisson (2002) note that there are few measures in the historical record that would allow us to achieve a consistent view of the evolution of well-being over two centuries. One such measure they report is life expectancy. Figure 10.3 shows average life expectancy at birth from 1820 to 2015 using data compiled by Bourguignon and Morrisson (2002) and the World Health Organization (2018). The United Nation's (2015) forecast of life expectancy in

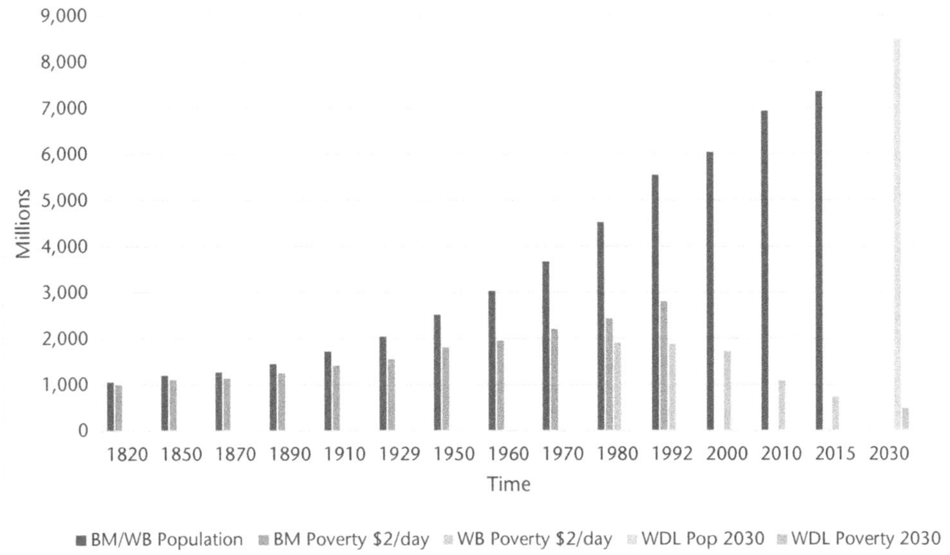

Figure 10.2 Global number of people in poverty.

2030 is also included in Figure 10.3. We will discuss that forecast later. Someone born in 1820 could expect to live twenty-seven years on average. We cannot know the joys, challenges, triumphs, and disappointments that characterized the life of the typical person born in 1820. We do know, however, that this person's life was short. Brevity would have circumscribed

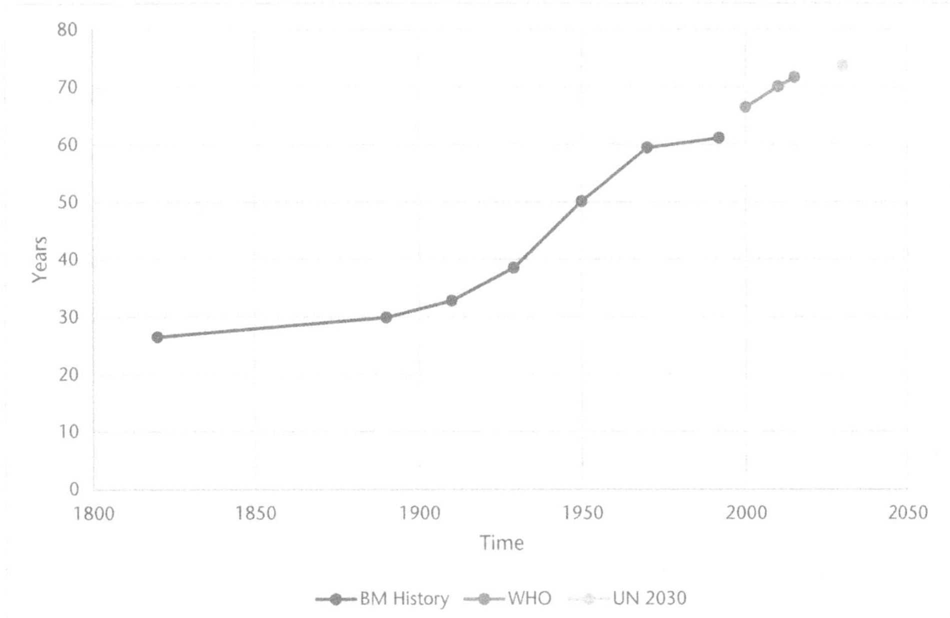

Figure 10.3 Global average life expectancy at birth.

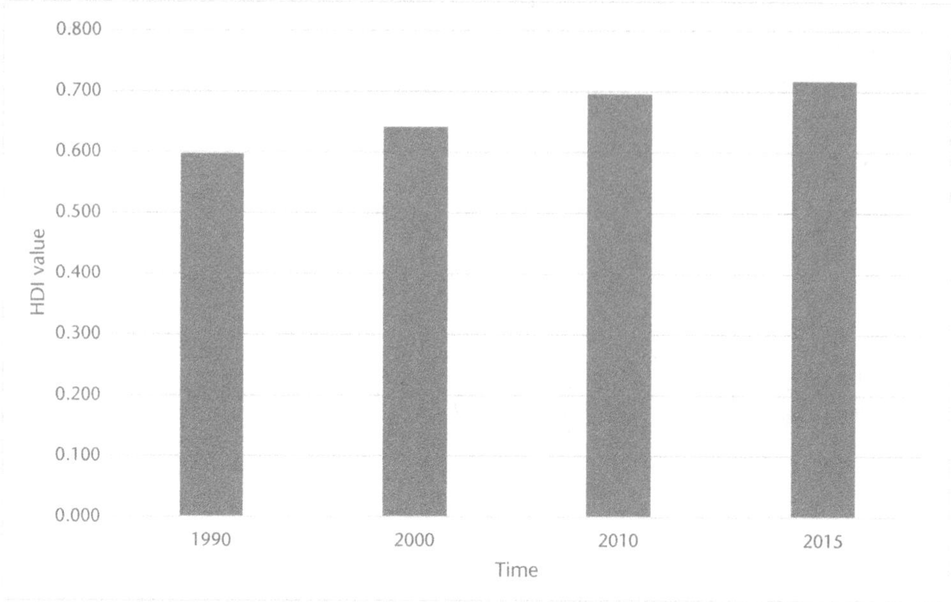

Figure 10.4 Global human development.

their well-being. The advance in life expectancy is unmistakable. The upward bend around 1910 corresponds to the surge in population around that same date. We will associate a longer life with an improvement in well-being. It is reasonable to assume that the better nutrition and health that extended years of life facilitated interactions and experiences that enriched the quality of life. By 2015, life expectancy had almost tripled to seventy-two years.

If we focus on a shorter time span, we can broaden our view of dimensions of well-being by combining information about life expectancy with information on educational attainment and income per capita. The United Nations Development Program (2016) does this. The result is the Human Development Index (HDI). Figure 10.4 shows the global HDI since 1990, the first year the United Nations produced it. The range of the HDI is zero to one with larger values indicating higher levels of well-being. The trend in Figure 10.4 is unmistakable. Over the past three decades, global well-being is improving.

Together, the historical trends in Figures 10.1 through 10.4 convey a clear message: we are winning the battle against extreme poverty. We cannot assure complete victory, however, without understanding why poverty was so prevalent in the past and why it has declined over the past two centuries.

Why were so many people living in poverty?

Every family's situation is unique. Therefore, no single narrative can explain why so many people lived in poverty in the past. In retrospect, however, we can identify factors that affected a large number of families adversely. Here, we highlight four of those factors: absence of industrialization, colonization, weak public support systems, and lack of accountability.

In 1820, the Industrial Revolution was already underway in Britain. It was also spreading to Western Europe. Most people alive at that time worldwide, however, did not feel its impact in terms of elevated income or consumption available to them on a daily basis. One reason for this is that most people worked in the agricultural sector and worked with limited amounts of physical capital. Thus, productivity was low. According to Maddison (2007), by 1820, Britain and Western Europe were already twice as rich as the rest of the world. Early industrialization accelerated productivity. An expansion of trade domestically and internationally permitted specialization according to comparative advantage. People in countries that were slow to industrialize and slow to join the world trading system remained poor throughout the 19th century.

Some countries participated in the expansion of trade in the 19th century but their indigenous populations did not reap the benefits of that participation. This was the result of colonization. Countries in the Caribbean, the Americas, Africa, and South Asia provided Western European colonial powers with primary products and labor. These vital inputs fueled industrialization in Western Europe. Normally, we would expect trade to be mutually beneficial. Trade between Western Europe and its colonies, however, was anything but because of the concomitant institutional arrangements. Systematic enslavement of peoples meant that labor was largely uncompensated. Colonists expropriated indigenous people's land via conquest and without compensation. Colonists did not share profits from trading with Western Europe equitably. They did not have to. Their political and social control of indigenous populations was virtually complete. The colonial system persisted well into the 20th century. It retarded industrialization and poverty reduction outside of Western Europe and its affiliates (North America and Australia) for centuries.

A defining characteristic of industrialization is structural change. We see this change as a reduction in the agricultural sector's share of output and employment. As structural change occurred during the Industrial Revolution in Western Europe and its affiliates, the agricultural sector released unskilled labor. Absorption of this labor into the nascent industrial sector was uneven and incomplete. Thus, there were large numbers of people without land to farm, shops to keep, or factories to staff. The English Poor Laws existed long before the Industrial Revolution but they were not substantive enough to provide meaningful relief to people living in poverty. In some cases, nor was that their intent. Rather, society left it to the church and other private charitable organizations to respond to prevalent deprivation. These entities, however, never had enough resources to support all of those in need. The reluctance of governments to intervene programmatically meant that millions of people would have to endure in poverty on their own. Not until late in the 19th century in Germany would we see government beginning to act at the national level to provide public insurance to individuals at risk of poverty for reasons beyond their control.

Measuring poverty on a global scale is a massive undertaking. Historically, the information gathering and coordination required for the task was not feasible. Although poverty was pervasive, no one had an accurate count. Therefore, it was not possible to hold governments accountable for poverty and its persistence. As Ravallion (2016) notes, it would not be until Booth's (1903) and Rowntree's (1902) attempts to tally the total number of people living in poverty in London and York that serious attention was paid to the task. Without measurement, it is impossible to know the scale and scope of a problem. It is difficult to design an appropriate response, be it public or private. The persistence of poverty we see historically was in part due to an insufficient response to a large-scale problem. In the absence of evidence, there was no consensus within countries or across countries about whose, if anybody's, responsibility it was to do something about the problem. Today, the World Bank performs this task. Doing it correctly requires the input of national statistical agencies worldwide and coordination across countries.

Measuring global poverty

The World Bank focuses on consumption per person when determining a person's poverty status. Consumption more closely correlates with well-being than income. The reason is that a person can decouple consumption from income if she receives assistance from other sources such as family, friends, government, or non-governmental organizations. This assistance can help her to enjoy her life more than she would have if she had to sustain herself on her income alone. Ferreira et al. (2016) provide the details of the World Bank's methods. They note that in some cases, such as Latin America, statisticians use income to determine a person's poverty status. Participating countries collect survey data at the household level. The surveys ask representative samples of households how much they consume per unit of time and the number of people living in the household. Then, statisticians monetize each household's reported amount of consumption, valuing it at market prices within the respective country.

Worldwide, there are many poverty lines. Countries set a level of consumption per capita such that we classify people who consume less than this amount as living in poverty. National poverty lines are denominated in the units of the national currency. Countries also have different price levels and inflation rates. Additionally, countries trade some goods and services internationally but not others. These facts make it difficult to count the number of people living in poverty across countries. We require some type of standardization in order to treat similarly situated people equally. The World Bank's International Comparison Project develops such a standard. The outcome of the program is a set of Purchasing Power Parities (PPP). PPP is the relative price of a common basket of goods where we set one country's basket as the numeraire.

Once PPP for a country is available, we use it to produce "international dollars" if the US dollar is chosen as the numeraire, as is customary. We also refer to international dollars as PPP dollars denoted symbolically as PPP$. Consider a stylized example of how to convert a national poverty line from national currency units into international dollars. Suppose that the poverty line in India in rupees is ₹1,000 per person per month. Let India's PPP equal 15. Here, the units of PPP are ₹/$. Then, India's poverty line in international dollars would be PPP$66.67 (= ₹1,000/15) per person per month or PPP$2.19 (= PPP$66.67/30.5) per person per day. This is a stylized example because, in practice, there are two poverty lines in India; a low one that covers rural areas and a higher one that covers urban areas. Such distinctions can be important in the developing country context.

Consumption and income are monetary measures of well-being. Sen (1999) argues, however, that many things make life fulfilling besides income and consumption; what people are capable of doing and being matters. To identify these qualities, we must consider non-monetary measures of well-being. In fact, the HDI is a step in that direction. The HDI puts weight on a measure of health (life expectancy) and educational attainment in addition to income. Therefore, declining (or stagnant) performances in health and education mitigate the impact of increasing income on well-being. The HDI encourages policymakers to look beyond per capita income as they think about development.

More recently, Alkire et al. (2015) advocate for expanding the dimensionality of measures of well-being exclusive of income per capita. Their multidimensional poverty index (MDI) has three dimensions: education, health, and standard of living. Each dimension has associated with it a set of indicators, weights on each indicator, and a threshold that signals deprivation if the household does not surpass that threshold. For example, the standard of living dimension has the following indicators, all with weight $\frac{1}{18}$ in the index: electricity, sanitation, water, floor, cooking fuel, and physical assets (including a radio, TV, bike, and refrigerator). Like the HDI, an intent of the MDI is to broaden the discussion about what we mean when we say that someone is living in poverty. It also reshapes our image of what remedies are relevant for improving well-being. See Chapter 4 in this *Handbook* for more on multidimensional poverty.

Understanding the decline in global poverty

Sustained economic growth reduces poverty. Using historical data from Bourguignon and Morrisson (2002) and the World Bank (2018a), Figure 10.5 shows average per capita income from 1820 to 2015. The Bourguignon and Morrisson data are in 1990 PPP dollars. The World Bank data are in 2011 PPP dollars. It took ninety years, from 1820 to 1910, for average income to double from its level of PPP$659 in 1820. After the turbulence of two world wars, it took only forty years from 1950 to 1992, for average income to double again. From 1992 onward, we see a dramatic growth in average income fueled by the emergence of China and India. Global average income more than doubles in a mere twenty-three years. According to the World Bank, global average income in 2015 was PPP$15,687. The impact of these three growth eras is evident in Figure 10.1 where we see a gradual decline in the poverty rate in the 19th century, a faster decline in the aftermath of World War II, and then a rapid decline post-1992. The observation that economic growth reduces poverty, however, begs the question, what fosters growth?

Acemoglu and Robinson (2012) provide ample historical evidence that the nature of a country's economic and political institutions determines its capacity to grow and to reduce poverty. Extractive institutions such as corruption and prohibition of private property distort incentives and sap people's desire to invest, take risks, and innovate. Inclusive institutions such as equal protection under the law and property right enforcement, encourage growth-friendly activities

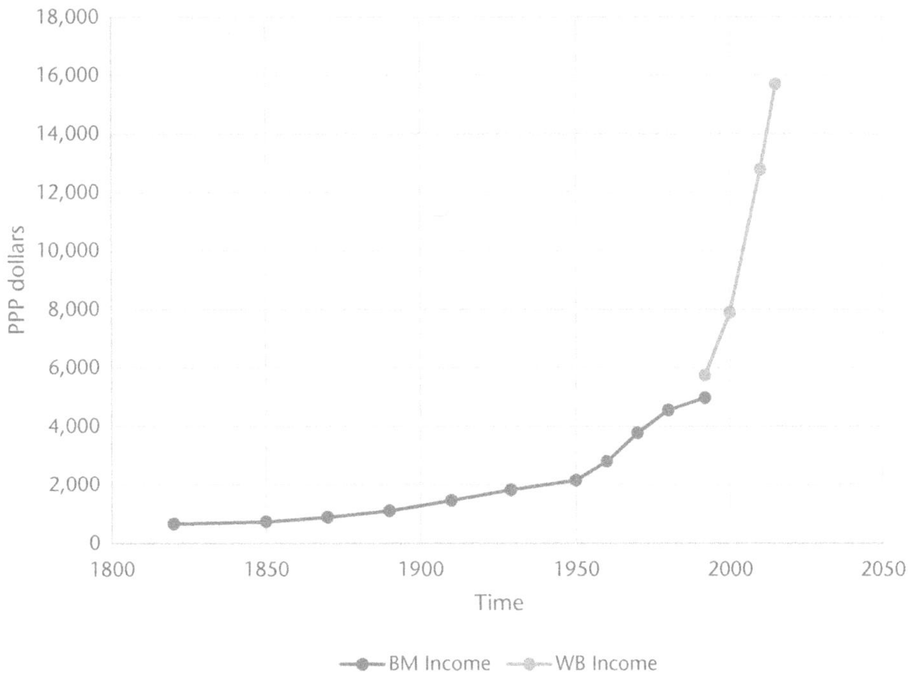

Figure 10.5 Average income per person.

such as entrepreneurship, civic engagement, and asset accumulation. They argue that countries are more likely to enjoy sustained economic growth if their economic and political systems are inclusive. If we extrapolate their thesis to the global level and look over the past two centuries, then we can conclude that, on average, the global institutional environment has been inclusive and favorable to growth and poverty reduction.

One byproduct of a favorable global institutional environment is the capacity for trade to occur between countries. If freedom of movement of people and financial capital accompany this trade, then we have globalization. Williamson (2011) documents the explosion of international trade in the 19th century. England was the most prosperous nation and it believed firmly in free trade. England promulgated this ethos throughout its empire and affiliated countries. Trade allowed for specialization according to comparative advantage. Each country could produce goods for which its opportunity cost was lowest. Specialization increased global output. Global income grew as a result.

Recognizing that trade is good does not mean that everyone benefits from trade. Trade may harm people who produce goods that compete with imports. If people lose their jobs due to trade, then they will be at increased risk of poverty. Such displacements are just one of many factors that can cause people to be at risk of poverty.

The vicissitudes of market economies can displace and marginalize people. In response, societies construct social safety nets. These are the web of programs and policies designed to provide support to people living in poverty. Typically, public and private entities do the provisioning of service. Beaudoin (2007) notes that public–private partnerships have been a hallmark of assistance to people living in poverty at least since the 16th century. The English Poor Laws empowered the church to collect taxes. The church then used these taxes to provide relief to people living in poverty locally. In the 19th century, social safety nets slowly evolved in Europe, culminating in the introduction of national social insurance for workers in Germany in the 1880s. Today, over one hundred countries have some type of social safety net program that assist people living in poverty. The examples range from Ethiopia's Urban Productive Safety Net Project that provides part-time employment and a stipend, to the United Kingdom's Universal Credit that provides a cash payment to adults with low income and without a job. According to the World Bank (2018b), social safety net spending is 1.5 percent of global GDP. That spending reduced the global poverty rate by 36 percent at the PPP$1.90 per day level. The World Bank bases these figures on underlying countries' most recent data between 2008 and 2016.

Obstacles to global poverty eradication

Milanovic (2016) asks us to consider the economic status of each person independent of where in the world that person lives. From this perspective, there is only one society, the global one. We can evaluate a person's position in the global income distribution. When we do this, the role of inequality in the persistence of poverty is more transparent. The rapid growth of China and India, two countries with huge populations, has created a large global middle class. People in the global middle class are far from rich, especially compared to the middle class in high-income countries. The former, however, are gaining on the latter. The global middle class is also leaving behind the global poor, people in the lowest quintile of the global income distribution. These people received only two percent of global income growth from 1988 to 2008.

Milanovic argues that the difficulty we face is not one of economic growth, per se. Rather, it is equitable distribution of that growth. The global elite, people in the top one percent of the global income distribution, are richer and more politically powerful than ever before. Increasingly, they have the capacity to influence public policy in countries where they reside.

They advocate for taxation and spending policies that preserve their status. Low taxes on capital income and reduced spending on social safety nets are examples. They fund campaigns of politicians who share their views. When elected, these politicians press for laws consistent with views of the elite. The net effect is that people in the lowest quintile of the global income distribution receive less support. The structure of society is likely to trap them in their position because they are more vulnerable to negative shocks related to climate, technology, and political and economic instability. This is especially true if limited access to quality education and healthcare for people living in poverty accompanies the resurgent political power of the global elite.

One goal of the Millennium Development Goals (MDGs) was to provide access to primary education for all school-age children. By 2015, the global primary school enrollment rate for eligible children was almost 90 percent according to the World Bank (2018a). On the surface, this outcome is praiseworthy. Education increases workers' productivity. It empowers women and girls. It enhances civic engagement. The difficulty, however, is that enrollment is not the same as learning. Testing from India to Mexico indicates that children are not performing up to grade level in mathematics and writing. Student and teacher absenteeism is a problem. Schools are under-resourced. Teacher preparation and training are uneven. These factors weaken the transformative power of education. This is particularly unfortunate because, as Psacharopoulos and Patrinos (2018) report, the private rate of return to an additional year of primary education in low-income and middle-income countries is over nine percent. Low-quality education perpetuates intergenerational poverty.

The World Health Organization and the World Bank (2017) estimate that at least 3.8 billion people (out of 7.3 billion people globally) did not have essential health services coverage in 2015. They define essential health services as interventions in four areas: (1) reproductive, maternal, newborn, and child health, (2) infectious diseases, (3) non-communicable diseases, and (4) service capacity and access. Restricted access to basic health services makes transition out of poverty very difficult. It can lead to absenteeism from school or work. Children who miss school due to illness fall behind their peers. They learn less. Therefore, they accumulate less human capital than they would otherwise. As adults, they are less productive. Their attachment to the formal labor force is tenuous. They earn less when employed. These outcomes increase the likelihood of intergenerational transmission of their childhood poverty status. The tragedy is that society can prevent or easily treat many childhood diseases via vaccination. Then, there are the public health implications of limited essential health services coverage. The health sector's limited capacity to respond in a timely manner to known threats exacerbated mortality and morbidity effects of the HIV/AIDS and ebola epidemics in sub-Saharan and Western Africa.

In 2018, rival factions within South Sudan signed a peace agreement that ended a civil war that began shortly after independence from Sudan in 2011 and lasted more than four years. Also in 2018, Ethiopia and Eritrea signed a peace agreement that ended a war between them that lasted almost twenty years. These three countries are among the poorest on Earth with income per capita of $995 or less in 2017. While there are multiple reasons why South Sudan, Ethiopia, and Eritrea are struggling, the persistent violence due to warfare surely ranks among the leading reasons. Violence and conflict are poverty-producing machines. They destroy almost everything of productive value including people, land, capital equipment, infrastructure, livestock, and structures. They create an environment where it is virtually impossible to invest in the future. They displace non-combatant populations. According to the United Nations High Commissioner for Refugees (2017), the forcibly displaced population worldwide stood at 66 million people in 2016. This figure is the cumulative effect of years of conflict, violence, persecution, or human rights violations. Often, these people are not prepared to support themselves. Nor are societies that receive them prepared to absorb them. The exigencies of warfare dominate most, if not all, plans for human development. Human development indicators, including life expectancy and infant mortality, get worse during periods of warfare. Poverty reduction ceases to be a priority.

The level and locus of future global poverty

Figures 10.1 and 10.2 report World Data Lab (2018) forecasts of the global poverty rate, the number of people living in poverty, and global population in 2030, respectively. Figure 10.3 reports the United Nation's (2015) forecast of life expectancy in 2030. Of course, forecasts of the future are fraught with uncertainty. These are no exception. Nevertheless, they provide some guidance about likely future implications of current policy. They predict that the global poverty rate and the number of people living in poverty will decline to six percent and 476 million, respectively. The good news is that these outcomes will be all-time lows. A rise in life expectancy to 74 years and population to 8.5 billion will accompany these poverty outcomes. The bad news is that almost half a billion people will still live in poverty. At our current rate of poverty reduction, we will not achieve the first SDG: eliminate extreme poverty everywhere by 2030.

Challenges in sub-Saharan Africa are likely to be a major retardant on the rate of poverty reduction over the next decade. According to the World Bank (2018a), the number of people living in poverty there rose from 278 million in 1990 to 413 million in 2015, countering a decline in that number in every other region of the world. Clearly, poverty reduction in sub-Saharan Africa represents a final frontier in our struggle against poverty.

Conclusion

The focus of this chapter is trends in global poverty. Four questions frame the discussion. Our answers to them provide a convenient summary of this chapter. First, the historical trend in the global poverty rate is negative. In 1820, the global poverty rate at two dollars a day was over ninety percent. Today it is ten percent. Second, we use monetary measures such as income per capita and consumption per capita to measure poverty. We also use non-monetary measures such as education, health, and life expectancy to capture other dimensions of well-being. The latter measures expand the scope of accountability and policymaking. Third, economic growth, sound institutions, trade, and social protection programs are leading causes of the negative trend in global poverty. Fourth, forecasters project that the global poverty rate will be around six percent in 2030. Unfortunately, that rate implies that almost half a billion people will still be living in poverty. Therefore, we have much more work to do. We know a lot about how to eradicate global poverty. Whether we have the political will to do it is unknown.

References

Acemoglu, Daron and James A. Robinson (2012): *Why Nations Fail: The Origins of Power, Prosperity, and Poverty*, Crown Business, New York.

Alkire, Sabina, James Foster, Suman Seth, Maria Emma Santos, Jose Manuel Roche, and Paola Ballon (2015): *Multidimensional Poverty Measurement and Analysis*, Oxford University Press, Oxford.

Beaudoin, Steven M. (2007): *Poverty in World History*, Routledge, New York.

Booth, Charles (1903): *Life and Labor of the People of London*, Macmillan and Co., London.

Bourguignon, Francois and Christian Morrisson (2002): "Inequality among World Citizens: 1820–1992," *American Economic Review*, Vol. 92, No. 4, September, pp. 727–744.

Ferreira, Francisco H. G., Shaohua Chen, Andrew Dabalen, Yuri Dikhanov, Nada Hamadeh, Dean Jolliffe, et al. (2016): "A Global Count of the Extreme Poor in 2012: Data Issues, Methodology and Initial Results," *The Journal of Economic Inequality*, Vol. 14, no. 2, pp. 141–172.

Jefferson, Philip N. (2018): *Poverty: A Very Short Introduction*, Oxford University Press, Oxford, United Kingdom.

Maddison, Angus (2007): *Contours of the World Economy, 1–2030 AD: Essays in Macro-Economic History*, Oxford University Press, New York.

Milanovic, Branko (2016): *Global Inequality: A New Approach for the Age of Globalization*, Harvard University Press, Cambridge, MA.

Psacharopoulos, George and Harry Antony Patrinos (2018): "Returns to Investment in Education: A Decennial Review of the Global Literature," *Policy Research Working Paper 8402*, World Bank, Washington DC.

Ravallion, Martin (2016): *The Economics of Poverty: History, Measurement, and Policy*, Oxford University Press, New York.

Rowntree, Benjamin S. (1902): *Poverty: A Study of Town Life*, Macmillan, London.

Sen, Amartya (1999): *Development as Freedom*, Alfred A. Knopf, New York.

United Nations (2015): "World Population Prospects: The 2015 Revision, Key Findings and Advance Tables," Department of Economic and Social Affairs, Population Division Working Paper No. ESA/P/WP.241. https://esa.un.org/unpd/wpp/Publications/Files/Key_Findings_WPP_2015.pdf; accessed 26 July 2018.

United Nations Development Programme (2016): *Human Development Report 2016: Human Development for Everyone*, United Nations Development Programme, New York.

United Nations High Commissioner for Refugees (2017): *Global Trends: Forced Displacement in 2016*, Geneva, Switzerland.

Williamson, Jeffrey G. (2011): *Trade and Poverty: When the Third World Fell Behind*, The MIT Press, Cambridge, MA.

World Bank (2018a): "PovcalNet: the on-line tool for poverty measurement developed by the Development Research Group of the World Bank." http://iresearch.worldbank.org/PovcalNet/home.aspx; accessed 12 October 2018.

World Bank (2018b): *The State of Social Safety Nets 2018*, World Bank, Washington DC. © World Bank. https://openknowledge.worldbank.org/handle/10986/29115 License: CC BY 3.0 IGO (accessed 7 August 2018).

World Data Lab (2018): "World Poverty Clock." http://worldpoverty.io/; accessed 23 July 2018.

World Health Organization and World Bank (2017): *Tracking Universal Health Coverage: 2017 Global Monitoring Report*, License: CC BY-NC-SA 3.0 IGO.

World Health Organization (2018): "Life Expectancy and Healthy Life Expectancy" Data by WHO region. http://apps.who.int/gho/data/view.main.SDG2016LEXREGv?lang=en; accessed 26 July 2018.

11

The discourse of poverty

Structural and behavioural approaches in the UK since 1900

John Welshman

Introduction

This chapter surveys how poverty has been understood historically in the UK since 1900. It argues that, on the one hand, understandings of poverty have been significantly advanced through social surveys, both in terms of empirical knowledge of poverty, locally and nationally, and how poverty was measured and defined. Significant developments have included the collection of empirical data, the elaboration of poverty lines, the use of random sampling, the move from concepts of absolute poverty to those of relative poverty, and the development of methodologies and theories based on poverty dynamics (see also Chapters 1 and 2). However, the chapter also notes that the development of understandings of poverty based on income, educational attainment, housing status and other structural factors has always been accompanied, at least in the UK, by a parallel emphasis on poverty as an individual or family problem (see also Chapters 22 and 23). In the modern period, these concepts have included (in the UK) the social residuum of the 1880s, the social problem group of the 1920s, the problem family of the 1950s, the cycle of deprivation of the 1970s, the underclass of the 1980s, the socially excluded of the 1990s, and the troubled families of the early 21st century. John Macnicol has argued correctly that underclass stereotypes have always been a part of the discourse on poverty in advanced industrial societies (Macnicol 1987, 296). The problem is that these strands have usually been considered separately. The chapter thus looks at three landmarks in the study of poverty – the Rowntree survey of York (1901); Peter Townsend's theory of relative poverty; and more recent research on poverty dynamics. In each case, it shows how each was both preceded by, and followed by, rival readings of poverty. In the UK at least, poverty has thus been viewed as both a residual personal or family problem, and a large-scale structural phenomenon.

The 1900s: Seebohm Rowntree

In the early 1900s, arguably the greatest advances in both the extent of poverty, and how poverty might be defined, came through the work of Seebohm Rowntree in York. Impressed by the work of Charles Booth in London, Rowntree (1871–1954) was determined to find out if poverty in York was as serious as Booth had found in London, and *Poverty: A Study of Town Life* was published in 1901. Rowntree said that his aim was to 'throw some light upon the conditions which govern the life of the wage-earning classes in provincial towns, and especially upon the problem of poverty' (Rowntree 1901, vii–x). The method chosen was a house-to-house survey carried out in 1899, of 11,560 families living in 388 streets. The families comprised a total of 46,754 people, or two-thirds of the overall population of the city. Rowntree included an enquiry into food, rent, and other expenditure, along with a study of social conditions, budgets, and diet. There was no doubt that serious poverty existed in York (Rowntree 1901, 5). Rowntree set out seven classes ranging from 'A' to 'G', and adopted a four-fold classification of the working-class family (A–D), according to the weekly income for a 'moderate' family of two adults and two to four children. The income ranges were less than 18 shillings; 18–21 shillings; 21–30 shillings; and more than 30 shillings.

Rowntree divided his class 'A' (the lowest) into those earning money and those earning no money. He estimated that in the case of 1,295 people (two-thirds of the total), the immediate cause of poverty was the fact that the main wage-earner had died or deserted the family, or was unable to work because of ill-health or old age. Economic causes, through lack of work or low wages, accounted for the poverty of 418 people (21 per cent). He concluded that 'after full allowance has been made for public and private charity, the people in class A are chronically ill-housed, ill-clothed, and underfed' (Rowntree 1901, 45).

Arguably the most important conclusion drawn by Rowntree was the distinction between primary and secondary poverty. Primary poverty was defined as 'families whose total earnings are insufficient to obtain the minimum necessaries for the maintenance of merely physical efficiency'. Secondary poverty, on the other hand, was defined as 'families whose total earnings would be sufficient for the maintenance of merely physical efficiency were it not that some portion of it is absorbed by other expenditure, either useful or wasteful' (Rowntree 1901, vii–x). Rowntree's conclusion was that there were 7,230 people in primary poverty (9.91 per cent of the total population); 13,072 people in secondary poverty (17.93 per cent); and 20,302 people were in poverty in total (27.84 per cent). This was comparable to the findings of Booth, who had estimated that 30.7 per cent of the population of London were in poverty. Rowntree concluded that more attention should be given to living standards, 'for no civilisation can be sound or stable which has at its base this mass of stunted human life' (Rowntree 1901, 295, 304).

The closest that Rowntree came to a behavioural explanation was in his discussion of what he termed secondary poverty. Rowntree estimated secondary poverty by calculating the amount of poverty in York, and then subtracting primary poverty from the total. He conceded that 'the point at which "primary" passes into "secondary" poverty is largely a matter of opinion, depending upon the standard of well-being which is considered necessary' (Rowntree 1901, 140–2). Rowntree argued that the causes of secondary poverty were in part in the control of individuals. They included 'drink, betting, and gambling. Ignorant or careless housekeeping, and other improvident expenditure, the latter often induced by irregularity of income' (Rowntree 1901, 140–2). Nevertheless, Rowntree argued that the causes of 'secondary poverty' were again primarily structural, in that they reflected the wider environmental circumstances within which much of the working class lived (Rowntree 1901, 144–5). Moreover, Rowntree argued that people moved in and out of poverty, and stressed that structural factors were the key causes. Rowntree argued, for example, that few people were likely to remain in class 'A'. At any time the poor might sink into it, through lack of work or the death or illness of the main wage-earner, but equally they would rise out of it when work was found, or when children began to earn money. Only older people would remain in class 'A', until they died or went into the workhouse (Rowntree 1901, 47). Thus Rowntree recognised that most people moved in and out of poverty. The main determinants of these movements were structural factors such as death, illness, unemployment, and low income.

Most secondary writing has centred on Rowntree's distinction between primary and secondary poverty. John Veit-Wilson has argued that Rowntree's work was of fundamental importance in the history of social investigation, in facilitating a shift from an absolutist to a relativistic model of poverty (Veit-Wilson 1986, 97–8). Peter Hennock has pointed out that Charles Booth relied on the School Visitors for his information, and that what he was counting were impressions. Rowntree, on the other hand, took a lot of trouble to collect information on household income, and used this to classify working-class households, and to calculate the number of households in primary poverty (Hennock 1987). So there were two main differences between Booth and Rowntree. Rowntree employed special investigators to undertake house-to-house visits, and surveyed the entire working-class population; and he classified his households by income and household composition rather than by 'conditions of poverty' (Hennock 1991, 191). Rowntree was particularly interested in comparing his findings to those of Booth. In this way, and in choosing to focus on York, he also challenged Charles Booth's earlier preoccupation with London. Hennock argues that this signalled an important change in the conception of poverty as a national rather than a local problem. Rowntree also broke free from Booth in calculating necessary expenditure to construct a poverty line, and it was this that was to dominate poverty surveys from then on (Hennock 1991, 200).

Rowntree's survey comes between the social residuum concept of the 1880s, and the social problem group theory of the 1920s. In the 1880s, the theory of the social residuum had been put forward by a range of commentators, including Henry Hyndman, Arnold White, Samuel Barnett, and perhaps most importantly Charles Booth. It drew on contemporary fears of social degeneration, inspired in part by Charles Darwin. Nevertheless while aspects of the social residuum were carried over into ideas about the unemployable in the early 1900s, including by William Beveridge, it had effectively died away by the First World War. Partly this was due to the Rowntree survey, but also to other surveys, most notably that of Arthur Bowley (1915) which employed the new technique of random sampling, and also because of full employment during the First World War (Welshman 2013, 15–56). As Gareth Stedman Jones has written, once employment opportunities became available, the unemployables could not be found; in fact 'they had never existed, except as a phantom army called up by late Victorian and Edwardian social science to legitimise its practice' (Stedman Jones 1984, 336).

Rowntree's methods and findings were criticised by some of his contemporaries. Helen Bosanquet, for instance, argued that questions about whether people were above or below poverty lines were rarely just about income (*The Times* 1902, 4). Moreover, the early 1900s were characterised by debates about unemployability – those allegedly unwilling to work – while the 1920s and 1930s were marked by the search for a social problem group, characterised by mental deficiency and inter-generational continuities. This latter concept was pushed and funded through the Eugenics Society, including its support for research on pauper pedigrees by E. J. Lidbetter, a Poor Law Relieving Officer working in the East End of London. Its efforts received added impetus following the report of the Wood Committee on Mental Deficiency (1929), which claimed that the number of mental defectives had increased markedly. Whereas the Rowntree survey had focused on the death or illness of the main wage-earner, large families, and low wages as causes of poverty, the Social Survey of Merseyside (1934), edited by David Caradog Jones, included much material relating to what he called 'subnormal types'. Thus, in fact, the Rowntree survey failed to kill off these rival theories. Rather, the social problem group, heredity, and voluntary sterilisation continued to be important currents in intellectual thought up to the outbreak of the Second World War (Welshman 2013, 57–77).

The 1960s: Peter Townsend (1928–2009)

Rowntree's methodological advances were arguably matched by Peter Townsend's conceptual advances in the 1960s. These came in the wider context of the 'rediscovery of poverty', and the establishment of the Child Poverty Action Group (1965), and were international in their impact. In 1962, Townsend questioned the assumption that the welfare state had abolished poverty. He argued that the proposition rested on three generalisations that had been accepted as facts – that full employment had brought prosperity to the mass of the population; that there had been a marked redistribution of income from rich to poor; and that the introduction of the welfare state had provided a net which prevented nearly all those who were sick, disabled, old or unemployed from falling below a civilised standard of subsistence. Various surveys had led to a greater readiness to concede the existence of residual poverty (Townsend 1962). Townsend noted from Ministry of Labour surveys on the expenditure and income of a random sample of 13,000 households in 1953 and 1954 that 5.4 per cent of the households, and 4.1 per cent of the people, were in poverty according to Rowntree's criteria. Another 10.6 per cent of persons were living at a standard lower than 40 per cent above the poverty line. Altogether, 14.7 per cent of the persons in the sample were in poverty or near-poverty. Applied to the whole population, these figures suggested that 2.1 million persons were in poverty, and another 5.4 million only marginally better off, or a total of 7.5 million. In terms of national assistance rates, Townsend found that 10.1 per cent of the households, and 7.8 per cent of persons, were living at a standard less than 40 per cent above the basic national assistance rates.

But Townsend also wrote that despite the work of Booth, Rowntree, Bowley and others, 'the study of poverty has not developed theoretically during the course of this century' (Townsend 1962, 218). The mistake was to look at physical efficiency, and to divorce that from people's psychological well-being and the organisation and structure of society. Thus Townsend argued that poverty was a dynamic, not a static, concept; 'man' was a social animal entangled in a web of relationships which exerted complex and changing pressures to which 'he' must respond, as much in 'his' consumption of goods and services as in any other aspect of his behaviour (Townsend 1962, 219). New approaches might be derived from various directions – more imaginative use might be made of nutritional studies; the living standards of individuals might be studied in relation to the standards those individuals had previously experienced; poverty could be defined on the basis of the number of households having a total income of less than two-thirds of the average; more study might be given to the distribution of non-monetary resources among individuals and families comprising the population; and the development of theories of poverty and deprivation could not be based solely on studies in Britain. Perhaps most importantly, Townsend argued that poverty was not an absolute state, but was relative deprivation. He wrote that individuals and families whose resources fell seriously short of those commanded by the average individual or family in the community in which they lived were, by definition, in poverty (Townsend 1962, 225).

With Brian Abel-Smith, Townsend had realised that there was little precise information about living conditions; they had the idea of re-analysing existing income and expenditure survey data to reveal more about poverty and income distribution. They used Ministry of Labour expenditure surveys for the years 1953–54 and 1960 to assess how many people were living at levels below the National Assistance Board rate, and how many were 40 per cent above it. This showed that it was not only older people who were in poverty, and the numbers included not only people receiving benefits, but some in full-time work. The book, *The Poor and the Poorest* (Abel-Smith and Townsend 1965), showed that extensive poverty still existed in Britain, and that even the introduction of family allowances had not abolished child poverty. Townsend subsequently argued that individuals, families, and groups were in poverty 'when they lack the resources to obtain the types of diet, participate in the activities and have the living conditions and amenities' which were customary, or at least widely encouraged or approved, in the societies to which they belonged (Townsend 1979, 31). Townsend's work on relative poverty did not go unchallenged (Sen 1985; Townsend 1985). Nevertheless, it was of profound importance in the study of poverty.

In the UK context, Townsend's work came in the context of, and partly as a response to, the debate about problem families which was the successor to the concept of the social problem group in the 1930s. In fact, he noted research on problem families in his 1962 article. Articles on problem families rarely mentioned income; they were essentially descriptions of household squalor; they paid little attention to how the problem family was defined; and they focused on the mother. It has been suggested that four professional interest groups had something to gain from the construction of the problem family – public health doctors; voluntary organisations called Family Service Units; members of the Eugenics Society; and social workers. The concept of the problem family was different to the social problem group in that it was more optimistic, in the sense that it was thought families could be rehabilitated rather than segregated or sterilised. Moreover, it led to actual interventions on the ground, with local authorities seeking to tackle problem families through health visitors and home helps. By the mid-1960s, however, the concept had fallen out of favour, partly because of the rediscovery of poverty, but also because of the realisation of the methodological flaws in much of the research; the belief that while the problem family was easy to recognise, it was hard to define (Welshman 2013, 79–97).

The equivalent concept in the US in the 1960s was the culture of poverty (Welshman 2013, 99–118). Moreover, while Townsend's work on both the concept of relative poverty and on the extent of poverty in the UK was clearly of profound significance, at the political level the 1970s were also marked by a debate about a cycle of deprivation, or transmitted deprivation. It was Sir Keith Joseph, Conservative Secretary of State for Health and Social Services, who proposed the theory of a cycle of deprivation in a speech given in June 1972. The theory acknowledged the importance of income, but was nevertheless linked more to behavioural factors, notably parenting, and to what Joseph saw as inter-generational continuities. Townsend himself was highly critical (Townsend 1974). However, unusually the Joseph speech led to a large-scale Research Programme, funded by his department, and organised by the Social Science Research Council (1974–82). The final report on the Research Programme on Transmitted Deprivation was rather inconclusive, and the theory faded away, only returning to the political stage in the UK with the election of the New Labour Government from 1997 (Welshman 2013, 119–37).

The 1990s: poverty dynamics

More recent methodological advances in the study of poverty have come in the area of poverty dynamics. The term 'dynamic analysis' can have several meanings. It can refer to studies of income fluctuations from one year to the next. It can cover life-course perspectives. And it can refer to studies of inter-generational continuities. It is recognised that poverty dynamics is not completely new. Rowntree noted that people could fall into poverty, and equally rise out of it, over the life course. However, despite the Rowntree survey, the life cycle approach fell away during the interwar period. It was only when new data sets became available from the 1970s, that people turned again to this approach (Bane and Ellwood 1986, 1–23). Gradually British commentators began to use longitudinal data sets to look more closely at income dynamics among the low-income population. As in the US, data from longitudinal studies have been recognised as playing a key role in debates about poverty, social exclusion, and social mobility.

As this work assumed greater importance from the 1990s, various claims were made in support of it. It was argued that making time more explicit in the way that poverty and social exclusion were conceptualised, defined, and measured helped to clarify the differences between them (Falkingham and Hills 1995). Qualitative research, too, seemed to indicate that the different patterning of poverty over time, and the varying trajectories that people followed, meant poverty had different social meanings and risks of social exclusion. In these cases, social exclusion could be a 'destination on a journey through poverty' (Walker 1995, 102–28). Lutz Leisering and Robert Walker, for example, claimed understandings of the nature of poverty were reframed by this work in four main ways. Poverty was more differentiated and dynamic than was allowed for in traditional accounts or public debate. Poverty and the receipt of social assistance were not restricted to marginal groups. One section of the population was less mobile and suffered long-term or recurrent spells of poverty. And although poor families risked being socially excluded, many of them retained some leverage over their circumstances. Dynamic research provided little support for models of dependency, and provided evidence of both social processes and agency, change, and choice. It tended to point to policies that built on the agency of people in need, pro-active policies that emphasised early intervention (Leisering and Walker 1998, 265–85; Jenkins 2000, 529–67).

The first main approach has been in terms of income fluctuations from one year to the next. The British Household Panel Survey (BHPS), for instance, seemed to indicate that there was much movement in and out of poverty. Steven Webb argued from a preliminary analysis of the data that 'there is not a single homogeneous group who are "the poor" and whose lot is permanently to remain poor. Rather, fluctuations in personal circumstances lead to considerable variations in living standards even from one year to the next' (Webb 1995, pp. 17–18). Others used the first two waves of the BHPS to argue that most income changes from one year to the next were not very great (Jarvis and Jenkins 1998, 428–43). Simon Burgess and Carol Propper agreed that any snapshot picture hid the degree of mobility that existed, and in general their analysis confirmed that of Jarvis and Jenkins. People move out of poverty, but generally to an income level that is not much higher (Burgess and Propper 2002).

The second main approach has argued that an understanding of income and poverty dynamics benefits from taking a life cycle perspective. This work explores the question of how life events affect the probability of moving up or down the income distribution: partnership formation and dissolution; having children; retirement; and the death of a spouse. Robert Walker, for example, found from longitudinal data for the Netherlands and Germany that although most spells of poverty were short, much poverty was accounted for by a small number of people who were in the midst of very long spells of poverty. He suggested that there was 'not one kind of poverty but many', with different implications for social exclusion (Walker 1995). Other data from the first ten waves of the BHPS (1991–2000) suggested that particular life events are closely associated with either falling or rising trajectories, but that there are differences in income trajectories following these events. Overall, life cycle factors do not explain as much of the variation in income trajectories as labour market factors, but they do have an important explanatory role: rising trajectories (partnership formation and children becoming independent); and falling trajectories (having children and partnership breakdown) (Rigg and Sefton 2004).

The third approach has been in terms of inter-generational mobility – the question of to what extent there is a correlation between a parent's position in the earnings distribution and that of his or her children. Researchers had earlier used data on children and their parents to assess the extent of inter-generational mobility (Atkinson et al. 1983). In the 1990s, researchers turned to longitudinal data from the National Child Development Study. They argued that the extent of inter-generational mobility was limited in terms of both earnings and schooling. There was a clear inter-generational correlation between fathers, and both sons and daughters, in terms of labour market earnings and years of schooling (Dearden et al. 1997). A further element of this research has been the relationship between childhood experiences and subsequent labour market performance as an adult. Paul Gregg and Stephen Machin have suggested that such studies of inter-generational mobility are important for looking for transmission mechanisms; they shed light on which pre-labour market factors are connected to labour market success or failure; and they can inform future policy on child outcomes (Gregg and Machin 2001, 146). This work has tended to suggest that initiatives to improve skills and employment opportunities are the most sensible way to tackle persistent poverty, and have highlighted the importance of the policy agenda to reduce child poverty and disadvantage (Blanden 2006). Overall, panel surveys have achieved much. However knowledge about the mechanisms involved in these issues remains unclear (Such and Walker 2002).

Research on poverty dynamics was preceded by the debate about the underclass in the 1980s, in both the US and the UK. In both, contributors can be divided into four broad categories. First, those, predominantly on the Right, who believed that an identifiable class below the working class did exist, and had a different culture and behaviour. Second, commentators, including many on the Left, who also believed that the underclass existed, but who linked it more to structural causes, such as unemployment, poverty, and technological change. Third, those whose position can be described as broadly agnostic, who thought that it was a theoretical possibility, but who found no empirical evidence. And fourth, a group who were hostile to the concept from the outset. Charles Murray was an important contributor to the debate on both sides of the Atlantic, but perhaps the biggest difference between the US and UK was that in the former the debate was essentially a debate about race. Again, the arguments had effectively petered out by the mid-1990s, when it was replaced by the theory of social exclusion – which came initially from France and the European Union (Welshman 2013, 139–207).

Moreover, despite the methodological advances evident in research on poverty dynamics, the policy landscape in the UK from around 2011 included interventions to tackle so-called troubled families. The origins of this were in some of the policies adopted by New Labour from 2006, including Family Intervention Projects and the Family Nurse Partnership. Furthermore, following the riots in the summer of 2011, a more focused intervention on troubled families was announced by the Coalition Government (2010–15). Prime Minister David Cameron said the government was committing £448 million to tackling 120,000 troubled families through a new Troubled Families Unit in the Department for Communities and Local Government. It was claimed that many social problems were caused by 120,000 troubled families, costing £6 billion, and local authorities were given funding to identify the families and to 'turn them around'. The policy continued under the Conservative government from 2015. Evaluations of the projects were critical, and at the time of writing troubled families have largely disappeared from political rhetoric (Welshman 2013, 209–27). Nevertheless, the key point is that in the political arena these concepts continued to have traction.

Conclusion

The history of poverty in the UK since 1900 has thus been characterised by parallel developments. First, poverty has been viewed as a large-scale structural phenomenon, with methodological advances that have included the collection of empirical data; the elaboration of poverty lines; the move from absolute to relative concepts of poverty; and the shift to theories based on poverty dynamics. This work has had a global impact. But, second, poverty has also been viewed repeatedly as a residual personal or family phenomenon, with alleged behavioural, individualistic, or cultural causes. It seems likely that there are important national differences here, with the histories of the UK (and the US) being marked more by behavioural or individualistic interpretations, than, for example, countries in the European Union. Moreover, it is important not to exaggerate the significance of some of these concepts, and it is arguable that some – the social problem group; the problem family; the cycle of deprivation – were short-lived, and of relatively minor importance. Researchers such as Rowntree and Townsend were rightly dismissive of such theories. Nevertheless, the persistence of the debate is striking, and points to deeper ideological or political differences; it is naive to suppose that moral or individualistic notions can be killed off by simple empirical research or investigation alone. In terms of the future, this history would lead us to anticipate further methodological advances, based on understandings of poverty as a large-scale structural issue, but also new concepts based on familiar readings of poverty as a residual personal or family phenomenon.

References

Abel-Smith, B. and Townsend, P. 1965. *The Poor and the Poorest: A New Analysis of the Ministry of Labour's Family Expenditure Surveys of 1953–54 and 1960*. London: G. Bell & Sons.

Atkinson, A. B., Maynard, A. K., and Trinder, C. G. 1983. *Parents and Children: Incomes in Two Generations*. London: Heinemann.

Bane, M. J. and Ellwood, D. T. 1986. 'Slipping into and out of poverty: The dynamics of spells'. *Journal of Human Resources*, 21: 1–23.

Blanden, J. 2006. 'Cycles of disadvantage'. *Poverty*, 124: 15–17.

Burgess, S. and Propper, C. 2002. 'The Dynamics of Poverty in Britain'. In *Understanding Social Exclusion*, edited by J. Hills, J. Le Grand, and D. Piachaud, 44–61. Oxford: Oxford University Press.

Dearden, L., Machin, S., and Reed, H. 1997. 'Intergenerational mobility in Britain'. *Economic Journal*, 107: 47–66.

Falkingham, J. and Hills, J. eds. 1995. *The Dynamic of Welfare: The Welfare State and the Life Cycle*. Hemel Hempstead: Prentice Hall/Harvester Wheatsheaf.

Gregg, P. and Machin, S. 2001. 'Childhood Experiences, Educational Attainment and Adult Labour Market Performance'. In *Child Well-Being, Child Poverty and Child Policy in Modern Nations: What do we Know?* edited by K. Vleminckz, and T. M. Smeeding, 129–50. Bristol: Policy Press.

Hennock, E. P. 1987. 'The measurement of urban poverty: From the metropolis to the nation, 1880–1920'. *Economic History Review*, XL, 2: 208–27.

Hennock, E. P. 1991. 'Concepts of Poverty in the British Social Surveys from Charles Booth to Arthur Bowley'. In *The Social Survey in Historical Perspective 1880–1940*, edited by M. Bulmer, K. Bales, and K. Kish Sklar, 189–216. Cambridge: Cambridge University Press.

Jarvis, S. and Jenkins, S. P. 1998. 'How much income mobility is there in Britain?' *Economic Journal*, 108: 428–43.

Jenkins, S. P. 2000. 'Modelling household income dynamics'. *Journal of Population Economics*, 13: 529–67.

Leisering, L. and Walker, R. eds. 1998. *The Dynamics of Modern Society: Poverty, Policy and Welfare*. Bristol: Policy Press.

Macnicol, J. 1987. 'In pursuit of the underclass'. *Journal of Social Policy*, 16, 3: 293–318.

Rigg, J. and Sefton, T. 2004. *Income Dynamics and the Life Cycle*. London: CASE, CASE paper 81.

Rowntree, B. S. 1901. *Poverty: A Study of Town Life*. London: Macmillan.

Sen, A. 1985. 'A sociological approach to the measurement of poverty: A reply to Professor Peter Townsend'. *Oxford Economic Papers*, 37: 669–76.

Such, E. and Walker, R. 2002. 'Falling behind? Research on transmitted deprivation'. *Benefits*, 10, 3: 185–92.

Stedman Jones, G. 1984. *Outcast London: A Study in the Relationship Between Classes in Victorian Society*. Oxford: Oxford University Press, 1971, Peregrine edition.

The Times. 1902. 16 September, p. 4, column f.

Townsend, P. 1962. 'The meaning of poverty'. *British Journal of Sociology*, 13, 3: 210–27.

Townsend, P. 1974. 'The cycle of deprivation: The history of a confused thesis'. In British Association of Social Workers, *The Cycle of Deprivation: Papers Presented to a National Study Conference, Manchester University, March, 1974*, 8–22. Birmingham: BASW.

Townsend, P. 1979. *Poverty in the United Kingdom: A Survey of Household Resources and Standards of Living*. Harmondsworth: Penguin.

Townsend, P. 1985. 'A sociological approach to the measurement of poverty: A rejoinder to Professor Amartya Sen'. *Oxford Economic Papers*, 37: 659–68.

Walker, R. 1995. 'The Dynamics of Poverty and Social Exclusion'. In *Beyond the Threshold: The Measurement and Analysis of Social Exclusion*, edited by G. Room, 102–28. Bristol: Policy Press.

Webb, S. 1995. *Poverty Dynamics in Britain: Preliminary Analysis from the British Household Panel Survey*. London: Institute for Fiscal Studies.

Welshman, J. 2013. *Underclass: A History of the Excluded Since 1880*. London: Bloomsbury.

Veit-Wilson, J. H. 1986. 'Paradigms of poverty: A rehabilitation of B. S. Rowntree'. *Journal of Social Policy*, 15: 69–99.

12
Poverty development in affluent welfare states

Kate Summers

Introduction

The country contexts brought together in this chapter are united by their status as 'affluent welfare states'; broadly defined as countries with high levels of national income and spending, with large, centralised states and developed welfare state apparatus. The systematic measurement of living standards and poverty first began in the countries included in this chapter; the studies of Rowntree (1901) and Booth (1903) in the English cities of York and London, respectively, are often cited as the first attempts to operationalise the concept of a poverty line. The main geographic scope of this chapter therefore covers Western European countries, Australia and New Zealand. Although there are unifying characteristics between these countries, there is also a great deal of variation across these national contexts, which this chapter aims to highlight.[1]

The aim of the chapter is to consider how poverty is currently measured in affluent welfare states; to observe poverty rates including over time, for specific subgroups, and using different measures; to identify relevant policy tools and approaches for tackling poverty; and to consider emerging challenges that, it is concluded, have the potential to seriously exacerbate poverty levels.

Statistical description of the development of poverty

This section provides an account of changes in poverty rates over time, as well as considering some competing definitions of poverty and related debates as applied to affluent welfare states.

The most widely used definition of poverty in affluent welfare states is a poverty line drawn at 50% or 60% of median income.[2] There are two things to note: this is a relative measure, meaning that changes in the income distribution that affect the median will in turn affect the poverty line level; and this is a money-metric, and more specifically income-based, measure (see Chapters 2–4). Figure 12.1 shows relative poverty rates from 2005 to 2017 across selected countries.

The trends in poverty across the period presented are related to the degree to which countries experienced economic contraction as a result of the 2008 financial crisis, and in turn the extent to which countries pursued austerity policies that cut social protection provision for low-income households (Ólafsson, Daly, Kangas, & Palme, 2019). Iceland is notable for its persistently low relative poverty rate across the time series.[3] Greece, Spain and Italy, on the other

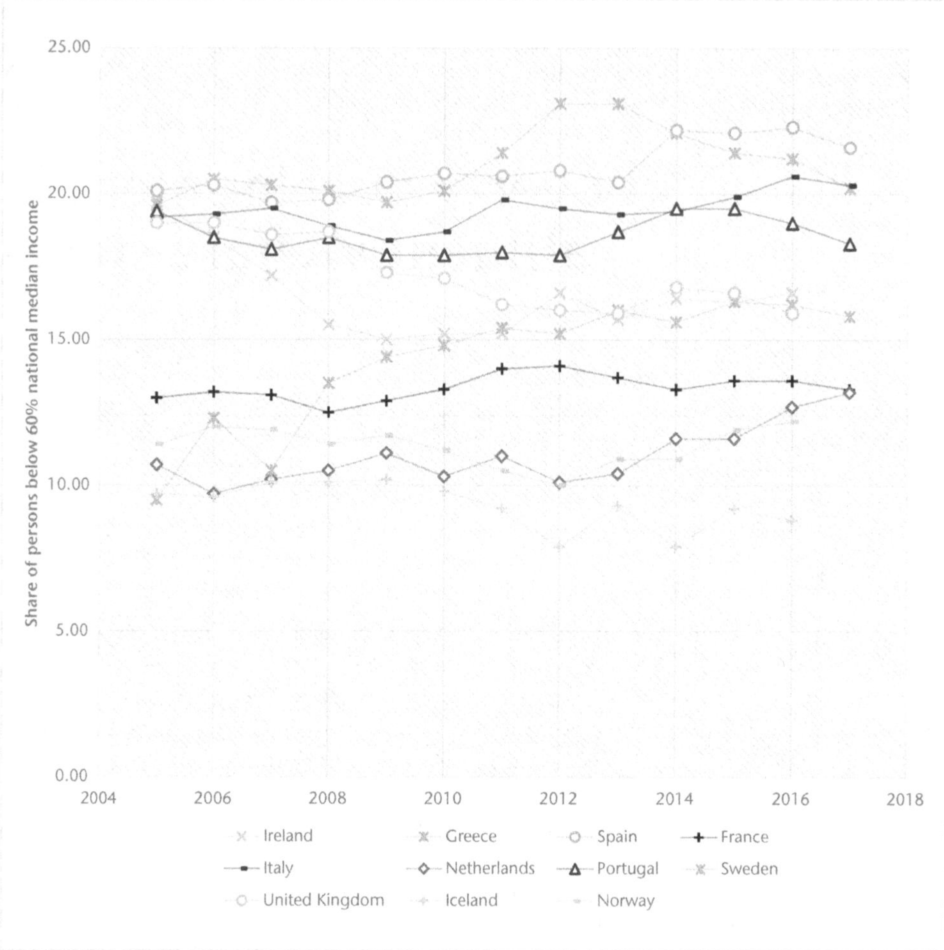

Figure 12.1 The share of persons with an equivalised disposable income below the risk-of-poverty threshold, which is set at 60% of the national median equivalised disposable income (after social transfers) across selected affluent welfare states.

Source: Eurostat.

hand, have the highest rates among the countries included, with Greece seeing a spike in the early 2010s, and Spain and Italy showing steadily increasing poverty rates across the time period. There are dramatic changes for some countries: Sweden begins with some of the lowest relative poverty rates and then jumps to the middle of the included countries by 2017,[4] while Ireland begins the period with some of the highest rates before falling to a middling position.

Looking at the relative poverty rate alone cannot tell us whether changes in the rate are because the median income level has changed, which therefore 'pulls up' or 'pushes down' where the 60% of median poverty line is drawn; or whether the median has remained the same but people in the bottom half of the distribution have seen a change to their incomes that has moved them to above or below the poverty line. Therefore, it can be useful to supplement relative measures with an anchored measure. Such a measure involves drawing a relative poverty line in a chosen 'anchor year' and then adjusting this line over time by inflation. Anchored poverty lines provide us with a 'weak relative' or closer to an absolute measure of poverty, and can be particularly useful when there have been periods of economic growth or contraction that have affected the income distribution in a country and make a relative poverty line more difficult to interpret in isolation (Morelli, Smeeding, & Thompson, 2015).

Figure 12.2 shows the anchored poverty rates, using a baseline year of 2005, for selected countries.

Using this anchored measure, Greece stands out for the dramatic increase in poverty from 2010 onwards. The financial crisis and austerity policies have had deep and protracted effects on living standards in Greece (Andriopoulou, Karakitsios, & Tsakloglou, 2018). When combined with the fluctuating but much more stable relative poverty line we can observe for Greece in Figure 12.1, we can conclude that the crisis had an adverse effect across the middle as well as the bottom of the income distribution. Relative poverty has not increased because households in the middle of the distribution saw a reduction in their living standards too, however, in more absolute terms using an anchored measure, poverty has increased. Similar, but less pronounced

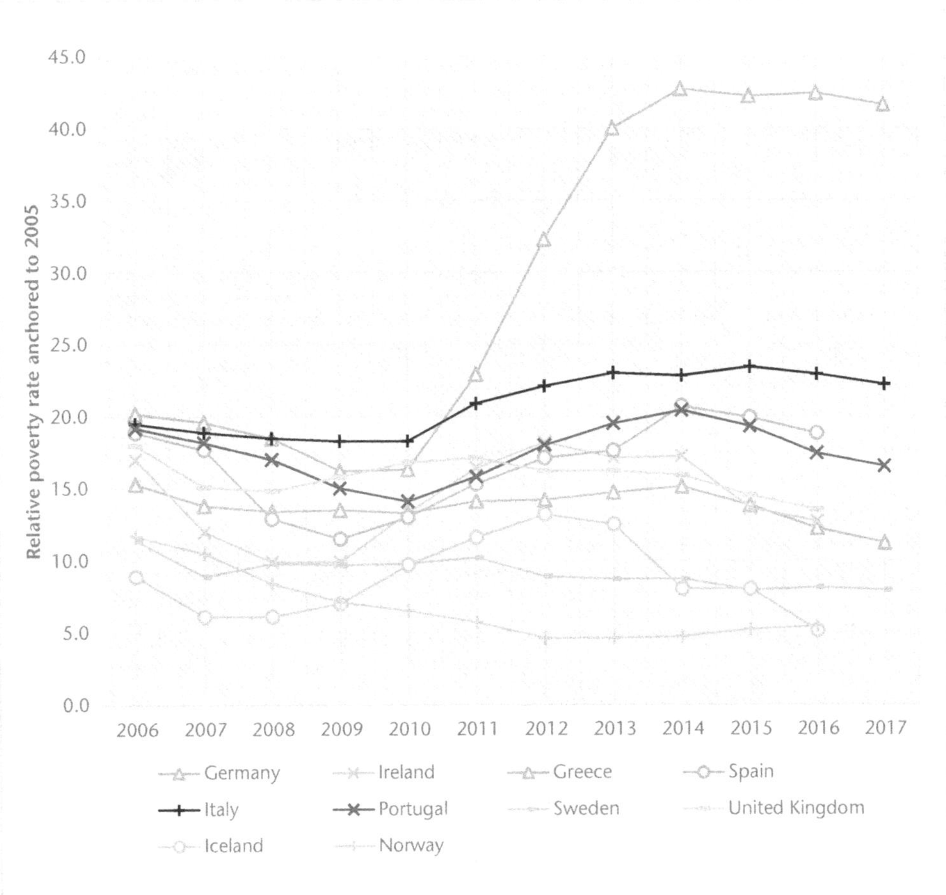

Figure 12.2 Anchored relative poverty rate across selected affluent welfare states.

Source: Eurostat.

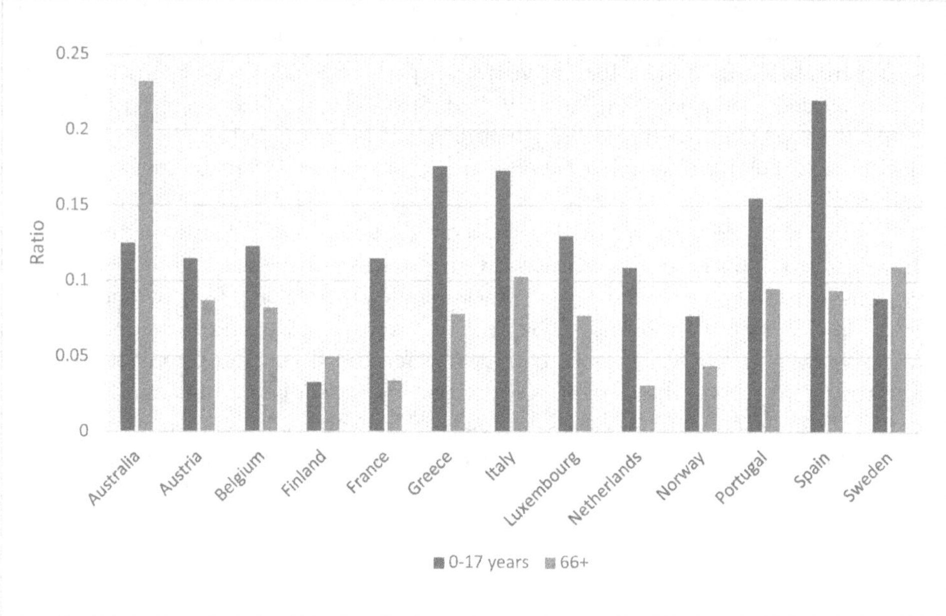

Figure 12.3 The ratio of the number of people (in age groups 0–17 years and 66 years and over) whose income falls below the poverty line; taken as half (50%) the median household income of the total population, 2016.

Source: OECD Social and Welfare Statistics: Income distribution.

trends can be observed in Italy and Spain as well. The Scandinavian countries of Sweden and Norway, on the other hand, show a steady decline in their anchored poverty rates over the period of measurement.

Turning to poverty rates among particular subgroups, Figure 12.3 compares relative poverty drawn at 50% of median income for children (aged between 0 and 17 years) and over 65s in 2016. Among the included countries, Finland has the lowest child poverty rate of 3.3%, while Spain has the highest child poverty rate of 22%. Among over 65s, the Netherlands has the lowest poverty rate of 3.1% and Australia has the highest rate of 23.2%. With the exception of Australia, Finland and Sweden, child poverty rates are higher than over 65 poverty rates within each country. In France, Greece, the Netherlands and Spain, child poverty rates are over double that of the over 65s poverty rate. This is a relatively recent trend whereby it is child poverty that is higher and rising as compared to poverty among older people which is generally lower and falling (Morelli et al., 2015: 614). In the last ten years, the increases in child poverty across many affluent welfare states have been closely associated to deleterious changes in parental income and earnings, as well as levels of social transfers (Thévenon, Manfredi, Govind, & Klauzner, 2018). On the other hand, poverty levels among older age groups are closely tied to the adequacy of safety-net retirement benefits (OECD, 2017b: 134).

With child poverty in particular, the measurement and interpretation of figures present additional challenges. Children overwhelmingly live in households with their parent(s), and the challenge is to get *inside* the household to understand how household-level measures of poverty relate to children's experiences. Assumptions have to be made about how resources are shared between household members (Chzhen, Nolan, Cantillon, & Sudhanshu, 2017: 20). Children do not tend to be responsible for providing economic resources for themselves, and so variations in child poverty, and ameliorative policies, generally focus on the roles of family structure (including lone parenthood), social transfers and parental employment (Bradbury, Jäntti, & Lindhal, 2018; Gornick & Jäntti, 2012).

For further summary statistics, the most accessible set of resources on poverty development across rich countries is the OECD's Income Distribution Database, which can be searched by indicator and by area (www.oecd.org/social/income-distribution-database.htm).

There are several qualifying points to be made about how poverty tends to be measured in affluent welfare states. The focus on relative income measures has both strengths and limitations. The strengths include that the approach is aligned with a well-established theoretical perspective on poverty that understands the experience of poverty as inherently relative: as dependent upon the social context within which one is living (Sen, 1983; Townsend, 1979). A relative measure of income deprivation tells us (according to some perspectives) about absolute deprivation in terms of social functioning or participation. In a rich country more income might be needed "to buy enough commodities to achieve the *same social functioning*, such as 'appearing in public without shame'" (Sen, 1992: 115).

The existence of reliable relative poverty data across affluent welfare state contexts is an important development in and of itself. It has only been quite recently that multiple sources of harmonised (comparable) household income and poverty data have become available (Morelli et al., 2015), most notably in the form of the Luxembourg Income Study database and the Organization for Economic Cooperation and Development's (OECD) data. The ability to compare across countries over time can be a powerful analytic tool, although there is also the risk that somewhat arbitrary country rankings, or 'league tables' are created. Creating internationally comparable data is undesirable if this encourages an abstracted perspective that forgets specific country contexts and conditions, and the detail of policy instruments available to address poverty. Indeed, it might even encourage complacency for those who 'rank' top or mid-table.

There are of course limitations to relative poverty measures. There are challenges in defining and measuring income, as well as deciding on the reference period, income unit, and assumptions about resource sharing that should be used (Morelli et al., 2015: 598–601; see also Chapters 2–4). As relative poverty measures tend to define the poverty line in reference to median income, measures of poverty can be particularly difficult to interpret in periods of dramatic economic contraction or growth that affect median income levels. Also, by drawing a poverty *line*, we learn nothing about the depth or distribution of poverty below that line: we cannot tell from a relative poverty line whether those in poverty are a little or a long way from the line, or how resources are distributed among those in poverty. We also cannot know about the persistence of poverty: a relative poverty line drawn annually does not tell us whether all those below the line are the same or different from those who were below the line in the previous year. There have been various refinements proposed and operationalised to address some of these limitations, including providing absolute, or anchored, poverty lines alongside relative lines (see, for example, the reporting of the UK's Households Below Average Income series (Department for Work and Pensions, 2018)); measuring the *depth* of poverty below a given line; and using longitudinal data to see how much 'churn' there is, as people move in and out of poverty between years (Hills, 2015).

The use of a money-metric measure has further advantages and drawbacks. A focus on money is both easy to measure, and perhaps also best aligns with policy interventions which involve cash transfers. A focus on income also means that we know what someone *has*, rather than assessing the outcomes they achieve through the choices they make: an income-based focus means we do not mix up voluntarily low levels of consumption with material deprivation.

However, arguably money-metric measures do not directly tell us what many might say we are interested in, namely whether people are indeed reaching some sort of acceptable living standard. This is particularly pertinent for, for example, people living with a disability, who might require a higher income to achieve the same ends as someone who does not (Zaidi & Burchardt, 2005).

Alternative approaches in affluent welfare state contexts have included multidimensional measures and consumption-based indicators (see Chapters 2–4). Many think that consumption is a better proxy for wellbeing than income (Fisher, Johnson, & Smeeding, 2012). Multidimensional measures (which have perhaps seen greater consensus in development contexts (Alkire et al., 2014)) are a response to both increasing data availability, but also the growing evidence base that income poverty is a weak proxy for material deprivation in rich country contexts (Nolan & Whelan, 2011). These alternative approaches arguably provide more direct measures of the aspects of poverty we are actually concerned with, while ensuring that a focus on material resources is maintained (Lister, 2017). However, one of the main strengths of relative income measures remains their comparability across countries: consumption data is not yet comparable (Morelli et al., 2015: 595), and while many affluent welfare states have developed measures of material deprivation, they are often not standardised in a way that makes it possible to compare across a wide range of contexts. As Sen concludes, relative income poverty, "gives a neat and well-defined measure, and it is not hard to see why it has been so widely used in the empirical literature on poverty and deprivation" (1992: 102).

There are ongoing efforts to refine and provide alternative, comparable, measures of poverty among affluent welfare states. From 2009, for example, material deprivation indicators were adopted by all 27 European Union (EU) countries (European Commission & Eurostat, 2012). The material deprivation measure is used alongside the standard relative poverty measure (60% of median income) and a measure of household work intensity as a formal definition of those at risk of poverty and social exclusion in the EU ('AROPA'). The material deprivation measure consists of nine items. If three items out of the nine cannot be afforded then a household is defined as 'materially deprived', if four items cannot be afforded then the household is 'severely materially deprived'. Figure 12.4 shows the rates of material, and severe material deprivation in the EU countries included in this chapter.

The southern European countries of Greece, Italy and Portugal stand out for their high levels of material deprivation. The northern European countries of Norway and Sweden have particularly low levels of material deprivation as compared to the other countries. The measures of material and severe material deprivation are constructed so as to distinguish between lacking but wanting an item, and lacking an item out of choice. However, the choice of items in such a list can be difficult to agree on, as can deciding when to change or adjust items as social norms change. Further, the specific EU measure has been critiqued for the small number of items on which it is based, and the weak robustness of some of the items (European Commission & Eurostat, 2012: 37–45).

There are also proposed refinements, or alternatives to official measures at the national level. In Australia the 'Henderson poverty line' is widely used, based on a benchmark income level established in 1973 that is updated periodically (Wilkins, 2018). New Zealand does not have an official poverty line, but in the government's Social Report, relative income poverty and material deprivation are measured (New Zealand Ministry of Social Development, 2016: 135–142). In the UK there is an established tradition of alternative poverty measurements. The long running 'breadline Britain' research programme (that began in 1983) employs a consensus-based approach to define the 'necessities of life' and then measures who cannot afford these necessities (Lansley & Mack, 2015; see also the work of the Minimum Income Standards programme that

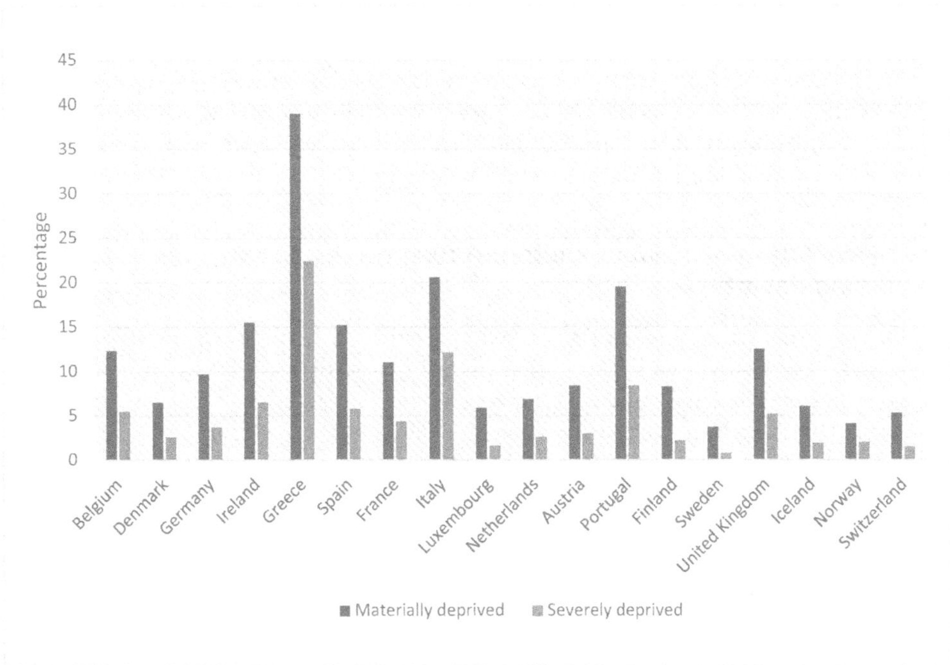

Figure 12.4 Percentage materially or severely materially deprived.

Source: Eurostat.

takes a consensual approach, Padley & Hirsch, 2017). A new poverty measure has recently been proposed for the UK, put forward by the government-appointed 'Social Metrics Commission' (Stroud, 2018). The measure aims to take account of all material resources (including wealth) and not just income; to include extra costs related to, for example, disability or childcare; and to account for housing (including by defining someone who is street homeless as being in poverty).

Alongside the development of multidimensional and consumption-based measures, contemporary debates around measuring poverty in affluent country contexts can be seen as pulling in two main directions. The first centres around a re-emerging debate on extreme poverty. Mirroring in some ways the 'rediscovery of poverty' moment in 1960s Britain (Abel-Smith & Townsend, 1975) whereby scholars 'rediscovered' the existence of poverty in a wealthy society, there has been a recent resurgence in researching and identifying minimalistic definitions. This can perhaps most clearly be seen in the recent body of scholarship around food poverty (Dowler & Lambie-Mumford, 2015; Riches & Silvasti, 2014), and work to identify specific minimalist circumstances such as 'destitution' (Fitzpatrick et al., 2016). The second is to move from concerns with 'relative poverty' to a more explicit concern with 'inequality' (Savage, 2014) (although there is a danger of overstating this paradigmatic shift: to be concerned with relative poverty is to be concerned with forms of inequality).

The motivations behind drawing a poverty line varies across the countries included in this chapter. There are longstanding 'official' measures of poverty across many of the countries included, and for Europe as a whole. Poverty measurement is particularly 'popular' in English-speaking countries, with the aim appearing to centre on a longstanding commitment to reporting and monitoring, although there are examples, including recently, of poverty measurement becoming highly politicised (see, for example, the recent radical redefinition of the official child poverty measure in the UK (Stewart & Roberts, 2018)). Northern European and Scandinavian countries, on the other hand, tend to more directly tie discussions of poverty measures to assessing and setting the levels of social welfare programmes (Bjorklund & Freeman, 1997; Marx & Nelson, 2013). How poverty is measured, and what it is measured for, can therefore tell us a lot about a country's political and policy outlooks and priorities.

The heavy lifting of affluent welfare states: successes and challenges in *reducing* poverty

The country contexts included in this chapter are unified in having relatively advanced state apparatuses for tackling poverty. This section considers what role these have played in reducing poverty, while remembering that there is a great amount of variation across the country contexts.

As Barr (2001) explains, welfare states combine the role of 'piggy bank' and 'Robin Hood' in varying forms and degrees. The piggy bank, collective insurance, function protects those who have contributed in some form against social risks. The Robin Hood, redistributive, function can be both horizontal across an individual's life course, and vertical between those with higher and lower incomes. It is important to remember throughout that poverty reduction, although often central, is only one among many aims of affluent welfare states.

In terms of poverty reduction, the evidence is clear that social spending at a high level is crucial. As Marx, Nolan and Olivera explain, "no advanced economy achieved a low level of inequality and/or relative income poverty with a low level of social spending, regardless of how well that country performed on other dimensions that matter for poverty" (Marx, Nolan, & Olivera, 2015: 2081). Specific policy design and details matter, but these cannot compensate for inadequate *amounts* of spending by the state.

Looking at the overall redistributive effort of different countries, and the effect this has on poverty outcomes, it is found that the direct effect of transfers and taxes on poverty rates varies significantly. Table 12.1 shows relative income poverty rates pre- and post-social transfers, and the extent to which social transfers reduce poverty. The extent to which post-social transfer poverty rates are lower than pre-transfer rates varies from a 15.8% reduction in the case of Greece, to a 56.9% reduction in the case of Finland. Broadly speaking, the southern European countries see the least amount of poverty reduction between pre- and post-transfer, while the Scandinavian countries (who have much higher levels of social spending) see the most.

The bases for these variations have motivated the development of a large literature. Korpi and Palme (1998) famously argued that, contrary to popular understandings, the efficient targeting of social transfers was the most successful strategy in reducing poverty in rich countries (Besley, 1990; Le Grand, 1982), greater poverty reduction is achieved by more universal transfers, as this encourages support for a larger welfare state (Nelson, 2004). This is termed the 'paradox of redistribution'. However, the very strong relationship between the extent of targeting and amount of spending has weakened (Kenworthy, 2011).

The paradox of redistribution has been revised and extended by Brady & Bostic (2015) into two new paradoxes: non-complementarity and undermining. The non-complementarity paradox emphasises the potential mismatch between what matters for poverty reduction and what matters for redistribution preferences: a high transfer share (share of household income from welfare transfers) is most robustly related to reducing poverty, but is not related to redistribution preferences; low-income targeting is negatively related to redistribution preferences but is not robustly related to poverty. Brady and Bostic also find that transfer share (i.e. the measure associated with poverty reduction) is positively associated with low-income targeting (i.e. the

Table 12.1 Relative poverty rates pre- and post-social transfers, 2017

	Relative poverty before social transfers	*Relative poverty after social transfers*	*Reduction in poverty (% point)*	*Reduction in poverty (%)*
Belgium	26.3	15.9	10.4	39.5
Denmark	25.3	12.4	12.9	51.0
Germany	24.1	16.1	8	33.2
Ireland (2016)	34.7	16.6	18.1	52.2
Greece	24	20.2	3.8	15.8
Spain	28.4	21.6	6.8	23.9
France	24.1	13.3	10.8	44.8
Italy	25.2	20.3	4.9	19.4
Luxembourg	29	18.7	10.3	35.5
Hungary	25	13.4	11.6	46.4
Netherlands	21.9	13.2	8.7	39.7
Austria	24.9	14.4	10.5	42.2
Portugal	23.6	18.3	5.3	22.5
Finland	26.7	11.5	15.2	56.9
Sweden	29.3	15.8	13.5	46.1
United Kingdom (2016)	28.1	15.9	12.2	43.4
Iceland (2016)	19.7	8.8	10.9	55.3
Norway (2016)	26.3	12.2	14.1	53.6
Switzerland (2016)	24.7	14.7	10	40.5

Note: The poverty rate is measured as the share of persons with an equivalised disposable income below 60% of the national median equivalised disposable income. Indicator is based on EU-SILC statistics.

Source: Eurostat.

measure negatively associated with support for redistribution), which they term the undermining paradox. Crucially the authors "confirm [that] transfer share is the paramount dimension for poverty" (Brady and Bostic, 2015: 292). The means-testing versus universalism debate is ongoing (Gugushvili & Hirsch, 2014); recent work using longitudinal data has provided further evidence that social transfers that are more concentrated at the bottom of the distribution are associated with lower reductions in poverty (McKnight, 2015).

The relationship between social spending and poverty reduction does not only vary according to the extent to which transfers are targeted or universal: further nuances are found across welfare state typologies (Maître, Nolan, & Whelan, 2012; Whelan, Nolan, & Maître, 2013).[5] As we have seen, welfare state effort, that is the amount of public social expenditure, is crucial to reducing poverty (Ferrarini & Nelson, 2003; Gottschalk & Smeeding, 1997; Kenworthy, 2011), which is why poverty rates tend to be lower in social democratic regimes that have higher social spending levels. Variation across typologies prompts us to recognise that it is not only transfer and tax systems that underpin variations in poverty levels, but also other institutional features. It has been found, for example, that minimum wage protection, unionisation and collective bargaining, state-funded or supported employment, investment in education, and so on, are all related to rates of poverty (Gornick & Smeeding, 2018).

Furthermore, this macro level perspective should not cause us to lose sight of *who* is most vulnerable to poverty within countries: generally, being younger, female, with a low level of education and a low level of work intensity, is associated with a higher probability of being poor (Caminada, Goudswaard, & Koster, 2010; Gornick & Smeeding, 2018; Kim, Lee, & Lee, 2010), and therefore are the groups and areas that need to be prioritised in policy formulation.

Turning to minimum income protection policies alone, these policies tend to take the form of means-tested social assistance, with social insurance and minimum wage legislation often providing a higher 'floor' above this minimum social safety net. Minimum income protection policies tell us about the most basic level of protection that citizens can rely on. It has been found that across European countries the social safety net falls (increasingly far) below the relative poverty line (Marchal, Marx, & Mechelen, 2014; Marchal, Marx, & Van Mechelen, 2016). In many cases minimum benefits are below 40% of median equivalised income (Cantillon, Mechelen, Pintelon, & Heede, 2013: 173). The decreasing adequacy of social assistance benefits holds not only for single persons, but also for households with children. Indeed, child benefit packages (unlike unemployment benefits) were not eroded dramatically during the 1990s, but since then have declined in the majority of countries (Van Mechelen & Bradshaw, 2013). Given the current prevalence of child poverty in affluent welfare states, restoring or protecting the incomes of children and their families should be a central policy priority. Recent work by Leventi, Sutherland and Tasseva (2018) confirmed that increasing the levels of child benefits and social assistance were the most cost effective options for reducing poverty in the European countries they studied.

Challenges for poverty levels in affluent welfare states

Looking to contemporary and future challenges for poverty in affluent welfare states, this final section highlights two main factors: the changing nature of the labour market and demographic shifts.

First, labour markets in the majority of affluent welfare states are undergoing shifts that threaten the adequacy of incomes and existing policies. The rise in non-standard employment, and underemployment is putting additional and new pressures on social protection schemes (Storrie, 2017). Furthermore, changes in the structure of the labour market have seen its 'hollowing out', resulting in jobs clustering toward the top and the bottom in terms of skills and wages. The rise of in-work poverty, and the accompanying introduction and expansion of in-work benefits schemes, is another ongoing development (Marx, 2018). Accompanying these shifts in labour market dynamics is what can be characterised as 'the activation turn' (Raffass, 2017). Working-age social security benefits are increasingly tied to, and contingent upon, participation or seeking participation in the labour market. The activation turn has in some countries been characterised by active labour market policies that focus on training, skills, and labour market insertion for disadvantaged groups, while in other country contexts the policy focus has not been on providing 'carrots' but, rather, on imposing 'sticks' through more stringent and minimal social security provision with the aim of impelling workforce participation.

Second, two main demographic shifts are relevant here: declining birth rates and ageing populations; and migration flows resulting from an increasingly interconnected and globalised world and a growing demand for migrant labour in ageing affluent societies. The age profile of affluent welfare states is putting pressure on an increasingly small working-age population to support an increasingly large retired population (OECD, 2008, 2011). So far affluent welfare states have been relatively successful in protecting the incomes of the retired, which in part stems from the high voter turnout and therefore representation of this group's interests in the policymaking process (Gardiner, 2016). One way of growing the working-age population is through encouraging migration into a society. However, increasing diversity within a population poses different challenges in terms of social cohesion and support for generous welfare benefits, and poverty rates are found to be particularly high among some immigrant populations (Taylor-Gooby, Leruth, & Chung, 2017).

Conclusion

This chapter has considered the development of poverty across affluent welfare states. Beginning with a description of key poverty trends, the widespread use of a relative poverty line is identified, and poverty rates across the last 12 years are presented for each country. Poverty rates for children and the over 65s are also presented. Refinements and alternatives to a relative poverty line are identified, including the use of anchored poverty lines, multidimensional measures, and measures of material deprivation. Next, the chapter considers the extent to which the countries included in this chapter have been successful in tackling poverty, and pre- and post-social transfer poverty rates are presented. Broadly speaking, high levels of social transfers, both in terms of total public social spending and the levels of transfers received by individual households, are crucial for effective poverty reduction. However, it is also crucial to remember that other institutional features are important for promoting or impeding lower poverty rates. The chapter ends by identifying dramatically changing labour markets, and demographic shifts, as key contemporary challenges to affluent welfare states' poverty reduction efforts. There is a danger of oversimplifying the experiences of all of the countries gathered together in this chapter with one concluding point: nevertheless, it is tentatively suggested that the re-emergence of extreme forms of poverty (such as food poverty and destitution), alongside evidence of the increasing inadequacy of the minimum income protection policies, and challenging labour market and demographic shifts, present a serious set of challenges for poverty in affluent welfare states that require urgent and ambitious action.

Notes

1 Further, there are some rich nations that this chapter does not focus on, including those on the North American and Asian continents, which are discussed in Chapters 15 and 18. The level of geographic definition here is the nation state, which leads us to not focus on autonomous regions such as Hong Kong (Lau, Pantazis, Gordon, Lai, & Sutton, 2015) or states with highly devolved and therefore great variation in welfare state development (see for example, Li & Piachaud (2004) on social policy development in China).

2 The Organisation for Economic Co-operation and Development (OECD), for example, uses a 50% of median income poverty line. The European Union uses 60% of median income to denote households 'at risk of poverty'.

3 Iceland stands out as a country that was hard-hit by the financial crisis, but then pursued a strategy of redistribution with the aim of protecting the most vulnerable, as opposed to an austerity agenda (Ólafsson, 2019).

4 The uprating of social security benefits below the rate of wage growth has been cited as an important factor driving this increase (OECD, 2017a).

5 The welfare states that developed across affluent countries throughout the 20th century and into the 21st have taken various forms, and various categorisations have been used to describe their diversity. Titmuss distinguished between three models of welfare state provision: a *residual* model where provision is highly selective and means tested; an *industrial achievement performance* model where benefits and services are tied to workforce participation and performance; and an *institutional redistributive* model where provision is universal and rights based (Titmuss, Titmuss, & Abel-Smith, 1974: 31). The welfare state typology developed by Esping-Andersen has been even more influential, whereby regimes are divided into *social democratic* (e.g. Sweden); *conservative corporatist* (e.g. Germany); and *liberal* (e.g. UK) (Esping-Andersen, 1989; see also Lewis (1992) for an influential gender-based critique).

References

Abel-Smith, B., & Townsend, P. (1975). *The Poor and the Poorest.* London: G. Bell & Sons.

Alkire, S., Foster, J., Seth, S., Santos, M. E., Roche, J. M., & Ballon, P. (2014). *Multidimensional Poverty Measurement and Analysis* (Chapter 1). Oxford: Oxford University Press.

Andriopoulou, E., Karakitsios, A., & Tsakloglou, P. (2018). Inequality and Poverty in Greece: Changes in Times of Crisis. In D. Katsikas, D. A. Sotiropoulos, & M. Zafiropoulou (Eds.), *Socioeconomic Fragmentation and Exclusion in Greece under the Crisis* (pp. 23–54). Cham: Springer International Publishing.

Barr, N. (2001). *The Welfare State as Piggy Bank : Information, Risk, Uncertainty, and the Role of the State.* Oxford: Oxford University Press.

Besley, T. (1990). Means Testing versus Universal Provision in Poverty Alleviation Programmes. *Economica, 57*(225), 119–129.

Bjorklund, A., & Freeman, R. B. (1997). Generating Equality and Eliminating Poverty: The Swedish Way. In R. B. Freeman, R. Topel, & B. Swedenborg (Eds.), *The Welfare State in Transition: Reforming the Swedish Model* (pp. 33–78). Chicago, IL: University of Chicago Press.

Booth, C. (1903). *Life and Labour of the People of London* (Vol. *5*). Macmillan and Co.

Bradbury, B., Jäntti, M., & Lindhal, L. (2018). Labour Income, Social Transfers and Child Poverty. *Social Indicators Research, Online First.*

Brady, D., & Bostic, A. (2015). Paradoxes of Social Policy: Welfare Transfers, Relative Poverty, and Redistribution Preferences. *American Sociological Review, 80*(2), 268–298.

Caminada, K., Goudswaard, K., & Koster, F. (2010). *Social Income Transfers and Poverty Alleviation in OECD Countries* (SSRN Scholarly Paper No. ID 1553826). Rochester, NY: Social Science Research Network. Retrieved 22 November 2018 from https://papers.ssrn.com/abstract=1553826

Cantillon, B., Mechelen, N. V., Pintelon, O., & Heede, A. V. den. (2013). *Social Redistribution, Poverty, and the Adequacy of Social Protection.* Oxford: Oxford University Press.

Chzhen, Y., Nolan, B., Cantillon, B., & Sudhanshu, H. (2017). Impact of the Economic Crisis on Children in Rich Countries. In B. Cantillon, Y. Chzhen, H. Sudhanshu, & B. Nolan (Eds.), *Children of Austerity: Impact of the Great Recession on Child Poverty in Rich Countries* (pp. 8–29). Oxford: Oxford University Press.

Department for Work and Pensions. (2018). *Households below average income: An analysis of the UK income distribution: 1994/95–2016/17* (p. 14).

Dowler, E., & Lambie-Mumford, H. (2015). Introduction: Hunger, Food and Social Policy in Austerity. *Social Policy and Society, 14*(03), 411–415.

Esping-Andersen, G. (1989). *The Three Worlds of Welfare Capitalism* (1st Edition). Cambridge, UK: Polity Press.

European Commission, & Eurostat. (2012). *Measuring material deprivation in the EU: indicators for the whole population and child-specific indicators.* Luxembourg: Publications Office. Retrieved 30 November 2018 from http://dx.publications.europa.eu/10.2785/33598

Ferrarini, T., & Nelson, K. (2003). Taxation of Social Insurance and Redistribution: A Comparative Analysis of Ten Welfare States. *Journal of European Social Policy, 13*(1), 21–33.

Fisher, J., Johnson, D. S., & Smeeding, T. (2012). Inequality of Income and Consumption: Measuring the Trends in Inequality from 1985–2010 for the Same Individuals. Presented at the Association for Public Policy Analysis and Management 2012 Fall Research Conference.

Fitzpatrick, S., Bramley, G., Sosenko, F., Blenkinsopp, J., Johnsen, S., Littlewood, M., … Watts, B. (2016). *Destitution in the UK.* Joseph Rowntree Foundation.

Gardiner, L. (2016). *Votey McVoteface* (Intergenerational Commission). Resolution Foundation. Retrieved 30 November 2018 from www.resolutionfoundation.org/app/uploads/2016/09/Generational-voting.pdf

Gornick, J. C., & Jäntti, M. (2012). Child Poverty in Cross-national Perspective: Lessons from the Luxembourg Income Study. *Children and Youth Services Review, 34*(3), 558–568.

Gornick, J. C., & Smeeding, T. M. (2018). Redistributional Policy in Rich Countries: Institutions and Impacts in Nonelderly Households. *Annual Review of Sociology, 44*(1), 441–468.

Gottschalk, P., & Smeeding, T. M. (1997). Cross-National Comparisons of Earnings and Income Inequality. *Journal of Economic Literature, 35*(2), 55.

Gugushvili, D., & Hirsch, D. (2014). *Means-Testing or Universalism: What Strategies Best Address Poverty?* Centre for Research in Social Policy.

Hills, J. (2015). *Good Times, Bad Times: The Welfare Myth of Them and Us.* Bristol: Policy Press.

Kenworthy, L. (2011). *Progress for the Poor.* Oxford: Oxford University Press.

Kim, K., Lee, Y., & Lee, Y. (2010). A Multilevel Analysis of Factors Related to Poverty in Welfare States. *Social Indicators Research: An International and Interdisciplinary Journal for Quality-of-Life Measurement, 99*(3), 391–404.

Korpi, W., & Palme, J. (1998). The Paradox of Redistribution and Strategies of Equality: Welfare State Institutions, Inequality, and Poverty in the Western Countries. *American Sociological Review, 63*(5), 661–687.

Lansley, S., & Mack, J. (2015). *Breadline Britain: The Rise of Mass Poverty*. London: Bloomsbury.
Lau, M., Pantazis, C., Gordon, D., Lai, L., & Sutton, E. (2015). Poverty in Hong Kong. *China Review; Hong Kong, 15*(2), 23–58.
Le Grand, J. (1982). *The Strategy of Equality: Redistribution and the Social Services*. London: G. Allen & Unwin.
Leventi, C., Sutherland, H., & Tasseva, I. V. (2018). Improving Poverty Reduction in Europe: What Works Best Where? *Journal of European Social Policy, 29*(1), 29–43.
Lewis, J. (1992). Gender and the Development of Welfare Regimes. *Journal of European Social Policy, 2*(3), 159–173.
Li, B., & Piachaud, D. (2004). *Poverty and Inequality and Social Policy in China*. Paper No. 087, Centre for Analysis of Social Exclusion.
Lister, R. (2017). *Poverty*. Cambridge: Polity Press.
Maître, B., Nolan, B., & Whelan, C. T. (2012). Low Pay, In-work Poverty and Economic Vulnerability: A Comparative Analysis Using EU-SILC. *The Manchester School, 80*(1), 99–116.
Marchal, S., Marx, I., & Van Mechelen, N. (2014). The Great Wake-Up Call? Social Citizenship and Minimum Income Provisions in Europe in Times of Crisis. *Journal of Social Policy, 43*(2), 247–267.
Marchal, S., Marx, I., & Van Mechelen, N. (2016). Minimum Income Protection in the Austerity Tide. *IZA Journal of European Labor Studies, 5*(1), 4.
Marx, I. (2018). Handbook on In-Work Poverty. Cheltenham: Edward Elgar.
Marx, I., & Nelson, K. (2013). *Minimum Income Protection in Flux*. Basingstoke: Palgrave Macmillan.
Marx, I., Nolan, B., & Olivera, J. (2015). The Welfare State and Antipoverty Policy in Rich Countries. In A. B. Atkinson & F. Bourguignon (Eds.), *Handbook of Income Distribution* (Vol. 2, pp. 2063–2139). Oxford and Amsterdam: Elsevier.
McKnight, A. (2015). *A fresh look at an old question: is pro-poor targeting of cash transfers more effective than universal systems at reducing inequality and poverty?* ImPRovE Working Paper No. 15/14, p. 31.
Morelli, S., Smeeding, T., & Thompson, J. (2015). Post-1970 Trends in Within-Country Inequality and Poverty. In A. B. Atkinson & F. Bourguignon (Eds.), *Handbook of Income Distribution* (Vol. 2, pp. 593–696). Oxford and Amsterdam: Elsevier.
Nelson, K. (2004). Mechanisms of poverty alleviation. *Journal of European Social Policy, 14*, 371–390.
New Zealand Ministry of Social Development. (2016). The Social Report *2016*, 332.
Nolan, B., & Whelan, C. T. (2011). *Poverty and Deprivation in Europe*. Oxford and New York: Oxford University Press.
OECD. (2008). Ageing OECD Societies. Retrieved 2 November 2018 from www.oecd.org/berlin/41250023.pdf
OECD. (2011). Sizing Up the Challenge Ahead: Future Demographic Trends and Long-term Care Costs. Retrieved 2 November 2018 from www.oecd.org/els/health-systems/47884543.pdf
OECD. (2017a). *OECD Economic Surveys: Sweden 2017* (Text). Retrieved 2 November 2018 from www.oecd-ilibrary.org/economics/oecd-economic-surveys-sweden-2017_eco_surveys-swe-2017-en
OECD. (2017b). *Pensions at a Glance 2017*. Retrieved 2 November 2018 from https://read.oecd-ilibrary.org/social-issues-migration-health/pensions-at-a-glance-2017_pension_glance-2017-en
Ólafsson, S. (2019). Iceland's Strategy of Redistribution. In S. Ólafsson, M. Daly, O. Kangas, & J. Palme (Eds.), *Welfare and the Great Recession: A Comparative Study* (pp. 132–153). Oxford: Oxford University Press.
Ólafsson, S., Daly, M., Kangas, O., & Palme, J. (2019). *Welfare and the Great Recession: A Comparative Study* (First edition). Oxford: Oxford University Press.
Padley, M., & Hirsch, D. (2017). *A Minimum Income Standard for the UK in 2017*. York: Joseph Rowntree Foundation.
Raffass, T. (2017). Demanding Activation. *Journal of Social Policy, 46*(02), 349–365.
Riches, G., & Silvasti, T. (2014). *First World Hunger Revisited: Food Charity or the Right to Food?* Basingstoke: Palgrave Macmillan.
Rowntree, B. S. (1901). *Poverty: A Study of Town Life*. London: Macmillan and Co.
Savage, M. (2014). Piketty's Challenge for Sociology. *British Journal of Sociology, 65*(4), 591–606.
Sen, A. (1983). Poor, Relatively Speaking. *Oxford Economic Papers, 35*(2), 153–169.
Sen, A. (1992). *Inequality Reexamined*. Oxford: Clarendon.
Stewart, K., & Roberts, N. (2018). Child Poverty Measurement in the UK: Assessing Support for the Downgrading of Income-Based Poverty Measures. *Social Indicators Research, 142*(2), 523–542.
Storrie, D. (2017). *Non-standard forms of employment: Recent trends and future prospects* (p. 42). Eurofound. Retrieved 2 November 2018 from www.eurofound.europa.eu/sites/default/files/ef_publication/field_ef_document/ef1746en.pdf

Stroud, P. (2018). *A new measure of poverty for the UK* (p. 147). Social Metrics Commission. Retrieved 22 November 2018 from https://socialmetricscommission.org.uk/MEASURING-POVERTY-FULL_REPORT.pdf

Taylor-Gooby, P., Leruth, B., & Chung, H. (2017). *After Austerity: Welfare State Transformation in Europe after the Great Recession*. Oxford: Oxford University Press.

Thévenon, O., Manfredi, T., Govind, Y., & Klauzner, I. (2018). *Child Poverty in the OECD: Trends, Determinants and Policies to Tackle it*. OECD Social, Employment and Migration Working Papers 218, OECD Publishing.

Titmuss, R. M., Titmuss, K., & Abel-Smith, B. (1974). *Social Policy : An Introduction* (2nd edition, rev. and expanded). London: Allen & Unwin.

Townsend, P. (1979). *Poverty in the United Kingdom: A Survey of Household Resources and Standards of Living*. London: Penguin Books.

Van Mechelen, N., & Bradshaw, J. (2013). Child Poverty as a Government Priority: Child Benefit Packages for Working Families, 1992–2009. In I. Marx & K. Nelson (Eds.), *Minimum Income Protection in Flux* (pp. 81–107). Basingstoke: Palgrave Macmillan.

Whelan, C. T., Nolan, B., & Maître, B. (2013). Analysing Intergenerational Influences on Income Poverty and Economic Vulnerability with EU-SILC. *European Societies*, *15*(1), 82–105.

Wilkins, R. (2018). *Poverty Lines: Australia* (p. 5). Melbourne Institute.

Zaidi, A., & Burchardt, T. (2005). Comparing Incomes When Needs Differ: Equivalization for the Extra Costs of Disability in the U.K. *Review of Income & Wealth*, *51*(1), 89–114.

13

Poverty in developing countries, 1990–2016

Some regional, temporal, and income level variations

Udaya R. Wagle

Introduction

Poverty measurement is a central exercise in thinking about the best ways poverty can be understood (see also Chapters 2 and 3) and tackled in both developed and developing countries. Whereas poverty has historically been measured using such monetary resources as income or consumption, comparing poverty measurements across countries has posed a major challenge for international development partners and policy practitioners. Questioning the core idea that poverty is always about monetary resources, recent developments in poverty measurement have operationalized multidimensional frameworks, which allow comparing measurement outcomes and progress in reducing poverty across countries as well as over time.

This chapter provides a snapshot of poverty across developing countries following the traditional monetary as well as the multidimensional frameworks of measurement. With the argument that poverty results from an inability to participate and harness resources available in the economy and society, the purpose is to link poverty with the way governments have made progress in bringing people to the economic and social processes. By tracking cross-national data since 1990, this chapter offers a comparative analysis of poverty across countries in some distinct ways: over time, by region, and by income groups. At some fundamental level, multiple frameworks of measurement must address the question of consistencies or differences in poverty outcomes. This comparative analysis, therefore, provides a more accurate picture of the degree and structure of poverty in developing countries, helping to assess the progress in poverty reduction at this point and rethink appropriate policy options moving forward. The role of government and especially social protection policies in helping the poor are also explored as a way to contextualize the picture of poverty in developing countries.

Various concepts and lines of poverty

Poverty has historically been measured with an exclusive focus on income or the ability to maintain a living standard considered acceptable in a given society. While the actual living standard can vary for a variety of reasons including geography and unique needs, the focus has primarily been on the *ability* to generate an income that is necessary for an objectively developed living standard or, more directly, to maintain the consumption of goods and services needed for such a standard. Since the idea of an acceptable living standard varies by time and context, specific poverty lines are developed and/or modified to accommodate those differences.

Conceptually, poverty can be absolute, relative, or even subjective depending on the role of the overall society or the concept of what it means to be poor. But the typical way of determining monetary poverty has been by focusing on the cost of basic needs, which mostly follows the absolute concept. Poverty measurement under this income or consumption-based monetary approach involves developing food poverty lines from the expenditures attached to an "economy food plan" or a "basket of goods" which yields the required nutritional intake using given price levels and adding nonfood allowances based on expenditures of families falling around the food poverty lines (Orshansky 1965; Ravallion 1998; Wagle 2008; World Bank Institute 2005). The first part of this process is seemingly technical whereas the latter draws from empirical observations and thus can be less objective.

Policy choice may enter in developing the economy food plan that ensures the requisite nutritional intake in one of several ways. Including meat, fish, poultry, or other high-quality products, for example, can elevate the expenditures needed to develop the food poverty line compared to other lower quality options. It is also a standard practice that food poverty lines are revised above and beyond incorporating changing consumer price indices so that the resulting estimates properly align with the customary food consumption patterns for a given time or context. Additionally, the allowances set aside for nonfood expenditures can involve even a greater degree of policy choice. Since variations are possible in determining the nonfood expenditures, whether they are determined directly from surveys empirically or by expressing as a percentage (or multiplier) of the food expenditures, even minor adjustments to them can lead to very different pictures of poverty. The case of the United States is illustrative. The official poverty lines developed from the expenditure patterns of the 1960s do not exactly hold today as the expenditures in housing, transportation, insurance, childcare, and even communication have drastically altered the fact of life over time (Citro and Michael 1995; Dalaker 2005; Haveman 1987).

Despite these reservations, these income or consumption based, monetary poverty lines have been used extensively throughout recent history. Also, what comes out of this exercise is essentially a geographically focused monetary poverty line typically at the national level for a given time but sometimes at the local or regional levels which are then aggregated for national purposes. Using extensive survey data and technical assistance from the World Bank (1996), developing countries started creating and using national poverty lines and adjusted them depending on the changes in cost of living and expenditure patterns.

While these country- and time-specific national poverty lines are not fully comparable across countries, the World Bank has also spearheaded the drive to develop and revise what are called international poverty lines. For the purpose of international comparison and monitoring, the international poverty line originally developed by the World Bank (Ravallion, Dutt, and van de Walle 1991) involved aggregating the international purchasing power parity (PPP) values of the national poverty lines across 15 of the poorest countries in 1985 United States dollars. This international poverty line set at one-dollar-a-day of income (or consumption) for 1985 prices has been adjusted multiple times, leading to $1.90 at 2011 prices (Cruz, Foster, Quillin, & Schellekens 2015; Ferreira et al. 2015). Since the per capita income has drastically improved in much of the developing world during the past 30 years, which has significantly reduced the purchasing power of incomes well beyond inflation, the traditional

$1.90 poverty line is now termed "extreme poverty." The World Bank has, therefore, used adjusted poverty lines set at $3.20 and $5.50 to monitor progress in poverty reduction across the different categories of developing countries.

No doubt, these international monetary poverty lines are seemingly arbitrary as the specific parameters—such as food energy requirements, food bundles, and nonfood allowances—used in developing them are rather arbitrary and can vary drastically by lifestyles and other circumstances across countries. Whereas multiple adjustments are made to capture the realities of countries with higher living standards, questions such as how they relate to the specific contexts and what kind of deprivation the poor are experiencing are debatable. Even the governments attempting to monitor progress in poverty reduction find these poverty lines not very useful. Moreover, the idea that the national poverty lines used in developing the international ones are expected to reflect the prevailing realities of living standard and poverty (Ravallion, Chen, & Sangraula 2009) is difficult to hold since the measurement exclusively focuses on income-based metrics, without any role of the person's unique circumstances or needs. With the notion that individual well-being depends on a host of personal and institutional factors, at the center of which is what's called "capability to function," the multidimensional poverty framework operationalized by the United Nations Development Program (1990) focuses on indices across three separate dimensions assessed separately.

In essence, this framework operationalizes the idea that development is about expanding people's freedom and opportunities and that people's capabilities and well-being must be at the center of the development agenda when it comes to measuring, tracking, and comparing progress in individual well-being (Sen 1987, 1999; UNDP 1990; Wagle 2008). Operationally, the counting-based multidimensional framework currently espoused by the UNDP (2016) assesses the well-being across education, health, and living standard, with each measured by using one or more indicators (Alkire and Foster 2011). Whereas the specific indicators can vary depending on data availability, years of schooling and school attendance are used as the indicators of education; nutrition and child mortality are used as the indicators of health; and six different indicators spanning cooking fuel, sanitation, drinking water, electricity, housing, and assets are used as the indicators of living standard. While questions arise regarding the relevance of these dimensions and indicators as well as their relative weights used in computation (Ravallion 2011; Wagle 2014), suffering deprivation in at least a third of the weighted indicators is used as the benchmark for multidimensional poverty, with deprivation in at least one-half of the weighted indicators used as the benchmark for severe multidimensional poverty (UNDP 2016).

Poverty measures: the overall picture

This section paints the overall picture of poverty following the three measurement frameworks outlined above. The measurement outcomes are presented by the international poverty lines following the World Bank approach, with those from the national poverty lines and multidimensional approaches drawing an alternative but important comparison. Covering all of the years and countries included in this analysis (using the World Bank classification of developing countries) to the extent that data are available from the World Bank World Development Indicators and the UNDP's Human Development databases, this overall picture focuses on how the different measures compare with each other in capturing poverty experiences.

Summarizing data from 667 developing country-years (see Appendix for the list of developing countries covered in this analysis by region) between 1990 to 2016, Table 13.1 reports that the average poverty headcount ratios measured at the international monetary poverty line of $1.90 were at 13 percent, with a low of zero and a high of 84 percent. This compares with the

Table 13.1 Poverty headcount ratios and gaps at various poverty lines (1990–2016)

Variable	*Obs.*	*Mean*	*Std. Dev.*	*Min.*	*Max.*
International poverty headcount ratios					
Poverty line US$1,90	667	12.99	18.37	0.00	84.10
Poverty line US$3.20	667	26.49	26.12	0.00	95.30
Poverty line $US5.50	667	45.86	29.23	0.40	98.90
International poverty gap					
Poverty line $US3.20	667	10.85	13.56	0.00	63.80
Poverty line $US5.50	667	21.63	19.22	0.00	77.70
Alternative poverty headcount ratios					
National poverty lines	512	28.74	16.79	0.60	83.30
Multidimensional poverty line[a]	179	34.55	29.55	0.30	93.40
Severe multidimensional poverty line[b]	179	18.77	20.83	0.00	86.10

Notes: a. Suffering deprivation in at least 33% of the weighted indicators; b. Suffering deprivation in at least 50% of the weighted indicators.

Data source: Author's calculations using data from the World Bank World Development Indicators.

averages of over 26 percent for the similar poverty line at $3.20 and close to 26 percent for the poverty line at $5.50. While Table 13.1 does not report these data by years, poverty headcount ratios run close to 100 percent when $3.20 and especially $5.50 of per capita income are used as the applicable poverty lines. It is not surprising that almost no poverty is reported for some of these countries even at the most stringent level of $5.50 per capita income since this analysis includes all developing countries. But the magnitude of poverty ranges very widely across these countries and perhaps over time as indicated by the relatively sizable standard deviations.

The data on poverty gap, or the degree of poverty experienced by the poor, are also interesting. While the poor on average experience a shortfall of income at close to 11 percent of the $3.20 poverty line income and at close to 22 percent for the $5.50 poverty line income, the average degrees of poverty do not vary very drastically across the two very different poverty lines. As expected, the range is quite large as indicated by the applicable standard deviations, with the $3.20 poverty line exhibiting an even wider range.

The alternative poverty headcount ratios provide an additional insight into the way poverty is experienced in the developing world. For one, the coverage of these data is different especially on multidimensional poverty drawn from the UNDP with only 179 country-years included and even that since 2005. But the aggregate picture provided by these data is not very different. At close to 35 and 19 percent, respectively, the average multidimensional and severe multidimensional poverty headcount ratios are right in between the most ($5.50) and least ($1.90) stringent measures of international, monetary poverty whereas those from the national poverty lines are slightly higher than the ones from the moderately stringent ($3.20) international, monetary poverty lines. Whereas the national poverty lines capture unique features of the specific countries and times since they are adjusted using survey data, poverty estimates using these cutoffs closely align with those from the international poverty lines at $3.20 of per capita income. Just as many countries with very low incomes are advancing to greater per capita income, thanks to their impressive record on economic growth, the $3.20 international poverty line comes on average very close to the incomes at the national poverty lines.

Albeit derived from very different processes, the magnitude of multidimensional poverty suggests that slightly over one-third of the population, on average, experiences deprivation in at least one-third of the weighted indicators, with close to 19 percent experiencing severe deprivation, signified by deprivations across 50 percent of the weighted indicators. Since the developing world includes a range of countries, the relatively sizable standard deviation is justifiable in each case, as also are the minimum headcount ratios ranging from zero to almost 100 percent. But these average poverty headcount ratios are measured very differently from those based on the national and international monetary poverty lines.

Poverty measures: some decompositions

Further insights into the structure of these aggregate poverty measurement outcomes necessitate some decomposition analysis. Table 13.2 reports basic decomposition analysis of the international poverty headcount ratios and gaps across six regions, three decades, and three income groups. It is clear from the regional analysis that Eastern Europe has the lowest poverty headcount ratios as well as gaps on average, followed by Latin America and the Caribbean and the Middle East, North Africa, and Central Asia. Interesting is the fact that whereas these latter two groups of countries have very similar poverty headcount ratios at around eight percent, the average headcount ratios for the Middle East, North Africa, and Central Asia are almost 50 percent higher than those for Latin America and the Caribbean. This and similar observation on the average poverty gap suggest that many people in the Middle East, North Africa, and Central Asia have incomes that are higher but not too distant from the $1.90 per day used for the least stringent income poverty measure.

Sub-Saharan Africa has the highest poverty headcount ratio, with South Asia a distant second, followed by East Asia and the Pacific. But the differences in poverty measures between East Asia and the Pacific and South Asia are very similar to the ones between Latin America and the Caribbean and the Middle East, North Africa, and Central Asia, with most of the incomes in South Asia hovering around the least stringent international income poverty lines. Somewhat different is the case of sub-Saharan Africa, where there are more stringent poverty headcount ratios, and the poverty gap is much greater and the most stringent poverty headcount ratios

Table 13.2 Decomposition of international poverty headcount ratios and gaps (1990–2016)

Country breakdown	*Obs.*	*Poverty headcount ratios*			*Poverty gap*	
		PL $1.90	*PL $3.20*	*PL $5.50*	*PL $3.20*	*PL $5.50*
Regions						
Sub-Saharan Africa	96	43.14	65.19	82.00	32.87	50.45
East Asia and the Pacific	83	15.46	36.85	60.37	13.22	28.51
Eastern Europe	200	3.42	10.71	27.93	3.38	9.95
Latin America and the Caribbean	196	8.16	17.40	34.48	7.14	15.05
Middle East, North Africa, and Central Asia	74	8.53	25.14	52.87	8.11	21.39
South Asia	18	18.12	52.04	80.51	17.01	38.70
Decades						
1990s	110	18.58	34.67	55.61	15.18	28.00
2000s	300	13.31	27.78	48.26	11.14	22.60
2010s	257	10.23	21.48	38.89	8.65	17.78
Income groups						
Low income countries	63	51.40	75.21	90.30	38.63	57.72
Low middle-income countries	275	14.01	32.21	56.39	12.21	26.02
High middle-income countries	329	4.78	12.37	28.55	4.39	11.06

Data source: Author's calculations using data from the World Bank World Development Indicators.

are almost identical to those of South Asia. It is important to note, however, that this regional decomposition analysis does not account for the differences in population. Since results are not weighted by population across countries, the fact that China and India's massive populations drive the estimates for East Asia and the Pacific as well as South Asia, respectively, does not apply here.

It is just logical to expect poverty headcount ratios and gaps to decline over time as economic growth helps not just the well-off but poor people as well. This holds true across the board, with the international poverty headcount ratios declining by eight percent at $1.90, 13 percent at $3.20, and 17 percent at $5.50. Similar changes occurred on the poverty gap statistics as well. But while the almost linear decrease in poverty is impressive, even more impressive are the relatively low and declining magnitudes of poverty gap, suggesting that the average shortfall in income during the 2010s was less than nine percent of the $3.20 of daily income and 18 percent of the $5.50 of daily income. The actual representation of countries from sub-Saharan Africa and South Asia pose a caveat, however, since the relative lack of data on them may have helped subdue the degree of poverty on average.

The decomposition by income groups is even more self-explanatory. The headcount ratios and gaps for low-income countries are, on average, over three times greater than those for high middle-income countries. But whereas the higher expected incomes dwarf the poverty headcount ratios in the latter group, the declining rates of difference for more stringent poverty suggests that the reach of the income differential is greater at the less stringent poverty lines. After all, higher average incomes lift the incomes for all, including those at the bottom (Wagle 2012).

Similar decomposition analysis is presented in Table 13.3, focusing on the alternative poverty headcount ratios. Averaged at close to 29 percent, the national poverty headcount ratios have a range of close to 20 percent in East Asia and the Pacific to over 46 percent in sub-Saharan Africa. This relatively compact range emanates from the fact that the income poverty lines in

Table 13.3 Decomposition of alternative poverty headcount ratios (1990–2016)

	Income poverty		*Multidimensional poverty*		
	Obs.	*National poverty lines*	*Obs.*	*MP line*	*Severe MP line*
Regions					
Sub-Saharan Africa	83	46.36	77	59.77	35.58
East Asia and the Pacific	71	19.69	18	22.63	9.47
Eastern Europe	163	21.18	17	1.57	0.15
Latin America and the Caribbean	127	33.09	31	14.00	4.86
Middle East, North Africa, and Central Asia	49	24.79	24	8.33	2.44
South Asia	19	31.49	12	42.87	19.87
Decades					
1990s	8	34.44	NA	NA	NA
2000s	232	31.48	81	34.32	19.45
2010s	272	26.23	98	34.75	18.21
Income groups					
Low-income countries	56	47.74	57	66.41	41.28
Low middle-income countries	222	32.60	70	29.18	13.23
High middle-income countries	234	20.48	52	6.86	1.57

Data source: Author's calculations using data from the World Bank World Development Indicators and UNDP 2018 Global Multidimensional Poverty Index.

use already account for the unique circumstances of income and needs so the incorporation of the relative concept mitigates extreme levels of poverty (at both higher and lower ends). But this decomposition is markedly different from that of its closest form of international poverty at $3.20 as East Asia and the Pacific have significantly lower poverty headcount ratios than do Eastern Europe, Latin America and the Caribbean, and the Middle East, North America, and Central Asia. A similar observation holds for the breakdown by income levels as the poverty headcount ratios for low-income countries at two-and-half times those of high middle-income countries is nowhere close to over six times in case of international poverty headcount ratios at $3.20. Additionally, while the poverty headcount ratios are declining over time, the declines do not appear to be as impressive as in the case of international poverty lines.

The decomposition analysis of multidimensional poverty headcount ratios has a specific context in which 39 of the 141 countries included here do not have these data. The more limited coverage, in that these data do not extend prior to 2005, also leads to perhaps even more unbalanced decomposition analysis when compared with the monetary poverty data. With these caveats in mind, the decomposition analysis of multidimensional poverty headcount ratios allows interesting observations. On one hand are the very low headcount ratios for Eastern Europe, effectively ruling out the existence of multidimensional poverty, followed by the Middle East, North Africa, and Central Asia and, somewhat distantly, Latin America and the Caribbean. On the other are South Asia and especially sub-Saharan Africa, the latter of which has a multidimensional poverty headcount ratio at close to 60 percent and the severe variant of it has close to 36 percent. These statistics provide stark differences in the rates of multidimensional poverty across regions, which are much broader than in the case of international and national poverty headcount ratios. It is particularly in sub-Saharan Africa, South Asia, and, to some extent, East Asia that the high levels of deprivation remain across multiple indicators of multidimensional poverty.

Data do not show any relevance of temporal decomposition as the poverty headcount ratios do not vary between the 2000s and 2010s. While the data do not include the years prior to 2005 and the combination of countries covered in each of the two periods may have been different, the fact that no discernible temporal differences exist in headcount ratios suggests that improvements in income or poverty measures observed earlier may not fully transfer into the well-being across different poverty dimensions.

The differences are markedly visible in case of the breakdown by income groups, however. The average multidimensional poverty headcount ratios, for example, are below seven percent across high middle-income countries, compared to 29 percent across low middle-income countries and 66 percent across low-income countries, with similar differences in the severe multidimensional headcount ratios as well. While there may be other explanations for these aggregate measures, this decomposition provides a more direct observation of the way income may interact with multidimensional poverty, suggesting that higher incomes may help improve individual well-being across many multidimensional poverty dimensions.

Similarities and differences in measurement

How similar or different are the different poverty measurement outcomes? Given the completely independent processes by which the monetary and multidimensional poverty are measured, it is important to ascertain how their measurement outcomes compare. Even in case of monetary poverty, measurement outcomes from the universally applied international poverty lines are expected to be different from those that account for unique national (or even regional) circumstances operationalized in national poverty lines. While the previous section has addressed

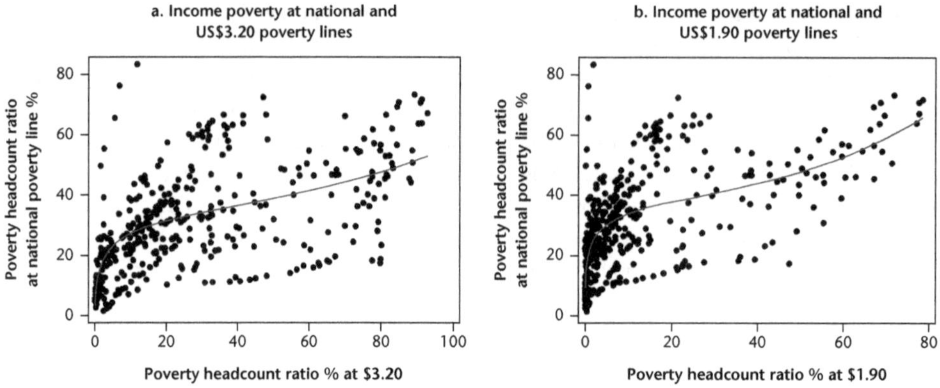

Figure 13.1 Income poverty headcount ratios at national and international poverty lines (1990–2016).

Data source: Author's calculation using data from the World Bank World Development Indicators.

this issue by using the aggregate poverty measurement outcomes, this section takes it one step further by examining the similarities and differences at the unit level of country-year directly.

Figure 13.1 presents two-way graphs of the poverty headcount ratios between national poverty lines and international poverty lines at both $3.20 and $1.90 for all developing countries and years. The two profiles are somewhat different, with many of the international poverty headcount ratios at $1.90 concentrated at the lower end, compared with those at $3.20. But the way these two sets of poverty headcount ratios interface with those from national poverty lines is very similar. As indicated by the fit lines overlaid on the scatterplots, the relationship is positive and nonlinear: Whereas countries with even a slight difference in international poverty headcount ratios can witness very different levels of national poverty headcount ratios at the lower end, countries at the moderate levels of national poverty headcount ratios can be all over with regard to international poverty headcount ratios. As with any data, however, some notable outliers exist, where national poverty headcount ratios are quite high despite having very low international poverty headcount ratios.

Figure 13.2 presents similar profiles interfacing poverty headcount ratios between multidimensional poverty and international monetary poverty. Noteworthy here is the effective number of observations, as the timing of the measurement of monetary poverty does not coincide with that of the multidimensional poverty, which already has a limited coverage to begin with. But the profiles are very instructive in that the relationships are positive and nonlinear. More specifically, while the profile of multidimensional poverty headcount ratios and international poverty headcount ratios at $3.20 fits the quadratic function, the one involving severe multidimensional poverty headcount ratios and international poverty headcount ratios at $1.90 fits the cubic function. The latter in particular is interesting as the severe multidimensional poverty headcount ratios may even be lower for countries experiencing higher poverty headcount ratios beyond somewhere close to 60 percent.

These two figures, in sum, paint a picture in which all three sets of poverty headcount ratios move in the same direction. They also suggest that the relationships may be rather nonlinear in which the rate of increase in one form of poverty varies across increasing units of another. While dissection of this nonlinear relationship is beyond the scope of this chapter, Table 13.4 helps quantify the relationships with the assumption of linearity. The correlations involving

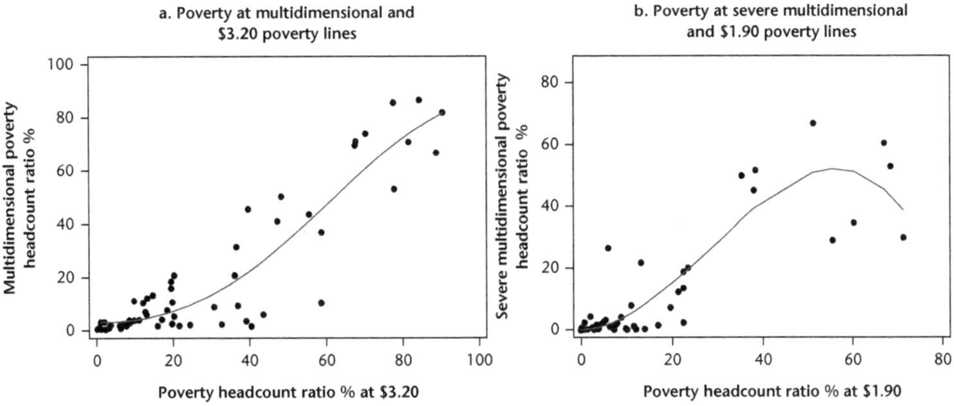

Figure 13.2 Poverty headcount ratios at multidimensional and international poverty lines (1990–2016).

Data source: Author's presentation using data from the World Bank World Development Indicators and UNDP 2018 Global Multidimensional Poverty Index.

Table 13.4 Correlation of poverty headcount ratios across various poverty lines

Variables	*Obs.*	*PHR US$1.90*	*PHR US$3.20*	*PHR US$5.50*	*PHR, NPL*
National poverty lines	453	0.60	0.59	0.59	1.00
Multidimensional poverty line	59/60	0.90	0.89	0.77	0.65
Severe multidimensional poverty line	59/60	0.86	0.85	0.72	0.57

national poverty headcount ratios hover consistently around 0.60, suggesting that they help predict international and multidimensional poverty headcount ratios in about 60 percent of the cases. This moderately high correlation is not surprising given that each dyad of the poverty headcount ratios either concentrates on monetary poverty or focuses on the specific national or regional contexts of countries and years. More surprising, however, is the relatively high correlation (>0.72) between multidimensional poverty and international monetary poverty, since each dyad includes two different forms of poverty. While the correlation of multidimensional poverty headcount ratios runs the highest (>0.89), when it comes to those from international poverty lines at $1.90 and $3.20, the observation that multidimensional and international concepts of poverty have this much in common is very insightful.

A link with social protection policies

With the above concepts of poverty and similarities and differences across the various poverty measurement outcomes, what actually explains why countries and years have different poverty outcomes? Some of the discussion has focused on regionality, temporal variations, and income levels as a way to understand how poverty outcomes have varied. But even such factors as economic growth and income alone may not fully explain the differences. While the international poverty headcount ratios and even multidimensional poverty headcount ratios were lower for low middle-income and especially high middle-income countries, their national poverty headcount ratios did not share this observation. This section offers deeper insights into the way poverty varies across countries and over time by interfacing poverty headcount ratios with

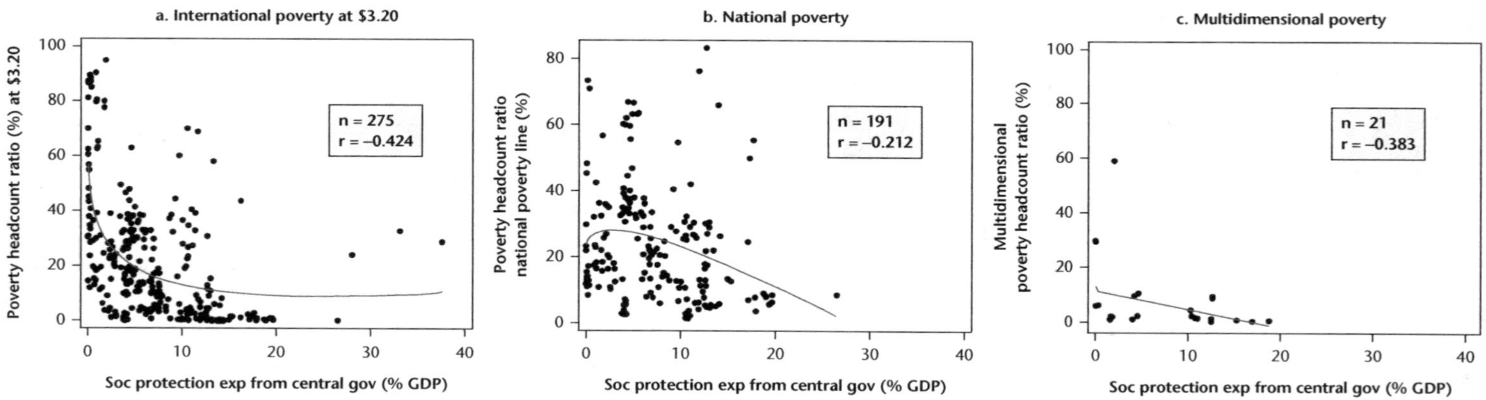

Figure 13.3 Poverty headcount ratios and social protection policies (1990–2016).

Data source: Author's presentation using data from the World Bank World Development Indicators and UNDP 2018 Global Multidimensional Poverty Index.

social protection policies. With the understanding that social protection policies help the poor, low income, and other socioeconomically disadvantaged groups more effectively benefit from opportunities provided by the increasingly competitive global market, policymakers and international development partners have largely embraced the push toward various social protection and active labor market policies (ILO 2014; OECD 2009; United Nations 2015; UNRISD 2010; World Bank 2012, 2014). The post-2015 Sustainable Development Goals of the United Nations (2015), for example, place social protection systems and policies at the core of the strategies devised to fight poverty and inequality worldwide.

Figure 13.3 presents profiles of the interaction of international (at $3.20), national, and multidimensional poverty headcount ratios with public social protection expenditures relative to GDP (drawn from the International Monetary Fund's Government Finance Statistics database) at the level of country-year. While issues remain about the consistency of measurement both over time and across countries, the data on public social protections capture the expenditures of central governments on various social insurance programs including social security, health insurance, and unemployment insurance as well as social assistance programs including housing, education, and other general-purpose or targeted supports to the poor and vulnerable groups. There is a reminder that the profile involving multidimensional poverty has a very limited number of observations. But the profiles are consistently negative, suggesting that social protection policies possess a significant power in reducing poverty. The magnitude of this relationship is not identical as the national poverty headcount ratios emanating from specific contexts may be swayed less by social protection policies, which understandably has to do with the incorporation of relative notions of poverty in creating and revising national poverty lines. The relationships are also not linear in each case, with the national poverty headcount ratios even increasing together with social protection expenditures, before starting to decline almost linearly, and the international poverty headcount ratios declining sharply with social protection expenditures before leveling off. But this limited exercise provides a corroborating evidence for the findings from many other studies (Barrientos 2011; Esping-Andersen 1990; Wagle 2017, 2015, 2013) that social protection policies can serve as a formidable force in reducing poverty across countries and over time.

Conclusion

Poverty measurement outcomes are expected to be different across different approaches. First, the monetary and multidimensional frameworks are very different by nature and therefore their measurement outcomes are expected to vary widely. Second, while the international and national approaches share a very similar frame of reference emanating exclusively from monetary resources, the nationally and sometimes even regionally circumscribed context of the national approach can yield poverty measurement outcomes that are very different from the "very rough" international approach. This chapter has examined these differences across developing countries and over time and attempted to link them with the evolving social protection coverages.

In a general sense, the poverty measurement outcomes from these approaches are not very different, with any variation justified in terms of the way the poverty lines, especially from the international approach, range from less to more stringent. The average poverty headcount ratios when all developing countries and years are included ranged from 13 to 46 percent depending on the specific poverty lines used, with the international monetary poverty lines at $1.90 and $5.50 registering the lowest and highest magnitudes, respectively. The poverty headcount ratios from the national poverty lines as well as the multidimensional approach fit somewhere between those resulting from the least stringent ($1.90) to most stringent ($5.50) international poverty lines. At a deeper level, however, the degree of consistency does not fully depend on the level of stringency of the poverty lines themselves neither do they depend on the ability to incorporate unique national contexts. This is evident in the moderately high correlation in poverty outcomes between international and national poverty lines and between national poverty lines and multidimensional poverty lines. But the relatively high correlations in poverty outcomes between international and multidimensional poverty lines suggest that these two completely independent approaches lead to relatively more consistent poverty outcomes. Seemingly coincidental, this observation has to do with the choice made by the architects of multidimensional poverty measurement framework at UNDP (Alkire and Foster 2011) as relaxing the definition of deprivation beyond in just one-third of the weighted indicators can lead to more widespread poverty headcount ratios.

Other insights include lower poverty headcount ratios and gaps applying to more recent periods, higher-income developing countries, and certain regions including Eastern Europe, Latin America and the Caribbean, and the Middle East, North Africa, and Central Asia. It is important to note, however, that this observation may not do full justice to the analytical insights provided here since multidimensional poverty as well as national monetary poverty estimates do not follow this pattern. Among many of the factors responsible for these deviations are the exclusive focus on access to development amenities in case of multidimensional poverty (Wagle 2014) and the use of modified poverty lines by incorporating the national (or regional) trends in monetary resources and especially consumption in case of national monetary poverty (Wagle 2008). Finally, there is very clear evidence that countries with more comprehensive social protection policies are able to reduce poverty in all these forms. This last observation is quite powerful in that countries struggling to reduce poverty can look for ways to expand the size and scope of their social protection with the aim of helping people that otherwise are not able to benefit from the changes associated with today's increasingly interconnected and competitive global market.

Appendix

Table A13.1 Developing countries by region

Sub-Saharan Africa	Tunisia	**Latin America and the Caribbean**
Benin	Uganda	
Burkina Faso	Zambia	Argentina
Burundi	Zimbabwe	Bolivia
Cabo Verde		Brazil
Cameroon	**East Asia and the Pacific**	Colombia
Central African Republic	China, P.R.: Mainland	Costa Rica
Chad	Indonesia	Ecuador
Comoros	Kiribati	El Salvador
Congo, Dem. Republic	Lao, People's Dem. Rep.	Haiti
Congo, Republic of	Malaysia	Honduras
Côte d'Ivoire	Mongolia	Mexico
Djibouti	Myanmar	Nicaragua
Ethiopia	Philippines	Peru
Gabon	Thailand	São Tomé and Príncipe
Gambia, The	Timor-Leste, Dem. Rep. of	
Ghana	Vanuatu	**Middle East, North Africa, and Central Asia**
Guinea	Viet Nam	
Guinea-Bissau		Egypt

Kenya
Lesotho
Liberia
Madagascar
Malawi
Mali
Mauritania
Mauritius
Mozambique
Namibia
Niger
Nigeria
Rwanda
Senegal
Sierra Leone
South Africa
South Sudan
Sudan
Tanzania
Togo

Eastern Europe
Albania
Azerbaijan, Republic of
Belarus
Bosnia and Herzegovina
Bulgaria
Croatia
Georgia
Kosovo, Republic of
Latvia
Macedonia
Moldova
Montenegro
Morocco
Romania
Russian Federation
Serbia, Republic of
Seychelles
Ukraine

Iran, Islamic Republic of
Iraq
Kazakhstan
Kyrgyz Republic
Lebanon
Morocco
Syrian Arab Republic
Tajikistan
Turkey
Uzbekistan
West Bank and Gaza
Yemen, Republic of

South Asia
Bangladesh
Bhutan
India
Maldives
Nepal
Pakistan

References

Alkire, Sabina and James Foster. 2011. Counting and Multidimensional Poverty Measurement. *Journal of Public Economics*, 95, 476–87.

Barrientos, Armando. 2011. Social Protection and Poverty. *International Journal of Social Welfare*, 20, 240–49.

Citro, Constance and Robert Michael. 1995. *Measuring Poverty: A New Approach*. Washington, DC: National Academy Press.

Cruz, Marcio, James Foster, Bryce Quillin, and Philip Schellekens. 2015. *Ending Extreme Poverty and Sharing Prosperity: Progress and Policies*. World Bank Policy Research Note # 15/03.

Dalaker, Joe. 2005. *Alternative Poverty Estimates in the United States: 2003*. Washington, DC: US Census Bureau.

Esping-Andersen, Gosta. 1990. *The Three Worlds of Welfare Capitalism*. Cambridge: Polity Press.

Ferreira, Francisco, Shaohua Chen, Andrew Dabalen, Yuri Dikhanov, Nada Hamadeh, Dean Jolliffe, et al. 2015. *A Global Count of the Extreme Poor in 2012: Data Issues, Methodology and Initial Results*. World Bank Policy Research Working Paper # 7432.

Haveman, R.H. 1987. *Poverty Policy and Poverty Research: The Great Society and Social Sciences*. Madison, WI: University of Wisconsin Press.

ILO. 2014. *World Social Protection Report: Building Economic Recovery, Inclusive Development, and Social Justice*. Geneva, Switzerland: International Labour Organization.

OECD (Ed.). 2009. *Promoting Pro-Poor Growth: Social Protection*. Paris, France: Organization for Economic Cooperation and Development.

Orshansky, Mollie. 1965. Counting the Poor: Another Look at the Poverty Profile. In L.A. Ferman, J.L. Kornbluh, and A. Haber (Eds.), *Poverty in America: A Book of Readings*, pp. 42–81. Ann Arbor, MI: The University of Michigan Press.

Ravallion, Martin. 1998. *Poverty Lines in Theory and Practice*. World Bank Living Standards Measurement Study Working Paper # 133.

Ravallion, Martin. 2011. *On Multidimensional Indices of Poverty*. World Bank Policy Research Working Paper # 5580.

Ravallion, Martin, Gaurav Dutt, and Dominique van de Walle. 1991. Quantifying Absolute Poverty in the Developing World. *Review of Income and Wealth*, 37(4), 345–61.

Ravallion, Martin, Shaohua Chen, and Prem Sangraula. 2009. Dollar a Day Revisited. *World Bank Economic Review*, 23(2), 163–84.

Sen, Amartya K. 1987. *Commodities and Capabilities* (Hennipman Lecture, University of Amsterdam, 1982). New Delhi, India: Oxford University Press.

Sen, Amartya K. 1999. *Development as Freedom*. New York, NY: Alfred A. Knopf.

UNDP. 1990. *Human Development Report 1990*. New York, NY: Oxford University Press.

UNDP. 2016. *Human Development Report 2016*. New York, NY: United Nations Development Programme.

United Nations. 2015. *Transforming Our World: The 2030 Agenda for Sustainable Development (A/RES/70/1)*. Resolution adopted by the General Assembly, 25 September. New York, NY: United Nations.

UNRISD. 2010. *Combating Poverty and Inequality: Structural Change, Social Policy, and Politics*. Geneva, Switzerland: United Nations Research Institute for Social Development.

Wagle, Udaya. 2008. *Multidimensional Poverty Measurement: Concepts and Applications*. New York, NY: Springer.

Wagle, Udaya. 2012. The Economic Footing of the Global Poor, 1980–2005: The Roles of Economic Growth, Openness, and Political Institutions. *Journal of International Development*, 24(S1), S173–S179.

Wagle, Udaya. 2013. *The Heterogeneity Link of the Welfare State and Redistribution: Ethnic Heterogeneity, Welfare State Policies, Poverty, and Inequality in High Income Countries*. New York, NY: Springer.

Wagle, Udaya. 2014. The Counting-Based Measurement of Multidimensional Poverty in the United States: The Focus on Economic Resources, Inner Capabilities, and Relational Resources. *Social Indicators Research*, 115(1), 223–40.

Wagle, Udaya. 2015. Limited but Evolving: The Political Economy of Social Protections in Nepal. *Journal of Contemporary Asia*, 45(1), 92–112.

Wagle, Udaya. 2017. The Role of Social Protection Policies in Reducing Poverty and Inequality: An Insight from Asian Experiences. *Global Social Policy*, 17(2), 137–67.

World Bank. 1996. *Poverty Reduction and the World Bank: Progress and Challenges in the Early 1990s*. Washington, DC: Poverty and Social Policy Department, The World Bank.

World Bank. 2012. *Resilience, Equity, and Opportunity: 2012–2022 Social Protection and Labor Strategy*. Washington, DC: The World Bank.

World Bank. 2014. *The State of Social Safety Nets 2014*. Washington, DC: The World Bank.

World Bank Institute. 2005. *Introduction to Poverty Analysis*. Washington, DC: The World Bank.

14

What contributes to a higher degree of voluntarism in China's rural displacement programmes?

Poverty Alleviation Resettlement as a case study

Tao Xue and Mark Wang

Anti-poverty programmes, resettlement, and voluntarism in China

Resettlement for reasons of development in China is a widespread practice, but has long been critiqued as effectively forcing powerless rural residents to settle elsewhere (Li et al. 2001; Wilmsen et al. 2011a). Labelled as involuntary Development-Induced Displacement and Resettlement (DIDR), this kind of resettlement in China and elsewhere has been found to raise a series of problematic issues including compensation inequity, land conflicts, vulnerable livelihoods and impoverishment (Akca et al. 2013; Cernea 2003; Cernea & Mathur 2008; Gebre 2003; Tan 2008; Webber & McDonald 2004). These problems are deeply entwined with China's authoritarian nature, particularly its institutions and governance of land (Lin 2009; Lin & Yi 2011; Rogers 2014; Wilmsen 2018).

Few studies have delved into the whole repertoire of resettlement in China, including Poverty Alleviation Resettlement (PAR) which is reported as one of the few successful examples of 'voluntary' resettlement (Lo et al. 2016; Xue et al. 2013). These 'voluntary' resettlements are an anti-poverty initiative involving physically relocating poor rural villagers away from highly impoverished and/or ecologically degraded areas. This state-led resettlement programme aims to improve living standards and increase access to modern infrastructure (transportation) and markets by moving them to developed areas. Since 2008, voluntary participation has been one of the four principles of PAR as released by the central government.[1] The feature of voluntarism presumably distinguishes PAR from mainstream resettlement practice in China.

In order to reconcile PAR's voluntary principle and government claims of success with the findings of studies of other kinds of DIDR, this chapter aims to understand the voluntary nature of PAR projects in China. It will examine the PAR initiative and explore the following three questions: (1) what is PAR and what are its characteristics? (2) How voluntary is the resettlement practice? (3) What are the independent variables for its voluntary nature and why? This chapter will proceed as follows. First, a brief literature review will be provided followed by the method for this study. Second, three sections will independently answer the proposed questions. Third, the implications of this study will be explored in a discussion. The last section of this chapter provides our conclusions about PAR in China.

China's resettlement studies

Resettlement studies, as a sub-category of the migration and development literature, has a long history dating from post-war community rehabilitation (Richardson & Sheldon 1948). In general, resettlement has been framed as three main types: refugee resettlement, natural disaster resettlement and displacement in the name of development (Oliver-Smith & Hansen 1982, p. 6). Development-induced resettlement refers to the resettlement caused by regional development (Elder 1976; Kinsey 1982), infrastructure provision (Colson 1971), or interventions for unemployment and economic depression (Clawson 1978). Another type is the resettlement for environmental response, arranged from natural disaster (Oliver-Smith 1991), drought alleviation (Howorth & O'Keefe 1999), protection for natural reserves (Karanth 2007) and animal habitat (Witter 2013). In addition, other initiated causes of resettlement include food security (Taye & Mberengwa 2013), spontaneous dislocation (Thapa & Weber 1988), and refugee settlement (Rogge 1981).

The most significant bodies of literature on China's DIDR focus on large infrastructure projects, such as resettlement caused by dam construction (Jackson & Sleigh 2000; Li et al. 2001; McDonald 2006). Environmental resettlement is another cause for resettling a huge number of people in China, especially in eco-vulnerable areas such as Inner Mongolia (Dickinson & Webber 2007; Rogers & Wang 2006). However, few studies have delved into other functions of resettlement, such as poverty alleviation (Lin 2003; Xue et al. 2013); there are several reasons for this.

First, mainstream resettlement studies have concentrated on post-resettlement impacts. The first systematic study was Colson's (1971) work on the sociocultural consequences of a dam resettlement project. The analysis on resettlement impacts has long been framed under a risk model of impoverishment analysing the post-resettlement impact for host and resettled population by way of: landlessness, joblessness, homelessness, marginalisation, morbidity, food insecurity, loss of access to common property and services and social disarticulation (Cernea 1999, 2000) with corresponding countermeasures (Cernea 2007).

In China, the focus of DIDR studies has also included the social-cultural impact, livelihood and risk models, participation and volition. Jackson and Sleigh (2000) identified the widespread social impact on the affected population in terms of insufficient compensation, farmland loss, inadequate rights to property and services, unemployment and health risk and potential institutional changes. Rogers and Wang (2006) examined the impoverishment risk of social disarticulation in Inner Mongolia, China, then argued that the resettlers' adaptive ability also suggests a few aspects of rearticulation rather than simply disarticulation. McDonald (2006) used the Three Gorges Dam (TGD) as a test case to explore whether 'Resettlement with Development' is a suitable model for livelihood restoration and improvement. She chose an anthropological approach following the TGD resettlement over time to investigate the long-term impacts upon the affected population (McDonald et al. 2008; McDonald-Wilmsen & Webber 2010; Wilmsen et al. 2011b).

Second, DIDR studies have highlighted that involuntary resettlement tends to result in social conflict and incidents, both of which drew great public and academic attention. The mass media also reported that resettlement in China created social tension and protest

(Johnson 2014; Ross 2014; Tu 2010). Tang, Mason and Sun (2012) explained the reasons that resettled populations' interests were encroached on by ambiguous property rights, abuse of public interest and malfunctioning in government agencies. In this regard, a few researchers, such as Wang, Zhang and Cheong (2014), asserted that bottom-up participation should be introduced for social stability and effective local administration during resettlement projects.

Finally, studies on voluntary resettlement showed that voluntary resettlement projects can also be flawed. Schmidt-Soltau and Brockington (2007), for example, examined resettlement projects in Cameroon and argue that many policies are intended to 'preclude the possibility of real voluntary resettlement'. Social tension also existed in spontaneous resettlement in Thailand when the resettled competed for marginal land (Hirsch 1989). Ong (2014) concluded that 'voluntary' resettlement in China is an instrument of state-led urbanisation for land revenue and can trigger social tension as well. In addition, Lo and Wang (2018) critiqued the PAR's voluntarism, showing that key information was concealed by local officials during the negotiation process with villagers.

Forced resettlement, therefore, creates a higher level of social anxiety and insecurity compared with voluntary projects (Cernea & Guggenheim 1993, p. 3) and is prone to failure (Barnett & O'Neill 2012). In contrast, voluntary cases showed that free choice of living location with support from resettlement agencies could positively influence livelihood restoration (Yoshida et al. 2013) at a lower cost (Thapa & Weber 1988).

Increasingly more scholars have noticed the significance of China's PAR and paid close attention to its practices and progress. Merkle (2003) concluded that PAR cases in Ningxia during the 1980s were a failure of poor government performance and ineffective administration. Lin (2003) conducted research in Yunnan and Ningxia and concluded that PAR has significant positive outcomes for poverty reduction, specifically in improving rural households' income after resettlement. However, the controversy over PAR's impacts was all concluded before voluntarism in PAR was given elevated priority in national policies since 2001 (PRC State Council 2011), and the central government has officially encouraged rural labour migration since the new millennium (Wang & Cai 2009). Moreover, recent studies have covered the barriers of PAR's voluntarism in terms of insufficient support to sustainable livelihoods for the poor (Liu et al. 2018; Lo & Wang 2018; Xue et al. 2013), and lack of participation in resettlement (Lo et al. 2016), but failed to systematically profile the quantitative and qualitative nature of the voluntarism in PAR.

In addition, the implementation of PAR has recently been accelerating since it was first piloted in the early 1980s. From 2001 to 2015, PAR programmes in China have resettled around 12 million rural residents and there are plans to resettle another 10 million of the poorest rural residents over the period of the 13th 'Five-Year Plan (2016–2020)'[2] (National Development and Reform Commission 2016). It is evident that nearly one-third of the poorest villages will engage in PAR in this same period (Ministry of Land and Resources 2017). By the end of 2016 there were 43.35 million people living below the national poverty line in central and western China (Liu et al. 2017). As such, further research into the voluntarism of PAR in China provides an evaluation of China's anti-poverty practice, which will offer practical implications for any country wishing to pursue similar programmes.

Research methods

To analyse PAR, we chose the Loess Plateau, one of the poorest areas in China and one of the target areas in the 13th 'Five-Year Plan' (2016–2020), as our case study. The Loess Plateau is located in north-western China and spans Shaanxi, Shanxi, Ningxia, and Gansu provinces,

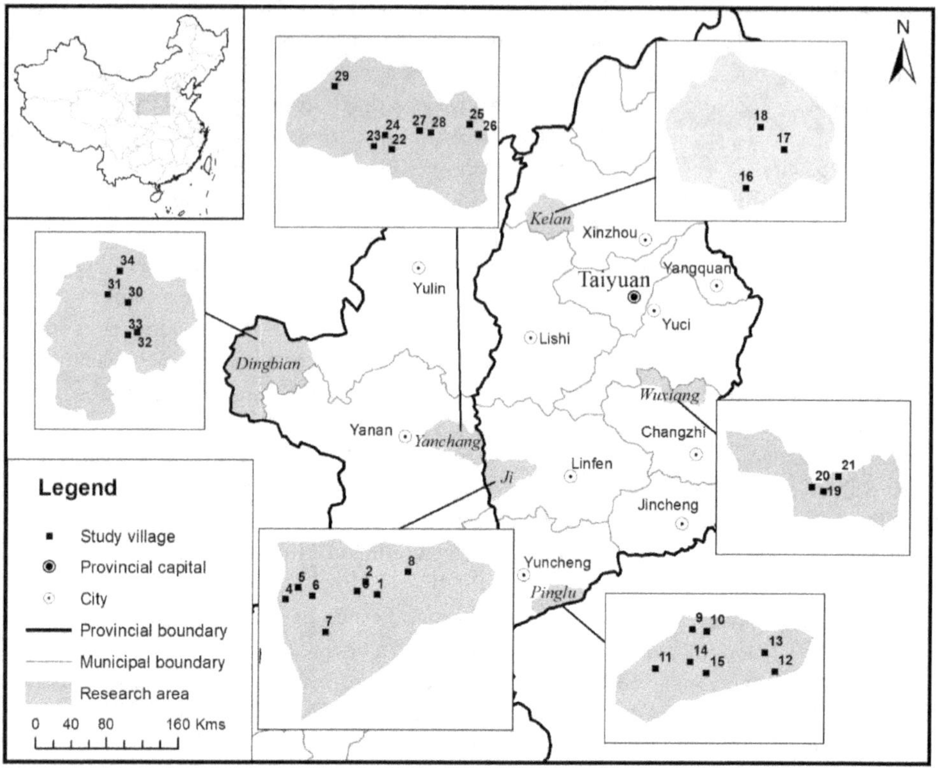

Figure 14.1 Fieldwork site map.

No. – village name (resettlement year):

1 – Checheng (2002); 2 – Baipodi (2002); 3 – Sangcun (2008); 4 – Guxian (2008); 5 – Wencheng (2008); 6 – Dageta (2008); 7 – Baidong (2007); 8 – Taidu (2009); 9 – Wali (2004); 10 – Zhangdian (2010); 11 – Tudimiao (2003); 12 – Jianping (2009); 13 – Houyao (2009); 14 – Zhenggou (2003); 15 – Fusheng (2003); 16 – Wujiazhuang (2009); 17 – Songjiagou (2010); 18 – Guanjiazhuang (2009); 19 – Xiaguan (2007); 20 – Hongtuwa (2005); 21 – Taoyu (2011); 22 – Angou (2011); 23 – Hujiahe (2009); 24 – Beiyang (2007); 25 – Huyan (2009); 26 – Baijiazhuang (2007); 27 – Zhangjitan (2011); 28 – Xiapanshi (2007); 29 – Heijiabao (2011); 30 – Magouquan (2011); 31 – Hongdunliang (2004); 32 – Yangjing (2011); 33 – Qinwan (2011); 34 – Yishiliang (2011).

and parts of Qinghai, Inner Mongolia and Henan (see Figure 14.1). Poverty in this region is a common phenomenon due to its severe natural and environmental conditions and overdevelopment, including arid land, land erosion, poor soil and water conservation and excessive farming (Nolan et al. 2008; Ostwald & Chen 2006; Shi & Shao 2000). Within the Loess Plateau our focus is on Shaanxi and Shanxi provinces.

In the selected provinces, we chose six national poverty counties[3] in Shaanxi and Shanxi. At least two townships within the selected counties were chosen, resulting in 34 PAR cases in 21 townships (see Figure 14.1). Most of the field data was collected in 2013 with further minor data collection in 2014 and 2015. Our target participants were resettled people but also local officials, who play a significant role in interpreting and implementing central policies (O'Brien & Li 2017). In total we conducted 753 questionnaires, 260 face-to-face semi-structured interviews with rural households and 39 interviews with local officials. The quantitative data collected provided a broad picture about PAR at each site and facilitated our selection of proposed interviews that, as the most important qualitative data, offered key information in exploring the questions posed in this chapter.

Resettlement as an anti-poverty instrument

Poverty policies in China

China's post-1978 Reform and Opening policy has served as a double-edged sword for poverty reduction. On the one hand, China's poverty problem has changed, largely from a so-called 'shared poverty' during the Mao period to poverty mainly stemming from income polarisation (Fan et al. 2004). On the other hand, sustained economic growth fuelling historically unprecedented poverty reduction has seen China's poverty rate fall from over 60 per cent in 1981 to less than 7 per cent in 2012 (Chen & Ravallion 2007; China's Poverty Alleviation Database 2015). PAR only contributes to the later stage of such poverty reduction – in 2001, 'fully voluntary' was mentioned for the first time as an instrument to address poverty issues in China: 'as to those minor rural households who suffered from severe subsistence and development problems, the implementation of developmental resettlement is possible'.[4] In 2001, the State Council proposed the *China's Rural Poverty Alleviation and Development Scheme (2001–2010)*, in which voluntary resettlement for poverty alleviation was listed as a key policy with the intention of relocating the rural poor away from highly impoverished or environmentally vulnerable areas (Ministry of Agriculture 2001). The support for those relocated has also been linked with the Grain for Green policy[5] under which rural farmers converted their land to forest and grassland with subsidies from the central government. This initiative has been further associated with and incorporated into three national programmes: the Western Development Programme, 'Poverty Alleviation in the New Century', and 'Building a New Socialist Countryside' (Li et al. 2011). It is anticipated that by the end of 2020, the remaining two per cent of China's poorest population will have been lifted out of poverty as 'scheduled' by the central government (Liu et al. 2017). PAR projects have certainly gained traction in the past few decades.

Poverty administration

In China, poverty alleviation, as a special project initiated by the central government, has a clear top-down administrative hierarchy. The Leading Group Office of Poverty Alleviation and Development (LGOPAD) in the State Council is the highest poverty alleviation administrative unit in China. The Poverty Alleviation Office (PAO) is the official government body which conducts the daily operations for poverty reduction policies and PAR programmes. At each level of China's governments below the central state, there are LGOPADs and PAOs, and the former is more powerful than the latter (See Figure 14.2).

According to the institutional description on the website of the State Council LGOPAD, the responsibilities of LGOPAD at a central level include: poverty investigation and its administration; design of poverty guidelines, policies and plans; coordination of potential problems; supervision and inspection of PAR projects. The subordinate PAO at the State Council is in charge of detailed administration and management, including human resources, policy and regulation, financial planning, international cooperation, social anti-poverty affairs, development guidance and party committee. The Development Guidance Office is the key administrative unit with responsibility for PAR administration. Provincial governments detail and administer

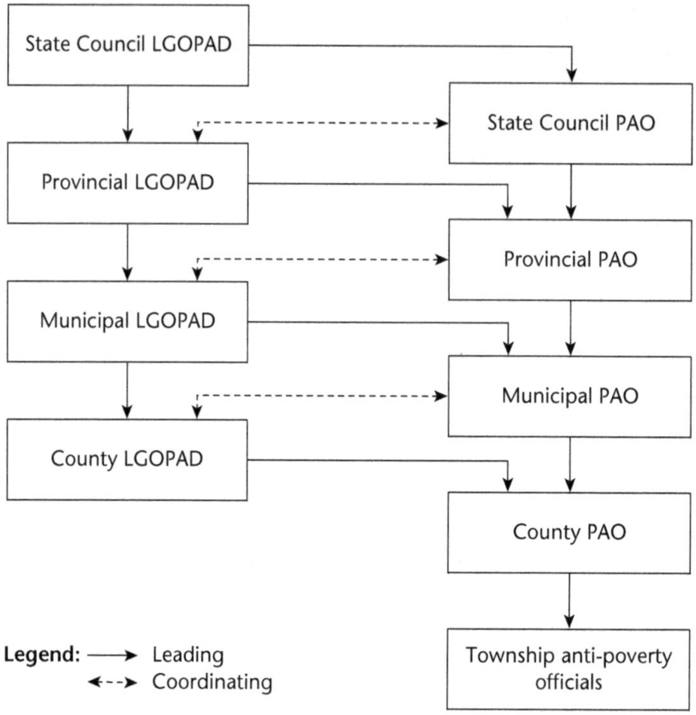

Figure 14.2 Poverty administration in China.

Source: China's State Council LGOPAD website: www.cpad.gov.cn/col/col282/index.html (in Chinese).

the implementation of PAR in accordance with central plans. At the grassroots level of this administrative system, it is the officials from county and township level governments that are effectively implementing PAR in China, and village cadres whose performance is assessed by the 'one vote veto' system: that is, if their village PAR project fails, they are 'accountable for mistakes' with *ex post* punishment (Chang 2018, p. 884). In the new era of Xi Jinping, the veto in PAR has also been incorporated into a Performance Evaluation System for the leading cadres at the other local government levels (Wang 2018). As such, the accomplishment of poverty goals has become an important aspect of evaluations linked to decisions about local officials' career promotion or financial bonuses (Manion 1985), which in turn enhances the central policies (Whiting 2017, p. 461).

PAR procedures in China

According to our data at the local[6] level in Shaanxi and Shanxi, PAR has three main stages: preparation, implementation and completion. Preparation commences with institutional establishment such as the formation of LGOPAD and PAO at county level and the appointment of township officials. They are the key actors in putting the national policies into practice, targeting PAR participants, propagandising national policy and organising and coordinating physical resettlement. Such implementation refers to the physical resettlement process, within which local agencies have responsibility for the investigation and monitoring of PAR's progress, publicity and funds management. The last stage of completion mainly involves archiving PAR households and reporting to upper-level government.

The process as summarised in Figure 14.3, arose from our early findings in Shanxi Province based on interviews with municipal and county officials and resettled households. The first step for local governments is the selection of candidate villages based on following criteria (Li et al. 2011):

- The overall gradient of the selected site should be less than 25 degrees;[7]
- Adjoining market and transportation facilities;
- Access to farmland and water resources;
- Minimisation of negative impacts for host places;
- Avoidance of resettling to an ecological area;
- Preferred short distance resettlement.

With feedback obtained from the candidate villages, local officials propose resettlement sites that will be approved by upper-level government. At the next stage, the proposed villages will hold a meeting with the participation of local officials and villagers, and the former will introduce resettlement rules and regulations, proposed resettlement sites and subsidy levels in order to reach consent with the latter. A proportion of 80 percent is the threshold for deciding whether the village is to take part in the PAR programme. Meanwhile, the agreement of half of the participants to the proposed resettlement site is a must in the first year. Furthermore, the villagers have voting rights to decide where to move, but are limited to a list of proposed sites. The proposed resettlement sites are planned at county levels with suggestions from township officials. The potential villages are not involved in the process of selecting preferred sites. The information provided to villagers is in fact limited. Besides a few key pieces of information, the detailed plan is not provided to the rural community, including when they will resettle and how they will be compensated. Our field data also confirms the so-called 'bureaucratic absorption' (Chuang 2014). At meetings, local officials have great enthusiasm to persuade attending villagers to move, as they may have a better chance of promotion if they demonstrate successful resettlement cases. For instance, one of our interviewed township officials in Zhangdian, Shanxi, Mr W, was promoted from the resettlement village as a reward after implementation of a successful programme. For those unwilling to move to a centralised living site, they will move to the place they choose, with the same amount of subsidy provided. They could still live in their houses even if they decided not to take part in the PAR programmes.

Once the villagers sign the agreement, it is collected by local officials and submitted to upper-level government for approval. The provincial government is the final administrative tier that authorises the county government to transfer subsidies directly into households' bank accounts with the aim of avoiding corruption. The other two transactions take place when new houses are built and people have moved in.

Indeed, the PAR procedure discussed here involves local villagers in the decision-making process. Our interview data showed, however, that the poor can say no but have limited alternative options. In cases where farmers are not given sufficient policy information by local officials and simply asked a yes or no question, they have poor engagement in the decision-making process. In other cases, such as Zhangjiatan in Shaanxi, engagement is deeper. Based on the interview with a head at Xia Pan Shi Village, the village committee has been positively involved in the site selection, planning, and construction works of

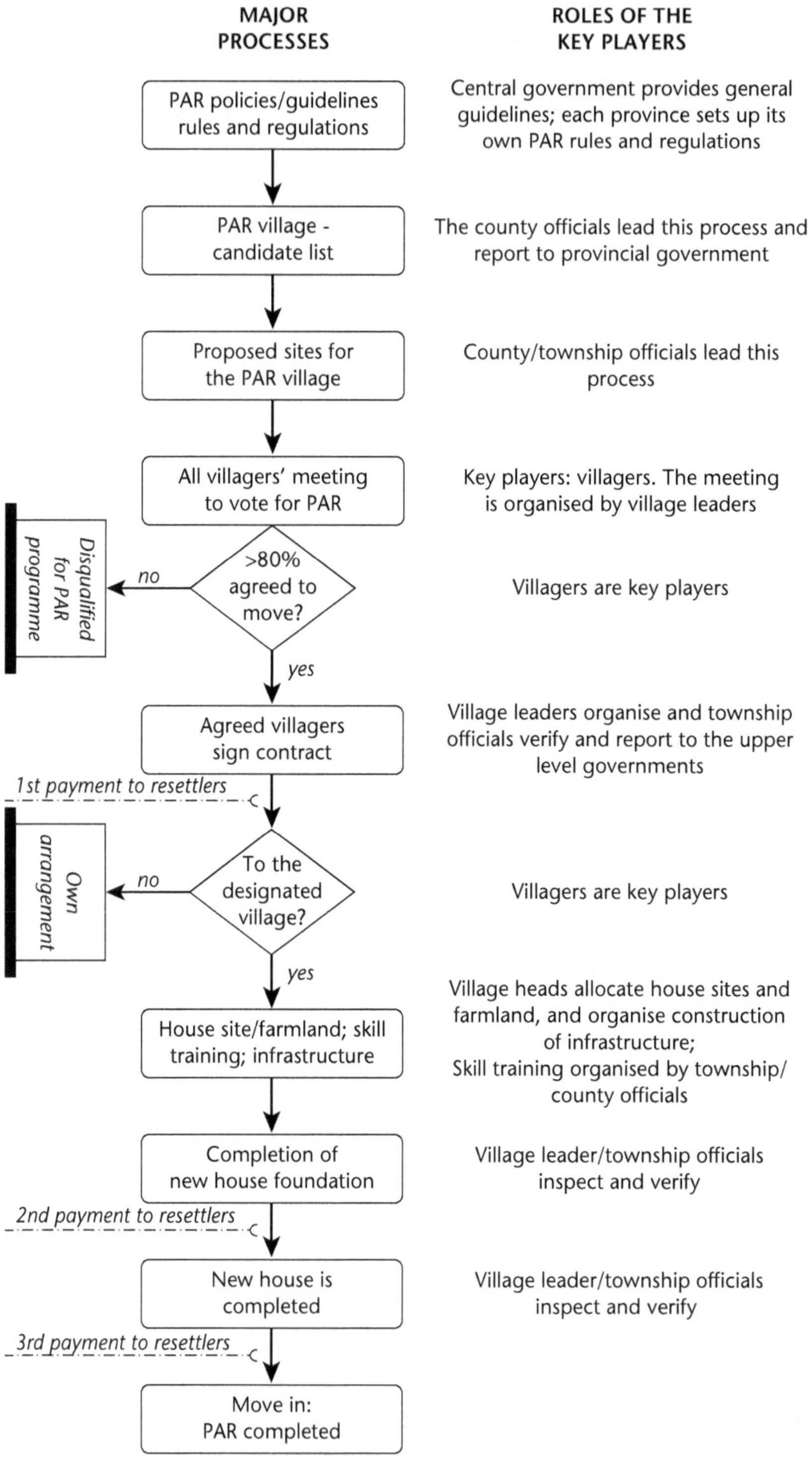

Figure 14.3 Major processes and key players.

Source: Xue et al. (2013).

the resettlement. As such, our data also confirmed that the voluntarism in Xia Pan Shi Village is higher than other cases. Despite the different levels of engagement, there is some evidence that – in some cases at least – resettled farmers are having some input into the resettlement project.

The rationale of PAR's voluntarism in China

Resettlement itself is a complex phenomenon and the binary division between voluntary and involuntary is problematic (Schmidt-Soltau & Brockington 2007; Wilmsen & Wang 2015; Xue et al. 2013). Gebre (2002) proposed another two features of resettlement from his observation of Ethiopian projects – induced voluntary and compulsory voluntary, which overcomes the rigid classification of voluntarism for resettlement projects. Drawing lessons from this study, we divided voluntarism into five categories: totally involuntary, relatively involuntary, neutral, relatively voluntary, fully voluntary, all of which have been marked from 1 to 5 provided in the questionnaires and interviews. This classification mainly considers the explanation for resettlement voluntarism.

Among 753 participant households, nearly 70 per cent can be classified as fully voluntary while only 1.7 per cent expressed their strong unwillingness to move (see Figure 14.4). Figure 14.4 also shows that over 86 per cent of total households were totally or relatively voluntary. It is evident that from the perspective of the resettled population, PAR in Shaanxi and Shanxi could be understood as a 'voluntary' practice.

Spatial variation

We can further examine the voluntarism of PAR from the perspective of spatial patterns and policy implementation environments. According to Long et al. (2012), the spatial-territorial reorganisation in rural China comprises mainly of three models: village–village, village–town, and village–city. In this study, we reclassified the division and added an analysis on an administrative level of the resettled sites. Given the spatial models of resettled houses, resettled sites have been divided into three types: rural settlement, urban fringe and urban area (see Table 14.1). Of all 753 resettlement participants, 627 households still moved to villages while 98 households resettled in an urban area and only 28 households lived on the outskirts of cities or towns.

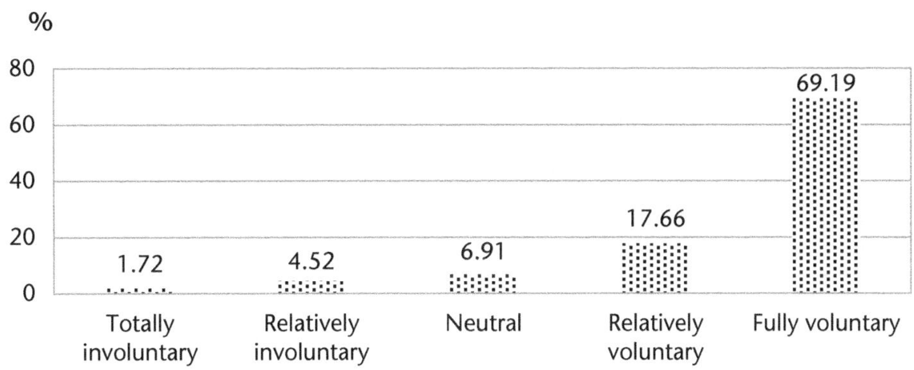

Figure 14.4 Household voluntarism to resettlement in Shaanxi and Shanxi.

Table 14.1 The voluntarism of different resettlement types

Resettlement type	*No. of households*	*Totally involuntary (%)*	*Relatively involuntary (%)*	*Neutral (%)*	*Relatively voluntary (%)*	*Fully voluntary (%)*
To rural	627	1.91	3.67	5.10	19.46	69.86
To urban fringe	28	0.00	3.57	3.57	0.00	92.86
To urban area	98	1.02	10.20	19.39	11.22	58.16

Table 14.1 shows that households that moved to urban outskirts areas tended to have higher voluntarism. Our interview respondents explained that the promise of higher household income was one of the most significant factors influencing their willingness. The number of people who chose to move to urban fringe areas was the smallest, but had the highest degree of willingness to move among the three groups. The majority of the households moving to the urban fringe have opportunities to engage in both non-farming work and farming for cash crops, which has easy access to the urban market.

We further add another spatial dimension into this part of analysis – destination. The moving destinations have been divided into four sections: moving within the administrative village, within the same township but other villages, within the same county but other townships, and within the same province but other counties (see Table 14.2). Most households (542) in the study regions still moved within their administrative boundary, such as from natural village to centralised village or other natural villages. The remaining 180 households moved to nearby villages within the jurisdiction of the same township. Only a few chose long-distance resettlement with 28 households moving to other townships and three households to other counties.

Unlike the voluntarism of moving to rural or urban areas, households that moved further away had a higher willingness to do so. Although only three households resettled in other counties, all of them are fully voluntary. Compared with the households moving further away, households resettled within township boundaries are relatively involuntary, around 5–9 per cent express their involuntary experience. This contradictory phenomenon results from the fact that most households moving further away are those who independently chose to move rather than move with other households in their village as part of a government-led project, which likely contributed to their higher voluntarism. Furthermore, almost all households that moved to other townships and counties either had support from their social networks, such as relatives

Table 14.2 The voluntarism of different moving destinations (administrative boundaries)

Moving destination	*No. of households*	*Totally involuntary (%)*	*Relatively involuntary (%)*	*Neutral (%)*	*Relatively voluntary (%)*	*Fully voluntary (%)*
Within village	542	1.48	4.06	6.46	20.66	67.34
Within township (other villages)	180	2.78	6.67	8.89	10.56	71.11
Within county (other townships)	28	0.00	0.00	3.57	7.14	89.29
Within province (other counties)	3	0.00	0.00	0.00	0.00	100.00

or friends, or expressed clear intentions to move, for example close to their workplace (meaning they were likely already working outside the village).

Voluntary variables

To identify the variables of a household's voluntarism, we employed principal component analysis to identify different sources of influence. Voluntarism is the dependent variable Z, valued from 1–5 (totally involuntary = 1; relatively involuntary = 2; neutral = 3; relatively voluntary = 4; fully voluntary = 5). Modelling the regression equation as follows:

$$Z = \beta_0 + \beta_1 Y_1 + \ldots + \beta_P Y_P$$

β_0 is constant, β_1 …, β_p are standard regression coefficients

Reason to resettle was classified into three categories: characteristics of the resettled household (household size, age composition, average education years per household, occupation, working place, children's education, plan to build a new house before PAR, average income per capita in one household, average area of farmland); resettlement policies (resettlement time; housing subsidies, policy understanding, participation, decision making); and the patterns of the resettlement process (resettlement organiser, resettlement distance, resettlement type, ways of moving out, ways of settling in), labelled from x_1 to x_{19} according to the above order. We adopted principal component methods, with maximum variance rotation, and identified six key components: economic measure to resettlement, policy understanding, personal characteristics, ways of moving out and settling in, resettlement type; household characteristics, and labelled from y_1 to y_6, respectively. The results are shown in Table 14.3.

The data has been put into SPSS with multi-factor linear regression model analysis. The contributions to voluntarism from high to low are as follows: economic measure to resettlement, policy understanding, personal features, moving out and settling in, resettlement type and household features (see Table 14.4).

Standard regression equation:

$$Z = 4.487 + 0.213 \times y_1 + 0.154 \times y_5 + 0.137 \times y_3 + 0.057 \times y_4 - 0.050 \times y_2 + 0.020 \times y_6$$

The results in Tables 14.3 and 14.4 indicate that apart from y_2 (resettlement type), all variables are positively correlated with voluntarism. First, the economic measure is of the most significance to resettlement voluntarism especially in subsidies and income after resettlement. Second, policy understanding is associated with resettlement time, subsidies, resettlement choice, moving out and resettling in. All the factors are highly related to voluntarism to resettlement. Third, personal features showed that working in other counties, long periods of education, and non-farming are related to income and living quality improvement after resettlement, all of which facilitate their voluntarism. Fourth, the ways of moving out and resettling in positively correlated to voluntarism. Moving out in batches and resettling at scattered locations contributed to high voluntary opinions and *vice versa*. The flexible choices provided to the proposed resettlement population to some extent increased their willingness to move. Next, resettlement type indicated that resettling to a rural area would improve voluntarism. This is because three-quarters of resettled households are rural farmers who have bonded with their land – resettlement to an urban area could become their concern before resettlement thereby reducing the degree of their voluntarism. Last, the weakest influence is household feature. Big family size increases the

Table 14.3 Voluntary factor analysis

Voluntary factors	*After rotation*						*Before rotation*
	y_1 *economic measure*	y_2 *resettlement type*	y_3 *personal features*	y_4 *moving out settling in*	y_5 *policy understanding*	y_6 *household feature*	*Communality*
x_{10} resettlement time	0.719						0.698
x_{11} housing subsidies	0.719						0.736
x_8 annual income/ person	0.690						0.667
x_{14} decision making							0.415
x_{17} resettlement type		0.831					0.740
x_{16} resettlement distance		0.729					0.642
x_7 housing plan							0.640
x_5 working place			0.751				0.593
x_3 educated years			0.652				0.620
x_4 occupation			0.643				0.590
x_6 children's education							0.776
x_{18} ways of moving out				0.764			0.733
x_{19} ways of resettling in				−0.731			0.642
x_{12} policy understanding					0.853		0.758
x_{13} participation					0.850		0.764
x_{15} resettlement organiser							0.690
x_2 age composition						0.775	0.719
x_1 household size						0.680	0.737
x_9 farmland size							0.636

possibility of resettlement as, in some counties, subsidies are measured relative to household size. The younger generation also finds it easier to accept new changes in their lives compared to the older generations as most of them have migration working experience.

Understanding the key variables

This section will interpret a few key variables in more detail with the support of our survey and interview analysis. First, our interview data verifies and confirms quantitative findings that economic measurement of the resettled is one of the most significant variables. In the field work

Table 14.4 Factor regression analysis

Model	*B*	*SD*	*Beta*	*t*	*Sig.*
Constants	4.487	0.033		135.946	0.000
y_1: economic measure	0.105	0.033	0.213	3.184	0.000
y_5: policy understanding	0.144	0.033	0.154	4.350	0.000
y_3: personal features	0.127	0.033	0.137	3.857	0.001
y_4: moving out and settling in settling in	0.053	0.033	0.057	1.611	0.003
y_2: resettlement type	−0.047	0.033	−0.050	−1.411	0.012
y_6: household features	0.019	0.033	0.020	0.573	0.018
$R = 0.658$; $R^2 = 0.433$; adjusted $R^2 = 0.448$; $F = 15.142$; sig. = 0.000					

period, we provided 12 reasons for their participation in PAR to the research participants, based on the current literature of PAR in China.

As shown in Figure 14.5, the three main reasons for resettlement are convenience to public services, consideration for children and living quality improvement. First, the selected study villages are in remote areas. It is reasonable for resettled farmers to consider their access to public services, such as easy transportation, proximity to clinics, recreation places and shopping. For instance, one elderly farmer in Ji County was reluctant to move at the beginning of resettlement, and finally moved to centralised village near his son one year later. He said, 'I am too old to live alone, and I have to live near my son with good public services'. Second, consideration of children is a frequent response, especially for those who have school-age children studying in central villages or towns. More than half of these respondents also mention that they have considerations for their children's marriage and possible job opportunities as well. Finally, living

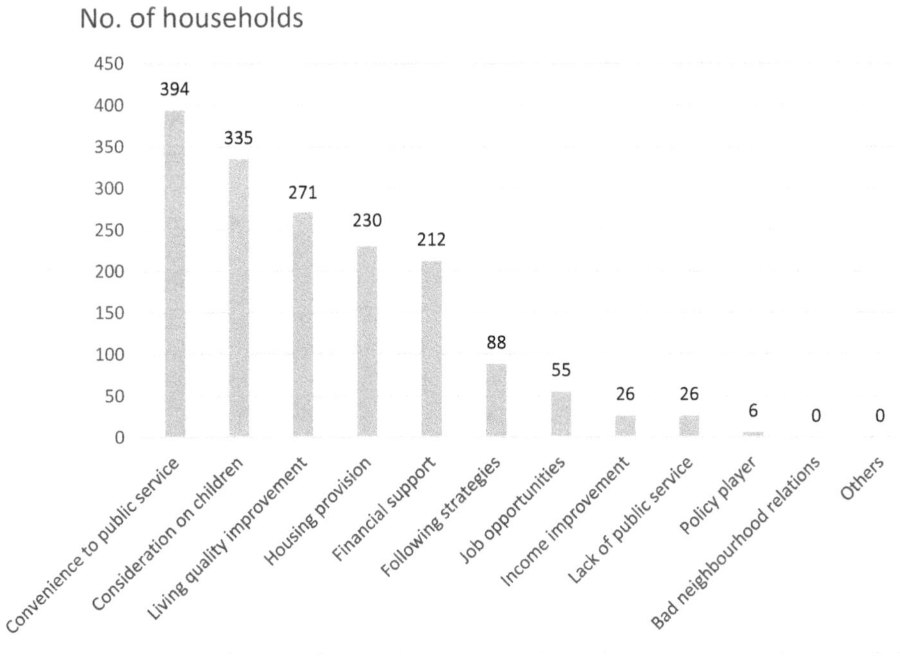

Figure 14.5 Households' multiple responses to voluntarism.

quality improvement is the third frequent response identified, as most villages have poor natural endowment for living, where there is exposure to low farming output, risks of natural disasters, and environmental degradation. One of the cases in point is Huyan village in Shaanxi, where villagers have lived for decades in cave houses and with limited agricultural output to consume.

These main reasons are relatively feasible via PAR because the majority of resettlement sites from our data are central villages, with a few moving to the urban fringe or even urban areas such as towns. The following two are housing and financial support. Of these five responses, quality of life improvement, housing and financial support are factors closely associated with the economic measurement of resettlement in regression analysis. Access to public services and consideration of children are common issues in resettlement, not only for PAR but also for other resettlement projects in China.

Besides, education level and occupation type are two personal features that exert influence on PAR's voluntarism. A person with higher education levels tended to have a higher degree of voluntarism. Of all survey respondents, around one-fifth of the population have studied for over nine years (equivalent to senior high or above) and among these, three-quarters are fully voluntary with only one per cent being totally involuntary. For those studying less than nine years, the proportion with fully voluntary opinions is ten per cent or less, while the totally involuntary population is two per cent higher than those with a higher education level.

Furthermore, employment status is another significant factor with a positive correlation to voluntarism. Those with stable urban jobs tended to have higher voluntarism although the majority of survey participants are subsistence farmers (28.55 per cent) or part-time workers (47.81 per cent). Around three-quarters are fully voluntary in participating in PAR projects. Interestingly, the unemployed have a higher voluntarism to resettlement projects, although there are only eight households falling into this category. The key reason for their voluntarism is the belief that they could benefit from PAR, whereby they described themselves as 'the poorest in the poor area'. In addition, all of them are young people, which will be further explained in the following paragraphs.

Finally, household size and average age are household features that have the least influence on voluntarism. We divided the household size into three groups: 1–2 persons (7.30 per cent), 3–4 persons (51.92 per cent) and over 4 persons (40.78 per cent). It is evident that 'nuclear' families and extended families are the two dominant family types in the surveyed population. Voluntarism is higher when household size is larger, although the differences among groups is less than five per cent with fully voluntary responses by 65.45 per cent, 69.05 per cent, and 71.66 per cent, respectively.

Another factor is the average age of the targeted households. We divided the households into three groups with age groups ranging from 18 to 90 years old: young group (18–44 years old) accounts for 34.53 per cent, medium group (45–60 years old) makes up 51.26 per cent; and senior group (61–90 years old) occupies 14.21 per cent of the total households. The data clearly shows a negative correlation between average age and voluntarism, with a similar effect on household voluntarism. Younger households are willing to move while older households tended to resist. Over 80 per cent of young households expressed voluntary responses and less than 5 per cent involuntary opinions. By contrast, over 10 per cent of senior households are involuntary resettlers; while approximately 75 per cent of senior households reply with voluntary responses.

Critical review on voluntary PAR

Our new data on PAR cases clearly shows a relatively high level of voluntarism. Compared to other forms of DIDR, the resettled in PAR programmes have a much higher level of willingness to move.

PAR's higher voluntarism is related to its flexibility and increased choices for villagers. We can summarise such flexibility in the following aspects: (1) 'opportunity to say no': individual household can choose whether to participate in the PAR or not; (2) 'majority choice': PAR will not be approved unless 80 per cent of villagers agree. Arguably, a proportion of 80 per cent indicating willingness to resettle does not constitute full consent; (3) unlike China dam-induced displacements, the officials have no rigid deadline for PAR project completion; and (4) the resettled could keep their land and old houses as their own property in the old village. For example, in Ji County, many PAR resettled farmers have two houses: one in the old village and the other in the resettlement site.

While the flexibility and appeal of PAR policy highlights its higher voluntarism, it should not be considered totally voluntary. First, the resettled were 'persuaded' or misled by the local officials. PAR is local officials' top priority task. With the pressure and potential rewards for successful PAR completion from superiors, local officials tended to reveal limited resettlement information and/or even exaggerate potential benefits for resettlement. Local officials selectively released information of positive aspects of the PAR project at village meetings so that villagers agreed to signing the contracts. For example, Mr Za in Zhangdian Township, Pinglu County, told us that he did not know the resettlement details even after he had signed the resettlement contract, and that he had indeed been encouraged to sign the resettlement contract when local officials had told him of the potential benefits, including government resettlement subsidies. Sometimes, the local officials mislead or even fabricated post-resettlement supports. Our fieldwork findings indicate that the promised job positions in the construction of resettlement site in Pinglu County and in village-owned enterprises in Dingbian County were never delivered. As such, many households feel that they were cheated after they resettled.

Second, those who decided not to move were later, to some extent, 'forced' to move because the left-behind population lived in ghost villages. Our analysis showed that 19 per cent of households in Checheng township refused to participate in PAR programmes at the consensus-making stage. Mr Su is one of those who decided not to move but later he and his household were forced to move since he could not conveniently live in the old village. As the majority of households moved away, he barely had access to the village service. In the government data file, he is shown as one who resettled voluntarily.

Third, many of the left-behind households in our PAR case studies are those who could not afford the resettlement expenditure. Although the Chinese government has gradually increased its PAR subsidy standards, the poorest households have no money to match the gap. For instance, Mr Qi, a single male living alone[8] in Checheng village, told us that 'the subsidy is not enough, (and I had) no money to resettle elsewhere'. Similarly, Ms Do also stated her family were short of financial capacity to resettle and to build a new house for five family members, but she further added that she would move when the subsidy standard was raised. As Lo, Xue and Wang (2016) pointed out, support and safeguards for the livelihood of those who choose not to move need to be addressed in future PAR policies.

Finally, local variations of PAR can result in inequity, which further deteriorates the voluntary nature of PAR. Those villages that participated in the PAR at a later stage received substantially higher subsidies as the government increased its subsidy standards over the years. In Ji County, the subsidy for PAR participants had been raised from 1,000 RMB per capita in 1997 to 4,200 RMB in 2013.

In this sense, the voluntarism of PAR solely demonstrates its nature at a confined level as it is still a top-down resettlement policy within the authoritarian bureaucratic system in China. Indeed, PAR as an anti-poverty instrument has presented efficacy, but its voluntary nature and the ways to achieve a better anti-poverty outcome are still questionable. As Wilmsen and Wang (2015) pointed out concerning the 'false dichotomy' of voluntarism, the point at issue should be the active engagement to settle for a better resettlement outcome. In this aspect, the studies on PAR's voluntarism call for enquiries into how to effectively fulfil anti-poverty goals with relevancy to limited participation of the resettled in PAR.

Conclusion

This chapter has outlined the nature of PAR in Shaanxi and Shanxi; that it is a top-down anti-poverty policy aimed at resettling populations in China's poorest areas. Over the turn of the new millennium, the Chinese government introduced 'fully voluntary participation' as one of the key PARs. In the implementation of PAR at local level, county, township, and village officials effectively negotiated with resettled villagers in terms of their attitude to moving and subsidies. The *in situ* procedures of PAR in Shaanxi and Shanxi showed that it offered more options and villagers had a higher level of willingness to move compared to the other DIDR programmes, but did not overcome the defects in local policy implementation, such as 'bureaucratic absorption' (Chuang 2014) via persuasion and selective behaviours of local officials (O'Brien & Li 2017).

Voluntarism shows spatial variation: higher voluntarism for those resettled in new resettlement villages in urban fringe areas than urban or rural areas. The key contributing variables are the economic measures, including household income, subsidy standard and resettlement time (the subsidy has been increasing annually). The understanding of the policy, urbanised jobs, scattered resettlement, big family, and young average age of a household also contributed to higher voluntarism among PAR participants.

Higher voluntarism is related to the flexibility and optional choices of the PAR programmes in Shaanxi and Shanxi provinces. However, the flexibility of PAR does not guarantee high voluntarism. With the efforts of local officials during negotiations, persuasively or fraudulently, our fieldwork shows that at least 10 per cent of the participants regret their move. Such an issue has many policy implications. To promote its effectiveness, central government should increase the support provided to the resettled population (Lo & Wang 2018) from a monetary and administrative level. Meanwhile, post-resettlement programmes should be initiated for sustainable livelihood restoration. Additionally, the findings of this study evidence that policy information should be effectively conveyed to proposed resettlers regarding PAR details such as subsidies, resettlement locations and scheduled timelines. Ningxia's PAR in the early 1980s showed precisely that participation correlates with the resettlement outcome (Lin 2003). Last, this chapter suggests that PAR should diversify its compensation flexibility away from solely monetary subsidies, given the lessons from DIDR in China (McDonald 2006, p. 333). This will enhance the resettled population's voluntarism and achieve the national anti-poverty goal.

Acknowledgements

The authors would like to thank Professor Bent Greve, the anonymous reviewer for insightful feedback, and Dr Sarah Rogers for her critical inputs and language polishing. This project was partially funded by China National Social Science Foundation (Project ID #: 12BJL076).

Notes

1 The four principles are *qunzhong ziyuan* (voluntary participation), *jiujin anzhi* (settlement in vicinity), *liangli erxing* (act according to the capability), *shidang buchang* (appropriate subsidies).
2 'The Five-Year Plan' is the legacy of China's planned economy since 1953. For more information about this plan see Emerson (1983) and Fan (2006).

3 Referring to poor counties as 'National Poverty Counties' is China's primary approach to fighting against poverty in the poorest rural areas by providing loans, grants and public works (Rogers 2014).
4 Details of this plan can be retrieved at www.cdpf.org.cn/ywzz/jyjyb/fp_241/zcwj_250/200711/t20071123_74845.shtml (in Chinese)
5 Grain for Green is a policy that aimed at rectifying the severe environmental problems in Western China, such as soil erosion, flooding, land degradation, with the provision of subsidies to rural farmers converting about 15 million ha of farmland into grassland or forest, and afforesting 17 million ha of wasteland (Feng et al. 2005).
6 Local here means the county level and below due to the fact that PAR has been effectively implemented by county agencies and below.
7 According to Li et al. (2011), the resettlement site's gradient is positively correlated to the resettlement's success due to the fact that 'migrants require the relatively flat land for living and farming after their move' (p. 470).
8 We employed the Expert Scoring Method to classify all households of six PAR villages in Chengcheng Township into five categories from richest to poorest. Given this classification of households in PAR villages, we could reach a clear conclusion on the numbered proportion of participants in PAR programme in each category.

References

Akca, E., Fujikura, R. & Sabbag, C. 2013. 'Ataturk Dam resettlement process: increased disparity resulting from insufficient financial compensation', *International Journal of Water Resources Development*, vol. 29, no. 1, pp. 101–8.

Barnett, J. & O'Neill, S. J. 2012. 'Commentary: islands, resettlement and adaptation', *Nature Climate Change*, vol. 2, no. 1, pp. 8–10.

Cernea, M. M. 1999. 'Why economic analysis is essential to resettlement: a sociologist's view', in M. M. Cernea (ed.), *The Economics of Involuntary Resettlement: Questions and Challenges*, World Bank, Washington, DC, vol. 34, pp. 2149–58.

Cernea, M. M. 2000. 'Risks, safeguards and reconstruction: a model for population displacement and resettlement', *Risks and Reconstruction: Experiences of Resettlers and Refugees*, vol. 35, no. 41, pp. 3659–78.

Cernea, M. M. 2003. 'For a new economics of resettlement: a sociological critique of the compensation principle', *International Social Science Journal*, vol. 55, no. 175, pp. 37–45.

Cernea, M. M. 2007. 'IRR: an operational risks reduction model for population resettlement', *Hydro Nepal: Journal of Water, Energy and Environment*, vol. 1, pp. 35–9.

Cernea, M. M. & Guggenheim, S. E. 1993. *Anthropological Approaches to Resettlement: Policy, Practice, and Theory*, Boulder, CO: Westview Press.

Cernea, M. M. & Mathur, H. M. (eds) 2008. *Can Compensation Prevent Impoverishment? Reforming Resettlement through Investments and Benefit-sharing*, New Delhi: Oxford University Press, 2008.

Chang, Y. 2018. 'The paradox of accountability system of grassroots cadres in China'. Paper presented to the 2018 International Conference on Educational Research, Economics, Management and Social Sciences (EREMS 2018), Changchun China, 24–25 December. <https://webofproceedings.org/proceedings_series/article/artId/5613.html#location>

Chen, S. & Ravallion, M. 2007. 'Absolute poverty measures for the developing world, 1981–2004', *Proceedings of the National Academy of Sciences*, vol. 104, no. 43, pp. 16757–62.

China's Poverty Alleviation Database 2015. *National Eight-Seven Anti-Poverty Plan*, Retrieved 20 November 2018 from <www.jianpincn.com/zgjpsjk/jpjxs/331769.html>.

Chuang, J. 2014. 'China's rural land politics: bureaucratic absorption and the muting of rightful resistance', *The China Quarterly*, vol. 219, pp. 649–69.

Clawson, M. 1978. 'Resettlement experience on nine selected resettlement projects', *Agricultural History*, vol. 52, no. 1, pp. 1–92.

Colson, E. 1971. *The social consequences of resettlement: the impact of the Kariba resettlement upon the Gwembe Tonga*, Kariba Studies IV, Manchester: The University of Manchester Press.

Dickinson, D. & Webber, M. 2007. 'Environmental resettlement and development, on the steppes of Inner Mongolia, PRC', *The Journal of Development Studies*, vol. 43, no. 3, pp. 537–61.

Elder, J. W. 1976. *Planned resettlement in Nepal's Terai: a social analysis of the Khajura*, Land Tenure Center Newsletter, University of Wisconsin.

Emerson, J. P. 1983. 'Urban school-leavers and unemployment in China', *The China Quarterly*, vol. 93, pp. 1–16.
Fan, C. C. 2006. 'China's eleventh five-year plan (2006–2010): from "getting rich first" to "common prosperity"', *Eurasian Geography and Economics*, vol. 47, no. 6, pp. 708–23.
Fan, S., Zhang, L. & Zhang, X. 2004. 'Reforms, investment, and poverty in rural China', *Economic Development and Cultural Change*, vol. 52, no. 2, pp. 395–421.
Feng, Z., Yang, Y., Zhang, Y., Zhang, P. & Li, Y. 2005. 'Grain-for-green policy and its impacts on grain supply in West China', *Land Use Policy*, vol. 22, no. 4, pp. 301–12.
Gebre, Y. D. 2002. 'Contextual determination of migration behaviours: the Ethiopian resettlement in light of conceptual constructs', *Journal of Refugee Studies*, vol. 15, no. 3, pp. 265–82.
Gebre, Y. 2003. 'Resettlement and the unnoticed losses: impoverishment disasters among the Gumz in Ethiopia', *Human Organization*, vol. 62, no. 1, pp. 50–61.
Hirsch, P. 1989. 'Settlement and resettlement on marginal land: a case study from Thailand', *Australian Geographer*, vol. 20, no. 1, pp. 80–9.
Howorth, C. & O'Keefe, P. 1999. 'Drought-induced resettlement: a case study from Burkina Faso', *Regional Environmental Change*, vol. 1, no. 1, pp. 15–23.
Jackson, S. & Sleigh, A. 2000. 'Resettlement for China's Three Gorges Dam: socio-economic impact and institutional tensions', *Communist and Post-Communist Studies*, vol. 33, no. 2, pp. 223–41.
Johnson, I. 2014. 'Move . . . or else: why is China's government forcing millions of farmers to move into cities?', *New York Times Upfront*, vol. 146, no. 11, pp. 10–17.
Karanth, K. K. 2007. 'Making resettlement work: the case of India's Bhadra wildlife sanctuary', *Biological Conservation*, vol. 139, nos. 3–4, pp. 315–24.
Kinsey, B. H. 1982. 'Forever gained: resettlement and land policy in the context of national development in Zimbabwe', *Africa*, vol. 52, no. 3, pp. 92–113.
Li, H. M., Waley, P. & Rees, P. 2001. 'Reservoir resettlement in China: past experience and the Three Gorges Dam', *Geographical Journal*, vol. 167, pp. 195–212.
Li, Y., Yin, H. & Liu, S. 2011. 'Relocation selection for poverty alleviation: factor analysis and GIS modeling', *Journal of Mountain Science*, vol. 8, no. 3, pp. 466–75.
Lin, G. C. 2009. 'Scaling-up regional development in globalizing China: local capital accumulation, land-centred politics, and reproduction of space', *Regional Studies*, vol. 43, no. 3, pp. 429–47.
Lin, G. C. & Yi, F. 2011. 'Urbanization of capital or capitalization on urban land? Land development and local public finance in urbanizing China', *Urban Geography*, vol. 32, no. 1, pp. 50–79.
Lin, Z. 2003. 'Voluntary resettlement in China: policy and outcomes of government-organised poverty reduction projects', Ph.D. thesis, Wageningen University, Wageningen, Netherlands.
Liu, W., Xu, J. & Li, J. 2018. 'The Influence of poverty alleviation resettlement on rural household livelihood vulnerability in the western mountainous areas, China', *Sustainability*, vol. 10, no. 8, p. 2793.
Liu, Y., Liu, J. & Zhou, Y. 2017. 'Spatio-temporal patterns of rural poverty in China and targeted poverty alleviation strategies', *Journal of Rural Studies*, vol. 52, pp. 66–75.
Lo, K. & Wang, M. 2018. 'How voluntary is poverty alleviation resettlement in China?', *Habitat International*, vol. 73, pp. 34–42.
Lo, K., Xue, L. & Wang, M. 2016. 'Spatial restructuring through poverty alleviation resettlement in rural China', *Journal of Rural Studies*, vol. 47, pp. 496–505.
Long, H., Li, Y., Liu, Y., Woods, M. & Zou, J. 2012. 'Accelerated restructuring in rural China fueled by "increasing vs. decreasing balance" land-use policy for dealing with hollowed villages', *Land Use Policy*, vol. 29, no. 1, pp. 11–22.
Manion, M. 1985. 'The cadre management system, post-Mao: the appointment, promotion, transfer and removal of party and state leaders', *The China Quarterly*, no. 102, p. 203.
McDonald, B. 2006. *From compensation to development : involuntary resettlement in the People's Republic of China*, PhD thesis, Melbourne University, Melbourne, Australia.
McDonald, B., Webber, M. & Yuefang, D. 2008. 'Involuntary resettlement as an opportunity for development: the case of urban resettlers of the Three Gorges Project, China', *Journal of Refugee Studies*, vol. 21, no. 1, pp. 82–102.
McDonald-Wilmsen, B. & Webber, M. 2010. 'Dams and displacement: raising the standards and broadening the research agenda', *Water Alternatives*, vol. 3, no. 2, pp. 142–61.
Merkle, R. 2003. 'Ningxia's third road to rural development: resettlement schemes as a last means to poverty reduction?', *The Journal of Peasant Studies*, vol. 30, nos. 3–4, pp. 160–91.

Ministry of Agriculture 2001. *China's Rural Poverty Alleviation and Development Plan (2001–2010)*, retrieved 20 November 2018 from <http://jiuban.moa.gov.cn/zwllm/zcfg/qtbmgz/200601/t20060123_540625.htm>.

Ministry of Land and Resources 2017. *Press Conference on Ministry of Land and Resource's support for Poverty Alleviation in Severe Poverty Regions*, retrieved 20 October 2018 from <www.mnr.gov.cn//dt/zb/2017/tpgj/>.

National Development and Reform Commission 2016. *The 13th 'Five Year' Plan of Resettlement for Poverty Alleviation*, viewed 20/11/2018, <www.gov.cn/xinwen/2016-10/31/5126509/files/86e8eb65acf44596bf21b2747aec6b48.pdf>.

Nolan, S., Unkovich, M., Yuying, S., Lingling, L. & Bellotti, W. 2008. 'Farming systems of the Loess Plateau, Gansu Province, China', *Agriculture, Ecosystems & Environment*, vol. 124, nos. 1–2, pp. 13–23.

O'Brien, K. J. & Li, L. 2017. 'Selective policy implementation in rural China', in K. E. Brødsgaard (ed.), *Critical Readings on Communist Party of China*, Leiden/Boston, MA: Brill, pp. 437–60.

Oliver-Smith, A. & Hansen, A. 1982. 'Introduction: involuntary migration and resettlement: causes and contexts', in A. Hansen & A. Oliver-Smith (eds), *Involuntary Migration and Resettlement: The Problems and Responses of Dislocated People*, Boulder, CO: Westview Press, pp. 1–9.

Oliver-Smith, A. 1991. 'Successes and failures in post-disaster resettlement', *Disasters*, vol. 15, no. 1, pp. 12–23.

Ong, L. H. 2014. 'State-led urbanization in China: skyscrapers, land revenue and "concentrated villages"', *China Quarterly*, no. 217, pp. 162–79.

Ostwald, M. & Chen, D. 2006. 'Land-use change: impacts of climate variations and policies among small-scale farmers in the Loess Plateau, China', *Land Use Policy*, vol. 23, no. 4, pp. 361–71.

Park, A. & Wang, S. 2010. 'Community-based development and poverty alleviation: an evaluation of China's poor village investment program', *Journal of Public Economics*, vol. 94, nos. 9–10, pp. 790–9.

PRC State Council (2011). 'White papers of the government: new progress in development oriented poverty reduction program for rural China', retrieved 27 April 2018 from <www.china.org.cn/government/whitepaper/node_7142125.htm>

Richardson, F. L. W., Jr. & Sheldon, R. C. 1948. 'Community resettlement in a depressed coal region III the problem of community change: from company town to planned resettlement', *Applied Anthropology*, vol. 7, no. 4, pp. 1–27.

Rogers, S. 2014. 'Betting on the strong: local government resource allocation in China's poverty counties', *Journal of Rural Studies*, vol. 36, pp. 197–206.

Rogers, S. & Wang, M. 2006. 'Environmental resettlement and social dis/re-articulation in Inner Mongolia, China', *Population and Environment*, vol. 28, no. 1, pp. 41–68.

Rogge, J. R. 1981. 'Africa's resettlement strategies', *International Migration Review*, vol. 15, nos. 1–2, pp. 195–212.

Ross, B. 2014. 'China's big move: why is the government forcing millions of farmers to move into cities?', *Junior Scholastic*, vol. 116, no. 12, pp. 6–9.

Schmidt-Soltau, K. & Brockington, D. 2007. 'Protected areas and resettlement: what scope for voluntary relocation?', *World Development*, vol. 35, no. 12, pp. 2182–2202.

Shi, H. & Shao, M. 2000. 'Soil and water loss from the Loess Plateau in China', *Journal of Arid Environments*, vol. 45, no. 1, pp. 9–20.

Tan, Y. 2008. 'Displacement and resettlement in the three gorges project: issues confronting women migrants', *Asian and Pacific Migration Journal*, vol. 17, no. 1, pp. 1–31.

Tang, Y., Mason, R. J. & Sun, P. 2012. 'Interest distribution in the process of coordination of urban and rural construction land in China', *Habitat International*, vol. 36, no. 3, pp. 388–95.

Taye, M. & Mberengwa, I. 2013. 'Resettlement: a way to achieve food security? A case study of Chewaka resettlement scheme, Oromia National Regional State, Ethiopia', *Journal of Sustainable Development in Africa*, vol. 15, no. 1, pp. 141–54.

Thapa, G. B. & Weber, K. E. 1988. 'Resettlement experiences and alternatives in Thailand', *Singapore Journal of Tropical Geography*, vol. 9, no. 2, pp. 141–50.

Tu, C. 2010. 'Withdrawing villages and enclosing land to pursue land finance in many provinces (Duosheng Checun Quandi Yi Zai Tudi Caizheng)', *The Beijing News (Xin Jing Bao)*, <http://news.sohu.com/20101102/n276943288_1.shtml>.

Wang, D. & Cai, F. 2009. 'Migration and poverty alleviation in China',in R. Murphy (ed.), *Labour Migration and Social Development in Contemporary China*, Oxford: Routledge, pp. 17–46.

Wang, Q. Y., Zhang, M. & Cheong, K. C. 2014. 'Stakeholder perspectives of China's land consolidation program: a case study of Dongnan Village, Shandong Province', *Habitat International*, vol. 43, pp. 172–80.

Wang, Z. 2018. 'Reassessing the performance evaluation system in the Xi Jinping era: changes and implications', *East Asia*, vol. 35, no. 1, pp. 59–77.

Webber, M. & McDonald, B. 2004. 'Involuntary resettlement, production and income: evidence from Xiaolangdi, PRC', *World Development*, vol. 32, pp. 673–90.

Whiting, S. H. 2017. 'The cadre evaluation system at the grass roots: the paradox of party rule', in K. E. Brødsgaard (ed.), *Critical Readings on Communist Party of China*, Leiden/Boston, MA: Brill, pp. 461–78.

Wilmsen, B. 2018. 'Is land-based resettlement still appropriate for rural people in China? A longitudinal study of displacement at the Three Gorges Dam', *Development and Change*, vol. 49, no. 1, pp. 170–98.

Wilmsen, B. & Wang, M. 2015. 'Voluntary and involuntary resettlement in China: a false dichotomy?', *Development in Practice*, vol. 25, no. 5, pp. 612–27.

Wilmsen, B., Webber, M. & Yuefang, D. 2011a. 'Involuntary rural resettlement: resources, strategies, and outcomes at the Three Gorges Dam, China', *Journal of Environment & Development*, no. 4, p. 355.

Wilmsen, B., Webber, M. & Yuefang, D. 2011b. 'Development for whom? Rural to urban resettlement at the Three Gorges Dam, China', *Asian Studies Review*, vol. 35, no. 1, pp. 21–42.

Witter, R. 2013. 'Elephant-induced displacement and the power of choice: moral narratives about resettlement in Mozambique's Limpopo National Park', *Conservation & Society*, vol. 11, no. 4, pp. 406–19.

Xue, L., Wang, M. Y. & Xue, T. 2013. '"Voluntary" poverty alleviation resettlement in China', *Development and Change*, vol. 44, no. 5, pp. 1159–80.

Yoshida, H., Agnes, R. D., Solle, M. & Jayadi, M. 2013. 'A long-term evaluation of families affected by the Bili-Bili Dam development resettlement project in South Sulawesi, Indonesia', *International Journal of Water Resources Development*, vol. 29, no. 1, pp. 50–8.

15

Dynamics of rural transformation and poverty and inequality in Asia and the Pacific[1]

Katsushi Imai, Raghav Gaiha and Fabrizio Bresciani

Introduction

While many countries in Asia – in particular, in East Asia and South Asia – have experienced rapid economic growth during the last decade, its rural areas have experienced structural transformation, induced by globalisation, industrialisation, and urbanisation. Despite economic growth, a large section of people in rural areas still suffer from abject poverty and malnutrition, implying that economic growth has bypassed many (IFAD, 2016).

The growth-inequality relationship is intricately associated with the relationship between structural transformation and inequality. If labour productivity in rural areas rises at a slower rate than in urban areas, the disparity between rural and urban areas will widen. Rural-to-urban migration, however, could have an offsetting effect if migration is temporary and benefits more rural households than before during the urbanisation process. While many of the rural regions have benefited from more integrated wholesale and retailing networks and supply chains (e.g. expansion of supermarket chains to rural areas, horticulture or contract farming with multinational firms, agricultural production and sales more integrated with urban regions and the developed world, and diversification of the rural non-farm sector), whether it decreases inequality is unclear and depends on geographical distributions of these networks. If structural transformation increases overall productivity and outputs in rural areas, the structural transformation would reduce income inequality at national levels. However, if for example backward regions (e.g. mountainous areas in north-east India or northern mountain regions in Vietnam) are left out of structural transformation, it is likely to increase inequality. One of the main objectives of this chapter is to understand better whether inequality and poverty have increased as the country experienced structural transformation, and the underlying reasons.

Of particular importance are farm and non-farm linkages and whether higher rural incomes are in part due to more diversified livelihoods and the emergence of high-value chains and the extent to which these have reduced rural–urban disparities and dampened migration. Apart from easier access to credit in order to strengthen farm/non-farm linkages, and smallholder participation in high-value chains, other major policy concerns relate to whether remittances – sent either from internal migrants from rural to urban areas or international migrants – could be allocated to more productive uses in rural areas, through higher risk-weighted returns, and whether returns could be enhanced in agriculture and rural non-farm activities while risks are reduced.

This study examines how the structural transformation in rural Asia and the Pacific dynamically influences poverty and inequality by applying econometric models to the cross-country panel data to capture the dynamic relationships among rural/agricultural transformations, growth/productivity, and poverty/inequality.

The rest of this chapter is organised as follows. After reviewing the concepts of agricultural transformation, we will discuss three different measures of agricultural transformation. We then outline an empirical model and discuss the results. The final section is devoted to concluding observations with policy implications.

Concepts and measurement of rural or agricultural transformation[2]

While 'rural transformation' (*RT*) is a broader concept than 'agricultural transformation' (*AT*) due to the non-negligible share of the non-agricultural sector, we will primarily focus on the transformation of the agricultural sector, drawing and building upon Dawe (2015). While Dawe discusses in detail the transformation of the agricultural sector of middle-income Asian countries,[3] he does not provide a clear definition of 'agricultural transformation'. Citing Reardon and Timmer (2014), Dawe first discusses 'the structural transformation of economies' and then argues that *AT* is one of the five key transitions as a result of sustained income, that is, (i) urbanisation, (ii) growth of the rural non-farm economy, (iii) dietary diversification, (iv) a revolution in supply chains and retailing, and (v) transformation of the agricultural sector. Consistent with the last transition, he argues that '[t]here are at least three key changes that might be expected to occur during the agricultural transition: *mechanization, increases in farm size*, and *crop/product diversification*' (Dawe, 2015, p. 5, emphasis added). Dawe then reviews some statistical evidence to show how mechanisation took place, farm size increased, and crop diversification took place in middle-income Asian countries, China, Indonesia, Malaysia, the Philippines, Thailand, and Vietnam. However, as Dawe did not define *AT* clearly, it is not clear what sort of transformation is envisaged. For instance, farm size did not increase uniquely in different areas of these countries (Dawe, 2015, Figures 14–15 on pp. 21–22), but it is not clear whether this heterogeneity implies *AT* took place in some parts of the country but not in other parts.[4] It is not clear either whether crop/product diversification took place consistently across these countries (e.g. Malaysia became more specialised in oil crops, as illustrated in Dawe (2015, Figure 17)).

In this chapter, we define *AT* as: fundamental changes in agricultural production and smallholders' livelihood in a developing economy as it is globalised, which are characterised as the three changes: (i) mechanisation and new agricultural technologies, (ii) changing cropping patterns with declining shares of grains and rising shares of non-grains, in particular, fruits, vegetables, dairy products, and meat, and (iii) new organisational forms (contract farming) as well as land and machinery rental markets that would enable smallholders to benefit from economies of scale (Barrett et al. 2012). While Dawe (2015) focuses mainly on the first and partly the second aspect, our study captures *AT* as a broader and more complex process covering the remaining aspects.

Measures of agricultural transformation (*AT*)

While *AT* should be defined from a broader perspective, it is not feasible to use a measure covering all the above aspects in *AT*. We will thus construct three measures, commercialisation index, agricultural openness and production diversification to capture salient features of *AT*.

Commercialisation index

To construct our commercialisation index, we use the production file (the value of agricultural production) (http://faostat.fao.org/site/613/default.aspx#ancor) as well as the price file (http://faostat.fao.org/site/703/default.aspx#ancor) in FAOSTAT to capture the extent to which processed agriculture and livestock products are produced in total agricultural and livestock production. The values are adjusted based on producer prices in the international US$ purchasing power parity (PPP) in 2004–2006. More specifically, the index is defined for all the years in the sample, 1960–2014, as follows.

$$\text{Commercialisation index} = (C + L)/(C + L + CP + LP)$$

where:

C = [Monetary value of production for aggregate crops processed (beer, cotton lint, cotton seed, margarine, molasses, oil (such as coconut oil, cottonseed oil, ground nut oil, linseed oil), palm kernels, sugar raw centrifugal, wine)]

L = [Monetary value of production for aggregate livestock processed (butter, cheese, milk, lard, yogurt)]

CP = [Monetary value of production for aggregate crop primary]

LP = [Monetary value of production for aggregate livestock primary]

This measure is based on the assumption that processed agricultural products are more likely to be commercialised. For instance, we assume that farmers producing maize oil are more commercialised than those producing maize. While this will be a reasonable assumption, it is noted that our measure captures only a part of the process where agricultural production of the country gets commercialised. This index reflects the overall structure of agricultural production in terms of whether the agricultural crops or livestock are sold as raw crops or processed crops. However, the index does not capture the increase in the production of, for instance, raw vegetables or plantation crops such as rubber, pineapple, bananas, which tend to be well commercialised. To partly overcome possible limitations of the index, we will use alternative indices.

We have examined whether our commercialisation index is correlated with the value added in food, beverage, and tobacco production. As expected, they are positively correlated with the correlation coefficient 0.37 (with p-value 0.0000) for the whole of Asia. Figure 15.1 shows the overall association between our commercialisation index and the value added in food, beverage, and tobacco production. At low levels of food production, our commercialisation index can be high or low with high variance, there is then a positive relationship at a slightly higher level of food production, and above a certain threshold, the commercialisation index becomes almost flat.

We have also examined the relationship between the commercialisation index and the index of mechanisation. Given that only crude measures are available from FAOSTAT, we have used the number of tractors per 100 km^2 of land. These are positively and significantly correlated with an overall correlation coefficient of 0.53 for the whole of Asia. Figure 15.2 confirms the positive correlation between the two variables.

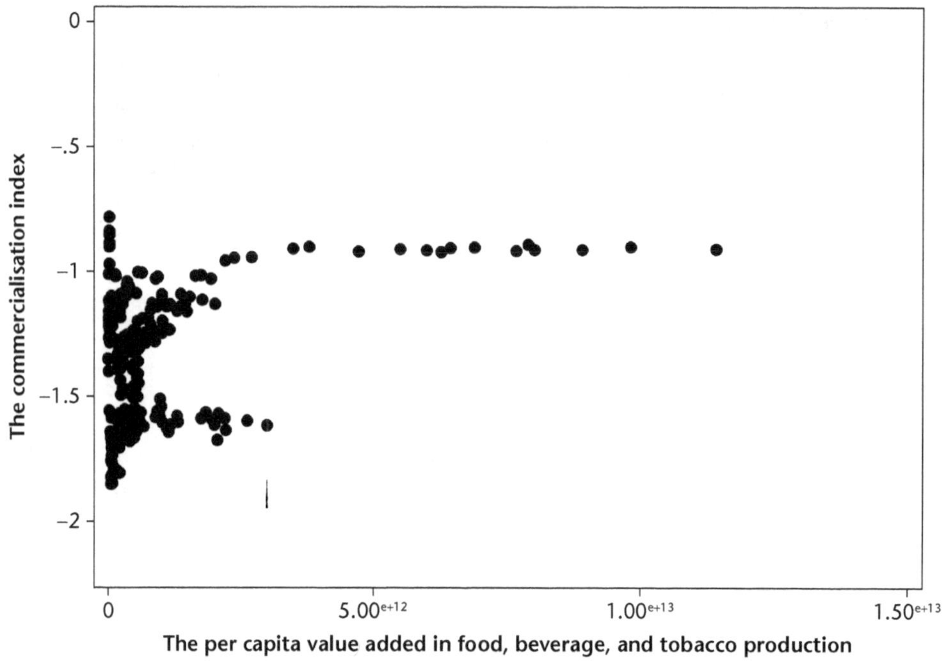

Figure 15.1 The relation between the commercialisation index and the per capita value added in food, beverage, and tobacco production.

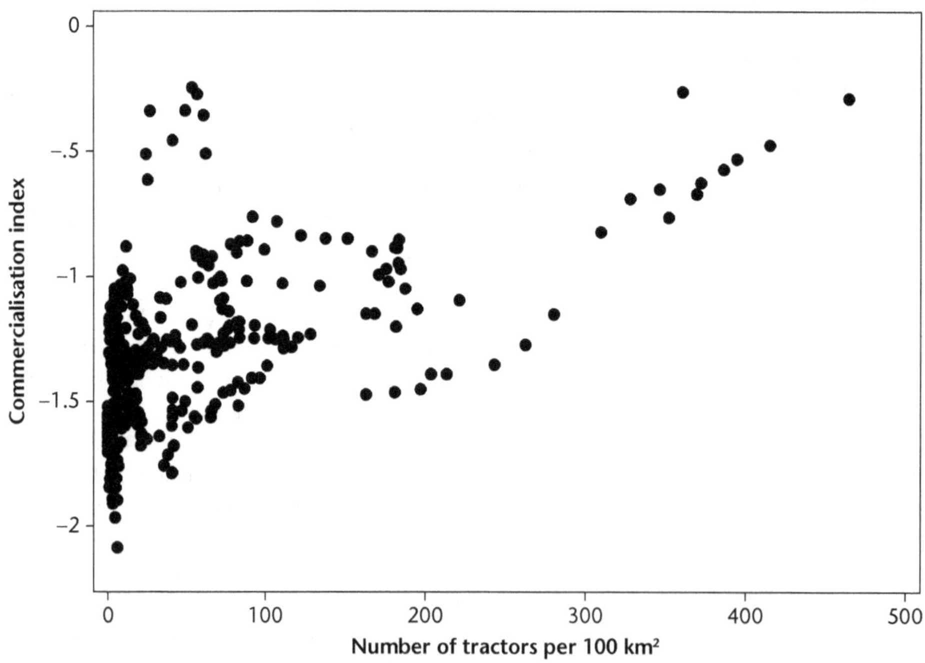

Figure 15.2 The relation between the commercialisation index and the number of tractors per 100 km^2.

Agricultural openness

Agricultural trade openness is simply defined as [aggregate agricultural export]/ [agricultural value added]. Agricultural export is based on the trade file of FAOSTAT (http://faostat.fao.org/site/535/default.aspx#ancor) (in the international US$ (PPP) in 2004–2006). The agricultural exports include food and non-food agricultural products. Here we do not include agricultural imports because the import of agricultural crops, while influenced by globalisation and influencing agricultural production systems to some extent, would mainly be demand-driven and does not reflect the transformation of the agricultural production systems we discussed earlier.[5] On the contrary, higher share of agricultural export tends to reflect more integration of agricultural production into the rest of the world and is deemed a more suitable proxy for the agricultural transformation. The agricultural value added is based on World Development Indicators (WDI) published and released in 2016. As the agricultural sector of the country gets structurally transformed (e.g. through mechanisation or contract farming), the relative competitiveness of the agricultural product improves and the agricultural openness index tends to be higher.

Product diversification

We propose to use the diversity index at the country level drawing upon Remans et al. (2014) who used an index called 'Shannon entropy diversity metric' to capture the production diversity at the country level using FAOSTAT. The index can be defined as:

$$H' = -\sum_{i=1}^{R} p_i \ln p_i$$

where R is the number of agricultural products and p_i is the share of production for the item i, available from FAOSTAT. The production share, p_i is defined in terms of the monetary value at a local price for each product, i. If the country produces more agricultural products, including processed and unprocessed crops and the monetary values of products are more evenly divided among different items, the diversity index, H', takes a larger value. On the contrary, if the country produces a smaller number of agricultural products and the monetary value of one or two specific products is large, H' is smaller. Figure 15.3 indicates that our product diversification index is highly correlated with the share of non-cereal production. The correlation coefficient for all the 21 sample countries in Asia is 0.41 – except the top end (above 90%) of non-cereal share where these two variables are negatively correlated for Malaysia. The correlation is stronger for the countries in South Asia with the correlation coefficient 0.74 (p-value 0.0000) and weaker for East and South East Asia with the correlation coefficient 0.22 (p-value 0.0003).

Data, empirical models and results

Data

Our empirical analysis is based mostly on FAOSTAT (http://faostat.fao.org/), World Development Indicators (WDI) 2016 (http://data.worldbank.org/data-catalog/world-development-indicators), the World Bank poverty database (PovCalNet, http://iresearch.worldbank.org/PovcalNet/), World Bank World Governance Indicators (WGI) (http://data.worldbank.org/data-catalog/worldwide-governance-indicators), and Quality of Government Dataset (http://qog.pol.gu.se/data). The agricultural TFP estimates are taken from Fuglie (2012, 2015). Table 15.1 summarises the main variables we will use in the econometric estimations.

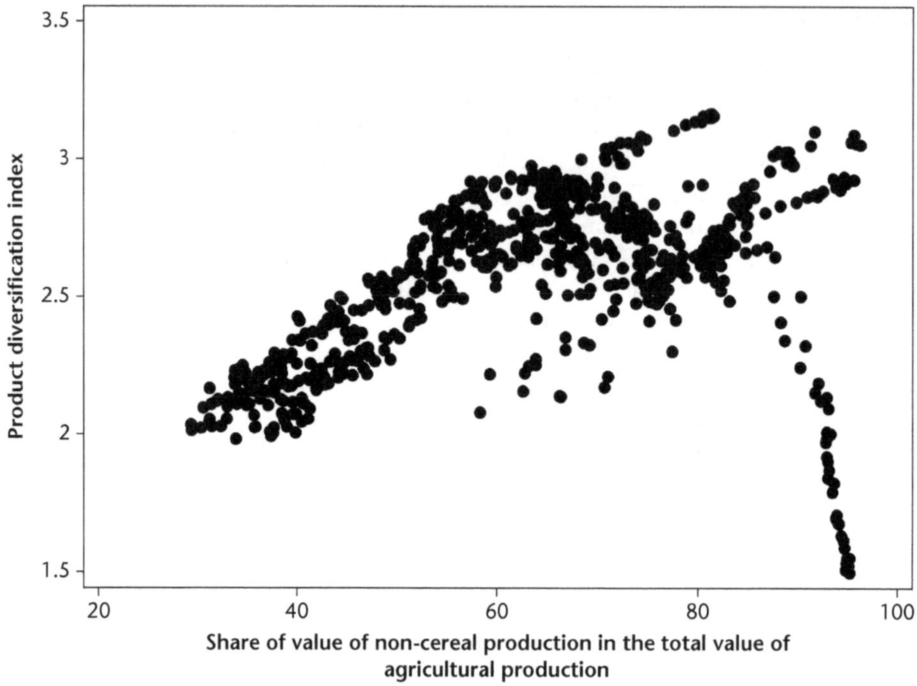

Figure 15.3 The relation between the product diversification index and the share of value of non-cereal production in the total value of agricultural production.

A few points are noted in Table 15.1. First, we will use both old and new World Bank poverty estimates. The first set of poverty estimates is based on the international poverty lines, US$1.25 and US$2.00 adjusted by 2005 PPP (Ravallion et al., 2009). The second set of poverty estimates are the revised World Bank estimates which were released in 2016 and based on US$1.90 and US$3.10 adjusted by 2011 PPP (World Bank, 2016). While the latter covers more countries and more years, our study primarily focuses on the former because these have been more widely used in the literature and have served as the basis for specification of the first of the Millennium Development Goals (MDGs) as well as Sustainable Development Goals (SDGs). We will also use rural poverty estimates which the Strategy and Knowledge Department of the International Fund for Agricultural Development obtained from the World Bank (see our earlier study (Imai et al., 2014) which used the same estimates). These were computed by using World Bank Living Standard Measurement Survey (LSMS) data. Second, we have used variables capturing institutional qualities, political stability, and state fragility. Institutional qualities and political stability are based on World Governance Indicators (WGI) which have been widely used in the literature. The degree of fragility is captured by 'fragility index' proxied by the rating of macroeconomic management and coping with fragility (1 = low to 6 = high). High value implies low fragility. We have also tried conflict indices, but prefer the 'fragility index' as the former does not cover many countries. Third, we have used the annual growth rates of agricultural and non-agricultural real value added per capita drawing upon WDI. It is noted here that non-agricultural value added is defined as the difference between national GDP and agricultural value added and this is admittedly a rough approximation.

Due to data limitations, the panel dataset covers only 21 Asian and Pacific countries,[6] namely, Bangladesh, Bhutan, Cambodia, China, Fiji, India, Indonesia, Kazakhstan, Lao PDR, Malaysia,

Table 15.1 Descriptive statistics of variables

Variable	*Definition (data source)*	*Obs.*	*Mean*	*Std. Dev.*	*Min.*	*Max.*
Dependent variables						
dlogagrivapc	Annual growth of agricultural value added per capita (WDI)	748	0.008	0.064	–0.692	0.341
logagTFP	Agricultural TFP index (log) based on FAOSTAT (Fuglie, 2012 and 2015)[a]	1,272	4.606	0.214	3.784	5.323
dlogagTFP	Growth rate of agricultural TFP	1,272	0.0092	0.035	–0.309	0.324
povertyhc200	Log of poverty headcount ratio based on US$2.00 (PPP at 2005) (WDI)	153	3.695	1.064	–2.813	4.583
povertyhc200_raw	Poverty headcount ratio based on US$1.25 (PPP in 2005) (WDI)	153	53.773	26.981	0.060	97.810
povertyhc190	Log of poverty headcount ratio based on US$1.90 (PPP at 2011) (WDI)	1,155	0.611	1.634	0.000	5.541
Poverty190_raw	Poverty headcount ratio based on US$1.90 (PPP in 2011) (WDI)	1,155	20.584	57.079	1.000	255.000
povertyhc310	Log of poverty headcount ratio based on US$3.10 (PPP at 2011) (WDI)	1,155	0.670	1.758	0.000	5.765
povertyhc310_raw	Poverty headcount ratio based on US$3.10 (PPP in 2011) (WDI)	1,155	27.392	74.400	1.000	319.000
Gini	Gini coefficient (in log)	191	3.594	0.156	3.248	4.113
Gini_raw	Gini coefficient (in raw value)	191	36.811	5.824	25.740	61.100
logweight_age	Log of malnutrition prevalence, weight for age (% of children under 5)	148	3.268	0.677	1.224	4.209
weight_age	Malnutrition prevalence, weight for age (% of children under 5)	126	31.248	16.013	3.400	67.300
epov_h_rur	Extreme rural poverty headcount ratio (% of rural population under $1.25 a day) (SKD, IFAD)	110	24.579	21.794	0.000	83.500
epov_gap_rur	Extreme rural poverty gap (% of rural population under $1.25 a day) (SKD, IFAD)	110	7.067	8.408	0.000	57.600
epov_gap2_rur	Extreme rural squared poverty gap (% of rural population under $1.25 a day) (SKD, IFAD)	110	2.994	5.116	0.000	45.560
gini_rur	Gini coefficient in rural areas (SKD, IFAD)	110	32.669	5.886	23.850	63.960
mpov_h_rur	Moderate rural poverty headcount (% of rural population under $2 a day) (SKD, IFAD)	110	47.900	30.966	0.190	93.040
mpov_gap_rur	Moderate rural poverty gap (% of rural population under $2 a day) (SKD, IFAD)	110	18.367	14.839	0.010	69.030
mpov_gap2_rur	Moderate rural squared poverty gap (% of rural population under $2 a day) (SKD, IFAD)	110	9.163	9.031	0.000	57.020

(continued)

Table 15.1 (continued)

Variable	*Definition (data source)*	*Obs.*	*Mean*	*Std. Dev.*	*Min.*	*Max.*
epov_h_urb	Extreme urban poverty headcount (% of urban population under $1.25 a day) (SKD, IFAD)	109	14.586	15.394	0.000	62.010
epov_gap_urb	Extreme urban poverty gap (% of urban population under $1.25 a day) (SKD, IFAD)	108	4.218	6.623	0.000	51.970
epov_gap2_urb	Extreme urban squared poverty gap (% of urban population under $1.25 a day) (SKD, IFAD)	107	1.878	4.906	0.000	47.080
gini_urb	Gini coefficient in urban areas	107	35.963	6.102	24.600	71.700
mpov_h_urb	Moderate urban poverty headcount (% of urban population under $2 a day)	107	31.949	25.782	0.030	86.640
mpov_gap_urb	Moderate urban poverty gap (% of urban population under $2 a day)	106	11.229	11.266	0.000	57.410
mpov_gap2_urb	Moderate urban squared poverty gap (% of urban population under $2 a day)	106	5.478	7.114	0.000	51.880
epov_h_rur	Extreme rural poverty headcount (% of rural population under $1.25 a day)	110	24.579	21.794	0.000	83.500
Explanatory variables						
Commercialisation index	Commercialisation index[b] (FAOSTAT)	861	−1.165	0.411	−2.202	−0.245
agopenness	[aggregate agricultural export]/ [agricultural value added] (FAOSTAT)	639	−8.682	2.526	−13.535	5.107
productdiversity	Production diversity index[c] (FAOSTAT)	861	0.943	0.128	0.403	1.152
Institution	Aggregate institutional quality (average of voice and accountability, government effectiveness, regulatory quality, rule of law, and control of corruption)	395	−0.524	0.464	−1.660	0.940
Political stability	Political stability and absence of violence (WGI)	388	−0.545	0.857	−2.810	1.330
Land	Land area is a country's total area (WDI)	1,155	3.815	1.166	0.000	5.118
Population_density	Population density (people per sq. km of land area)	1,155	6.302	1.641	0.000	7.636
Fragility index	CPIA rating of macroeconomic management and coping with fragility (1 = low to 6 = high)	1,176	7.618	1.193	1.000	8.000
Openness	Imports and exports (value added)/GDP (WDI)	1,155	4.543	2.846	0.000	7.146
Ethnic fractionalisation	Ethnic fractionalisation index[d]	697	−1.059	0.706	−3.091	−0.308
lab_with_secondary	Labour force with secondary education	1,155	0.150	0.706	0.000	5.209
Riskinland	The degree to which a country is landlocked	455	−1.856	1.722	−4.605	0.000

primary_yrs	Average years of schooling at primary school	1,155	3.700	1.522	1.000	7.000
second_years	Average years of schooling at secondary school	1,155	3.740	1.502	1.000	6.000
populati~_14	Population below 14 years old	1,155	1495.045	405.122	205.000	2116.000
populati~65_	Population above 14 years old	1,155	1225.122	366.004	2.000	2080.000
SA	Whether in South Asia	1,155	0.286	0.452	0.000	1.000
EAP	Whether in East Asia and Pacific	1,155	0.524	0.500	0.000	1.000
LOWI	Whether in low-income countries	588	0.413	0.493	0.000	1.000
LOWERMI	Whether in lower middle-income countries	588	0.412	0.493	0.000	1.000
UPPERMI	Whether in upper middle-income countries	588	0.094	0.291	0.000	1.000
ICLASS	Income class (0 for low-income countries; 1 for lower middle-income countries; 2 for upper middle-income countries)	540	0.652	0.657	0.000	2.000
Gnipcadj	Adjusted GNI per capita based on World Atlas Method (adjusting for local and world price and exchange rate fluctuations)	827	1189.746	1596.007	50.000	11850.000
Logagriemp	Log of agricultural employment	192	3.057	0.732	0.182	4.388
gA	Annual growth rate of agricultural output	119	−0.086	0.721	−3.367	3.217
Logmanuemp	Log of manufacturing employment	209	2.795	0.365	0.993	3.384
gN	Annual growth rate of non-agricultural output	155	0.018	0.116	−0.817	0.615
Logseremp	Annual growth rate of service output	209	3.443	0.325	2.573	4.009
gS	Annual growth rate of service output	155	0.016	0.064	−0.274	0.322

Notes:

a Presents agricultural TFP indexes (based year 1992 = 100) over 1961–2012 using primarily FAO data, supplemented in some cases by national statistics. The output is FAO gross agricultural output (GAO) smoothed using the Hodrick-Prescott Filter (lambda = 6.25). Input growth is the weighted-average growth in the quality-adjusted land, labour, machinery power, livestock capital, synthetic NPK fertilisers, and animal feed, where weights are input (factor) cost shares. Agricultural TFP indexes are estimates by country and for groups of countries aggregated by geographic region and income class (Fuglie, 2012 and 2015).

b This is defined as {[Aggregate Crops Processed (beer, cotton lint, cottonseed, margarine, molasses, oil (such as coconut oil, cottonseed oil, ground nut oil, linseed oil), palm kernels, sugar raw centrifugal, wine)] + [Aggregate livestock processed (butter, cheese, milk, lard, yogurt)]}/{[Aggregate Crops Processed (same as above)] +[Aggregate livestock processed (same as above)] + [(Raw) Crops] + [Aggregate Livestock Primary] + [Aggregate Livestock, Primary (eggs, skins, wool)]}

c The index can be defined as $H' = \sum_{i=1}^{R} p_i \ln p_i$, where R is the number of items of agricultural products and p_i is the share of production for item i, available from FAOSTAT.

d Ethnic fractionalisation index reflects the probability that two randomly selected people from a given country will not belong to the same ethnolinguistic group. The higher the number, the more fractionalised the society. The definition of ethnicity involves a combination of racial and linguistic characteristics. The result is a higher degree of fractionalisation than the commonly used ELF-index (see el_elf60) in, for example, Latin America, where people of many races speak the same language.

Federated States of Micronesia, Nepal, Pakistan, Papua New Guinea, the Philippines, Sri Lanka, Tajikistan, Thailand, Timor-Leste, Turkmenistan, and Vietnam for 1960–2014. However, the data availability varies considerably depending on the choice of variables. As a result, only a subset of the data is used for the main econometric analyses (e.g. 15–19 countries).[7]

An empirical model

The main purpose of our empirical model is to assess the effect of *AT* on poverty and inequality. To do so, we take a two-stage approach. In the first stage, we estimate the effect of *AT* on a measure of agricultural production or agricultural productivity by treating the former as endogenous. In the second stage, we estimate the effect of agricultural production on poverty and inequality. We have used the dynamic panel model, or the linear dynamic panel model based on System GMM (Blundell and Bond, 1998). Given a small n, a number of samples in the cross-sectional component, and a relatively small sample size, a finite sample correction has been made for the variance by using the robust estimator when two-step estimations are feasible (Windmeijer, 2005). In the second stage, a measure of poverty or inequality, disaggregated into rural and urban areas, is estimated by the agricultural production or productivity predicted in the first stage.[8]

Results

We will first discuss whether *AT* influenced agricultural output.[9] First, the commercialisation index positively increases agricultural value added per capita with a year's lag after taking account of the reverse causality from the latter to the former. If the share of processed agricultural and livestock products in the total agricultural and livestock products increases by 1%, agricultural value added per capita tends to increase by 0.47% in the next year, other things being equal. Given the limitation of the index as a proxy for commercialisation, we can confirm that the commercialisation – in terms of the higher share of processed crops – significantly increases agricultural production. The commercialisation in terms of the higher share of processed crops also accelerates the growth of agricultural value added per capita with a time lag after taking account of the reverse causality. Second, agricultural openness does not significantly increase agricultural production or its growth rate after taking account of the reverse causality. Third, product diversity tends to increase the level of agricultural production as well as its growth rate after taking account of the reverse causality. Overall, the *AT* would increase agricultural value added per capita with some lag.

As an extension, we have examined the effects of *AT* on TFP. The results are broadly consistent with those for agricultural value added per capita. First, a commercialisation index positively influences TFP with the first lag. Second, the effects of agricultural openness on TFP are ambiguous. Third, increased product diversity tends to improve TFP with the first lag. Turning to other variables, a higher population density tends to dampen both TFP and its growth rate, a fragility index is negatively and significantly associated with TFP, and education in terms of labour force with secondary education being positively correlated with TFP growth.

Based on the estimates of agricultural value added and agricultural productivity as a function of *AT*, we have examined the effect of agricultural transformation indices (namely, the commercialisation index and the product diversity index) on poverty or inequality. In Table 15.2 we report the results on rural and urban poverty for the international poverty thresholds, US$1.25 and US$2.00 (based on PPP in 2005). Here the predicted value of log agricultural value added is based on the case in which the commercialisation index is used as a main explanatory variable. Panel A shows the results for rural poverty, Panel B for urban poverty. Panel A of Table 15.2 indicates that as the agricultural sector grows, not only will the share of poor people in rural areas be reduced, but also

Table 15.2 Effect of predicted agricultural TFP on poverty

Panel A: Rural poverty

Variables	*Case 1*	*Case 2*	*Case 3*	*Case 4*	*Case 5*	*Case 6*
	Extreme rural poverty	*Extreme rural poverty*	*Extreme rural poverty*	*Moderate rural poverty*	*Moderate rural poverty*	*Moderate rural poverty*
Poverty threshold	US$1.25	US$1.25	US$1.25	US$2.00	US$2.00	US$2.00
Definition	P0 (headcount)	P1 (gap)	P2 gap squared	P0 (headcount)	P1 (gap)	P2 gap squared
Model	FE	FE	FE	FE	FE	FE
Variables						
plogagrivapc	**–4.787*****	**–5.544*****	**–5.370*****	**–2.929*****	**–3.877*****	**–4.527*****
Predicted log agricultural value added per capita	**(0.926)**	**(1.014)**	**(1.150)**	**(0.619)**	**(0.756)**	**(0.863)**
Observations	80	80	78	80	80	80
R-squared	0.5	0.56	0.565	0.412	0.497	0.53
Number of code1	17	17	17	17	17	17
Hausman test for selecting Random Effects (RE) or Fixed Effects (FE) model	FE	FE	FE	FE	FE	FE

Note: Standard errors in parentheses *** $p<0.01$, ** $p<0.05$, * $p<0.1$.

Panel B: Urban poverty

Variables	*Case 1*	*Case 2*	*Case 3*	*Case 4*	*Case 5*	*Case 6*
	Extreme urban poverty	*Extreme urban poverty*	*Extreme urban poverty*	*Moderate urban poverty*	*Moderate urban poverty*	*Moderate urban poverty*
Poverty threshold	US$1.25	US$1.25	US$1.25	US$2.00	US$2.00	US$2.00
Definition	P0 (headcount)	P1 (gap)	P2 gap squared	P0 (headcount)	P1 (gap)	P2 gap squared
Model	FE	FE	FE	FE	FE	FE
Variables						
plogagrivapc	**–4.019*****	**–4.979*****	**–4.032*****	**–3.856*****	**–4.532*****	**–5.012*****
	(10.44)	**(1.184)**	**(1.211)**	**(0.730)**	**(0.878)**	**(0.995)**
Observations	79	77	74	77	76	76
R-squared	0.608	0.561	0.575	0.621	0.62	0.6
Number of code1	17	17	17	17	17	17
Hausman test for selecting Random Effects (RE) or Fixed Effects (FE) model	FE	FE	FE	FE	FE	FE

the severity of poverty and inequality among the rural poor will be reduced. This study is the first, to our knowledge, to show that agricultural growth has reduced poverty in rural areas, after taking into account the endogeneity of agricultural value added per capita, and using a cross-country panel data with a dynamic model. For instance, if the agricultural value added per capita increases by 1%, extreme poverty headcount ratio is reduced by 2.59% points. We can infer the relative magnitude of the effect of *AT* on rural poverty by combining the first- and the second-stage results. If the ratio of commercialised output to the total agricultural output increases by 1%, agricultural value added per capita will increase by 0.47% next year, and this will correspond to 1.22% reduction in poverty (= 2.59*0.47) based on the mean value of rural poverty headcount (e.g. 20% to 19.76% = 20% − 20*1.22%) next year, other things being equal (Panel A of Table 15.2 and Case 1 of Panel A of Table 15.2). Poverty gap, as well as its square at the poverty threshold US$1.25 are significantly reduced as agricultural value added per capita increases (Cases 2 and 3).[10] The relative magnitudes are small, but the poverty headcount, the depth of poverty, and the severity of poverty at the US$2.00 poverty line have also been significantly reduced.

In Panel B of Table 15.2, we have examined the effect of agricultural value added per capita on urban poverty based on the commercialisation index. Panel B shows that, as the agricultural value added per capita increases, the headcount (only at the poverty line of US$2.00, not US$1.25), the poverty depth, and the severity of poverty (at both US$1.25 and US$2.00) have been significantly reduced. It is particularly noted that the magnitude of reduction is larger for urban poverty than for rural poverty, implying a substantially larger indirect effect of *AT* on urban poverty, for example, as a positive effect of rural-to-urban migration (e.g. through finding a job in the urban non-farm sector with real wages much higher than in rural areas) exceeds its negative effect (e.g. expanding urban slums with low-paying jobs as a result of migration).

That is, agricultural growth also reduces urban poverty in terms of the share of poor people based on the headcount index (P0). It is also found that agricultural growth decreases the depth of urban poverty which is based on the poverty gap index (P1) and inequality among the urban poor based on the squared poverty gap index (p2), a weighted sum of poverty gaps where the weights are the proportionate poverty gaps themselves. For instance, a 1% increase in agricultural value added is associated with a 2.73% decrease in the moderate poverty headcount ratio (based on Case 5 of Panel B). A positive externality of agricultural growth is an expansion of processing firms in urban areas and thereby employment which then reduces poverty.

In the regression based on the product diversity index *H'*, we find similar results with the coefficient estimate statistically significant in all the cases for both rural and urban poverty. That is, if the agricultural production is more diverse, poverty in both rural and urban areas is significantly reduced.[11]

We have estimated the effects of (predicted) agricultural TFP on rural and urban poverty and the overall results remain broadly unchanged. We have found that improvement in agricultural TFP significantly reduces rural poverty. For instance, a 1% improvement in TFP tends to decrease rural poverty headcount ratio based on US$1.25 a day by 4.78%, keeping other factors constant. If we combine the first-stage and the second-stage results, we can infer that a 1% increase in commercialisation index TFP tends to reduce rural poverty by 0.54%. This appears to be quite large in terms of the absolute magnitude of the effect of increase in TFP on poverty. We have found that a rise in agricultural TFP significantly reduces urban poverty as well. A 1% increase in TFP tends to decrease the urban headcount ratio based on US$1.25 a day by 4.02%, keeping other factors constant. If we combine the first- and second-stage results, we can infer that a 1% improvement in commercialisation index tends to reduce rural poverty by 0.45%.[12]

We have also examined the effect of (predicted) agricultural value added per capita on poverty and child malnutrition in Table 15.3 where in the first stage the commercialisation index is used as a main explanatory variable.[13] The poverty-reducing effect of agricultural value added

Table 15.3 Effect of predicted agricultural value added per capita on poverty and child malnutrition

	Case 1	*Case 2*	*Case 3*	*Case 4*	*Case 5*	*Case 6*
	Poverty headcount	*Poverty headcount*	*Poverty headcount*	*Poverty headcount*	*log child underweight*	*log child underweight*
	US$1.25	US$1.25	US$2.00	US$2.00		
	Based on Case 2 of Table 15.2	Based on Case 5 of Table 15.2	Based on Case 2 of Table 15.2	Based on Case 5 of Table 15.2	Based on Case 2 of Table 15.2	Based on Case 5 of Table 15.2
Variables	Trans index	Product diversity	Trans index	Product diversity	Trans index	Product diversity
Plogagrivapc	**–0.497**	**–0.347**	**–0.897****	**–0.803***	**–0.888*****	**–0.653*****
	(0.825)	**(0.885)**	**(0.402)**	**(0.435)**	**(0.155)**	**(0.171)**
Observations	142	136	142	136	143	126
R-squared	0.248	0.241	0.324	0.305	0.743	0.77
Number of code1	18	15	18	15	18	15
Hausman test for selecting Random Effects (RE) or Fixed Effects (FE) model	FE	FE	FE	FE	FE	FE

Note: Standard errors in parentheses *** p<0.01, ** p<0.05, * p<0.1.

per capita is statistically significant for moderate poverty but not for extreme poverty. Here, if agriculture is transformed and this transformation leads to agricultural growth, then the status of child nutritional conditions will improve, for instance, because the household has more agricultural products and food availability will improve, or additional income due to the agricultural growth can be used for food consumption for children.

Our results suggest that agricultural growth tends to reduce child underweight prevalence. That is, a 1% growth in agricultural value added per capita tends to reduce child underweight prevalence by 0.65% to 0.89%. If the first- and second-stage results are combined, we can infer that agricultural growth reduces child underweight prevalence by 0.07% to 0.10%. It is noted that this is an annual estimate and the commercialisation will have a substantial impact on child nutrition over time.[14]

Finally, we have examined the relationship between agricultural value added per capita and inequality by replacing poverty in the second stage by inequality. We have used log of Gini coefficients for rural areas (called 'rural Gini') and for urban areas (called 'urban Gini'). However, in none of the cases is (predicted) log of agricultural value added per capita statistically significant in explaining variation in inequality. This could be due to either the fact that *AT* or agricultural growth does not reduce inequality or a non-linear relationship between rural Gini and agricultural value added per capita. So we examined whether there is any non-linear relationship between agricultural value added per capita and its square and found that statistically significant coefficients are found only for rural Gini when we restrict the sample to low-income countries only. We have found that as the agricultural sector grows, inequality of low-income countries tends to fall, but if it grows beyond a certain point, inequality tends to increase. So the inequality-reducing effect of the agricultural growth (induced by commercialisation) is observed only at the initial stage of development. This may be due to the stronger poverty-reducing effect at the lower poverty threshold than at the higher poverty threshold for rural areas.

Concluding remarks

This chapter has analysed the dynamics of transformation of agriculture in rural Asia and the Pacific with a focus on its effect on poverty, based on the up-to-date country panel dataset for the region. We have examined the effects of *AT* on various measures of poverty and inequality, where the dynamic effect of *AT* on agricultural growth is modelled by a dynamic panel model and then poverty is estimated by the predicted agricultural value added per capita using the static panel model. *AT* is defined by three different indices, namely, agricultural openness index, commercialisation index to capture the share of processed agricultural and livestock production in the total production, and the agricultural production diversity index based on how agricultural production is diversified into different products. Our study is important because, as far as we know, this is the first study to quantify the *AT* – albeit in a limited manner – and evaluate its effect on agricultural output, growth, and productivity in the Asian and Pacific context. We have also assessed the effect of these terms on rural and urban poverty and on inequality in Asia using cross-country panel data.

Transformation of the agricultural sector in terms of commercialisation and product diversity has dynamically increased agricultural value added per capita and consequently reduced both rural and urban poverty significantly. Our results show that even a small change in the process of *AT*, such as a 1% increase in commercialisation index or in product diversity index, reduces both rural and urban poverty substantially. However, the effect of agricultural openness has not significantly impacted on agricultural growth.[15] Presumably, this is linked to slow adaptation to growing competitiveness of integrated markets. The effect of *AT* in reducing child malnutrition has also been observed, while inequality in rural areas is reduced only at the initial stage of development of agriculture for low-income countries. As an extension, we have examined the effect of *AT* on TFP. Our analysis confirmed that *AT*, in terms of commercialisation and product diversification, has promoted TFP with lags. This reinforces the positive relationship between agricultural value added and *AT*. We have also found that the predicted TFP significantly reduced rural and urban poverty.[16]

Some policy implications are delineated below. First, there is a case for promoting synergy between public and private investment in rural areas. A priority is to strengthen rural infrastructure. Although our analysis does not focus on smallholders, their inclusion in the transformation process through easier access to credit, land, and output markets, and upgradation of product quality could lead to significantly larger poverty and inequality reduction. As prospects of absorption of growing rural labour force in manufacturing and services and other activities are limited, it is important for policymakers to create enough jobs in rural areas (e.g. through expanding Rural National Employment Guarantee Schemes in remote areas). Some of the preceding proposals would help create more employment in rural areas, raise wage rates and dampen rural–urban migration. Land rental markets would facilitate the redistribution of land in favour of more efficient small farmers and help consolidation of small farms into more viable units. Finally, in view of the demographic transition, expansion of education and training facilities in rural areas would help reap the dividend flowing from a larger workforce.

Notes

1 This study is funded by Asia and the Pacific Division (APR), IFAD (International Fund for Agricultural Development). The authors are grateful for valuable comments from one internal reviewer at IFAD, Kostas Stamoulis (FAO), Andrea Cattaneo (FAO), and other participants in 'Expert Consultation on Focusing Agricultural and Rural Development Research and Investment on Achieving SDGs 1 and 2: A joint initiative of FAO, IFAD, CGIAR, and the World Bank: In partnership with the EU' in Rome in January 2017. The second author acknowledges valuable advice from David Bloom. The authors also thank Bilal Malaeb for his advice on data processing and econometric estimations. The opinions expressed in this publication are those of the authors and do not necessarily represent those of IFAD.
2 This sub-section draws upon Imai (2017) where the analysis has been carried out for all developing countries using a similar model.
3 It is taking place in low-income countries too, but not quite as visibly.
4 The overall trend in Asia has been that of declining farm size. For example, in Bangladesh, average farm size declined drastically from 1.4 ha in 1976/77 to 0.3 ha in 2005. Similarly, India, Pakistan, and the Philippines also experienced significant declines in average farm size over time (Thapa, 2016).
5 We could construct the share of the input import in the input consumption, but the data on the fertiliser and pesticides import are available only after 2002 from FAOSTAT and unsuitable for the present purpose.
6 These 21 countries cover only 43% of the total 48 countries in terms of country numbers, but 84% of the population of all the countries in the region.
7 We have used the data based on the maximum number of sample countries for each specification. However, when we restrict our sample to 15 countries in all the cases, the coefficient estimates of key explanatory variables are more or less the same.
8 See Imai (2017) for technical details of the model.
9 Tables detailing the results will be provided by the first author on request.
10 It is noted that the Foster-Greer-Thorbecke (1984) (FGT) class of poverty measures are used in our study. The headcount index (P0) measures the proportion of the population that is poor (Haughton and Khandker, 2009, p. 67). The poverty gap index (P1) measures the extent to which individuals fall below the poverty line as a proportion of the poverty line, while the squared poverty gap index (P2) averages the squares of the poverty gaps relative to the poverty line (ibid., p. 67).
11 The results will be provided on request.
12 The results will be provided on request.
13 The results are broadly similar if they are based on the product diversity index as a main covariate.

14 This is of course subject to the caveat that intra-household distribution of income and food is often not equitable (Dreze and Sen, 1995).

15 One possibility is that the agricultural openness effect is manifested through agricultural commercialisation and product diversity.

16 Barrett et al. (2017) argues that ending extreme poverty will require structural change in agriculture sectors in sub-Saharan Africa. Future research should extend our research to all developing countries.

References

Barrett, C. B., Bachke, M. E., Bellemare, M. F., Michelson, H. C. and Narayanan, S. (2012). Smallholder participation in contract farming: comparative evidence from five countries. *World Development*, 40(4), pp. 715–730.

Barrett, C. B., Christiaensen, L., Sheahan, M. and Shimeles, A. (2017). 'On the structural transformation of rural Africa', Policy Research Working Paper 7938, The World Bank, Washington DC.

Blundell, R. and Bond, S. (1998). Initial conditions and moment restrictions in dynamic panel data models. *Journal of Econometrics* 87, pp. 115–143.

Dawe, D. (2015). Agricultural transformation of middle-income Asian economies: diversification, farm size and mechanization. *Korea*, 6(7.5), pp. 1–6.

Dreze, J. and Sen, A. K. (1995). *India Economic Development and Social Opportunity*. Oxford University Press, New Delhi.

Foster, J., Greer, J. and Thorbecke, E. (1984). A class of decomposable poverty measures. *Econometrica*, 32(3), pp. 761–766.

Fuglie, K. O. (2012). 'Productivity Growth and Technology Capital in the Global Agricultural Economy.' In: Fuglie, K., Wang, S. L. and Ball, V. E. (eds.) *Productivity Growth in Agriculture: An International Perspective*. CAB International, Wallingford, UK, pp. 335–368.

Fuglie, K. O. (2015). Accounting for growth in global agriculture. *Bio-based and Applied Economics*, 4(3), pp. 201–234.

Haughton, J. and Khandker, S. R. (2009). *Handbook on Poverty and Inequality*. World Bank, Washington, DC.

IFAD (2016). *Rural Development Report 2016: Fostering inclusive rural transformation*, IFAD, Rome.

Imai, K. S. (2017). 'Roles of agricultural transformation in achieving sustainable development goals on poverty, hunger, productivity, and inequality', RIEB Discussion Paper Series, No. DP2017-26, Kobe University.

Imai, K. S., Abekah-Nkrumah, G. and Purohit, P. (2014). 'Is rural contribution to aggregate poverty reduction substantial? New evidence'. Brooks World Poverty Institute Working Paper Series 208/14, BWPI, The University of Manchester.

Ravallion, M., Chen, S. and Sangraula, P. (2009). Dollar a day revisited. *World Bank Economic Review*, 23(2), pp. 163–184.

Reardon, T. and Timmer, C. P. (2014). Five inter-linked transformations in the Asian agrifood economy: food security implications. *Global Food Security*, 3(2), pp. 108–117.

Remans, R., Wood, S. A., Saha, N., Anderman, T. L, and DeFries, R. S. (2014). Measuring nutritional diversity of national food supplies. *Global Food Security*, 3(3–4), pp. 174–182.

Thapa, G. (2016). 'Land markets in Asia: a synthesis of issues, lessons and policy implications'. APR, IFAD. Mimeograph.

Windmeijer, F. (2005). A finite sample correction for the variance of linear efficient two-step GMM estimators. *Journal of Econometrics*, 126, pp. 25–51.

World Bank (2015). *Staying the Course: World Bank East Asia and Pacific Economic Update October 2015*. The World Bank, Washington DC.

World Bank. (2016). *World Development Indicators 2016*. The World Bank, Washington DC.

16
Poverty in Africa

Felicitas Becker and Ewout Frankema

Introduction: a continent defined by poverty

Africa is the poorest region of the world today. This statement is supported by several indicators capturing different dimensions of poverty, including the poverty headcount rate, per capita GDP, child mortality and life expectancy estimates, educational attainment rates and indicators of access to vital (re)productive resources such as basic health care, nutrition, clean drinking water and electricity (see data provided by the World Bank 2018; UNESCO 2018). It is therefore not surprising that much of the development literature refers extensively to the causes and consequences of African poverty, including studies that are explicitly framed by questions as to why Africa 'lags behind' the rest of the world (Sachs & Warner 1997; Collier & Gunning 1999; Acemoglu & Robinson 2010).

The systematic portrayal of Africa in terms of poverty in both academic studies as well as development policy reports contributes to a deep, but rather understudied, notion that there is something 'African' in the nature of poverty in Africa that goes beyond the plain geographical delineation. Considering the comparative statistics of various poverty dimensions, this focus is certainly justifiable. Even though the share of extremely poor people in the total population has been on the decline since the early 1990s, the decrease is slower than elsewhere and has therefore retained higher levels than in other (former) developing regions, as we will show below.

However, defining a continent in terms of its poverty can also lead to serious misconceptions that prevent a balanced perspective on the changing nature of poverty. This has become apparent in the resurging optimism on African economic development since the mid-2000s, which followed upon a long period of 'Afro-pessimism' that dominated public and academic writings during the last quarter of the 20th century. A telling example is the issue of *The Economist* that portrayed Africa as 'The hopeless continent' in 2000. In 2011 the editors apologized for using the term 'hopeless' and overshot in the other direction with an issue entitled 'The hopeful continent: Africa rising'.[1] After three decades of crisis and stagnation, the past two decades of rapid growth have made a significant number of development specialists believe that Africa is the new 'growth miracle' (Young 2012). Indeed, short-term trends are all too often confused with long-term patterns of change in the nature and incidence of poverty.

Both the old 'pessimist' and renewed 'optimist' narratives reveal a lack of historical consciousness and both are related to a second misconception: the assumption that Africa has always been poorer than the rest of the world, and that researchers' primary task is to identify 'structural impediments' to growth, to explain the causes of retardation and the exceptional rigidity of 'extractive' or 'exclusive' institutions. In view of this literature, it is worth emphasizing that less than half a century ago, poverty rates in Asia were at least as high as in Africa, and that regions such as West and Southern Africa, were significantly richer in terms of GDP per capita than Asian giants such as India, Indonesia and China (Maddison 2010). Available evidence on the purchasing power of urban and rural wages also suggests that the majority of Africans were better off than the majority of Asians (Frankema & van Waijenburg 2012, 2018).

These misconceptions in the African poverty debate underline the need for greater temporal and contextual depth. Poverty is not primarily an African phenomenon, it is a global historical phenomenon, even though the *nature* of poverty in Africa may indeed contain a number of 'African' features. These features are dynamic, rather than static. This chapter will summarize part of these dynamic aspects in order to enhance context-aware research and balanced policy debates. We will start with a brief quantitative overview of comparative developments. We then examine the predominant dynamics causing poverty in Africa. This means, first, examining the effects of increasing but uneven shortage of land, which has very recently displaced the problems connected to relative abundance of land, but shortage of people. Second, it means examining the effects of rapid population growth in a context of stalled industrialization. Next, we discuss the way policy debates in international institutions have grappled, or at times failed to grapple, with these problems. Finally, we comment on popular views on poverty in an age of rising inequality.

The incidence of African poverty in comparative perspective

Defining, measuring and comparing human poverty over time and space are complicated issues. Poverty has various dimensions ranging from structural deprivation to temporary subsistence crises, from experiences of physiological and psychological stress to social exclusion, pervasive discrimination and inter-personal violence. In Amartya Sen's capabilities approach the human freedom to achieve a basic level of well-being is defined as a set of human capabilities to access food, health care, education and so on (Sen 2000). What is essential though in all definitions of, and approaches to poverty, is that lack of access to such basic human needs is related to low levels of income. For instance, gender discrimination can happen in very rich families and societies, but in this case it is not seen as a dimension of poverty. On the other hand, a child that cannot attend school because its parents cannot do without the revenues from child labour, is a critical aspect of human poverty. In this section we confine ourselves to an income approach, focusing on the concept of the absolute *poverty headcount ratio*. Today's standard for international comparisons is $1.90 per person per day (expressed in 2011 PPPs). The absolute poverty headcount rate is thus defined as the percentage share of a given population having an income below $1.90 per day.[2]

Apart from the question whether these poverty rates can be measured with acceptable degrees of accuracy – a question we will put aside here (see Chapters 2–4) – it is important to note that both poverty rates tend to be measured on the basis of annual average income levels, thus disregarding the temporal, often season-bound, volatility in incomes and associated risk of subsistence crisis. These data tend to be available for benchmark years in which household surveys or population censuses have been conducted, yielding nation-wide survey data on personal or household income and/or expenditure levels. The main advantage of using these measures is that they are intuitively appealing and, at least in theory, comparable across time and space.

Figure 16.1 shows the poverty headcount ratios for a selection of African regions as recorded in several years between 1980 and 2015. This figure demonstrates that the incidence of poverty in Africa varies enormously from region to region, with South Africa and North Africa & Middle East having much lower rates than the sub-Saharan African aggregate. The figure also shows that the post-1980 decline in poverty in Africa has been much more modest than in East and South Asia. Within Africa, country-to-country variation is large. With over 70% of the total population living in extreme poverty, Malawi and Madagascar rank among the poorest countries in the world. Africa's most populous country, Nigeria, has over half its population in extreme poverty. In contrast, poverty rates in Côte d'Ivoire have been between 20 and 30% and in Ghana they dropped from around 50% in 1991 to 12% in 2012, a huge fall if we can trust the numbers. Given the huge difference in the headcount ratio of North Africa, South Africa and the rest of Africa south of the Sahara, it is useful to consider these regions separately in international comparisons.

Figure 16.2 reveals another crucial dimension of the spatial distribution of poverty into rural and urban areas. It shows a very consistent pattern of poverty rates being substantially higher in the countryside than in the city. This is true for almost all developing countries in the world, but the differences in rates tend to be larger in African countries than elsewhere in the world. In part this is the result of a selection effect in rural–urban migration, where the most capable and educated young people move to the city to make a living there, while the more vulnerable

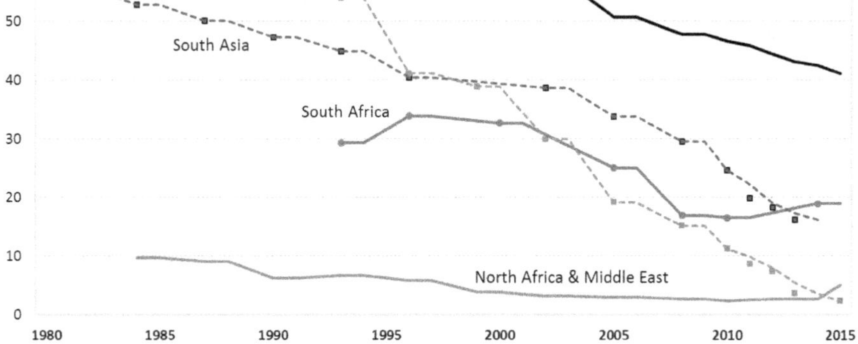

Figure 16.1 Poverty headcount ratio for selected regions, 1980–2015.

Source: World Bank, *World Development Indicators 2018*, poverty headcount ratio, latest update 04-11-2018.

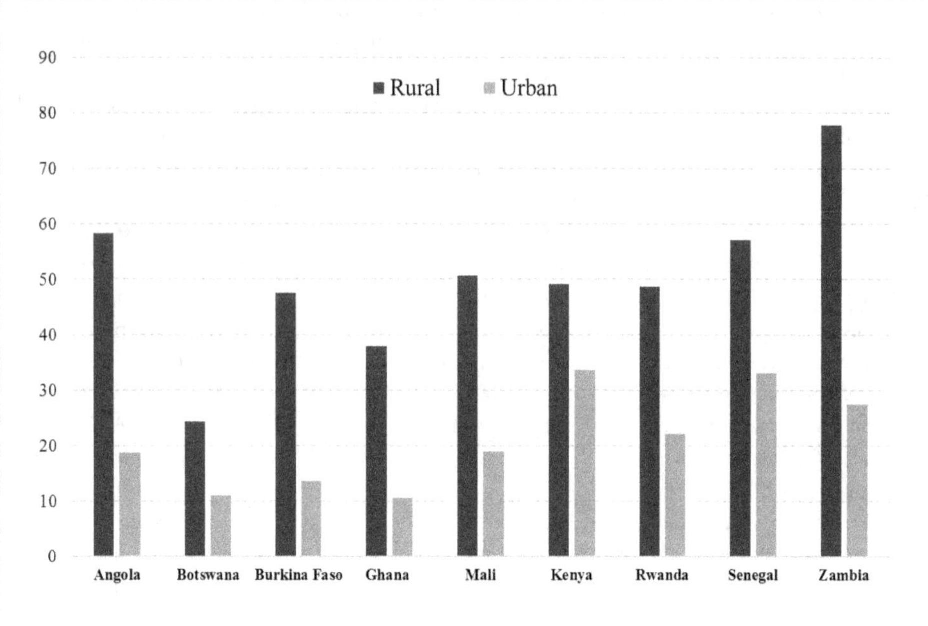

Figure 16.2 Poverty headcount ratio in rural and urban areas in a selection of African countries, *c.* 2010.

Source: World Bank, *World Development Indicators 2018*, urban and rural poverty headcount ratio at national poverty lines in %, latest update 23-03-2017.

family members stay behind in the village. Earning opportunities are also better in cities, where there are more jobs in the formal sector, including in government, administration and larger (international) enterprises.

Even though average income levels in cities may be higher, the costs of living are also higher in cities (which are not always corrected for, e.g. when nation-wide PPPs are used to deflate both rural and urban incomes), and social safety nets may be worse in cities than in 'home' villages. Further, income earned in cities may be transferred to the countryside to aid family members, or to be invested in a safety net for urban migrants. On the other hand, access to capability-enhancing services such as schooling, health care, electricity and the internet tends to be higher in cities. These figures thus show that incomes in urban areas tend to be higher than in rural areas, but are less useful for inferences on comparative levels and dimensions of human deprivation.

Figure 16.3 shows an interpolated and extrapolated poverty headcount ratio in sub-Saharan Africa between 1980 and 2020. The share of people living on less than \$1.90 a day – at 2011 PPPs – rose from 51.5% in 1981 to 59.4% in 1993, and after 1993 declined to 41.1% in 2015 – the last year for which we have a region-wide benchmark estimate. Figure 16.3 also shows that the total number of extreme poor in sub-Saharan Africa has increased dramatically, from 185 million in 1980 to 450 million at present. These contrasting trends are explained by the fact that over the past 40 years, population growth rates have outpaced the decline of the poverty rate. The average rate of population growth in sub-Saharan Africa has been around 2.7%, whereas the decline in the share of extreme poor has been about 0.5% on average between 1993 and 2010.

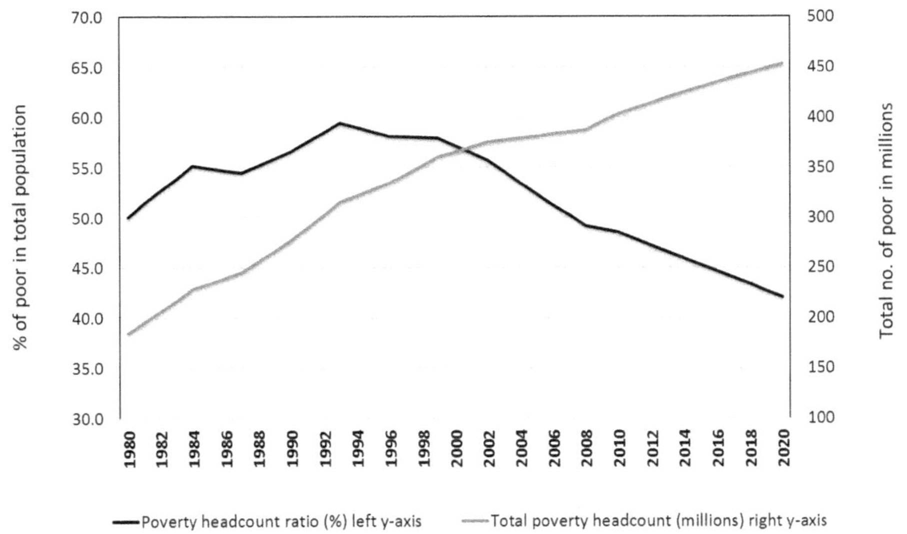

Figure 16.3 Contrasting poverty trends in sub-Saharan Africa, 1980–2020.

Source: Poverty headcount ratio from World Bank, *African Development Indicators 1960–2012*; linear interpolations and extrapolations of missing values by the authors. Population data for calculation of total poverty headcount from UN, *World Population Prospects 2017*, accessed 27-10-2017.

The vast gap in the pace of demographic growth and poverty decline suggests that this pattern may continue for several more decades, before absolute numbers of poor will be decreasing as well. Figure 16.4 shows future projections of both poverty measures based on the assumption that the annual rate of decline in poverty will remain constant at about 0.5%. In this scenario, the peak in the absolute number of extreme poor in sub-Saharan Africa will be reached in 2040.

In other regions of the world, and especially in Asia, poverty rates have tended to decrease faster in recent decades, while population growth has almost everywhere been significantly lower. As a result, this contrast between a declining headcount ratio and increasing total numbers of extreme poor may be regarded as an 'African' phenomenon, even though it has not been uncommon in other parts of the world. In Table 16.1 we offer the available World Bank estimates of the annual average decline of the poverty headcount ratio along with population growth rates for China, India and Indonesia, three of the most populous countries in Asia. This table shows that only in India has the absolute number of poor been on the rise, but at a much more modest rate than in sub-Saharan Africa.

These different trends have resulted in a major shift in the gravity centre of global poverty out of East Asia, and toward Africa south of the Sahara. In 1990 half of the world's extreme poor lived in East Asia, China in particular, and less than 15% lived in sub-Saharan Africa. In 2015, these rates were reversed, with more than half of the world's extreme poor living in sub-Saharan Africa, and less than 10% in East Asia. The share of South Asia, and in particular India, Pakistan and Bangladesh, has remained more stable at 28% in 1990, 38% in 2005 and back to 29% in 2015.[3]

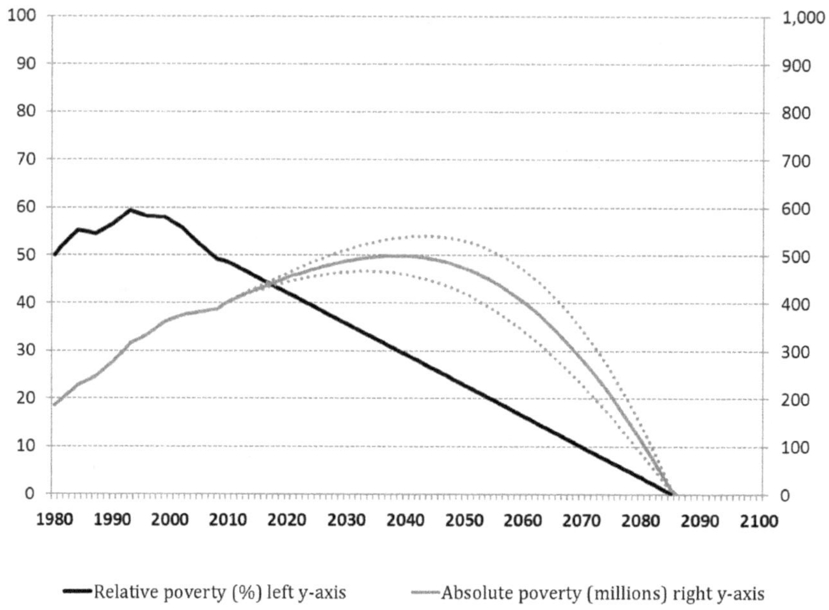

Figure 16.4 Future projections of poverty trends in sub-Saharan Africa, 1980–2100.

Source: Author's own estimations. The defining assumption in this scenario is that the headcount poverty rate will continue to decline at the pace of 1993–2010, i.e. 0.5% per annum. Total headcount forecasts are based on mid-fertility population projections from the UN, *World Population Prospects 2017*, accessed 27-10-2017. The dotted lines indicate the low and high fertility scenarios.

Table 16.1 Poverty rates and population growth in China, Indonesia, India and sub-Saharan Africa, 1977–2017

Country	*Period*	*Average annual poverty decline (%)*	*Average annual population growth (%)*
China	1990–2015	−2.6	0.7
Indonesia	1984–2017	−2.0	1.5
India	1977–2011	−1.2	1.9
Sub-Saharan Africa	1993–2010	−0.5	2.7

Source: World Bank, *World Development Indicators 2018*; United Nations, World Population Prospects

Continuity and changes in the nature of African poverty

There is an important distinction to be made between the incidence of poverty and the nature of poverty. The former can be phrased in questions of 'how much' and studied by quantitative indicators, the latter can only be qualified, and relates to questions such as 'who are the poor?', 'where do they live?', 'what makes them poor?', 'how do they cope?' and 'how do they perceive their own condition vis-à-vis others?' To get a better understanding of the changing nature of poverty, it is useful to adopt a longer historical view. In the 1980s, Iliffe summarized the starting situation for a discussion of contemporary poverty in Africa as follows:

> The incapacitated, the aged, unsupported women [with young children], and the young were still the bulk of the structural poor. They were supplemented by the new poor of the twentieth century – inhabitants of neglected regions, the unemployed, and especially the ill paid – and by growing numbers who, although able-bodied, were barred from resources by the competition of a growing population or by a more ruthless use of power and wealth.
>
> *(Iliffe 1987, 230)*

In addition to the changing nature of poverty, the last 20–30 years, in particular, have been characterized by dramatic reversals in policy approaches to, and political rhetoric around poverty. Nevertheless, patterns can be distinguished in both causes of and policy on poverty. To explain them, it is helpful to start with how poverty in most of Africa has historically differed from the experience of much of Europe and Asia. This entails examining Africa's recent transition out of 'land-rich' poverty, and its experience of population explosion in a context of stalled industrialization.

A fundamental change: the decline of 'land-rich' poverty

Widespread concern about current levels of population growth in Africa must be seen against the fact that historically, population densities in Africa have been low (Iliffe 1987, 2007; Acemoglu et al. 2002). The continent did not participate in the expansion of population seen elsewhere before the twentieth century (Acemoglu et al. 2002). Concomitantly, poverty was not, until recently, typically a function of lack of access to land. The exceptions to this rule were found in agriculturally favoured areas, above all Ethiopia and the East African Great Lakes Region (Uganda, Rwanda and Burundi) (Iliffe 2007; Doyle 2013). Rather than being landless, the very poor tended to be those who lacked individual labour power or were burdened with young children, while also lacking the social support that could have mitigated their problems: the incapacitated and isolated. This form of poverty continues in parts of Africa where pressure on land remains limited (Becker 2019).

Yet due to the dramatic growth of populations in Africa since the mid-twentieth century, combined with the alienation of land to settlers and increasingly to corporations and national elites, the internal frontiers of settlement that were a distinctive feature of Africa have closed, or are closing (Kopytoff 1987, on internal frontiers). In 1997, for example, Murton found that in Kenya's Machakos District, people pushed out of favourable locations in the hills could no longer move into agriculture on the surrounding plains instead (Murton 1999). Their only recourse was the city. In this way, Africa is currently undergoing the formation of a landless proletariat. Against this background, the relationship between town and countryside is crucial for shaping the dynamics of poverty in the latter.

Poverty in land and poverty in resources in the countryside

Both geography and politics are important determinants of rural poverty in contemporary Africa (Boone 2003). Granted, most rural producers face problems with low and fluctuating agricultural productivity on one hand, and unpredictable movements in global markets on the other (World Bank 2013b). But topographical, historical and political factors lead to great variations in different regions' access to markets and technical support. Thus many of Africa's rural poverty 'hotspots' are in areas that lack adequate transport links rather than agricultural potential (Iliffe 1987; Boone 2003). Moreover, even within better-connected locations, the economic status of individual households depends strongly on the nature of their links to the city, with the less-connected more likely to be poor (Murton 1999).

Rural–urban linkages have acquired particular importance with economic liberalization since the 1990s. This is because liberalization has led to a reduction in free input provision for cultivators, thus greater dependence on private incomes. Bryceson (2002) has characterized this period as one of 'de-agrarianization' of the countryside, as rural producers scrambled for non-agricultural income sources to add to their livelihood strategies. The importance of rural–urban linkages in this context is demonstrated by the already-mentioned study of Machakos, Kenya. Here, researchers found that the wealthiest, most productive rural households were also those with the highest *non-farm*, typically urban-generated, income (Murton 1999). Their ability to thrive agriculturally was a function of their access to resources provided by incomes remitted from the city. Conversely, inability to access the same resources further reduced the productivity of the poorest households with the smallest landholdings. Poverty in land and poverty in resources reinforced each other, and the poorest producers worked the poorest soils.

Similar correlations between the poverty of cultivators and that of their soils was observed in locations as diverse as semi-arid Zimbabwe and Northern Rwanda (Franke et al. 2016; Rusinamhodzi et al. 2013). For both maize in Zimbabwe and climbing bans in Rwanda, a crucial determinant of yield variations was found to be cultivators' ability, or lack of it, to access cattle manure. Only wealthier households could afford to keep cattle, thus use their dung. As in Machakos, poorer cultivators found themselves trapped by declining landholdings and declining productivity caused by lack of inputs. To be clear, here as in Machakos, poor households did not necessarily lack personal connections to the city. But they lacked connections to well-earning urbanites who could have afforded to reinvest income into improvements to rural landholdings. In this manner, relative agricultural prosperity and dire poverty can exist in close proximity, and the gradations of want are endless.

This is true also of the differences between countries and regions. Figure 16.2 above showed both that rural poverty in Africa remains very widespread, and that its incidence varies significantly over space. Many factors contribute to this variation: Botswana's relatively low rate of rural poverty reflects the fact that much of its countryside is uninhabited, while Ghana's is owed to relatively profitable cash crops. That politics are a factor is most brutally evident in the intentional creation of 'rural slums' of displaced city dwellers under South Africa's apartheid regime. Elsewhere, once-prosperous regions have suffered neglect for political reasons, entrenching vicious circles of lack of access to markets and education (Iliffe 1987; Boone 2003; Moore and Vaughan 1994). Yet the absence of these structural disadvantages is not enough for a rural region to escape poverty. To be relatively prosperous, rural regions need both good connections to markets, infrastructural as well as institutional, *and* favourable environmental conditions. A number of studies have found that cultivators can influence their environments positively (Tiffen et al. 1994; Fairhead and Leach 1996; Leach and Mearns 1996), but overall knowledge of the behaviour of soils and climates in Africa remains limited. Raising agricultural productivity remains a challenge, especially with climate change on the horizon.

Stalled industrialization, jobless growth and urban poverty

Meanwhile in the cities, any positive effects of the strong economic growth of the last two decades has been counterbalanced by demographic growth. Despite Africa's marginal role in the global economy, its cities serve as bridgeheads for such extractive and export industries as do exist (Lall et al. 2017; Ferguson 2006). These extractive industries have seen rapid, if not always sustained, expansion due to rising demand from newly industrializing countries. This has been a main driver of the strong growth rates that many African economies have been posting since ca. 2000. Combined with incomes from the 'aid industry', they have enabled an expansion of professional, settled urban middle classes (Ellis 2011; Green 2014). Yet their four-wheel-drive vehicles compete for urban space with the ramshackle minibuses run for and by the urban poor, whose numbers have been increasing faster still (Rizzo 2017). This combination of economic, demographic and spatial expansion means that the positive growth figures have not translated into better living conditions for the urban poor, or a reduction in their numbers.

Central to this stalemate is the lack of formal urban employment. Much of the growth observed recently has been in extractive industries such as mining and logging, and in tourism (Africa Development Bank 2017). These industries create only limited linkages to the wider urban economy, as much of their expertise and inputs are imported, and their proceeds exported. As Austin, Frankema and Jerven (2017) show, much of Africa has seen a pattern of stalled industrialization, with attempts at import-substituting industrialization in the mid-twentieth century failing due to unfavourable factor costs and institutional weaknesses. The mass consumer goods that might sustain industrialization based on local markets, from shoes to mobile phones to cars, continue to be imported. Although the wave of retrenchments that came with liberalization in the 1980s/90s is over, the public sector is in no position to fill the gap. With the gradual growth of a middle class and transport links in the last two decades, there are glimmers of hope for future industrialization (Frankema and van Waijenburg 2018). For now, though, the urban poor remain heavily dependent on the much-vaunted informal sector; a far from dependable means of coping.

Processes, effects and living standards in the un-enumerated, informal economy are by definition hard to trace. Albeit pervasive, Africa's informal sectors have given rise to wildly conflicting assessments. They can be treated as testament to Africans' initiative and entrepreneurialism, perhaps even with the potential to 'scale up' into the formal economy (Tripp 1997). Such optimistic assessments underlay the enthusiasm for micro-credit provision in the 2000s. By now, though, it has become clear that micro-credit is often used for consumption rather than investment, and that the effects of its availability are mixed rather than unequivocally positive (van Rooien et al. 2012). African urban planners and security forces, for their part, continue to treat much informal economic activity as a nuisance or downright illegal (an approach that also enables security personnel to collect bribes). Detailed studies are less frequent than general judgements.

The studies that do exist make clear that vast amounts of effort and ingenuity are expended daily in the informal sector (Rizzo 2017). Without it, the urban poor would be unable to get themselves housed, fed, groomed or shod. Any passing researcher knows that it can produce goods of unimpeachable quality. Yet it is also clear that the people working in the informal sector operate with minuscule margins of profit. The constant threat of shocks from ill health, police interference or shifts elsewhere in the economy makes them intensely precarious. Idiosyncratic combinations of luck and skill characterize those who manage to thrive, while lack of formal schooling, training and credit makes attempts to transition into the formal sector perilous (Rizzo 2017).

Public goods provision and the poor

With the heyday of 'state roll-back' in the past, the importance of access to public goods for the most vulnerable has been recognized again in recent years. The imposition of fees on education and healthcare has been scaled back, and vouchers have been used to provide fertilizer for those least able to afford it. These vouchers have been credited with greatly reducing rural malnutrition in Malawi, among other places, though the extent and causal dynamics of this welcome reversal have been questioned (Mkwara and Marsh 2011). In healthcare, concerted action to improve maternal care has enabled a decline in rates of maternal and neonatal mortality (WHO 2015). The fairly successful roll-out of antiretroviral drugs for Africa's many HIV-positive citizens is another significant success (Iliffe 2007).

While these interventions clearly save lives, they are no recourse against the continuing growth in the number of the absolute poor. They resemble running in order to stand still, or go backward more slowly. If, as is possible, the episode of slower growth in the numbers of the poor in the early 2000s reflected more of them dying of AIDS before the roll-out of antiretrovirals, then arguably the faster increase since is a positive sign. Evidently, figures can be misleading. Moreover, while the poor are particularly dependent on public goods, their poverty is also liable to interfere with their access to them. The poor are least able to pay bribes, and unlikely to mount legal or political challenges to measures that marginalize them, whether legally or, as in the case of demands for bribes, illegally. Here, the problems of the poor give reality to the broad policy discourse on 'good governance' as central to poverty reduction in Africa. This discourse forms part of large-scale arguments we turn to next.

Policy debates: grand claims and modest aims

The fact that the world's poor are becoming more and more concentrated in Africa gives extra urgency to the question how to reduce it here (African Development Bank 2017; Frankema and van Waijenburg 2018). Debates on how to do this exhibit a marked dualism. On one hand, large-scale 'grand claims' tend to focus on a limited number of critical factors, with sharp disagreements over which these critical factors are (Sachs 2005; Easterly 2001, 2013) and ambitious competing prescriptions for intervention (Collier 2007). On the other, development experts planning concrete, limited practical interventions work with a great variety of 'mid-range' concepts that may or may not align themselves with the schools of thought behind the grand claims (Banerjee & Duflo 2011). The following paragraphs organize these parallel and competing discourses around two sets of problems; problems whose centrality is widely debated.

Political reform, basic needs and environmental constraint

The highest-profile argument about poverty alleviation in Africa this century pitted calls for fundamental political reform against calls for massive investment into overcoming environmental, geographic and human resource constraints. For the former camp, Easterly argues that the primary cause of Africa's poverty is the corrupt and parasitic nature of its elites, especially those officially responsible for reducing its poverty. This line of thought aligns itself with the 'institutionalist' claim that a society's poverty or wealth is a function of its institutions (Acemoglu et al. 2002; North 1990). For the latter, Sachs sought to demonstrate through his 'millennium village' project that coordinated and well-funded investment in health care, transport, basic services such as water and electricity, and education could lead to self-sustaining growth even in unfavourable locations such as the Northern Kenyan drylands.

As funding for the 'millennium villages' faltered and their prosperity gains have not become self-sustaining, Easterly has declared himself the winner of this argument (Munk 2013; Easterly 2013). The focus in public debate on corruption and dysfunction in the aid sector as factors perpetuating Africa's poverty shows his public influence (Moyo 2009). But a more pragmatic focus on improvements to service delivery in specific locations, involving routine reliance on state authorities such as they are, remains central to many individual development projects (Banerjee & Duflo 2011). It has been crucial to achieving some of the most clearly measurable gains in welfare for the African poor in recent years, such as the advances against maternal mortality and HIV/AIDS mentioned above.

At the conceptual level, economic historians have spoken up in defence of the 'geography hypothesis', which holds that Africa faces distinctive problems in overcoming poverty (Austin 2008). They specify climate, soils, topography and demographics as imposing constraints that cannot be put down only to human institutions. Others make the point that Africa's institution did not develop in a vacuum; that they owe their shape partly to the continent's history of interaction with the rest of the world and cannot necessarily be changed by Africans' efforts alone (Akyeampong et al. 2015). Notwithstanding the exclusivism that characterizes some stances in this debate, there is no logical reason to play these strands of causation off against each other; the tendency to do so rather reveals the political nature of this debate.

Trade and production

As noted, much of Africa's recent economic growth is due to export trade. This is in line with the expectations of the proponents of economic liberalization, who argued that over-regulation perpetuated poverty by strangling trade, and with institutionalism more broadly, which takes 'entrepreneurial' (very often, trading) behaviour as crucial to growth and thus poverty reduction (Bates 2014). In effect, this export-led growth has helped cement the dominance of institutionalist approaches, increased acceptance of the roll-back of the state, and reduced the scope for capitalism-critical rhetoric and economic nationalism. This hegemonic position, though, has recently entered a state of flux with the revival of economic nationalism and capitalism-critical rhetoric (under the vague label of 'populism') in the West. It is finding swift imitators in Africa.

Discontent with the market-optimist orthodoxy is fed by the fact that the conditions under which Africans participate in these exchanges, and their ability to profit from them, remain highly stratified. Workforces in the extractive industries have been brutally disciplined where they were recognized as employees, and elsewhere been re-defined as pseudo-independent subcontractors who labour under dangerous and precarious conditions. In agricultural produce trade, state institutions retain much de-facto importance, partly by choice and partly because poor infrastructure and services deter private investors (Ponte 2002; Cooksey 2011). Nevertheless, development planners have taken the focus on individual entrepreneurialism on board, offering training in marketing and financial administration.

Both rural and urban poor remain cash-starved, and the kind of trading that serves them daily, where tea leaves are sold by the spoonful and cigarettes singly, profits from export trading only if marketing conditions for a particular rural commodity improve, or urban employment is created; in other words, via rising incomes. In consequence, the conditions of and constraints on *production* for trade remain crucial to poverty mitigation. Institutionalists recognize this inasmuch as they emphasize the importance of education for creating a better workforce, and the need to fight corruption so as to ensure that the benefits from the marketing of produce reach producers. They have also argued for the privatization ('titling') of land to encourage entrepreneurial producers (Englert & Daley 2008).

The concrete problems surrounding Africa's low agricultural productivity, though, garner little attention in these policy debates. Instead, they are the focus of geographers, overstretched agricultural extension services and non-governmental aid organizations such as Oxfam. In concert with critical anthropologists of development and proponents of 'fair trade', these organizations tend to be highly sceptical of the ability of Africa's poor to capture their share of the benefits of global trade (Ferguson 2006). In recent years, 'value-chain' analysis has emerged as a tool to trace where the profits from global commodity trading go, and to try to nudge more of them toward poor producers (Ponte 2002). Typically, this involves shifting more of their processing toward primary producers, again emphasizing the importance of improving productive capacities, and particularly industrialization, in poverty mitigation.

Conclusion: poverty in an era of rising inequality

Evidently, recent changes in poverty in Africa have been contradictory. Expanding urban middle classes coexist with growing numbers of desperately poor people, lacking prospects in either agriculture or the job market. Not only the number of absolute poor, but also that of billionaires in Africa is at an all-time high. Strengthened access to global consumer goods, owed to strong growth in recent years and China's active expansion into African markets, combines with the explosive growth of social media to provide the 'haves' with ever more ways to flaunt their wealth. Africa, then, is in the mainstream of global economic trends in the sense that here, too, inequality is on the rise.

A long-standing discourse in the social sciences holds that peasant societies, African ones included, tend to be inherently egalitarian (Scott 1977), which would make protest against increasing, and increasingly visible, inequality likely. It has even been argued that 'redistributive pressures' exerted on the economically successful by envious neighbours and relatives, cause poverty by dis-incentivizing entrepreneurial behaviour (Platteau 2015). But attitudes to wealth and poverty are more diverse than the cliché of egalitarianism allows. Suspicions of zombie-keeping or witchcraft by the economically successful coexists with the lionization of 'big men' and elaborate fantasies about what being rich might be like in popular culture (Geschiere 1997; Ellis & ter Haar 2003; Chabal & Daloz 2010; Weiss 2009).

It is nevertheless clear that many people in Africa, not all of them poor, tend to think of economic matters in moral terms (Ferguson 2006; Becker 2019). Given how crushing absolute poverty is, this is perhaps nearly inevitable. But the variety of the claims and counter-claims about poverty on Africa's streets and village squares are also a study in the resourcefulness of its poor. There is reason to think that poor people, too, have bought into the institutionalist discourses about entrepreneurialism and self-improvement that have been peddled widely in recent years (Brown & Green 2015). But assertions that poor people can have virtue and dignity, and that the rich are at fault for disregarding them, also abound. 'The tears of the wretched have their payment with God', says a Tanzanian pop song (Becker 2013). The same term for 'wretched', *wanyonge*, occurs more threateningly in the words of a Muslim preacher who called on the privileged to 'fear the tears of the wretched', because they have the power to call down God's wrath on those who abuse them. Even without considering their eternal salvation at stake, it is a warning that policy-makers might want to heed.

Notes

1 See *The Economist*, 13 May 2000, for the cover 'The hopeless continent' and the issue of 3 December 2011, for the cover 'The hopeful continent: Africa rising', in which the editors suggest that Africa has a real chance to follow in Asia's footsteps.

2 The *relative poverty headcount ratio* is a context-specific measure. It compares a person's or household's income to the income distribution of the country of residence. It thus refers to the minimum amount of income required to enjoy an acceptable living standard in the country of reference (Ravallion et al. 1991).

3 See for a visualization of the data: http://datatopics.worldbank.org/world-development-indicators/stories/where-do-the-worlds-poorest-people-live-today.html

References

Acemoglu, D. & J. Robinson. 2010. Why is Africa poor? *Economic History of Developing Regions* 25(1), 21–50.

Acemoglu, D., S. Johnson & J. Robinson. 2002. Reversal of fortune: geography and institutions in the making of modern world income distribution. *Quarterly Journal of Economics* 117, 1231–1294.

Africa Development Bank. 2017. *Africa sustainable development report: tracking progress on agenda 2063 and the sustainable development goals*. Addis Ababa: Africa Development Bank.

Akyeampong, E., R. Bates, N. Nunn & J. Robinson (eds.). 2015. *Africa's Development in Historical Perspective*. Cambridge: Cambridge University Press.

Austin, G. 2008. Resources, techniques and strategies south of the Sahara: revising the factor endowments perspective on African economic development, 1500–2000. *Economic History Review* 61(3), 587–624.

Austin, G., E. Frankema & M. Jerven. 2017. Patterns of Manufacturing Growth in Sub-Saharan Africa: From Colonization to the Present. In K. O'Rourke & J. G. Williamson (Eds.), *The Spread of Modern Industry to the Periphery since 1871* (pp. 345–373). Oxford: Oxford University Press.

Banerjee, A. V. & E. Duflo. 2011. *Poor Economics: A Radical Rethinking of the Way to Fight Global Poverty*. New York: Public Affairs.

Bates, Robert. 2014. *Markets and States in Tropical Africa: the Political Basis of Agricultural Policies*. Berkeley, CA: University of California Press.

Becker, F. 2013. Remembering Nyerere: political rhetoric and dissent in contemporary Tanzania. *African Affairs* 112, 238–261.

Becker, F. 2019. *The Politics of Poverty: Development and Local Politics in East Africa*. Cambridge: Cambridge University Press.

Boone, Catherine. 2003. *Political Topographies of the African State: Territorial Authority and Institutional Choice*. Cambridge: Cambridge University Press.

Brown, H. & M. Green. 2015. At the service of community development: the professionalization of volunteer work in Kenya and Tanzania. *African Studies Review* 85(2), 63–84.

Bryceson, D. 2002. The scramble in Africa: reorienting rural livelihoods. *World Development* 30(5), 725–739.

Chabal, P. & J. P. Daloz. 2010. *Africa Works: Disorder as a Political Instrument*. London: James Currey.

Collier, D. & J. W. Gunning. 1999. Why has Africa grown slowly? *The Journal of Economic Perspectives* 13(3), 3–22.

Collier, P. 2007. *The Bottom Billion: Why the Poorest Countries Are Failing and What Can Be Done About It*. Oxford: Oxford University Press.

Cooksey, Brian. 2011. Marketing reform? The rise and fall of agricultural liberalization in Tanzania. *Development Policy Review* 29(1), 57–81.

Doyle, S. 2013. *Before HIV: Sexuality, Fertility and Mortality in East Africa, 1900–1980*. Oxford: Oxford University Press for the British Academy.

Easterly, W. 2001. *The Elusive Quest for Growth: Economists' Adventures and Misadventures in the Tropics*. Boston, MA: MIT Press.

Easterly, W. 2013. *The Tyranny of Experts: Economists, Dictators and the Forgotten Rights of the Poor*. New York: Basic Books.

Ellis, S. 2011. *Season of Rains: Africa in the World*. London: Hurst.

Ellis, S. & G. ter Haar. 2003. *Worlds of Power: Religious Thought and Political Practice in Africa*. London: Hurst.

Englert, B. & E. Daley. 2008. *Women's Land Rights and Privatization in Eastern Africa*. Oxford: James Currey.

Fairhead, J. & M. Leach. 1996. *Misreading the African Landscape: Society and Ecology in a Forest-Savanna Mosaic*. Cambridge: Cambridge University Press.

Ferguson, J. 2006. *Global Shadows: Africa in the Neoliberal World Order*. Durham, NC: Duke University Press.

Franke, A. C., F. Baijukya, S. Kantengwa, M. Feckling, B. Vanlauwe & K. E. Giller. 2016. Poor farmers – poor yields: socioeconomic, soil fertility and crop management indicators affecting climbing bean productivity in Northern Rwanda. *Experimental Agriculture* 1, 1–20.

Frankema, E. & M. van Waijenburg. 2012. Structural impediments to African growth? New evidence from real wages in British Africa, 1880–1965. *Journal of Economic History*, 72(4), 895–926.

Frankema, E. & M. van Waijenburg, 2018. Africa rising? A historical perspective. *African Affairs* 117, 543–568.

Geschiere, Peter. 1997. *The Modernity of Witchcraft: Politics and the Occult in Postcolonial Africa*. Charlottesville and London: University Press of Virginia.

Green, Maia. 2014. *The Development State: Aid, Culture and Civil Society in Tanzania*. Woodbridge: James Currey.

Iliffe, John. 1987. *The African Poor: A History*. Cambridge: Cambridge University Press.

Iliffe, John. 2007. *Africans: The History of a Continent*. Cambridge: Cambridge University Press.

Kopytoff, I. (ed.). 1987. *The African Frontier: The Reproduction of Traditional African Societies*. Bloomington and Indianapolis: Indianapolis University Press.

Lall, S. V., J. V. Henderson & A. J. Venables. 2017. *Africa's Cities: Opening Doors to the World*. Washington, DC: The World Bank.

Leach, M. & R. Mearns. 1996. *The Lie of the Land: Challenging Established Wisdom on the African Environment*. Oxford: James Currey.

Maddison, A. 2010. *Historical Statistics on World Population, GDP and Per Capita GDP, 1-2008 AD*. www.ggdc.net/maddison/. Retrieved 04-01-2019.

Mkwara, B. & D. Marsh. 2011. Effects of maize fertilizer subsidies on food security in Malawi. Hamilton, New Zealand: University of Waikato Economics Working Paper 14/11.

Moore, H. & M. Vaughan. 1994. *Cutting Down Tress: Gender, Nutrition and Agricultural Change in Northern Zambia, 1890–1990*. Portsmouth, NH: Heinemann.

Moyo, D. 2009. *Dead Aid: Why Aid Is Not Working and How There Is Another Way for Africa*. London: Penguin.

Munk, N. 2013. *The Idealist: Jeffrey Sachs and the Quest to End Poverty*. New York: Anchor Books.

Murton, J. 1999. Population growth and poverty in Machakos district, Kenya. *Geographical Journal* 165, 37–46.

North, Douglass. 1990. *Institutions, Institutional Change and Economic Performance*. Oxford: Oxford University Press.

Platteau, J.-P. 2015. Redistributive Pressures in Sub-Saharan Africa: Causes, Consequences and Coping Strategies. In E. Akyeampong, R. Bates, N. Nunn & J. Robinson (Eds.), *Africa's Development in Historical Perspective* (pp. 153–207) Cambridge: Cambridge University Press.

Ponte, S. 2002. *Farmers and Markets in Tanzania*. Oxford: James Currey.

Ravallion, M., G. Datt & D. Van De Walle. 1991. Quantifying absolute poverty in the developing world. *Review of Income and Wealth* 37(4), 345–361.

Rizzo, M. 2017. *Taken for a Ride: Grounding Neoliberalism, Precarious Labour, and Urban Transport in an African Metropolis*. Oxford: Oxford University Press.

Rusinamhodzi, L., M. Corbeels, S. Zingore, J. Nyamangara & K. Giller. 2013. Pushing the envelope? Maize production intensification and the role of cattle manure in recovery of degraded soils in smallholder farming areas of Zimbabwe. *Field Crops Research* 147, 40–53.

Sachs, J. 2005. *The End of Poverty: Economic Possibilities for our Time*. London: Allen Lane.

Sachs, J. D. & A. M. Warner. 1997. Sources of slow growth in African economies. *Journal of African Economies* 6(3), 335–376.

Scott, J. 1977. *The Moral Economy of the Peasant: Rebellion and Subsistence in Southeast Asia*. New Haven, CT: Yale University Press.

Sen, A. 2000. *Development as Freedom*. New York: Anchor Books.

Tiffen, M., M. Mortimore & F. Gichuki. 1994. *More People, Less Erosion: Environmental Recovery in Kenya*. New York: Wiley-Blackwell.

Tripp, A. M. 1997. *Changing the Rules: The Politics of Liberalization and the Informal Urban Economy in Tanzania*. Berkeley: University of California Press.

UNESCO. 2018. *Data for the Sustainable Development Goals*. UNESCO Institute for Statistics, UIS.Stat, http://data.uis.unesco.org/

Van Rooien, C., R. Stewart & C. de Wet. 2012. The impact of microfinance in Sub-Saharan Africa: a systematic review of the evidence. *World Development* 40(11), 2249–2262.

Weiss, Brad. 2009. *Street Dreams and Hip Hop Barbershops: Global Fantasy in Urban Tanzania*. Bloomington, IN: University of Indiana Press.

World Bank. 2013a. *African Development Indicators 1960–2012*. Washington, DC: The World Bank.

World Bank. 2013b. *Unlocking Africa's Agricultural Potential*. Washington, DC: The World Bank.

World Bank. 2018. *World Development Indicators 2018*. Washington, DC: The World Bank.

World Health Organization. 2015. Trends in maternal mortality: 1990 to 2015. Estimates by WHO, UNICEF, UNFPA, World Bank Group and the UN Population Division. Available at http://apps.who.int/iris/bitstream/10665/194254/1/9789241565141_eng.pdf?ua=1.

Young, A. 2012. The African growth miracle. *Journal of Political Economy* 120(4), 696–739.

17

Poverty and social policy in Latin America

Key trends since *c.* 2000

Camila Arza and Roxana Maurizio

Introduction

Since the new millennium Latin America[1] has experienced high rates of economic growth – especially before the international crisis – and improvements in social and labour market indicators. A larger fiscal space facilitated the expansion of public social expenditures, the extension of social security coverage, and the implementation of new non-contributory benefits for informal workers and low-income families. Income inequality fell, average household income increased, and the incidence of poverty and extreme poverty reduced. These trends were not only associated to economic growth and rising employment, they were also an outcome of economic and social policies implemented during these years in a political context characterized by the ascendance to power of governments with more progressive public policy agendas.

Despite the progress achieved during this expansionary phase, Latin American countries continue to show significant social deficits. Poverty rates remain above 20 per cent in most countries, and in some of them poverty reaches more than one-third of the total population. The end of the latest phase of economic growth by about 2014 already shows the fragilities of recent achievements. In only three years (between 2014 and 2017) most of the progress made in the reduction of extreme poverty over the previous period (2.4 out of 3.4 percentage points) was lost. This shows the risks and challenges that remain in a highly unequal and heterogeneous region.

This chapter presents recent poverty trends in Latin America, identifying both shared patterns across countries and regional heterogeneity, and discusses key features of labour markets and social policies associated to them. We take an absolute criterion for poverty identification and use poverty estimates made by the UN Economic Commission of Latin America and the Caribbean (ECLAC). In 2018 ECLAC updated poverty and extreme poverty estimates using a new methodology.[2] Poverty lines are made up of a basic food basket (BFB) and a non-food component. In order to calculate the value of the BFB, ECLAC first estimates the caloric requirements considering the FAO/WHO/UNU recommendations for persons by sex, age and level of physical activity. Those caloric requirements are then converted into goods and services, based on the expenditure structure of a "reference population" (which is the first quintile of the population).

Finally, the BFB is valued with the prices of the official consumer price index. The resulting measure is the extreme poverty line. In order to estimate the total poverty line, the BFB is multiplied by the inverse of the Engel's coefficient, to incorporate the non-food component. In the new methodology, ECLAC considers country-specific values for the Engel's coefficient, which are based on the price structure of each country.

Poverty lines thus estimated reflect the cost of a basket of goods and services that is deemed necessary to satisfy the same set of basic needs in each country, taking into account each country's consumption patterns. In terms of Sen's conceptualization, the different poverty lines are similar in the space of capabilities but different – i.e. country-specific – in the space of goods and services (Sen 1983). Households are identified as poor (or extremely poor) if their total income (corrected for non-response) is below the total poverty line (or the extreme poverty line).

The chapter is structured as follows. First we present poverty trends in Latin America since 1980 and contextualize these trends into the broad macroeconomic and labour market context of the period. The next section focuses on labour market issues associated to poverty, including informal employment and low wages, as well as labour institutions. Then we deal with social policies implemented in Latin America to provide income security over the life-course, focusing on cash benefits for families and children, working-age adults and older adults, and briefly discuss their role for poverty reduction. In the last section we present some final remarks.

Poverty trends in Latin America

Since the 1980s Latin America has experienced profound changes in macroeconomic policy as well as in social and labour market indicators. The "Lost Decade" of the 1980s was characterized by important capital outflows for the payment of the external debt services accumulated mainly in the late 1970s, when the region became part of financial globalization. The domestic consequences of this process were high levels of inflation, high macroeconomic instability and average GDP growth rates close to zero.

Faced with this regional outlook, the market-friendly recommendations of the Washington Consensus[3] promised the region stability and economic growth. Based on the argument that the negative socioeconomic outcomes of the previous years were largely due to state inefficiency, the prescriptions were to reduce state participation in the economy and to deregulate markets. Several Latin American countries began to implement measures such as commercial and financial liberalization, privatization of public companies, tax reform and labour market flexibility. In parallel, at the beginning of the 1990s the region entered the international capital market once again, experiencing an important increase in capital inflows. In several Latin American countries, a growing deficit in the balance-of-trade, associated mainly to the appreciation of the national currencies, was accompanied by a deficit in the balance-of-payment. Countries managed to stabilize high inflation, but a rising external debt became unsustainable, leading to important macroeconomic crises (Mexico 1994–1995, Argentina 1995, Brazil 1998–1999 and again Argentina 2001–2002).

After these crises, the international context improved with the commodity price boom and the renewal of capital inflows to the region. The largest countries (Argentina, Brazil and Mexico) shifted their exchange rate regimes and combined intervention in the foreign exchange market and management of the domestic interest rate. A new political context also brought social and labour regulation policies back to the agenda, in contrast to the model of the 1990s, which was geared toward the retreat of state from many of these functions. Several Latin American countries promoted greater state intervention and the expansion of social protection systems (Huber and Stephens 2012; Pribble 2013).

In this new environment, Latin America experienced a sustained period of economic growth: GDP increased at an average annual rate of 2.5% between 2003 and 2014, an unprecedented pace for such a long period.[4] This economic performance was accompanied by a positive behaviour of labour market indicators as well as by social policy expansion. It was a period of job creation, reduction of unemployment, more formal jobs and a modest recovery in average wages. Between 2003 and 2018 employment rates increased from 52.3% to 56.7%, unemployment fell from 11.2% to 8.4% (ILO 2010, 2018a), and income inequality declined in most countries (Beccaria et al. 2015a; Cornia 2014; Cruces and Gasparini 2010; Soares 2006; Maurizio 2015; Maurizio and Vázquez 2016).

Higher rates of employment and higher incomes contributed to the reduction of poverty and extreme poverty. In contrast to what happened in the 1980s (when poverty rates rose by about 8 percentage points [pp] on average), between 2002 and 2017 Latin America experienced an impressive drop of 14.3 pp in poverty (from 44.5% to 30.2%) and a more modest reduction of 1 pp in extreme poverty (from 11.2% to 10.2%) (Figure 17.1).

Since *c.* 2002, poverty trends show three phases. During the first one (between 2002 and 2008) poverty sharply fell in line with improvements in the labour market and the extension of coverage of social security and social assistance. In the second phase (between 2008 and 2014) the poverty decline was less pronounced, mostly as a result of the local impacts of the 2008 international crisis. Finally, during the third phase (from 2015 on), in a context of significantly lower (even negative) economic growth rates and worsening labour market indicators in several countries, both poverty and extreme poverty rose.

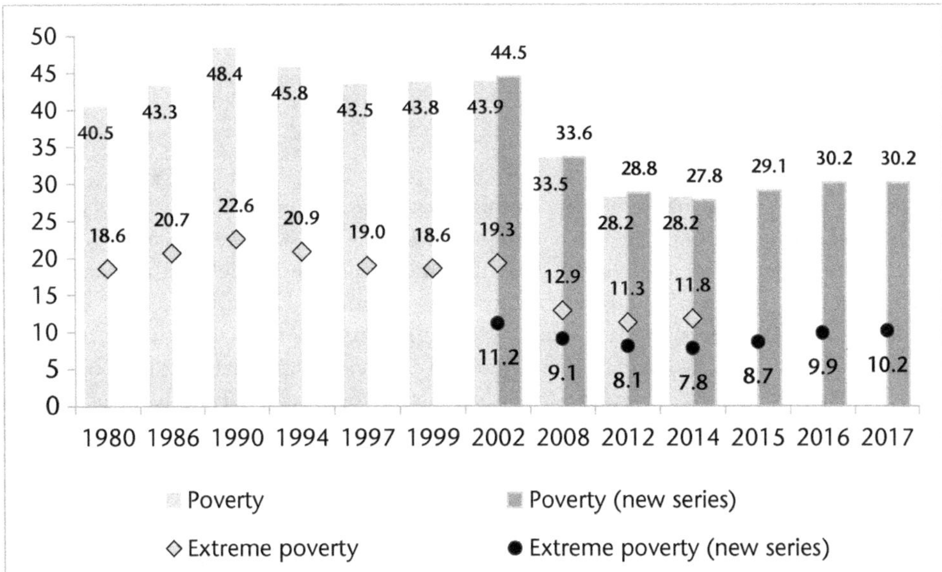

Figure 17.1 Poverty and extreme poverty in Latin America, regional average (% of total population, 1980–2017).

Notes: ECLAC's weighted average of 18 countries: Argentina, Bolivia, Brazil, Chile, Colombia, Costa Rica, Dominican Republic, Ecuador, El Salvador, Guatemala, Honduras, Mexico, Nicaragua, Panama, Paraguay, Peru, Uruguay and Venezuela.

Source: Authors' elaboration based on ECLAC (2018, 2019a).

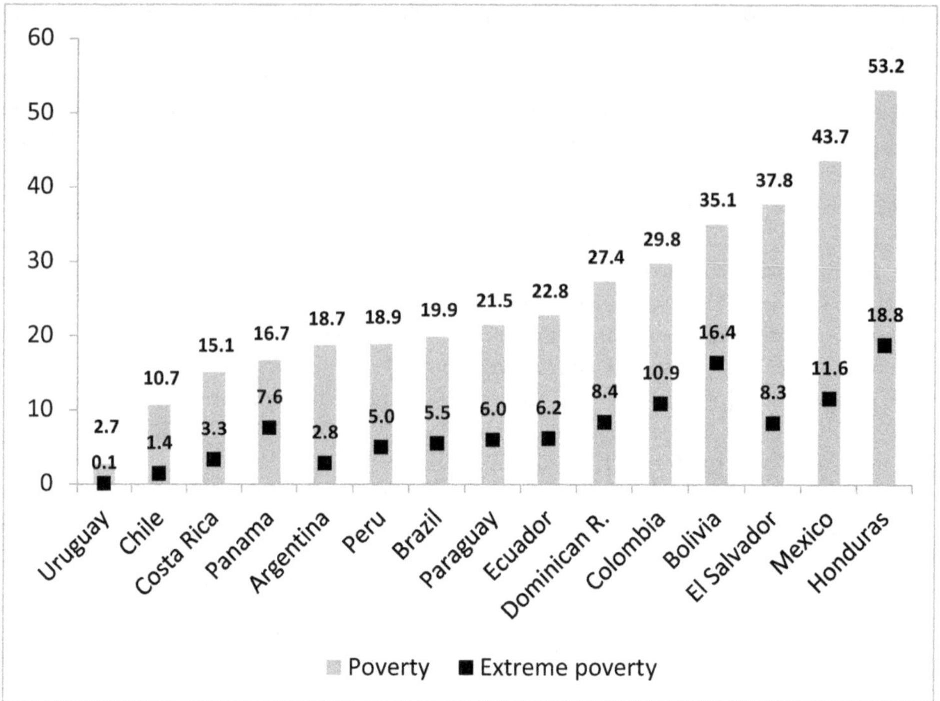

Figure 17.2 Poverty and extreme poverty in Latin America, by country (% of total population, *c.* 2016/17).

Note: Year 2017 for all countries except for Dominican Republic, Mexico and Honduras (2016).

Source: Authors' elaboration based on ECLAC (2019b).

Behind this general outlook there is high heterogeneity across countries. Following ECLAC's estimates, at one extreme is Uruguay with a very low poverty rate (around 3%), while at the other extreme is Honduras with more than 50% of the total population living in poverty. In terms of trends, several countries experienced important reductions in the incidence of poverty over the past one and a half decades: Argentina, Bolivia, Brazil, Chile, Colombia, Costa Rica, Panama, Paraguay, Peru and Uruguay cut poverty rates by about half or more between around 2001/3 and 2016/17. In contrast, countries like Honduras and Mexico, experienced virtually no poverty reduction over the same period, and remain among the Latin American countries with the highest incidence of poverty and extreme poverty. In between these two groups, countries like El Salvador and Dominican Republic had a moderate reduction of poverty (about 20%) over the period (ECLAC 2019b).

This cross-country heterogeneity suggests that regional generalization should be done with caution, and point to the domestic drivers of poverty trends, including macroeconomic and social policies implemented in each country (see below in the section on poverty and social protection systems). In a recent study, Beccaria et al. (2015b) evaluate the relative importance of labour markets and public cash benefits in the outflows of poverty in Argentina, Brazil, Costa Rica, Ecuador and Peru. They find that 30 to 40% of initially poor households exited poverty the following year, and that the "positive" labour market events they experienced (e.g. an increase in the number of paid workers, in the hourly wages, in the working hours), alone or in combination with increases in non-labour income (pensions, cash transfers or other non-labour income), accounted for 70–80% of those exits. A rise in income from pensions was the most important non-labour event in Argentina and Brazil (the two countries with the most developed pension systems among the five included in their study), while an increase in other non-labour income (mainly transfers from other households such as remittances) was more relevant in Costa Rica, Ecuador and Peru.

Besides these cross-country variations, there are shared patterns of poverty concentration in certain populations. Children are overrepresented among poor and extremely poor populations: they represent one-quarter of the total population of Latin America and 38% of the population living in poverty, and 42% of the population living in extreme poverty (ECLAC 2018). Indeed, the incidence of poverty among children (aged 0–14) is estimated at 46%, compared to 27% for the middle-aged adult population (aged 35–44) (ECLAC 2019a). Poverty also concentrates among rural and indigenous populations. People living in rural areas account for 18% of the total population of Latin America, and for 29% and 41% of the population living in poverty and extreme poverty, respectively (ECLAC 2018). In rural areas, almost half of the population is poor, compared to 26% in urban areas. Something similar happens with indigenous populations, 51% of whom are estimated to be poor (compared to 28% of the population who are not indigenous or afro-descendent) (ECLAC 2019a).

Poverty and the labour market: informal employment, labour institutions and the "working poor"

Labour informality is one of the categories of analysis that most contributes to the characterization of labour conditions in Latin America. There are two main approaches to informality. On the one hand, the concept of *informal sector* emerged in the early 1970s, in ILO documents on Africa (ILO 1972). It was then developed in Latin America by the Regional Employment Program for Latin America and the Caribbean (PREALC). The informal sector refers to small productive units with low levels of productivity, which aim at survival rather than at capital accumulation. Under this "productive approach", employment in the informal sector reflects the inability of countries' economies to generate sufficient employment in the formal sector to absorb the entire labour force.

On the other hand, the concept of informal employment, which emerged in more recent years, takes a different perspective and focuses on jobs rather than on firms. Under this "legal approach", informality is associated with the lack of compliance with labour regulations: informal employment is defined as "all remunerative work (i.e. both self-employment and wage employment), that is not registered, regulated or protected by existing legal or regulatory frameworks, as well as non-remunerative work undertaken in an income-producing enterprise" (ILO 2019). Informal workers have no secure employment contracts, are not registered in the social security system, and are not entitled to workers' benefits.[5] This chapter adopts this second approach distinguishing between formal (registered workers with social security rights) and informal workers.

Over the 2000s, the incidence of informal employment fell in several countries due to the combination of a context of sustained economic growth and employment creation and policies to promote labour formalization.[6] In parallel, wage concentration reduced and accompanied wage recovery and, in some countries, also the strengthening of minimum wages and collective bargaining. Real minimum wages increased especially in Argentina, Brazil, Ecuador and Uruguay (Marinakis 2014; Maurizio and Vázquez 2016).

Despite this progress, the region continues to show significant deficits in the labour dimension, with persistently high rates of unemployment and informality, income inequality and low wages. The average unemployment rate in the region is 8.4% and informal employment ranges from 24% of total employment in Uruguay to over 70% in Bolivia, Paraguay, Nicaragua, Honduras and Guatemala (ILO 2018b). At the same time, the self-employed remain a significant share of total employment (27.7% on average, and 40.9% and 36.6% in countries such as Peru and Ecuador, respectively), much higher than in developed countries (ILO 2018a). This large incidence of informality and self-employment (mainly non-professional own-account worker) clearly narrows the scope for labour institutions and regulations.

In this labour context, the phenomenon of the "working poor" is also widespread. In Latin America having a job is no guarantee against poverty. Poverty rates are considerably higher for informal and own-account workers than for other types of workers.[7] In the case of informal wage-earners, this is a direct outcome of the lower wages they receive. The "penalty" of monthly labour income on informal wage-earners was estimated at about 66% in Argentina, 32% in Peru and 25% in Brazil (Maurizio 2014),[8] which reflects both fewer hours of work per month by informal workers, and lower hourly wages. The wage gap associated with informality is not constant across the income distribution: it is larger at the lower income tail, strengthening the connection between informality and poverty.

On the other hand, wage gaps between formal and informal wage-earners are associated to workers' observed attributes but not wholly. Indeed, these informal workers have a vector of personal characteristics that are usually linked to lower wages: they have lower levels of formal education, are younger, and concentrate in economic sectors such as commerce, construction and domestic service. However, Maurizio (2014) shows that informal workers' lower wages are not totally explained by these observed attributes, and suggests that the unexplained difference is likely to be associated to the different impact that labour market institutions (such as minimum wage legislation and collective bargaining) have for formal and informal workers. Informal workers' jobs are not protected by these and other labour regulations (e.g. concerning layoffs, working hours, or the 13th month salary[9]), and experience higher occupational turnover (Beccaria and Maurizio 2018), income instability and, consequently, higher exposure to poverty risks.

Poverty and social protection systems over the life-course

Over the 2000s, social expenditures grew in most countries, rising from 11.0 to 14.5 per cent of GDP on average between 2000 and 2015 (ECLAC 2016). These higher expenditures went to the development of existing and new social programmes for both formal and informal workers. Informal workers and low-income families, typically not covered by contributory social security systems, were incorporated into non-contributory programmes providing modest cash benefits, especially for families with children and older adults, which contributed to reduce economic insecurity for them. However, large gaps remain both in coverage and in the sufficiency of the benefits that these populations have obtained.

Conditional cash transfers for families with children

Conditional cash transfer (CCT) programmes emerged in Latin America by about the mid-1990s (in Brazil and Mexico) and expanded throughout the region over the following decade. In a context where child-centred social policies (beyond education) have traditionally had limited development, the expansion of CCTs brought a considerable improvement in the coverage of children, especially of children in lower income households. Across countries, these programmes have different designs, scopes, legal frameworks and eligibility criteria,[10] but they share the aim to reduce the current incidence of poverty and extreme poverty and to break the intergenerational transmission of poverty. Key features are a focus on families and children (rather than on workers, as in previous workfare programmes), the targeting of poor or extremely poor families, and the establishment of a set of behavioural conditions, normally associated to children's health monitoring and education, that beneficiaries must fulfil to receive the benefits.

Currently virtually all Latin American countries have some sort of CCT programme operative, and these programmes have become the main social assistance policy in most of these countries. Coverage increased considerably over the first decade of the 2000s, and by 2016, it is estimated that CCTs reached almost 130 million people (about 20% of the population) (Cecchini and Atuesta 2017; see Figure 17.3). CCT programmes provide households with a regular income that does not depend on macroeconomic or labour fluctuations. This can be particularly important for the poorest, who tend to have more unstable incomes. Cash transfers can also partly cushion income loss, for instance when a member of the household loses a job or leaves the household, reduce barriers of entry into certain productive activities, and increase the cash circulating in poor communities where beneficiaries live, thus favouring local economies (ECLAC 2010).

Conditionalities are a characteristic feature of these programmes. In order to get the cash (or to continue receiving it) families normally must certify that children attend school, get required vaccinations and make regular doctor visits to monitor their health. This is, in theory, associated to the aim to break the transmission of poverty and inequality by enhancing children's human capital. However, from the region's empirical evidence, it is not possible to identify the independent role of the conditionalities beyond the impact of the cash transfer. Quite often, the existence of conditionalities is justified more by the social consensus this generates on CCT programmes than by the independent effect that conditionalities have

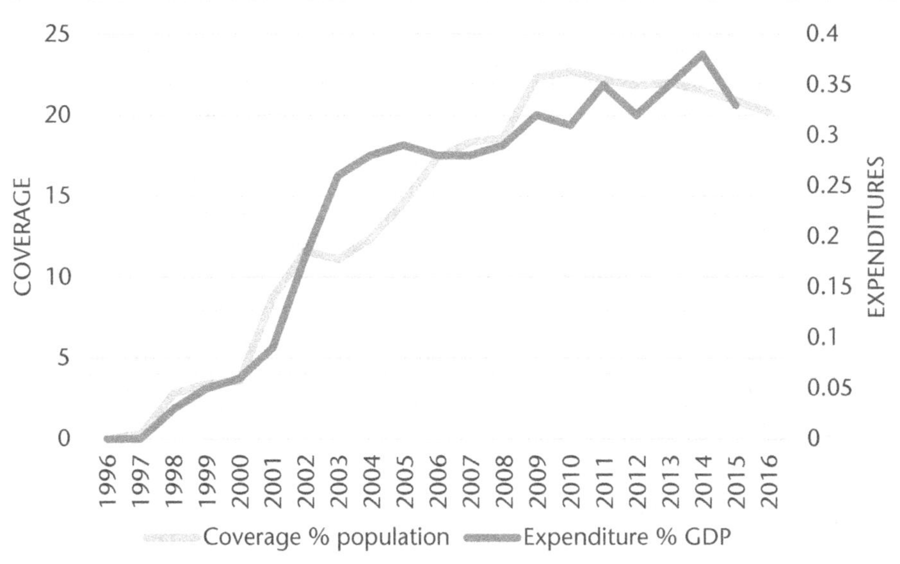

Figure 17.3 Coverage rates and total spending in conditional cash transfer programmes.

Source: Authors' elaboration based on Cecchini and Atuesta 2017, Table A.II.15.

on outcomes. Another key related issue has to do with whether countries go beyond simply introducing incentives for families to invest in the health and education of their children (i.e. CCT conditionalities) and effectively guarantee universal access to quality healthcare and education for all, by increasing public investment in these services, particularly in the areas where low-income families live.

The impact of CCTs on labour market participation of beneficiary households has also been much debated. It is often argued that cash transfers discourage participation in the labour market because they increase household income, thus reducing the need for household members to seek paid employment. However, cash transfers can also have the opposite effect, lifting the cash constraint to seek for a job (e.g. to pay for transport and communication) or to get the supplies needed to start a small productive activity. Therefore, the impact of CCTs on labour market participation is an empirical matter. Recent evidence for Latin American countries tends to find no significant disincentives of CCTs on labour market participation.[11] On the other hand, a reduction of labour market participation could be a positive outcome from a social investment perspective in some cases, for instance when young adults withdraw from the labour force to go back to education or training, or when the cash transfer can free workers to take very low-quality, dangerous and exploitative jobs. In fact, cash transfers can contribute to increase the "reservation wage" of beneficiaries, and thus the minimum wages effectively paid in informal jobs.

Another key issue of these programmes is the means-testing applied and the rules for benefit suspension and "graduation". If means-testing is very narrow or benefits are easily discontinued, there is a risk that vulnerable (but maybe not extremely poor) families will fail to obtain these benefits or cease to receive them. Income fluctuation, especially in lower income households, means that some may manage to obtain income above the eligibility threshold at one point in time, but not necessarily to secure a stable improvement in their socioeconomic position over time.

After over a decade of development and expansion, CCT programmes seem to have become a stable component of current social protection systems. They have reached millions of poor and vulnerable families, but still face significant limitations to operate as a platform for equal opportunities and to reduce the intergenerational transmission of poverty – a key aim of these programmes. Indeed, while most quantitative studies find a positive impact of CCTs on poverty, the size of the poverty reduction achieved as a result of these benefits remains relatively small. Benefits improve household incomes, but the amounts paid are often low (sometimes even below extreme poverty lines), coverage is incomplete, and the public budget dedicated to these programmes remains relatively limited. By around 2015, CCT programmes reached about 20% of the population, and on average paid USD 153 per year per person in beneficiary households, accounting for only 3.1% of public social spending and 0.33% of the countries' GDP (Cecchini and Atuesta 2017; Figure 17.3). Child poverty fell over the period when these programmes developed, but the drop was less marked than for the adult population, and – as mentioned above – across countries, children continue to be poorer than any other age group.

Social security for working-age adults

Labour market regulations as well as social security systems are key instruments to reduce the incidence of labour market risks or help workers to cope with them. However, in Latin America, the large share of informal and own-account employment and the limited capacity of states to enforce labour regulations, drastically reduces the effectiveness of these policies to cushion labour market risks and avoid poverty. For instance, all Latin American countries have a programme to protect workers in case of work injury, but coverage gaps are large, and only about three-quarters of workers in Chile (the country with the highest rate of effective coverage in this programme), and less than one-third of workers in El Salvador, Honduras and Bolivia are effectively protected against work injury (ILO 2017; ISSA 2018). A similar pattern is found in terms of paid maternity leave. For unemployment insurance the picture is even worse: only eight out of the 18 Latin American countries have such a programme and effective coverage is very low (less than 10% of workers in Argentina, Brazil and Ecuador, and less than one-third in Chile and Uruguay, the two countries with the highest coverage) (ILO 2017; ISSA 2018). Thus, a large share of Latin American workers remains unprotected in the event of unemployment, maternity or work injury.

Beyond contributory social security, which only covers formal workers, there are specific labour market programmes to offer work training and income support for more vulnerable, informal and lower income workers. While CCT programmes discussed above normally target families with children, some countries have also developed cash transfer programmes for young adults to encourage the completion of formal education or the take-up of work training (e.g. "*Progresar*" in Argentina and "*Jóvenes en Acción*" in Colombia). Other programmes include those oriented to improve the employability of vulnerable populations by offering tax incentives or subsidies for firms to hire workers from vulnerable families, intermediation policies for jobseekers, and economic support for self-employment and micro-enterprises (Cecchini et al. 2015). The main weaknesses of these programmes often have to do with their narrow targeting and small scale, as well as with the difficulties to secure a stable incorporation in the formal economy for the target population of these programmes.

Contributory and non-contributory pensions for older adults

All Latin American countries have a pension system to provide economic security in old age and in the case of disability or widowhood. These systems have been traditionally designed following a social insurance model of work-related, contributory, and publicly managed benefits. In some countries, these programmes went through structural reforms in the 1980s (Chile), 1990s or early 2000s, shifting partly or fully to privately managed individual savings accounts (Mesa-Lago 2004). During the late 2000s some of these countries implemented new reforms that increased the role of the state in pension administration. The most structural of these post-privatization reforms was the Argentinian (2008), which did away with individual accounts established in 1993/4 and shifted back to a fully public pay-as-you-go system (Arza 2012; also Kritzer et al. 2011; Mesa-Lago 2014).

Since in contributory pension systems eligibility for a retirement pension depends on past contributions, the high incidence of informal employment in Latin America puts effective coverage down, and many workers have no access to a contributory old-age pension. Furthermore, in some countries, pension enrolment for workers in some occupations (such as the self-employed or domestic workers) is voluntary and therefore very low, while unpaid family workers either have voluntary affiliation or are not included in contributory social security programmes.

All these factors reduce the ability of contributory pension systems to guarantee economic protection for the elderly population in Latin America. While in some countries non-contributory pension programmes already existed before recent expansion (e.g. Argentina, Brazil, Chile – see Bertranou 2002), these programmes had low coverage and were unable to significantly narrow the old-age protection gap. Over the 2000s, the reach of non-contributory benefits increased considerably across Latin America as several countries created new non-contributory or semi-contributory schemes or expanded existing ones. Non-contributory pension programmes varied in kind and scope across the region, some countries offered rather residual means-tested benefits, while others established universal or pension-tested benefits, or expanded coverage by relaxing contributory requirements for social insurance pensions (Arza 2017, 2019; Rofman et al. 2013). As a result, the share of older adults receiving a contributory or non-contributory benefit increased markedly in many countries (Figure 17.4).

The incidence of poverty among older adults in Latin America varies across countries. In countries with the most advanced pension systems in terms of both coverage and sufficiency (Argentina, Brazil, Chile and Uruguay, and to a lesser extent Costa Rica and Panama) old-age poverty rates are consistently lower than among working-age adults. In other countries with high total pension coverage but low benefits (Bolivia, Mexico), as well as in countries where pension systems suffer from both limited coverage and low benefits (Honduras, Guatemala, El Salvador), old-age poverty rates remain high.

In the region as a whole, old-age poverty almost halved between 2002 and 2016, dropping from 29.4% to 15.1% (ECLAC 2019b). As Figure 17.4 shows, this was also a period of old-age pension coverage expansion, as a result of policies specifically oriented to incorporate older adults with no access to existing contributory programmes.

In addition to coverage, pension benefit sufficiency is key to keeping older adults out of poverty. Contributory pensions tend to provide higher benefit amounts: it is estimated that over 90% of these benefits were above the poverty line in 2016 (up from 79% in 2002) (ECLAC 2018). In contrast, non-contributory benefits are considerably lower, and below the official poverty

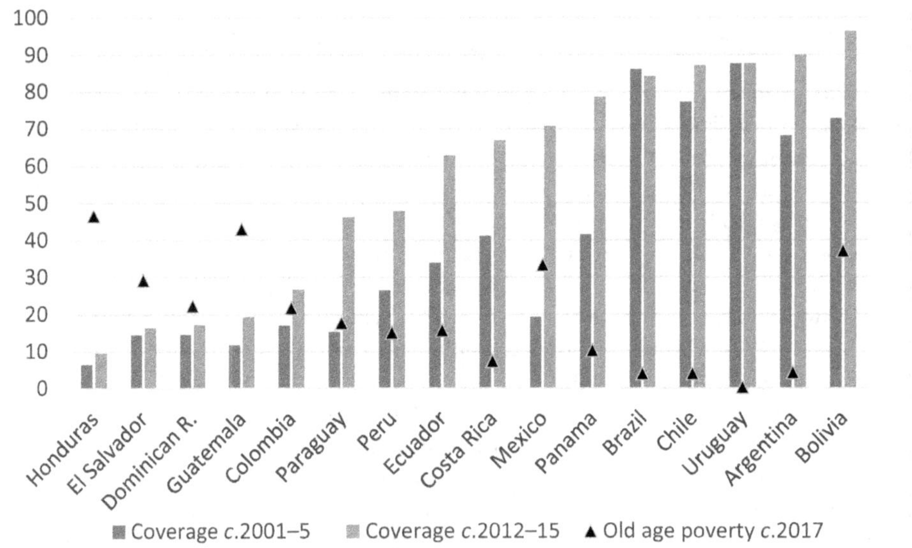

Figure 17.4 Total pension coverage (contributory and non-contributory) and poverty rates among older adults (65+).

Notes: Old-age pension coverage is measured by the share of older adults aged 65 and over who receive a contributory or non-contributory benefit (where data are available). Old-age poverty rates of 2017, except for Honduras, Dominican Republic and Mexico (2016), and Guatemala (2014).

Source: Own elaboration based on data from ECLAC (2018, 2019b).

line in several countries. Indeed, the very low value of some non-contributory pensions means that while many more elderly people now have access to a benefit their socioeconomic position remains precarious and their economic autonomy is at best only partial.

Final remarks

Over the first one and a half decades of the 2000s, the social conditions of the population in Latin America improved, including a considerable drop in poverty rates. Economic growth, the expansion of social policies and better labour conditions have been key underlying factors for these trends. Poverty reduced across countries, dropping by about 14 pp on average between 2002 and 2017.

Despite improvements, important labour and social deficits still characterize the region. These deficits are mostly linked to three structural features: (1) high income inequality, both among workers and households; (2) very low systemic competitiveness and productivity, and high productive heterogeneity; (3) insufficient levels of social protection due to the limited reach of contributory-based social security and the residual character of most non-contributory schemes. Inequality in the distribution of labour income partly reflects the productive heterogeneity where highly efficient and competitive sectors and companies coexist with activities and firms that operate under a survival rationale. Thus, most informal employment is linked to small, unstructured productive units where it is frequently easier to conceal labour relations. This also entails low and unequally distributed access to social security and labour regulations that could effectively protect against labour market and life-course risks.

In this context, a more profound and stable reduction of poverty requires a better distribution of income, jobs and social security rights and benefits. Enhancing formal employment and labour institutions, including minimum income and collective bargaining, are important for that purpose. But given the structural character of labour market informality in the region, the development of a comprehensive social protection system grounded on universal social rights (based not only on traditional social insurance pillars but also on non-contributory components) is also essential to guarantee access to income security and basic social services over the life-course for the population at large. This approach clearly differs from those strategies that narrowly target the poor and rely on safety nets. Indeed, the very high levels of poverty and inequality that persist in the region demand a broader role for the social protection system as a fundamental part of a social development strategy. This must come hand in hand with a strengthening of governments' fiscal and redistributive capacities, through a more progressive taxation structure and improved revenue raising power.

Notes

1 In this chapter we focus on 18 Latin American countries (excluding the Caribbean) (for a listing see note to Figure 17.1).
2 These new series only span from 2002 to 2018; therefore, comparable estimates for the 1980s and 1990s are not available. For further information, see ECLAC (2018, 2019a).
3 The so-called "Washington Consensus" refers to a set of economic policy measures for market reform, promoted for Latin America by the US, the IMF, the World Bank and others, over the 1980s and 1990s (see Williamson 1990).
4 In the following two years economic growth rates for Latin America were negative (−0.2% in 2015 and −1.1% in 2016). In 2017 the growth rate was positive again but low (1.2%) (ECLAC 2019b).
5 ILO (2019, 2002), Hussmanns (2004).
6 For further information about these processes, see, for instance, Maurizio (2015), Bertranou et al. (2013), Corseuil and Foguel (2012), Berg (2011).

7 The poverty rate for informal wage-earners is about five times higher than for formal wage-earners in Argentina and three times higher in Brazil, Ecuador or Peru. Among own-account workers, poverty rates are between two times higher than for formal workers in Brazil and 4.5 times higher in Argentina (Maurizio 2017).
8 Another study on this topic is Tannuri-Pianto and Pianto (2002).
9 The 13th month salary is an additional remuneration that wage-earners must receive from their employers (normally equivalent to one-month salary per year).
10 For more details on these programmes see, for instance, ECLAC (2019c), World Bank (2009), ILO/IPEC (2007), Perez Rivas et al. (2008), Villatoro (2008), Ibarrarán et al. 2017, among others.
11 See, for example, Alzúa et al. (2010), Parker and Skoufias (2000), Foguel and Paes de Barros (2010), Maurizio and Vázquez (2014), Maurizio and Monsalvo (2017).

References

Alzúa, M., G. Cruces and L. Ripani (2010). "Welfare programs and labor supply in developing countries: experimental evidence from Latin America", CEDLAS Working Paper. 95, La Plata.

Arza, C. (2012). "Policy change in turbulent times: The nationalization of pension funds in Argentina." In P. Utting, S. Razavi and R. Buchholz (eds.), *The Global Crisis and Transformative Social Change*. New York: Palgrave, pp. 123–140.

Arza, C. (2017). "The expansion of economic protection for older adults in Latin America: Key design features of non-contributory pensions", United Nations University, WIDER Working Paper 2017/29, Helsinki.

Arza, C. (2019). "Basic old age protection in Latin America: non-contributory pensions, coverage expansion strategies and ageing patterns across countries", *Population and Development Review*, Early View at https://onlinelibrary.wiley.com/doi/abs/10.1111/padr.12267

Beccaria, L., R. Maurizio and G. Vázquez (2015a). "Recent decline in wage inequality and formalization of the labor market in Argentina", *International Review of Applied Economics*, vol. 29, no. 5, pp. 677–700.

Beccaria, L., R. Maurizio, G. Vázquez and M. Espro (2015b). "Factors associated with poverty and indigence mobility in five Latin American countries", *Research on Economic Inequality*, vol. 23, pp. 71–107.

Beccaria, L. and R. Maurizio (2018). "Labor turnover in Latin America: How intensive is it and how differently does it behave across countries?", *International Labour Review*, (forthcoming).

Berg, J. (2011). "Laws or Luck? Understanding rising formality in Brazil in the 2000s." In S. Lee and D. McCann (eds.), *Regulating for Decent Work: New Directions in Labour Market Regulations*, Geneva: ILO and Palgrave Macmillan, pp. 123–150.

Bertranou, F. (2002). *Pensiones no contributivas y asistenciales: Argentina, Brasil, Chile, Costa Rica y Uruguay*. Santiago: International Labour Office.

Bertranou, F., L. Casanova and M. Saravia (2013). "How, why and in what sectors employment informality decreased in Argentina from 2003 to 2012", MPRA Paper 47467. Munich: University Library of Munich.

Cecchini, S. and B. Atuesta (2017). "Programas de transferencias condicionadas en América Latina y el Caribe. Tendencias de cobertura e inversion", Serie Políticas Sociales No. 224, Santiago: Economic Commission for Latin America and the Caribbean

Cecchini, S., F. Filgueira, R. Martínez and C. Rossel (eds.) (2015). *Towards Universal Social Protection: Latin American Pathways and Policy Tools*. Santiago: Economic Commission for Latin America and the Caribbean.

Cornia, G. (ed.) (2014). *Falling Inequality in Latin America: Policy Changes and Lessons*, UNU-Wider, Oxford: Oxford University Press.

Corseuil, C. and M. Foguel (2012). "Economic expansion and increase in labour market formality: A poaching approach", *Revista Brasileira de Economia*, vol. 66, no. 2, pp. 207–224.

Cruces, G. and L. Gasparini (2010). "A distribution in motion: the case of Argentina." In L. López-Calva and N. Lustig (eds.), *Declining Inequality in Latin America: A Decade of Progress?* Washington, DC: Brookings Institution, pp. 100–133.

ECLAC (2010). *Time for equality: closing gaps, opening trails*. Report of the thirtieth session of ECLAC. Santiago: Economic Commission for Latin America and the Caribbean.

ECLAC (2016). *Social panorama of Latin America 2015*. Santiago: Economic Commission for Latin America and the Caribbean.

ECLAC (2018). *Social panorama of Latin America 2017*. Santiago: Economic Commission for Latin America and the Caribbean.

ECLAC (2019a). *Social panorama of Latin America 2018*. Santiago: Economic Commission for Latin America and the Caribbean.
ECLAC (2019b). *CEPALSTAT: Databases and statistical publication*. Economic Commission for Latin America and the Caribbean, available at http://estadisticas.cepal.org/cepalstat/Portada.html, accessed 19 March 2019.
ECLAC (2019c). *Non-contributory Social Protection Programmes Database: Latin America and the Caribbean*. Economic Commission for Latin America and the Caribbean, available at https://dds.cepal.org/bpsnc/cct, accessed 3 August 2019.
Foguel, M. and R. Paes de Barros (2010). "The effects of conditional cash transfer programmes on adult labour supply: an empirical analysis using a time-series-cross-section sample of Brazilian municipalities", *Estudos Econômicos*, vol. 40, no. 2, pp. 259–293.
Huber, E. and J. Stephens (2012). *Democracy and the Left*. Chicago/London: University of Chicago Press.
Hussmanns, R. (2004). *Measuring the Informal Economy: From Employment in the Informal Sector to Informal Employment*. Geneva: ILO Working Paper, 53.
Ibarrarán, P., V. Medellín, F. Regalia and M. Stampini (2017). *Así funcionan las trasnferencias condicionadas. Buenas prácticas a 20 años de implementación*, Washington, DC: Inter-American Development Bank.
ILO (1972). *Employment, income and equality: a strategy for increasing productive employment in Kenya*. Geneva: International Labour Office.
ILO (2002). *Resolution concerning decent work and the informal economy*. Governing Body, 285th Session, Seventh item on the agenda, Geneva.
ILO (2010). *Labour overview 2010: Latin America and the Caribbean*. Lima: Regional Office for Latin America and the Caribbean.
ILO (2017). *World social protection report 2017/19: Universal social protection to achieve the Sustainable Development Goals*. Geneva: International Labour Office.
ILO (2018a). *Panorama Laboral 2018: Latin America and the Caribbean*. Lima: Regional Office for Latin America and the Caribbean.
ILO (2018b). *Mujeres y hombres en la economía informal: un panorama estadístico* (3rd ed.), Geneva: International Labour Office.
ILO (2019). "Informal employment." ILO Thesaurus, available at http://ilo.multites.net/default.asp (accessed 18 March 2019).
ILO/IPEC (2007). *Trabajo Infantil y los programas de transferencias en efectivo condicionadas en América Latina*. San José: International Labour Office.
ISSA (2018). *Social security programs throughout the World: The Americas, 2017*. Geneva: ISSA/US Social Security Administration.
Kritzer, B. E., S. J. Kay, et al. (2011). "Next generation of individual account pension reforms in Latin America", *Social Security Bulletin*, vol. 71, no. 1, pp. 35–76.
Marinakis, A. (ed.) (2014). *Incumplimiento con el salario mínimo en América Latina. El peso de los factores económicos e institucionales*. Santiago: International Labour Office.
Maurizio, R. (2014). "Labor informality and poverty in Latin America: The case of Argentina, Brazil, Chile and Peru." In J. Cling, S. Lagrée, M. Razafindrakoto and F. Roubaud (eds.), *The Informal Economy in Developing Countries*, Abingdon and New York: Routledge, pp. 21–49.
Maurizio, R. (2015). "Transitions to formality and declining inequality: The case of Argentina and Brazil in the 2000s", *Journal of Development and Change*, vol. 46, no. 5, pp. 1047–1079.
Maurizio, R. (2017). "In-work poverty in Latin America: prevalence, driving forces and trends." In H. Lohmann and I. Marx (eds.), *Handbook of Research on In-work Poverty*, Cheltenham UK: Edward Elgar Publishing, pp. 365–394.
Maurizio, R. and P. Monsalvo (2017). "Evaluación de los impactos de la AUH en el comportamiento laboral de los adultos y en la generación de ingresos." In *Análisis y propuestas de mejoras para ampliar la Asignación Universal por Hijo*. Buenos Aires: ANSES-UNICEF, pp. 115–176.
Maurizio, R. and G. Vázquez (2014). "The impacts of a child allowance program on the behavior of adults in the labor market: the case of Argentina", *CEPAL Review*, no. 113, pp. 115–137.
Maurizio, R. and G. Vázquez (2016). "Distribution effects of the minimum wage in four Latin American countries: Argentina, Brazil, Chile and Uruguay", *International Labour Review*, vol. 155, no. 1, pp. 97–131.
Mesa-Lago, C. (2004). "An appraisal of a quarter-century of structural pension reforms in Latin America", *CEPAL Review*, vol. 84, no, pp. 57–81.

Mesa-Lago, C. (2014). "Reversing pension privatization: the experience of Argentina, Bolivia, Chile and Hungary", *Extension of Social Security*, Working Paper 44, Geneva: International Labour Office.

Parker, S. and E. Skoufias (2000). "The impact of PROGRESA on work, leisure, and time allocation", Working Paper, Washington, DC: International Food Policy Research Institute.

Perez Ribas, R., F. V. Soares and G. Hirata (2008). "The Impact of CCTs: What we know and what we are not sure about", *Poverty in Focus* "Cash Transfers: Lesson from Africa and Latin America", International Poverty Centre, Brazil.

Pribble, J. (2013). *Welfare and Party Politics in Latin America*, Cambridge: Cambridge University Press.

Rofman, R., I. Apella, and Evelyn Vezza (eds.) (2013). *Más allá de las pensiones contributivas: Catorce experiencias en América Latina*. Buenos Aires: World Bank.

Sen, A. (1983). "Poor, relatively speaking", *Oxford Economic Papers*, no. 35, pp. 153–169.

Soares, S. (2006). "Distribuição de renda no Brasil de 1976 a 2004 com ênfase no período entre 2001 e 2004", IPEA Dicussion Paper 1166, Brasilia.

Tannuri-Pianto, M. and D. Pianto (2002). "Formal-informal differentials in Brazil: A semi-parametric approach." Paper presented at Graduate School of Economics, Getulio Vargas Foundation, University of Brasılia.

Villatoro, P. (2008). "CCTs in Latin America: human capital accumulation and poverty reduction", *Poverty in Focus* "Cash Transfers: Lesson from Africa and Latin America", International Poverty Centre, Brazil.

Williamson, J. (ed.) (1990). *Latin American Adjustment: How Much Has Happened?* Washington, DC: Institute for International Economics.

World Bank (2009). *Transferencias monetarias condicionadas: Reducción de la pobreza actual y futura*, Bogota: Mayol Ediciones.

18

Poverty around the world

North America

Emily W. Kane

Introduction

Across Canada, Mexico, and the United States, poverty is a persistent social problem. Though these nations vary significantly in their income levels, languages, and historical connections to colonial powers, they share a common geographic context as North American nations. This chapter considers the extent and predictors of poverty, as well as tracing a brief history of poverty policy in each nation. Attention is also devoted to common themes in the literature across the three nations, including rhetoric about poverty in mass media and public opinion, and the importance of recognizing low-income people's capacity for decision-making, creativity, and accomplishment.

Statistical overview

Measuring poverty is complex, as previous chapters have detailed. According to comparative data published in the USA's World Factbook (2018), 9.4% of Canadians, 15.1% of Americans, and 46.2% of Mexicans live in poverty. But as that source documents, each of these North American nations uses a different approach to measuring poverty, making precise comparisons difficult. As I consider more fully below, Canada calculates a "Low Income Cut-off," the U.S. calculates an official poverty line, and for Mexico, a country with lower income levels overall, a food-based measure of poverty is used for this comparative purpose.

Canada defines no official poverty line:

> Statistics Canada . . . use the term "after-tax Low Income Cut-Offs" or LICO to refer to the level below which a Canadian's income is considered to be low. Most social scientists and advocacy organizations consider this measure to be the poverty line.
>
> *(Harding 2016, 28)*

According to MacKinnon (2013, 20), "While it continues to be the measure most commonly used, the LICO is not a perfect measure and it is often criticised for its flaws." Aspects questioned in the literature include its lack of adjustment for varying cost of living across regions, its relative rather than absolute calculation basis, and the argument by some that it overstates the level of poverty relative to measures used in other nations (MacKinnon 2013). The level of poverty, and trends over time, vary depending on the measure used, but overall analysts estimate the poverty rate in Canada at between 9% and 14%, and conclude that poverty levels have generally declined over the last 50 years, and have continued to decline a bit or remain steady in recent years (Myles 2015; Smith-Carrier and Lawlor 2017).

The United States federal government defines an official poverty line and that measure is contested as well, with critics arguing it relies too much on an outdated set of necessities for defining a minimum living standard, and fails to capture regional variations in the cost of living or the impact of public assistance (Waldfogel 2014). With varying definitions taken into account, overall poverty estimates for the United States range between 15% and 20%. Most analysts conclude the poverty rate has mostly declined over the past 50 years but has been increasing a bit after the financial crisis of recent years (AEI and Brookings 2015; Waldfogel 2014).

In Mexico, defining and measuring poverty has been shaped by broader Latin American debates, with official definitions overseen by the Consejo Nacional de Evaluación de la Política de Desarrollo Social (CONEVAL) (Castillo Fernández and Arzate Salgado 2016). CONEVAL takes a multidimensional approach that considers three elements: "monetary income . . . the fundamental rights of individuals in regards to social development . . . communitarian and geographical aspects of poverty" (Barahona 2018, 601). Calculations focused on monetary income, food availability, and assets estimate the overall poverty rate in Mexico in the mid-40% range, with a bit of increase in poverty in recent years due to the impact of the USA's financial crisis (Castillo Fernández and Arzate Salgado 2016; Ziccardi 2014).

Within each nation, these overall rates vary notably by other factors as well. For example, poverty rates for all three countries tend to be higher for single-parent families, children, people with disabilities, rural residents, and marginalized racial/ethnic groups (AEI and Brookings 2015; Castillo Fernández and Arzate Salgado 2016; MacKinnon 2013; UNICEF 2017). Especially frequent is attention to the role of race or ethnicity, with people of color and indigenous or Aboriginal people substantially more likely to suffer poverty in all three nations (Castillo Fernández and Arzate Salgado 2016; Davis, Roscigno and Wilson 2016; Fording, Soss and Schram 2011; Livingstone and Weinfeld 2015; MacKinnon 2013; Smith-Carrier and Lawlor 2017; Thiede, Kim and Slack 2017; Ziccardi 2014). Gender has also received attention, with women increasingly more likely to live in poverty, especially if raising children alone, a phenomenon some have termed the feminization of poverty (Collins and Mayer 2010; Edin and Kefalas 2011; Hallgrimsdottir, Benoit and Phillips 2013; Hryciuk 2017; Lopreite and Macdonald 2014; Smith-Carrier and Lawlor 2017). With some variation by nation, there is a general recognition that rural areas have particularly high rates of poverty while urban areas have significant poverty alongside greater economic security and even wealth, as well as attention to ways the experience and predictors of poverty vary in rural versus urban contexts (Castillo Fernández and Arzate Salgado 2016; Dolson 2015; Gilderbloom, Squires and Wuerstle 2013; Ryser and Halseth 2017; Small and Newman 2001; Smith, Koikkalainen and Casanueva 2014; Ziccardi 2014).

Poverty policy across North America

Specific policies developed to address poverty vary across the three nations, based on their demographics, politics, and history. But scholars identify a clear commonality too, one that is considered in greater detail elsewhere in this handbook: neoliberal approaches to poverty governance and economic policy more broadly. This approach to poverty policy is especially evident in the popularity of various types of conditional cash transfer programs, and I focus in particular on these as key examples of poverty policy. In a review of scholarship on neoliberal poverty governance, I have argued that it tends to emphasize three key elements: privatization, individualism, and punitive orientation (Kane 2018). Rather than conceptualizing public assistance as a right, neoliberal poverty governance expects each individual to "earn" economic citizenship through market activity, and motivates that activity through incentives but especially sanctions. Relatively little recognition is made of structural obstacles or structured inequalities, nor of the social value of family carework, and markets are viewed as the most appropriate distributors of social resources.

Fording, Soss and Schram (2011, 1611) argue that US "[w]elfare programs today are administered and implemented through a decentralized network of actors, organized by quasi-market relations, and charged with the task of bringing discipline to the lives of the poor." Mazelis (2017, 6) argues that "deep poverty has been increasing since the mid-1970s . . . (when) the United States began to embrace neoliberalism, a theory that a free market can best solve social problems." The result is that among ten affluent Western nations (including Canada), the U.S. safety net is "dead last when it comes to the core task of poverty relief" (Grusky, Mattingly and Varner 2016, 8). Though perhaps most pointed in the United States, scholars emphasize this neoliberal logic in Canada and Mexico as well. It flows, as detailed below, from somewhat different origins in each case, differentiated by links to Latin American policy in Mexico and western European trends in Canada and the U.S., and is also shaped differently by the varying income levels of Mexico versus the U.S. and Canada. But neoliberal approaches are clearly highlighted by researchers focused on all three of these North American nations. Johnstone, Lee, and Connelly (2017, 1443) claim that Canadian social policy has become dominated by "the meta-discourse of neoliberalism, which results in time-limited programs, divorced from community needs, with an ad hoc development of services." And Bayón (2017, 99) offers a similar assessment: "in Mexico there has been no break or adjustment in the neoliberal model that started to take shape in the mid-1980s." Echoing the three defining features of neoliberal poverty governance that I outline above, Bayón (2017, 114–115) goes on to note that in Mexico, "The ideal of a commodified society emphasizes individual responsibility; redistribution is replaced by the reeducation of the poor from stigmatizing, punitive, and discriminatory approaches."

Poverty policy in the United States

Over 50 years ago, at a time of postwar expansion in the economy and growing political activity among marginalized communities, social conditions were ripe for U.S. President Lyndon Johnson's declaration of a "War on Poverty." This initiative involved a range of ambitious programs designed to significantly reduce poverty, including increased food assistance, early childhood education programs, and expanded access to housing and health care. Orleck and Hazirjian (2011, 2) document the way "the poorest of the poor, despite daunting obstacles, transformed themselves into effective political actors who insisted on being heard." In recent years, various U.S. poverty scholars have compared that moment of possibility with current policy. "Fifty years after the War on Poverty, America's low-income families and children must rely on a tattered, minimal safety net" (Waldfogel 2013, 2). Santiago (2015, 6) concurs:

> Markedly different from the beginnings of the War on Poverty are the political and social contexts shaping our current approaches to addressing poverty in America . . . we have moved from waging an unconditional war on poverty to an unconditional war on the poor.

Though it took over a decade for organized political opposition to the War on Poverty to gain ascendance, the rhetoric of opposition emerged the same year the war was declared. At the 1964 Republican National Convention, California politician Ronald Reagan introduced a racialized line of attack he would eventually turn into a centerpiece of his successful run for the U.S. presidency in 1980. "Reagan's rise to national political prominence was tied directly to the backlash against the War on Poverty that he helped to foment" (Orleck 2011, 446–447). In subsequent years, public assistance has been framed as primarily supporting people of color, despite the fact that most recipients are White, and the rhetoric surrounding it has focused on protecting taxpayer dollars rather than providing security to economically vulnerable families. Many scholars see the culmination of that new approach as captured in the 1996 Personal Responsibility and Work Opportunity Reconciliation Act (PRWORA).

Colloquially referred to as "welfare reform," the Act replaced cash assistance to poor families ("Aid to Families with Dependent Children") with close surveillance of recipients and a range of punitive sanctions organized as TANF ("Temporary Assistance to Needy Families"). Recipients are required to check-in regularly with government officials, and often required to attend training programs focused not only on "job readiness" but dictating approaches to family life and relationships as well (Randles and Woodward 2018). Edin and Shaefer (2015, 25) document that "under the new plan, no one with children would have the legal right to receive a dime of cash welfare from the government, even if the family had no other means of support." The PRWORA combined strict work requirements and a five-year lifetime limit on benefits with often inadequate education, job training and child care subsidies (all through TANF), as well as marriage promotion programs and other interventions designed to reshape individual-level values. The result was a strong push for low-income parents to accept unstable, low-wage employment, an outcome Fording, Soss and Schram (2011) argue is more consistent with the interests of low-wage employers than with the interests of low-income citizens. For some previous recipients, the surveillance and rigid sanctions left no safety net at all, a trend Edin and Shaefer (2015) document in their study of the rising number of Americans living on $2 a day or less in the wake of welfare reform. Though TANF is largely funded by the federal government, the PRWORA allowed flexibility across states in how strict the surveillance is, how many activities "count" as work, and how adequate funding is for support programs. Despite these state-level variations, with some more generous than others, the trend has been reduced benefits for those living in poverty.

Under what Collins and Mayer (2010) call "market fundamentalism," the focus of public assistance policy shifted "to the bottom line, the short-term, and the individual" (148), with people living in poverty, especially people of color, framed as "civic failures" for their supposedly inadequate participation in the labor market (Soss, Fording and Schram 2011, 44). This was "part of a much broader political campaign . . . traced to the same political forces that have worked to deregulate industries, cut taxes, shift risks onto private actors, and weaken social protections for the middle class" (Soss, Fording and Schram 2011, 19). Individuals struggling with poverty are assumed to lack discipline, morals, and capacities. Consequently, interventions such as marriage promotion programs and other required training for PRWORA participants are designed to enhance individual work ethic, traditional family values, and specific work skills. The punitive focus flows logically from the preoccupation with market forces and individual choice, both of which imply the need for discipline and surveillance. That discipline can take the form of incentives but is more often structured through penalties and stigma. Collins and Mayer (2010, 149) argue that neoliberal poverty policy treats people receiving public assistance as failed market actors, for whom "citizenship was not the birthright of everyone but had to be earned through productive labor" enforced through punitive sanctions.

Another key poverty-reduction program in the United States is the Earned Income Tax Credit (or EITC). This program is consistent with neoliberalism's individualist market orientation, but operates through incentives rather than punitive sanctions, because it is available only to people already employed in the paid labor force. It allows some low-income workers with children to receive a federal tax refund up to and beyond the amount they paid in federal taxes, in effect providing a cash subsidy. Sykes et al. (2015, 245) summarize its impact: "TANF benefits are typically so low that recipients remain below the poverty line, whereas the EITC currently lifts nearly 7 million individuals out of poverty, including 3.3 million children." This government transfer of funds is offered without stigma or surveillance, processed through the system all U.S. tax-payers use. Therefore, researchers argue it fosters social inclusion rather than exclusion: "Although both programs proffer cash benefits to claimants who struggle to make ends meet, in stark contrast to TANF, EITC receipt connotes conformity with social norms, self-sufficiency, and even pride" (Sykes et al. 2015, 259).

Poverty policy in Canada

Researchers chart a similar trajectory in Canada.

> The ideological shift from Keynesian to neoliberal government policies began in the 1980s . . . Since then policies that emphasise market mechanisms and individual rather than collective approaches to solving or handling economic and social problems have become commonplace . . . (and) take a narrow approach to poverty and social exclusion through policies aimed at the labour supply in direct response to labour market need.
>
> *(MacKinnon 2013, 22)*

Harding (2016, 26) asserts that "Canadians have witnessed the dismantling of the welfare state and a gradual decline in social entitlements." As in the PRWORA in the U.S., national level policy in Canada in the late 1990s and early 2000s coupled cutbacks through work incentives with plans for increased investment to stimulate opportunity, plans that were never realized. "It is not difficult to understand why the stick succeeded and the carrot failed. Cutting passive social expenditures saves money; new social investments in education, training, and active labor market policy cost money" (Myles 2015, 8), money that Myles argues no political party supports allocating due to neoliberal "tax phobia." Myles (2015, 14–16) also notes that, like state variation in the United States, poverty-reduction and public assistance policies in Canada have varied by province, with particularly notable contrasts between Alberta and Ontario, on the one hand, and Quebec on the other.

Ontario is Canada's largest province in terms of population, and represents key elements of the neoliberal policy many scholars claim characterizes the nation overall. Smith-Carrier and Lawlor (2017, 106) view neoliberalism as a process, and argue that "this process has reduced the effectiveness of the social safety net in helping to curb poverty . . . declining effectiveness is most pronounced in Ontario." They offer a discourse analysis of Ontario's 2008 provincial "Poverty Reduction Strategy" (PRS), as well as annual reports made in the following years and the updated PRS launched in 2014. The 2008 PRS included specific goals, like a 25% reduction in child poverty over five years and a promise to end homelessness, neither of which were realized; in the updated PRS, similar goals were offered but without deadlines. Throughout the official documents analyzed, Smith-Carrier and Lawlor (2017, 121) argue that

> the individual, nearly stripped of agency, is assumed to have ultimate responsibility to obtain the skills, education and willingness necessary to exit poverty and enter the realm of the (venerable, employed) socially included . . . (neoliberalisation) has created the structures and conditions that perpetuate and sustain poverty, while rendering people culpable for the systemic failures that accompany neoliberal restructuring.

Dolson (2015, 116) posits that "Ontario Works" is based on neoliberal logic: "'participants'-in order to receive social assistance-must engage in a documentable effort to pursue employment, practical education or skills-development leading to entry into the labor market," generally into low-wage, precarious work. These policies follow patterns similar to those noted by scholars of poverty governance in the USA, with cash assistance increasingly conditional on activity in the labor market regardless of the quality of employment available and with only limited regard for the obstacles individuals may face in maintaining stable employment.

But along with these similarities, there are some aspects of social provision in Canada that are more generous and universally available, which means they provide greater support to people struggling with poverty too. In other words, due to strong social provision overall, those living in poverty are less marginalized in some ways in Canada. Health care is an example:

> universality has remained stronger in the field of healthcare than in the one of cash benefits, a trend related to the wide popularity of universal healthcare, which explains why conservatives have been extra careful when dealing with this policy area closely tied to citizenship.
>
> *(Béland and Waddan 2014, 83)*

Hallgrimsdottir, Benoit, and Phillips (2013, 27) also argue that Canada is generous in some regards, though they criticize limited support for child care: "Canada's welfare state is lopsided: while leading the world in some areas of social investment – most notably health care and higher education – it is a laggard in other areas of social welfare spending, including childcare policies." In addition, Ontario has just recently suspended a three-year pilot program offering universal basic income payments (non-conditional cash benefits) to 4,000 low-income residents, moving away from this universal program back toward more conditional approaches (Ontario Ministry of Children, Community, and Social Services 2018).

Poverty policy in Mexico

Poverty levels are higher in Mexico, and the economic context quite different in some regards, but the pattern of increasingly neoliberal approaches to poverty is evident here as well. Castillo Fernández and Arzate Salgado (2016, 97) claim that in the 1970s Mexican poverty policy "sought to increase employment rates and improve relative salary redistribution" with "efforts to form and implement social policies based on the principles of social solidarity, universalism, and general social welfare needs;" but by the end of the 1980s, the "free market began to be seen as the key to social welfare." This shift is directly connected to shifts in Canada and the United States, but in Mexico the process is even more responsive to increased involvement in global markets, as part of a Latin American "transition to a new development model based on free trade, a residual role of the State in the provision of social services, and, in general, a full integration into the global economy" (Bayón 2017, 115). The policy adjustments required for that integration led, according to Castillo Fernández and Arzate Salgado (2016, 101), to increasing levels of poverty and employment instability: "The neoliberal economic model adopted at the beginning of the 1980s has led to a complex situation of helplessness and growing social vulnerability. Unemployment, job informality, deteriorating work conditions, poverty and social inequality have become serious challenges."

A prominent poverty-reduction policy in Mexico is Opportunidades, a conditional cash transfer program somewhat consistent with the neoliberal logic of the USA's TANF and Canada's Ontario Works but also, in some ways, more inclusively oriented. "The Mexican government launched this program in order to tackle poverty throughout the country . . . by making cash payments to the poorest families in the country in return for regular school attendance and periodic revisions of health and nutritional habits" (Barahona 2018, 602). Some analysts report successes:

> The Oportunidades program has . . . been evaluated more than any other government program in Mexico. The main external evaluation . . . found significant positive results: increased school attendance, lengthening of educational careers, better nourishment, and improved health among the program participants.
>
> *(Smith, Koikkalainen and Casanueva 2014, 11)*

Given that all of these outcomes are ones negatively associated with poverty, these results suggest the program is in some ways successful in alleviating the effects of poverty. In their analysis, Smith, Koikkalainen, and Casanueva (2014, 10) also argue that while the program is infused with individualistic rhetoric and stigmatizing sanctions, making it popular with elites politically, in practice it operates more inclusively, like "a traditional welfare program that redistributes income to families in extreme poverty and increases their probability of attaining a minimum level of consumption."

Those who report successes are joined by analysts critical of Opportunidades, who focus on tensions similar to those questioned in the United States and Canada. "The program has been criticized for being too technocratic, overlooking civil society participation, and excluding many who would deserve assistance" (Smith, Koikkalainen and Casanueva 2014, 19). Bayón (2017, 114–115) highlights the "extensive poverty that still affects one half of the Mexican population and the low quality services offered" and argues that "though blurring the structural causes of poverty, blaming the poor legitimates inequality and the concentration of privileges." And Castillo Fernández and Arzate Salgado (2016, 100) conclude that while Opportunidades has had some positive effects, especially for children and youth, its impact is limited: "due to the demands of the labor market, the level of training offered by the program is insufficient to obtain well paid jobs, especially in light of the free market economic model and the resulting devaluation of human capital." Though not directly connected to Opportunidades, Lopreite and Macdonald (2014) offer a similar critique about Mexican policy that pushes low-income women into precarious employment without providing adequate support for child care, a criticism also offered of U.S. welfare reform by scholars such as Collins and Mayer (2010).

> Mexican policies continue to be implemented in a manner that reflects neoliberal assumptions about the need for human capital development, and that requires parents to pay a significant share of the costs for low-quality care that will free up women to work in the paid labor force.
>
> *(Lopreite and Macdonald 2014, 98)*

Related to its higher levels of poverty and lower income levels overall, migration patterns also differentiate Mexico from the two more affluent nations. Poverty prompts migration to the United States as a survival strategy and, as Zavella (2011) documents, that migration often involves remittances sent back to Mexico and movement back and forth across the border. Torres and Carte (2016) review previous literature that claims remittances help alleviate poverty, and agree that there are some positive impacts. But in their own analysis of ethnographic data they contend that those left behind also "bear the burden of 'externalities' or hidden costs of neoliberal restructuring and transnational migration" (Torres and Carte 2016, 400). Bayón (2017) also considers migration in relation to poverty in Mexico, as one of the few sources of hope. "Crossing the border undocumented, el otro lado, emerges . . . as the (only?) way to fulfill—at least partially and temporarily—aspirations for better life chances," but that route comes with many negative consequences for migrants, their families, and their home communities (Bayón 2017, 114).

Other themes in the literature

Along with these sketches of poverty policy in the USA, Canada, and Mexico, with their common foundation of neoliberalism, other themes are evident across the literature. Rhetoric and beliefs are referenced commonly, and are sometimes the central focus of research. Analysis of how poverty is framed in U.S. media indicates a predominance of what Rose and Baumgartner (2013, 23) call "stingy frames," with the poor often represented "as cheaters, as lazy or unwilling to work," and with governmental support represented as dysfunctional or dependence-inducing. Harding (2016, 26) draws a similar conclusion in Canada, with an analysis of newspapers that documents "the prominence of established and emerging poverty discourses that blame poor people for their plight or cast them in a negative light." Public opinion about poverty and related social policy has also prompted interest. Campbell (2016) finds that U.S. public opinion is predominated by negative attitudes toward public assistance, especially among people who came of age during the "welfare reform" era. Harell, Soroka, and Ladner (2014) investigate attitudes toward public assistance in Canada. They argue Canadians are less individualistic in their explanations for poverty than those in the United States, but they still find substantial proportions of the general population with negative attitudes toward "welfare" and especially so when respondents are primed to think about indigenous Canadians as the recipients. Though not studied as much directly in Mexico, the same kind of neoliberal framings and beliefs evident in U.S. and Canadian studies are noted by scholars, such as Bayón's (2017, 114) claim that Mexican poverty policy is "based on a discourse focused on personal deficits of those suffering deprivation."

The active agency of the poor is another theme in literature across all three nations. Rather than viewing low-income people only as passive recipients in need of correction by neoliberal policy regimes, scholarship documents their active capacity to participate in collective action and the design and execution of policy. Cazenave (2007) traces low-income people's successful organizing and cooperative development of local poverty-reduction organizations during the U.S. War on Poverty, while Dominguez (2011) and Mazelis (2017) offer case studies of social networks among people living in poverty in the United States that allowed them to creatively respond to economic hardship. Price (2014) documents the collective work of an indigenous women's weaving cooperative in rural Mexico, while Fletes-Ocón and Bonanno (2013) investigate local political organizing among poor farmers to resist neoliberal restructuring in Mexican agriculture. Harding (2016) outlines successful advocacy by low-income Canadians and their allies in pushing for more comprehensive and specific anti-poverty strategies, and Dolson (2015, 116) studies resistance among street youth in London, Ontario, exploring their "creative interpretation and manipulation of (Ontario Works) rules" to craft "an alternative moral economy (that) reveals the limits of the state's reach and effort to domesticate marginalized youths."

Conclusion

There is far more to consider in an overview of poverty in North America, from the specifics of child poverty and elder poverty, to the way increasing income inequality throughout the region is linked to the experiences of both rich and poor people, to the rapidly shifting politics of each nation. But the topics considered here paint a clear picture of commonalities and variations across Mexico, Canada, and the United States in the levels of poverty experienced, the approaches to defining poverty employed and debated, and trends in policy for addressing poverty. Though the variations are important, the region is interconnected economically, with Canada and Mexico especially affected by the U.S. economy. And all three nations are connected to a global economy characterized by neoliberal policy in economic, social, and political arenas. There is greater incidence of poverty in Mexico relative to the United States and Canada, as documented above, tied to the nation's lower overall income levels and its placement within the global economy. But given the differences in overall income across these three nations, it is striking that levels of extreme poverty (and levels of income inequality) in the United States remain so high. The common emphasis poverty scholars place on neoliberalism, conditional approaches to public assistance, and dismissive attitudes toward the poor, as well as the particular impact of poverty on marginalized racial/ethnic groups and on women raising children, are striking commonalities too. Many scholars emphasize the political agency and creativity of people living in poverty too, pointing to potentially more inclusive approaches. As Santiago (2015, 10) argues, "If we move beyond our shortsighted perceptions of poor people as needy and undeserving, we will uncover different narratives that reveal resourcefulness, capability, and initiative" and recognize "the necessity of including poor people in developing the options that work best for them."

References

AEI/Brookings Working Group. 2015. Opportunity, Responsibility, and Security. www.brookings.edu/wp-content/uploads/2016/07/Full-Report.pdf

Barahona, Igor. 2018. "Poverty in Mexico." *Social Indicators Research* 135 (2): 599–627.

Bayón, Maria Cristina. 2017. "Accumulating Disadvantages, Multiplying Inequalities: Biographies of Poverty in Mexico City." *Journal of Poverty* 21 (2): 97–119.

Béland, Daniel and Alex Waddan. 2014. "Conservatives, Partisan Dynamics and the Politics of Universality: Reforming Universal Social Programmes in the UK and Canada." *Journal of Poverty & Social Justice* 22 (2): 83–97.

Campbell, Colin. 2016. "The Formative Years, Economic Hardship, and Beliefs about the Government's Role in Lessening Poverty." *Social Problems* 63: 244–265.

Castillo Fernández, Didimo and Jorge Arzate Salgado. 2016. "Economic Crisis, Poverty and Social Policy in Mexico." *Critical Sociology* 42 (1): 87–104.

Cazenave, Noel A. 2007. *Impossible Democracy*. Albany: SUNY Press.

Collins, Jane L. and Victoria Mayer. 2010. *Both Hands Tied*. Chicago: University of Chicago Press.

Davis, James J., Vincent J. Roscigno, and George Wilson. 2016. "American Indian Poverty in the Contemporary United States." *Sociological Forum* 31: 5–28.

Dolson, Mark S. 2015. "By Sleight of Neoliberal Logics: Street Youth, Workfare, and the Everyday Tactics of Survival in London, Ontario, Canada." *City & Society* 27 (2): 116–135.

Dominguez, Silvia. 2011. *Getting Ahead*. New York: New York University Press.

Edin, Kathryn and Maria Kefalas. 2011. *Promises I Can Keep*. Berkeley: University of California Press.

Edin, Kathryn and Luke Shaefer. 2015. *$2 a Day*. New York: Houghton-Mifflin.

Fletes-Ocón, Hector B. and Alessandro Bonanno. 2013. "Responses to the Crisis of Neo-liberal Globalization: State Intervention in Palm Oil Production in Chiapas, Mexico." *International Journal of Sociology of Agriculture & Food* 20 (3): 313–334.

Fording, Richard C., Joe Soss, and Sanford F. Schram, 2011. "Race and the Local Politics of Punishment in the New World of Welfare." *American Journal of Sociology* 116: 1610–1657.
Gilderbloom, John I., Greogory Squires, and Margaret Wuerstle. 2013. "Emergency Homeless Shelters in North America." *Housing & Society* 40 (1): 1–37.
Grusky, David B., Marybeth Mattingly, and Charles Varner. 2016. "The Poverty and Inequality Report: Executive Summary." *Pathways*, special issue, 3–9.
Hallgrimsdottir, Helga K., Cecilia Benoit, and Rachel Phillips. 2013. "The Mother-Citizen and the Working Girl: First-Wave Feminist Citizenship Claims in Canada and Discursive Opportunities for Twenty-First Century Childcare Policy." *Canadian Review of Sociology* 50 (1): 27–51.
Harding, Robert. 2016. "Limited and Limiting Conversations about the Poor: Elizabethan Prescriptions to Poverty in the Canadian Press." *Canadian Review of Social Policy* 76: 25–51.
Harell, Allison, Stuart Soroka, and Kiera Ladner. 2014. "Public Opinion, Prejudice and the Racialization of Welfare in Canada." *Ethnic & Racial Studies* 37 (14): 2580–2597.
Hryciuk, Renata E. 2017. "Mothering for Neoliberal Times: Mazahua Women, Poverty and the Cultural Politics of Development in Central Mexico." *Polish Sociological Review* 200: 523–543.
Johnstone, Marjorie, Eunjung Lee, and Jo Connelly. 2017. "Understanding the Meta-discourse Driving Homeless Policies and Programs in Toronto, Canada." *International Social Work* 60 (6): 1443–1456.
Kane, Emily W. 2018. "The Neoliberal Baseline? A Community-Based Exploration of Beliefs about Poverty and Social Policy." *Journal of Poverty* 22: 65–87.
Livingstone, Anne-Marie and Morton Weinfeld. 2015. "Black Families and Socio-economic Inequality in Canada." *Canadian Ethnic Studies* 47 (3): 1–23.
Lopreite, Debora and Laura Macdonald. 2014. "Gender and Latin American Welfare Regimes." *Social Politics* 21 (1): 80–102.
MacKinnon, Shauna. 2013. "The Politics of Poverty in Canada." *Social Alternatives* 32 (1): 19–23.
Mazelis, Joan Maya. 2017. *Surviving Poverty*. New York: NYU Press.
Myles, John. 2015. "The Fading of Redistributive Politics in Canada." *Canadian Review of Sociology* 52 (1): 1–21.
Ontario Ministry of Children, Community, and Social Services. 2018. "Ontario's Government for the People Announces Compassionate Wind Down of Basic Income Research Project." Press Release available at https://news.ontario.ca/mcys/en/2018/08/ontarios-government-for-the-people-announces-compassionate-wind-down-of-basic-income-research-projec.html; accessed February 19, 2019.
Orleck, Annelise. 2011. "The War on Poverty from the Grassroots Up." In *The War on Poverty*, edited by Orleck, Annelise and Lisa Gayle Hazirjian. Athens: University of Georgia Press, pp. 1–28.
Orleck, Annelise and Lisa Gayle Hazirjian, eds. 2011. *The War on Poverty*. Athens: University of Georgia Press.
Price, Cassandra. 2014. "Community Murals: Strength for the Struggle." *Journal of Poverty* 18 (1): 103–107.
Randles, Jennifer and Kerry Woodward. 2018. "Learning to Labor, Love, and Live: Shaping the Good Neoliberal Citizen in State Work and Marriage Programs." *Sociological Perspectives* 61: 39–56.
Rose, Max and Frank R. Baumgartner. 2013. "Framing the Poor." *The Policy Studies Journal* 41: 22–53.
Ryser, Laura and Greg Halseth. 2017. "Opportunities and Challenges to Address Poverty in Rural Regions: A Case Study from Northern BC." *Journal of Poverty* 21 (2): 120–141.
Santiago, Anna Maria. 2015. "Fifty Years Later: From a War on Poverty to a War on the Poor." *Social Problems* 62: 2–14.
Small, Mario L. and Katherine Newman. 2001. "Urban Poverty after the Truly Disadvantaged." *Annual Review of Sociology* 27: 23–45.
Smith, Michael Peter, Saara Koikkalainen, and Leticia Casanueva. 2014. "The Oligarchic Diffusion of Public Policy." *Urban Affairs Review* 50 (1): 3–33.
Smith-Carrier, Tracy and Andrea Lawlor. 2017. "Realising Our (Neoliberal) Potential? A Critical Discourse Analysis of the Poverty Reduction Strategy in Ontario, Canada." *Critical Social Policy* 37 (1): 105–127.
Soss, Joe, Richard Fording, and Sanford Schram. 2011. *Disciplining the Poor*. Chicago: University of Chicago Press.
Sykes, Jennifer, Katrin Križ, Kathryn Edin, and Sarah Halpern-Meekin. 2015. "Dignity and Dreams: What the EITC Means to Low-Income Families." *American Sociological Review* 80: 243–267.
Thiede, Brian C., Hyojung Kim, and Tim Slack. 2017. "Marriage, Work, and Racial Inequalities in Poverty." *Journal of Marriage & Family* 79 (5): 1241–1257.

Torres, Rebecca M. and Lindsey Carte. 2016. "Migration and Development? The Gendered Costs of Migration on Mexico's Rural 'Left Behind'." *Geographical Review* 106 (3): 399–420.
UNICEF Office of Research. 2017. "Building the Future: Children and the Sustainable Development Goals in Rich Countries." *Innocenti Report Card 14*, UNICEF Office of Research – Innocenti, Florence.
USA's World Factbook. 2018. (www.cia.gov/library/publications/resources/the-world-factbook/); accessed July 8, 2019.
Waldfogel, Jane. 2013. "Fifty Years after the War on Poverty, the Safety Net for America's Families with Children Is Frayed." Scholars Strategy Network Key Findings Brief. www.scholarsstrategynetwork.org
Waldfogel, Jane. 2014. "New Measures Reveal the True Impact of America's Antipoverty Programs." Scholars Strategy Network Key Findings Brief. www.scholarsstrategynetwork.org
Zavella, Patricia. 2011. *I'm Neither Here Nor There: Mexicans' Quotidian Struggles with Migration and Poverty*. Durham, NC: Duke University Press.
Ziccardi, Alicia. 2014. "Poverty and Urban Inequality: The Case of Mexico City Metropolitan Region." *International Social Science Journal* 65 (1/2): 205–219.

Part III

Policies toward poverty

19
The working poor

Ive Marx

What this chapter is about and why it matters

This chapter is about the working poor in the rich world. That makes sense because most of the world's poor people actually work in some capacity or another. The term 'working poor' as a specific subcategory is almost by definition confined to advanced welfare states where people can survive without working thanks to social benefits and other provisions. For much, if not most, of the world's population that option simply does not exist and hence they are simply called the poor.

As we will see, even in the rich world the distinction between the working and the non-working poor is actually not that clear-cut. This has to do with definitional issues. The 'working' part in the expression usually refers to the labour market status of the people under focus. It usually denotes the fact that the people in question spend a sizeable amount of activity in paid work. That still allows for a lot of variation when it comes to their actual work intensity. Hence, part-time workers or temporary workers may qualify as 'working' even if for their income they draw in large part on other household members or on state benefits, or both. The 'poor' part usually refers to the living standard of the household in which the individual under focus lives. That means that the incomes that others bring into the household, or not, matter a lot. And of course the number of people and children living on that income or those combined incomes matters. So, as with poverty in general, a lot of factors come into play, making it a causally complex phenomenon. A key message of this chapter is that it is not useful to regard the working poor, or 'in-work poverty' as it is alternatively referred to, as a problem that is clearly distinct from the wider poverty phenomenon. That distinction is rarely really useful for analytical purposes and it is certainly not useful for policy purposes.

And yet attention on the working poor as a specific issue worthy of academic and policy attention has grown fast (Marx and Verbist, 1998; Andreß and Lohmann, 2008; Fraser et al., 2011; Crettaz, 2013; Marx and Nolan, 2014; Lohmann and Marx, 2018). Which is not to say, of course, that the phenomenon is in any way new. Friedrich Engels (1848) wrote about the impoverished working classes during early industrialization, as did Seebohm Rowntree (1901) in his classic study on poverty among working families in York.

But the expression 'working poor' is relatively new outside of the United States, where it has been commonly used for a long time (Fields, 2012). One would be hard pressed to find studies referring to 'the working poor' pertaining to Europe prior to the 1990s. In rich countries in-work poverty is usually linked to the demise of industrial employment and the assumed proliferations of low-paid, insecure service sector jobs, epitomized by the proverbial McDonalds jobs. The contrast is often drawn with the golden years of welfare capitalism when manufacturing industry provided stable, well-paid employment to the majority of the work force, even to those with little or no formal education. As Gosta Esping-Andersen et al. (2002: 28) once put it:

> We no longer live in a world in which low-skilled workers can support the entire family. The basic requisite for a good life is increasingly strong cognitive skills and professional qualifications … Employment remains as always the sine qua non for good life chances, but the requirements for access to quality jobs are rising and are likely to continue to do so.

Guliano Bonoli (2007: 496) said it this way: 'Postindustrial labour markets are characterized by higher wage inequality with the result that for those at the bottom end of the wage distribution, access to employment is not a guarantee of a poverty-free existence.' Meanwhile, some have even gone further. Guy Standing has put forward the thesis that the combined forces of globalization and neoliberalism have brought a new social class which he labels the 'the precariat', consisting of several different social groups, notably immigrants, young educated people, and those who have fallen out of the old-style industrial working class (Standing, 2011). He projects a world in which wages will continue to decline and job insecurity will continue to grow. Whether the actual evidence bears out such dystopian views is another matter. But the perception that such trends are real is certainly feeding popular and also policy discourse. Governments and international organizations like the OECD have paid increasing attention to the working poor. The European Pillar of Social Rights, a declaration signed by all European Union Member States in 2017 states that "In-work poverty shall be prevented."

The very latest source of concern comes from the emergence of the platform economy. Workers in the platform economy – for example people working for Uber or Deliveroo – are more likely to be categorized as self-employed contractors rather than employees or workers. This classification as self-employed means that many are excluded from social and employment protections that are available to other workers. Also, there is concern that pay levels are significantly lower than normal wages for similar jobs and even lower than national minimum wages. Hence, the fear that the platform economy is a new source of in-work poverty. In what follows, I first discuss definitional and measurement issues. I then say something about levels and trends across industrialized countries. The typical profile of the working poor is discussed next. I conclude with some policy considerations.

Defining and measuring the working poor

The literature on the working poor uses a variety of definitions (for an overview see: Crettaz, 2013; Lohmann, 2018).

The most common approach builds for one part on the labour market status of the individual under focus and for another on the living standard of the household in which that individual resides. For example, Eurostat defines the working poor as those individuals who have been mainly working during the reference year (either in employment or self-employment) and whose household equivalized disposable income is below 60 per cent of the median in the country in question. Employment status is measured on the basis of monthly calendars completed by survey respondents, with 'in work' taken to mean that the status he/she declares to have occupied for at least seven months is employee or self-employed.

For the self-employed particular problems exist (Horemans and Marx, 2017). This is not a trivial point of methodology since the self-employed are at a particularly high risk of being poor, or at least being counted as such. They also tend to make up a significant part of the working poor. But there are serious measurement challenges as far as this group is concerned. Complex accounting practices and tax optimization schemes often make it difficult for the self-employed to provide an accurate estimation in surveys like those used for EU-SILC of their personal as opposed to their (incorporated) business income, which are often intertwined. In addition, the self-employed tend to be less likely to respond to income surveys. Their income variables are subjected to higher levels of item non-response as well as under-reporting. Additional problems arise when self-employment is a secondary activity for employees.

Clearly, combining two levels of analysis – the individual's labour market status and the household's income (adjusted for household size) – inherently complicates interpretation, since the labour market status of other persons in the household, rather than that of the individual being considered, may be crucial. It usually is. For one's living standard it makes a huge difference whether one lives in a household with other earners or not. The number of dependent children, if any, also has a big impact on living standards. Furthermore, using a year as the reference period also complicates interpretation. Those working for part but not all of the year may be in poverty on an annual basis for that reason even if they were not poor while working.

Note that this common approach to measuring in-work poverty puts relatively high weight on overall household work intensity as a driving factor (Marx and Nolan, 2014; Ponthieux, 2010). Note also that the most precarious workers, those with volatile and marginal labour market attachment during the income reference period, are not included (Crettaz, 2011). On the other hand, as periods of not working (up to five months) are allowed to be considered 'in-work', it is possible that in-work poverty can be, at least partially, seen as an unemployment problem (Halleröd et al., 2015).

All this has important policy implications. Take, for example, a two-adult household with two dependent children. There is a sole breadwinner working in a relatively low-paid job and a non-working partner. Child benefits are modest in the country where they live. The household finds itself living in financial poverty.

Whether, and to what extent, the poverty status of that household is seen as a problem of insufficient breadwinner earnings, or as a problem of partner non-participation in work, or as a problem of insufficient child support makes a fundamental difference as to what type of policy action is to be examined and possibly favoured. Some will claim that the problem here is insufficient or low earnings. They will call for a decent 'living wage' (Horton and Wills, 2018). Another section of opinion in Europe would brand our example of a traditional breadwinner family with insufficient earnings as a problem of partner under-participation in the labour market.

That may be clear in this case, but in other cases it may be less clear-cut. Even if in-work poverty is construed as largely a problem of low household work intensity, the question arises what can be deemed to be a sufficient level of work intensity. It is not self-evident that this is equal to all working-age, work-capable adults in the household being in full-time work the whole year round. Societal norms on this issue may differ across countries. In countries like the Netherlands, for example, a $\frac{4}{5}$ job per adult appears to be closer to the norm of full work intensity. Also, household composition may be deemed to matter. It is not self-evident that a lone parent with young children is expected to work full-year, full-time before additional income support is considered legitimate if his or her earnings fall short of the poverty threshold.

Levels and trends

There is considerable variation in the prevalence of in-work poverty across the developed world. If we look at Eurostat figures as calculated from the harmonized EU-SILC database, we can see that the prevalence of in-work poverty ranges from a low of 4–5 per cent in countries such as Belgium, the Czech Republic, Denmark and Finland to highs of up to 17 per cent in Romania. Romania is a bit of an outlier though. In a few countries that percentage is much higher than 13 per cent, including Greece, Spain and Italy. That is less variation than we observe for overall poverty rates, let alone for some other subcategories like the unemployed.

The OECD, employing a different definition and a range of different data sources, finds similar variation across a wider set of rich and emerging economies. The OECD defines the working poor as those living in households with a working-age head and at least one worker, and having an income below the poverty line, which the OECD sets at 50 per cent of the national median equivalized disposable income. Interestingly, this still yields lower levels of in-work poverty in countries such as the United States and Canada than in places like Spain, Greece or Italy.

Looking at trends, there is again striking cross-country variation. The common perception that 'in-work poverty is on the rise' is certainly not supported by the facts. While it is true that in-work poverty rates for the EU for the latest available year tend to be higher as compared to the start of the series in 2006, there is no universal trend. In-work poverty rates have remained relatively stable in countries such as Belgium, Denmark, the Czech Republic, Greece, the Netherlands or Portugal. There are even countries where there has been a decline, as in Latvia. However, it is still true that the EU average has increased by just over one percentage point since 2007.

However, it is crucial to remind ourselves of the difference between risks and shares. People who have a job tend to be far less exposed to poverty than, say, unemployed people. But then workers tend to be far more numerous than unemployed people. The consequence is that among the total population of people living in poverty at working age, workers may still make up a larger share than the unemployed. Additionally, it is worth keeping in mind that the number of working poor will rise, even if poverty risks remain stable, when more people transition from non-employment as their dominant status into employment. So while it is true that poverty risks for workers have remained relatively steady in many countries, the working poor may still have become more numerous in countries where employment levels increased.

It is worth focusing on two groups: part-time workers and the self-employed.

Part-time workers tend to have higher poverty risks than full-time workers (Horemans et al., 2016). But much depends on the motives for working part-time. While some reasons for working part-time can simply be labelled as either voluntary or involuntary, this is sometimes more ambiguous. Working part-time because of caring, for example, can either be classified as voluntary or involuntary.

At any rate, it is clear that workers who clearly work part-time for lack of full-time employment face significantly higher poverty risks. Involuntary part-time employment increased quite considerably in most countries during the recent financial crisis, in several countries rising by more than ten percentage points. This rise was accompanied by an increase, on average, in the poverty risk associated with working part-time.

The self-employed also face significantly higher income poverty risks (Horemans and Marx, 2017). About 15 percent of European workers in self-employment can be labelled as working poor as compared to 10 per cent of contracted employees. Remarkably, however, while income poverty levels are quite significant among the self-employed, material deprivation rates are generally much lower. The discrepancy between income poverty measures and material deprivation measures is much larger for the self-employed than it is for employees. One possible explanation is that the self-employed can more often draw on assets accumulated over the life cycle or on business assets they control. This said, the self-employed constitute a very mixed segment of the workforce. Within-group inequality is quite significant. One group that emerges as being particularly at risk of poverty are own-account workers, substantiating worries about the rise of this form of self-employment.

Drivers and patterns of in-work poverty across the rich world

Drivers of in-work poverty can be categorized in terms of needs, resources and restrictions (Lohmann, 2009). Needs increase with the size of a household and also the age of its members. Resources refer to the earnings potential of household members, but also access to transfers. Restrictions refer to the obstacles to realizing that earnings potential or accessing benefits.

These play at the individual as well as the household level. Whether people and households are in a position to earn a decent income in the labour market obviously depends on a host of factors. Macro-economic and monetary policies affect the availability of jobs, especially in certain localities and sectors, as well as the skills required. On the supply side, education and training policies matter for earnings capacity since more highly educated, better skilled people earn more. Wage-setting mechanisms, including minimum wages, directly affect the returns to work effort. Taxes and social security contributions impact on the difference between gross pay and take-home pay. Then there are policies that affect whether people can actually realize their earnings potential. There may be restrictions on working times or contract forms, or on access to certain professions. The availability, quality and cost of child care provision greatly affects the capacity of those with care responsibilities to realize their earnings capacity (Van Lancker and Horemans, 2018).

Government transfers matter, obviously. Income replacement benefits for periods not in work may compensate for the inability to work full-time, such as in the case of partial unemployment, sickness or old-age. Income replacement benefits provided to non-working household members may affect living standards. And then there are household income supplements, usually to compensate for the cost of children. In some countries housing allowances are available.

This list is not even near exhaustive, but it does go to illustrate that variations in in-work poverty across countries or across time are not easily understood as outcomes of a handful of factors. I have not even listed the 'exogenous' changes impacting on in-work poverty. Economic globalization, trade liberalization and technological change are affecting labour markets in rich countries. There is considerable debate among labour economists as to exactly how. While for a long time the consensus was that globalization and technological change were particularly detrimental to the potential earnings of low-skilled workers, the dominant view now is that the tendency is toward job polarization (Buyst et al., 2018). That implies that many people in previously middle skilled professions (or with the education and skills levels for such jobs) are increasingly left with no other option than to take up (very) low-paid jobs requiring few skills, unless they can upskill (Maître et al., 2018).

Socio-demographic trends also matter. They matter more for in-work poverty than is the general perception. The notion of in-work poverty often conjures up stereotypical images of poorly paid service sector workers toiling away in fast-food chains, hotels and supermarkets. But socio-demographic trends are at least an equally important driver.

On the one hand there has been a trend toward double earnership among couples (Nieuwenhuis, 2014). Female employment rates have increased dramatically over the past couple of decades. The proliferation of double earnership has been an important factor in rising living standards, pushing up median household income even where wages were relatively stagnant. On the other hand, there has been a rise in the number of single-person and single-parent households. These face an inherent disadvantage in societies where dual earner living standards have increasingly come to determine the norm. Single earners with dependent children are at a particular disadvantage.

As Nieuwenhuis and Maldonado (2018) have put it, single parents face a triple bind of inadequate resources, employment and policies. Single parents have no partner at home, depriving them of potential income as well as care support to maximize their own earnings potential. Women face additional challenges in that they face disadvantages in the labour market, including a gender pay gap and motherhood pay gap, discrimination, specialization in lower earning occupations, fewer opportunities for promotion, and less accumulation of experience over their life course. And they often face inadequate policies. Without available, affordable and quality childcare it is particularly difficult for single parents to negotiate work and family responsibilities. Lone parents constitute the core of the working poor in many countries in the rich world.

As I have tried to stress throughout this chapter, institutions and policies matter for in-work poverty. There is immense diversity across the rich world in this respect. However, welfare states do not represent random collections of institutions and policies, but rather there are more or less coherent clusters of institutional arrangements which embody distinct values and rationales, as has been stressed in the concept of welfare regimes. While there have been a lot of justifiable critiques of welfare state 'regimes' as overstylized simplifications, they remain a useful device for synthesis nevertheless (Lohmann and Marx, 2008).

The Nordic welfare states all share low levels of in-work poverty. These systems have been shaped by strongly egalitarian aspirations and are (still) characterized by comparatively high degrees of both decommodification and defamilization. The main institutional features include strong collective wage-setting mechanisms ensuring high effective wage floors. These go together with high employment rates thanks to well-performing education systems and extensive active labour market policies focused on continuous education and training. In addition, there are comparatively plentiful public employment opportunities. Extensive childcare and career interruption provisions facilitate high levels of labour market participation across the board. Social insurance and social assistance provisions are comparatively generous, including child benefits for those in work. These factors account for the comparatively low incidence of in-work poverty in these countries, despite high levels of labour market flexibility and a high prevalence of non-standard work. To the extent that in-work poverty exists, it mostly affects single-earner households in the context of almost generalized double earnership and no preferential tax/benefit treatment for single-earner households. Single young adults are also at a relatively high risk, since they tend to become economically self-reliant at a relatively early age.

In many ways the mirror image of the Nordic cluster is the Anglo-Saxon one. These countries have the least egalitarian or decommodifying ambitions. Here, a rather non-interventionist approach is taken to the labour market and the economy as a whole, and the emphasis is on individual economic self-reliance. Gender equality is ensured through legislation, but the state takes no strong role in facilitating equal participation through providing or subsidizing childcare, etc. Social protection is heavily means tested and aimed at minimum income protection. Collective wage bargaining is not widespread and wage floors are ensured through minimum wages. At the same time, however, the Anglo-Saxon countries have gone the furthest by far in implementing in-work benefits (tax credits in particular) aimed at households with low earnings – specifically single-parent households (Marchal et al., 2018; Marchal and Marx, 2018).

As a consequence, in-work poverty rates in countries such as the UK, Ireland or even the US are not as high as one might expect on the basis of the large numbers of workers in relatively low-paid work and the extent of poverty overall. That is mainly because these countries have gone relatively far in 'making work pay' through targeted income supplements, mainly through the tax system. In the United States, for example, the Earned Income Tax Credit is now the largest redistributive programme for the working aged. But such in-work benefits are also very important in the United Kingdom and Ireland.

Moving to the northern part of mainland Europe, the situation becomes (even) more heterogeneous and hybrid. Income maintenance tends to be comparatively generous, but strongly tied to labour market status and even occupational category. Defamilization is more limited than in Scandinavia but the traditional breadwinner/caretaker division has faded (see, for example, Greve (2012) on Germany). Some countries can be said to be pluralist in nature in that a remaining breadwinner bias in taxation and social security is accompanied by extensive spending on family policies and childcare provisions (this is particularly true for France and Belgium).

Employment conditions tend to be strongly regulated although there are peripheral labour market segments mainly occupied by young people, part-time workers, migrants, etc. Collective wage bargaining results in a fairly high degree of wage compression and a comparatively low incidence of low-paid work in some countries. While collective wage bargaining remains important in countries such as Germany and the Netherlands, its importance has strongly eroded, resulting in strong growths in low-paid employment, which in the case of Germany has been accompanied by rising in-work poverty.

Levels of in-work poverty remain moderately low to average in countries such as Belgium, the Netherlands, France and even Germany, although there has been a significant rise there. In contrast to the Anglo-Saxon countries, most transfer spending is still directed to those not in work. Apart from child benefits there is little additional income support for workers. The Netherlands is a bit of an outlier in this respect in the sense that its labour market has acquired clear Scandinavian flexicurity traits. There is a lot of non-standard employment there, including a relatively large low-pay sector, but policy has also shifted toward supplementing workers on low incomes, especially if they are sole earners with dependent children.

Moving toward the southern European countries, these retain many institutional features that foster strong labour market inequalities – such as those that prevail between core, permanent (male) employees and others, such as temporary or part-time workers. Parts of the labour market are particularly strongly regulated, as seen for example from indicators on dismissal protection. And whereas countries in the north are committed to providing at least some form of universally accessible minimum protection, this is still not the case in southern Europe. Income protection remains fragmented, catering well to particular segments, while not at all to other segments.

It would be a far stretch to say that women are still principally seen as mothers and caretakers. There has been a strong shift in this respect over recent decades. It is increasingly recognized that the state has at least some substantial role to play in the conflict women, in particular, face in combining care and work. The number of young children entering formal care has risen strongly in countries such as Portugal and Italy. Yet family and inter-generational solidarity continue to play a strong role, not only in accommodating work/care conflicts but also in providing protection against social risks. It is well documented that young people in southern Europe move out of the parental home at a relatively late age, when they acquired some level of economic independence and security.

This may account for the fact that in-work poverty rates in southern Europe are only moderately high, in the range of 10 to 13 per cent. In-work poverty is, to a large extent, related to single earnership, due to the evident difficulties women face in gaining access to the labour market. There is also a high incidence of involuntary part-time work. Limited public spending on family benefits increases the need to work full-time, while limited spending on childcare puts a constraint on the ability to do so, making part-time work more of an imposed choice.

The post-communist countries are often discussed as a group but they represent quite different sets of institutions and policies. They do share, by and large, a history of exceptionally egalitarian wage distributions and high levels of female labour participation (on comparatively equal terms compared to men). Their transitions toward market economies happened in quite varied ways, however, with some countries, such as the Baltic countries, making rapid transitions and other countries making smoother ones, for example Hungary and the former Czechoslovakia.

Whatever the path, the situation is clearly quite different these days. The highest shares of low-paid work (in relative as well as absolute terms in Europe) are to be found in the post-communist countries, with levels of close to 25 per cent of the work force in places such as Latvia, Lithuania and Romania, and a level upwards of 20 per cent almost everywhere else. On the other hand, minimum wages have tended to increase and so have various social transfers, including child-related benefits (Marchal and Marx, 2018). But in terms of social transfer spending the post-communist countries still lag behind the richer European economies. Policies to support the combination of work and care also remain relatively underdeveloped (Greve, 2012).

In-work poverty rates vary quite a bit across the post-communist countries, with countries such as the Czech Republic, Slovenia, Slovakia and Croatia at Scandinavian levels. The Baltic countries, Hungary and Poland are at EU average levels. Romania is the country with the highest incidence of in-work poverty in the EU.

Policies for the working poor

As we discussed in the section on conceptual and measurement issues, the extent to which the poverty status of households with at least one worker is seen as a problem of insufficient earnings, or as a problem of underemployment, or as a problem of insufficient child support makes a fundamental difference as to what type of policy action is to be examined and possibly favoured. This requires normative choices on the part of the policy maker.

We have also seen that a host of institutions and policies affect poverty outcomes, including for workers or households mainly reliant on earnings. This means that the policy maker can potentially pull many levers. Deeply engrained institutions may not prove particularly malleable but tax and benefit policies ought to be more responsive.

Policy makers face trade-offs here. Some policy choices may yield effective and immediate poverty relief, for example in-work benefits, but they may come at the cost of supply and earnings-mobility disincentives. Policy choices aimed at longer term, structural improvements, for example through training programmes that boost earnings, possibly come at the cost of less effective immediate poverty relief.

If the resources are not available to pursue both policy courses at the same time a choice has to be made. Again, this choice can only be made as a function of political priorities.

Space constraints do not allow an in-depth discussion here (we refer to Marchal et al. (2018) and Horemans and Marx (2018)) but it is worth highlighting a couple of points.

Minimum wages tend to feature prominently in any debate about what to do about in-work poverty. The connection is made almost immediately in the public mind. However, because of the limited overlap between individual low pay and poverty, any policy aimed at improving the earnings of low-paid individuals will directly benefit only a minority of poor households. Studies suggest that even where the overlap between low pay and household poverty is the greatest, increases in the minimum wage have a relatively limited impact on poverty or income inequality and a substantial spillover to the non-poor. Moreover, boosting minimum wages to the upper prevailing ranges (relative to average earnings) would not be sufficient to eradicate in-work poverty in any country, even without any negative employment effects. Essentially that is because minimum wages have become inherently constrained in providing minimum income protection to sole breadwinner households in countries where relative poverty thresholds are strongly determined by dual earner living standards. All in all, as an isolated measure, higher minimum wages – within realistically feasible ranges – cannot contribute much toward fighting in-work poverty. And yet minimum wages matter, for example by helping to contain the budgetary cost of state income support and to counter the possible wage erosion effects of low earnings subsidization.

Governments provide income support to workers in a variety of ways. Child benefits are particularly important for working families with children. These tend to come in two forms: child benefits and tax advantages linked to the presence of children in the household. Studies show that the best performing countries in terms of poverty reduction tend to have systems that are not particularly strongly targeted. Universal child benefits have the great advantage of having an immediate impact on poverty without adversely affecting work incentives between workers and non-workers.

Governments offer support in other ways. Some countries have introduced tax rebates and allowances for low-wage earners in previous years, thus increasing the income progressivity of social contributions and taxes. The prime objective here, however, has in general not been to alleviate in-work poverty but to increase work incentives, particularly the net pay-off to making the transition from dependence on a social assistance or unemployment benefit to a low-paid job.

Increasingly countries have invested in in-work tax benefits and tax credits, with the most well-known examples being the measures taken in the United States (the Earned Income Tax Credit, EITC) and the United Kingdom (the Working Tax Credit, currently being integrated with other tax credits into the Universal Credit) (Immervoll and Pearson, 2009). Over the past decades, various European countries have experimented with this type of policies. They are attractive as they aim to enhance work incentives for disadvantaged groups, as well as to provide extra income to support their living standards. However, the design of the in-work benefit plays a big role. They are most suitable in countries with dispersed income distributions.

In order to be effective as an anti-poverty device and at the same time affordable within reasonable limits, such tax credits need to be strongly targeted. However, strong targeting at households with low earnings is bound to create mobility traps, which can only be avoided if taper-off rates are sufficiently flat. That comes at a very considerable cost if the lower end of the household earnings distribution is densely populated, as is the case in many European countries. This cost can only be avoided by making the amount of the tax credit itself smaller, but in that case the anti-poverty effect is reduced. Studies by Bargain and Orsini (2007) for Germany, France and Finland, by Figari (2010) for four southern European countries (Italy, Spain, Portugal and Greece) and by Marx et al. (2012) for Belgium, illustrate that tax credits may not be equally effective everywhere.

Conclusion

The 'working poor' was an expression that was rarely used in Europe until a decade or so ago. Since then attention on the phenomenon has proliferated and the term has become common currency in European debates.

This has happened for a number of reasons. Deindustrialization, economic globalization and technological change are seen to threaten the capacity of the less skilled and less talented to make a decent living in rich economies geared toward high value added products and service. In addition, such structural economic shifts are seen to be exacerbated by trends toward trade liberalization, deregulation, the decline of union power and neoliberalism. The most recent source of concern derives from the development of the platform economy. Many of these fears are overblown. Employment levels have reached historical highs in many countries and there is not much evidence of a universal decline in wages or work standards, although this has happened in some countries.

This chapter has stressed that socio-demographic changes, the proliferation of double earnership on the one hand and the spread of single-person and single-parent households on the other has been the more important and real driver of in-work poverty. As double-earner living standards have become the norm, those having to make ends meet on a single-earner income have become inherently disadvantaged. For single earners with dependent children, even well above minimum wage jobs will often not suffice to achieve a minimally acceptable standard of living. There is a very considerable overlap between in-work poverty and child poverty.

This points to the responsibility of states to providing additional support. There are a great many levers to provide support in direct and indirect ways. Adequate education and training will boost the earnings potential of people, and provisions such as available and affordable childcare and adequate public transport can help them to realize that earnings potential. But in order to reach a decent living standard for themselves and their children many workers will still need additional and structural income support through redistribution. A strong claim can be made that people who do their utmost to be productive and financially self-reliant members of society support such support.

Bibliography

Andreß, H.-J. and Lohmann, H. (2008). *The Working Poor in Europe: Employment, Poverty and Globalisation.* Cheltenham, UK and Northampton, MA, USA: Edward Elgar Publishing.

Bargain, O. and Orsini, K. (2007). Beans for breakfast? How exportable is the British workfare model? In O. Bargain (Ed.), *Microsimulation in Action: Policy Analysis in Europe Using EUROMOD* (pp. 165–198). Oxford: Elsevier.

Bonoli, G. (2007). Time matters: postindustrialization, new social risks and welfare state adaptation in advanced industrial democracies. *Comparative Political Studies* 40(5), 495–520.

Buyst, E., Goos, M. and Salomons, A. (2018). Job polarization: an historical perspective. *Oxford Review of Economic Policy* 34(3), 461–474.

Crettaz, E. (2011). *Fighting Working Poverty in Post-Industrial Economies: Causes, Trade-offs and Policy Solutions.* Cheltenham: Edward Elgar.

Crettaz, E. (2013). A state-of-the-art review of working poverty in advanced economies: theoretical models, measurement issues and risk groups. *Journal of European Social Policy* 23(4), 347–362.

Engels, F. (1848). *Die Lage der arbeitenden Klasse in England.* Leipzig: Otto Wiegand.

Esping-Andersen, G., Gallie, D., Hemerijck, A. and Myles, J. (2002). *Why We Need a New Welfare State.* Oxford: Oxford University Press.

Fields, G. S. (2012). *Working Hard, Working Poor.* Oxford University Press: Oxford.

Figari, F. (2010). Can in-work benefits improve social inclusion in the southern European countries? *Journal of European Social Policy* 20(4), 301–315. doi:10.1177/0958928710374375

Fraser, N., Gutiérrez, R. and Peña-Casas, R. (2011). *Working Poverty in Europe: A Comparative Approach.* Houndmills: Palgrave Macmillan.

Greve, B. (2012). *Reconciliation of work and family life in four different welfare states.* Neujobs Working Paper No. D 5.5.

Halleröd, B., Ekbrand, H. and Bengtsson, M. (2015). In-work poverty and labour market trajectories: poverty risks among the working population in 22 European countries. *Journal of European Social Policy* 25(5), 473–488. (On line first (October 7)).

Horemans, J. (2016). *Half a job, twice as poor: Empirical investigations into the role of earnings, family composition, and institutions as factors underlying the poverty risk of part-timers across Europe*, doctoral dissertation, University of Antwerp, Antwerp.

Horemans, J. and Marx, I. (2017). *Poverty and material deprivation among the self-employed in Europe: an exploration of a relatively uncharted landscape*, IZA DP No. 11007.

Horemans, J. and Marx, I. (2018). Doesn't anyone else care? Variation in poverty among working single parents across Europe. In Laurie C. Maldonado and Rense Nieuwenhuis (Eds), *The Triple Bind of Single-Parent Families: Resources, Employment, and Policies to Improve Well-being* (pp. 195–222). Bristol: Policy Press.

Horemans, J., Marx, I. and Nolan, B. (2016). Hanging in, but only just: part-time employment and in-work poverty throughout the crisis. *IZA Journal of European Labor Studies* 5:5.

Horton, A. and Wills, J. (2018). Impacts of the living wage on in-work poverty. In H. Lohmann and I. Marx (Eds), *Handbook of Research on In-Work Poverty* (pp. 228–244). Cheltenham: Edward Elgar.

Immervoll, H. and Pearson, M. (2009). *A good time for making work pay? Taking stock of in-work benefits and related measures across the OECD*. OECD Social, Employment and Migration Working Papers No. 81. Paris: OECD Publishing.

Lohmann, H. (2009). Welfare states, labour market institutions and the working poor: a comparative analysis of 20 European countries. *European Sociological Review* 25(4), 489–504.

Lohmann, H. (2018). The concept and measurement of in-work poverty. In H. Lohmann and I. Marx (Eds), *Handbook of Research on In-Work Poverty* (pp. 7–25) Cheltenham: Edward Elgar.

Lohmann, H. and Marx, I. (2008). The different faces of in-work poverty across welfare state regimes. In H. J. Andrez and H. Lohmann (Eds), *The Working Poor in Europe: Employment, Poverty and Globalization* (pp. 17–46). London: Edward Elgar.

Lohmann, H. and Marx, I. (Eds.). (2018). *Handbook on In-Work Poverty*. Cheltenham: Edward Elgar.

Maitre, B., Nolan, B. and Whelan, C. (2018). Low pay, in-work poverty and economic vulnerability. In H. Lohmann and I. Marx (Eds), *Handbook on In-Work Poverty* (pp. 124–145). Cheltenham: Edward Elgar.

Marchal, S. and Marx, I. (2018). Stemming the tide: what have EU countries and the US done to support low-wage workers in an era of downward wage pressures? *Journal of European Social Policy* 28(1), 18–33.

Marchal, S., Marx, I. and Verbist, G. (2018). Policy options for the working poor. In H. Lohmann and I. Marx (Eds), *Handbook on In-Work Poverty* (pp. 000–000). Cheltenham: Edward Elgar

Marx, I. and Nolan, B. (2014). In-work poverty. In B. Cantillon and F. Vandenbroucke (Eds.), *Reconciling Work and Poverty Reduction: How Succesful Are European Welfare States?* (pp. 131–156). Oxford: Oxford University Press.

Marx, I. and Verbist, G. (1998). Low wage employment and poverty: curse of cure? In S. Bazen, M. Gregory and W. Salverda (Eds), *Low-wage Employment in Europe* (pp. 63–86). London: Edward Elgar.

Marx, I., Vanhille, J. and Verbist, G. (2012). Combating in-work poverty in continental Europe: the potential impact of higher minimum wages and targeted tax relief. *Journal of Social Policy* 41(1), 19–41. doi: 10.1017/s0047279411000341

Nieuwenhuis, R. (2014). *Family policy outcomes: combining institutional and demographic explanations of women's employment and earnings inequality in OECD countries: 1975–2005*, Stockholm University, Stockholm.

Nieuwenhuis, R. and Maldonado, L. C. (Eds) (2018). *The Triple Bind of Single-Parent Families: Resources, Employment, and Policies to Improve Well-being*. Bristol: Policy Press.

OECD. (2011). *Taxation and employment*. Paris: OECD Publishing.

OECD. (2015). *Minimum wages after the crisis: making them pay*. OECD Employment Outlook. Paris: OECD Publishing.

Ponthieux, S. (2010). *In-work poverty in the EU*. Eurostat-Methodologies and Working Papers. Luxembourg: Publications Office of the European Union.

Rowntree, Seebohm (1980 [1901]). *Poverty: A Study of Town Life*. New York: Garland.

Standing, G. (2011). *The Precariat: The New Dangerous Class*. London: Bloomsbury.

Van Lancker, W. and Horemans, J. (2018). Childcare policies and in-work poverty. In H. Lohmann and I. Marx (Eds), *Handbook on In-Work Poverty* (pp. 261–276). Cheltenham: Edward Elgar.

20
Poverty in old age

Bernhard Ebbinghaus, Kenneth Nelson and Rense Nieuwenhuis

Introduction

The reduction of old-age poverty was a major aim in the post-war development of welfare states. However, income protection in old age is currently facing many challenges as a consequence of population ageing and economic changes. While the financial sustainability of pension systems has been high on reform agendas in many affluent countries (sometimes referring to the 'demographic time bomb'), the social sustainability of retirement income has only recently come into focus (Grech, 2013, 2014; Ebbinghaus, 2015). Financial sustainability is concerned with costs and affordability of future pensions, and it advances pension reforms that often include an emphasis on defined contributions, prefunding, private responsibility, extended retirement ages, and stricter access to early retirement and disability benefits (for more details, see Chapter 29). Social sustainability relates to issues of low income, economic hardship, and poverty, and is addressed in this chapter.

Most OECD countries have made important changes to their pension systems in order to make public expenditures more sustainable in ageing societies (for a review see Hinrichs & Lynch (2010), and for analyses outside the OECD, see Chapters 12–18). While these reforms may have been necessary for financial reasons, concerns are raised about the re-emergence of old-age poverty and low income among the elderly. All affluent countries have old-age safety nets in place that are intended to raise the incomes of the poorest elderly who have not been able to allocate sufficient contributions to secure an acceptable pension (Goedemé & Marchal 2016). However, available evidence indicates that these minimum pension benefits sometimes fail to protect the elderly from falling into poverty (OECD, 2015). There are different types of pension systems. Some combine universal basic benefits and supplementary occupational and private pensions, while others are based on contributory earnings-related benefits, often complemented with supplementary pensions and means-tested social assistance. Both types of pension systems are crucial for poverty prevention in old age. However, funded occupational or private pensions are more likely to affect elderly incomes above the poverty line. For old-age poverty, we therefore expect public pensions to be more important.

Little is known about the income position of the elderly across different countries. While the literature on poverty is extensive, the specific focus on old-age poverty is limited – particularly when it comes to recent trends. In this chapter we therefore take stock of income developments among the elderly, focusing on changes in the lower part of the income distribution. It is well known that income distributions grew wider between the mid-1980s up to the mid-2000s, and poverty increased in the majority of countries in the Western hemisphere. However, old-age poverty diverged from these overall trends with fewer elderly people in poverty, which in part has been attributed to the success of pension policies to redistribute income between the rich and the poor, and over the life cycle (OECD, 2008).

Is poverty among the elderly still declining, thus showing a different trend compared to the working-age population? Or is it possible to observe a shift in poverty statistics as countries have reformed their pension policies? Which elderly population subgroups carry elevated poverty risks, and how are incomes changing as cohorts of elderly people are growing older? Is it possible to identify universal trends and patterns in old-age poverty that transcend national borders, or are developments in old-age incomes more nation-specific?

Concepts, measurements and data sources

The conceptualization and measurement of poverty is continuously discussed in research, and is acknowledged to be only one of many relevant aspects of quality of life (Walker, 2005). In analyses of high-income OECD countries, scholars often apply a relative perspective on economic hardships and evaluate whether incomes are adequate to maintain an average (or close to average) standard of living that in principle should allow people to participate in society (Townsend, 1979). Whether or not a person is defined as relatively 'income poor' is determined in relation to median incomes and their household composition. Persons living in households with incomes below a certain 'poverty line', defined as a particular fraction of median income, are classified as relatively income poor. Since relative income poverty is sensitive to the exact yardstick used to define when households are poor, in this chapter we use three poverty lines, measured as 40, 50 and 60 per cent of median income. People living in households with incomes lower than these thresholds are considered to be poor, relatively speaking. The poverty threshold at 60 per cent of median income is used by the European Commission to monitor social inclusion processes in the member states (i.e. the so-called 'at-risk-of-poverty', or AROP, threshold). Outside the EU, it is more common to use the poverty threshold at 50 per cent of median income. The threshold at 40 per cent of median income is sometimes used to analyse more severe forms of economic hardships.

In all our analyses, poverty counts are at the individual level, although income as such is measured at the household level. To adjust incomes for economies of scale within households, we divide household incomes by the square root of household size. The square root equivalence scale is commonly used in comparative research, and it is also used by the Luxembourg Income Study (LIS) to generate their key figures on poverty and income inequality. Alternative scales developed by the OECD and Eurostat differ, particularly in the weights attached to dependent children. Obviously, this is of less relevance for calculating old-age poverty rates. All our analyses apply sampling weights, though we need to take notice that older institutionalized people and those who are frail are commonly not included or are underreported in socio-economic surveys.

Relative poverty tells us how low-income households compare to those in the middle of the income distribution, irrespective of changes in real incomes (i.e. their purchasing capacity). We will therefore also analyse so-called anchored poverty rates, capturing changes in poverty while keeping developments in living standards constant (Atkinson et al., 2002). Instead of analysing how people compare to current median income, we here compare elderly incomes for all years to the poverty line observed in the mid-1980s (the first year of observation in our analyses of poverty trends).

Poverty lines for subsequent years are only updated according to price developments. This estimation strategy allows us to compare how elderly incomes have developed in more absolute terms.

Comparative research on income distributions requires high-quality cross-national data. The empirical analyses in this chapter are based on LIS data. LIS is an international research infrastructure that harmonizes national micro-level income datasets to a common template, in order to optimize comparability between countries and over time. Although great efforts have been made to include middle-income countries in LIS, several of these middle-income countries have LIS data for only one or two years. Since we will analyse developments over a longer time period, the empirical analyses are restricted to longstanding OECD countries for which data are available in LIS from the mid-1980s and onwards. No alternative comparative data source allows for such an extended analysis of old-age poverty, spanning almost three decades in most of our countries.

We analyse LIS data in five-year intervals from 1985 until 2015 (or closest year available). Austria, France, and Switzerland lack data for one of these time points. Greece and Ireland lack data for two time points. For these particular countries, data have been interpolated when possible. For Sweden, data for the two most recent time points were drawn from the Swedish income register (HEK). Sample sizes vary across countries, between 347,907 and 3,254 observations for Norway in 2013 and Ireland in 1987, respectively. More information about LIS, including years and countries in their database, is available online at their webpage.

Poverty trends

The relative income position of the elderly has improved over recent decades. Defining the elderly as 65 years and older, Figures 20.1a–c show relative old-age income poverty as an average of 19 OECD countries for the period 1985–2015. As reference, the figures also show poverty rates for the working-age population (25–64 years). The lower-bound age restriction excludes many students and apprentices from the analysis.

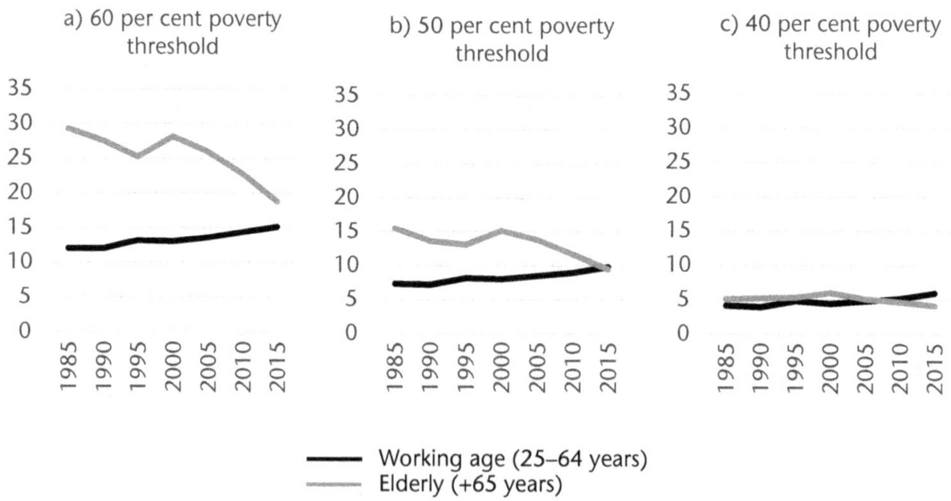

Figure 20.1 Relative income poverty in the working-age (25–64 years) and elderly (65+ years) population, averages of 19 OECD countries, 1985–2015. (a) 60 per cent poverty threshold; (b) 50 per cent poverty threshold; (c) 40 per cent poverty threshold.

Source: LIS.

The relative income position of the elderly has improved substantially since the mid-1980s. With the exception of a short period around the turn of the millennium, old-age poverty shows a steady decline from its peak levels in the mid-1980s. This decline is particularly notable after the year 2000. At the 60 per cent threshold, old-age poverty declined from around 30 per cent in the mid-1980s, to slightly below 20 per cent in more recent years. At the 50 per cent threshold, the decline in old-age poverty is somewhat less pronounced, but still substantial, with poverty being reduced from 15 per cent in the mid-1980s to 10 per cent in the mid-2010s. At the 40 per cent threshold, old-age poverty is even lower, down to less than 5 per cent at the end of the period.

The working-age population showed the opposite trend, with a slight increase in poverty. Relative income poverty used to be higher among the elderly than among those of working age, and this pattern was still observable in the mid-1980s. However, due to their different trends in poverty, the relative income positions of the elderly and those of working age have converged. Today, old-age poverty at the 50 per cent threshold is actually on par with the poverty rate observed in the working-age population. At the 40 per cent poverty threshold, the elderly even do slightly better.

Cross-country averages conceal differences between countries. Figure 20.2 shows old-age poverty in each of our 19 OECD countries at three points in time, around 1985, 2000, and 2015. In this analysis we only show results based on the 50 per cent poverty threshold. Old-age poverty is in the middle range between five and ten per cent in Canada, Finland, France, Germany, Greece, Ireland, Italy, the United Kingdom, Spain, and Sweden. Lower poverty rates of less than five per cent are observed in Denmark, Luxembourg, the Netherlands, and Norway. At the other end, we find Australia, Austria, Israel, Switzerland, and the United States. In these countries, more than one out of every ten elderly people live in a household defined as relatively income poor.

Only three countries diverged from the overall decline in old-age poverty observed above. In Australia, Switzerland, and the United Kingdom old-age poverty has increased by two or

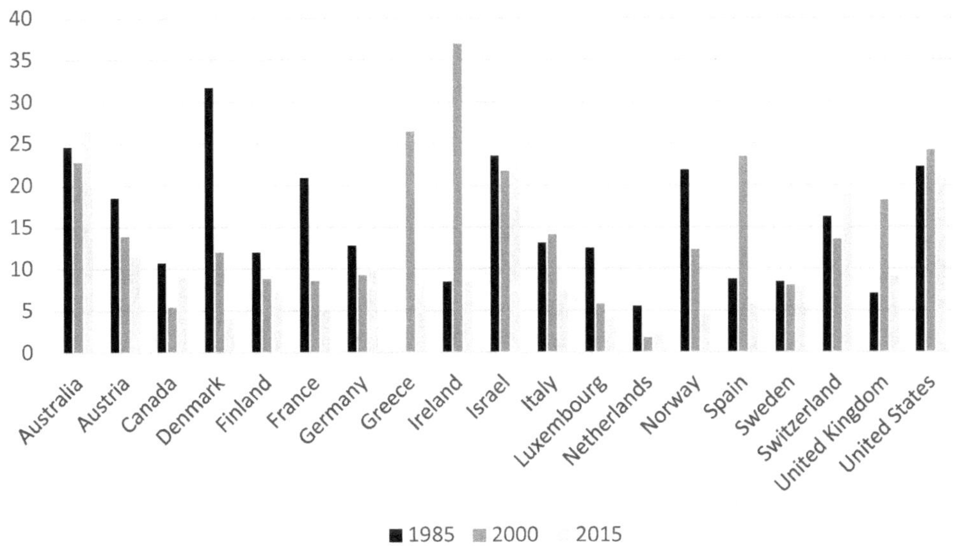

Figure 20.2 Old-age poverty 1985, 2000, and 2015 (or closest years) in 19 OECD countries (50% poverty threshold).

Source: LIS.

three percentage points since the mid-1980s. A few countries managed to reduce old-age poverty quite substantially. In Denmark, France, Greece, and Norway, poverty declined by more than 20 percentage points. Denmark developed an effective combination of generous universal basic pension benefits and growing supplementary funded pensions (Anderson, 2004). Unskilled public sector workers were the first to negotiate a pension deal in the late 1980s, followed by metalworkers in the early 1990s. The coverage rate for occupational pensions rose from about one-third in the 1970s, to nearly 90 per cent in the late 1990s (Andersen, 2011). France made several adjustments to their pension policies in the 1970s, making policies toward the elderly more generous and inclusive. The maximum replacement rate used to calculate pension benefits was raised, pension credits were provided to mothers, and participation in occupational schemes was made compulsory for private firms (Naczyk & Palier, 2011).

The sharp decline in Greece, though we lack data before the mid-1990s, is to some extent a consequence of the economic crisis and mass unemployment since the late 2000s, which exerted a downward pressure on household incomes in the working-age population and lowered the median income used in the calculation of relative income poverty. Norway substantially reformed their pension system in 2011 by introducing clear elements of defined contributions. Although minimum pension benefits have become more generous in Norway, the substantial decline in old-age poverty observed in our analysis is most likely due to the continued maturation of the old national insurance pension system, in combination with higher labour force participation of new female cohorts entering retirement (Pedersen, 2017).

Ireland and Spain also show extraordinary developments. In both countries, relative income poverty peaked among the elderly at the turn of the new millennium, after which there were substantial declines in old-age poverty. During the economic boom of the Irish economy from the mid-1990s up to 2001, pension benefits fell short of developments in incomes from work and capital, making many elderly households relatively less well-off economically (Layte et al., 2004). The reversal of the poverty trend in Ireland is difficult to fully explain. However, it should be noted that in the mid-1990s Ireland initiated a process to strengthen the basic state pension, which over time became more effective in reducing old-age poverty (Russell et al., 2010). The rise in old-age poverty in Spain up to the mid-2000s is very much related to a growing number of pensioners with insufficient contributions for a full pension. Many older people were also left behind due to a rapid growth of real wages prior to the global financial crisis beginning in 2007/2008 (OECD, 2011).

Anchored poverty

A common objection against the use of purely relative measures of income poverty is that they do not take into account possible increases in living standards. Figure 20.3 shows the 'anchored' poverty rate as an average of 19 OECD countries (1985–2015), where poverty lines are anchored according to the median income in the first year of observation (mid-1980s or first available wave). We plot the anchored poverty rate for the elderly and those of working age separately.

Anchored poverty has declined substantially among the elderly, also in those countries where (relative) old-age poverty increased (Figure 20.4). In all countries, elderly incomes seem therefore to have benefited positively in real terms, despite austerity measures that slowed down benefit increases in some countries. However, Greece shows a peak in anchored poverty in the 2000s, something that probably reflects the scale and depth of the sovereign debt crisis faced by Greece in the aftermath of the financial crisis of 2007/08. Due to missing data for the earliest years, poverty in Greece is here anchored to median incomes in the mid-1990s. Anchored poverty shows a more moderate decline among those of working age, suggesting that the purchasing capacity of the elderly has caught up with developments in the working-age population.

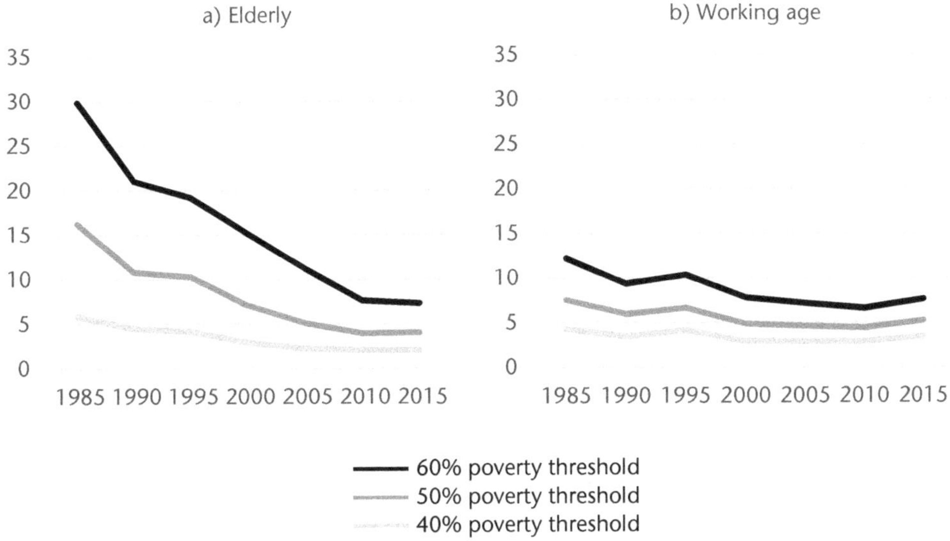

Figure 20.3 Anchored poverty 1985–2015 in the elderly population (65+ years) and among those of working age (25–64 years) at various thresholds in 19 OECD countries: (a) elderly; (b) working age.

Source: LIS.

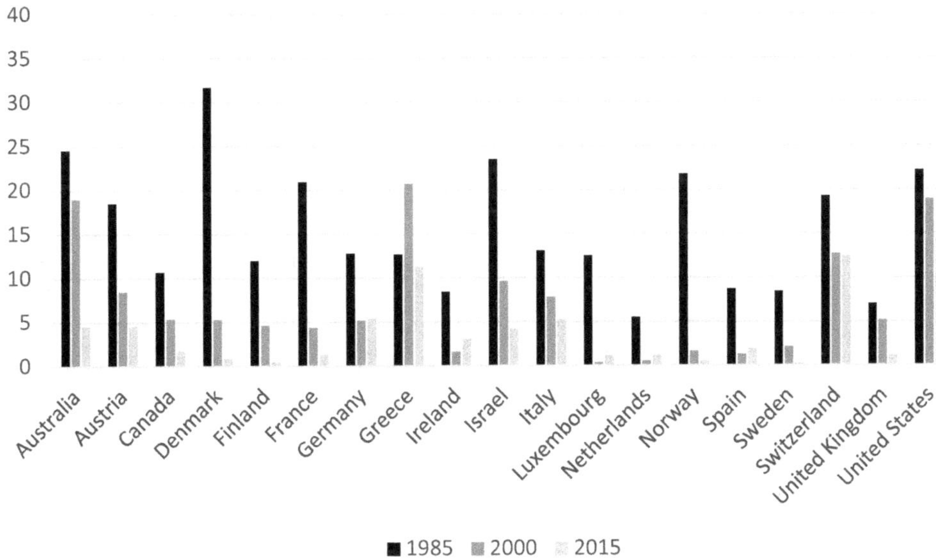

Figure 20.4 Anchored old-age poverty 1985, 2000, and 2015 (or closest years) in 19 OECD countries (50% poverty threshold).

Source: LIS.

Old-age risk groups

Poverty risks are not equally distributed among the elderly. Figure 20.5 shows old-age poverty by major risk groups in 19 OECD countries (around 2015 or the most recent year). Once again, we present the 50 per cent relative poverty threshold. Using boxplots that order poverty rates from the highest to the lowest scores along the vertical axis, the horizontal line in the box represents the median. The lower edge of the box is represented by the 1st quartile, and the top by the 3rd quartile. Thus, the box represents the middle half (50%) of our countries. The upper vertical line shows the range of scores that is within 2.5 times the width from the median to the top of the box (the inter-quartile range), while the lower vertical line shows the opposite. The circular dots outside the box represent countries that do not fit the general pattern observed in our data.

Relative income poverty among the elderly is higher among those with lower education, something that probably reflects differences in earnings and pension contributions during economically active years. It also increases with age, being higher for the oldest old (75+ years) who were economically active in periods when pension systems were less matured. Relative income poverty in old age is particularly high among single persons. Widows are overrepresented in this group due to greater longevity than men (not shown). Elderly migrants are more likely to be relatively income poor than natives, something that probably reflects shorter contribution spells of first-generation migrants, but potentially also the commonality of precarious employment in this group. Another

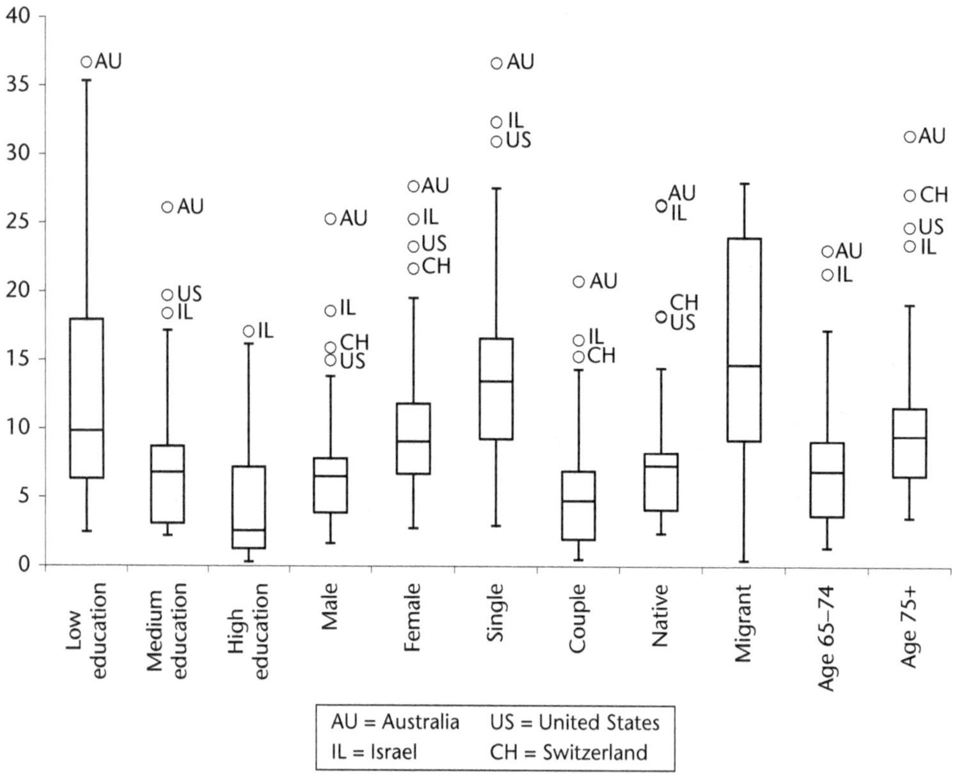

Figure 20.5 Boxplots of relative income poverty (50% threshold) by old-age risk group in 19 OECD countries (around 2015 or most recent available data).

Source: LIS.

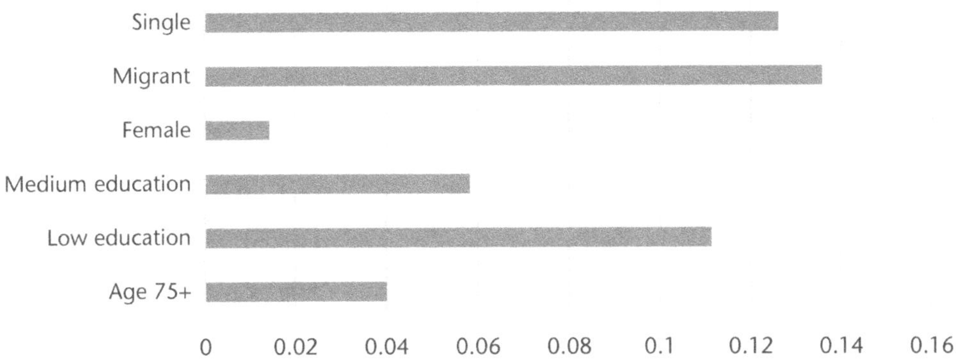

Figure 20.6 Linear probabilities of relative income poverty (50% threshold) in different elderly (65+) risk groups in 19 OECD countries, around 2015.

Source: LIS.

risk group is elderly women, which has brought attention to the gender dimension of pension reform (Daly, 2011). Gender differences in old-age incomes reflect several factors, including different labour force participation rates of men and women, gender differences in work, interruptions and part-time work due to caring responsibilities, gender pay gaps, lower participation of women in occupational pensions and private pension plans, the greater likelihood of early retirement of women, gender differences in longevity noted above, and cutbacks to survivors' pensions.

As already noted, several of the social risk factors above are interrelated. To assess the net contribution of each factor, we estimated a simple linear probability model pooling all country data for the most recent waves (around 2015). Figure 20.6 shows the beta coefficients, using the same definition of relative income poverty as above. All coefficients are statistically significant at the 1 per cent level. The beta coefficients (multiplied by 100) can be interpreted as the additional poverty risk in percentage points associated with each factor – net of the effects of the other variables.

Education, migration background and household composition (single vs. couple) are all strongly associated with old-age poverty. By comparison, the net effect of gender is much smaller, which can be explained by the substantial overlaps between risk factors (women are overrepresented in single elderly households, elderly women are less educated than elderly men, and so forth). In Figure 20.7, we therefore show relative income poverty by gender in different elderly risk groups, using the 50 per cent poverty threshold. The results indicate that old-age poverty is strongly gendered. For all risk factors, elderly women are, on average, more likely to be relatively income poor than elderly men.

Cohort analysis

Is the decline in old-age poverty in most of our countries uniform across all elderly cohorts, or does the overall downward trend reflect that younger and more economically strong cohorts are entering old age? There are at least two fundamentally different mechanisms through which cohort replacement can contribute to an overall reduction in old-age poverty. More recent cohorts either can enter old age at lower risks of poverty, or can see a slower increase of their poverty risk as they grow older. For our analyses of elderly cohorts (Figure 20.8), we used all

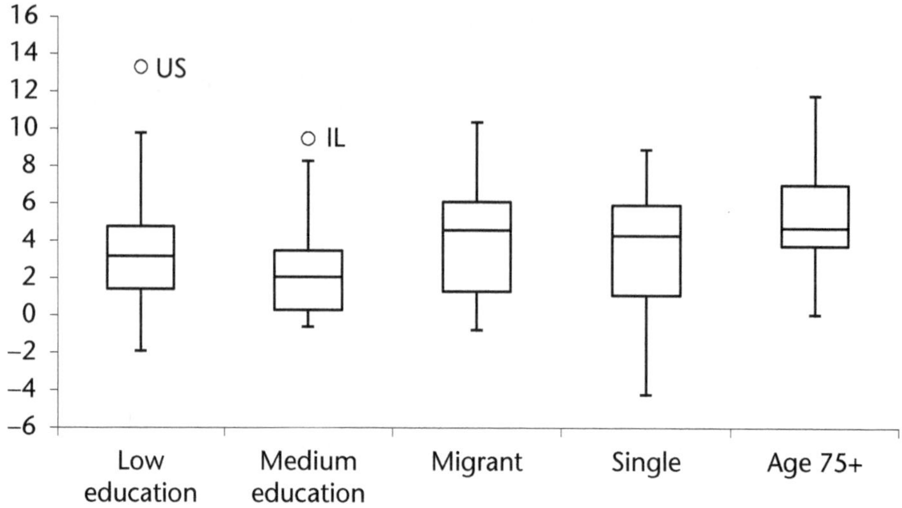

Figure 20.7 Difference between poverty rates (50% threshold) of women and men, by risk group in 19 OECD countries (around 2015 or most recent available data).

Source: LIS.

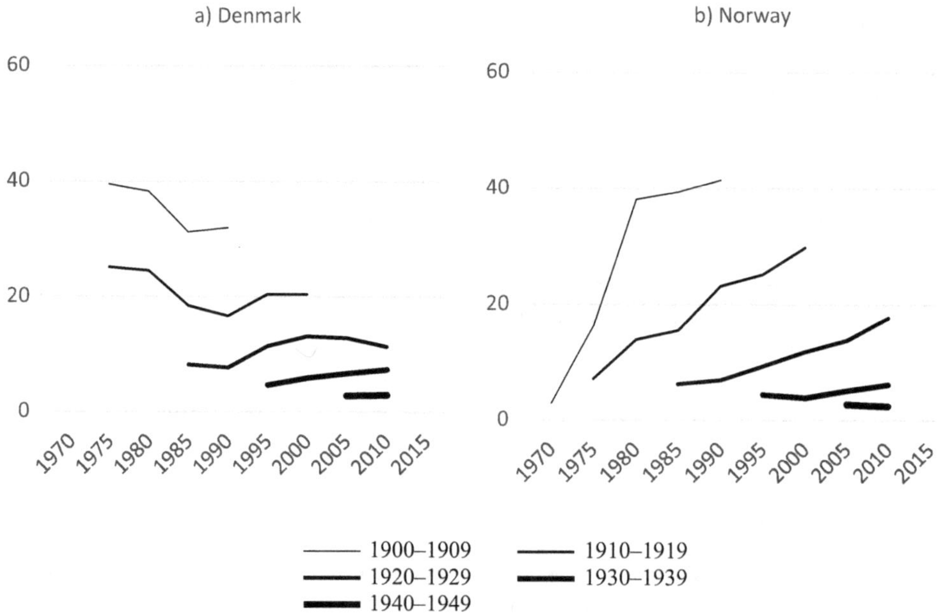

Figure 20.8 Relative income poverty (50% poverty threshold) in different synthetic old-age (65+ years) cohorts by year in selected OECD countries.

Source: LIS.

available LIS datasets for our 19 OECD countries. It should be noted that in this analysis we use synthetic cohorts, defined by birth year and analysed across successive waves of independent cross-sections of data (Deaton, 1985). Thus, we do not follow the same individuals as they grow older. Analyses of synthetic cohorts are sensitive to compositional changes and results should, therefore, be interpreted cautiously. In our analysis, compositional changes may, for example, occur due to differences in life expectancy across elderly cohorts.

The first mechanism of lower poverty risks of new cohorts entering old age is illustrated in Figure 20.8a, showing how relative income poverty in different synthetic cohorts of elderly people developed in Denmark since 1970. Similar patterns can be observed in Canada, France, Greece, Israel, and Luxembourg. Figure 20.8b uses Norway as an example of the latter mechanism of poverty risks increasing more slowly among recent elderly cohorts as they grow older. Countries with similar patterns as Norway are Australia, Finland, Germany, the United Kingdom, and the United States.

Conclusion

We surveyed income developments in old age and among the working-age population across high-income economies with a particular focus on changes in old-age poverty. Overall, relative income poverty in old age fell in the three decades between 1985 and 2015 in the majority of the 19 OECD countries studied here. Notable exceptions were the slight increases in old-age poverty in Australia, Switzerland, and the United Kingdom. The elderly used to be at greater risk of poverty than those of working age, however, in the last three decades, poverty rates among the elderly and in the working-age population have converged. At lower poverty thresholds, old-age poverty today is either on a par or slightly lower than for the working-age population. These patterns were largely confirmed using an anchored measure of poverty as well, suggesting that the purchasing capacity of elderly incomes grew faster than those of the working-age population.

In times of high and rising inequality, our observation that poverty in old age is going down in most of our countries is reassuring. It seems to suggest that developments in recent decades to ensure the financial sustainability of pension systems have not necessarily created additional problems of assuring adequate minimum incomes in old age – at least not in the short run. However, three important clarifications should be made, that require further attention in academia as well as in policymaking.

First, our findings clearly show that elderly from older cohorts are at greater risk of poverty than elderly from younger cohorts in a large number of countries. The results for the older cohorts are most likely due to the belated expansion of pension benefits for the oldest elderly, including the provision of adequate minimum pension benefits for those groups who cannot realize the full potential of the pensions reforms introduced in the immediate post-war decades. Younger cohorts not only entered old age at lower poverty risks, in some countries their incomes deteriorated less substantially as they reached their 'third age' and grew older after retirement. In countries where old-age poverty is strongly associated with cohort replacement, special attention to those at a very advanced age ('fourth age' at 75+) is warranted – particularly as this group is substantially less likely to have the capability to supplement their pension with income from work. With the increase in pensionable age and improvements in longevity, more people work beyond age 65. However, it should be noted that for some of the elderly, employment is enforced by lack of adequate pensions (Scherger, 2015).

Second, the same set of risk factors that is strongly associated with poverty in working age, is also present among the elderly. Market inequalities are often reproduced in old age due to the employment-pension link in contributory systems, as well as in individual savings schemes.

Vulnerable groups with a more limited contribution record are those with low education, migrants, and women. It is well established in research that women's work histories are shorter and more precarious than men's (Pettit & Hook, 2009; Andringa et al., 2015). Women also tend to earn less (Charles & Grusky, 2005; Cukrowska-Torzewska, 2017; Gornick & Meyers, 2003), and contribute less to household income than men (Nieuwenhuis et al., 2017). These differences in working careers and earnings between men and women seem to be reproduced in many pension systems, thus increasing the poverty risks of elderly women. In the short term, the only effective remedy to reduce poverty risks of elderly women may be to strengthen the minimum pension benefits. In relation, as women live longer than men, adequate indexation of pensions is particularly important to the income position of women in old age (Falkingham & Rake, 2001). Other strategies include compensation for care giving through pension credits (currently mainly used in public schemes). Individual pension benefits of married couples are sometimes recalculated at time of divorce or death of partner, thus adjusting for the fact that elderly women may have lower benefits due to family-related inactivity.

Third, many of the elderly cohorts analysed in this chapter were of working age in the 1960s and 1970s. The labour market was very different in those days. Full employment was a reality in many countries, and for those in work, full-time employment was often a realistic option. How current trends of more precarious work (Kalleberg, 2018) and in-work poverty (Lohmann & Marx, 2018) resonate in future contribution histories remains an issue of concern in many pension reforms (Hinrichs & Jessoula, 2012). Further research is needed in predicting future poverty trends among the elderly using a typical agent or micro-simulation approach (Meyer et al., 2007). Enforcing stronger links between contribution history and pension rights, as introduced in several OECD countries (Ebbinghaus, 2011), poses a real threat to the social sustainability of old-age incomes. Without effective minimum income pension benefits in place that are able to sustain or raise elderly incomes above commonly agreed poverty thresholds, we cannot simply expect the recent decline in old-age poverty to continue to hold for future generations.

References

Andersen, J. G. 2011. Denmark: the silent revolution towards a multipillar pension system. In: Ebbinghaus, E. (ed.) *The Varieties of Pension Governance: Pension Privatization in Europe* (pp. 183–209). Oxford: Oxford University Press.

Anderson, K. M. 2004. Pension politics in three small states: Denmark, Sweden and the Netherlands. *The Canadian Journal of Sociology*, *29*(2): 289–312.

Andringa, W., R. Nieuwenhuis, and M. Van Gerven. 2015. Women's working hours: the interplay between gender role attitudes, motherhood, and public childcare support in 23 European countries. *International Journal of Sociology and Social Policy*, *35*(9/10): 582–599.

Atkinson, Anthony B., Bea Cantillon, Eric Marlier, and Brian Nolan. 2002. *Social Indicators: The EU and Social Inclusion*. Oxford: Oxford University Press.

Charles, M., and D. B. Grusky. 2005. *Occupational Ghettos: The Worldwide Segregation of Women and Men* (Vol. 71). LIT Verlag Münster.

Cukrowska-Torzewska, E. 2017. Cross-country evidence on motherhood employment and wage gaps: the role of work–family policies and their interaction. *Social Politics: International Studies in Gender, State & Society*, *24*(2): 178–220.

Daly, M. 2011. What adult worker model? A critical look at recent social policy reform in Europe from a gender and family perspective. *Social Politics*, *18*(1): 1–23.

Deaton, A. 1985. Panel data from a time series of cross-sections. *Journal of Econometrics*, *30*(1–2): 109–126.

Ebbinghaus, B. 2011. *The Varieties of Pension Governance: Pension Privatization in Europe*. Oxford: Oxford University Press.

Ebbinghaus, B. 2015. The privatization and marketization of pensions in Europe: a double transformation facing the crisis. *European Policy Analysis*, *1*(1): 56–73.

Falkingham, J. and Katherine Rake. 2001. Modelling the gender impact of British pension reforms. In: Ginn, J., Street, D. and Arber, S. (eds.) *Women, Work and Pensions: International Issues and Prospects* (pp. 67–85). Milton Keynes: Open University Press.

Goedemé, T. and S. Marchal. 2016. Exploring a blind spot in comparative pension reform research: long-term trends in non-contributory pensions in Europe. *International Journal of Social Welfare, 25*: 161–175.

Gornick, J. C. and M. K. Meyers. 2003. *Families that Work: Policies for Reconciling Parenthood and Employment.* New York: Russell Sage Foundation.

Grech, A. G. 2013. Assessing the sustainability of pension reforms in Europe. *Journal of International and Comparative Social Policy, 29*(2): 143–162.

Grech, A. G. 2014. Evaluating the possible impact of pension reforms on elderly poverty in Europe. *Social Policy & Administration, 49*(1): 68–87.

Hinrichs, K. and M. Jessoula. 2012. *Labour Market Flexibility and Pension Reform: Flexible Today, Secure Tomorrow?* Basingstoke, UK: Palgrave.

Hinrichs, K. and J. Lynch. 2010. Old-age pensions. In: Castles, F. G., Leibfried, S., Lewis, J., Obinger, H. and Pierson, C. (eds) *The Oxford Handbook of the Welfare State* (pp. 353–366). Oxford: Oxford University Press.

Kalleberg, A. L. 2018. *Precarious Lives: Job Insecurity and Well-being in Rich Democracies.* John Wiley & Sons.

Layte, R., B. Nolan and C. T. Whelan. 2004. Explaining poverty trends in Ireland during the boom. *Irish Banking Review* (Summer): 2–14.

Lohmann, H. and I. Marx. 2018. *Handbook on In-Work Poverty.* Cheltenham: Edward Elgar Publishing.

Meyer, T., P. Bridgen and B. Riedmüller. 2007. *Private Pensions Versus Social Inclusion? Non-State Provision for Citizens at Risk in Europe.* Cheltenham, UK: Edward Elgar.

Naczyk, M. and B. Palier. 2011. France: promoting funded pensions in Bismarckian corporatism? In: Ebbinghaus, E. (ed.) *The Varieties of Pension Governance: Pension Privatization in Europe* (pp. 89–118). Oxford: Oxford University Press.

Nieuwenhuis, R., H. van der Kolk and A. Need. 2017. Women's earnings and household inequality in OECD countries, 1973–2013. *Acta Sociologica, 60*(1), 3–20.

OECD. 2008. *Growing Unequal? Income Distribution and Poverty in OECD Countries.* Paris: OECD.

OECD. 2011. *OECD Perspectives: Spain Policies for a Sustainable Recovery.* Paris: OECD.

OECD. 2015. *In it Together: Why Less Inequality Benefits All.* Paris: OECD.

Pedersen, A. 2017. *ESPN Thematic Report: Assessment of Pension Adequacy in Norway 2017.* Brussels: European Commission.

Pettit, B. and J. L. Hook. 2009. *Gendered Tradeoffs: Women, Family, and Workplace Inequality in Twenty-one Countries.* New York: Russell Sage Foundation.

Russell, H., B. Maître and B. Nolan. 2010. *Monitoring Poverty Trends in Ireland 2004–2007: Key Issues for Children, People of Working Age and Older People.* ESRI Research Series No. 17. Dublin: The Economic and Social Research Institute.

Scherger, S. 2015. *Paid Work Beyond Pension Age: Comparative Perspectives.* Basingstoke: Palgrave.

Townsend, P. 1979. *Poverty in the United Kingdom: A Survey of Household Resources and Standards of Living.* Berkeley: University of California Press.

Walker, A. (2005). A European perspective on quality of life in old age. *European Journal of Ageing, 2*(1), 2–12.

21

Poverty and access to welfare benefits

Caroline Dewilde

Introduction

Most welfare states attempt to alleviate poverty, though some more successfully than others. This chapter discusses why some welfare states invest more in social policies that reduce the level of poverty. Welfare states in so-called 'advanced welfare democracies' are the product of century-long processes of social transformation and struggle for power between organized interests (e.g. Korpi, 1974; de Swaan, 1989; Esping-Andersen, 1990). The first claim of this chapter is therefore that – even though welfare states nowadays consist of myriad transfer programmes and social services, which are in turn based on several redistributive principles (see further) – 'history' still matters. The second claim is that changes in welfare states, from the early origins (ca. 1880) to recent developments, are driven by coalition politics. As historical variations in the balance of power between organized interests crystallized in various decision-making arenas relevant to social policy-making, ensuing systematic differences in the nature, workings and strategic development of such political coalitions arose. Even though modern-day social policy-making has become ever more complex and 'multidimensional' (e.g. Bonoli and Natali, 2012b; Häusermann, 2012; Hemerijck, 2013), giving rise to political coalitions of a very different kind than in the past, recent research continues to demonstrate that 'history' and 'politics' matter. This implies that outcomes regarding 'poverty and the access to welfare benefits' are explainable by social science, as well as amenable to change. Poverty, arising from a lack of access to sufficiently generous welfare transfers and services for those who cannot derive the bulk of economic resources from the labour market, is the child of political choice.

To complicate matters, the welfare state forms the object of study for different social science disciplines, analysing its development and outcomes through various theoretical and analytical frameworks. Given the importance of coalition politics driving welfare reform in parliamentary democracies, the latter decision-making arena is a prime topic of study for *political scientists*. They tend to focus on political system features, electoral dynamics and partisan politics (e.g. Esping-Andersen, 1990; Pierson, 1996; Korpi and Palme, 2003; Allan and Scruggs, 2004; Gingrich and Häusermann, 2015), i.e. the decision-making arena where social policies are 'voted'. For *comparative political economists* (CPE), the welfare state forms part of a broader 'package' referring to the regulation of capitalism. Because of theoretically hypothesized institutional complementarities leading to comparative advantages, different '*Varieties of Capitalism*' (VOC) beg their own type of system, which all tend to be organized along similar lines: social policy regime; industrial relations system; educational system, etc. (Hall and Soskice, 2001; Schröder, 2008). For CPE scholars, 'organized interests' and 'coalition politics' pertain to the decision-making arena of (corporatist) coordination between employers, unions and the state – i.e. where social policies are 'negotiated'. Political scientists and VOC scholars are indirectly interested in poverty as the assumed outcome of social policies resulting from such coalition politics – they hence engage less with empirical poverty research. The latter is the domain of *sociologists and social policy* researchers. They focus on poverty measurement, adequacy of welfare benefits, within- and between-country variations in poverty risks (e.g. Dewilde, 2008; Dewilde and Raeymaeckers, 2008), and related topics such as solidarity, 'deservingness', welfare attitudes, and stigmatization (e.g. van Oorschot et al., 2017). Getting a grasp on these different research traditions is a daunting task, given the spectrum of theoretical and methodological approaches. However, when it comes to explaining recent developments related to the theme of this chapter, the most fruitful analyses have been made by scholars that draw on *accumulated knowledge across different traditions* (e.g. Palier and Thelen, 2010; Thelen, 2011; Hemerijck, 2013, 2017; Rueda, 2014; Ebbinghaus and Naumann, 2018).

Across disciplines, there is furthermore a running debate on the pros and cons of different ways of 'operationalizing' the welfare state (and welfare reform), in particular in terms of its impacts through the provision of welfare benefits generally aimed at improving households' income situation, including the prevention of poverty. While some analyse trends in 'disaggregated' (programmatic) social expenditure, sometimes in relation to caseloads (e.g. Vandenbroucke and Vleminckx, 2011; de la Porte and Jacobsson, 2012; Kuitto, 2016), others focus on the 'actual' uptake of benefits and their levels of generosity/capacity to reduce poverty, at the macro- or micro-level (see De Deken and Clasen (2013) on the use of caseload data, Otto and van Oorschot (2018) on actual benefit recipiency, and the EUROMOD-project[1]). Political scientists and VOC scholars, who less often directly address the issue of poverty, are more focused on codifying (changes in) the legal reality of social rights entitlements (Esping-Andersen, 1990; Scruggs et al., 2017). As various operationalizations of the welfare state indicate different aspects of the same phenomenon, they are positively associated with one another: "actual benefit receipt can be considered the result of social rights [. . .] and the driver of social expenditure" (Otto and van Oorschot, 2018: 3). Given that this review aims to point at general trends, it relies on research using diverse operationalizations.

The chapter starts by laying out some basic concepts pertaining to the blueprint of all welfare states. It then goes on to explain *why* welfare states came to differ from each other in terms of poverty and the access to welfare benefits, combining theoretical and empirical insights across disciplines. Next, the same tools are used to review how recent welfare reform has come to be associated with worsening poverty outcomes. The chapter concludes by singling out some issues for future research.

Why history matters

What welfare states have in common

While welfare provision in pre-industrial times was based on either charitable poor-relief or reciprocity-based solidarity within confined groups, welfare states developed as collective and nation-wide systems of compulsory, 'institutionalized', *social* solidarity (de Swaan, 1989).

They can be understood as a rational-economic response to mass urban misery caused by unfettered early industrial capitalism. Welfare states 'emerged' through a long process of amalgamation of workers' and employers' interests at subsequently higher levels of integration, promoted by an ever-growing 'activist' state. Interests in the collective good of *social* solidarity were driven by the shared understanding of both 'capital' and 'labour' of its positive externalities, and of the negative externalities of more exclusionary alternatives. Income security, education, health care, and social mobility became gradually recognized as key to national competitiveness (e.g. Titmuss, 1974; de Swaan, 1989). This synergy between social policy and economic growth continues to be a main strategic goal for international institutions and organizations, such as the European Union (EU) and the Organization for Economic Cooperation and Development (OECD).

All welfare states are hence committed to alleviating poverty by providing 'a basic modicum of economic welfare as a social right' to their citizens.[2] Historically, they first and foremost aimed to provide social protection against the 'old' life-course risks typical for industrial capitalism. *Horizontal redistribution* – between groups differentiated by risk (e.g. men–women, young–old, employed–unemployed, with–without children), or over one's own life course (e.g. by paying social contributions to finance future pensions) – is dominant (Figure 21.1). Such horizontal redistribution is mostly insurance-based, i.e. risks are reapportioned within groups of similar socio-economic standing (e.g. Veit-Wilson, 1992; De Deken et al., 2006). Social insurance finances (mostly) earnings-related transfers out of (mostly) employees' and employers' contributions (the redistributive principle of *equity*). Social corrections leading to *vertical redistribution* from rich to poor are 'in-built' through the modulation of contributions, taxes, and transfers according to income. For those who – through lack of contributions

Contributory schemes ('funded' by employers' and employees' contributions)	**Non-contributory schemes (general taxes)**	**Social services (general taxes)**	**Fiscal welfare (tax deductions)**
- Earnings-related social insurances for different groups of workers (e.g. employees, workers, civil servants, self-employed, ...) - Occupational schemes (e.g. mandatory occupational pensions)	- Universal or categorical schemes not targeted toward the poor (e.g. child allowance, 'universal' state pensions) - Means-tested schemes targeted toward the poor (e.g. social assistance, housing allowances)	- Universal or means-tested - Health care, education, social housing, childcare, social work, ...	- Mortgage interest deduction, tax credits for the working poor, tax allowances for childcare, occupational or private pensions...

Figure 21.1 Blueprint of the welfare state.

Source: Adapted from various sources, in particular MISSOC (www.missoc.org/missoc-database/comparative-tables/) and ILO (www.ilo.org/global/topics/social-security/).

or exhaustion of rights – do not qualify for social insurance, most welfare states operate a residual safety net that distributes means-tested social assistance (based on the redistributive principle of *need*). Welfare states furthermore redistribute through social services and fiscal welfare. Social services are judged to be more vertically redistributive when means-tested, and less vertically redistributive or even regressively redistributive from poor to rich[3] when access is universal (e.g. Jensen, 2011). Overall, social services have been found to boost the income of those with higher poverty risks (Verbist et al., 2012). Fiscal welfare on the other hand is judged to disproportionally benefit higher-income groups. Overall, individuals in high-risk groups (who are more likely to be poor) tend to contribute (somewhat) less and receive (somewhat) more over the life course (e.g. Falkingham and Hills, 1995). Such a pattern is, however, far from clear-cut and may vary between countries.

How welfare states differ

Notwithstanding their common blueprint, differences between welfare states determine access to welfare benefits of different types, their generosity, and therefore whether these benefits can (theoretically) lift people out of poverty (or not). In *The Three Worlds of Welfare Capitalism*, Esping-Andersen (1990) explains how different 'worlds of welfare' emerged out of the divergent strategies of ruling elites to accommodate 'socialist' threats posed by the commodification of labour under industrial capitalism. Such strategies diverged for reasons of ideology/power, social structure, and religion, but also because of more mundane factors such as the timing and scale of industrialization (e.g. de Swaan, 1989; Kahl, 2005).

Esping-Andersen distinguishes between three responses, leading to the crystallization of particular types of welfare states with particular consequences for the level of 'de-commodification'[4] and the nature of social stratification, and hence inequality and poverty. The aim of the *liberal welfare state* is to 'strengthen the commodity status of labour' by minimalist state intervention aimed at reducing the worst instances of poverty (*need*). Eligibility rules are strictly confined, 'basic' benefits (e.g. old-age pensions) are universal but low and flat-rate, and means-tested social assistance is preferred. Market-solutions for social risks are encouraged. This leads to a dualist welfare state, as the middle classes rely on occupational or private welfare to augment transfer income. The distinctive nature of the *conservative-corporatist welfare state* concerns the organization of mutualistic insurance within social classes reflective of the 'old' divisions of hierarchy, status, and (occupational) class. This results in differentiated social rights with earnings-related benefits strongly tied to contribution records (*equity*). Until recently, a preference for the male-breadwinner family prevailed. The *social-democratic welfare state* consists of a ground floor of fairly generous universal social rights based on citizenship (the redistributive principle of *equality*), to which an earnings-related top floor has been added over time. The state strives toward full employment for both genders and provides comprehensive public services, socializing care for children and elderly people. Social spending tends to be higher in both the Scandinavian social-democratic welfare states and the conservative-corporatist welfare states of continental Europe, compared with the Anglo-Saxon liberal welfare states (see Table 21.1). The main contribution of Esping-Andersen and others involved in the Social Citizenship Indicator Program[5] (SCIP, 1930–2005), as well as its several successors, pertains to the idea that the quality of social rights in terms of coverage, income replacement, and the rules of entry and exit regarding the access to (more generous) social insurance benefits matters more than spending per se. At similar levels of social spending, social-democratic welfare states are more redistributive and 'de-commodifying' than their conservative-corporatist counterparts.

Table 21.1 Overview of key indicators, ca. 1980–1985 or earliest available (A) and latest year available (ca. 2010–2015) (B)

Country/ welfare state type	*Total social expenditure as % of GDP*[(a)]		*Social expenditure in kind (social services) as % of GDP*[(a)]		*Welfare generosity index (total)*[(b)]		*EPL, standard contracts (0–6)*[(a)]		*Union density %*[(a),(c)]		*Union centralization (0-8)*[(c)]		*Centra-lization wage bargaining (0–1)*[(c)]		*Gini-index of prefiscal income, 18–64 years*[(a)]		*Gini-index of disposable income, 18–64 years*[(a)]		*% Reduction in Gini-index*		*Relative poverty rate (60% median)*[(d)]	
	A	*B*	*A*	*B*	*A*	*B*	*A*	*B*	*A*	*B*	*A*	*B*	*A*	*B*	*A*	*B*	*A*	*B*	*A*	*B*	*A*	*B*
Liberal																						
Australia	10.3	20.4	4.2	9.3	20.5	20.9	1.17	1.67	49.6	19.0	3.0	2.0	0.55	0.52	35.2	41.2	26.5	30.4	−24.7	−26.2	18.3	21.3
Canada	13.3	16.8	6.4	7.9	24.6	25.7	0.92	0.92	34.0	29.5	2.0	2.0	0.27	0.30	33.3	41.0	26.5	31.3	−20.4	−23.7	18.9	21.0
Ireland	15.7	20.2	7.3	7.3	25.8	35.3	1.44	1.40	57.1	33.7	1.0	1.0	0.36	0.46	47.0	51.4	31.4	28.2	−33.2	−45.1	20.0	16.6
New Zealand	16.7	19.4	5.2	9.4	22.4	21.4	1.24	1.39	69.1	19.4	1.0	0.0	0.25	0.30								
Switzerland	14.5	25.1	3.8	8.2	36.4	37.1	1.60	1.60	27.5	16.2	0.0	0.0	0.35	0.35	33.0	34.3	29.6	28.0	−10.3	−18.4	13.5	14.8
United Kingdom	15.8	22.8	5.5	10.9	31.5	27.5	1.10	1.10	51.7	25.7	0.0	0.0	0.09	0.11	32.8	45.8	24.4	32.9	−25.6	−28.2	16.8	17.4
United States	13.2	19.1	4.7	9.6	21.3	21.7	0.26	0.26	22.1	11.4	0.0	0.0	0.12	0.18	37.7	46.1	29.1	36.5	−22.8	−20.8	21.3	24.3
Conservative-corporatist																						
Austria	23.3	28.4	5.6	8.5	32.5	34.3	2.75	2.37	56.7	27.4	6.0	5.0	0.92	0.88		39.3	20.4	26.2		−33.3	11.7	14.2
Belgium	23.2	29.3	5.4	10.4	37.4	42.6	1.85	1.89	51.3	55.1	4.5	4.5	0.48	0.48	34.7	35.8	22.0	25.8	−36.6	−27.9	10.5	16.1
France	20.2	31.7	6.6	11.4	34.2	38.0	2.59	2.38	18.3	7.7	2.0	2.0	0.25	0.23	37.8	42.6	29.9	28.7	−20.9	−32.6	17.0	15.5
Germany	23.6	26.2	7.0	10.4	35.8	32.0	2.58	2.68	34.9	17.7	0.0	0.0	0.41	0.47	30.7	41.3	23.1	28.6	−24.8	−30.8	10.6	16.7
Japan	10.3	23.7	4.9	10.7	23.6	25.7	1.70	1.37	31.1	17.8	1.0	2.0	0.18	0.32		34.5		30.4		−11.9		17.6
Luxembourg	19.2	24.1	4.6	8.0				2.25	50.8	32.8	2.0	2.0	0.34	0.31	30.6	40.1	22.4	27.5	−26.8	−31.4	10.9	16.4
Netherlands	23.7	23.6	6.1	10.2	38.1	38.6	3.07	2.82	34.8	18.0	4.0	3.0	0.48	0.57	43.8	37.2	25.7	25.5	−41.3	−31.5	10.3	12.4
Social-democratic																						
Denmark	20.3	31.5	9.8	13.4	40.0	34.1	2.18	2.20	78.6	66.8	4.0	3.0	0.53	0.42	31.3	36.7	21.7	23.1	−30.7	−37.1	17.3	12.4
Finland	17.7	29.5	6.7	10.9	29.3	34.1	2.79	2.17	69.4	69.0	3.0	4.0	0.41	0.43	31.5	38	18.9	24.5	−40.0	−35.5	10.7	14.0

Iceland	16.1	22.8	7.8	9.8				1.73	66.2	80.7						32.9		23.0		−30.1		11.5
Norway	16.4	23.0	6.7	10.4	40.7	43.9	2.33	2.33	58.3	52.1	6.0	5.0	0.58	0.51	28.3	35.8	20.3	23.5	−28.3	−34.4	12.1	13.6
Sweden	24.8	27.8	11.9	14.0	44.1	35.2	2.80	2.61	78.0	67.4	5.0	4.0	0.56	0.52	30.4	37.1	18.8	22.1	−38.2	−40.4	9.1	12.0
Southern-European																						
Cyprus		21.4		3.7					76.0	45.2	2.0	2.0	0.26	0.29								
Greece	9.9	28.0	3.2	7.4	24.5	29.2	2.85	2.12	39.0	21.5	2.0	1.0	0.34	0.27	38.9	47.8	33.0	33.9	−15.2	−29.1	21.5	20.1
Italy	18.2	29.3	5.6	7.8	24.9	29.6	2.76	2.68	49.6	37.3	3.0	3.0	0.33	0.38	38.0	39.7	30.9	32.3	−18.7	−18.7	17.4	19.9
Malta		17.3		6.3					53.4	52.9	4.0	4.0	0.40	0.33								
Portugal	9.7	25.8	3.0	6.6		35.1	5.00	3.18	54.8	18.5	1.0	2.0	0.29	0.35								
Spain	15.0	26.3	4.1	8.2	28.0	35.6	3.55	2.05	13.5	16.9	3.0	3.0	0.34	0.38	37.3	47.0	30.8	34.6	−17.4	−26.4	19.4	22.7
Baltic																						
Estonia		15.9		5.4				1.81	93.9	6.5	2.0	2.0	0.35	0.32	43.9	41.5	43.0	33.3	−2.1	−19.8		23.0
Latvia		14.7		4.1				2.69	46.0	13.1	2.0	2.0	0.55	0.51								
Lithuania		14.8		4.8				2.45	31.3	9.0	2.0	2.0		0.36		41.5		33.0		−20.5		20.1
Central- and Eastern-European																						
Bulgaria		17.3		5.3					99.0	17.5	2.0	2.0	0.29	0.29								
Croatia		20.7		6.7				2.48		30.9		0.0										
Czech Republic	14.2	20.6	4.1	7.1			3.31	2.92	64.4	12.7	4.0	0.0	0.28	0.25	31.9	36.5	19.6	25.1	−38.6	−31.2	6.8	11.3
Hungary		22.1		6.9			2.00	1.59	94.0	10.7	4.0	1.5	0.25	0.26	41.7	37.4	27.9	26.0	−33.1	−30.5	15.7	13.1
Poland	20.5	19.0	4.8	5.3			2.23	2.23	65.7	12.7	4.0	2.0	0.40	0.17	38.3	43.7	26.0	31.2	−32.1	−28.6	17.0	14.5
Romania		14.3		4.1					100	19.8	4.0	1.0	0.21	0.23	34.3		27.4		−20.1		15.2	
Slovakia		18.2		6.8			2.47	1.84	67.3	13.3	2.0	2.0	0.53	0.50	34.0	35.4	18.3	26.6	−46.2	−24.9	6.3	13.8
Slovenia		24.0		7.3				2.16	91.5	21.2	2.0	2.0	0.57	0.32	30.7	36.0	21.7	25.7	−29.3	−28.6	12.5	15.9

Notes: (a): Armingeon et al. (2018); (b): Scruggs et al. (2017); (c): Visser (2016), union centralization is summary measure; (d) Luxembourg Income Study – Key Figures (2018).

A note on welfare state types. Over the years, Esping-Andersen's typology has been heavily criticized. Important additions for this chapter are the Southern-European and the 'post-socialist' countries. The former are characterized by: unsupported (rather than supported) familialism reinforced by patchy social assistance; a fragmented and corporatist system of income maintenance; universal health care; a low degree of state influence in the welfare sector; and clientelism and patronage, resulting in the selective distribution of benefits and services (e.g. Ferrera, 1996; Saraceno, 2017). It is unjustified to conceive of the 'post-socialist' countries as a homogeneous cluster. While the Baltics have followed an outspoken liberal trajectory upon the implosion of communism, other countries combine a varying mix of 'conservative-corporatist' and liberal traits (Kuitto, 2016; Kovács et al., 2017). This chapter does not engage with a detailed review of this literature (see e.g. Arts and Gelissen, 2002). It is merely pointed out that welfare programmes across countries strike a different balance between the redistributive principles of need, equity and equality, reflective of how welfare provision is divided by markets, states and families, and which actors have, historically, been more powerful.

VOC scholars argue that systematic differences in social policy form part of a broader 'policy package' of social and economic regulation, which can be traced back to similar historical-institutional roots (Schröder, 2008, 2017). This is of theoretical importance, because it diverts attention away from the decision-making arena of partisan politics (where social policies are 'voted') to cross-national variations in the industrial relations system (where social policies are 'negotiated'). Owing to their protestant/liberal heritage of a pervasive distinction between the 'deserving' and 'undeserving' poor undermining collective action in favour of a more encompassing notion of solidarity, liberal welfare states ended up with a weaker form of economic regulation. In liberal market economies (LMEs), production is organized through competitive market arrangements that are easily accommodated to changes in supply and demand. Individual workers bargain with individual employers in a labour market that is lightly regulated. Employment protection legislation (EPL) is weak and unionization is low. In coordinated market economies (CMEs), coordination through collective bargaining is much higher. What is lost in flexibility is gained through higher strategic cooperation based on trust embedded in collaborative networks (e.g. within sectors, between social partners) (Hall and Soskice, 2001). While LMEs operate a low-skill/low-wage equilibrium, CMEs operate a high-skill/high-wage equilibrium: labour markets are more strictly regulated and employment protection is high. The type of coordination, however, differs between the social-democratic and 'conservative-corporatist' countries. In the former, economic coordination is more centralized at the national level, and "employers and unions try not to destroy, but to mutually stabilize each other into nationally encompassing peak level associations" (Schröder, 2017: 48). In the latter countries, collective bargaining is segmented along sectoral and/or regional lines, with limited solidarity between segments.

Concluding, while all welfare states aim to alleviate poverty, not all welfare states are committed to substantially reducing inequality. Although liberal welfare states aim to prevent poverty, they in fact have the highest poverty rates. This is, first and foremost, the result of political choice – liberal welfare states tend to be more concerned about reduced work incentives associated with higher welfare benefits (e.g. Veit-Wilson, 1992). Korpi and Palme (1998) furthermore pointed at the 'paradox of redistribution': while targeted welfare is more efficient in terms of redistributing resources to those who need them most, more stingy welfare states operate a smaller overall redistributive budget in comparison with welfare states that involve the middle classes. Finally, Titmuss (1968) already argued that more selectivity results in loss of status, dignity, and self-respect. Stigmatization, in combination with discretionary assessments of needs and resources by so-called 'street-level bureaucrats', has been associated with lower take-up rates of (means-tested) welfare benefits, and thus higher poverty (e.g. Lipsky, 1980; Van Mechelen and Janssens, 2017).

The politics of welfare reform

Welfare states emerged out of a struggle for power between large, fairly homogeneous social classes (represented by organized interests) regarding the introduction and expansion of social rights. Assuming a close link between organized interests and their 'associated' political parties, Esping-Andersen (1990) and others (e.g. Korpi, 1974) explain how the nature of welfare state expansion was driven by which political parties were able to capture workers' votes, and by the variegated political coalitions parties from different ideological strands were able to forge. Over time, such political-coalitional dynamics became more diverse and complex. Pierson (1996) was among the first to point out how the oil crises of 1973–1979 and ensuing 'interdependent' processes of economic globalization and 'skill-biased technological change' – resulting in the outsourcing of low-skilled work to low-wage countries, the transition to a post-industrial 'low growth'-employment structure in the west, and the decline of 'labour' (e.g. DiPrete et al., 2006; Kalleberg, 2018) – combined with socio-demographic change (e.g. individualization, population ageing) to produce a new context of fiscal austerity undermining the financial viability of welfare states. The mature welfare state, however, creates its own, new constituencies of interest groups (e.g. welfare state beneficiaries such as the elderly (e.g. Pampel and Williamson, 1985), public service workers). In this new context, 'new politics' limiting the potential for welfare state roll-back arose, as elected officials will mostly avoid retrenchment or try to 'spread the blame' for such unpopular measures. As Pierson (1996: 151) puts it: "the weakening of organized labour need not translate automatically in a commensurate weakening of the welfare state".

Some point at the declining power of organized interests, in particular 'labour', to influence social policy-making. It may be the case that, in LMEs in particular (where union power has declined more), electoral dynamics and party politics have become more directly relevant for social policy reform (e.g. Taylor-Gooby, 2016). On the other hand, political fragmentation on both the left and the right have as a consequence that these 'new' politics of welfare reform overall became more variable and changeable (e.g. Häusermann, 2012; Gingrich and Häusermann, 2015). Further complexity arose as 'supra-national' social policy models (e.g. Social Investment, see further) promoted by government bureaucrats (e.g. Jenson, 2012) have been added to the mix of reform recipes.

More VOC-inspired research, however, focuses on the 'opposite' idea that out of the struggle for social rights, an industrial relations system crystallized that has gained its own, more or less independent momentum as driver of social policy reform (where social policies are 'negotiated'), with perhaps only weaker links to what happens in the decision-making arena of electoral dynamics and partisan politics (where social policies are 'voted'). In CMEs, social policy reform has been linked to the extent to which different interest groups collectively bargain for more universal, 'encompassing' policies (i.e. in social-democratic welfare states) rather than for 'sector'-specific insider interests (i.e. in conservative-corporatist welfare states). The recent (as yet patchy) integration of VOC and social policy research has resulted in the so-called 'dualization' thesis (Palier and Thelen, 2010; Thelen, 2011; Emmenegger et al., 2012; Palier, 2012; Rueda, 2014), which is a modernized version of the idea that 'history' and 'politics' – through the diversified reproduction of institutions over time – continue to explain differences and trends in the access to welfare benefits and hence poverty rates.

Though the welfare state has proven to be remarkably resilient, this has, in fact, hinged on adaptability. Welfare reform has been substantial. Modern-day social policy-making has become ever more 'multidimensional': policy reforms are often the result of intricate 'package deals' negotiated between organized interests and other actors active throughout the spectrum of social and economic regulation. Furthermore, this development seems more 'intense' in the conservative-corporatist countries, for the reasons outlined above (e.g. Thelen, 2011; Bonoli and Natali, 2012a; Crouch and Keune, 2012; Häusermann, 2012; Hemerijck, 2013). This hugely complicates research, as one needs to delve into the 'black box' of how such coalitional, negotiated reforms are forged. Systematic cross-national research – linking welfare reform and resulting poverty outcomes to trends over time regarding the balance of power between different decision-making arenas (where social policies are 'voted' vs. where social policies are 'negotiated'), and analysing the conditions under which welfare reform is pushed through in one way or another – is currently lacking. Nevertheless, the state-of-the-art does allow for a structured discussion regarding the recent deterioration in terms of poverty and the access to welfare benefits – in particular for the population of working age – across different welfare state types and the systems of social and economic regulation in which these are embedded (see Figure 21.2).

'Downward dualization drift' rather than 'social investment'

Given that unemployment is the most difficult life-course risk to insure (de Swaan, 1989), it is no surprise that welfare benefits for the population of working age have been at the heart of welfare reform. The stylized trends and policy trade-offs for different welfare state types are by now well documented (e.g. Iversen and Wren, 1998; DiPrete et al., 2006). Where the more lightly regulated LMEs responded to macro-economic pressures by lowering wages and welfare benefits, CMEs – until recently, and given stronger EPL and more restrictions to lower the social wage – responded with increased labour market flexibility in terms of employment contracts and working conditions. Over time, however, the number of people in 'flexible', 'insecure', 'a-typical' or 'non-standard' labour market positions had increased to such an extent that the financial capacity of social insurance programmes to 'be social' became undermined. Governments have therefore been forced to gradually restrict access to (generous) contributory benefits, by tightening the rules of entry/exit, increasing conditionality and decreasing generosity. 'Downward dualization drift' thus not only refers to a growing divide between 'insiders' and 'outsiders' on the labour market,[6] but also to increasing welfare gaps and reduced income security due to a concomitant erosion of social insurance rights for 'outsiders' (i.e. those with incomplete contribution records) (Rueda, 2014). As more people have been transferred from unemployment to social assistance, poverty levels have increased – not only in the liberal countries, but also on the continent (Cantillon, 2011; Vandenbroucke and Vleminckx, 2011). The real value of minimum benefits has furthermore also declined (Nelson, 2010): across welfare states, social assistance levels are below the commonly accepted income poverty thresholds (Cantillon et al., 2018).

In line with the claim that 'history' and 'politics' matter, the extent and nature of 'dualization' differ between welfare states. In more liberal welfare states, where low-paid service-sector jobs abound, the main social issue relates to the swelling numbers of 'working poor'. In conservative-corporatist countries, where collective bargaining and (social) solidarity are segmented along labour market/regional divisions, recent history of negotiated social policy reform has been characterized by a growing insider-outsider divide, as a (shrinking) group of 'insiders'

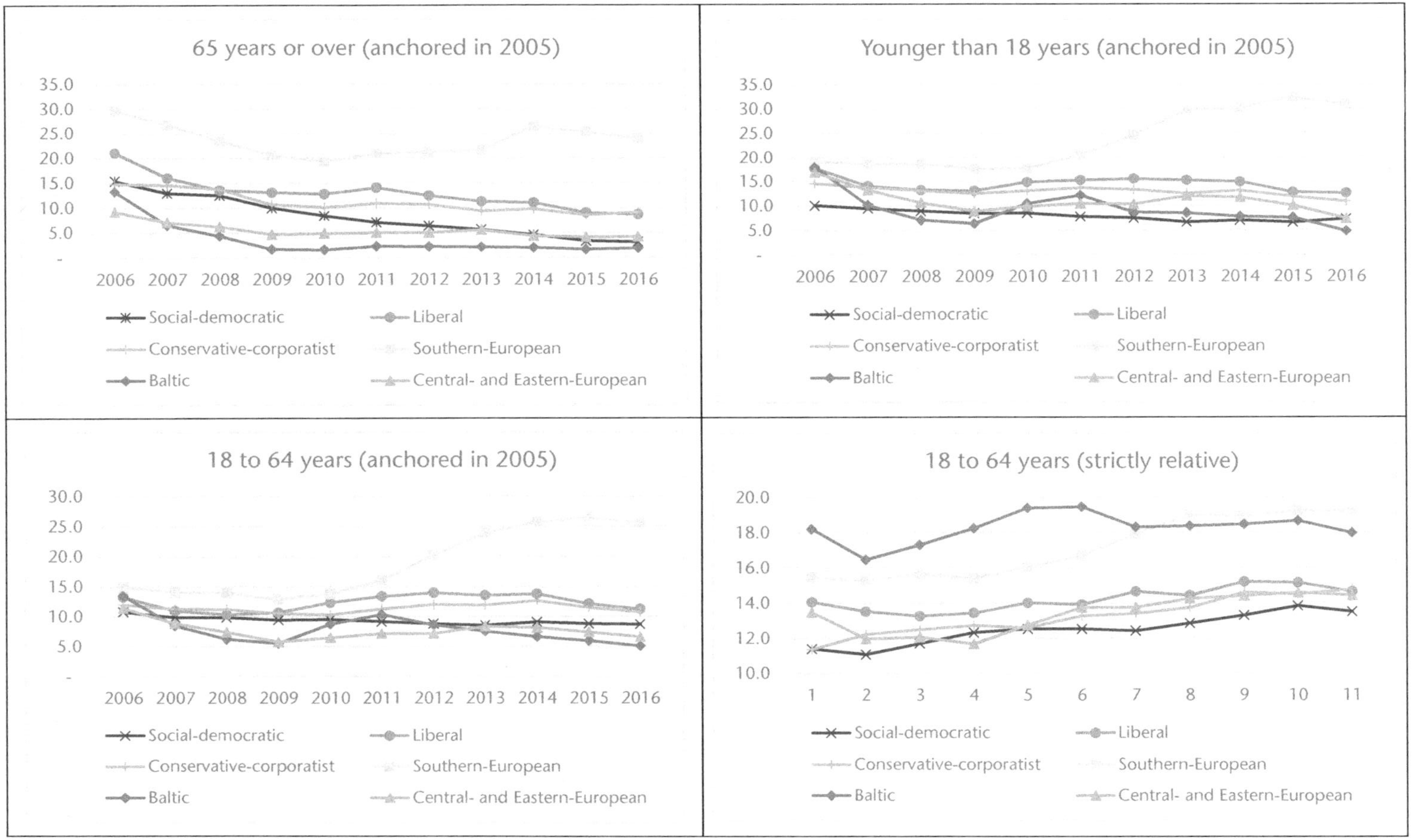

Figure 21.2 Trends in relative poverty (%, poverty threshold [60% of median equivalized disposable household income] anchored in 2005), by welfare state type (mean of country-level poverty rates).

Source: EUROSTAT – Statistics by Theme: Population and Social Conditions (retrieved 18/02/2019).

manages to successfully mobilize in order to protect high-standard employment conditions and social insurance, mostly at the expense of 'outsiders'. Over time, expensive 'labour shedding'-strategies (e.g. early retirement) have been replaced by stronger labour market flexibilization, though some countries (e.g. Germany) have pursued the latter more successfully than others (e.g. France). In these countries, increases in poverty following from declined access to (more generous) welfare benefits seem traceable to the fact that "what has disappeared is the capacity of the model to be encompassing and to cover all citizens under one type of work contract and social protection" (Palier and Thelen, 2010: 139). In social-democratic welfare states, characterized by more centralized collective bargaining allowing for 'quasi-universal' social solidarity, labour market deregulation has been 'socially embedded' (Thelen, 2011): the unemployed can count on both generous replacement benefits and on *active labour market policies* (ALMP) (e.g. (re)training, counselling) so as to promote a quick labour market re-entry. Fiscal imbalance has, however, been the 'Achilles heel' of the social-democratic welfare state for decades (Iversen and Wren, 1998).

The Scandinavian approach featured as the blueprint for the so-called 'social investment'-turn promoted by the EU. Social investment was put forward as a response to 'new social risks' arising in post-industrial societies: in-work poverty; the combination of work and care; obsolete or low skills; lack of social protection (e.g. Bonoli, 2005). While employers attempted to reduce the cost of labour through pursuing labour market deregulation, welfare states aimed to render more individuals better 'employable', so as to increase economic security of households and reduce welfare burdens. Social investment policies aim to "increase people's skills and capacities so that they are either prevented from entering situations resulting in social problems or are empowered to exit such situations" (Kvist, 2017: 83). Theoretically, social investments over the life course, when pursued in a 'coherent' way permeating all social policy domains (i.e. with an eye to long-term returns), are hypothesized to even have the potential to break cycles of intergenerational disadvantage (Esping-Andersen et al., 2002; Kvist, 2017).

In practice, however, recent accounts indicate that in most welfare states, social investment either did not happen or was 'incomplete' – potentially giving birth to *more rather than less* inequality (e.g. Taylor-Gooby, 2008; Cantillon, 2011; Vandenbroucke and Vleminckx, 2011; van Kersbergen and Hemerijck, 2012). In particular conservative-corporatist welfare states adopted only specific social investment policies: more workfare-type *ALMP* and family policies aimed at increasing female labour market participation (Häusermann, 2012; Palier, 2012; Hemerijck, 2017; Kuitto, 2016). The latter were, however, taken up to a higher extent by higher-educated women, thus contributing to perverse effects in terms of income inequality and poverty. In liberal and also in Central- and Eastern-European welfare states, social investment was never on the agenda (e.g. de la Porte and Jacobsson, 2012; Dukelow and Heins, 2017). Post-crisis reform trajectories in the latter are characterized by "residualizing welfare provision at the expense of the most disadvantaged and the maintenance of a relatively generous welfare system for the middle classes" (Kovács et al., 2017: 213). The disadvantaged resolve welfare gaps through increasing informality and familialization. While the Southern-European welfare states did attempt to cure a number of well-known ills (e.g. by tackling over- and under-protection and introducing some minimum income provisions), these attempts were neither particularly systematic nor successful (with welfare retrenchment outweighing expansion), leading to only small improvements for some disadvantaged groups (e.g. de la Porte and Jacobsson, 2012; Saraceno, 2017). Furthermore, these countries were hit hard by the 2008–2009 economic downturn, which makes it difficult to disentangle the combined impacts of austerity packages and other welfare reforms, in a context of intensified family support. Finally, even the Scandinavian commitment to social investment has started to give way to more liberal (less costly) 'workfare' policies (e.g. control and counselling rather than (re)training/investment) (de la Porte and Jacobsson, 2012), resulting in more poverty following from declined access to more generous social insurances (Cronert and Palme, 2017; Greve, 2017). Recent literature thus leads to the conclusion that social investment as an 'overall' policy model for Europe has failed.

The impacts of increased selectivity on stigmatization, deservingness, and non-take-up

As access to social insurance has become more selective and more people came to rely on means-tested welfare transfers, one would expect an increase over time in terms of stigmatization and non-take-up of welfare benefits, in combination with less favourable public perceptions regarding 'welfare deservingness'. 'Deservingness theory' postulates that in particular those reliant on targeted welfare (with some variation related to different deservingness criteria) tend to be perceived as less deserving (van Oorschot et al., 2017). Evidence regarding the impact of institutional change on deservingness perceptions is, however, mixed (reflective of the 'confusing' empirical patterns regarding welfare attitudes across welfare states in general, see Svallfors (2010)). Comparative studies investigating the impact of actual social policy changes are scarce. Using repeated cross-sections for the Netherlands (1975–2006), Jeene, van Oorschot, and Uunk (2014) find that the long-term trend in deservingness is rather *stable and upward*; effects of policy reforms remain limited. In liberal countries, there are more indications that in particular the unemployed, social assistance beneficiaries and immigrants are increasingly stigmatized as 'less deserving' (Dukelow and Heins, 2017). For the UK, Taylor-Gooby (2016) relates this to the fact that the Conservative Party (in power since 2010) financially depends on the rich and powerful, and in order to safeguard (electoral) support, aims to legitimize reduced welfare benefits for the least powerful through pursuing 'divisive' social policies that resonate in public debate. Taking better account of 'whether social policies are voted rather than negotiated' might move this literature forward.

It is unclear how increased selectivity has impacted on non-take-up of welfare benefits, given the lack of comparative longitudinal research. Apart from stigmatization, non-take-up may also result from other factors, such as increasing complexity of policy design (Van Mechelen and Janssens, 2017). Overall, the vast majority of even the most conservative estimates of non-take-up in Table 21.1 are above 40%, suggesting that the phenomenon is far from marginal. All countries included in Table 21.1 have at least one benefit for which the estimate is 40% or higher (EUROFOUND, 2015: 21). Potential trends toward higher non-take-up might furthermore be offset by the fact that in many countries administrative data are increasingly available. Data coupling across government departments facilitates detection of benefit fraud, but also the identification of non-take-up. This would consequently allow for automated enrolment of those vulnerable groups that fail to claim their entitlements (e.g. Buysse et al., 2017). Developments in e-government services (e.g. online application procedures) might also contribute to diminishing diverse 'costs' (time, travel, effort, stigma) of application (EUROFOUND, 2015).

The rise of 'anti-poverty policies' as a response to increased welfare gaps

For Palier and Thelen (2010: 133), the 'institutionalization of dualism' across labour markets and welfare systems discussed previously has resulted in an emerging 'secondary world of welfare', characterized by non-contributory (tax-financed) means-tested compensatory arrangements aimed at lifting the growing group of outsiders out of poverty. *In-work benefits* (employment-conditional earnings subsidies) are a prime example. Such benefits have been around since the

1970s in liberal welfare states, but have spread across the western world. Kenworthy (2018) finds that such programmes boost the absolute incomes of poor households in the UK and the United States, but also that 'regular' social policies in CMEs were comparatively more effective in combating poverty. In-work benefits may furthermore suppress wages, and thus benefit employers more than employees. Other types of 'anti-poverty policies' range from promoting bottom-up initiatives of *social innovation* to forms of *decentralization to local levels* of governance (urban development programmes, local social policy) and the *'institutionalization' of foodbanks* as a more or a less accepted (sometimes even means-tested)[7] element of social assistance. Efforts to *reduce non-take-up* of social benefits were already discussed.

The combination of all these measures seems to work to some extent, though this varies across countries. Gábos et al. (2018), for instance, find no evidence that the 'EU-wide' association between unemployment and poverty rates became stronger after the economic crisis, while Matsaganis and Leventi (2018) conclude that in the 'European periphery' changes in taxes and benefits contributed to poverty increases. From a policy perspective, it furthermore becomes a difficult task to ensure that resources mobilized through a wider range of 'anti-poverty policies' are distributed in a fair and equitable way across the poor – some groups may be targeted disproportionally, while others are left behind. The century-old distinction between the 'deserving' and 'undeserving' poor might furthermore reappear with a new vengeance. There is also a risk that new 'overarching' policies will be called for to 'integrate' the growing array of initiatives in an 'intersectoral' fashion – we know that such attempts are often less successful. A final issue relates to the argument that, while in practice the welfare state in recent decades has redistributed a growing amount of resources in a more vertical fashion toward those at the bottom (see Table 21.1, Cantillon et al., 2018), the development of 'encompassing' universalistic welfare states has historically hinged on notions of equity and reciprocity – horizontal redistribution with a social element. This renders 'verticalist' anti-poverty policies, which are located in the decision-making arena 'where social policies are voted' rather than 'where social policies are negotiated', vulnerable for political-electoral dynamics. The long-term sustainability of this policy strategy is hence questionable.

Conclusion

This chapter has explained how welfare states crystallized out of historical power struggles between organized interests, and how the resulting institutions of social and economic regulation *continue to determine how present-day policy trade-offs are resolved*. Different welfare state types are associated with variegated policy trajectories regarding the access to welfare benefits, and hence poverty outcomes. It has discussed the recent stabilization or even increase in poverty rates and concomitant policy responses, as well as future challenges. Although 'path dependency' remains key, it is important to recognize that muddled-through adaptations such as 'policy drift' and 'institutional layering' can – under certain circumstances – give way to so-called 'critical junctures' resulting in more systemic policy change (Ebbinghaus, 2015). This is, for instance, the case when the balance of power shifts from corporatist negotiation to the political arena (see e.g. van der Veen and Trommel (1999) on the liberalization of the Dutch welfare state).

A final note pertains to broader social and economic trends affecting the poor. Changes in social and economic regulation have not only affected welfare states and therefore welfare benefits of the poor, but have also impacted on the *expenditures* of the poor. Political decisions have rendered the tax system overall more regressive, e.g. by reducing wealth taxation (Förster et al., 2014) or increasing VAT – which is known to disproportionally disadvantage the poor (e.g. Taylor-Gooby, 2016). Changes in housing markets and policies have strongly impacted on the stratification of wealth accumulation (Ronald and Dewilde, 2017) and the costs of housing, in particular for urban poor (Dewilde, 2018). Consequently, compared to a decade ago, the income of poor households seems to stretch less far. Social disarray (e.g. '*les gilets jaunes*') finds its origins in social-structural changes indeed.

Acknowledgements

The author thanks Dr. Tim Goedemé for suggestions, as well as several colleagues and cohorts of students in the Department of Sociology (Tilburg University).

Notes

1 www.euromod.ac.uk/
2 Goodin et al. (1999: 22) identify a wider range of welfare state goals: reducing poverty and promoting efficiency, social equality, social inclusion, social stability, and autonomy.
3 The 'Matthew-effect in social policy' arises from the fact that higher socio-economic groups are better able to take advantage of, and advocate for, universally available services that serve their needs (Deleeck et al., 1983).
4 De-commodification is defined as: "when a service is rendered as a matter of right, and when a person can maintain a livelihood without reliance on the market" (Esping-Andersen, 1990: 22).
5 See for instance www.sofi.su.se/spin/ or www.lisdatacenter.org/resources/other-databases/.
6 Regarding pensions, negotiated reforms also point at increased 'dualization' (i.e. between those with pensions from different pillars and those dependent on public pensions), but on top of that, a generational divide is unfolding as welfare reform has been passed on to future generations (Bonoli, 2012; Palier, 2012).
7 As is the case in the Netherlands.

References

Allan J.P. and Scruggs L. (2004) Political Partisanship and Welfare State Reform in Advanced Industrial Societies. *American Journal of Political Science* 48(3): 496–512.

Armingeon K., Wenger V., Wiedemeier F., Isler C., Knöpfel L., Weisstanner D. and Engler S. (2018) *Comparative Political Data Set 1960–2016*, University of Bern: Institute of Political Science.

Arts W. and Gelissen J. (2002). Three Worlds of Welfare Capitalism or More? A State-of-the-Art Report. *Journal of European Social Policy* 12(2): 137–158.

Bonoli G. (2005) The Politics of the New Social Policies: Providing Coverage Against Social Risks in Mature Welfare States. *Policy and Politics* 33(3): 431–449.

Bonoli G. (2012) Blame Avoidance and Credit Claiming Revisited. In: Bonoli G. and Natali D. (eds) *The Politics of the New Welfare State*. Oxford: Oxford University Press, pp. 93–110.

Bonoli G. and Natali D. (2012a) The Politics of the 'New' Welfare States: Analysing Reforms in Western Europe. In: Bonoli G. and Natali D. (eds) *The Politics of the New Welfare State*. Oxford: Oxford University Press, pp. 3–17.

Bonoli G. and Natali D. (eds) (2012b) *The Politics of the New Welfare State*, Oxford: Oxford University Press.

Buysse L., Goedemé T., Van der Heyden M., Van Mechelen N., Janssens J., De Spiegeleer T. and Nisen L. (2017) De automatische toekenning van rechten in de Belgische sociale bescherming. In: Lahaye W., Pannecoucke I., Vranken J., et al. (eds) *Armoede in België. Jaarboek 2017*. Gent: Scribis, pp. 73–99.

Cantillon B. (2011) The Paradox of the Social Investment State: Growth, Employment and Poverty in the Lisbon Era. *Journal of European Social Policy* 21: 432–449.

Cantillon B., Goedemé T. and Hills J. (eds) (2018) *Decent Incomes for All? Improving Policies in Europe*, Oxford: Oxford University Press.

Cronert A. and Palme J. (2017) *Approaches to Social Investment and Their Implications for Poverty in Sweden and the European Union*, Bergen: University of Bergen.

Crouch C. and Keune M. (2012) The Governance of Economic Uncertainty: Beyond the 'New Social Risks' Analysis. In: Bonoli G. and Natali D. (eds) *The Politics of the New Welfare State*. Oxford: Oxford University Press, pp. 45–66.

De Deken J. and Clasen J. (2013) Benefit Dependency: The Pros and Cons of Using 'Caseload' Data for National and International Comparisons. *International Social Security Review* 66(2): 53–78.

De Deken J., Ponds E. and Van Riel B. (2006) Social Solidarity. In: Clarck G.L., Munnell A.H. and Orszag J.M. (eds) *The Oxford Handbook of Pensions and Retirement Income*. Oxford: Oxford University Press, pp. 141–160.

de la Porte C. and Jacobsson K. (2012) Social Investment or Recommodification? Assessing the Employment Policies of the EU Member States. In: Morel N., Palier B. and Palme J. (eds) *Towards a Social Investment Welfare State? Ideas, Policies and Challenges*. Bristol: The Policy Press, pp. 117–149.

Deleeck H., Huybrechs J. and Cantillon B. (1983) *Het Matteüseffect: De ongelijke verdeling van de overheidsuitgaven in België*, Antwerpen: Kluwer.

de Swaan A. (1989) *In Care of the State. Health Care, Education and Welfare in Europe and the USA in the Modern Era*, Cambridge: Polity Press.

Dewilde C. (2008) Individual and Institutional Determinants of Multidimensional Poverty: A European Comparison. *Social Indicators Research* 86(2): 233–256.

Dewilde C. (2018) Explaining the Declined Affordability of Housing for Low-Income Private Renters across Western-Europe. *Urban Studies* 55(12): 2618–2639.

Dewilde C. and Raeymaeckers P. (2008) The Trade-Off between Home-Ownership and Pensions: Individual and Institutional Determinants of Old-Age Poverty. *Ageing & Society* 28(6): 805–830.

DiPrete T.A., Goux D., Maurin E. and Quesnel-Vallee A. (2006) Work and Pay in Flexible and Regulated Labor Markets: A Generalized Perspective on Institutional Evolution and Inequality Trends in Europe and the U.S. *Research in Social Stratification and Mobility* 24: 311–332.

Dukelow F. and Heins E. (2017) The Anglo-Saxon Welfare States: Still Europe's Outlier – Or Trendsetter? In: Kennett P. and Lendvai-Bainton N. (eds) *Handbook of European Social Policy*. Cheltenham: Edward Elgar, pp. 230–247.

Ebbinghaus B. (2015) Welfare Retrenchment. In: Wright J.D. (ed.) *International Encyclopedia of the Social and Behavioral Sciences*. 2nd Edition. Amsterdam: Elsevier, pp. 521–527.

Ebbinghaus B. and Naumann E. (eds) (2018) *Welfare State Reforms Seen from Below: Comparing Public Attitudes and Organized Interests in Britain and Germany*, London: Palgrave Macmillan.

Emmenegger P., Häusermann S., Palier B. and Seeleib-Kaiser M. (eds) (2012) *The Age of Dualization: The Changing Face of Inequality in Deindustrializing Societies*, Oxford: Oxford University Press.

Esping-Andersen G. (1990) *The Three Worlds of Welfare Capitalism*, Cambridge: Polity Press.

Esping-Andersen G., Gallie D., Hemerijck A. and Myles J. (eds) (2002) *Why We Need a New Welfare State*, Oxford: Oxford University Press.

EUROFOUND (2015) *Access to Social Benefits: Reducing Non-Take-Up*, Luxembourg: Publications Office of the European Union.

Falkingham J. and Hills J. (eds) (1995) *The Dynamic of Welfare: The Welfare State and the Life Cycle*, New York: Prentice Hall/Harvester Wheatsheaf.

Ferrera M. (1996) The 'Southern Model' of Welfare in Social Europe. *Journal of European Social Policy* 6(1): 17–37.

Förster M., Llena-Nozal A. and Nafilyan V. (2014) *Trends in Top Incomes and Their Taxation in OECD Countries*, Paris: OECD.

Gábos A., Branyiczki R., Lange B. and Tóth I.G. (2018) Employment and Poverty Dynamics Before, During and After the Crisis. In: Cantillon B., Goedemé T. and Hills J. (eds) *Decent Incomes for All? Improving Policies in Europe*. Oxford: Oxford University Press.

Gingrich J. and Häusermann S. (2015) The Decline of the Working-Class Vote, the Reconfiguration of the Welfare Support Coalition and Consequences for the Welfare State. *Journal of European Social Policy* 25(1): 50–75.

Goodin R.E., Headey B., Muffels R. and Dirven H.-J. (1999) *The Real Worlds of Welfare Capitalism*, Cambridge: Cambridge University Press.

Greve B. (2017) Reflecting on Nordic Welfare States: Continuity or Social Change? In: Kennett P. and Lendvai-Bainton N. (eds) *Handbook of European Social Policy*. Cheltenham: Edward Elgar, pp. 248–262.

Hall P. and Soskice D. (2001) *Varieties of Capitalism: The Institutional Foundations of Comparative Advantage*, Oxford: Oxford University Press.

Häusermann S. (2012) The Politics of Old and New Social Policies. In: Bonoli G. and Natali D. (eds) *The Politics of the New Welfare State*. Oxford: Oxford University Press, pp. 111–132.

Hemerijck A. (2013) *Changing Welfare States*, Oxford: Oxford University Press.

Hemerijck A. (2017) Continental Welfare States in Transition: The Incomplete Social Investment Turn. In: Kennett P. and Lendvai-Bainton N. (eds) *Handbook of European Social Policy*. Cheltenham: Edward Elgar, pp. 169–193.

Iversen T. and Wren A. (1998) Equality, Employment, and Budgetary Restraint: The Trilemma of the Service Economy. *World Politics* 50(4): 507–546.

Jeene M., van Oorschot W. and Uunk W. (2014) The Dynamics of Welfare Opinions in Changing Economic, Institutional and Policy Contexts: An Empirical Analysis of Dutch Deservingness Opinions, 1975–2006. *Social Indicators Research* 115: 731–749.

Jensen C. (2011) The Forgotten Half: Analysing the Politics of Welfare Services. *International Journal of Social Welfare* 20: 404–412.

Jenson J. (2012) A New Politics for the Social Investment Perspective. In: Bonoli G. and Natali D. (eds) *The Politics of the New Welfare State*. Oxford: Oxford University Press, pp. 21–44.

Kahl S. (2005) The Religious Roots of Modern Poverty Policy: Catholic, Lutheran, and Reformed Protestant Traditions Compared. *European Journal of Sociology* 46(1): 91–126.

Kalleberg A.L. (2018) *Precarious Lives: Job Insecurity and Well-Being in Rich Democracies*, Cambridge: Polity.

Kenworthy L. (2018) Do Employment-Conditional Earnings Subsidies Work? In: Cantillon B., Goedemé T. and Hills J. (eds) *Decent Incomes for All: Improving Policies in Europe*. Oxford: Oxford University Press.

Korpi W. (1974) Conflict, Power and Relative Deprivation. *American Political Science Review* 68(4): 1569–1578.

Korpi W. and Palme J. (1998) The Paradox of Redistribution and Strategies of Equality: Welfare State Institutions, Inequality, and Poverty in the Western Countries. *American Sociological Review* 63(October): 661–687.

Korpi W. and Palme J. (2003) New Politics and Class Politics in the Context of Austerity and Globalization: Welfare State Regress in 18 countries, 1975–95. *American Political Science Review* 97(3): 1–22.

Kovács B., Polese A. and Morris J. (2017) Adjusting Social Welfare and Social Policy in Central and Eastern Europe: Growth, Crisis and Recession. In: Kennett P. and Lendvai-Bainton N. (eds) *Handbook of European Social Policy*. Cheltenham: Edward Elgar, pp. 194–217.

Kuitto K. (2016) From Social Security to Social Investment? Compensating and Social Investment Welfare Policies in a Life-Course Perspective. *Journal of European Social Policy* 26(5): 442–459.

Kvist J. (2017) Social Investments over the Life Course: Ending European Social Policy as We Know It? In: Kennett P. and Lendvai-Bainton N. (eds) *Handbook of European Social Policy*. Cheltenham: Edward Elgar, pp. 75–89.

Lipsky M. (1980) *Street-Level Bureaucracy: Dilemmas of the Individual in Public Service*, New York: Russell Sage Foundation.

Matsaganis M. and Leventi C. (2018) Distributive Effects of the Crisis in the European Periphery. In: Cantillon B., Goedemé T. and Hills J. (eds) *Decent Incomes for All? Improving Social Policies in Europe* (pp. 133–153). Oxford: Oxford University Press.

Nelson K. (2010) Social Assistance and Minimum Income Benefits in Old and New EU Democracies. *International Journal of Social Welfare* 19: 367–378.

Otto A. and van Oorschot W. (2018) Welfare Reform by Stealth? Cash Benefit Recipiency Data and Its Additional Value to the Understanding of Welfare State Change in Europe. *Journal of European Social Policy*. (Published Online) https://doi.org/10.1177/0958928718796299

Palier B. (2012) Turning Vice into Vice: How Bismarckian Welfare States Have Gone from Unsustainability to Dualization. In: Bonoli G. and Natali D. (eds) *The Politics of the New Welfare State*. Oxford: Oxford University Press, pp. 233–253.

Palier B. and Thelen K. (2010) Institutionalizing Dualism: Complementarities and Change in France and Germany. *Politics and Society* 38(1): 119–148.

Pampel F.C. and Williamson J.B. (1985) Age Structure, Politics, and Cross-National Patterns of Public Pension Expenditures. *American Sociological Review* 50(6): 782–799.

Pierson P. (1996) The New Politics of the Welfare State. *World Politics* 48(January): 143–179.

Ronald R. and Dewilde C. (2017) Why Housing Wealth and Welfare? In: Dewilde C. and Ronald R. (eds) *Housing Wealth and Welfare*. Cheltenham: Edward Elgar, pp. 1–34.

Rueda D. (2014) Dualization, Crisis and the Welfare State. *Socio-Economic Review* 12: 381–407.

Saraceno C. (2017) Southern European Welfare Regimes: From Differentiation to Reconvergence? In: Kennett P. and Lendvai-Bainton N. (eds) *Handbook of European Social Policy*. Cheltenham: Edward Elgar, pp. 218–229.

Schröder M. (2008) Integrating Welfare and Production Typologies: How Refinements of the Varieties of Capitalism Approach Call for a Combination of Welfare Typologies. *Journal of Social Policy* 38(1): 19–43.

Schröder M. (2017) Varieties of Capitalism and Welfare States: Eroding Diversity? In: Kennett P. and Lendvai-Bainton N. (eds) *Handbook of European Social Policy*. Cheltenham: Edward Elgar, pp. 45–59.

Scruggs L., Detlef J. and Kuitto K. (2017) *Comparative Welfare Entitlements Data Set 2, Version 2017-09*. University of Connecticut and University of Greifswald.

Svallfors S. (2010) Public Attitudes. In: Castles F.G., Leibfreid S., Lewis J., et al. (eds) *The Oxford Handbook of the Welfare State*. Oxford: Oxford University Press, pp. 241–251.

Taylor-Gooby P. (2008) The New Welfare State Settlement in Europe. *European Societies* 10(1): 3–24.

Taylor-Gooby P. (2016) The Divisive Welfare State. *Social Policy & Administration* 50(6): 712–733.

Thelen K. (2011) Varieties of Capitalism: Trajectories of Liberalization and the New Politics of Social Solidarity. *Annual Review of Political Science* 15: 137–159.

Titmuss R.M. (1968) *Commitment to Welfare*, London: George Allen and Unwin.

Titmuss R.M. (1974) *Social Policy*, London: Allen and Unwin.

van der Veen R. and Trommel W. (1999) Managed Liberalization of the Dutch Welfare State: A Review and Analysis of the Reform of the Dutch Social Security System, 1985–1998. *Governance: An International Journal of Policy and Administration* 12(3): 289–310.

van Kersbergen K. and Hemerijck A. (2012) Two Decades of Change in Europe: The Emergence of the Social Investment State. *Journal of Social Policy* 41(3): 475–492.

Van Mechelen N. and Janssens J. (2017) *Who is to Blame? An Overview of Factors Contributing to the Non-Take-Up of Social Rights*, Antwerp: Herman Deleeck Centre for Social Policy.

van Oorschot W., Roosma F., Meuleman B. and Reeskens T. (eds) (2017) *The Social Legitimacy of Targeted Welfare. Attitudes to Welfare Deservingness*, Cheltenham: Edward Elgar.

Vandenbroucke F. and Vleminckx K. (2011) Disappointing Poverty Trends: Is the Social Investment State to Blame? *Journal of European Social Policy* 21(5): 450–471.

Veit-Wilson J. (1992) Muddle or Mendacity? The Beveridge Committee and the Poverty Line. *Journal of Social Policy* 21(3): 269–301.

Verbist G., Förster M. and Vaalavuo M. (2012) *The Impact of Publicly Provided Services on the Distribution of Resources: Review of New Results and Methods*, Paris: OECD.

Visser J. (2016) *ICTWSS Data base. Version 5.1*, Amsterdam: Amsterdam Institute for Advanced Labour Studies.

22

Coping with poverty in everyday life

Jane Gray, Jennifer Dagg and Clíona Rooney

Introduction

This chapter discusses recent developments in qualitative research on how people experience, and cope with, poverty in their everyday lives, and on how those experiences and practices lead to the reproduction of poverty and inequality. There has been renewed interest in understanding the everyday experience of poverty in recent years, associated with a revival of interest in qualitative approaches. There are a number of factors associated with this trend. First, the emergence of new theoretical perspectives on culture has reopened questions about the relationship between cultural practices, poverty and the reproduction of inequality in ways that transcend earlier, discredited approaches to the 'culture of poverty'. Second, there has been a flourishing of research on the (lived) experience of poverty in everyday life in the contexts of welfare state reform, and of the impact of the Great Recession and associated policies of austerity in some countries. Third, there has been growing interest in documenting poor people's voices and the application of qualitative methods within the field of development studies (Morrow and Crivello 2015; Shaffer 2013).

These trends have been supported by developments in qualitative research methodology, notably a growing interest in longitudinal qualitative research and the revival of ethnography and community studies. Ethnographic research has helped to bring the challenges faced by poor people, and how they address them, into the public domain. Longitudinal and biographical approaches have increased the potential for qualitative research to address questions about processes of vulnerability and resilience to poverty within and across lives. However, the resurgence of qualitative research has also been accompanied by debates about how different styles of qualitative research portray people living in poverty and about their value for sociological research. Finally, recent qualitative scholarship has renewed interest in how processes of stigma and shame inform experiences of and responses to poverty. The chapter concludes with a discussion of the potential for qualitative research to inform policy.

Core concepts in the study of life for people in poverty

The fortunes of the concept of *culture* within sociological research on poverty have altered alongside theoretical changes in how culture itself is understood. Contemporary qualitative researchers (often implicitly) deploy an understanding of culture as a '"toolkit" for constructing "strategies of action"' (Swidler 1986: 277), rather than as coherent sets of norms and values that are internalized by different groups of people. This way of thinking about culture (also often implicitly) draws on the concept of *experience* to understand how culture, in the form of 'skills, habits and attributes', guides established patterns of behaviour or informs responses to new challenges.

Many qualitative studies set out to document the experience or 'lived experience' of people in poverty. Such research tends to emphasize the value of attending to the (often hidden or unnoticed) experiences of *everyday life* (Back 2015). Through its focus on everyday life, qualitative research tends to foreground practices of coping, 'getting by', and in some cases, *resilience* (see e.g. Dagdeviren and Donoghue 2018), in contrast to the emphasis on risk and the reproduction of poverty within the quantitative research tradition. Thus, the key contributions of qualitative approaches centre on their emphasis on agency and on their potential to distinguish variations in how people respond to poverty. Nevertheless, qualitative research also shows how the *stigma* of poverty, and associated feelings of *shame*, affect people's experiences and their capacity for coping and resilience (Lamont 2009; Sherman 2013).

Qualitative research and the revitalization of culture

In a widely cited article, Small et al. (2010) argued that culture was 'back on the poverty research agenda', following an extended period in which sociologists eschewed consideration of cultural factors due to their perceived association with negative images of the poor. Associated mainly with the work of Oscar Lewis (and with the Moynihan (1965) report), the idea that sustained poverty gave rise to 'a set of cultural attitudes, beliefs, values, and practices' – that is, to a 'culture of poverty' that tended to perpetuate itself over time – was heavily criticized by scholars in the 1960s and 70s on the grounds that this was a form of 'blaming the victim'. Urban ethnographic research in the United States during the 1960s aimed 'to shatter pejorative stories about marginalized Black and Brown communities and demystify their lives', and to show how larger structural forces shaped the prevalence of 'risk behaviours' (Ray and Tillman 2019). Research within the British 'community studies' tradition emphasized the social cohesiveness and practices of mutual support that characterized poor, working-class communities (Crow and Allan 1994). Nevertheless, qualitative research on the everyday life experiences and practices of people living in poverty fell out of fashion in the 1970s. However, with the publication of *The Truly Disadvantaged*, Wilson (1987) reopened the question of culture through a 'structuralist' lens (Small and Newman 2001). While arguing that poverty in inner-city areas was caused by the loss of jobs due to deindustrialization, Wilson also suggested that social isolation led to the exclusion of people living in poor communities from mainstream values and to feelings of low individual and community efficacy.

Especially in the United States, subsequent qualitative research on poverty developed under the auspices of the new 'sociology of culture'. Drawing on a wide range of overlapping concepts drawn from diverse theoretical traditions, this way of thinking about culture emphasizes how different 'frames' or 'repertoires' inform people's perceptions of events and circumstances, and the variety of ways in which they respond. Small and Lamont (2010) identify as many as seven different 'analytical devices' through which questions about culture and poverty have been addressed. Within their list, concepts deriving from the work of Erving Goffman and Pierre Bourdieu have probably been most influential in international qualitative research on poverty. In practice, most qualitative scholarship continues to focus on examining the 'life worlds' of people living in poverty – how they make sense of and manage their socio-economic conditions (Rodríguez-Muñiz 2015).

Leading authors continue to emphasize the importance of this contribution of qualitative research to the understanding of poverty. Thus for example, Lister (2016) noted the importance of moving beyond statistics, of 'listening' to people living in poverty in order to ground the conceptualization of poverty in 'lived experience'. Daly and Kelly (2015: 8–9) argued that qualitative research gets to the 'core' of poverty by revealing 'what it means to be poor'. However, other scholars have been critical of what they perceive as failure to move beyond a narrow focus on 'the poor' to include more systemic, relational and inter-sectional understandings of poverty (Ray and Tillman 2019; Rodríguez-Muñiz 2015; Branch and Scherer 2013). The next sections in this chapter discuss some recent findings from qualitative research on poverty under two broad headings: (1) research showing the agency of poor people in coping with lived experiences and discursive constructions of poverty, including experiences of stigma and shame; and (2) research that attempts to identify the mechanisms through which poverty is reproduced or through which people exhibit resilience and capacities to escape from poverty.

Coping with poverty

Many studies document how people living in poverty engage in practices of 'constant struggle' to meet basic needs. Poor people expend considerable labour deploying strategies of budgeting, cutting back, and taking on short-term debt in order to 'get by' (O'Brien and Kyprianou 2017). Narayan et al. (2000: 45) documented how, in conditions of precariousness, poor people around the world

> struggle to diversify their sources of income and food: they work on the land and in quarries and mines; they hunt down temporary jobs and sell an endless variety of goods on the streets; they do piecework in factories and from homes; they patch together remittances; and they cultivate home gardens.

Patrick (2014) described the 'hard work' involved in 'getting by' on benefits, including practices of doing without, engaging in informal economic activities and seeking out bargains and low-cost items alongside searching for, and moving in and out of low-paid work. She also showed the extent to which poor people engaged in non-waged but socially valuable work, such as volunteering and care work. Whereas some participants in her study viewed volunteering as a stepping stone to formal employment, for others it was critical for improving confidence and self-esteem. Parents – and lone parents in particular – prioritized caring activities over the expectations and demands of state welfare agencies, even in the face of perceived stigmatization of lone parenthood and undervaluation of caring activities within the wider society (Patrick 2014: 714–716; see also the references to volunteering in McKenzie 2012: 467–469). In a thematic qualitative analysis of online social media, Caplan et al. (2017: 441–443) identified the extent to which poverty was experienced as *arduous*, requiring strenuous activities to get by and the mobilization of an *arsenal of survival strategies and skills*. Similarly, Pemberton et al. (2017) documented the extent to which life on a low income required 'unrelenting effort' and how, in the context of the 'Great Recession' and associated policies of austerity, the effectiveness of past strategies had diminished.

Drawing on findings from a nine-country European study, Dagdeviren and Donoghue (2018) identified three categories of 'adjustment to hardship' in the context of the recent 'Great Recession'. Efforts to *reduce the cost of living* included cutting back on consumption, relentlessly pursuing bargains, substituting self-provision for purchased goods and services, planning day-to-day life and drawing on an intricate web of social and informal economies of exchange, including kinship relations. Participants also engaged in *efforts to protect or stabilize their incomes* by taking on work for which they were over-qualified, 'patching together' spells of insecure and/or informal work, migration and (often unsuccessfully) attempting to take on further education or training. Third, participants engaged in efforts to *make better use of assets and resources*, by remaining in or returning to the family home, taking on debt or using public resources such as parks and libraries. Estêvão et al. (2017: 17) summarized these practices as *mobilizing resources* and *shifting risks*.

Many authors argue that it is important to document the unrelenting effort involved in attempting to make ends meet, and the emotional and physical strain that this effort entails, in order to counter negative discursive constructions of poor people as 'skivers' (see, for example, the discussion in Patrick 2016). However, qualitative research also provides critical insights into how poor people themselves experience, construct and respond to wider cultural understandings of poverty and inequality. For instance, Back (2015: 831) uses the example of 'excessive' multi-coloured Christmas decorations – contrary to 'good taste' – to illustrate how working-class people refuse 'the "authority of judgments" that have their origin in middle-class respectability'. Hamilton (2012) by contrast, used the example of purchasing branded goods to argue that poor people's attempts to address threats to their identity through conspicuous consumption, paradoxically reproduced negative stereotypes. McKenzie (2012) described how a sense of community belonging – 'being St. Ann's' – provided residents of an impoverished neighbourhood with an alternative source of feeling valued. Milbourne (2014) similarly argued that in poor rural communities, 'senses of inclusion within the social, cultural, and natural fabric of rural places' acted as 'compensatory factors . . . capable of offsetting some of the material problems associated with life on a low income'. However, other studies have described how poor people may themselves participate in the construction of negative images of poverty and 'welfare' through a process of 'defensive othering' which manages stigma by seeking to deflect it onto a different group judged less deserving of state support (Patrick 2016).

Stigma, shame and social devaluation

Experiences of stigma and shame have remained a central theme in both historical accounts of poverty and in contemporary poverty research (Sutton et al. 2014). Indeed, Sutton et al. (2014) refer to Adam Smith's early observations that 'poverty has been associated with an inability to observe customary norms relating to dress, tastes and styles of living and has been explicitly framed in terms of avoiding social disgrace and opprobrium' (in Sutton et al., 2014: 143). Writing in the 1970s, Peter Townsend (in Walker and Bantebya-Kyomuhendo 2014: 2), referred to poverty as the 'social shame of those with little money' and in the context of claiming benefits, the desire of potential applicants 'to avoid the shame of pleading poverty', while Amartya Sen (in Walker and Bantebya-Kyomuhendo 2014: 2) asserts that shame is at the 'irreducible absolutist core' of the idea of poverty. Goffman (1963 [2009]: 12–13) described shame as 'an attribute that is deeply discrediting' in which the subject is reduced in our minds from a whole and usual person to a tainted, discounted one'. Walker and Bantebya-Kyomuhendo (2014: 2) claim that the 'salience of poverty-related shame is arguably intensifying as social status and personal identity become progressively more determined by individual economic success in societies that are increasingly individualistic and market oriented'.

Recently, the scientific literature on poverty research understands the shame felt by people in poverty as co-constructed: they are being shamed and they are feeling shame (Chase and Walker 2013; Walker and Bantebya-Kyomuhendo 2014; Sutton et al. 2014; Garthwaite 2016). This approach argues that shame is not only present within the psychosocial dimension, or internally felt, but also within the objective dimension, through society and societal structures, or social relationships. Shame is taken to be externally imposed by society, via individuals and through social institutions, and internalized to create negative emotions such as 'pretence, withdrawal, self-loathing, "othering", despair, depression, thoughts of suicide and generally to reductions in personal efficacy' (Walker et al. 2013: 216; Scheff 2003: 255). For some, a distinction is drawn between shame and stigma, where stigma 'reflects an external process through which the social "contribution" or "value" of those on low incomes is actively denigrated by the pejorative labels that are attached to specific aspects of life on a low income' (Sutton et al. 2014: 144). Shame then refers to 'the internalisation of stigmatising labels that force an individual to view themselves "negatively through the eyes of others"' (Sutton et al. 2014: 145). Reutter et al. (2009: 302) refer to this internalization process as 'stigma consciousness', the 'belief that they are viewed negatively as a burden to society, and essentially deserving of what they get'. Chase and Walker (2013: 743) observe how the words 'awkward', 'embarrassed', 'guilty', 'rotten', 'degraded', 'crap', 'useless', 'worthless', 'a failure', 'uncomfortable', 'funny', and 'dirty', were all used to convey how people in poverty felt about themselves or were made to feel in certain social interactions.

Although poverty is culturally nuanced, there is evidence to suggest 'that shame experienced as a consequence of poverty is widespread across different cultures' (Narayan et al. 2000 in Walker et al. 2013: 217). Indeed, in Walker et al.'s (2013: 226) study across seven countries (including rural Uganda and India, urban China, Pakistan, South Korea, United Kingdom and small town and urban Norway), they found that the 'juxtaposition of internalised shame with the explicit shaming of people in poverty by society was present in every one of the seven national settings'. Those experiencing poverty reported feelings of stigma and shame at the social, personal and institutional levels (Sutton et al. 2014: 146). This included: social hostility associated with benefit receipt; individual level stigma arising from an enforced inability to buy things taken for granted by others; being unable to effectively perform social roles; and institutional stigma when in receipt of particular benefits for services (Sutton et al., 2014: 146).

Reutter et al.'s (2009) study exploring low-income people's perceptions of and responses to 'poverty stigma', highlighted the micro-level processes involved in addressing the discrepancies between how other people perceive you, and who you perceive yourself to be (Reutter et al. 2009: 298). Their analysis reveals that the coping strategies used to manage stigma include confronting discrimination directly, disregarding responses from others, helping other low-income people, withdrawing and isolating themselves from others, engaging in processes of cognitive distancing, and concealing their financial situation (Reutter et al. 2009: 297). Using life history interviews, Shildrick and MacDonald (2013) explored how poor people talk about poverty. They found that paradoxically, interviewees succumbed to dominant discourses that resulted in them either denying their poverty or morally condemning 'the poor'.

Garthwaite's (2016) ethnographic exploration of foodbank use in the UK from the perspective of residents highlighted how stigma, shame and embarrassment are created and reproduced. She argued that the growing dominant discourse, moral judgement and misconceptions characterized those accessing food banks as the 'undeserving poor' resulting in many 'hidden costs' (Purdam et al. 2016) associated with their use. He detailed how those in need waited until they had exhausted all other avenues of support before they asked for a foodbank voucher, while the dominant discourse in the UK continues to question the lifestyles and personal attitudes of people using foodbanks (Garthwaite 2016: 11). Additionally, Sutton et al. (2014), explored the qualitative evidence on poverty in Japan and the UK to conclude that 'stigma is a central feature of the experience of poverty in diverse societies' (Sutton et al. 2014: 149). They suggested that the

> affective impacts of the internalisation of stigma are reflected in feelings of guilt, embarrassment, humiliation, disrespect, assault on self-esteem, and shame, and that the nature and intensity of these effects reflects the differing social roles, responsibilities and statues attributed to different populations on the basis of their social and demographic characteristics (for example, age, ethnicity, gender, social class).

Responses to manage shame included strategies such as withdrawal from social relationships and social participation and concealing aspects of their circumstances from others.

A number of studies have documented the distinctive experiences of coping with poverty, and with feelings of stigma and shame, among those who found themselves newly poor in the context of the Great Recession. In an analysis of findings from a nine-country European study, Dagdeviren et al. (2017) distinguished between the 'narratives of hardship' provided by participants classified as the 'old poor', for whom the crisis meant simply a continuation of the struggle to make ends meet (see also Emmel and Hughes, 2010), and those provided by the 'new poor', who confronted hardship generated by the crisis without the same reservoir of knowledge and skills with which to 'get by'. The authors found that 'individuals with no experiences of hardship in the past tend to feel more vulnerable, more deprived and more stigmatized' (Dagdeviren et al. 2017: 374). In a study carried out in the United States, Sherman (2013: 427) found that, among people who were downwardly mobile into poverty, the stigma of receiving aid was so severe that they went without basic necessities to save face among families and friends, avoided social contacts leading to social isolation and greater emotional distress, and in many cases 'created symbolic boundaries through vilifying others in their same situation, drawing on divisive discourses based in racial stereotypes'. Lempidaki and Kalerante (2015: 173) similarly elaborated on the pervasiveness of feelings of 'anxiety, fear, shame and disappointment' amongst those experiencing new poverty in Greece. Their participants used comparisons with others perceived to be worse off as a way of alleviating distress.

Relationships between coping, vulnerability and resilience

As the summary above shows, many qualitative studies document the 'lived experience' of coping with poverty, including dealing with the psychosocial consequences of stigma. However, qualitative research also aims increasingly to address questions about the *mechanisms* giving rise to vulnerability and resilience to poverty within biographies and in different community contexts (Harding and Hepburn 2014). These questions reflect a growing interest among scholars and policy makers in moving beyond a 'deficit model' of poverty toward an understanding of the factors giving rise to variations, including 'unexpectedly' positive outcomes (Canvin et al. 2009). Instead of focusing on how everyday life experiences and practices tend inevitably toward the 'reproduction of poverty' across lives and generations, the literature on resilience aims to identify the conditions under which people are able to exercise agency in ways that lead to sustainable improvements in their lives (see Dagdeviren and Donoghue (2018) for a recent review).

While welcoming how questions about resilience foreground poor people's *agency*, many scholars have criticized the literature for treating resilience as an attribute of individuals (Estêvão et al. 2017) and for failing to take sufficient account of the structural and 'path-dependent' processes that limit people's capabilities (Dagdeviren et al. 2016). Other critics have argued that the language of resilience shifts responsibility for poverty and crisis away from those in power and underestimates the costs associated with 'bouncing back' (Andres and Round 2015; Harrison 2013). Recent sociological research, therefore, treats resilience as an attribute of the collective social context that 'conditions the possibility of action and available resources, which is also affected by the social position of the subjects and groups' (Revilla et al. 2018: 105). Hall and Lamont (2013: 2–3) characterize 'social resilience' as the capacities for societies – rather than individuals – to cope with many kinds of challenges, and they suggest that the sources of social resilience may be found in 'the institutional and cultural resources that groups and individuals mobilize to sustain their well-being'. Promberger (2017: 29–30) summarized those resources under three headings: *common goods*, ranging from natural resources to collective goods provided by voluntary organizations, to welfare state provisions; *cultural resources*, including knowledge, skills and alternative values; *social networks* of exchange and support.

Many qualitative case studies have demonstrated the importance of support networks or family ties to help resolve financial issues when government assistance is insufficient (see e.g. Gabriel Silva et al. 2014). Kinship and community relationships can encourage positive adjustments (Theron and Theron 2013). According to Revilla et al. (2018: 104), '[t]he level of integration in a community and the diversity of relations mark an important difference in the capacity for resilience'. These findings are consistent with an earlier literature on social capital, which, however, found that while local social networks were indispensable for coping with poverty, they could also play a part in entrenching social inequality (MacDonald et al. 2005). Similar to Sampson et al'.s (1999) argument that collective efficacy – a set of shared beliefs in conjoint capability for action – is necessary to convert social ties into desired outcomes, scholars suggest that social resilience requires alternative 'collective imaginaries' that provide the cultural tools with which people make sense of the challenges they face and imagine solutions to them (Hall and Lamont 2013: 18).

In the absence of longitudinal research designs, it may be difficult to trace the relationships between practices of coping with poverty and social outcomes. Indeed, in their analysis of the 'resilience practices' documented within a recent nine-country European study, Dagdeviren and Donoghue (2018) concluded that almost none of the practices observed were *transformative* (actions that move people to a new level where they are better off and less vulnerable on a long-term basis); the great majority were *absorptive* (short-term actions taken in response to a shock with negative and potentially harmful consequences) or *adaptive* (actions that 'lock people in' to certain practices in the medium to long term). They attributed this pattern to 'the prominence of structural constraints such as labour market conditions and initial conditions of families (e.g. their assets and resources), limiting the participants' "degrees of freedom" or "autonomy" and hence the nature of their agency' (Dagdeviren and Donoghue 2018: 16). In general, then, this research tends to confirm Seccombe's (2002) earlier conclusion that money is what families principally need to beat the odds – or, more broadly, the social, economic and institutional environments that enable them to secure and keep a greater quantity of material resources.

Understanding the extent and circumstances under which actions have the potential to be transformative for individual lives may require a life course perspective. Elder (1998: 9) noted that the central theme of his classic study, *Children of the Great Depression*, 'is not the harsh legacy of a deprived family through enduring limitations . . . Rather, it is the story of how so many women and men successfully overcame disadvantage in their lives'. There has been growing interest in, and (availability of) qualitative longitudinal research data that extends findings from quantitative longitudinal analyses by focusing on 'the active ways in which people are (or are not) able to respond to their situations and in particular their responses to risk events, and the resources that they are able to call upon to deal with these' (Millar 2007: 534). In a recent analysis, based on a fifteen-year qualitative longitudinal study of lone parents and their families, Millar and Ridge (2018) noted how their lack of material resources and of wider family support networks left 'no margin for error' to parents and young adults as they tried to improve their lives. Using a retrospective, biographical approach, Bayón (2017) documented how disadvantage accumulated across the lives of poor people in Mexico City. Her participants' lives were characterized by: 'Frustrations, truncated projects, and a limited structure of opportunities that persistently weaken the efforts and possibilities to escape poverty' and 'those who manage to twist (at least temporarily) their "destinies" of precarity, do not do it thanks to (or because of) [public] institutions, but, precisely in spite of them' (Bayón 2017: 114). Identifying the contexts within which transformative resilience occurs will require a focus on those 'turning points' within biographies that allow people not only to take actions to cope with adversity, but also to imagine – and believe in the possibility of – alternative futures (Gray and Dagg 2018).

In addition to insights from biographical and life course perspectives, recent ethnographic research has raised new questions about how cultural mechanisms might link the experience of growing up in poor areas to individual outcomes. In a review and analysis of the literature, Harding and Hepburn (2014) surveyed the wide variety of ways in which studies informed by the new 'sociology of culture' have explained 'neighbourhood effects'. These include:

- *Cultural heterogeneity*. People living in poor neighbourhoods acquire a mix of 'mainstream' and 'oppositional' cultural 'repertoires' that make it more challenging to plan and implement effective life strategies. (On the other hand, cultural heterogeneity might provide scope for creativity in improving one's circumstances by 'looking beyond the culture of everyday life' (Kumar 2010: 354).)
- *Weak collective efficacy*. Subjective beliefs about their neighbours and the cultural frames through which people living in poor neighbourhoods understand and respond to local and external institutions – such as police and the legal system – affect their capacity for social organization and impact on individual behaviour.
- *Cultural capital and imagined futures*. Neighbourhood contexts may restrict poor people's access to mainstream forms of cultural capital that 'signal' high status and affect how people construct narratives of identity and hopeful expectations about the future.

Despite recent developments, the authors conclude that social science understanding of cultural mechanisms in neighbourhood effects remains limited and that significant conceptual and methodological work remains to be done.

Qualitative research on poverty and social policy

As we have seen throughout this chapter, much of the qualitative research on life for people in poverty has documented the extent to which encounters with institutional and state actors are characterized by processes of stigmatization and shame. Across the world, according to Narayan (2017: 19):

> Institutions mediate [poor people's] access to resources and opportunities. But the individuals with whom they must interact in the private sector, state, and, to a much lesser extent, civil society are often exclusionary, rude and uncaring, as well as corrupt and exploitative.

In the context of an emerging 'social investment' paradigm (Kersbergen and Hemerijck 2012), social security systems within advanced welfare regimes have become increasingly 'targeted', thereby increasing the potential for stigmatization by weakening the 'feedback loop between personal experience and social values' (Hudson et al. 2016: 220), by exacerbating feelings of inferiority and shame among those who are unable to meet increased expectations for 'self-reliance' (Simons et al. 2018) and by 'pathologizing' poverty (Hansen et al. 2014).

In these contexts, Hudson et al. (2016) argue, qualitative research has an important role to play in promoting social solidarity by documenting the lived experience of 'welfare' and by showing how different institutional designs affect processes of stigmatization and othering. For example, Halpern-Meekin et al. (2016: 53) argued that, in the United States, the system of 'Earned Income Tax Credit' provides effective support for low-income families without 'the humiliation and shame so many describe experiencing when receiving other means-tested cash and in-kind benefits'. As Hudson et al. (2016) note, there remain considerable differences across states in public attitudes toward, and experiences of, social welfare. Nevertheless, Underlid (2005) demonstrated that, even in advanced welfare systems, people living in poverty are cognizant of failure to live up to prevailing cultural ideals and values, and experience social devaluation.

This chapter has documented a resurgence of interest in qualitative understandings of the everyday lives of people in poverty, especially in the context of new approaches to understanding culture within social science. Important questions remain, however, about the usefulness of such approaches for research and practice in social policy. In a recent article, McIntosh and Wright (2018: 1) suggested that social policy scholarship 'may be on the cusp of a large-scale adoption of the notion of *lived experience* . . . unaccompanied by discussion of what [the term] may mean or imply', especially in the context of the growth of qualitative longitudinal research. Tracing the evolution of the term through phenomenology, feminist scholarship and ethnography, they suggest that the value of the idea of lived experience may inhere in its potential to: give voice, 'making the invisible visible as a response to subordination'; to open a window onto the 'shared typical' or 'constellation of motives' at work in the practices of people living in poverty, as well as in those of policy makers, managers and frontline workers; as a basis for critique from multiple standpoints.

Focusing on the usefulness of *cultural analysis* for policy, Lamont and Small (2010: 170) suggested that policy makers should take account of the 'worldviews of the poor', not in terms of 'what they are not', but in order to understand 'how the living conditions of the poor limit the range of choices available to them, as well as which of the available paths would be most productive for them to take, given their situation'. Cultural diversity, they argued, should be supported as a basis for collective empowerment, understanding stigma, maximizing capabilities and increasing moral concern about poverty.

Finally, focusing on qualitative *methodology*, Edin and Pirog (2014) suggested its value for policy research on three grounds: through its inductive approach, generating new hypotheses to inform new questions and interventions; getting 'underneath' quantitative findings to identify (or challenge assumptions about) potential underlying processes and mechanisms; understanding the meanings behind practices and behaviours. It should be noted, however, that the 'cultural turn' has also led to some vigorous debate about the value and rigour of qualitative methodology. For example, scholars have argued that much qualitative research fallaciously assumes a connection between people's articulation of cultural meanings and their behaviour (on qualitative interviewing see the debates between Vaisey 2009 and Pugh 2013; on ethnography see Jerolmack and Khan 2014 and Cerulo 2014) and is flawed by being wrapped in 'a thick coat of moralism' (Wacquant 2002: 1469; for a rebuttal see Duneier 2002).

Conclusion

This chapter has situated recent scholarship on life for people in poverty within theoretical developments in the sociology of culture, the emergence of a longitudinal sensibility in qualitative research and the current popularity of questions about resilience, especially in the context of increased experiences of hardship and deprivation associated with the 'Great Recession' and associated policies of austerity in some countries.

Much of this research has uncovered patterns of lived experience that might look very familiar to an older body of scholarship on poverty and everyday life: the relentlessness of the work involved in getting by; the importance of networks of social support and a shared community identity; the impact of stigma and feelings of shame, leading often to attempts to establish a positive sense of self-identity by othering 'less worthy' groups. However, the recent literature claims to invoke a more dynamic, less fixed understanding of cultural processes and poverty, one that prioritizes understanding agency, creativity and the transformative potential of poor people's practices given the right institutional and societal contexts.

Critics of this new scholarship argue that in practice much of this research fails to move beyond documenting the 'lifeworld' or 'lived experiences' of poverty. Nevertheless, there remains considerable potential for longitudinal, mixed-method research designs to identify the mechanisms linking cultural experiences and practices to different outcomes at the level of both communities and individuals. And, perhaps equally importantly, this research may play a part in the construction of the 'alternative collective imaginaries' necessary to create the potential for change (Hall and Lamont 2013).

References

Andres, L., and J. Round. 2015. 'The Role of "Persistent Resilience" within Everyday Life and Polity: Households Coping with Marginality within the "Big Society"'. *Environment and Planning A: Economy and Space* 47 (3): 676–690. https://doi.org/10.1068/a46299.

Back, Les. 2015. 'Why Everyday Life Matters: Class, Community and Making Life Livable'. *Sociology* 49 (5): 820–836. https://doi.org/10.1177/0038038515589292.

Bayón, María Cristina. 2017. 'Accumulating Disadvantages, Multiplying Inequalities: Biographies of Poverty in Mexico City'. *Journal of Poverty* 21 (2): 97–119. https://doi.org/10.1080/10875549.2016.1141385.

Branch, Enobong Hannah, and Mary Larue Scherer. 2013. 'Mapping the Intersections in the Resurgence of the Culture of Poverty'. *Race, Gender & Class* 20 (3/4): 346–358.

Canvin, Krysia, Anneli Marttila, Bo Burstrom, and Margaret Whitehead. 2009. 'Tales of the Unexpected? Hidden Resilience in Poor Households in Britain'. *Social Science & Medicine* 69 (July): 238–245. https://doi.org/10.1016/j.socscimed.2009.05.009.

Caplan, Mary A., Gregory Purser, and Peter A. Kindle. 2017. 'Personal Accounts of Poverty: A Thematic Analysis of Social Media'. *Journal of Evidence-Informed Social Work* 14 (6): 433–456. https://doi.org/10.1080/23761407.2017.1380547.

Cerulo, Karen A. 2014. 'Reassessing the Problem: Response to Jerolmack and Khan'. *Sociological Methods & Research* 43 (2): 219–226.

Chase, Elaine, and Robert Walker. 2013. 'The Co-Construction of Shame in the Context of Poverty: Beyond a Threat to the Social Bond'. *Sociology* 47 (4): 739–754.

Crow, Graham, and Graham Allan. 2013 [1994]. 'The Way Things Were: Community Life in Past Generations'. In *Community Life: An Introduction to Local Social Relations*. London: Routledge, pp. 24–44.

Dagdeviren, Hulya, and Matthew Donoghue. 2018. 'Resilience, Agency and Coping with Hardship: Evidence from Europe during the Great Recession'. *Journal of Social Policy*, 1–21. https://doi.org/10.1017/S0047279418000624.

Dagdeviren, Hulya, Matthew Donoghue, and Lars Meier. 2017. 'The Narratives of Hardship: The New and the Old Poor in the Aftermath of the 2008 Crisis in Europe'. *The Sociological Review* 65 (2): 369–385. https://doi.org/10.1111/1467-954X.12403.

Dagdeviren, Hulya, Matthew Donoghue, and Markus Promberger. 2016. 'Resilience, Hardship and Social Conditions'. *Journal of Social Policy* 45 (1): 1.

Daly, Mary, and Grace Kelly. 2015. *Families and Poverty: Everyday Life on a Low Income*. Bristol: Policy Press.

Duneier, Mitchell. 2002. 'What Kind of Combat Sport is Sociology?' *American Journal of Sociology* 107 (6): 1551–1576.

Edin, Kathryn, and Maureen A. Pirog. 2014. 'Special Symposium on Qualitative and Mixed-Methods for Policy Analysis'. *Journal of Policy Analysis and Management* 33 (2): 345–349. https://doi.org/10.1002/pam.21756

Elder, Glen H. 1998. 'The Life Course as Developmental Theory'. *Child Development* 69 (1): 1–12.

Emmel, Nick, and Kahryn Hughes. 2010. 'Recession, it's all the same to us son': the longitudinal experience (1999–2010) of deprivation'. *Twenty-First Century Society*, 5 (2): 171–181. DOI: 10.1080/17450141003783413

Estêvão, Pedro, Alexandre Calado, and Luís Capucha. 2017. 'Resilience: Moving from a "Heroic" Notion to a Sociological Concept'. *Sociologia, Problemas e Práticas*, no. 85 (September): 9–25. https://doi.org/10.7458/SPP20178510115.

Gabriel Silva, Pedro, Hermínia Gonçalves, and Octávio Sacramento. 2014. 'Economic Crises and Resilience Strategies of Women: A Case Study from the Portuguese Northern Inland'. *Procedia – Social and Behavioral Sciences*, 161: 24–28. ISSN 1877-0428, https://doi.org/10.1016/j.sbspro.2014.12.005.

Garthwaite, Kayleigh. 2016. 'Stigma, Shame and 'People Like Us': An Ethnographic Study of Foodbank Use in the UK'. *Journal of Poverty and Social Justice* 24 (3): 277–289.

Goffman, Erving. 2009. *Stigma: Notes on the Management of Spoiled Identity*. New York: Simon and Schuster.

Gray, Jane, and Jennifer Dagg. 2018. 'Using Reflexive Lifelines in Biographical Interviews to Aid the Collection, Visualisation and Analysis of Resilience'. *Contemporary Social Science*. Published online before print. doi: 10.1080/21582041.2018.1459818

Hall, Peter A., and Michèle Lamont. 2013. *Social Resilience in the Neoliberal Era*. Cambridge: Cambridge University Press.

Halpern-Meekin, Sarah, Laura Tach, Jennifer Sykes, and Kathryn Edin. 2016. 'A Hand Up for Low-Income Families'. *Contexts* 15 (2): 52–57. https://doi.org/10.1177/1536504216648155.

Hamilton, Kathy. 2012. 'Low-Income Families and Coping through Brands: Inclusion or Stigma?' *Sociology* 46 (1): 74–90. https://doi.org/10.1177/0038038511416146.

Hansen, Helena, Philippe Bourgois, and Ernest Drucker. 2014. 'Pathologizing Poverty: New Forms of Diagnosis, Disability, and Structural Stigma under Welfare Reform'. *Social Science & Medicine*, Structural Stigma and Population Health, 103 (February): 76–83. https://doi.org/10.1016/j.socscimed.2013.06.033.

Harding, David J., and Peter Hepburn. 2014. 'Cultural Mechanisms in Neighborhood Effects Research in the United States'. *Sociologica Urbana e Rurale* 103: 37–73. doi: 10.3280/SUR2014-103004

Harrison, Elizabeth. 2013. 'Bouncing Back? Recession, Resilience and Everyday Lives'. *Critical Social Policy* 33 (1): 97–113. https://doi.org/10.1177/0261018312439365.

Hudson, John, Ruth Patrick, and Emma Wincup. 2016. 'Introduction to Themed Special Issue: Exploring "Welfare" Attitudes and Experiences'. *Journal of Poverty and Social Justice* 24 (3): 215–226. https://doi.org/10.1332/175982716X14721954315048.

Jerolmack, Colin, and Shamus Khan. 2014. 'Talk Is Cheap: Ethnography and the Attitudinal Fallacy'. *Sociological Methods & Research* 43 (2): 178–209.

Kersbergen, Kees Van, and Anton Hemerijck. 2012. 'Two Decades of Change in Europe: The Emergence of the Social Investment State'. *Journal of Social Policy* 41 (3): 475–492. https://doi.org/10.1017/S0047279412000050.

Kumar, Mukul. 2010. 'Poverty and Culture of Daily Life'. *Psychology and Developing Societies* 22 (2): 331–359. https://doi.org/10.1177/097133361002200205.

Lamont, Michèle. 2009. 'Responses to Racism, Health, and Social Inclusion as a Dimension of Successful Societies'. In *Successful Societies: How Institutions and Culture Affect Health*, edited by Peter A. Hall and Michèle Lamont. Cambridge, UK and New York: Cambridge University Press, pp. 151–168.

Lamont, Michèle, and Mario Luis Small. 2010. 'Cultural Diversity and Anti-Poverty Policy'. *International Social Science Journal* 61 (199): 169–180. https://doi.org/10.1111/j.1468-2451.2010.01754.x.

Lempidaki, Maria, and Evaggelia Kalerante. 2015. 'Days of the Memorandum: Understanding Experiences of New Poverty in Greece Using Interpretative Phenomenological Analysis'. *International Review of Social Sciences and Humanities* 9 (1): 164–177.

Lister, Ruth. 2016. '"To Count for Nothing": Poverty beyond the Statistics'. In *British Academy Lectures 2014–15*, edited by Janet Carsten and Simon Frith, 139–166. British Academy. https://doi.org/10.5871/bacad/9780197265987.003.0005.

MacDonald, Robert, Tracy Shildrick, Colin Webster, and Donald Simpson. 2005. 'Growing Up in Poor Neighbourhoods: The Significance of Class and Place in the Extended Transitions of "Socially Excluded" Young Adults'. *Sociology* 39 (5): 873–891. https://doi.org/10.1177/0038038505058370.

McIntosh, Ian, and Sharon Wright. 2018. 'Exploring What the Notion of "Lived Experience" Offers for Social Policy Analysis'. *Journal of Social Policy* 1–19. https://doi.org/10.1017/S0047279418000570.

McKenzie, Lisa. 2012. 'A Narrative from the Inside, Studying St Anns in Nottingham: Belonging, Continuity and Change'. *The Sociological Review* 60 (3): 457–475. https://doi.org/10.1111/j.1467-954X.2012.02094.x.

Milbourne, Paul. 2014. 'Poverty, Place, and Rurality: Material and Sociocultural Disconnections'. *Environment and Planning A: Economy and Space* 46 (3): 566–580. https://doi.org/10.1068/a45336.

Millar, Jane. 2007. 'The Dynamics of Poverty and Employment: The Contribution of Qualitative Longitudinal Research to Understanding Transitions, Adaptations and Trajectories'. *Social Policy and Society* 6 (4): 533–544.

Millar, Jane, and Tess Ridge. 2018. 'No Margin for Error: Fifteen Years in the Working Lives of Lone Mothers and Their Children'. *Journal of Social Policy*, 1–17. https://doi.org/10.1017/S0047279418000752.

Morrow, Virginia, and Gina Crivello. 2015. 'What Is the Value of Qualitative Longitudinal Research with Children and Young People for International Development?' *International Journal of Social Research Methodology* 18 (3): 267–280. https://doi.org/10.1080/13645579.2015.1017903

Narayan, Deepa. 2017. 'Poverty Is Powerlessness and Voicelessness'. *Development Ethics*. 15 May 2017. https://doi.org/10.4324/9781315258003-9.

Narayan, Deepa, Robert Chambers, Meera K. Shah, and Patti Petesch. 2000. *Voices of the Poor: Crying out for Change*. New York: Oxford University Press for the World Bank.

O'Brien, Mark, and Paul Kyprianou. 2017. *Just Managing? What it Means for the Families of Austerity Britain*. Open Book Publishers. https://doi.org/10.11647/OBP.0112.

Patrick, Ruth. 2014. 'Working on Welfare: Findings from a Qualitative Longitudinal Study into the Lived Experiences of Welfare Reform in the UK'. *Journal of Social Policy* 43 (4): 705–725. https://doi.org/10.1017/S0047279414000294.

Patrick, Ruth. 2016. 'Living with and Responding to the "Scrounger" Narrative in the UK: Exploring Everyday Strategies of Acceptance, Resistance and Deflection'. *The Journal of Poverty and Social Justice* 24 (3): 245–259. http://dx.doi.org/10.1332/175982716X14721954314887.

Pemberton, Simon, Eldin Fahmy, Eileen Sutton, and Karen Bell. 2017. 'Endless Pressure: Life on a Low Income in Austere Times'. *Social Policy & Administration* 51 (7): 1156–1173. https://doi.org/10.1111/spol.12233.

Promberger, Markus. 2017. 'Resilience among Vulnerable Households in Europe: Questions, Concept, Findings and Implications'. IAB-Discussion Paper 12/2017, Nürnberg. Available at: www.iab.de/966/section.aspx/Publikation/k170412301 (accessed 12 July 2019).

Pugh, Allison J. 2013. 'What Good Are Interviews for Thinking about Culture? Demystifying Interpretive Analysis'. *American Journal of Cultural Sociology* 1 (1): 42–68.

Purdam, Kingsley, Elisabeth A. Garratt, and Aneez Esmail. 2016. 'Hungry? Food Insecurity, Social Stigma and Embarrassment in the UK'. *Sociology* 50 (6): 1072–1088. https://doi.org/10.1177/0038038515594092.

Ray, Ranita, and Korey Tillman. 2019. 'Envisioning a Feminist Urban Ethnography: Structure, Culture, and New Directions in Poverty Studies'. *Sociology Compass* 13 (1): e12652. https://doi.org/10.1111/soc4.12652.

Reutter, Linda I., Miriam J. Stewart, Gerry Veenstra, Rhonda Love, Dennis Raphael, and Edward Makwarimba. 2009. '"Who Do They Think We Are, Anyway?": Perceptions of and Responses to Poverty Stigma'. *Qualitative Health Research* 19 (3): 297–311.

Revilla, Juan Carlos, Paz Martín, and Carlos de Castro. 2018. 'The Reconstruction of Resilience as a Social and Collective Phenomenon: Poverty and Coping Capacity during the Economic Crisis'. *European Societies* 20 (1): 89–110. https://doi.org/10.1080/14616696.2017.1346195.

Rodríguez-Muñiz, Michael. 2015. 'Intellectual Inheritances: Cultural Diagnostics and the State of Poverty Knowledge'. *American Journal of Cultural Sociology* 3 (1): 89–122. https://doi.org/10.1057/ajcs.2014.16.

Sampson, Robert J., Jeffrey D. Morenoff, and Felton Earls. 1999. 'Beyond Social Capital: Spatial Dynamics of Collective Efficacy for Children'. *American Sociological Review* 64 (5): 633–660. https://doi.org/10.2307/2657367.

Scheff, Thomas J. 2003. 'Shame in Self and Society'. *Symbolic Interaction* 26 (2): 239–262. https://doi.org/10.1525/si.2003.26.2.239

Seccombe, Karen. 2002. '"Beating the Odds" Versus "Changing the Odds": Poverty, Resilience, and Family Policy'. *Journal of Marriage and Family* 64 (2): 384–394. https://onlinelibrary.wiley.com/doi/abs/10.1111/j.1741-3737.2002.00384.x.

Shaffer, Paul. 2013. 'Ten Years of "Q-Squared": Implications for Understanding and Explaining Poverty'. *World Development* 45 (May): 269–285. https://doi.org/10.1016/j.worlddev.2012.12.008.

Sherman, Jennifer. 2013. 'Surviving the Great Recession: Growing Need and the Stigmatized Safety Net'. *Social Problems* 60 (4): 409–432. https://doi.org/10.1525/sp.2013.60.4.409.

Shildrick, Tracy, and Robert MacDonald. 2013. 'Poverty Talk: How People Experiencing Poverty Deny Their Poverty and Why They Blame "the Poor"'. *The Sociological Review* 61 (2): 285–303. https://doi.org/10.1111/1467-954X.12018.

Simons, Audrey M. W., Inge Houkes, Annemarie Koster, Daniëlle A. I. Groffen, and Hans Bosma. 2018. 'The Silent Burden of Stigmatisation: A Qualitative Study among Dutch People with a Low Socioeconomic Position'. *BMC Public Health* 18 (1): 443. https://doi.org/10.1186/s12889-018-5210-6.

Small, Mario Luis, David J. Harding, and Michèle Lamont. 2010. 'Reconsidering Culture and Poverty'. *The ANNALS of the American Academy of Political and Social Science* 629 (1): 6–27.

Small, Mario Luis and Katherine Newman. 2001. 'Urban Poverty after the Truly Disadvantaged: The Rediscovery of the Family, the Neighborhood and Culture'. *Annual Review of Sociology* 27 (1): 23–45. https://doi.org/10.1177/0002716210362077.

Sutton, Eileen, Simon Pemberton, Eldin Fahmy, and Yuko Tamiya. 2014. 'Stigma, Shame and the Experience of Poverty in Japan and the United Kingdom'. *Social Policy and Society* 13 (1): 143–154.

Swidler, Ann. 1986. 'Culture in Action: Symbols and Strategies'. *American Sociological Review* 51 (2): 273–286. https://doi.org/10.2307/2095521.

Theron, L. C., and A. Theron. 2013. 'Positive Adjustment to Poverty: How Family Communities Encourage Resilience in Traditional African Contexts. *Culture & Psychology* 19(3): 391–413. https://doi.org/10.1177/1354067X13489318.

Underlid, Kjell. 2005. 'Poverty and Experiences of Social Devaluation: A Qualitative Interview Study of 25 Long-Standing Recipients of Social Security Payments'. *Scandinavian Journal of Psychology* 46 (3): 273–283. https://doi.org/10.1111/j.1467-9450.2005.00457.x.

Vaisey, Stephen. 2009. 'Motivation and Justification: A Dual-process Model of Culture in Action'. *American Journal of Sociology* 114 (6): 1675–1715.

Wacquant, Loic. 2002. 'Scrutinizing the Street: Poverty, Morality, and the Pitfalls of Urban Ethnography'. *American Journal of Sociology* 107 (6): 1468–1532.

Walker, Robert, and Grace Bantebya-Kyomuhendo. 2014. *The Shame of Poverty*. Oxford: Oxford University Press.

Walker, Robert, Grace Bantebya Kyomuhendo, Elaine Chase, Sohail Choudhry, Erika K. Gubrium, Jo Yongmie Nicola, et al. 2013. 'Poverty in Global Perspective: Is Shame a Common Denominator?' *Journal of Social Policy* 42 (2): 215–233.

Wilson, W. J. 1987. *The Truly Disadvantaged: The Inner City, the Underclass, and Public Policy*. Chicago: University of Chicago Press.

23
Poverty and crime

David Denney

Introduction

> I think we deal with the symptoms and the outcomes, but society at large has got to think about how we solve some of the other issues about what has been causing the crime in the first place. I don't think children are born bad. I don't believe that for one moment.
>
> *(Assistant Commissioner Pat Galan Metropolitan Police,* The Guardian, *June 2018)*

> Narrowing the income and wealth gap to restore some degree of status and respect to vital but ill-rewarded workers is a precondition for lasting front-line crime reduction. All of which helps to explain why, despite a decade of falling crime, the fear of crime remains so high.
>
> *(Downes, 2004: 5)*

Both the above quotations, one from a senior British police officer and another from a criminologist, reflect the importance and contemporary significance of the relationship between crime and poverty. Reiman and Leighton's *The Rich Get Richer and the Poor Get Prison*, now in its eleventh edition asks why prisons appear to be occupied by poorer people. The US criminal justice system is seen from this perspective as failing to protect vulnerable people from the scheming of the rich who create widespread societal harm through the machinations and consequences of global capitalism (Reiman and Leighton, 2016).

A cursory examination of the social characteristics of the adult prison population would appear to reinforce the position taken by Reiman and Leighton, revealing clear linkages between complex manifestations of various forms of social deprivation and the committing of crime. In the UK, for instance, some 31% of the female and 24% of the male prison population were taken into care as children, compared with 2% in the general population. A disproportionate number of adult prisoners (47%) have no formal qualifications, compared with 15% of the working-age population outside prison. Although 3.9% of the general population has never had a job, this rises to 13% among adult prisoners. Periods of unemployment immediately preceding imprisonment are stark at 68% (81% for women, 67% for men), whereas in the general population 7.7% of the economically active population are unemployed. Some 15% of the prison population is homeless on the point of entering custody which is considerably higher than the 4% who have at some point been homeless or in temporary accommodation (Bromley Briefings, 2017). A similar picture emerges in the US where there is evidence that ex-prisoners fare badly in the labour market both pre- and post-incarceration and that the barriers to education and employment occur early in life. Prisoners live in low-income families and reside in areas of extreme material hardship (Looney and Turner, 2018).

The Nordic countries have been frequently cited as an exception to the general rule of increasing incarceration and punitiveness within criminal justice systems. More recently scholarship has focused on the ways in which prisons are integrated into the inclusive and well-established state welfare systems (Ugelvik, 2016). Thus, Nordic prisons are less a place of last resort but more a place where individuals can be restored to full societal membership. Significantly, Nordic prison inmates appear to have higher levels of educational attainment and potential future employability when compared with the situation described above. A relatively low proportion of Nordic prisoners, some 7–16%, have failed to finish compulsory schooling. These regimes offer more systematic educational programmes than in other jurisdictions taking a more long-term view of rehabilitation (Eikeland, Manger, and Asbjorusen 2009). In many respects the Nordic states are exceptional in that they have not developed punitive criminal justice policies. Pratt has linked Nordic 'exceptionalism' in criminal justice to unique geopolitical social and economic factors that are particular to the region. These states are not structured around rigid social class distinctions, while egalitarian traditions have led to a more humanitarian and ultimately effective approach to criminal justice (Pratt, 2008). Levels of crime in Norway, Denmark and Iceland are low when compared to other countries, while Sweden has moderately high crime rates (Numbeo, 2019).

While the existing literature points to some association between crime and poverty, a direct causal relationship is not easy to establish. In a report published by the Equality and Human Rights Commission (EHRC, 2015) it was argued that during the financial crisis between 2008 and 2013 there were increased levels of unemployment and significant declines in wages, with almost one-third of those between the ages of 16 and 24 living in poverty. The same group of young people were also more likely to be stopped and searched by the police and likely to be victims of sexual crime and violent crimes. However, there is no available data to indicate that this group is more likely to commit crime, which could run contrary to the idea that economic hardship is the cause of crime. On the contrary, there appears to have been a decline in convictions for those aged up to 20 during the same period. However, these data, according to some commentators, are insufficiently comprehensive, reliable and consistent to make any unequivocal judgements, leaving the relationship between unemployment and poverty open to a number of interpretations (Fergusson, 2015).

A further complicating factor when considering crime and its relationship to poverty is the social impact of new technologies. Social media has impacted on the reporting of crime providing a severe challenge to traditional media outlets over the last two decades (Trottier, 2012; van Dijk, 2013; Viner, 2016; Wajcman, 2015). Globalised crime is now becoming more digitalised and less terrestrial. This is particularly evident in offences related to drug and people trafficking, fraud, slavery, identity crime, kidnap, money laundering and theft (National Crime Agency, 2019).

Digital technologies have also created new forms of surveillance. Electronic surveillance methods can compound social exclusion by targeting groups who are categorised as undesirable by virtue of race, ethnicity, social class, geographical location or criminal record by subjecting selected individuals to more intense surveillance (Lupton, 2015). Such techniques can exclude individuals from some regions' particular spaces and particular public places. The use of increased electronic surveillance also operates unequally in society, affecting target groups and, in some respects, compounding social inequality (Henman and Marston, 2008; Goddard, 2012; Hannah-Moffatt, 2016; Ajana, 2013).

In mainstream media, crime is often reported in terms of a series of discrete events rather than paying any attention to correlations between crime and structural deprivation (Reiner, 2007). The causes of poverty and consequences are rarely explored, while detailed prurient descriptions of 'evil' are frequently presented (McKendrick et al., 2008.). Crime is thus often conceptualised as resulting from the negligent actions of a victim and an opportunistic attacker, constituting a cautionary tale (Moore, 2010). News stories relating to crime now have more diverse, including online, sources. This rapidly changing series of transformative complexities forms a backdrop to understanding the relationship between crime and poverty.

Core concepts

There is a lack of clarity as to the meaning of poverty and how it can be identified and addressed (Saunders, 2019) Poverty exists '[w]hen people do not have the resources to obtain the items necessary to meet their basic needs' Saunders, 2019).

In absolute terms 736 million people globally live on less than one dollar a day (World Bank, 2018), see also Chapters 2–4.

In relative terms, poverty

> Is where some people's way of life and income is so much worse than the general standard of living in the country or region in why they live that they struggle to live a normal life and participate in ordinary economic social and cultural activities.
>
> *(European Anti-Poverty Network, 2014: 13 quoted in Saunders, 2019)*

The differential impact of the digital age, as suggested above, has created new layers of inequality. The rapid digitalisation of the global south has opened up new vulnerabilities within this region and beyond. The pace at which these technologies have developed, although having benefits in terms of information availability and communications, has developed at a rate which has outpaced the abilities of state institutions and legal regulations to manage enormous data flows and the criminal consequences that arise from big data (Schia, 2018). Rapid rises in identity fraud are partly attributable to the misuse of information obtained about a victim online. Unlawful sales of assets, applications for a product using false information, false insurance claims and the abuse of personal data are some of the ways in which fraud facilitated by online criminals can often differentially impact on the most vulnerable in society (The Fraudscape, 2018). Big data, and more specifically algorithms, can reinforce and extend already established inequalities, reinforcing existing forms of discrimination. The authority of the algorithm is often based upon the fallibilities and biases in software applications (O'Neil, 2016).

Research and speculation about crime causation will often involve description, classification, causal theory and suggested solutions to crime which do not include poverty (Cohen, 1988). Crime itself has a number of dimensions and can be seen as a criminal law violation, as a violation of moral codes, and as social construct, as a form of ideological censure, as an historical invention or a social harm (Muncie, 2001). Explanations of the relationship between crime and poverty have, to some extent, become bifurcated across right and left political spectrums. However, it will be argued that other analyses of crime move beyond rigid ideological orthodoxies.

Individualised neo liberalism and crime

There are a number of variants of this position which locates the responsibility for crime with the individual perpetrator. Some proponents of rational choice theory have argued that crime is committed on the basis of expected utility and expected gain (Becker, 1968). Other variants of rational choice theory suggest that this is a bounded form of rationality since individuals who commit crime are often not in full possession of the facts and consequences of crime. Thus, there is an immediacy and spontaneity about the commissioning of crime based on the possible benefits rather than the potential risks involved. Explanations of individual criminal behaviour is often embedded in the individual characteristics of the offender. These attributes are differentially ascribed but include measurable intelligence, lack of self-control and poor parenting. Individuals make a rational choice to commit crime based upon the possibility of a positive and profitable outcome. In order to avoid criminal activity in later life self-control needs to be inculcated at an early age by parents who are able to recognise the need for self-control (Gottfredson and Hirschi, 1990).

Nilsson (2003) found in a population of 346 Swedish offenders that an accumulation of different types of resource problems were correlated with recidivism. In particular, offenders sentenced to prison had a reduced opportunity to lead a conventional life with a legitimate income once released. The correlation with unemployment suggests that lack of money is important, but where it is independently predictive, this may be due to poor financial management, which could be linked to poor coping skills generally. Many people on low incomes do not offend and therefore factors such as peer pressure, lifestyle and social-status needs, and poor financial coping skills may help to explain the link between poverty, social disadvantage and offending.

The theme of faulty parenting and poor socialisation is also present in another variant on this form of thought. Charles Murray, who has perhaps been one of the most outspoken and controversial figures in this debate, evokes distinctions between the deserving and undeserving poor. The deserving simply live on low incomes and make do, while a handful of poor people are defined by their own behaviour as undeserving (Murray, 1990). Criminality is intimately connected to an underclass living off but not participating or contributing to society, who have a destructive impact on local communities, creating social fragmentation and fear. Crime does not result from social deprivation and material poverty but from a form of moral poverty characterised by lax family discipline, permissiveness and the dissolution of traditional values. Empirical social research into the causes of crime is regarded as an interesting intellectual activity but ultimately a luxury. For Murray, attention needs to be directed toward practical solutions to crime which can impact on government in more direct and feasible ways in order to reduce the victimisation created by criminal behaviour. The only possible and inevitable endpoint for members of the undeserving underclass who continually indulge themselves in crime is incarceration in order to protect the functioning majority of the population (Wilson, 1975).

There is also a biologically determined element to this line of thinking which suggests that some individuals have a genetic predisposition to offending. Intelligence as measured through IQ scores can, from this perspective, be seen as a determinant of criminal behaviour. Those with a lower IQ score are more likely to be involved in crime for reasons that are not relatable to poverty or other structurally based social determinants. The research analysed US income and cognitive test scores on 12,686 individuals collected from the 1979 National Longitudinal Survey of Youth throughout the 1980s. Herrnstein and Murray (1994) concluded that those with lower IQs were more likely to be involved in criminal activity. This marked an emphasis toward a correlation between lower intelligence and crime.

Emphasis on individual responsibility and public protection has led to technologically determined risk assessment tools permeating criminal justice systems internationally. Such systems can reinforce existing social divisions by focusing on blame, fault and individual weakness underplaying the possible impact of social inequalities and deprivation on offending. When the logic of risk is unravelled in relation to criminal justice, social inequality is not high on the list of policy priorities. However, there is now widespread and international evidence to suggest that risk assessment fails to predict the future likelihood of crime with any accuracy, although risk assessment tools are increasingly used within criminal justice systems. Risk assessments should be more accurately matched to different social contexts of application. More attention needs to be given to protection against problematic forms of discrimination and stigmatisation within risk assessment processes (Denney, 2006, 2019; Douglas et al., 2017).

At the other end of the ideological spectrum, links between Marxist theory became part of criminological discourses in the 1960s and 70s. Based upon a study of European crime rates in the late nineteenth century Bonger reached the conclusion that capitalism was the exploitative system in which acts harming the interests of a dominant ruling class were selectively punished (Bonger, 1969). Crime was an entirely rational response to the inequalities and excesses of capitalist exploitation (Chambliss and Seidman, 1971; Taylor, Walton, and Young, 1975). People living in poverty, it is argued, are subjected to the harms of the rich through the workings of global capitalism (Reiman and Leighton, 2016). Individuals in more privileged socio-economic positions engage in a considerable amount of criminal activity which is distinct from crime committed by more socially deprived individuals (Sutherland, 1983). Moreover, it is often the case that the rich are strategically situated to commit crimes which are unpunished. Affluent white-collar criminals, however, will often plan their crimes and operate from the relative safety of an organisation. Offenders are often legitimately present at the scene of the crime and it takes place in private within an organisation (Croall, 2001).

The positions articulated above from the right and the left have been criticised by writers who claim that criminality is an integral part of the dynamic of global neoliberalism. Criminology should encompass new harms which are not always criminalised. Such harms include ecological catastrophe, the power of global capital and new securitisation processes which have the power to disrupt lives (Winlow and Hall, 2016).

Toward a middle way

Situated between the reductionism of Marxist theory and the social decontextualisation of the neoliberal theorists are those who emphasise social inequalities and deprivation in communities as contributing to criminal behaviour. In a landmark text which laid the foundations for 'left realism', Lea and Young aimed to show the reality of crime in socially deprived areas. Crime impacts negatively on individuals living in areas of social deprivation. Unlike the structural critique of the radical criminologists mentioned above, Lea and Young drew attention to the impact of crime on victims while paying attention to the causes of crime, many of which were rooted in various forms of social deprivation and poverty. Left realist thought emphasised the need for research into the causes of crime while also focusing on patterns of crime and the uniqueness of local communities. Unlike the right realists, Lea and Young advocated the minimal use of prison (Lea and Young, 1984).

In an extensive longitudinal study of pathways to offending involving 4,300 respondents published over three decades later, the influence of left realism is still felt. This study concluded that serious offending is associated with victimisation and social adversity. The early identification of at-risk children is not always effective while critical moments in the early teenage years are key to pathways out of offending. Diversionary strategies facilitate the desistence process and form the basis for youth justice policies that are more holistic in orientation (McAra and McVie, 2010).

Tough on crime and the causes of crime

Some policy approaches to crime appear to combine elements of individualism with an acknowledgement of the need to address social deprivation. When conceptualising the 'third way' politics, Anthony Giddens who greatly influenced Blair's New Labour polices in the UK, wrote of the construction of a new social contract: 'No rights without responsibilities. Those who profit from social goods should use them responsibly and give something back to the wider social community in return' (Giddens, 2000: 53).

What followed the elevation of New Labour to government in 1997 was what Garland called a 'responsibilities strategy' which has been reflected in criminal justice and other policies. Instead of using the apparatuses of the state to act upon crime directly, a new form of indirect control is exerted by the state on non-state actors and organisations to act responsibly against crime (Garland, 2001).

Blair claimed that the left in the 1980s had come to be associated with the belief that the causes of crime are entirely structural and had in the process eliminated individual responsibility. Crime was set apart from other social policies since there was an element of culpability, and to some extent blame, to be attributed to those who committed crime. From this position it was argued that an unemployed person dependent on benefits might find the '[r]elative rewards of illegitimate activity higher than someone earning legitimate wages' (Reiner, 2007: 357).

On this basis, Tony Blair promised to tackle both 'crime and the causes of crime' while also aiming to reduce poverty among families and children and pensioners. The policies designed to ameliorate and support families were bolstered by significant public spending on tax credits and benefits for families. Government-financed measures such as *Every Child Matters* and the 2003 Children Act aimed to create more coordinated services for children. Sure Start was launched in 1998 which aimed to provide children and families with emotional, educational and material support. These initiatives bore similarities to projects which had previously been launched in the US, Australia and Canada. By 2010 the National Evaluation of Sure Start indicated significant positive benefits for families in the UK (DFE, 2010). Although income equality changed little during these years, child and pensioner poverty fell significantly (Joyce and Sibieta, 2013).

Despite this lasting legacy to tackle deprivation, New Labour policies resulted in one of the biggest increases in the prison population since the Second World War. Between June 1993 and June 2012, the prison population in England and Wales increased by 41,800 prisoners to over 86,000 (Ministry of Justice, 2013). A significant part of this rise occurred during the Blair premiership between 1997 and 2007. England and Wales now have the highest prison population rate in western Europe at 141 per 100,000 of the population. This compares with 57 per 100,000 for Finland and Sweden (Clarke, 2013).

Situational crime and access to justice

More recently there has been increasing interest in the research which moves from ascribing individual characteristics of potential offenders as a cause of crime toward a situational conceptualisation of crime. The literature turns on a move from individual experiences of poverty toward social situations, attachments, networks and contexts in which crime occurs (Sharkey, Besbris, and Friedson, 2016). These writers also note that there is a bias in the literature toward 'street crime' which occurs in low-income communities.

In the US context, Philip Alston, United Nations Special Rapporteur on extreme poverty and human rights, following a visit to the US, reported on high levels of homelessness in many

US cities. Alston argues that American homeless people are effectively criminalised for sleeping rough, sitting in public places and public urination. The use of warrants, incarceration and fines and the stigma of a criminal conviction make future employment prospects problematic. In many US cities the criminal justice system acts to keep the poor in poverty, and raising revenue through fines and fees effectively keeps the poor in poverty (Alston, 2017).

Another practice that affects the poor disproportionately in the US is setting high bail bond conditions. Large bail bond conditions mean that wealthy defendants can secure their freedom while awaiting trial, while poor defendants are more likely to be held in custody. This has a disproportionate impact on poor people within the criminal justice system (Mayson, 2018). Recent changes to legal aid in the UK are an example of this and had a direct impact on the ability of some potential litigants to gain access to due process in law (Moore and Newbury, 2017).

Other recent policy developments have been driven by individualised privatised welfare, resulting in entitlements being framed within purely economic terms. It represents a marketised attempt to reduce the cost of criminal justice services which impact directly upon those in greatest need. In the case of probation, services designed to work constructively toward the rehabilitation of offenders have in certain respects diluted the service on offer by cost cutting and deprofessionalisation (Vanstone and Priestly, 2016).

Poverty, individualisation and the decontextualisation of poverty

This chapter has sought to demonstrate that poverty is one factor which is important when considering crime. The social characteristics of the prison population and the deprivation indicators identified at the outset of this chapter are not simply coincidental. However, the causes of crime are not entirely determined by poverty but stem from differentiated complex sources.

One of the major changes to be considered is the coming of a digital age which has created not only numerous benefits but also other new technologically determined risks which can have a disproportionate impact on socially deprived areas and particular regions of the world. The over-reliance on actuarial and inaccurate risk instruments has come to dominate many aspects of criminal justice processes, disproportionately affecting the poorest in society.

The nature of crime and policies related to crime have ebbed and flowed with the dominant political ideas of the day. With some notable Nordic exceptions tough policies on crime appear to have been normalised with an emphasis on public protection and not rehabilitation of the offender. While targeted welfare management policies can reduce some aspects of poverty, tough crime policies seem to dominate political agendas.

Over recent decades there has been a growth in the use of imprisonment as a response to crime disorder. One recent report found that over 10 million people are imprisoned worldwide, while in the United States the total prison population has increased from 500,000 in 1980 to its peak of over 2.3 million in 2008. Brazil has seen prisoner numbers increase twenty-fold from around 30,000 in 1973 to over 600,000 in 2017 (Jacobson, Heard, and Fair, 2017). At the time of writing, in the UK, some level of cross-party consensus around being 'tough on crime' appears to be questioned as the prison population spirals out of control. In the UK, ex home secretaries from both sides of the political spectrum have called for a reduction in the prison population (*The Guardian*, 2016). The decline of Keynesian 'welfare social management' has given way to the rise of neoliberalism which dominates the globalised political economy (Reiner, 2007). However, to demand justice for people living in poverty from a global society dominated by market competition is unrealistic.

References

Ajana, B. (2013) *Governing through Biometrics: The Biopolitics of Identity*, Basingstoke, Palgrave Macmillan.
Alston, P. (2017) *Report on Severe Poverty in the US. United Nations Human Rights Office of the High Commissioner.* www.ohchr.org/EN/NewsEvents/Pages/DisplayNews.aspx?NewsID=22533&LangID=E
Becker, G. (1968) Crime and punishment: an economic approach. *Journal of Political Economy* 76, 169–217.
Bonger, W. (1969) *Criminality and Economic Conditions*, Boston, Little Brown and Co.
Bromley Briefings (2017) *Prison Fact File*, London, Prison Reform Trust.
Chambliss, W. and Seidman, R. (1971) *Law, Order and Power*, Massachusetts: Addison-Wesley.
Clarke, S. (2013) Trends in crime and criminal justice 2010. *Eurostat* (18/2013) Luxembourg: European Commission.
Cohen, S. (1988) *Against Criminology*, New Brunswick, Transaction Books.
Croall, H. (2001) *Understanding White Collar Crime*, Buckingham, Open University Press.
Equality and Human Rights Commission (2015) *Is Britain Fairer?* www.equalityhumanrights.com/en/britain-fairer
Denney, D. (2006) *Risk and Society*, London, Sage.
Denney, D. (2019) Risk and the Management of Crime. In Greve, B. (ed.) *Routledge Handbook of the Welfare State* second edition, London and New York, Routledge, pp. 457–467.
Department for Education (2010) *The impact of Sure Start programmes on five year olds and their families*, Research Brief DFE-RB867. www.ness.bbk.ac.uk/impact/documents/RB067.pdf
Douglas, T., Pugh, J., Singh, I., Savulescu, J., and Fazel, S. (2017) Risk assessment tools in criminal justice and forensic psychiatry: the need for better data. *European Psychiatry* 42: 134–137.
Downes, D. (2004) New Labour and the lost causes of crime. *Criminal Justice Matters*, 55 (spring).
EHRC (Equality and Human Rights Commission) (2015) *Is Britain Fairer? The state of equality and human rights 2015*, London, Human Rights Commission.
Eikeland, O., Manger, T., and Asbjorusen, A. (2009) Education in Nordic prisons: prisoners' educational backgrounds, preferences and motivation. TemaNord 508. Nordic Council of Ministers. www.diva-portal.org/smash/get/diva2:702625/FULLTEXT01.pdf
European Anti-Poverty Network (2014) Poverty and Inequality in the EU, EAPN, Explainer 6, Brussels EAPH. Quoted in Saunders, P. (2019) Poverty. In Greve, B. (ed.) *Routledge Handbook of the Welfare State* second edition, London and New York, Routledge, pp. 58–71.
Fergusson, R. (2015) Is there a link between youth poverty and crime? Centre for Crime and Justice Studies. www.crimeandjustice.org.uk/resources/there-link-between-youth-poverty-and-crime)
Garland, D. (2001) *The Culture of Control: Crime and Social Order in Contemporary Society*, Oxford, Oxford University Press.
Giddens, A. (2000) *The Third Way and its Critics*, Cambridge, Polity.
Goddard, T. (2012) Post Welfarist risk managers? Risk crime prevention and the responsibilities of community-based organizations. *Theoretical Criminology* 16(3): 347–363.
Gottfredson, M.R. and Hirschi, T. (1990) *A General Theory of Crime*, Stanford, Stanford University Press.
Hannah-Moffat, K. (2016) Risk Knowledge(s), Crime and Law. In Burgess, A., Alemanno, A. and Zinn, J.O. (eds) *Routledge Handbook of Risk Studies*, London Routledge, pp. 241–252.
Henman, P. and Marston, G. (2008) The social division of welfare surveillance. *Journal of Social Policy* 37(2): 187–205.
Herrnstein, R. and Murray, C. (1994) *The Bell Curve: Intelligence and Class Structure in American Life*, New York, The Free Press.
Jacobson, J., Heard, C., and Fair, H. (2017) *Prison: Evidence of its rise and over-use from around the world.* London, Institute for Criminal Policy Research. www.prisonstudies.org/sites/default/files/resources/downloads/global_imprisonment_web2c.pdf
Joyce, R. and Sibieta, L. (2013) Labour record on poverty and social inequality, London, Institute for Fiscal Studies. www.ifs.org.uk/publications/6738
Lea, J. and Young, J. (1984) *What Is to Be Done about Law and Order?* London, Penguin Books.
Looney, A. and Turner, N. (2018) Work and opportunity before and after incarceration, The Brookings Institution, Economic Studies at Brookings. www.brookings.edu/wp-content/uploads/2018/03/es_20180314_looneyincarceration_final.pdf
Lupton, D. (2015) *Digital Sociology*, London and New York, Routledge.
Mayson, S.G. (2018) Dangerous defendants. *Yale Law Journal* 127(3): 490–569.
McAra, L. ad McVie, S. (2010) Youth crime and justice: key messages from the Edinburgh study of youth transitions and crime. *Criminology and Criminal Justice* 10(2): 179–209.

McAra, L. and McVie, S. (2013) Delivering Justice for Children and Young People: Key Messages from the Edinburgh Study of Youth Transitions and Crime. In Dockley, A. (ed.) *Justice for Young People: Papers by Winners of the Research Medal 2013*. Howard League for Penal Reform, pp. 3–14.

McKendrick, J.H., Sinclair, S., Irwin, A., Scott, G., and Dobbie, L. (2008) *The Media, Poverty and Public Opinion in the UK*, York, Joseph Rowntree Foundation.

Ministry of Justice (2013) The Story of the Prison Population 1993–2012. London, Ministry of Justice. www.gov.uk/government/statistics/story-of-the-prison-population-1993-to-2016.

Moore, S. (2010) Cautionary tales: drug facilitated sexual assault in the British media. *Crime Media and Culture: An International Journal* 5(3): 3015–3020.

Moore, S. and Newbury, A. (2017) *Legal Aid in Crisis*, Bristol, Polity.

Muncie, J. (2001) The Construction and Deconstruction of Crime. In Muncie, J. and McLaughlin, E. (eds) *The Problem of Crime*, London, Sage, pp. 7–71.

Murray, C. (1990) *The Emerging British Underclass*, London, IEA Health and Welfare Unit.

National Crime Agency (2019) National Strategic Assessment of serious and organized crime. https://nationalcrimeagency.gov.uk/who-we-are/publications/296-national-strategic-assessment-of-serious-organised-crime-2019/file

Nilsson, A. (2003) Living conditions, social exclusion and recidivism among prison inmates. *Journal of Scandinavian Studies in Criminology and Crime Prevention* 4, 57–83.

Numbeo (2019) Crime Index by Country. www.numbeo.com/crime/rankings_by_country.jsp?title=2019&region=150

O'Neil, C. (2016) *Weapons of Math Destruction: How Big Data Increases Inequality*, New York, Crown.

Pratt, J. (2008) Scandinavian exceptionalism in an era of penal excess. Part 1: The nature and roots of Scandinavian exceptionalism. *British Journal of Criminology* (48): 119–137.

Reiman, R. and Leighton, P. (2016) *The Rich Get Richer and the Poor Get Prison: Ideology Class and Criminal Justice*, London, Routledge.

Reiner, R. (2007) Political Economy and Criminal Justice. In Maguire, M., Morgan, R., and Reiner, R. (eds) *The Oxford Handbook of Criminology*, Oxford, Oxford University Press, pp. 341–380.

Saunders, P. (2019) Poverty. In Greve, B. (ed.) *Routledge Handbook of the Welfare State*, second edition. London and New York, Routledge, pp. 58–71.

Schia, Niels Nagelhus (2018) The cyber frontier and digital pitfalls in the Global South. *Third World Quarterly* 39(5): 821–837.

Sharkey, P., Besbris, M., and Friedson, M. (2016) Poverty and Crime. In Braby, D. and Burton, L. (eds) *The Oxford Handbook of Social Science and Poverty*, Oxford, Oxford University Press, pp. 623–637.

Sutherland, E.H. (1983) *White Collar Crime: The Uncut Version*, New Haven, CT, Yale University Press.

Taylor, L., Walton, P., and Young, J. (1975) *Critical Criminology*, London, Routledge Kegan Paul.

The Fraudscape (2018) www.cifas.org.uk/secure/contentPORT/uploads/documents/External-Fraudscape%202018-Final.pdf

The Guardian (2016) 'Chakrabarti pledges to end "authoritarian arms race" over UK prisons'. 23 December. www.theguardian.com/society/2016/dec/23/shami-chakrabarti-end-authoritarian-arms-race--uk-prisonseds (accessed 23 October 2018).

The Guardian (2018) 'Rising crime is symptom of inequality, says senior Met chief.' 14 June. www.theguardian.com/uk-news/2018/jun/14/rising-is-symptom-of-inequality-says-senior-met-chief

Trottier, D. (2012) *Social Media as Surveillance: Rethinking Visibility in a Converging World*, Farnham, Ashgate.

Ugelvik, Thomas (2016) Prisons as Welfare Institutions? Punishment and the Nordic Model. In Bennett, J., Jewkes Y., and Crewe, B. (eds) *Handbook on Prisons*, 2nd edition, London, Routledge, pp. 388–403.

van Dijk, J. (2013) *The Culture of Connectivity: A Critical History of Social Media*, Oxford, Oxford University Press.

Vanstone, M. and Priestly, P. (eds) (2016) *Probation and Politics*, London, Palgrave Macmillan.

Viner, K. (2016) 'How technology disrupted the truth', *The Guardian* 12 July.

Wajcman, J. (2015) *Pressed for Time: The Acceleration of Life in Digital Capitalism*, Chicago, University of Chicago Press.

Wilson, J.Q. (1975) *Thinking about Crime*, New York, Vintage.

Winlow, S. and Hall, S. (2016) Realist criminology and its discontents. *International Journal for Crime, Justice and Social Democracy* 5(3): 80–94.

World Bank (2018) *Decline of global extreme poverty continues but has slowed*. www.worldbank.org/en/news/press-release/2018/09/19/decline-of-global-extreme-poverty-continues-but-has-slowed-world-bank

24
Taxes and duties and their impact on poverty

Bent Greve

Introduction

This chapter focuses on how, by using taxes and duties, policy makers might be able to influence those living at risk of poverty. Measuring and understanding who is living in poverty will not be discussed, see instead Chapters 2–4. Instead, the focus is on presenting central issues related to financing of the welfare states, as the ability to finance welfare states has, and presumably will continue to be one of the important ways of being able to do something about the level of poverty in a country. In fact taxes and transfers are "the most direct and powerful instrument to redistribute income" (OECD 2015, p. 48).

In the next section a short empirical overview of the present situation with regard to financing of welfare states within OECD will be given. This is followed in the next section by looking into the different instruments and how they might influence the economic distribution. Thereafter is a discussion on user charges, although not a tax, often used as an instrument to finance at least part of the public sector spending and/or reduce demand for public services. This is followed by issues related to the administrative capacity to ensure compliance and reduce the risk that multinational companies do not pay tax, and finally some concluding remarks.

The chapter will not go into the two other classical roles of financing welfare states (allocation and stabilization) (Musgrave and Musgrave 1989; Greve 2010). The chapter will not delve into how the money is spent, albeit the way this is done can influence the degree of poverty (see instead Chapters 20, 21 and 25), and descriptions of poverty and measures to tackle this in different regions around the globe can be found in several chapters across the book.

How are welfare states financed today?

Before embarking upon the more theoretical and principle issues in how to finance welfare states, Appendix 24.1 shows the structure of overall financing of welfare states, split in the way OECD presents the main structures of taxes and duties (OECD 2017). Taxes and duties are defined as payment where you do not have the right to anything in return. This has the advantage that when later discussing the pros and cons and principles of the main taxes and duties it is possible to use Appendix 24.1 as a reference for how different OECD countries use the instruments available. This is without discussing what purpose they actually are using the money to achieve.

Appendix 24.1 depicts that financing of the expenditures is mainly through general tax revenue, earmarked payroll or income tax see also (Mossialos, Wenzl, Osborn, and Sarnak 2016), with differences across countries in the way income tax, duties and social security contributions play a role. There are also differences in the overall level as percentages of GDP, ranging from 17.2% in Mexico to 45.9% in Denmark. Overall, the trend has been toward broadening the tax-base, lowering of the top marginal tax-rates and making duties more uniform across countries and also to focus on taxation of the consumption of final goods (Mankiw, Weinzierl, and Yagan 2009; European Union 2015). This also reflects the impact of globalization and regionalization of economies, reducing the possible national options to have strong diversities in the tax-structures compared to other countries, and especially countries close by. The overall level of taxes and duties cannot, by itself, inform on the disposable income of persons to buy goods and services, as this will also depend on what a person has to pay for different kinds of welfare services, such as health and education. Thus in the field of health care if a person has to pay for insurance and/or pay a high level of user charges, see further below, then this can influence households' disposable income as well as the level of taxes and duties. Thus, even if this chapter focuses on ways of financing, it is in principle also important to look at what the individual gets by the payment of taxes and duties, and whether this reduces the need for that individual to pay for a variety of services (education, care, health, infrastructure) or take out insurance to cover specific social contingencies (unemployment, sickness and pensions, for example).

Principles of taxation

Taxes and duties have been central topics and open for discussion for a long time, also with regard to what would be the optimal taxation (Mankiw et al. 2009). Optimal taxation mainly exists theoretically as there are conflicting goals and aims of welfare policy. Optimal taxation is further based on the implicit assumption that the market is always the best way to allocate resources. The focus here will mainly be on the overall impact on the ability to finance public sector spending, whereas more detailed analysis of the impact of the different instruments is not included (see instead Stiglitz and Rosengaard 2015; Greve 2014).

Taxation has three important objectives, as pointed to already by Musgrave and Musgrave (1973) in the first edition of their book on public finances. These are to help in allocation, distribution and stabilization of the economies. Furthermore, it has been important to do it in a transparent way, although an invisible tax might be more popular than a tax individuals can see directly, such as income tax. A central issue has also been to collect taxes and duties with the fewest distortions possible, such as in relation to work/leisure and spending/saving. This is not an easy task and the aim is, at the same time, to ensure a sufficiently large amount of money to finance the activities and avoid having, at least over time, a public sector deficit, which will then need to be financed by future generations. Another central issue is the impact on distribution.

The trend in most countries has been to broaden the tax-base (OECD 2011, 2017; European Union 2015), including a way to reduce tax-avoidance. At the same time, there has been a tendency for narrowing the tax-base to give incentives to investment, and also lower income tax on companies, at least in the EU-countries (see www.skm.dk/skattetal/statistik/generelskattestatistik/kattesats-e-eucountries, obtained August 18, 2018, showing that from 1995 to 2017 the average rate in the EU has fallen from 35% to barely 22%). The implication is that taxes on profits and capital, despite increasing, have provided a lower part of the overall revenue.

Recent years' tax reforms in Europe have focused not only on the level, but also how they might enhance growth (European Union 2015) as economic growth might enable better options to pursue social policy. However, there is no documentation for a "trickle down" from those gaining from tax-reform that enhances growth in such a way as to improve living conditions for poor people. Still, there are taxes, such as taxes on immovable property, that could be both less distortive, and provide a revenue for the welfare states, albeit they are only used to a limited degree (see also Appendix 24.1).

Taxes to improve environment can be growth friendly, but if they fall on essential aspects of consumption for people living in poverty such as water, electricity or heating, this can have a negative impact on their living standard. This is another example of where consumption taxes might, if not enacted appropriately, have a negative impact on those living in poverty. Thus, a consumption tax, such as value added tax (VAT), is, if controlled effectively, a good instrument to ensure revenue for those living in a country, and, also from the tourist industry. It can thereby represent a stable income revenue for a state, but the possible risk is that those who spend all their income on daily goods and services will have to pay more than they otherwise would have to and at the risk of not being able to afford those goods and services. Consumption taxes tend thus to have a negative impact on distribution, even though duties on luxury goods can have a positive impact.

Finally, there are income tax and social security contributions. These will, depending on the way they are structured, have a different kind of impact.

The income tax system can thus, for example, be proportional, progressive or regressive (Musgrave and Musgrave 1989; Stiglitz and Rosengaard 2015). However, even a proportional tax might be progressive if there is basic deduction before having to pay the tax. However, not only is the rate important but also the possible deductions within the system, such as deductions for different expenses. Even the Earned Income Tax Credit, seemingly first introduced in the US in 1995 (Marx, Salanauskaite, and Verbist 2013), can influence the total tax to be paid by the individual. Use of fiscal welfare (Sinfield 2019) can thus be a way of giving incentives to take out insurance to cover health care, but this might at the same time reduce the fiscal revenue for the state. So, at the outset the impact of income tax on poverty and distribution cannot be decided, only an empirical analysis can do that (Sandmo 1995).

Social security contributions can, in principle, be done in the same way as income taxes. The distributional outcome might thus not in itself be influenced by the choice between these two, however, it can be influenced by whether or not payment has an impact on access to different kinds of social insurance. For this reason, it is not the financing per se, but more the possible impact on access to benefits and services that can have an impact.

An analysis indicates that, at least within the OECD countries, increasing the tax burden on labour or consumption relative to capital leads to higher income inequality, as one could expect due to the unequal distribution of capital income. On the other hand, a stronger focus on income taxes relative to consumption taxes can imply a more just distribution (Iosifidi and Mylonidis 2017). This effect likely stems from the redistributive objectives of social security contributions incorporated in labour taxes, especially in a progressive income tax system. However, the overall effect will depend on the mix of different types of taxes and duties, as well as whether and how user charges are included and, furthermore, how and in what way they interact with the social security system (Morel and Palme 2018).

An important issue is to structure the tax system in such a way that the combined tax to pay and reduction in social security benefits, if there is an increase in the wage income, does not mean that there will no increase in disposable income, or even a reduction. This is labelled a poverty trap where even if people get a job or start to work more, the combined tax-rate and decrease in benefit result in their income not increasing, or possibly even decreasing. Many commentators also mention the extra expenditure needed in order to earn the income, such as extra transport costs.

The overall relation between poverty and choice of taxation instruments is that, on the one hand, a taxation of even a very low or limited income can be beneficial for those groups to have consumption possibilities if this implies access to welfare services. On the other hand, at the same time, overall low levels of taxation can result in less money being available for the public sector to finance welfare policies.

User charges

User charges are used to a varying degree in most countries in order to access different kinds of welfare services. It is conventional in economics to argue that such charges are a way of ensuring that users are revealing their true preferences. Overall the discussion in relation to user charges revolves around to what degree this is in fact the case. In general it can be argued that user charges, besides regulating demand, help in raising revenues to pay for the services, the size depending on criteria for paying and the level of the charges, but also on the impact on demand from using user charges. If they regulate demand effectively, this can also improve the allocative efficiency. Finally, it can be argued that this might reduce abuse/overuse of the system.

There are many different possible ways to have user charges, which can be co-payment, co-insurance, deductive directly, but also indirectly by reference pricing (for example, in relation to drugs) and extra billing (Thomson, Foubiser, and Mossialos 2010). They can be a fixed amount, a proportion of the cost of delivering the service, there can be a maximum to pay and, finally, they might depend on the income/wealth of those using the system. Furthermore, they may vary across the different parts of the public sector; for example, in most countries access to public hospital is free of charge whereas there are strong differences across countries with regard to the existence and size of payments for visiting general practitioners, dentists, and part or all costs of medicine, day-care for children, long-term care and parts of the educational systems.

From a poverty perspective a problem with user charges is that poor people will often not be able to afford it, and in terms of health care this means they will not get the treatment they need in time. If it results in more expensive treatment being needed later, and this is available in the country, then this will increase costs in systems later, and also, presumably, increase inequality in access to public sector services. There is also the risk of less education, less care for children and the elderly depending on the way the system is enacted, at least for people at risk of living in poverty.

The consequence with regard to poor people will depend on the precise way the user charges are enacted. Thus, if, for example, low-income earners do not have to pay, then the impact will be less negative related to poor people than if they have to pay the same amount as high-income earners.

User charges can be part of the way one can finance welfare states, although there is "no theory of fairness in tax policy that permits targeting the ill in this way" (Thomson et al. 2010, p. 1.), and further, there is a high risk that those at risk of poverty will not be able to pay, and thus it can have a negative impact on their living standards, especially those user charges that are related to payment for health care.

Overall, even if user charges might be a way to know the demand for public sector services, it might have grave impact on access to important parts of the welfare services for poor people.

Administrative and compliance issues

Even the most theoretically well-designed tax system will only work if it is possible to administer it, and this includes taxation of multinational companies, and reducing the ability to avoid paying taxes – or more precisely the compliance with the tax-rules, including the issue of controlling the tax paid – whether income tax or different kinds of duties.

Overall the compliance literature with regard to paying taxes and duties is a combination of moral/norms, trust in government and enforcement of administrative procedures to collect taxes and duties, including the risk that one is caught trying to evade paying taxes (Torgler 2007; Weber, Fooken, and Herrmann 2014). Tax compliance thus seemingly is a result of the complicated interaction between tax-morale and deterrence measures (Schneider 2011). Trust in society that tax-enforcement takes place also influences compliance, and thus a fair treatment of tax-payers also has a role. For an overview of the literature in the field, see Torgler (2011), who also points to that people from Northern Europe have a higher tax-morale than in Southern Europe (p. 23). This helps to explain the limited size also in this study of the tax evasion in different countries, it being the case that more progressive tax systems imply higher tax-morale, although declining with income (Doerrenberg and Peichl 2013).

Several factors are at stake as to whether or not tax evasion is viewed as immoral: the impact of moral appeal, being a friend of someone cheating, perception of unfair treatment, and compliance seem to be higher in countries with stronger social cohesion (Alm and Torgler 2011). Compliance will be lower if it is generally accepted as being legitimate to practise tax evasion. If you know someone cheating this can also influence the individual's perception about how to react. The risk and waiting time for a tax-audit also influences compliance (Alm et al. 2012).

It is naturally difficult to measure and estimate the influence on compliance as it might vary due to different behaviour within the group, but also compared to other groups (Fortin et al. 2004), and lack of reliable information is central (Alm 2013).

The reason to include and discuss compliance is that this might be one of the ways to make it possible to reduce the prevalence of tax evasion while at the same time increasing the revenue for the public sector.

The Allingham-Sandmo approach was that people would only pay tax when an individual cost-benefit analysis or expected utility maximization implies it (Allingham and Sandmo 1972). Tax-morale has been argued to help in providing a rational explanation for paying tax as the original Allingham-Sandmo approach seemed to underestimate the observed rate of tax compliance. Intrinsic motivation (e.g. driven by internal rewards) also seems to play a role with regard to compliance within the tax system. For example, related to Italy it seems that "tax-morale was positively associated with social capital, political participation and immigration" (Russo 2013, p. 114), and further that migrants' positive attitude to paying tax implies a monetary contribution to the overall tax-income by setting a good example. Measurement of tax-morale has been done by looking into the percentage of survey respondents who agree with statements such as: "Citizens should not cheat on their taxes", "Cheating on taxes is justifiable if there is the opportunity to do so", or "Managing to avoid tax payments is legitimate". Thus, this analysis being an indication of that social capital, including moral, trust (in the public, including tax, authorities) and social capital can be elements having an impact on the degree of compliance with the tax system.

Other studies also focus on how an approach using behavioural insight can foster or prevent tax evasion, as for example, "tax behavior is embedded in and influenced by social structure norms and roles" (Pickhardt and Prinz 2014, p. 2). Thus, as also argued above, the trust and morale of tax-payers' influence in connection with the tax-authorities audits the willingness to pay and be compliant. It is further possible that tax-payers cooperate in tax evasion and also inform each other on the tax-authorities' behaviour. However, this will be reduced if there is high trust in the public administration. Furthermore, it seems that tax-payers' morale might be influenced by how the money is spent, and this may indicate that redistributive usage is not necessarily the highest aim (Doerrenberg 2015).

Behavioural issues in general thus seem to be important (Alm 2013). Behavioural issues that are important include:

a the cost of evasion;
b not only monetary cost, but also psychological costs due to fear of detection;
c perception of fairness.

Social customs also have an impact and thus there is a need to integrate behavioural aspects into models of tax evasion as there might be a loss of social prestige after being detected as a tax-evader. Finally, perceptions of fairness influence compliance behaviour (Hashimzade, Myles, and Tran-Nam 2017; Weber et al. 2014).

Overall, in general it can be argued that tax evasion increases the degree of inequality (for a case study, see Barrios et al. 2017). So, policy that can reduce tax evasion should increase the scope of money available also to do something about the level of poverty.

The economics of crime approach focuses on the impact of enforcement on compliance, and, the greater enforcement the better compliance (Alm 2013). Thus, this also points to the fact that the risk of being caught will have an impact on compliance and, thereby, that public sector auditing of tax-returns is an important aspect related to compliance. Auditing is also an important aspect of how to cope with multinational companies and reduce the possible impact of using transfer prices as a way of reducing tax-payment in a country with higher taxes and then paying less in a country with a lower level of taxation. The impact of transfer pricing and multinational companies can be substantial (Alstadsæter, Johannesen, and Zucman 2018), and not only reduce revenue for the states, but also increase the degree of inequality.

Finally, uncertainty about the tax-rules and differences and regular changes in the system among countries in the tax system can also have an impact on tax compliance, but also on investment and growth (Zangari, Caiumi, and Hemmelgarn 2017).

Some concluding remarks

Public sector spending including for the purpose of social policy, and also in relation to poverty reduction, has to be financed. It can thus be important to be aware of how financing has an impact on distribution, including its consequnces for those at risk of poverty. Still, the main aim of taxes and duties in relation to poverty is to fund interventions and support those in need.

There might be contradictions with regard to the possible impact of different forms of taxation. For example, taxes on consumption might be more difficult for the poor to cope with, while at the same time they can be a stable revenue with less possible distortion of other goals. They might even, in the case of duties on issues related to the environment, smoking, alcohol and healthy food, have other positive externalities associated with them.

Therefore, at the end of the day there is, and might be, a trade off between the different tax-instruments available and the goals one wants to achieve by using these different kinds of interventions. It is also a question of the administrative resources available to tax-audits and willingness to increase the level of tax compliance.

In recent years, increased global trade has made it more difficult for nations to implement different tax systems from other, especially neighbouring, countries. Therefore, international collaboration with regard to taxation of global companies, including their use of transfer pricing has also the implication that taxation is no longer just a national issue, but is increasingly an international one.

Finally, choice of instruments and the size of taxes and duties are, at the end of the day, political issues for decision makers, while at the same time if the goal is to alleviate poverty, then this will have implications for both the structure and the level of taxation.

Appendix 24.1

Table A24.1 Structure of taxes and duties in 2016 in OECD countries (in percentage of GDP)

Tax revenue	*Total tax revenue*	*1000 Taxes on income, profits and capital gains*	*2000 Social security contributions (SSC)*	*3000 Taxes on payroll and workforce*	*4000 Taxes on property*	*5000 Taxes on goods and services*	*6000 Taxes other than 1000, 2000, 3000, 4000 and 5000*
Austria	42.7	11.9	14.9	3.0	0.6	12.0	0.2
Belgium	44.2	15.7	13.7	0.0	3.5	10.8	0.0
Canada	31.7	15.1	4.8	0.7	3.8	7.4	0.0
Chile	20.4	6.8	1.5	0.0	1.0	11.1	–0.1
Czech Republic	34.0	7.4	14.7	0.0	0.5	11.3	0.0
Denmark	45.9	28.7	0.1	0.3	1.9	14.9	0.0
Estonia	34.7	7.8	11.6	0.0	0.3	14.9	0.0
Finland	44.1	15.3	12.8	0.0	1.4	14.5	0.0
France	45.3	10.6	16.7	1.6	4.1	11.1	1.1
Germany	37.6	12.0	14.1	0.0	1.1	10.2	0.0
Greece	38.6	9.1	11.0	0.0	2.6	15.8	0.0
Hungary	39.4	7.1	13.6	0.6	1.1	16.7	0.1
Iceland	36.4	17.8	3.6	0.3	1.9	12.1	0.6
Ireland	23.0	10.0	3.9	0.1	1.3	7.5	0.0
Israel	31.2	9.8	5.2	1.2	3.3	11.8	0.0
Italy	42.9	13.7	13.0	0.0	2.8	12.1	1.2
Japan	..	9.5	..	0.0	2.5	6.2	0.1
Korea	26.3	8.2	6.9	0.1	3.0	7.4	0.7

(continued)

Table A24.1 (continued)

Tax revenue	*Total tax revenue*	*1000 Taxes on income, profits and capital gains*	*2000 Social security contributions (SSC)*	*3000 Taxes on payroll and workforce*	*4000 Taxes on property*	*5000 Taxes on goods and services*	*6000 Taxes other than 1000, 2000, 3000, 4000 and 5000*
Latvia	30.2	8.0	8.3	0.0	1.1	12.6	0.0
Luxembourg	37.1	13.7	10.6	0.0	3.5	9.1	0.1
Mexico	17.2	7.3	2.2	..	..	..	..
Netherlands	38.8	10.6	14.8	0.0	1.5	11.5	0.0
New Zealand	32.1	17.8	0.0	0.0	2.0	12.3	0.0
Norway	38.0	14.0	10.6	0.0	1.2	12.1	0.0
Poland	33.6	6.7	12.8	0.0	1.4	10.7	1.8
Portugal	34.4	9.9	9.2	0.0	1.3	13.6	0.4
Slovak Republic	32.7	7.3	14.1	0.0	0.4	10.7	0.0
Slovenia	37.0	6.9	14.7	0.1	0.6	14.6	0.0
Spain	33.5	9.4	11.4	0.0	2.6	9.8	0.1
Sweden	44.1	15.7	10.0	4.7	1.1	12.4	0.0
Switzerland	27.8	13.0	6.8	0.0	1.9	6.0	0.1
Turkey	25.5	5.4	7.3	0.0	1.2	11.1	0.4
United Kingdom	33.2	11.9	6.3	0.0	4.2	10.7	0.0
United States	26.0	12.7	6.2	0.0	2.7	4.4	0.0

Source: Data extracted on 28 June 2018 09:06 UTC (GMT) from OECD.Stat

References

Allingham, M. G., and A. Sandmo. 1972. "Income Tax Evasion: A Theoretical Analysis." *Journal of Public Economics* 1 (3–4): 323–338.

Alm, J. 2013. "Measuring, Explaining and Controlling Tax Evasion: Lessons from Theory, Experiments and Field Studies." Working Papers 1213, Tulane University, Department of Economics.

Alm, J., and B. Torgler 2011. "Do Ethics Matter? Tax Compliance and Morality." *Journal of Business Ethics* 101: 635–651.

Alm, J., E. Kirchler, S. Muehlbacher, K. Gangl, E. Hofmann, C. Kogler, and M. Pollai. 2012. "Rethinking the Research Paradigms for Analysing Tax Compliance Behaviour." Working Papers 1210, Tulane University, Department of Economics.

Alstadsæter, Annette, Niels Johannesen, and Gabriel Zucman. 2018. "Tax Evasion and Inequality." *SSRN*. https://doi.org/10.2139/ssrn.3109300.

Barrios, S. et al. 2017. "Measuring the Fiscal and Equity Impact of Tax Evasion: Evidence from Denmark and Estonia." JRC Working Papers on Taxation and Structural Reforms, No. 5. Seville.

Doerrenberg, Philipp. 2015. "Does the Use of Tax Revenue Matter for Tax Compliance Behavior?" *Economics Letters*. https://doi.org/10.1016/j.econlet.2015.01.005.

Doerrenberg, Philipp, and Andreas Peichl. 2013. "Progressive Taxation and Tax Morale." *Public Choice*. https://doi.org/10.1007/s11127-011-9848-1.

European Union. 2015. "Tax Reforms in EU Member States: 2015 Report." Luxembourg.

Fortin, B. et al. 2004. "Tax Evasion and Social Interactions." IZA Discussion Paper No. 1359.

Greve, B. 2010. "Taxation, Equality and Social Cohesion European Experiences." In *Challenges of Social Cohesion in Times of Crisis: Euro-Latin American Dialogue*, edited by M. Zupi, and E. Estruch Puertas, 307–32. Madrid: FIIAPP.

——. 2014. "Financing the Welfare States: Changes and Challenges." In *Innovation in Social Services: The Public-Private Mix in Service Provision, Fiscal Policy and Employment*, edited by T. Sirovátka and B. Greve, 55–76. Farnham: Ashgate.

Hashimzade, Nigar, Gareth D. Myles, and Binh Tran-Nam. 2017. "Applications of Behavioural Economics to Tax Evasion." *Journal of Economic Surveys* 5: 941–77.

Iosifidi, M., and N. Mylonidis. 2017. "Relative Effective Taxation and Income Inequality: Evidence from OECD Countries." *Journal of European Social Policy* 27 (1): 57–76.

Mankiw, N. Gregory, Matthew Weinzierl, and Danny Yagan. 2009. "Optimal Taxation in Theory and Practice." *Journal of Economic Perspectives*. https://doi.org/10.1257/jep.23.4.147.

Marx, I., L. Salanauskaite, and G. Verbist. 2013. "The Paradox of Redistribution Revisited: And That It May Rest in Peace?" IZA Discussion Paper No. 7414. Bonn.

Morel, N., and J. Palme. 2018. "Financing the Welfare State and the Politics of Taxation." In *The Routledge Handbook of the Welfare State*, edited by B. Greve, 2nd ed., 467–76. Oxon: Routledge.

Mossialos, E., M. Wenzl, R. Osborn, and D. Sarnak. 2016. *2015 International Profiles of Health Care Systems*. Commonwealth Fund.

Musgrave, R., and P. Musgrave. 1989. *Public Finance in Theory and Practice*. New York: McGraw Hill.

Musgrave, Richard Abel, and Peggy B. Musgrave. 1973. *Public Finance in Theory and Practice*.

OECD. 2011. "OECD's Current Tax Agenda." Paris: OECD.

——. 2015. *In It Together: Why Less Inequality Benefits All*. Paris: OECD Publishing.

——. 2017. *Revenue Statistics: 1965–2016*. Paris: OECD.

Pickhardt, Michael, and Aloys Prinz. 2014. "Behavioral Dynamics of Tax Evasion: A Survey." *Journal of Economic Psychology*. North-Holland. https://doi.org/10.1016/j.joep.2013.08.006.

Sandmo, A. 1995. "Welfare Economics of the Welfare State." *Scandinavian Journal of Economics* 97 (4): 469–76.

Schneider, Friedrich. 2011. "The Shadow Economy and Shadow Economy Labor Force : What Do We (Not) Know ?" IZA Discussion Paper No. 5769.

Sinfield, A. 2019. "Fiscal Welfare." In *The Routledge Handbook of the Welfare State*, edited by B. Greve, 2nd ed., 23–33. Oxon: Routledge.

Stiglitz, J., and J. Rosengaard. 2015. *Economics of the Public Sector*. 4th ed. London: W. W. Norton & Company.

Thomson, Sarah, Thomas Foubiser, and Elias Mossialos. 2010. "Can User Charges Make Health Care More Efficient?" *BMJ (Online)*. https://doi.org/10.1136/bmj.c3759.

Torgler, Benno. 2011. “Tax Morale and Compliance : Review of Evidence and Case Studies for Europe.” World Bank Policy Research Working Paper Series, no. 5922: 1–81. https://doi.org/10.1596/1813-9450-5922.

Torgler, T. 2007. *Tax Compliance and Tax Morale: A Theoretical and Empirical Analysis.* Cheltenham: Edward Elgar.

Weber, Till Olaf, Jonas Fooken, and Benedikt Herrmann. 2014. “Behavioural Economics and Taxation.” Taxation Paper, No. 41. Luxembourg. https://doi.org/10.2778/32009.

Zangari, Ernesto, Antonella Caiumi, and Thomas Hemmelgarn. 2017. “Tax Uncertainty: Economic Evidence and Policy Responses.” Taxation Paper, No. 67. Luxembourg. https://doi.org/10.2778/620293.

25

Social cash transfers in the global South

Individualizing poverty policies

Lutz Leisering

Reducing poverty in countries of the global South has been an overriding concern of development politics from the beginnings in the 1950s. But in the early decades, this referred to the collective poverty of countries, to be overcome by economic growth and rising national income. Only from the 1990s did development politics zoom in on individual poverty. This new perspective led to the idea of tackling poverty, among others, by way of individualized welfare benefits to poor persons and households. The idea 'just give money to the poor' (Hanlon et al. 2010, title) had been rejected by international organizations from all political leanings well into the 1990s. From the late 1990s, continuing till the present day, 'social cash transfers'—regular non-contributory monetary public transfers to poor persons or households in view of general subsistence, mostly means-tested (that is, a variety of social assistance)—have mushroomed in the global South and on agendas of international organizations. Social cash transfers—in short, cash transfers—extend social security to informal workers and rural populations who had been excluded from public provisions.

This chapter enquires: What 'are' social cash transfers (first section), how widespread are cash transfers in the global South (second section), how inclusive are they (third section), what varieties of cash transfers can be identified (fourth section), what effects do they have (fifth section), and how does the new instrument transform poverty policy, and, as we argue, the very concept of poverty (conclusion)?

The chapter is based on a major study of cash transfers, FLOOR (summary monograph, Leisering 2019),[1] and the database FLOORCASH, which was the first to cover all countries in the global South and all identifiable programmes.[2] Social cash transfers have rarely been theorized, and then mostly from the perspectives of welfare economics (Barrientos 2013) and political economy (Lavinas 2013). By contrast, the FLOOR study adopts a sociological approach, which emphasizes processes of social construction, complementing the extant approaches. The first monographs on social cash transfers were based on data from other publications (Leisering et al. 2006) or on exemplary evidence (Hanlon et al. 2010; Barrientos 2013).

Concepts

Since the turn of the millennium, the number of social cash transfer programmes has increased more than any other type of social protection across the global South. For example, cash transfers account for the bulk of the rise of pension coverage in the South since 2000 (ILO 2017: 82–84). The term 'social protection', which has increasingly superseded the older term 'social security' (see ILO 2017), refers to individualized rights-based provisions, mainly social insurance, social assistance, and non-contributory allowances, and also to labour rights. There are four normative models of social protection (see Figure 25.2): provisions for civil servants, which are legitimized by merit; social insurance for formal workers, legitimized by achievement; 'universal' benefits, based on the notion of citizenship; and social assistance for the poor, based on the principle of need and means testing. The four ways of legitimizing public provisions indicate different notions of deservingness. The term 'social cash transfers' has become common currency in the development community since 2005 (von Gliszczynski 2015: 28–30; DFID 2005), mainly denoting varieties of social assistance, but also including some non-means-tested non-contributory programmes (e.g. for older persons); such programmes are often called 'universal' (e.g. by Kidd 2015). Social cash transfers are 'social' since they involve redistribution rather than market principles. 'Conditional cash transfers' (CCT) have received most attention in public debates, but they only account for less than a fifth of all programmes.

While the literature analyses single programmes (programme approach), this chapter also looks into 'national cash transfer regimes' (Leisering 2019: 153f.), that is, the ensemble of all social cash transfer programmes in a given country. Such a *systemic approach* measures the contribution of cash transfers to fighting poverty or, more generally, to social inclusion more adequately than a programme approach. We speak of 'national inclusiveness profiles' to denote the coverage of the poor under national cash transfer regimes.

Besides programmes, we take '*target categories*'—persons who are legally designated as entitlement-bearers under cash transfer programmes—as units of analysis *(entitlement approach)*. While the systemic approach addresses the macro configuration of cash transfer programmes, the entitlement approach reflects a micro perspective on programmes. Programme names like 'social pensions' and 'Child Support Grant' seem to suggest the target categories they address, but there is no full match between programmes and target categories. A programme may cater for more than one target category and, vice versa a target group may be served by more than one programme in a country. Moreover, as we argue, the range of target categories is much broader than the categories commonly discussed.

The spread of social cash transfer programmes in the global South

Since the 1990s, social cash transfer programmes have been mushrooming in the global South. The spread has been massive, and it has been fast and in waves, already suggesting that diffusion processes, flowing from international organizations and/or from other states, might have played a role. The programmes have spread to all types of states—poor and better-off, democratic and authoritarian—suggesting that the introduction of the new instrument cannot be attributed to the economic resources of a country. Rather, international diffusion processes as well as domestic politics have played a role. Still, democracies and middle-income countries have been more likely to install cash transfers than authoritarian regimes and low-income countries. The coverage of Southern populations is significant; up to 1 billion people are estimated to receive benefits (Barrientos 2013: 4). Around 9.5% of the populations in Africa receive benefits, 16.4% in Asia and the Pacific, and 39.2% in Latin America and the Caribbean (Leisering 2019: 310, compiled from imperfect data for 2015 by ILO 2017). Referring to the broader concept of 'social safety nets' of the World Bank (which includes cash transfers and other programmes such as school feeding, fee waivers, and in-kind transfers), spending increased from 0.4% of GDP in 2003 to 1.3% in 2015 in Latin America and the Caribbean; across the global South, spending averaged 1.5% of GDP in the mid-2010s (World Bank 2018: 26, 17).

Social cash transfers reach the majority of countries in the global South, namely 113 countries, as of 2012/2013, that is 76.4% of Southern countries, with 282 programmes (data from the FLOOR project). The biggest rise occurred after 2002. However, the spread of programmes is uneven, with regional patterns already hinting at heterogeneous determinants of the spread. Africa has 31 countries with cash transfer programmes (which is 57.4% of all 54 African countries); Latin America has 32 programmes (which is 97% of the 33 Latin American countries); Asia has 44 programmes (91.7% of the 48 Asian countries); and Oceania has six programmes (46.2% of 13 Oceanian countries). In short, cash transfers are found almost everywhere, but with limited spread in Africa.

There seems to be no unitary explanatory model that would explain the rise of all types of cash transfers and in all regions (Leisering 2019: 283–84). For social pensions across the global South, a complex model has been tested successfully (event history analysis, Böger and Leisering 2019). The African countries without cash transfer programmes tend to be non-democratic and former French, rather than British, colonies. Moreover, donor-driven programmes are particularly widespread in Africa, as are pilot programmes. In Africa, one out of four programmes is a pilot. Pilot programmes make up 9% of all programmes in the global South, and 64% of all pilot programmes are in Africa. So the colonial past and the presence of donors matter.

The spread of programmes in Latin America has been strongly influenced by policy diffusion between countries and by ideas from international financial institutions, especially the World Bank. The former Soviet Union member states in Central Asia adopted cash transfer programmes during the 1990s that responded to problems of post-socialist transformation. This is another instance of historical legacies. Asia as a whole is too heterogeneous to give overarching explanations of the spread of cash transfers.

How inclusive are social cash transfer programmes?

We investigate three dimensions of the inclusiveness of programmes: coverage, conditions of access, and benefit levels and standards.[3] We measure inclusiveness in terms of entitlements laid down in legal regulations. While legal entitlements do not necessarily result in actual receipt of benefits, entitlements reflect ascriptions of deservingness and indicate political commitments. That is, entitlements reveal the normative basis of programmes, irrespective of deficiencies in the administration and delivery of benefits.

Coverage

With the spread of cash transfer programmes across the global South, coverage has increased massively. Social cash transfers cover six main target categories, on which entitlements are bestowed: children, persons of working age, older persons, persons with disabilities, various 'small groups', and 'poor people'. Some countries have only programmes for some of these categories or no programmes at all. If a country has established a programme for a certain category, we interpret this as an attribution of deservingness to this category, while categories not covered are seen as undeserving (for deservingness as reflected in targeted benefit programmes in European countries, see van Oorschot et al. 2017). The ensemble of categories covered in a country can be interpreted as an order of deservingness, reflecting political priorities of governments, the influence of external donors, and political struggles between marginal groups, NGOs, and ruling elites. Figure 25.1 shows the overall order of deservingness in income security across the global South. For each target category, the figure shows the number of programmes that target the category, as a percentage of all programmes in the South. Multiple references are possible, since programmes may target more than one category (this applies to 38.8% of all programmes).

Children and older persons are the most frequently targeted categories, both are life-cycle groups. By contrast, persons of working age are much less frequently covered. They may profit from other welfare benefits shared in their households, such as child benefit, but our analysis refers to own entitlements of persons of working age. The exclusion of (non-disabled) persons of working age is a major entitlement gap in the global South, indicating that the workers' question is not at the forefront of Southern social security agendas—contrary to social assistance in Northern welfare states which focuses on the unemployed. Adults with disabilities score only slightly lower than older persons. 'Small groups'—such as war veterans, divorced women, pregnant women, martyrs, discharged prisoners—figure fairly frequently, testifying further to the diversity of the world of cash transfer programmes between and within countries.

'Poor people' as beneficiaries refers to programmes that define their target group as poor persons or households, without singling out specific categories of persons like children or older persons, i.e., these are non-categorical programmes. Poor people programmes operate in one way or other according to ascribed need, based on a means test, but half of these programmes define their target populations only vaguely, and only 20% come close to need orientation for everybody.

How is need assessed in cash transfer programmes? In the European ideal type of social assistance, the means test is an income test (plus an asset test), and it is also a needs test, since need is defined as the difference between the means of the applicant and the minimum standard defined by law. Considering the low degree of monetarization and limited administrative capacities in many countries of the global South, Southern means testing rarely works this way, and benefits (reflecting ascribed need) may only be loosely related to means. 'Ascribed poverty targeting' (Leisering 2019: 234–35) is widespread, that is, local elites designate persons or households as poor or non-poor by applying pre-defined broad or informal selection criteria; or, more formally, eligibility depends on how applicants score in a questionnaire that covers 13 dimensions of welfare or deprivation (in India); or fixed quotas limit the range of persons to be recognized as needy. Regarding older persons, 15 countries have universal social pensions, and 20 have pension-tested pensions, that is, only income from a prior pension is counted as means.

Zooming in on world *regions*, we find distinct patterns. For example, South Asia and South East Asia do not attend much to the income needs of older persons, whereas East Asia and Oceania are heavily biased toward older persons, in conjunction with a striking scarcity of programmes for children. Latin America's order of deservingness is roughly similar to the global order described above. Sub-Saharan Africa stands out by a strikingly even pattern of entitlements: most of the six main target categories are addressed to a similar extent. However, programmes for persons of working age are rare in all regions, except in the Middle East and North Africa (MENA).

The uneven coverage of the main target categories—uneven already in law, not only benefit receipt—demonstrates that cash transfer programmes involve inclusions as well as exclusions already at the programme level. If we look more closely, we even find that 'categorical' benefits are often restricted to a sub-category of the target category, such as orphaned children. We call this '*within-target category exclusions*'. That is, national cash transfer regimes may fall short of universal coverage not only by excluding certain target categories, but also through exclusions within target categories. These exclusions may make a big difference, but in the political discourse they tend to be hidden.

To measure these micro exclusions (within target categories), we define an *inclusion index* which measures for each target category the restrictions on entitlements, in three dimensions: social characteristics of the members of the target group (e.g. do child grants cover all children or only orphaned, disabled, or single-parent children?), age of the addressees (e.g. age of retirement in the case of social pensions), and geographic range (Weible 2016: 180f.;

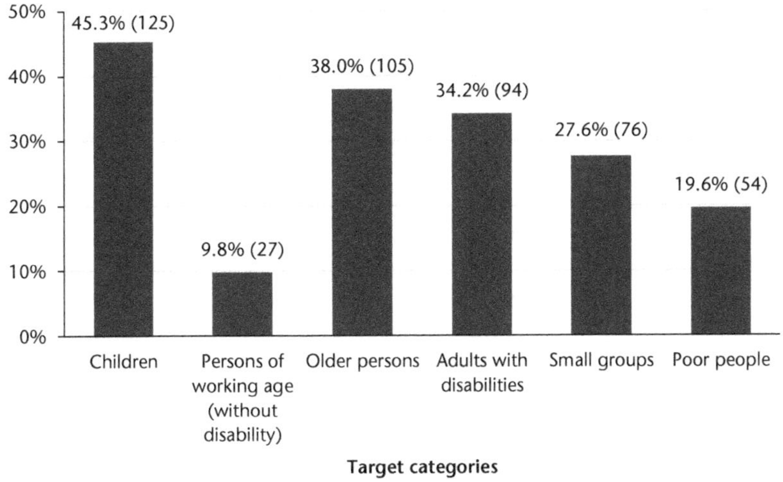

Figure 25.1 Social cash transfer programmes, by target categories (programmes that target the respective category, in % of all programmes in the global South; multiple references possible).

Source: The FLOOR project (Katrin Weible) (Leisering 2019: 161); database FLOORCASH, N = 276 (six missing values; for adults with disabilities and small groups one more missing value).

Leisering 2019: 168). Children, for example, are the most frequently targeted category, as shown in Figure 25.1, but have a very low inclusion score. That is, the political rhetoric of attending to children may eclipse the exclusion of substantial sections of the group of children and families with children. Programmes for children also score low with regard to institutionalization. For some social pensions, the legal age of retirement is so high that most persons die before qualifying.

Access

Two conditions may constrain access to benefits. First, CCTs, which are widespread in Latin America and have been advocated particularly by the World Bank, require the recipients to show a certain kind of behaviour, mostly sending children to school and to regular health check-ups. Of these programmes, 29% impose behavioural conditions (including programmes not normally grouped as CCT). Second, around 80% of all programmes apply a means test, and the percentage is similar across programme types. Countries with universal social pensions are mostly small or very small (in terms of population). 'Poor people programmes' are, by definition, means-tested. The issue of means testing vs. 'universalism' is hotly contested in the development community (for advocacy of universalism see, e.g., Kidd 2015; UN 2018: 114–15).

Benefits

Benefit levels under cash transfer programmes tend to be low, mostly far below a subsistence minimum, and programmes are not even designed to secure a minimum. Moreover, benefit standards are rare. Mainly social pensions tend to have comparatively high benefits, often based on benefit standards. If standards exist, they are often defined as a percentage of a more general standard such as the minimum wage. International organizations rarely refer to or even specify benefit levels, let alone benefit standards—calls for 'universalism' refer mainly to coverage.

How inclusive are national cash transfer regimes (the ensemble of all cash transfer programmes in a country)? National cash transfer regimes are even more diverse than cash transfer programmes. The general picture is that most cash transfer regimes are far from being comprehensive, that is, relevant sections of the population are excluded. Only 16 national social cash transfer profiles, making up 11% of the 148 Southern countries in our data set, are fully inclusive by design, that is, they include all life-cycle categories (children, persons of working age, older persons) and disabled adults, with a maximum inclusion score, or they include 'poor people' with a maximum inclusion score. Such inclusive basic protection can be found in several former Soviet Union member states, such as Armenia and Azerbaijan, in a few Latin American countries, such as Brazil, Chile, and Jamaica, in some East Asian countries and territories, especially South Korea and China, with qualifications also in Hong Kong, and in Mauritius in Africa. Uruguay comes close. A second general finding is that most cash transfer regimes in the global South are highly fragmented, ramifying into categorical programmes, sometimes complemented by poor people programmes.

Looking at continents, we find distinct national inclusiveness profiles (Leisering 2019: 196–99). Even in the group of low-income countries, which all have a weak inclusiveness profile, we find considerable variation (Leisering 2019: 202–04). Poorer countries not only have fewer cash transfer programmes, but these programmes also tend to be less inclusive than in better-off countries.

Varieties of social cash transfer programmes

There is a bewildering variety of cash transfer programmes, even more than in the global North, which has more standardized programmes. In debates, three big models are commonly referred to—CCTs, child grants or family allowances, and 'social' (non-contributory) pensions—but these labels eclipse the diversity of the programme types found in the global South. Many writers focus on CCT and only distinguish CCT and 'non-conditional cash transfers' (e.g. Brooks 2015). National cash transfer regimes, that is, the ensemble of all programmes in a country, are even more variegated.

There are many more than the three common programme types—a maze of entitlements. First, there are at least seven main types rather than three. Out of a total of 275 programmes in the global South (plus seven with missing values), 53 programmes are CCT, 27 are non-conditional family allowances, and 78 are social pensions (plus three mixed programmes that include a social pension; Leisering 2019: 176–77). The four types that come on top of these three types include: transfers related to work or employability (17 programmes; not to be mixed up with public work programmes, which do not provide regular cash payments irrespective of employment); programmes for persons with disabilities (22); programmes for various 'small groups' (21); and cash transfers for 'poor people' (54).

Second, some programmes only address sub-categories of the main target categories. Third, several programmes are hybrid, addressing more than one target group, and these target groups may be treated differently under the same programme. So the broad label of a programme, e.g. 'child benefit', may be misleading, because the programme may have fairly different sub-programmes or programme components. Inclusive rhetoric that highlights a certain target group may be decoupled from the actual range of entitlements. Similarly, under a CCT, some target groups covered by the programme may not be subject to conditions.

Effects of social cash transfers

Most studies give an overall positive evaluation of the effects of cash transfer programmes. Some programmes miss their target: persons who ought to be covered are not covered—called 'exclusion errors' in the literature—while persons outside the designated target population may receive benefits—referred to as 'inclusion errors'. But many programmes work to the benefit of the recipients and of society at large.

First of all, cash transfers may reduce extreme *poverty*. Studies on the effects of social safety nets (which include cash transfers) show that these transfers lifted 36% of households out of extreme poverty (measured by the $1.90/day threshold of extreme poverty), and the poverty gap was reduced on average by 45% (World Bank 2018: 60, referring to a sample of 79 Southern countries; mid-2010s). Relative poverty, defined as the poorest 20% of the welfare distribution, was also reduced to a degree. However, poverty reduction is smaller in poorer countries. In some countries the redistributive effects are diminished by regressive taxation.

Second, cash transfers also have immaterial effects on people's lives—they are not only about resources, but also about the social *recognition* of the poor. Entitlements to benefits indicate that older persons, children and parents, persons with disabilities, and various other social groups are considered worthy of public support. Cash transfers may help them to participate in social life, to become social citizens at least to a degree. Millions of poor persons have turned from objects of charity into individual rights-holders. Studies found that cash transfers enhance the social status of the beneficiaries in their families, in the local economy, and in society (Leisering 2019: 311). For example, beneficiaries are seen as credit-worthy, and the status of older persons is enhanced if they can support their children or grandchildren from their social pension. Cash transfers also help grandmothers in Southern Africa to look after their grandchildren whose parents have died of AIDS. Studies have shown positive effects of cash transfers on school attendance and grades of the children, on economic and political inclusion, on women's empowerment, and on health (for a literature review see ODI 2016, for sub-Saharan Africa see FAO and UNICEF 2016).

Third, social cash transfers may have wider effects on the local and national economy and on social *development*, by enabling the poor to contribute to society. The idea of cash transfers rests on the new notion of the poor as agents rather than victims of economic development. Some programmes provide more than cash. Barrientos (2013: 108f.) distinguishes pure income transfers, income transfers combined with asset accumulation, and integrated poverty reduction programmes. Barrientos argues that the former are only geared to reducing monetary poverty and alleviating consumption deficits of the poor, while the latter two address broader dimensions of poverty and deficits in productive assets. But in discourses by international organizations, pure cash transfers were also advocated on grounds of developmental effects (von Gliszczynski 2015: 34f., 132f.), and studies of cash transfer programmes suggest likewise. Linking poverty and cash transfers to economic growth and development emphasizes a collective utility of cash transfers. In the history of Northern social policy, reference to the collective, mostly economic utility of social security, rather than just doing good to the beneficiaries, was a major driver of social policy expansion.

Conclusion: the individualization of poverty policies

Over the last 25 years, social cash transfers have emerged in most countries of the global South and on agendas of international organizations as a new instrument for combating poverty. The massive expansion of the new instrument across the global South has brought a modicum of welfare and dignity to sizeable sections of Southern populations that had been left behind—persons who had been excluded from even the most basic public provisions. This was a significant, if limited, step toward extending the scope of human rights in the field of social security. Cash has come to be recognized as a useful instrument by most international actors and has even been spreading to humanitarian aid and to support for migrants.

Besides diminishing poverty, the programmes have enhanced the social recognition of the poor, including the view that the poor can contribute to the collective advance of society. Apart from the collective utility of cash transfers, cash also creates a space of autonomy and freedom for the beneficiaries, in contrast to benefits in kind. Hanlon et al. (2010: 10–11) even see cash transfers as a road to self-determination of the poor, challenging development strategies imposed from above by donors and international organizations (similarly, Ferguson 2015).

Bestowing individual entitlements to social security benefits on the poor reflects an *individualization of poverty policies*, which contrasts with earlier approaches to poverty (Figure 25.2): with poor relief without a rights base; with claims under traditional arrangements of charity or patronage, even if these claims may be quasi-rights-based (Simmel 1965: 119–20); with community development and infrastructural policies; and with strategies of economic development that seek

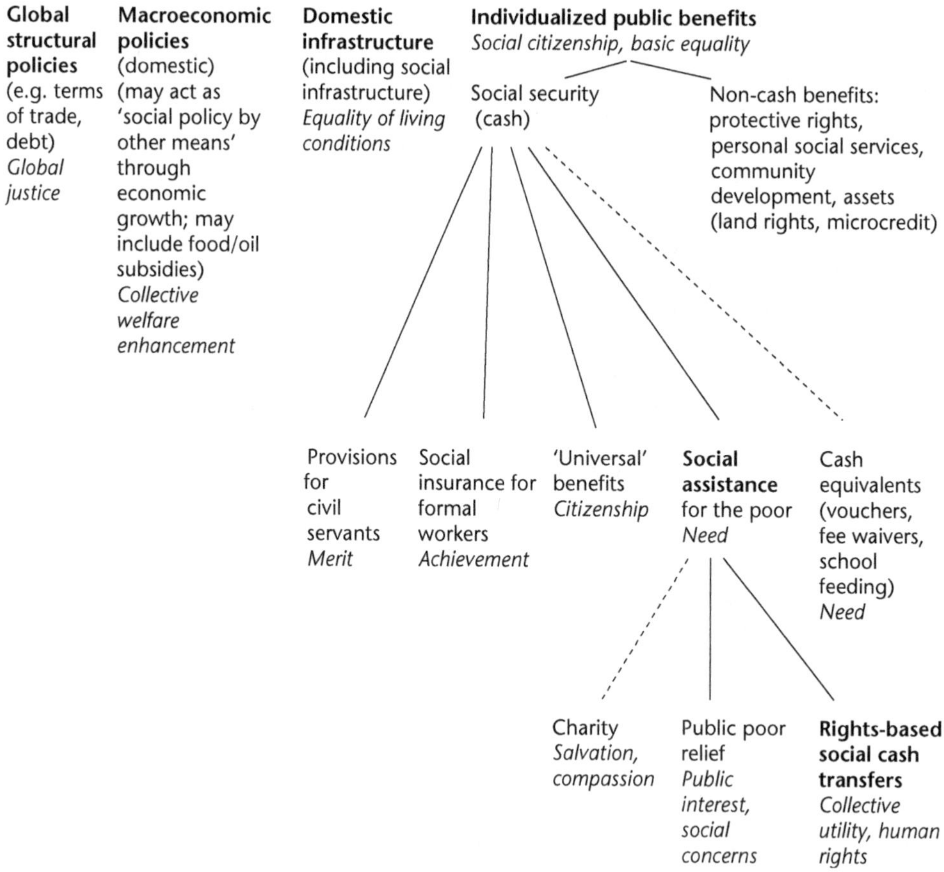

Figure 25.2 Strategies for fighting poverty in the global South.

Note: Italics: normative basis.

Source: the author.

to reduce the collective poverty of countries by macroeconomic policies rather than by individual welfare rights. Means-tested social cash transfers are sometimes criticized for 'targeting' the poor, entailing inclusion and exclusion errors and stigmatization of the poor (e.g. Kidd 2015). But our analysis suggests that targeting is just an aspect of the more fundamental process of individualizing poverty policies, which basically means to bestow individual entitlements to (means-tested or non-means-tested) public social security provisions on the poor.

The individualization of poverty policies is predicated on a redefinition, reframing and re-theorizing of poverty: For one, the emphasis has shifted from the collective poverty of states (as measured by GDP) to the poverty of individuals (as measured by person-related indicators, especially the $*x*/day indicator which was introduced in 1990; Berten and Leisering: 154–56). This amounts to an '*individualization of poverty*'. For another, a new conception of individual poverty has emerged since the 1990s. Poor persons are no longer conceived merely as victims of social change or as objects of charity, but as agents who can use public transfers responsibly and who have the potential to contribute to economic growth and development (see the analysis of changing discourses of international organizations by von Gliszczynski 2015: ch. 4.1). This is linked to a new, individualized concept of development (von Gliszczynski 2015: ch. 4.2; Leisering 2019: 255–60). From this point of view, it makes sense to kindle the potential of the poor through individualized public payments of cash. 'Individualization' does not mean that the household contexts are disregarded; rather, bestowing entitlements on individuals may take account of the households in which poor persons live, to identify need, e.g. the absence of labour capacity in a household (Schubert 2018).

Still, cash transfers are limited and may have negative impacts. They only help to alleviate extreme poverty and mostly do not provide a minimum and are not even designed to do so. Many programmes exclude sizeable large and small groups from entitlements and even create new social divisions ensuing from categorical fragmentation. Limitations of policy designs hint at limitations of politics (for the key role of domestic politics see Niño-Zarazúa et al. (2012) and Ulriksen (2012); for the limitations of the consensus on cash transfers among international organizations see von Gliszczynski and Leisering (2016: 339f.)). Regarding the delivery of benefits, cash transfers have become a new playground for clientelism in some places. Moreover, there may be opportunity costs of cash transfers. Hall (2017: 156), for example, raises the question if investments in social infrastructure could be more productive than increasing spending on cash transfers.

What future for social cash transfers? There is ample space for enhancing cash transfers in terms of coverage, generosity, and implementation. But cash transfers remain attached to a poverty agenda. In view of the renewed concern about social inequality, the next step could be to conceive of cash transfers as the bottom tier of a more comprehensive and composite arrangement of social protection programmes that would also address the near-poor and the emerging middle classes.

Notes

1 For other publications by the FLOOR project see www.floorcash.org. The research group FLOOR-B, Bielefeld University, Germany, was funded by the German Research Council (*Deutsche Forschungsgemeinschaft*; principal investigator Lutz Leisering). I am indebted to the research team, especially to Katrin Weible, John Berten, and Tobias Böger for constructing the database FLOORCASH, and to Katrin Weible, Tobias Böger, and Moritz von Gliszczynski for the data analyses on which this chapter is based.

2 FLOORCASH (www.floorcash.org) focuses on the structure of legal entitlements to cash transfers (for first analyses see Böger 2013; Weible 2016). Other comprehensive databases have been created by

Barrientos (2018), as yet unanalysed, by UNU-WIDER (2018; similar to Barrientos), and by Dodlova, Giolbas, and Lay (2018). For various other, less comprehensive databases see Leisering (2019: 151–53). FLOORCASH also includes qualitative data on the discourses of international organizations (for analyses, not reported here, see von Gliszczynski 2015; von Gliszczynski and Leisering 2016; Leisering 2019: chs 4 and 7).

3 For a fourth dimension (institutionalization—how benefits are administered and delivered to the beneficiaries) see Leisering (2019: 158, 165–66).

References

Barrientos, Armando (2013) *Social Assistance in Developing Countries*, Cambridge: Cambridge University Press.

Barrientos, Armando (2018) The Informational Basis of Emerging Social Assistance in Low and Middle-Income Countries, GDI Working Paper 2018-023, Manchester: The University of Manchester.

Berten, John and Lutz Leisering (2017) Social Policy by Numbers: How International Organisations Construct Global Policy Proposals, *International Journal of Social Welfare*, 26(2), 151–67.

Böger, Tobias (2013) Diffusing Social Citizenship at the Margins? The Spread of Social Pensions in the Global South, FLOOR Working Paper No. 28, Bielefeld: Bielefeld University, https://uni-bielefeld.de/soz/floorcash/publications.html (accessed 29 July 2019).

Böger, Tobias and Lutz Leisering (2019) A New Pathway to Universalism? Explaining the Spread of "Social" Pensions in the Global South, 1967–2011, *Journal of International Relations and Development* (forthcoming).

Brooks, Sarah M. (2015) Social Protection for the Poorest: The Adoption of Antipoverty Cash Transfer Programs in the Global South, *Politics & Society*, 43(4), 551–82.

DFID (2005) *Social Transfers and Chronic Poverty: Emerging Evidence and the Challenge Ahead*, DFID practice paper, London: DFID.

Dodlova, Marina, Anna Giolbas, and Jann Lay (2018) Non-Contributory Social Transfer Programs in Developing Countries: A New Dataset and Research Agenda, *Data in Brief*, 16, 51–64.

FAO and UNICEF (2016) *From Evidence to Action: The Story of Cash Transfers and Impact Evaluation in Sub-Saharan Africa*, ed. Benjamin Davis, Sudhanshu Handa, Nicola Hypher, Nicola Winder, Paul C. Winters, and Jennifer Yablonski, Oxford: Oxford University Press.

Ferguson, James (2015) *Give a Man a Fish: Reflections on the New Politics of Distribution*, Durham, NC and London: Duke University Press.

Hall, Anthony (2017) Cash Transfers as Social Investment: The Brazilian Case, in James Midgley, Espen Dahl, and Amy Conley Wright, eds., *Social Investment and Social Welfare: International and Critical Perspectives*, Cheltenham: Edward Elgar, 141–59.

Hanlon, Joseph, Armando Barrientos, and David Hulme (2010) *Just Give Money to the Poor: The Development Revolution from the Global South*, Sterling: Kumarian Press.

ILO (2017) *World Social Protection Report 2017–19: Universal Social Protection to Achieve the Sustainable Development Goals*, Geneva: ILO.

Kidd, Stephen (2015) The Political Economy of "Targeting" of Social Security Schemes, *Pathways' Perspectives on Social Policy in International Development*, Issue No. 19.

Lavinas, Lena (2013) 21st Century Welfare, *New Left Review*, 84, 5–40.

Leisering, Lutz (2019) *The Global Rise of Social Cash Transfers: How States and International Organizations Constructed a New Instrument for Combating Poverty*, Oxford: Oxford University Press.

Leisering, Lutz, Petra Buhr, and Ute Traiser-Diop (2006) *Soziale Grundsicherung in der Weltgesellschaft. Monetäre Mindestsicherungssysteme in den Ländern des Südens und des Nordens. Weltweiter Survey und theoretische Verortung*, Bielefeld: Transcript.

Niño-Zarazúa, Miguel, Armando Barrientos, Samuel Hickey, and David Hulme (2012) Social Protection in Sub-Saharan Africa: Getting the Politics Right, *World Development*, 40(1), 163–76.

ODI (2016) *Cash Transfers: What Does the Evidence Say? A Rigorous Review of Programme Impact and of the Role of Design and Implementation Features*, by Francesca Bastagli, Jessica Hagen-Zanker, Luke Harman, Valentina Barca, Georgina Sturge, and Tanja Schmidt, with Luca Pellerano, London: ODI.

Schubert, Bernd (2018) *Quantitative Assessment of the Social Assistance System in the Kingdom of Eswatini*, Mbabane: UNICEF.

Simmel, Georg (1965) The Poor, *Social Problems*, 13(2), 118–40.

Ulriksen, Marianne S. (2012) Welfare Policy Expansion in Botswana and Mauritius: Explaining the Causes of Different Welfare Regime Paths, *Comparative Political Studies*, 45(12), 1483–509.

UN (2018) *Promoting Inclusion through Social Protection. Report on the World Social Situation 2018*, New York: UN.

UNU-WIDER (2018) Social Assistance, Politics, and Institutions (SAPI) database [online] Helsinki: United Nations University World Institute for Development Economics Research, www.wider.unu.edu/project/sapi-social-assistance-politics-and-institutions-database (accessed 11 March 2019).

van Oorschot, Wim, Femke Roosma, Bart Meuleman, and Tim Reeskens eds. (2017) *The Social Legitimacy of Targeted Welfare: Attitudes to Welfare Deservingness*, Cheltenham: Edward Elgar.

von Gliszczynski, Moritz (2015) *Cash Transfers and Basic Social Protection: Towards a Development Revolution?* Basingstoke: Palgrave Macmillan.

von Gliszczynski, Moritz and Lutz Leisering (2016) Constructing New Global Models of Social Security: How International Organizations Defined the Field of Social Cash Transfers in the 2000s, *Journal of Social Policy*, 45(2), 325–43.

Weible, Katrin (2016) What Social Cash Transfer Programmes Do Not Do in Middle Income Countries: Identifying Entitlement Gaps in Basic Social Protection, in United Nations System Staff College and Hertie School of Governance, eds., *UN Reflection Series 2016: Development Cooperation, Policy Advice and Middle Income Countries*, Berlin: Neopubli, 173–92.

World Bank (2018) *The State of Social Safety Nets 2018*, Washington, DC: World Bank.

26

International migration and poverty

Meltem Yilmaz Sener

Introduction

As mentioned in the World Migration Report 2018, there were about 244 million international migrants in the world in 2015, which was equal to 3.3 percent of the world population (IOM 2018). Therefore, only a very small percentage of the world's population is composed of international migrants; the majority remain in the countries where they were born. However, migration has social, political, and economic impacts that go far beyond what the numbers of migrants may suggest. Contrary to rising negative opinions in many countries, international migration can help to improve people's lives in both origin and destination countries. During a period when many developed country governments are taking extensive measures against international migration, and citizens of those countries are increasingly voting for parties that are against immigration and immigrants, it is becoming more and more important to talk about the benefits of international migration. The current chapter has such a perspective. This essay will mainly present a review of the literature that discusses the relationship between migration and poverty, especially focusing on those approaches that discuss the benefits that international migration can bring to the lives of people in migrant-sending countries.

A review of the literature demonstrates that it is hard to generalize about the relationship between migration and poverty; there are ambivalent relations between the two. However, when we make an overall evaluation, international migration is a process that can bring advancements in living standards for the migrants themselves, their families, and societies. Following Ellis (2003), among others, this chapter looks at the role of migration in improving livelihoods and reducing poverty. For the migrants from developing countries, migration is a central strategy to improve their livelihoods. Migration can bring not only economic benefits, but it can also bring improvements in terms of other human development indicators, such as education and health. It can become a tool for redistribution of wealth within and between countries. As Crush and Frayne (2010) argue, in the debates on migration, poverty, and development, migrant lives and livelihoods should be at the center. However, this does not necessarily mean a neglect of the states' roles. This chapter agrees with the critique by de Haas about perspectives "celebrating migration as self-help development 'from below'" as they "shift the attention away from structural constraints and the vital role of states in shaping favorable conditions for positive development impacts of migration to occur" (2010: 227). Therefore, while talking about the positive potential of migration for migrants' livelihoods, this chapter also points out the crucial roles that states and policy makers can play in helping the migrants benefit more from the migration process.

> The adverse experience of being a migrant is in part created by public stances and policies, both internally and internationally, that result in migration being viewed in negative terms. These are susceptible to reversal by policy changes aimed specifically at protecting migrants' rights and raising their social status.
>
> *(Ellis 2003: 7)*

On the one hand, poverty and vulnerability can be factors behind the migration decision. This chapter looks at those theoretical and empirical studies which discuss in what contexts and under what circumstances poverty and/or vulnerability stirs international migration, or whether international migrants are the ones who are relatively better off compared to the ones who remain in the home countries/non-migrants. On the other hand, the chapter will also focus on the positive roles that migration can play in reducing poverty. In this part, there will be a discussion on the question of whose migration brings the highest benefits for alleviating poverty in the origin countries and whether it is the migration of the highly educated, highly skilled or the lower skilled that makes more difference. Here, we will discuss to what extent the migration of the highly skilled from the developing and underdeveloped countries brings improvements in terms of poverty in their origin countries.

The emigration of highly skilled from the developing countries is often discussed as brain drain in the literature because of the loss of "human capital", referring to the negative impact of this type of migration on the development of the origin country. On the other hand, remittances they send back to the home countries are considered as an important source of income for the ones who are left behind and also a contribution to the home country's economy. However, there is also research which shows that highly skilled migrants remit less than the unskilled, so the negative impact of the brain drain cannot be counterbalanced by higher remittances (Faini 2007; see also Docquier and Rapoport 2012). The chapter will conclude with a discussion on the conditions under which international migration can become a beneficial process for poverty alleviation.

Poverty as a cause of migration

Although currently international migration is mostly discussed with reference to its impacts on the receiving developed countries, the impact of international migration on the development of origin countries of migrants is also a crucial question. A major component of these development discussions is the relationship between migration and poverty. As Skeldon (2002) argues, there is an ambivalent relationship between poverty and migration. Migration can be both a consequence and also a cause of poverty, and also, migration can have varied impacts on poverty in different contexts. Although it is not possible to make easy generalizations about the relationship between the two, we can argue that the relationship between poverty and migration very much depends on the level of development of the country/locality that we are focusing on. Migration is often considered as motivated by the will to escape from poverty. The idea is that there are not enough local opportunities for people to improve their situation, so they move to other places to earn a living for themselves and their families. There are certainly cases in which people move to other areas, for instance, for escaping from famine situations, and for certain countries there is strong evidence that poverty is an important motivator for migration (Kothari 2003; Siddiqui 2003). However, there is also evidence which shows that this is largely restricted to the poorest country contexts; at an international scale, the link between poverty and migration does not necessarily apply. There is research which shows that internal migration is a much more beneficial process for poverty alleviation and inclusion of the excluded than international migration. Deshingkar (2006: 88) argues that this is because: (i) internal migration depends on a broader base and more people benefit from internal remittances, whereas international remittances reach fewer people; (ii) internal migration will most probably increase at a faster rate than international migration; (iii) internal migration, in comparison with international migration, involves poorer people from poorer regions; (iv) internal migration becomes an important driver of growth in many sectors.

There are studies which argue that the poorest are the least likely to migrate internationally (de Haas 2005; Skeldon 2008, 2002, 1997). As Skeldon (2002: 49) suggests, "survival migration of the poorest is likely to be mainly local, or regional at most, and primarily within country." Therefore, especially if we are discussing international migration, the ones who move are usually not the poorest, but the ones who have at least a certain level of access to some resources (McKenzie 2017; Ellis 2003). International migration involves costs especially related, but not limited to, transportation, and it is not the poorest who can afford them.[1] Although migration often increases income and reduces poverty, there are fewer migrants among the poor, and the poor can only travel to those destinations which can bring lower returns (Murrugarra et al. 2011). Migrants usually do not come from the poorest districts (de Haan 1999). This is not to suggest that poverty is not a cause behind international migration. However, as research shows, rather than conditions of absolute poverty, people's perception of themselves as poor compared to the others is a major factor behind international migration. As Stark's (1991) findings about Mexico demonstrate, deprivation plays an important role in migration decisions, and relatively deprived households are much more likely to migrate internationally than better-off households. Stark et al (2009) also demonstrate that there is a correlation between relative poverty and international migration. Similarly, de Haas states:

> Rather than absolute poverty, a certain level of socioeconomic development, combined with relative deprivation in the form of global inequality of development opportunities, seems to be the most important cause of migration. To a large extent this can also explain why leading emigration countries (eg Mexico, Morocco, Turkey, the Philippines) typically do not belong to the group of least developed countries.
>
> *(de Haas 2005: 1271)*

Sabates-Wheeler et al.'s (2008) findings that the poor and the very poor are more likely to migrate internationally than the non-poor in Ghana, and the poor are more likely to migrate than other groups in Egypt, can be explained with reference to the fact that they are looking at subjective poverty. They focus on "people/households who *feel that* they are unable to meet their basic needs requirements" (p. 325). Also, there are usually other factors at work in addition to subjective poverty, which can explain the decision to migrate internationally.

Positive or negative impact of migration on poverty and inequality

Although the main focus of this chapter is the impact of international migration on poverty and inequality in home countries, it is also important to mention those studies that look at the impact on the host countries. Siddiqui (2012) argues that there is insufficient knowledge about the poverty impacts of migration on destination countries. Nevertheless, there is a body of literature which argues that immigration is increasing poverty in the host country. There are a number of studies which use the term "importing poverty" to discuss immigration-related poverty especially in the US (see Camarota 1999; Rector 2006; Martin and Taylor 1998; Martin et al. 2006; Martin 2014). Camarota (1999), for instance, argues that the immigration policy in the US has significantly increased the size of the poor population, and the growth in the immigration-related poverty has been caused by both an increase in the poverty rates of immigrants and high levels of immigration. Rector (2006) relates increased immigration-related poverty to the increase in low-skill immigration to the US. He argues that today's immigrants, on average, have very low skill and education levels if we compare them with non-immigrants, and they impose high costs on taxpayers as they consume high levels of government services. For this reason, he argues that "US immigration policy should encourage high-skill immigration and strictly limit low-skill immigration" (Rector 2006: 29). Martin et al. (2006) look at the rising Mexico–United States migration, and they argue that it has a big impact on the new rural poverty. Martin (2014) also argues that the current business-labor model in the US only attracts poor and uneducated immigrants, who are then caught in a vicious circle of poverty and welfare dependency. These studies approach immigration mostly from an economic point of view and discuss under what conditions immigration can be beneficial for the US, without focusing on immigrants' experiences or perceptions about their situation in the host country[2] or the positive impact of the migration of the unskilled workers for poverty alleviation in their home countries. As McKenzie (2017: 13) argues, "poverty falls more when migration policies provide more options for unskilled migrants to migrate." There are also studies that look at the relationship between immigration and poverty in different European contexts: Vargas-Silva et al. (2016) look at the impact of international migration on poverty in the UK. De Bustillo and Anton (2011) demonstrate that both moderate and severe poverty are more acute among immigrants than nationals in Spain. Lelkes (2007) argue that migrants from outside the EU usually have higher poverty rates than the indigenous populations. She states that, in Belgium, over half of those who have non-EU citizenship live in poverty, and the figure reaches 45% in France and Luxembourg.

In particular, the literature on the migration–development nexus discusses the implications of migration for poverty alleviation especially in the home country (Nyberg-Sørensen 2012; Murrugarra et al. 2011; Faist et al. 2011; Mazzucato 2011; de Haas 2010; Piper 2009; Faist 2008; Davies 2007; Nyberg-Sørensen et al. 2002; Olwig and Sørensen 2003; Gundel 2002; Sriskandarajah 2002; Jazayery 2002). As de Haas (2010) argues, in the debates on the migration–development nexus, there are migration optimists and pessimists. Optimists think that migrants play a positive role in the development efforts of their countries in several ways. The remittances that they send back to their countries of origin stimulate economic growth. Remittances improve income distribution and quality of life (Keely and Tran 1989: 500). Return migrants are considered as important agents of innovation. They are expected to bring back not only money or other material resources, but also knowledge and new ideas. Therefore, both during their period of migration and also after their return, the migrants play positive roles in the development of their countries, according to optimists.

On the other side, according to pessimistic views, migration increases inter-regional and international disparities in developmental levels. Migration provides individuals an escape from misery that is caused by capitalist relations, but cannot change those structural conditions which, in fact, lead to migration. Therefore, migration worsens the problems of underdevelopment and inequality in the developing countries. Sunam and McCarthy (2016), using the case of rural Nepal, argue that international migration leads to commodification of land, and while it offers an escape from poverty for some people, it brings processes of deeper impoverishment for others. Pessimistic perspectives also emphasize the negative consequences of brain drain. The emigration of educated people from the developing countries leaves those countries deprived of the human skills of which they are very much in need (Papademetriou 1985). As mentioned before, although the development contribution of remittances sent by migrants is recognized, there are also concerns that remittances only fuel consumption, but are not used for productive purposes in the origin countries. Therefore, according to this perspective, "migration undermines regional and local economies by depriving communities of their most valuable labor force, increasing dependence on core countries . . . and stimulating further out-migration" (de Haas 2010: 234).

As Skeldon (2002) argues, migrants are usually a selected group from a population; they are usually the most dynamic and innovative members of their community. When these dynamic and innovative members of the society/community leave, it may lead to a brain drain, which can have broader consequences in terms of the extension of poverty. However, it is really difficult to prove empirically that there is a negative economic impact when the educated members leave the country. This is not only because of the difficulty of measuring the extent of the economic loss because of the departure of the educated; there is also a lot of return migration, which arguably leads to *brain gain*, rather than a brain drain in these countries. Nevertheless, many of the arguments stated here are, in fact, context-dependent. If there are relatively smaller numbers of educated people in a country, their loss can lead to a decline in growth rates and an increase in poverty, which is the situation for the countries in sub-Saharan Africa. As Katseli et al. (2006: 19) argue, the regions with high rates of brain drain are Central America and the Caribbean Islands, Southwest Asia, parts of Indochina, East Europe and the Balkans, but above all, sub-Saharan Africa. As they state, for sub-Saharan Africa, almost the entire region has high rates of brain drain.

As mentioned before, especially the international migration of the highly educated members of a developing country to a developed one is considered as brain drain (Docquier and Rapoport 2012; Docquier et al. 2007; Beine et al. 2001, 2008; Stark 2004; Adams 2003; Cervantes and Guellec 2002; Stark et al. 1997; Mountford 1997; Carrington and Detragiache 1999). Here, the idea is that the developing country loses the highly needed human capital when these skilled people leave the country to put their skills and experiences into use in the developed country context. Many developing countries put into implementation programs and policies to attract these highly educated and highly skilled migrants back to their countries of origin with the belief that they can contribute to the development efforts in these countries. However, even after the implementation of these programs and policies, it is still worth asking whether there is really something for those migrants to return to in their countries of origin. Moreover, it is another crucial question worth answering whether the ones who actually return can find the environment in which they can make a meaningful contribution to the development efforts of their countries of origin.

Although there are a lot of discussions on the negative impact of international migration in terms of poverty in the developing country contexts, there is more evidence which suggests the opposite: Migration can, in many cases, lead to positive outcomes in terms of improving the situation of the migrant households in the developing countries. Through migration, not only people, but also goods and money flow back and forth between the origin and destination countries. Migration can broaden the resource base of a household (Skeldon 2002). There are empirical findings about a variety of countries which show the positive impact of international migration on poverty: According to the research by Lokshin et al. (2010), one fifth of the poverty reduction in Nepal which took place between 1995 and 2004 was related to higher levels of work-related migration and remittances. They also demonstrate that the increase in international work-related migration has been the leading factor in this poverty reduction. Bertoli and Marchetta's (2014) empirical analysis shows that the Ecuadorian migration decreased poverty among migrant households by an estimated 17.4–20.8%. Nguyen et al. (2011) demonstrate that both work migration and non-work migration have a positive effect on per-capita expenditures of migrant-sending households. They also show that both non-work and work migration decrease poverty, although the impact of work migration on poverty is smaller. Finally, a World Bank publication that includes case studies from Albania, Nepal, Nicaragua, and Tanzania shows "how migration expands the choices available to poor people and how it can contribute significantly to alleviating poverty" (Murrugarra et al. 2011).

Especially when migration is circular in nature, with return migration taking place after a period of time, it usually provides more support for the migrants' communities of origin, whereas extended periods of stay in the host country can leave the communities left behind in dire circumstances. However, even in the cases of long-term stay, migrants can have regular contacts with their countries of origin. They not only frequently visit the countries of origin, but also send money and goods to their families or relatives. For this reason, the subject of remittances has a central importance in the discussions on migration and poverty.

Remittances

Remittances are one of the most important features of migration, especially for the origin countries. It is generally argued that the remittances sent by international migrants to their home countries have a significant impact on the living standards of people in the developing countries (de Haas 2005). There are also studies which show that "migration and remittances tend to have an overall positive impact on origin countries' long-run economic performance" (Rapoport and Docquier 2005: 75). Although the amount and extent of remittances is really hard to measure, currently there are some estimates of remittances by international migrants. As Adams and Page (2003: 2) emphasize, the amount of international remittances to developing countries is around $US80 billion per year, which is higher than the amount of total official aid to the developing countries. However, it is important to emphasize that these estimates depend on the remittances sent through official channels; there are also goods and money sent through unofficial channels, which these estimates cannot really capture (de Haan 1999). However, regardless of the differences between what is estimated and what actually is transferred, the issue of remittances has been a crucial factor in the discussions on development and poverty alleviation. Remittances have historically functioned as a very important source of income for many developing countries. There is research which argues that international migration and remittances significantly reduce the level, depth, and severity of poverty in developing countries:

> After instrumenting for the possible endogeneity of international migration, and controlling for various factors, results suggest that on average, a 10% increase in the share of international migrants in a country's population will lead to a 2.1% decline in the share of people living on less than 1 USD per person per day.
>
> *(Adams and Page 2005: 1645)*

It is important to stress here that these studies approach international migrants as a homogeneous group, not making distinctions between migrants from different classes and with different educational credentials. The emigration of the people with high educational credentials will certainly have negative implications in terms of the growth potential of the developing country.

Moreover, it is not easy to measure the impact of this kind of brain drain on poverty levels. There are also important debates on which group provides more regular and higher amounts of remittances to their countries/communities of origin. According to one position, skilled migrants can remit more because of their higher earning potential. However, there is also research which suggests that skilled migrants remit less and less frequently compared to the other groups of migrants (Niimi et al. 2010; Faini 2007).

A second important subject with regard to the remittances is the kind of use to which they can be put in the developing country contexts. It makes a crucial difference whether remittances are used for conspicuous consumption or whether they are used as an investment, or in ways which can have more productive potential. According to Lipton (1980), for instance, more than 90% of remittances is spent on everyday consumption; the remittance money is spent especially to reinforce status in the forms of construction of luxurious houses, high payments for feasts, or household items. Unproductive use of remittances for consumption purposes is argued to weaken local economies and increase dependency. However, there is also research which shows the positive impact of remittances. For instance, for rural Mexico, Taylor and Wyatt (1996) show that remittances are distributed almost evenly across income groups and have an equalizing impact in terms of economic inequality. Pant (2008) argues that remittances create the most direct, immediate, and far-reaching benefits to the migrants and their countries. He discusses the positive macro impact of remittances: "Whether remittances are utilized for consumption or for purchasing houses, or other investments, they produce positive impact on the economy by stimulating demand for other goods and services" (Pant 2008: 4).

Of particular importance is the question of whether remittances can help to alleviate poverty and decrease inequality. Pant (2008) argues that remittances have a significant impact on poverty reduction, as the recipients of remittances are often low-income families. Rapoport and Docquier (2005) demonstrate that the household members who are left behind use remittances for a variety of purposes, such as paying back loans received for financing migration or education, for insurance or other strategic motives. Adams and Page (2005), by using household surveys of 71 developing countries, show that both international migration and remittances have a strong, statistically significant impact on reducing poverty in developing countries.

However, there is evidence which suggests that while migration can decrease poverty, it can have a worsening impact on inequality. As discussed at the beginning, migrants are usually the better-off, not the poorest members of their communities. After international migration, when migrants support their own families and relatives in the form of remittances, it increases the already existing inequalities within those communities. "Because migrants tend to be the already employed, more entrepreneurial, open-minded, and relatively better-educated people, remittances and other benefits of migration would also disproportionately accrue to the already better-off" (de Haas 2010: 236). If only a limited number of people who have wealthier backgrounds migrate, it will serve to worsen inequalities (Cattaneo 2009). Moreover, as Skeldon (2002) argues, it can increase the sense of relative deprivation for the non-migrant families. However, as Cattaneo argues, there may also be spillover effects from migrant to non-migrant families. The remittance that the migrants send back to their countries can have impacts on the economy through an increase in consumption, which may also indirectly benefit the non-migrant households (Cattaneo 2009: 1182). Therefore, in spite of these multifaceted findings, we can still argue that migrants not only generate opportunities for themselves, but also help to generate wealth and employment for the other locals.

The empirical research that has appeared during the last three decades shows that the developmental effects of migration are largely heterogeneous. However, they also demonstrate that, if there are favorable economic and political conditions, migration can play a very important positive role in the development of countries. De Haas (2010: 240), for instance, argues that in countries such as Spain, Italy, Malaysia, and South Korea, migrants have played an important role in the development of their countries through remittances, investments, entrepreneurship, and contributions to public debates. As Rapoport and Docquier (2005: 76) discuss, to increase the amount of remittances, some countries have designed financial incentives, like the accounts in foreign currency in India, Sri Lanka, and Pakistan, and bonus on the official exchange rate in Egypt and Turkey. Also, several countries have implemented special programs for channeling remittances into productive uses, suchc as free managerial training for potential entrepreneurs in the cases of Korea and Sri Lanka, and reduced tariffs on imported equipment goods in Pakistan. To point out states' and policy makers' proper role in helping the migrants to benefit more from the remittance and the migration process, we will finish this section with a quote from Durand et al. (1996: 261), which we will further elaborate on in the conclusion:

> As they elevate a family's standard of living, contribute to business formation, and lead to community improvements, [remittances] represent a tangible accomplishment [. . .]. The way for policy makers to encourage productive investment is not to harangue migrants about their excessive consumption or to attempt to change their micro-level behavior. Rather, the best way is to pursue macroeconomic policies that yield a stable and propitious investment climate and to make expenditures on infrastructures [so as to] . . . make investments an attractive, profitable proposition.

Conclusion

As the above review demonstrates, it is hard to talk about a simple relationship between migration and poverty. Depending on the context, and also on factors like level of development or poverty, we have different findings about how poverty affects migration, or vice versa. Considering these multiple factors, we can still talk about some general findings. First, there is empirical research which shows that internal migration can be a more beneficial process for poverty alleviation and inclusion of the excluded than international migration. Therefore, international migration should be debated considering also the possibility of internal migration. Second, when we reflect on the question of whether the poor migrate, we see that the ones who migrate are not those who live in conditions of absolute poverty, but rather the ones who are relatively deprived. It is due to the fact that especially international migration requires at least a certain level of resources. Hence, this suggests that international migration does not directly function for the benefit of those who live in absolute poverty, but can be useful for the ones who feel deprived compared to the other groups in their societies.

Third, the impact of migration on poverty is multifaceted. On the one hand, migrants can play positive roles in development and poverty alleviation efforts of their countries of origin. The remittances that they send back to their countries of origin can improve the living standards of the ones who remain behind. If they decide to return, return migrants can become important agents of innovation. They can bring back material resources, knowledge, and new ideas, all of which can serve to increase the quality of life in those countries. On the other hand, migration can increase international inequalities in terms of development. It can worsen the problems of underdevelopment and inequality in the developing countries. Migration of individuals or households can improve their own living standards or that of their immediate communities, but cannot change the structural conditions that actually lead to migration. Not only skilled migrants, but many migrants in general are the more dynamic and educated members of their societies. Their emigration leaves those countries deprived of the human skills that they require.

To what extent migration leads to brain drain, or to what extent it is counterbalanced by brain gain are context-dependent questions. For regions that have both high rates of poverty and also high rates of brain drain, such as sub-Saharan Africa, the negative impact of emigration in terms of both development and poverty alleviation is obvious.

Finally, the findings about remittances suggest that they have a significant positive impact on the living standards of people in the developing countries. There is also research which demonstrates that remittances significantly reduce the level, depth, and severity of poverty in developing countries. However, there is evidence that while remittances decrease poverty, they lead to an increase in inequality. When migrants support their own families and relatives by sending remittances, it increases the already existing inequalities within their communities. It can intensify the sense of relative deprivation for non-migrant families. However, there may also be spillover effects from migrant to non-migrant families. Remittances can have impacts on the economy through an increase in consumption, which may also indirectly be useful for non-migrant households.

There is a lot of research which shows that a major proportion of remittances is used for consumption, rather than productive or investment purposes. This has been an issue that has been largely criticized both in the literature and also by policy makers. However, as stated in the quote from Durand et al. (1996: 261), as long as remittances contribute to the improvement of life standards for the migrant families and their communities, we can consider it a significant accomplishment. If policy makers have aims other than these, such as channeling these remittances to more productive activities or investments, what they need to do is to come up with macro economic policies that can create a better investment environment so that making investment become an appealing option for migrant families. As Durand et al. emphasize in the quote above, it is not policy makers' (and hence scholars') job to criticize migrants about their individual/household choices and consumption.

While it is important to talk about the potential contributions of migration to development and poverty alleviation, it is crucial to take into consideration the kind of critique that de Haas (2010) raises when he argues that the intensified debates on the development potential of migration also has an ideological dimension, as it is very much aligned with neoliberal political philosophies. As Kapur (2003) also argues, the current stress on remittances can also be explained with reference to this ideological element, as development or poverty alleviation by remittances fits very well with the notion of self-help: "Immigrants, rather than governments, then become the biggest provider of 'foreign aid'" (Kapur 2003: 10). As de Haan (2011) emphasizes, although migration is very important for the livelihoods of many households, it does not by itself bring structural change. This is a point that is relevant for both the potential of remittances and also migration for poverty alleviation: States and policy makers of both developing and also developed countries still have crucial roles in helping the migrants benefit more from the migration process. Making a case for the positive contribution of migration to poverty alleviation does not suggest replacing the key roles of policy makers by the benefits gained through mobility and money transfers of migrant individuals and families.

Notes

1 There is also research that shows the immobility of the poor in developed country contexts. The research by Fielding (1997) about England and Wales shows that the poor are extremely immobile and the unemployed are only averagely mobile, while the managers, professionals, and the owner-occupiers are highly mobile.

2 For an account of Latina immigrants' narratives on immigration and poverty in the US, see Cleaveland (2013).

References

Adams, Jr., Richard H. "International Migration, Remittances, and the Brain Drain: A Study of 24 Labor-Exporting Countries." World Bank Policy Research Working Paper No. 3069 (June 2003). Available at SSRN: https://ssrn.com/abstract=636431.

Adams, Richard H. and John Page. "Do international migration and remittances reduce poverty in developing countries?" *World Development* 33, no. 10 (2005): 1645–1669.

Beine, Michel, Frédéric Docquier, and Hillel Rapoport. "Brain drain and human capital formation in developing countries: winners and losers." *The Economic Journal* 118 (2008): 631–652. doi:10.1111/j.1468-0297.2008.02135.x.

Beine, Michel, Frédéric Docquier, and Hillel Rapoport. "Brain drain and economic growth: theory and evidence." *Journal of Development Economics* 64, no. 1 (2001): 275–289.

Bertoli, Simone and Francesca Marchetta. "Migration, remittances, and poverty in Ecuador." *The Journal of Development Studies* 50, no. 8 (2014): 1067–1089.

Camarota, Steven A. "Importing Poverty: Immigration's Impact on the Size and Growth of the Poor Population in the United States." Center for Immigration Studies, Paper no. 15 (1999): 1–65.

Carrington, W. J. and E. Detragiache. "How extensive is the brain drain?" *Finance and Development, 36* (1999): 46–49.

Cattaneo, C. "International migration, the brain drain and poverty: a cross-country analysis." *World Economy* 32 (2009): 1180–1202. doi:10.1111/j.1467-9701.2009.01178.x

Cervantes, Mario and Dominique Guellec. "The brain drain: old myths, new realities. (Brain drain)." *OECD Observer* (2002) Academic OneFile, https://link.galegroup.com/apps/doc/A85012950/AONE?u=googlescholar&sid=AONE&xid=b7b7f6a3. Accessed 14 Dec. 2018.

Cleaveland, Carol L. "'I stepped over a dead body': Latina immigrant narratives of immigration and poverty." *Journal of Human Behavior in the Social Environment* 23, no.1 (2013): 1–13.

Crush, Jonathan and Bruce Frayne (eds.) *Surviving on the Move: Migration, Poverty and Development in Southern Africa*, SAMP and DBSA, Cape Town and Midrand (2010).

Davies, Rebecca. "Reconceptualising the migration–development nexus: diasporas, globalisation and the politics of exclusion." *Third World Quarterly* 28, no. 1 (2007): 59–76. doi:10.1080/01436590601081823.

de Bustillo, Rafael M. and Jose-Ignacio Anton. "From Rags to Riches? Immigration and Poverty in Spain." *Population Research and Policy Review* 30 (2011): 661–676.

de Haan, Arjan. "Inclusive growth? Labor migration and poverty in India." *The Indian Journal of Labor Economics* 54, no. 3 (2011): 387–409.

de Haan, Arjan. "Livelihoods and poverty: the role of migration – a critical review of the migration literature." *The Journal of Development Studies* 36, no. 2 (1999): 1–47. doi:10.1080/00220389908422619.

de Haas, Hein. "Migration and development: a theoretical perspective." *International Migration Review* 44 (2010): 227–264. doi:10.1111/j.1747-7379.2009.00804.x.

de Haas, Hein. "International migration, remittances and development: myths and facts." *Third World Quarterly* 26, no. 8 (2005): 1269–1284.

Deshingkar, P. "Internal migration, poverty and development in Asia: including the excluded." *IDS Bulletin*, 37 (2006): 88–100. doi:10.1111/j.1759-5436.2006.tb00272.x

Docquier, Frédéric and Hillel Rapoport. "Globalization, brain drain, and development." *Journal of Economic Literature* 50, no. 3 (2012): 681–730.

Docquier, Frédéric, Olivier Lohest, and Abdeslam Marfouk. "Brain drain in developing countries." *The World Bank Economic Review* 21, no. 2 (2007): 193–218.

Durand, Jorge, William Kandel, Emilio A. Parrado, and Douglas S. Massey. "International migration and development in Mexican communities." *Demography* 33, no. 2 (1996): 249–264.

Ellis, F. "A livelihoods approach to migration and poverty reduction." Paper commissioned by the Department for International Development (DFID) Contract No: CNTR 03 4890 (2003).

Faini, Riccardo. "Remittances and the brain drain: do more skilled migrants remit more?" *World Bank Economic Review* 21, no.2 (2007): 177–191.

Faist, Thomas. "Migrants as transnational development agents: an inquiry into the newest round of the migration–development nexus." *Population, Space and Place* 14 (2008): 21–42.

Faist, Thomas, Margit Fauser, and Peter Kivisto (eds.). *The Migration-Development Nexus: A Transnational Perspective*. London: Routledge (2011).

Fielding, Tony. "Migration and poverty: a longitudinal study of the relationship between migration and social mobility in England and Wales." *IDS Bulletin* 28 (1997): 48–57. doi:10.1111/j.1759-5436.1997.mp28002005.x.

Gundel, J. "The migration–development nexus: Somalia case study." *International Migration* 40, no. 5 (2002): 255–277.

International Organization for Migration. *World Migration Report 2018*. Geneva: IOM (2018).

Jazayery, Leila. "The migration–development nexus: Afghanistan case study." *International Migration* 40 (2002): 231–254. doi:10.1111/1468-2435.00218

Kapur, Devesh. "Remittances: The New Development Mantra?" Paper prepared for the G24 Technical Group Meeting, September 15–16. New York and Geneva: United Nations (2003).

Katseli, Louka T., Robert Lucas and Theodora Xenogiani. *Effects of Migration on Sending Countries: What Do We Know?* Paris: OECD (2006).

Keely, Charles and Bao Nga Tran. "Remittances from labor migration: evaluations, performance, and implications." *International Migration Review* 23, no. 3 (1989): 500–525.

Kothari, Uma. "Staying put and staying poor?" *Journal of International Development* 15, no. 5 (2003): 645–657.

Lelkes, Orsolya. "Poverty among Migrants in Europe." European Center Policy Brief (April 2007).

Lipton, M. "Migration from rural areas of poor countries: the impact on rural productivity and income distribution." *World Development*, 8, no. 1 (1980): 1–24.

Lokshin, Michael, Mikhail Bontch-Osmolovski, and Elena Glinskaya. "Work-related migration and poverty reduction in Nepal." *Review of Development Economics* 14, no. 2 (2010): 323–332.

Martin, Philip. *Importing Poverty? Immigration and the Changing Face of Rural America*. New Haven, CT: Yale University Press (2014).

Martin, Philip and J. Edward Taylor. "Poverty amid prosperity: farm employment, immigration, and poverty in California." *American Journal of Agricultural Economics* 80, no. 5 (1998): 1008–1014.

Martin, Philip, Michael Fix, and J. Edward Taylor. *The New Rural Poverty: Agriculture and Immigration in California*. Washington, DC: Urban Institute Press (2006).

Mazzucato, Valentina. "Reverse remittances in the migration–development nexus: two-way flows between Ghana and the Netherlands." *Population, Space and Place* 17 (2011): 454–468. doi:10.1002/psp.646

McKenzie, David. "Poverty, inequality, and international migration: insights from ten years of migration and development conferences." *Revue D'Economie Du Developpement* 25, no. 3–4 (2017): 13–28.

Mountford, Andrew. "Can a brain drain be good for growth in the source economy?" *Journal of Development Economics* 53, no. 2 (1997): 287–303.

Murrugarra, Edmundo, Jennica Larrison, and Marcin Sasin. *Migration and Poverty: Toward Better Opportunities for the Poor*. Directions in Development; Poverty. World Bank (2011).

Nguyen, Cuong Viet, Marrit van den Berg, and Robert Lensink. "The impact of work and non-work migration on household welfare, poverty, and inequality." *Economics of Transition and Institutional Change* 19, no. 4 (2011): 771–799.

Niimi, Yoko, Cağlar Ozden, and Maurice Schiff. "Remittances and the brain drain: skilled migrants do remit less." *Annals of Economics and Statistics* No. 97/98 (January/June 2010): 123–141.

Nyberg-Sørensen, Ninna. "Revisiting the migration–development nexus: from social networks and remittances to markets for migration control." *International Migration* 50 (2012): 61–76. doi:10.1111/j.1468-2435.2012.00753.x.

Nyberg–Sørensen, Ninna, Nicholas van Hear, and Poul Engberg-Pedersen. "The migration–development nexus: evidence and policy options." *International Migration* 40 (2002): 49–73. doi:10.1111/1468-2435.00211.

Olwig, K. F. and N. N. Sørensen. *Work and Migration: Life and Livelihoods in a Globalizing World*. Oxon: Routledge (2003).

Pant, Bhubanesh. "Mobilizing remittances for productive use: a policy oriented approach." *NRB Working Paper no. 4* (2008): 1–13.

Papademetriou, Demetrios. "Illusions and reality in international migration: migration and development in post World War II Greece." *International Migration* XXIII, no. 2 (1985): 211–223.

Piper, Nicola. "The complex interconnections of the migration–development nexus: a social perspective." *Population, Space and Place* 15 (2009): 93–101.

Rapoport, Hillel and Frédéric Docquier. "The economics of migrants' remittances." Discussion Paper No. 1531 (2005). Bonn: Institute for the Study of Labor (IZA).

Rector, Robert. *Importing Poverty: Immigration and Poverty in the United States*. Heritage Special Report: Heritage Foundation (2006): 1–29.

Sabates-Wheeler, Rachel, Ricardo Sabates, and Adriana Castaldo Source. "Tackling poverty-migration linkages: evidence from Ghana and Egypt." *Social Indicators Research* 87, no. 2 (June 2008): 307–328.

Siddiqui, Tasneem. "Impact of Migration on Poverty and Development." Migrating Out of Poverty Research Program Consortium, Working Paper 2 (September 2012): 1–44.
Siddiqui, Tasneem. "Migration as a Livelihood Strategy of the Poor: the Bangladesh Case." Sussex: Development Research Centre on Migration, Globalisation and Poverty, Sussex University. Working Paper Series WP-C1 (2003).
Skeldon, Ronald. "International migration as a tool in development policy: a passing phase?" *Population and Development Review* 34, no. 1 (2008): 1–18.
Skeldon, Ronald. "Migration and poverty." *Asia–Pacific Population Journal* 17, no. 4 (2002): 67–82.
Skeldon, Ronald. *Migration and Development: A Global Perspective*. Harlow: Longman (1997).
Sriskandarajah, Dhananjayan. "The migration–development nexus: Sri Lanka case study." *International Migration* 40 (2002): 283–307. doi:10.1111/1468-2435.00220.
Stark, Oded. "Rethinking the brain drain." *World Development* 32, no. 1 (2004): 15–22.
Stark, Oded. *The Migration of Labour*. Cambridge, MA: Harvard University Press (1991).
Stark, Oded, Maja Micevska, and Jerzy Mycielski. "Relative poverty as a determinant of migration: evidence from Poland." *Economic Letters* 103, no. 3 (2009): 119–122.
Stark, Oded, Christian helmenstein, and alexia prskawetz. "a Brain Gain with a Brain Drain." *Economics Letters* 55, no. 2 (1997): 227–234.
Sunam, Ramesh K. and John F. McCarthy. "Reconsidering the links between poverty, international labor migration, and agrarian change: critical insights from Nepal." *The Journal of Peasant Studies* 43, no. 1 (2016): 39–63.
Taylor, Edward and T.J. Wyatt. "The shadow value of migrant remittances, income and inequality in a household-farm economy." *Journal of Development Studies* 32, no. 6 (1996): 899–912.
Vargas-Silva, Carlos, Yvonni Markaki, and Madeleine Sumption. "The impacts of international migration on poverty in the UK." Joseph Rowntree Foundation (July 2016): 1–38.

27

Neoliberalism and poverty

An unbreakable relationship

Guy Feldman

Introduction

Popular understandings of why people are poor and how poverty should be addressed reflect the broader political-economic dynamics and relations that prevail at a particular historical moment. Critical poverty scholars have argued that the dominant dynamics and relations in recent decades are best defined as *neoliberal* (Garrett 2013). Twenty or 30 years ago, the term "neoliberalism" had been barely used in academic and political debates. Today, however, it has become an ascendant phrase that is used in a variety of fields, from academia and art to popular media and politics. According to Google Scholar, only 111 articles and books were published in 1990 with the word "neoliberalism" mentioned in them, compared to 24,800 articles and books in 2017. The term has been so commonly mentioned and deployed that a growing number of scholars and commentators have recently begun to question and even attack it. Some critics question its relevance as a theoretical concept, arguing that it is a generic, catch-all phrase that does not explain much of our current political moment (Chait 2017; Venugopal 2015). Others point out that there is nothing "new" about neoliberalism; it is simply a form of capitalism or, at best, a new stage in the development of capitalism (Ehrenreich 2016). These critics argue that the idea of the unfettered market that legitimates business power is not a new idea. Neoliberalism in this sense is a new concept that intellectuals on the Left use to explain old political-economic forces, relations and problems. A third criticism argues that neoliberalism was perhaps once relevant, but it has become irrelevant because we currently live in a post-neoliberal era or we are at least on the brink of this new era (Jacques 2016; Peters 2018; West 2016). According to this strand of critique, the success of, on the one hand, right-wing populist leaders such as Donald Trump in the U.S. and Viktor Urban in Hungary and, on the other hand, the rise of Left-wing progressive leaders such as Bernie Sanders in the U.S. and Jeremy Corbyn in the U.K. – many of them call for policies that in some ways undermine the neoliberal doctrine – represents a repudiation and even the death of neoliberalism. This means that other concepts need to be developed (e.g., authoritarian nationalism), concepts that better articulate and explain our current political moment.

To be sure, "neoliberalism" is a slippery concept that is not free of flaws. Yet the premise of this chapter is that neoliberalism is still relevant and useful as an analytic concept that can help us understand the relationship between the state, the market and citizens in the current era.

Neoliberalism is particularly vital for understanding how the problem of poverty and people who live in poverty are governed today. Building on this premise, the aim of this chapter is to examine the relationship of neoliberalism to poverty and social welfare policies that affect poor people's opportunities. The chapter will argue that the ascendance of neoliberalism has introduced changes that are continuous with and simultaneously different from past discourses and interventions targeted at the poor. After defining what neoliberalism is, the chapter will highlight three interconnected features of neoliberalism and discuss their implications for poor people and antipoverty policy. These features include: the restructuring of the welfare state (Schram 2015), growing precarity and inequality (Alvaredo et al. 2018), and the fabrication of entrepreneurial subjectivity (Brown 2015). The chapter will conclude by highlighting the kind of poverty politics that could emerge in response to processes of neoliberalization.

What is neoliberalism?

In general, neoliberalism is discussed in the literature as an ideology, an intellectual movement, an economic theory and a political project that has far-reaching implications. The concept was originally developed and articulated by Austrian economist Friedrich Hayek during the 1940s and 1950s, and by economists of the Chicago School led by Milton Friedman from the 1950s onwards (Jones 2014). In particular, Friedrich Hayek's *Road to Serfdom*, published in 1944, proved to be catalytic in the rolling out of neoliberalism as a political-economic regime. Some also situate the origins of neoliberalism in a group of German economists, known as Ordoliberals, who were active from the 1930s to the 1950s (Foucault 2008). Much like 19th-century classical economic liberalism, neoliberalism champions markets and valorizes the pursuit of individual freedom (Gray et al. 2015). Neoliberalism, however, is much more than simply laissez-faire capitalism and the unfettered accumulation of capital, free from state control (Mirowski 2014). David Harvey (2005: 2), in one of the best-known introductions to neoliberalism, maintains that it

> is in the first instance a theory of political economic practices that proposes that human well-being can best be advanced by liberating individual entrepreneurial freedoms and skills within an institutional framework characterized by strong private property rights, free markets and free trade.

Under neoliberalism, then, the economic logic of the market is extended to ever-growing domains of human life previously thought of as nonmarket domains (Brown 2015; Garrett 2013; Schram 2015). Government bureaucracies, non-profit organizations, communities and individuals are reconfigured as economic actors who are expected to compete in order to maximize profit and buttress market operations. As Wendy Brown (2015: 10) aptly notes, in the neoliberal era, "[a]ll conduct is economic conduct; all spheres of existence are measured by economic terms and metrics." The power of the state is used to achieve this goal of the economization of everything (Garrett 2013; Mirowski 2014; Peck 2010). Market rationalities and practices have been imported into the state, which is charged with the task of promoting market expansion and imposing market discipline. In other words, although it is often confused with small government, the neoliberal doctrine does not advocate for the withering or weakening of the state but rather calls for a new mode of state intervention in which the state is deployed to create and preserve market rule (e.g., through policies of deregulation and free trade). In the process, neoliberalism has a highly gendered dimension, privileging male-identified market behavior over female-identified homemaking and caregiving (Gupta 2012).

To be sure, there is a disjuncture between neoliberalism in theory and neoliberalism in practice, on the ground. As Peck and Whiteside (2017: 183) argue, although "it is marked by family resemblances, recurring tropes, and patterned routines," neoliberalism is "variegated, mutating, unevenly developed, shape-shifting, and site-shifting." The reason for this is that neoliberal ideas and reforms usually do not circulate or operate on a bare landscape; they are confronted and influenced by institutional arrangements and political expectations which often pose challenges for a pure neoliberal transformation.

The impact of neoliberalism on the poor

Neoliberalism has shaped and structured poverty in the U.S., the U.K. and elsewhere. Its treatment of poor people is somewhat contradictory. On the one hand, neoliberalism positively conceives of the poor as free agents who have the ability to escape poverty via the market (Katz 2013). In this sense, it rejects pathological theories of poverty and sees the poor as equal to the rest of mainstream society. Since everyone is expected to make market-based decisions that would improve their lives, the poor are logically called out to do the same. On the other hand, neoliberalism constructs the poor, especially women, as deficient and immoral individuals who do not take full responsibility for their own fate. For example, the figure of the welfare queen, which identifies African-American mothers as cheats and delegitimizes welfare use by them, has become a cultural icon of the neoliberal era (Gustafson 2011). As a result, neoliberalism often offers extremely harsh and punitive treatment for poor people (Schram 2015).

The impact of neoliberalism on poor people is expressed in several interrelated features, including the restructuring of the welfare state, growing precarity and inequality, and the fabrication of entrepreneurial subjectivity.

The restructuring of the welfare state

The welfare state in western societies has undergone a major transformation in the neoliberal era (Schram 2015). In the pre-neoliberal era, particularly following the Second World War, the economics of John Maynard Keynes and the policy prescriptions of the Beveridge Report influenced the creation and expansion of the welfare state. In this postwar era, the basic institutions of the welfare state were designed to redistribute income and offer protection to diverse populations (but not all populations) from the insecurities of the market. However, neoliberals, such as Hayek and Friedman, depicted the ideas and policies of Keynes and Beveridge as a serious threat to a free and prosperous society. They argued that the interventionist welfare state, as envisioned by Keynes and Beveridge, harms economic growth, costs too much, breeds passivity and dependence, and threatens individual freedom. While their ideas had not garnered much attention in the years following the Second World War, it was the economic crisis during the first half of the 1970s (especially problems of inflation and stagnation that accompanied it) that provided a fertile ground for neoliberal ideas and reforms, turning them into a dominant force in many western societies (Jones 2014). Eventually, with the help of politicians who were sympathetic to its ideas (e.g., Margaret Thatcher, Ronald Reagan, Bill Clinton and Tony Blair), the neoliberal project rolled back the Keynesian programs that countered the market and, in their place, rolled out programs that were structured to serve the market and impose its logic (Peck 2010). When it comes to addressing poverty, Charles Murray's influential 1984 book *Losing Ground* epitomized the neoliberal approach. Murray, who is both a conservative and a neoliberal, argued that the welfare state does not help the poor; rather, it reinforces and increases poverty because it creates perverse incentives that lead poor people not to work and not to be productive and responsible citizens. In light of such hostile attacks, the welfare state in the neoliberal era has shifted away from an emphasis on income redistribution and providing basic social services to the poor toward one that focuses on facilitating effective market participation by them in order to utilize what is seen as the potential of markets to improve human lives (Katz 2013). In short, neoliberalism has not led to the repeal of social welfare programs targeted at the poor but to their reconfiguration, negating their redistributive and decommodifying functions. As a result, people on the bottom of the socio-economic ladder have been less protected and have many needs that remain unmet (Schram 2015).

At the frontlines of welfare provision, neoliberalism has also transformed the environment in which service providers (social workers in particular) operate. Processes of neoliberalization in general have contributed to the rise of the New Public Management approach, which pressures social service providers to adopt business- and competition-based practices that focus on the measured dimensions of work (Gray et al. 2015). Through privatization, contracting out, outsourcing and benchmarking, market logic has become an organizing principle in the management and delivery of social welfare programs for the poor. Le Grand (2003) famously argued that service providers in the neoliberal era are seen as self-interested (knaves), while service users are regarded as consumers (queens). This has led him to suggest that the provision of welfare services should be based on competition. Adopting a more critical perspective, Dominelli (2002: 46) argued that social service providers "have become highly regulated in a society that espouses deregulation. Managerially imposed procedures have repositioned [them] as technocrats whose capacity to exercise independent judgment is severely curtailed through bureaucratic procedures." In turn, service providers within various welfare settings have intensified their efforts to regulate their clients' behavior so that it aligns more closely with the narrow requirements and procedures of the neoliberal welfare system, especially that they accept responsibility for their poverty and practice market-consistent behavior. In the case of U.S. welfare reform, for example, Soss, Fording and Schram (2011) find that case managers in welfare agencies work in a highly competitive performance system and use sanctions as a disciplinary tool to ensure that clients comply with harsh welfare rules. In the Netherlands, Suvarierol (2015) shows how civic integration programs discipline migrants to become responsible citizens who look and apply for a job. Neoliberalism, therefore, involves an effort to immerse both professionals as well as their low-income clients in market experiences so that they will conduct themselves in ways that serve market actors and interests.

One of the most significant changes in welfare policy, both in North America and Western Europe, has been the move toward a work-based path out of poverty (Brodkin and Marston 2013; Peck 2001). Starting in the 1980s, efforts to address poverty have increasingly focused on one institution – the labor market. Workfare programs, also known as welfare-to-work programs, focus on increasing the participation of low-income families in the labor market, mainly by requiring them to engage in work-related activities as a condition of receiving benefits (Peck 2001). By the end of the 1990s, 14 out of 21 OECD countries had introduced some form of workfare programs (Bradbury 2004). In the U.S., for example, since 1996, people living in poverty are no longer entitled to welfare as a right, as the receipt of benefits is conditioned on work or participation in work-related activities (Edin and Shaefer 2015). In the U.K., from 2011 to 2017, the government rolled out the "Work Programme," which aimed to move the long-term unemployed into the workforce and rescue them from the "cycle of dependency" (Jordan 2018). Thus, while Beveridge suggested that the welfare state should provide social security so that poor people (and other groups) would be protected from the "cradle to the grave," the common consensus among policymakers today is that a key goal of the welfare state is to increase the participation of the poor in the labor market. As John Hutton, who served as the Secretary of State for Work and Pensions in the British Cabinet, explained: "Our approach has been based on the principle that the best welfare policy of all is work" (quoted in Jones 2010). Interestingly, Handler (2004) draws on a large body of evidence on workfare programs to argue that these programs are contradictory – they aim to incorporate low-income clients in the labor market, but they do so in ways that reinforce the exclusion of many clients, in particular those who fail to navigate tough program requirements and, as a result, drop from the program or those who get temporary, low-wage jobs that keep them in poverty. Indeed, the move from welfare to workfare has led to an increase in the number of U.S. families living in "extreme poverty" (Edin and Shaefer 2013). This reflects the duplicity of neoliberalism writ large. While it embraces laissez-faire and promotes the market as an ideal to be championed in all spheres of life, in practice it offers harsh treatment for those at the bottom of the socio-economic order, who do not meet the threshold requirements for being able to be successful market actors. Irrespective of their problematic aspects, the welfare state in countries around the world continues to promote the primacy of work and to limit the provision of welfare benefits. However, given increasing numbers of working poor, there has been some recognition by policymakers that work alone is often not enough to escape poverty (Reich 2015; see also Chapter 19).

The response to the global financial crisis is another example of the changing direction of the welfare state. In order to fix its debt problems and restore its economy to growth, countries such as Ireland implemented an austerity program in 2008 that, among other things, introduced a series of welfare cuts, such as a reduction in Child and Unemployment Benefits, that intensified the hollowing out of the welfare state (Oxfam 2013). Ireland also recapitalized its failed banks, which had carried high levels of debt, by using public funds (e.g., funds that were available through the National Pension Reserve Fund). The cuts had adverse consequences for low-income Irish families with children; according to Fanjul (2014), child poverty in Ireland grew from 18 percent in 2008 to 28.6 percent in 2012. The U.K. has also imposed significant austerity measures in response to the financial crisis. A recent report estimates that spending on welfare benefits for the poor in the U.K. will shrink by £37 billion by 2021 (Butler 2018). By dismantling social safety nets that serve to protect the poor and replacing them with market-based antipoverty interventions, neoliberalism has transformed social welfare programs and what they do.

Growing precarity and inequality

One of the outcomes of the transformation of the welfare state in recent decades has been a general sense of social insecurity and rising inequality. Garrett (2013: 86) claims that one of the main characteristics of neoliberalism "can be associated with the aspiration to inject new forms of insecurity into society." According to Gill and Pratt (2008), the concepts of "precariousness" and "precarity" emblematize neoliberalism, signifying "the multiplication of precarious, unstable, insecure forms of living" (p. 3). Elsewhere, Standing (2011: 1) argues that neoliberalism has created "a global 'precariat', consisting of many millions around the world without an anchor of stability."

The state of precarity has taken place in a growing number of social-economic arenas. One of the main arenas is the labor market. The concept of "precarious employment" is often used by those who are critical of the neoliberal project to describe an ascendant type of employment that is insecure, unprotected and flexible (e.g., temporary positions and fixed-term contracts that come with very few or no benefits) (Olsthoorn 2014). This type of employment has mostly affected workers in low-wage jobs. Among OECD countries, the average rate of temporary employment, which is defined as jobs that have a pre-determined termination date, was roughly

12 percent of all workers in 2017 (Organization for Economic Cooperation and Development 2018). In the U.K., the number of contracts without a minimum number of guaranteed hours ("zero-hours contracts") was 1.8 million in 2017, representing roughly 6 percent of all employment contracts (Office for National Statistics 2018). The development of these new forms of employment has stemmed from the neoliberal idea that they will increase the autonomy of employers and incentivize them to hire more workers. It implies new flexibility that facilitates the flow of workers and expertise according to the changing needs of the market, bypassing the rigid demands of unions and reducing organizational overhead expenditures. This precarious nature of work in the neoliberal era has resulted in a large number of working people in poverty. For example, in 2016, there were around 7.6 million people who the U.S. Bureau of Labor Statistics defined as "working poor," i.e., people who spent at least six months either working or looking for employment but their incomes were still below the poverty line (Desmond 2018).

Relatedly, the neoliberal agenda has contributed to the expansion of social-economic inequalities (Ehrenreich 2016). Neoliberal thinkers, such as Hayek and Friedman, are unconcerned about inequality. They suggest that inequality within societies is not a bad thing because it is necessary for society to prosper (although there is no agreement on the ideal level of inequality) (Mirowski 2014). Regardless of the circumstances, the government should not intervene in order to achieve equality because its actions would only undermine freedom and would not produce more equality. On this, Friedman argued: "A society that puts equality—in the sense of equality of outcome—ahead of freedom will end up with neither equality nor freedom" (Friedman and Friedman 1980: 140). While rejecting equality of outcomes, neoliberals are more sympathetic to the idea of equality of opportunity. Yet, this type of inequality is also something that requires no government intervention because, for neoliberals, only the market can create opportunities.

Perhaps unsurprisingly, an ever-growing body of social science work on inequality has shown that income and wealth inequality around the world has significantly increased in recent decades. The trends that these studies show are troubling and draw attention to the devastating consequences of neoliberal ideas and reforms for those on the bottom of the socio-economic ladder. The World Inequality Report, which was recently published by the world's leading researchers of inequality, shows how in one country after another, the state has orchestrated an uninterrupted transfer of income and wealth from the poor and the middle-class to the upper-class (Alvaredo et al. 2018). The report claims that "[i]n recent decades, income inequality has increased in nearly all countries, but at different speeds" (p. 5). In the U.S. and Canada, for example, the income of the top 10 percent was 47 percent of the total income in these countries in 2016, compared to 34 percent in 1980. In Europe, the income of the top 10 percent was 37 percent of the total income in 2016, compared to 32 percent in 1980. Examining the U.S. and Western Europe together, the report finds that the share of total income of the bottom 50 percent of individuals has *decreased* from 20.5 percent in 1980 to 13.5 percent in 2015. For the top 1 percent, the share of total income has *increased* from 10.5 percent in 1980 to 20 percent in 2015.

At the same time, according to the report, wealth inequality has also increased since the 1980s. In the U.S., the top 1 percent wealth share increased from 22 percent in 1980 to 39 percent in 2014. In the U.K., the rise in wealth inequality was more moderate – the top 1 percent wealth share increased from 19 percent in 1980 to 20 percent in 2014. The authors of the report predict that if recent trends continue without any intervention, inequality around the world will further increase. Elsewhere, Wilkinson and Pickett (2011) find that a host of health and social problems – such as mental illness, low life expectancy, obesity and violence – are more common in countries with greater levels of inequality. In short, policies of deregulation and welfare state reform have produced widening economic precarity and inequality, leading to a great deal of hardship for families with low income.

The fabrication of entrepreneurial subjectivity

Along with the restructuring of the welfare state and growing precarity and inequality, neoliberalism has also changed conceptions of citizenship and what it means to be a "good citizen" in the U.S. and many European countries (Brown 2015). In the postwar period, alongside the economic contributions they were expected to make, citizens also had civic responsibilities and were expected to act collectively to advance the common good (Crenson and Ginsberg 2002). In the current neoliberal era, however, citizens are viewed as nothing other than autonomous market actors who compete against one another and pursue ways to increase their value in the market. Michel Foucault is one of the strongest proponents of this third feature of neoliberalism. Making an important contribution to the literature on neoliberalism, he moves beyond an understanding of neoliberalism as an economic theory and theology promoting market rule and unfettered accumulation of capital. Foucault (2008) conceives of neoliberalism as an "art of government" and a form of political rationality that operates by means of discourses to produce the mentalities and modes of self-discipline required for the continued operation of the neoliberal project. He argues that, in the neoliberal era, the state deploys various techniques in order to fabricate a distinctive political figure conceptualized as an "entrepreneur of himself." He writes:

> In neo-liberalism . . . there is also a theory of homo oeconomicus, but he is not at all a partner of exchange. Homo oeconomicus is an entrepreneur, an entrepreneur of himself . . . the stake in all neoliberal analyses is the replacement every time of homo oeconomicus as partner of exchange with a homo oeconomicus as entrepreneur of himself, being for himself his own capital, being for himself his own producer, being for himself the source of [his] earnings.
>
> *(Foucault 2008: 226)*

For Foucault, neoliberalism is a disciplinary project dedicated to producing, through behavior manipulation, an entrepreneurial subject who invests in himself and takes risks in a future-oriented way. Extending Foucault's work, Brown (2015: 10) claims that the entrepreneurial subject "is an intensely constructed and governed bit of human capital tasked with improving and leveraging its (monetary and nonmonetary) competitive positioning and with enhancing its portfolio value across all of its endeavors and venues." In other words, neoliberalism is a political rationality, constituting people as self-governing and atomized subjects who bear full responsibility for themselves and participate in various entrepreneurial activities in order to enhance their own human capital, which is the primary source of their earnings and satisfaction.

Some of neoliberalism's strong interest in entrepreneurship can be traced back to Austrian economist Joseph Schumpeter (1947), who argued that entrepreneurs are the prime movers of the capitalist economy. He referred to them as "wild spirits" and "fiery souls," suggesting that the creativity and innovation they demonstrate in using current resources and knowledge can lead to new solutions to old problems. Since Schumpeter first made this argument, neoliberalism has turned entrepreneurship to a meta-narrative and elevated the image of the entrepreneur to the level of a social symbol (Marttila 2013). People today, irrespective of their economic circumstances or their position in society, are expected to see themselves and act as Schumpeterian entrepreneurs who leverage existing resources to enhance their value in every domain of life.

The prevalence of an entrepreneurial approach to social relations and human activity has penetrated into contemporary discourses of poverty and shaped social welfare policy. It suggests that the sources of complex social problems such as poverty are attributed to a lack of personal motivation and creativity among the poor. The remedy for poverty, therefore, lies in the sphere of individual, entrepreneurial initiatives. This means that people in poverty are expected to look for an individualized solution to their problems based on their entrepreneurial skills. To be sure, the emphasis on the lack of motivation and creativity among the poor existed in other economic periods. However, neoliberal political rationality promotes the solo entrepreneur as an ideal that needs to be championed and as the only identity that matters for the poor. For example, they are expected to build wealth through "house flipping," an exceedingly popular practice which involves buying a house, renovating it and reselling it for a profit (Feldman and Schram 2018). The entrepreneurial ideal is inextricably connected to the idea of personal responsibility, a neoliberal trope which suggests that the poor are responsible for overcoming their adverse situation. Traditional social welfare benefits and services are seen as opposed to the establishment of an entrepreneurial culture and spirit because they generate "dependency," "passivity" and "laziness." Instead, neoliberalism supports government-based programs that develop an entrepreneurial mindset. As Antony Giddens (1998: 99), who called for a "third way" between capitalism and social democracy, suggested, "[g]overnment has an essential role to play in investing in the human resources and infrastructure needed to develop an entrepreneurial culture." In such a culture, the poor are taught how to be good solo participants in the prevailing mainstream capitalist economy as opposed to effective partners acting collectively.

At the policy level, the valorization of an entrepreneurial culture has led to the rollout and implementation of new policies that cultivate the identity of the entrepreneur among the poor. A prime example is the growing financial inclusion movement that aims to increase low-income families' access to mainstream financial services and institutions (Chibba 2009). An important part of this movement is asset-building, which includes a set of programs designed to address poverty through savings and building wealth (Schreiner and Sherraden 2007). Given the crisis that has engulfed public assistance programs, asset-building has become increasingly prevalent in many parts of the world, including the U.S., the U.K. and Canada. The rationale for asset-building as an antipoverty strategy stems from the idea that people are trapped in poverty because they lack savings and assets which tend to increase in value. Given the central role of savings and assets, asset-building strategies were developed to help the poor save money and accumulate assets for long-term financial stability. Asset-building proponents argue that asset-building and public assistance programs are two distinctive approaches to reducing poverty. While public assistance programs are important, they are not effective in reducing poverty over the long run because they emphasize the maintenance of an income needed to continue consuming at a particular level. In order to move people out of poverty and promote their economic security, welfare policy should incentivize savings and asset accumulation. One of the primary interventions that incentivize the poor to save and accumulate assets is Individual Development Accounts (IDAs), which is a matched savings program where participants receive match money for every dollar they save. The savings accrued can be used only for asset-based goals that develop the family, including purchasing a home, acquiring post-secondary education or professional training, or opening a small business. Asset-building suggests that the solution to poverty requires low-income families to take on the identity of the entrepreneur, learning how to become savvy market actors who recognize the opportunities available for them in the market and seize upon them. These opportunities, in turn, would yield high returns and produce better future economic outcomes. For example, findings show that clients in IDAs in the U.S. are expected to demonstrate their entrepreneurial spirit by finding creative ways to save money out of their meager incomes, while making smart investments in the housing market or developing innovative products or goods that they can sell as small business owners (Feldman and Schram 2018). In short, asset-building policies participate in the work of remaking the poor in the image of the entrepreneur, who one way or another acquires wealth so as to become an effective market actor. The microfinance movement serves as another example of how contemporary antipoverty programs cultivate the identity of the entrepreneur among the poor. Microfinance focuses on lending poor women in the Global South money to start their own businesses. When they pay back the loan, organizations cycle the money to other borrowers. Microfinance elevates the entrepreneurial subjectivity above other subjectivities which are rooted in solidarity and collectivism (Brigg 2001).

Conclusion: neoliberalism in crisis?

Addressing the question whether neoliberalism is dead or alive today, Jamie Peck, among the most influential writers on neoliberalism today, argued: "It's both . . . it exists in a kind of an undead state" (Peck 2017). This seems like an accurate assessment of the current state of neoliberalism and its impact on the poor. On the one hand, neoliberalism has proven to be sticky, continuing to demonize the poor and blame them for their own poverty, while rolling back certain parts of the welfare state. On the other hand, neoliberalism's harsh treatment of the poor is being contested almost every day. The election of very progressive candidates for political office, especially women and people of color whose radical agenda runs counter to neoliberalism, is just one example. The French Yellow Vests movement, protesting against economic hardship caused by neoliberal policies, is another recent example. Yet a radical and transformative change does not happen overnight and neoliberalism remains ascendant these days.

What kind of poverty politics are needed to continue to scale back the harsh impact of neoliberalism on economically marginalized populations? It is perhaps first useful to think of neoliberalism in *relational* terms, i.e., as social-economic relations between the poor and powerful actors (e.g., employers, landlords or urban renewal authorities) that reproduce and sustain poverty and impoverishment. Conceiving of neoliberalism as a social relationship draws inspiration from the field of relational poverty studies, which was recently created by a group of critical geographers who were concerned about the overemphasis on individualistic and economistic conceptions of poverty (Lawson and Elwood 2018). If neoliberalism is to be understood as a relationship, then confronting it requires people (poor and nonpoor) to carry out activities that disrupt poor people's everyday interactions with those who dominate and exercise power over them. For example, the reproduction of material exploitation in a local community can be disrupted by pressuring employers to reduce their reliance on outsourcing, which involves the transfer of employees (who carry out activities for the employer) to for-profit or non-profit organizations. Or the exploitation that often prevails in the relationship between low-income tenants and their landlords can be interrupted by resisting evictions and pressuring municipalities to revoke the rental license of landlords who rent sub-standard houses. Given the key role that the state plays in normalizing neoliberal relations, resisting neoliberalism also requires targeting the state and pressuring it to create new policies and rules that introduce and institutionalize change in the existing neoliberal order. The Yellow Vests movement in France, including the concessions that it demanded from the government, provides a good example. These are some of the ways to resist neoliberalism's harsh treatment of the poor and to pave the road to the enhancement of forms of social protection that adequately address the risks and problems they face.

References

Alvaredo, Facundo, Lucas Chancel, Thomas Piketty, Emmanuel Saez, and Gabriel Zucman. 2018. *World Inequality Report*. Paris: World Inequality Lab.

Bradbury, Bruce. 2004. "Targeting Social Assistance." *Fiscal Studies 25*(3): 305–324.

Brigg, Morgan. 2001. "Empowering NGOs: The Microcredit Movement through Foucault's Notion of Dispositif." *Alternatives: Global, Local, Political 26*(3): 233–258.
Brodkin, Evelyn Z., and Gregory Marston (eds). 2013. *Work and the Welfare State: Street-Level Organizations and Workfare Politics.* Washington, DC: Georgetown University Press.
Brown, Wendy. 2015. *Undoing the Demos: Neoliberalism's Stealth Revolution.* New York: Zone Books.
Butler, Patrick. 2018. "Welfare Spending for UK's Poorest Shrinks by £37bn." *The Guardian*, [online] September 23. Available at: www.theguardian.com/politics/2018/sep/23/welfare-spending-uk-poorest-austerity-frank-field
Chait, Jonathan. 2017. "How 'Neoliberalism' Became the Left's Favorite Insult of Liberals." *New York Magazine*, [online] July 16. Available at: http://nymag.com/intelligencer/2017/07/how-neoliberalism-became-the-lefts-favorite-insult.html
Chibba, Michael. 2009. "Financial Inclusion, Poverty Reduction and the Millennium Development Goals." *The European Journal of Development Research 21*(2): 213–230.
Crenson, Matthew A., and Benjamin Ginsberg. 2002. *Downsizing Democracy: How Americans Sidelined Its Citizens and Privatized Its Public.* Baltimore, MD: Johns Hopkins University.
Desmond, Matthew. 2018. "Americans Want to Believe Jobs Are the Solution to Poverty. They're Not." *New York Times*, [online] September 11. Available at: www.nytimes.com/2018/09/11/magazine/americans-jobs-poverty-homeless.html
Dominelli, Lena. 2002. *Feminist Social Work Theory and Practice.* Basingstoke, UK: Palgrave Macmillan.
Edin, Kathryn J., and H. Luke Shaefer. 2015. *$2.00 a Day: Living on Almost Nothing in America.* Boston, MA: Houghton Mifflin Harcourt.
Ehrenreich, John. 2016. *Third Wave Capitalism: How Money, Power, and the Pursuit of Self-Interest Have Imperiled the American Dream.* Ithaca, NY: Cornell University Press.
Fanjul, Gonzalo. 2014. *Children of the Recession: The Impact of the Economic Crisis on Child Well-Being in Rich Countries.* Florence: Unicef.
Feldman, Guy, and Sanford F. Schram. 2018. "Entrepreneurs of Themselves: How Poor Women Enact Asset-Building Discourse." *Journal of Social Policy.* doi.org/10.1017/S0047279418000764
Foucault, Michel. 2008. *The Birth of Biopolitics: Lectures at the Collège de France, 1978–1979 (Lectures at the College de France).* New York: Palgrave Macmillan.
Friedman, Milton, and Rose Friedman. 1980. *Free to Choose: A Personal Statement.* New York: Houghton Mifflin Harcourt.
Garrett, Paul Michael. 2013. *Social Work and Social Theory: Making Connections.* Bristol, UK: Policy Press.
Giddens, Anthony. 1998. *The Third Way: The Renewal of Social Democracy.* Cambridge, UK: Polity Press.
Gill, Rosalind, and Andy C. Pratt. 2008. "In the Social Factory? Immaterial Labour, Precariousness and Cultural Work." *Theory, Culture & Society 25*(7–8): 1–30.
Gray, Mel, Mitchell Dean, Kylie Agllias, Amanda Howard, and Leanne Schubert. 2015. "Perspectives on Neoliberalism for Human Service Professionals." *Social Service Review 89*(2): 368–392.
Gupta, Rahila. 2012. "Has Neoliberalism Knocked Feminism Sideways?" *50.50 Inclusive Democracy*, [online] January 4. Available at: www.opendemocracy.net/5050/rahila-gupta/has-neoliberalism-knocked-feminism-sideways
Gustafson, Kaaryn S. 2011. *Cheating Welfare: Public Assistance and the Criminalization of Poverty.* New York: NYU Press.
Handler, Joel F. 2004. *Social Citizenship and Workfare in the United States and Western Europe: The Paradox of Inclusion.* Cambridge, UK: Cambridge University Press.
Harvey, David. 2005. *A Brief History of Neoliberalism.* New York: Oxford University Press.
Jacques, Martin. 2016. "The Death of Neoliberalism and the Crisis in Western Politics." *The Guardian*, [online] August 21. Available at: www.theguardian.com/commentisfree/2016/aug/21/death-of-neoliberalism-crisis-in-western-politics
Jones, Daniel S. 2014. *Masters of the Universe: Hayek, Friedman, and the Birth of Neoliberal Politics, Updated Edition.* Princeton, NJ: Princeton University Press.
Jones, N. 2010. "Work: The Best Route out of Poverty?" *Poverty Magazine 137*: 15–17.
Jordan, John D. 2018. "Welfare Grunters and Workfare Monsters? An Empirical Review of the Operation of Two UK 'Work Programme' Centres." *Journal of Social Policy 47*(3): 583–601.
Katz, Michael B. 2013. *The Undeserving Poor: America's Enduring Confrontation with Poverty, second edition.* New York: Oxford University Press.
Lawson, Victoria, and Sarah Elwood. 2018. *Relational Poverty Politics: Forms, Struggles, and Possibilities.* Athens, GA: University of Georgia Press.

Le Grand, Julian. 2003. *Motivation, Agency, and Public Policy: Of Knights and Knaves, Pawns and Queens*. New York: Oxford University Press.
Marttila, Tomas. 2013. *The Culture of Enterprise in Neoliberalism: Specters of Entrepreneurship*. New York: Routledge.
Mirowski, Philip. 2014. *Never Let a Serious Crisis Go to Waste: How Neoliberalism Survived the Financial Meltdown*. New York: Verso.
Office for National Statistics. 2018. *Contracts that do not guarantee a minimum number of hours: April 2018*. Accessed on February 4, 2019. Available at: www.ons.gov.uk/employmentandlabourmarket/peopleinwork/earningsandworkinghours/articles/contractsthatdonotguaranteeaminimumnumberofhours/april2018#future-of-the-experimental-business-survey
Olsthoorn, Martin. 2014. "Measuring Precarious Employment: A Proposal for Two Indicators of Precarious Employment Based on Set-Theory and Tested with Dutch Labor Market-Data." *Social Indicators Research 119*(1): 421–441.
Organization for Economic Cooperation and Development. 2018. *Temporary Employment*. Accessed on December 13, 2018. Available at: https://data.oecd.org/emp/temporary-employment.htm
Oxfam. 2013. *The True Cost of Austerity and Inequality: Ireland Case Study*. Oxford: Oxfam.
Peck, Jamie. 2001. *Workfare States*. New York: Guilford Publications.
——. 2010. *Constructions of Neoliberal Reason*. New York: Oxford University Press.
——. 2017. *Neoliberalism: Dead or Alive?* YouTube Video, 1:19:12, January 8, 2018. Accessed on December 13, 2018. Available at: www.youtube.com/watch?v=DL1pxtzxIHA
Peck, Jamie, and Heather Whiteside. 2017. "Neoliberalizing Detroit." In Sanford F. Schram and Marianna Pavlovskaya (eds.), *Rethinking Neoliberalism: Resisting the Disciplinary Regime* (pp. 181–198). New York: Routledge.
Peters, Michael A. 2018. "The End of Neoliberal Globalisation and the Rise of Authoritarian Populism." *Educational Philosophy and Theory 50*(4): 323–325.
Reich, Robert. 2015. "The Rise of the Working Poor and the Non-Working Rich." *Common Dreams*, [online] March 31. Available at: www.commondreams.org/views/2015/03/31/rise-working-poor-and-non-working-rich
Schram, Sanford F. 2015. *The Return of Ordinary Capitalism: Neoliberalism, Precarity, Occupy*. New York: Oxford University Press.
Schreiner, Mark, and Michael W. Sherraden. 2007. *Can the Poor Save? Saving & Asset Building in Individual Development Accounts*. New Brunswick, NJ: Transaction Publishers.
Schumpeter, Joseph. A. 1947. "The Creative Response in Economic History." *Journal of Economic History* 7(2): 149–159.
Soss, Joe, Richard C. Fording, and Sanford F. Schram. 2011. *Disciplining the Poor: Neoliberal Paternalism and the Persistent Power of Race*. Chicago, IL: University of Chicago Press.
Standing, Guy. 2011. *The Precariat: The Dangerous New Class*. New York: Bloomsbury Academic.
Suvarierol, Semin. 2015. "Creating Citizen-Workers through Civic Integration." *Journal of Social Policy 44*(4): 707–727.
Venugopal, Rajesh. 2015. "Neoliberalism as Concept." *Economy and Society 44*(2): 165–187.
West, Cornel. 2016. "Goodbye, American Neoliberalism. A New Era Is Here." *The Guardian*, [online] November 17. Available at: www.theguardian.com/commentisfree/2016/nov/17/american-neoliberalism-cornel-west-2016-election
Wilkinson, Richard G., and Kate Pickett. 2011. *The Spirit Level: Why More Equal Societies Almost Always Do Better*. London: Bloomsbury Press.

28
Poverty and health inequality

Mel Bartley

Introduction

This chapter will describe health inequality and explore the evidence that poverty may play a role in creating this widespread public health problem.

Most studies of health inequality use measures of socio-economic position such as social class, social status or education. As such, they do not directly measure the impact of poverty. An additional problem is that of defining poverty. Different countries have widely varying ways of defining who is "poor" (www.worldbank.org/en/topic/poverty/overview). Some measures are absolute, that is, they set out what is thought to be the minimum income that is needed for a certain standard of living. In studies of developing nations, absolute poverty is likely to be defined in terms of the availability of enough food, water and shelter to avoid starvation or death by exposure. In developed nations, there is, again, a variety of income standards. Some of the most commonly used ones derive from research that asks citizens what they consider to be essential goods and services, and cost these into a "decency standard" or something similar (Bradshaw et al., 2008). There is one measure that has used extensive evidence from medical and public health research to define a "minimum cost of a healthy life". This standard omits any cost that is held to be irrelevant or even harmful to healthy living such as cigarettes, motor cars and cable TV. But it does include the full cost of a healthy diet rich in fruit, grains and vegetables and that of regular exercise. It also includes the costs of a "round" of drinks for friends once a week and basic television, because these are part of being able to participate in social interaction, which is known to be helpful for social integration, which in turn is known to be a major influence on both physical and mental health (Morris, Donkin, Wonderling, Wilkinson, & Dowler, 2000). However, there is little research as yet that attempts to relate this type of poverty measure to health.

What is health inequality?

The pioneering work on social inequality in health came from a unique series of British official statistics published since 1931 ("Editorial: Occupational Mortality: The Registrar-General's Decennial Supplement, England and Wales, 1931," 1939). These were first analysed by Black et al. and Townsend in the 1980s (Black, Morris, & Townsend, 1982; Townsend, Davidson, & Whitehead, 1986) and have been brought up to date by Bartley (2016). In these studies, the measure of social inequality used was "social class" as defined by the British official statistical agency the Office of Population Censuses and Surveys and later the Office for National Statistics. However, the explanations for health inequality put forward by Black, Townsend et al., included reference to "material factors" such as poverty and its consequences such as poor quality, cold, damp or unhygienic housing, and poor diet.

Figure 28.1 shows the differences in mortality risk between members of more and less advantaged social classes in England and Wales from 1931 to 1991

The Standardised Mortality Ratio (SMR) is a measure that was used for many decades by British official statisticians in the Office of Population Censuses and Surveys (OPCC, now Office of National Statistics or ONS). It is no longer used but can easily be understood as the amount above or below the average for the population of the same age and sex (set to be 100). So for example, in 1931 mortality among men in professional occupations (Class I) was about 10% below the average for all men, and mortality among unskilled workers was about 10% above. This is contrasted to the figures for 1991 where mortality for Class I was almost 40% below the average and that for Class V was over 80% above. This was an enormous increase, and set the problematic for much research and policy effort. What made the increase even more problematic is that in the intervening period, poverty had fallen, wage differences between the social classes had reduced, and the UK had seen the introduction of a welfare state and free National Health Service.

Similar observations can be made in all European nations where research has been done, as shown in Figure 28.2 (Toch-Marquardt et al., 2014).

Here the figures are not SMRs but rather rates of death per 100,000 men, standardised to the European Standard Population to ensure that differences are not due to the age distributions in the different social classes. So, the rates in the different nation-specific social class groups can be directly compared to each other, showing that, for example, Finland had the highest and Netherlands the lowest mortality rates for the least advantaged men. Mortality of the most advantaged social classes shows far less national variability.

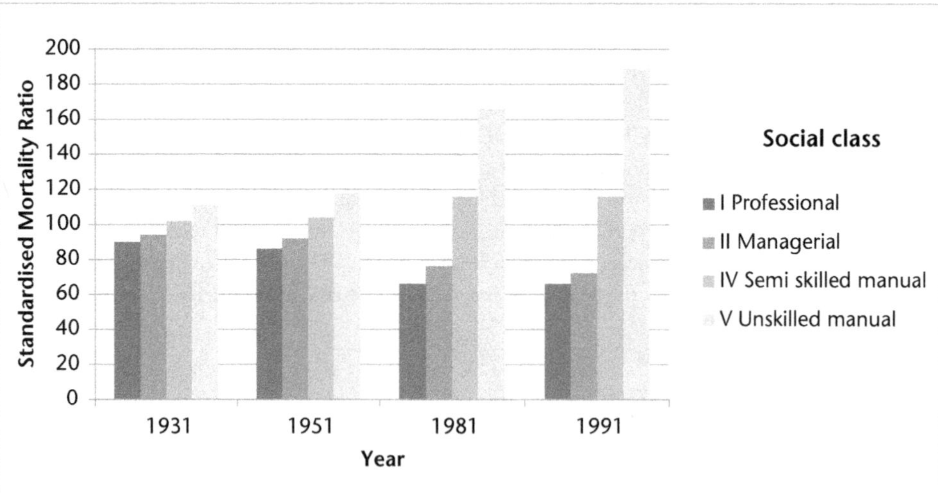

Figure 28.1 Trend in social inequality in mortality over a 60-year period in England and Wales.

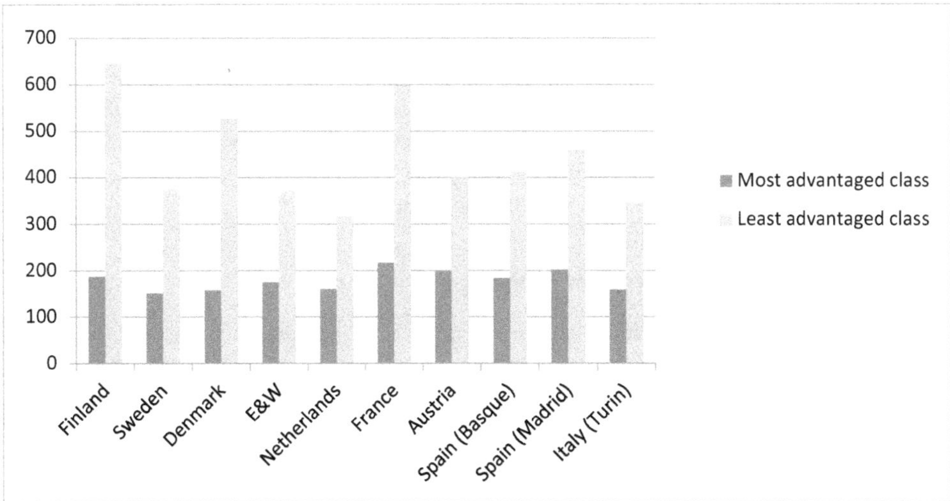

Figure 28.2 Age standardised death rates for men per 100,000 in European nations, early 2000s.

In the United States, it is not possible to easily classify people into "social classes", so education tends to be used as the standard measure of social advantage or disadvantage in official and academic work on health inequality. Figure 28.3 shows the relationship between education and life expectancy in the USA in 1996 and 2006.

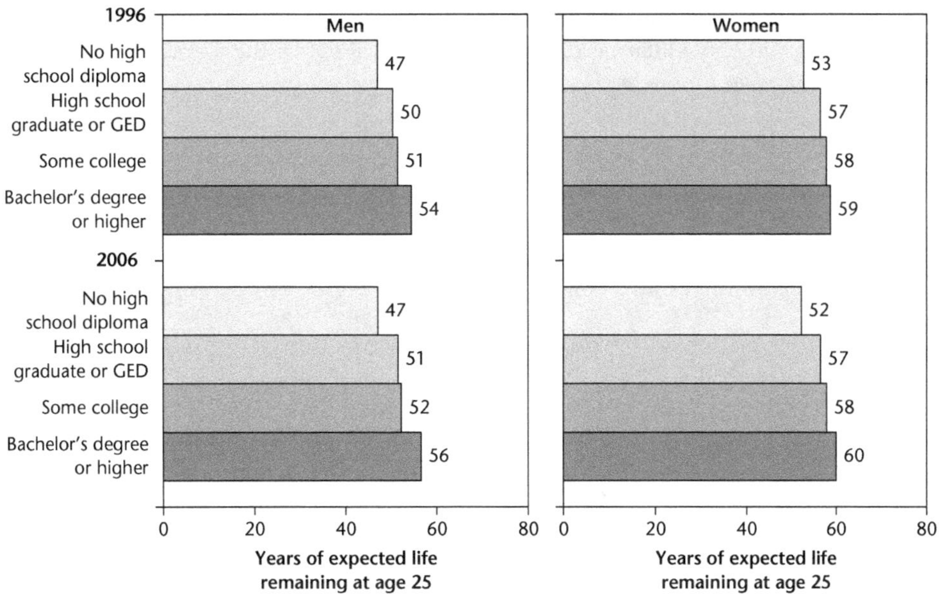

Figure 28.3 Education and life expectancy at age 25 in the USA in 1996 and 2006.

Note: GED is General Educational Development high school equivalency diploma.

Source: CDC/NCHS, *Health United States* 2011, Figure 32. Data from the National Health Interview Survey Linked Mortality File.

The advantage of using education as the indicator of socio-economic position is evident here in that it can also be applied to women. Because of intermittent labour force participation, samples of women able to state a classifiable occupation are biased toward those in better health. However, it requires a long series of assumptions to garner any evidence from these figures to the effect of poverty. In general, those with lower levels of education will earn less money and be more susceptible to periods in poverty, and this relationship has strengthened over time. But having a degree is no guarantee of an income above the poverty line.

Poverty and life expectancy in global perspective

Figure 28.4 shows the relationship between income and life expectancy at the global level, taking in nations where average income is far lower and severe poverty far higher than in developed industrial nations.

The African nations are clustered at the lower end of both the income and life expectancy distributions, with Europe and the Americas toward the higher end. The Asian nations are more widely spread, reflecting the range between India, China and "Pacific Tigers" such as Japan. The sizes of the circles represent population size. The African nations are clustered toward the bottom of the distributions of both income and life expectancy (in the lower left-hand corner of the graph). The Americas and Europe appear more toward the top right-hand of the graph. The Asian nations are far more spread out, both in terms of income and of life expectancy. Overall, there is a clear relationship between income and lifespan. But these figures tell us nothing about the relationship between national income and inequality in life expectancy; that is a more complex question.

A prominent contribution to the literature on health and social inequality has been made by Richard Wilkinson and Kate Pickett (Wilkinson & Pickett, 2010; Wilkinson, 1996). Their work argues that after a certain level of average income per capita, health and life expectancy in different nations are more influenced, not by income itself but by the distribution of income. So if we imagine two nations, each with an average annual income per capita of £30,000, the

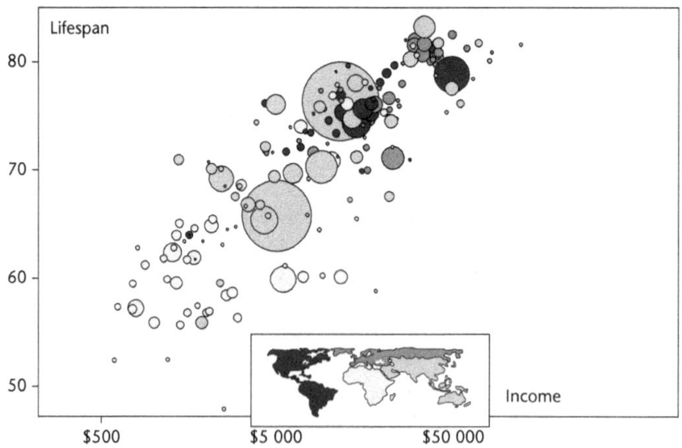

Figure 28.4 Income and life expectancy for all nations.

Source: Free material from gapminder.org. Available at: www.gapminder.org/answers/how-does-income-relate-to-life-expectancy/ (accessed 5/2/2019).

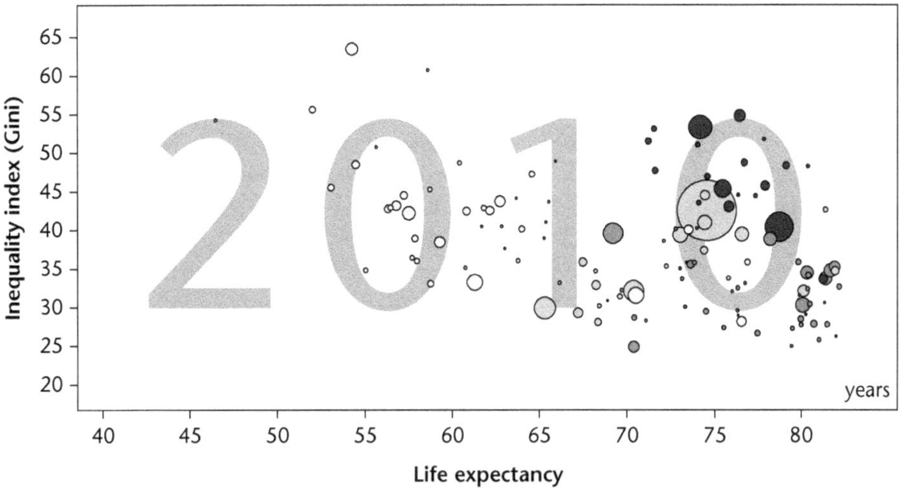

Figure 28.5 Income inequality and life expectancy in 2010.

Source: www.gapminder.org/tools/#$state$time$value=2010;&marker$axis_x$which=life_expectancy_years&domainMin:null&domainMax:null&zoomedMin:40&zoomedMax:null&scaleType=linear&spaceRef:null;&axis_y$which=inequality_index_gini&domainMin:null&domainMax:null&zoomedMin:20&zoomedMax:null&spaceRef:null;;;&chart-type=bubbles

Created 7 March 2019. Free material from www.gapminder.org

nation in which this was more equally distributed (often represented as a "Gini Coefficient") would be expected to have longer life expectancy. Figure 28.5, using the same convention as Figure 28.4 for representing world regions and national populations, shows some relationship of this kind, high inequality being associated with lower life expectancy and vice versa.

Once again, the European nations appear in the graph at both the lower level of income inequality and the higher life expectancy. In contrast, the African nations, while widely scattered, include the extremes of both variables. However, the relationship is a great deal less clear than that between income and life expectancy. It is also important to make the distinction between research on "health inequality", which compares different social groups within nations, and the work of Wilkinson and colleagues, which compares overall health indicators between nations with higher and lower levels of *income* inequality.

Explanations for health inequality: health care, health behaviours and stress

The literature on health inequality classifies possible explanations into five types: health care, behavioural, psychosocial, selection and material. It is widely agreed that, important as it is to be able to access health services, lack of health care cannot explain the vast majority of the observed health inequality. For one thing, health inequality is about the same in nations with all kinds of different health service arrangements, include the free British NHS. Second, as will be clear from Figure 28.1, health inequality did not decrease in England and Wales after the inception of the free NHS in 1946, on the contrary it increased greatly.

The behavioural explanation is perhaps the most popular one for the existence and persistence of health inequality (Goldberg, 2012; Katikireddi, Higgins, Smith, & Williams, 2013;

Lantz et al., 1998). Most "unhealthy" behaviours such as smoking, high-fat high-calorie diet, and lack of leisure time exercise follow a similar social gradient to that shown above for mortality risk (Lantz, Golberstein, House, & Morenoff, 2010). Some of the historical time trends in such behaviours are also consistent with this explanation for health inequality (Berkman et al., 2004). The decline in smoking after the various public health reports of the 1960s (Doll & Peto, 1981; Peto et al., 2000) was much faster in the more advantaged and higher educated social groups, at least in men. Obesity also tends to have a "social gradient" although this is more pronounced in women (Mackenbach, 2011; Sarlio-Lahteenkorva & Lahelma, 1999). The behavioural explanation would, of course, not be entirely consistent at first sight with an influence of poverty, as cigarettes are expensive. The role of poverty in explanation of "unhealthy diet" is nowadays more debated: fresh food may be cheaper to buy than "fast food" with high fat and sugar content, but costs more in both time and money to prepare. Although one might imagine that people unable to afford a motor car would be at an advantage due to the exercise involved in walking or cycling, evidence has long shown that car ownership is more strongly related to measures of *good* health and *longer* life expectancy (Fox & Goldblatt, 1982).

But the pre-eminence of the behavioural explanation for health inequality is neither uncontroversial nor supported by all the evidence. Van Rossum and colleagues used longitudinal follow-up data from a large study of London civil servants, the Whitehall I Study, to show that only around a third of the differences in mortality risk between those with the highest income and status and the best working conditions (the 'Administrative grade') and those in the least advantaged occupations such as catering staff and messengers, was explained by differences in health-related behaviour (van Rossum, Shipley, van de Mheen, Grobbee, & Marmot, 2000). A series of studies carried out by Lantz and colleagues in a more representative (all different kinds of occupations, not just civil servants) sample of the American population, found similar results (Lantz et al., 1998, 2001; Woolf & Laudan, 2013), as have studies in Norway (Skalická, van Lenthe, Bambra, Krokstad, & Mackenbach, 2009) and the Netherlands (van Oort, van Lenthe, & Mackenbach, 2005). Even smaller estimates of the importance of behaviour were found in two other multinational European studies (Gallo et al., 2012; McFadden, Luben, Wareham, Bingham, & Khaw, 2008).

Present day social epidemiology is moving away from regarding behavioural explanations for health inequality as competing with material or, even more so, psychosocial processes. It has dawned on researchers that the close relationship of social position to certain types of behaviour itself needs explanation if more effective policies are to be designed and implemented. Psychosocial explanations in the past have focused on employment conditions, contrasting those characterised by higher versus lower levels of control and satisfaction (Rosengren et al., 2004; Siegrist, Peter, Junge, Cremer, & Seidel, 1990; Torén et al., 2014). In the modern, post-industrial context the psychosocial consequences of unemployment and work insecurity have become far more important (Sverke, Hellgren, & Naswall, 2002). But recent research has considered the possibility that the psychosocial stresses associated with disadvantaged social and economic conditions may, in turn, be an important factor in risky health behaviour (Kouvonen, Kivimäki, Virtanen, Pentti, & Vahtera, 2005; Mulder, de Bruin, Schreurs, van Ameijden, & van Woerkum, 2011).

The psychosocial explanation for health inequality more broadly focuses on the ways in which mental stresses may directly influence the workings of the body and thereby increase the risk of heart disease (the major cause of early death in industrial nations until very recently). In the "fight or flight" model, for example, fear or anger prepare us physiologically for just that, to fight or to run away (Brunner, 1997). The changes involved include an increase in the heart rate, a narrowing of the tiny blood vessels in the skin (capillaries) along with the release of clotting factors into the blood (to prevent too much bleeding if wounded) and the release of fats and sugars into the blood to feed the muscles for effort. Theoretically these physiological changes would have been beneficial in the evolutionary past, so they are found more or less universally in human beings. However, when the sources of anger or fear (stresses) are of a more modern kind such as being bullied at work or being stuck in a traffic jam, any physical reaction actually to fight or run away is inappropriate. The excess fats and sugars therefore tend to build up in the blood vessels instead of being used up, and eventually may block the supply of blood to the heart muscle, resulting in a heart attack (Aiello & Kaplan, 2009).

Psychosocial explanations, particularly those which focus on work stresses, have become controversial in recent years. This is partly because of the increasing availability of rich data on larger numbers of study participants which fails to replicate earlier results, or show that health behaviours are far more important (Kivimäki & Kawachi, 2013; Kivimäki et al., 2012). The decline of interest in work stress can also be partly attributed to the wide ranging changes that are taking place in the labour markets of advanced industrial economies. These changes have seen large increases in work insecurity, economic inactivity and in the prevalence of low paid jobs (Kässi & Lehdonvirta, 2018). In consequence, the importance of work stress has fallen, and that of poverty as a cause of health inequality has grown considerably.

Explanations for health inequality: low income and poverty

In 1944, Morris (who would later co-author the Black Report) and Titmuss in their discussion of physical health in areas hard hit by the 1930s recession in Great Britain wrote of the "poverty complex", the tendency of low income, job insecurity and poor housing to be clustered in certain geographical areas and to be experienced by the same groups of people. They admitted the difficulties involved in separating out the effects of any single aspect of this complex from the others, but nevertheless felt that: "We are not . . . absolved from the attempt to break up the poverty complex and assess the role of the different component elements" (Morris & Titmuss, 1944).

Subsequently Blane and Davey Smith began to assess the relative importance to health inequality of what came to be known as the "cultural-behavioural" (smoking, diet, exercise, etc.) versus the "material" (poverty and associated risk exposures) factors. This was, and remains, an important task because until very recently, health behaviours have been seen as self-chosen risks within the free will of the individual (Oliver, Healey, & Grand, 2002; Mackenbach, 2010), whereas material factors are seen as produced as a consequence of the individual's position in the social structure and not subject to personal decisions (Blane, 1985). The differences in policy implications need hardly be elaborated, but some authors have reflected on the tendency of both research and policy responses toward "lifestyle drift" (Katikireddi et al., 2013; Popay, Whitehead, & Hunter, 2010) regardless of the evidence.

In these earlier studies, and still today in most studies, social position (more or less advantage or disadvantage) is measured in terms of social class, education and, more rarely, social status. Income (and hence poverty) only enters as one possible pathway (the "material" pathway) among others.

Studies of income (and therefore poverty) and health were later to appear in the epidemiological literature and at first used data from the United States. Income is asked about in US Censuses, unlike in the UK. But one of the earliest papers in fact used a geographical measure, the median family income of a US postal zip code (Davey Smith, Neaton, Wentworth, Stamler, & Stamler, 1998; Smith, Neaton, Wentworth, Stamler, & Stamler, 1996) finding, in white men, a death rate of nearly double where income was below $10,000 that where income was above $34,000. Later work on income and health was mostly carried out by health economists, and it is this which will largely be considered here.

There are several problems involved in considering income as a measure of social position (advantage and disadvantage). Unlike social class or education, income can be measured continuously on an interval scale. Changes in income can be measured in very small increments. There are, in many nations, agreed thresholds for the definition of poverty, enabling research on the associations with health of being above or below such a threshold. However, changes in income are much more frequent than changes in social class, and changes in education during adult life are quite unusual (though not non-existent). Using income in conventional regression models also has the disadvantage of assuming that the difference between, for example, earning $100,000 a year and $150,000 is "the same" as the difference between earning $10,000 and $60,000. It has been shown that this assumption is unjustified (Backlund, Sorlie, & Johnson, 1996; Rehkopf, Berkman, Coull, & Krieger, 2008). Whereas a steady stepwise gradient can be seen when relating social class or education measures to health outcomes (see Figures 28.1 and 28.2), this is not the case for income. As one would expect, the "effect" of a given increase in income is considerably greater among people with lower levels than for those with higher levels (Ecob & Davey Smith, 1999; Rehkopf et al., 2008).

Arising from the changeability of income in the lives of individuals is another problem: that any cross-sectional association of low income to ill-health or mortality might come about by means of "reverse causation", that is, because declining health results in declining income (Deaton, 2002; Hofoss, Dahl, Ivar Elstad, & Cvancarova, 2013; Kröger, Pakpahan, & Hoffmann, 2015). Deaton laments that the potential for health to cause low income is neglected in the public health literature but acknowledges that disabling illness is itself far more common among people whose working lives have involved low income. In his study using the US National Longitudinal Mortality Study, doubling income reduced mortality risk by 17% after 5–9 years of follow up, even controlling for education. By only measuring mortality several years after measuring income, this study guards against the problem that people who are already sick would both have low income and poor health. By controlling for education, it takes account of the possibility that people with both low income and a high risk of mortality might have other characteristics and experiences that confounded the relationship of income to mortality.

There are two separate debates here: whether low income and poverty might be a result of poor health resulting in lower opportunities in the labour market; and whether there are third factors (confounding variables) which might be the "causes" of both poverty and ill-health or early mortality. Most scholars seem to agree now that ill-health itself can result in poverty, but this is not a common enough phenomenon to account for the strong observed relationship (Deaton, 2002; Hofoss et al., 2013). Some cleverly designed studies have used exogenous sources of income increases such as lottery wins, and found evidence for a causal relationship to improved health (Adda, von Gaudecker, & Banks, 2009; Lindahl, 2005).

Perhaps a more pervasive issue when considering the role played by poverty in health inequality is what might be called "indirect selection". This approach does not propose that poor health itself causes low income or poverty, but that there are third variables in operation which produce the appearance of a relationship where none is in fact present. Hence, the pervasive tendency, when examining relationships between health and social class or income, to adjust for multiple variables such as education (Elo, Martikainen, & Smith, 2006), and various forms of health behaviour. Underlying these methods, but almost never stated, is the notion that citizens with "inferior" characteristics such as low intelligence, low conscientiousness (Pluess & Bartley, 2015), or external locus of control both earn less money and engage in health-damaging behaviours

(Mackenbach, 2012). One reason for this line of argument is that health inequality is no less in those nations whose social security arrangements are more effective in protecting citizens unable to earn by working. Figure 28.2, as well as demonstrating the pervasiveness of health inequality throughout Europe, for example, also shows that the mortality "gap" is no greater in the less than the more egalitarian nations. Figure 28.6 shows that, if anything, the nations with the lowest poverty rates have *higher* health inequality.

As a result, we are left with something of a paradox. Low income is associated with poorer health in all studies. Studies designed to show the effects of purely exogenous changes in income, such as lottery wins, indicate they are associated with health improvements. But nations in which poverty is more unusual have, at the very least, no less inequality in mortality than those where poverty is more common. Of course, it may be that what matters is not just how much money a person has, but what the money will buy. In Spain and Italy (whose persistently low levels of health inequality have been termed "the Mediterranean paradox" (Mackenbach, 2012; Mackenbach et al., 2014)), it may be that a healthy life is just cheaper. This might be because of climate, the widespread availability of fresh fruit and vegetables, or the fact that smoking does not yet have as sharp a social gradient as in the Nordic nations (Federico et al., 2013). Mackenbach, whose research group has done the leading comparative studies of health inequality for many years, has moved toward the position that in the more equal nations, the school system more effectively selects individuals with higher intelligence and other favourable personality characteristics into the higher earning jobs (and vice versa) (Mackenbach, 2010, 2012). This would potentially result in a greater concentration of health-damaging characteristics and behaviours among those with low earnings. Such an explanation will be extremely controversial for many people. However, further progress will depend on the emerging field of life course research (Katikireddi et al., 2013; Östlin et al., 2011). It is now possible to measure the social circumstances, cognitive function, behavioural development and educational progress

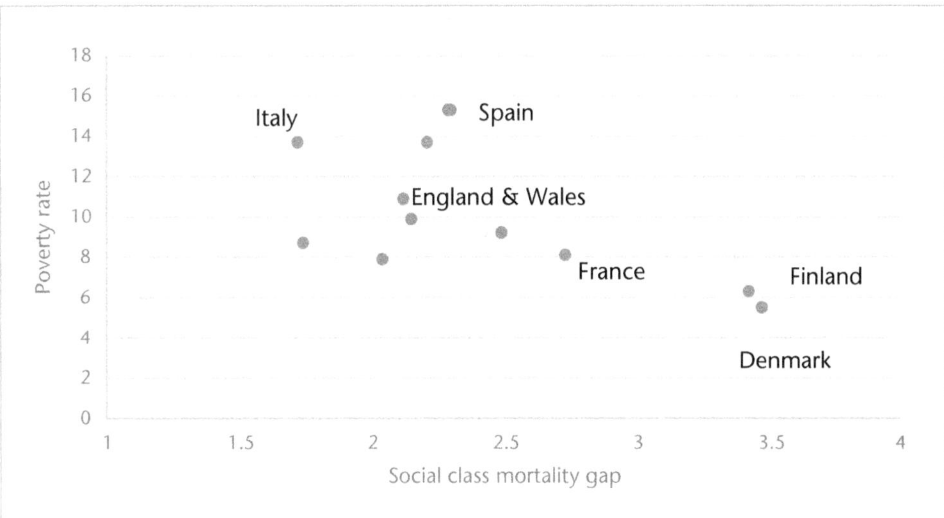

Figure 28.6 Relationship between national poverty rates and inequality in mortality in men.

Sources: OECD statistic_id233910_poverty-rates-in-oecd-countries-2015 accessed 9/11/2018 (Toch-Marquardt et al., 2014).

in cohorts of children from their earliest years. We can then see the extent to which such individual characteristics predict earnings in adult life. Or, alternatively, the extent to which a life history may accumulate different experiences of early socio-economic advantage or adversity with personal development, education, health behaviours and adult circumstances (Alwin, 2016; Pampel, Mollborn, & Lawrence, 2014). Only in this way can the paradox be resolved.

References

Adda, J., von Gaudecker, H. M., & Banks, J. (2009). The impact of income shocks on health: evidence from cohort data. *Journal of the European Economic Association*, 7(6), 1361–1399.

Aiello, A. E., & Kaplan, G. A. (2009). Socioeconomic position and inflammatory and immune biomarkers of cardiovascular disease: applications to the Panel Study of Income Dynamics. *Biodemography and Social Biology*, *55*(2), 178–205.

Alwin, D. F. (2016). Commentary: It takes more than one to tango: life course epidemiology and related approaches. *International Journal of Epidemiology*, *45*(4), 988–993.

Backlund, E., Sorlie, P. D., & Johnson, N. J. (1996). The shape of the relationship between income and mortality in the United States: evidence from the National Longitudinal Mortality Study. *Annals of Epidemiology*, *6*(1), 12–20.

Bartley, M. (2016). *Health Inequality: an introduction to concepts, theories and methods*. Chichester: John Wiley & Sons.

Berkman, L. F., Melchior, M., Chastang, J.-F., Niedhammer, I., Leclerc, A., & Goldberg, M. (2004). Social Integration and mortality: a prospective study of French employees of Electricity of France–Gas of France: The GAZEL Cohort. *American Journal of Epidemiology*, *159*(2), 167–174.

Black, D., Morris, J. N., & Townsend, P. (1982). Inequalities in Health: The Black Report. In P. Townsend & N. Davidson (Eds.), *The Black Report and the Health Divide* (pp. 39–233). Harmondsworth, UK: Penguin.

Blane, D. (1985). An assessement of the Black Report's explanations of health inequalities. *Sociology of Health & Illness*, 7, 231–264.

Bradshaw, J., Middleton, S., Davis, A., Oldfield, N., Smith, N., Cusworth, L., & Williams, J. (2008). *A minimum income standard for Britain: What people think*. Loughborough University.

Brunner, E. (1997). Socioeconomic determinants of health: stress and the biology of inequality. *British Medical Journal*, *314*(7092), 1472–1476.

Davey Smith, G., Neaton, J. D., Wentworth, D., Stamler, R., & Stamler, J. (1998). Mortality differences between black and white men in the USA: contribution of income and other risk factors among men screened for the MRFIT. MRFIT Research Group. Multiple Risk Factor Intervention Trial. *Lancet*, *351*(9107), 934–939.

Deaton, A. (2002). Policy implications of the gradient of health and wealth. *Health affairs*, *21*(2), 13–30. doi:http://dx.doi.org/10.1377/hlthaff.21.2.13

Doll, R., & Peto, R. (1981). The causes of cancer: appendix E. *Journal of the National Cancer Institute*, *66*, 1291–1305.

Ecob, R., & Davey Smith, G. (1999). Income and health: what is the nature of the relationship? *Social Science & Medicine*, *48*(5), 693–705. doi:https://doi.org/10.1016/S0277-9536(98)00385-2

Editorial: Occupational Mortality: The Registrar-General's Decennial Supplement, England and Wales, 1931. (1939). *The American Journal of Cancer*, *36*(1), 110–116. doi:10.1158/ajc.1939.110

Elo, I. T., Martikainen, P., & Smith, K. P. (2006). Socioeconomic differentials in mortality in Finland and the United States: the role of education and income. *European Journal of Population/Revue européenne de Démographie*, *22*(2), 179–203. doi:10.1007/s10680-006-0003-5

Federico, B., Mackenbach, J. P., Eikemo, T. A., Sebastiani, G., Marinacci, C., Costa, G., & Kunst, A. E. (2013). Educational inequalities in mortality in northern, mid and southern Italy and the contribution of smoking. *Journal of Epidemiology and Community Health*, *67*(7), 603–609.

Fox, A. J., & Goldblatt, P. (1982). *Longitudinal Study: Socio-Demographic Mortality Differentials: A First Report on Mortality in 1971–1975 According to 1971 Census Characteristics, Based on Data Collected in OPCS Longitudinal Study*. HMSO.

Gallo, V., Mackenbach, J. P., Ezzati, M., Menvielle, G., Kunst, A. E., Rohrmann, S., et al. (2012). Social inequalities and mortality in Europe: results from a large multi-national cohort. *PloS one*, 7(7), e39013.

Goldberg, D. S. (2012). Social justice, health inequalities and methodological individualism in US health promotion. *Public Health Ethics*, *5*(2), 104–115.

Hofoss, D., Dahl, E., Ivar Elstad, J., & Cvancarova, M. (2013). Selection and mortality: a ten-year follow-up of income decile mortality in Norway. *European Journal of Public Health*, *23*(4), 558–563.

Kässi, O., & Lehdonvirta, V. (2018). Online labour index: measuring the online gig economy for policy and research. *Technological Forecasting and Social Change*, *137*, 241–248. doi:https://doi.org/10.1016/j.techfore.2018.07.056

Katikireddi, S. V., Higgins, M., Smith, K. E., & Williams, G. (2013). Health inequalities: the need to move beyond bad behaviours (editorial). *Journal of Epidemiology and Community Health*, *67*, 715–716.

Kivimäki, M., & Kawachi, I. (2013). Need for more individual-level meta-analyses in social epidemiology: example of job strain and coronary heart disease. *American Journal of Epidemiology*, *177*(1), 1–2.

Kivimäki, M., Nyberg, S. T., Batty, G. D., Fransson, E. I., Heikkilä, K., Alfredsson, L., et al. (2012). Job strain as a risk factor for coronary heart disease: a collaborative meta-analysis of individual participant data. *Lancet*, *380*(9862), 1491–1497.

Kouvonen, A., Kivimäki, M., Virtanen, M., Pentti, J., & Vahtera, J. (2005). Work stress, smoking status, and smoking intensity: an observational study of 46 190 employees. *Journal of Epidemiology and Community Health*, *59*(1), 63–69.

Kröger, H., Pakpahan, E., & Hoffmann, R. (2015). What causes health inequality? A systematic review on the relative importance of social causation and health selection. *European Journal of Public Health*, *25*(6), 951–960. doi:10.1093/eurpub/ckv111

Lantz, P. M., Golberstein, E., House, J. S., & Morenoff, J. (2010). Socioeconomic and behavioral risk factors for mortality in a national 19-year prospective study of U.S. adults. *Social Science & Medicine*, *70*(10), 1558–1566.

Lantz, P. M., House, J. S., Lepkowski, J. M., Williams, D. R., Mero, R. P., & Chen, J. (1998). Socioeconomic factors, health behaviors, and mortality results from a nationally representative prospective study of US adults. *JAMA*, *279*(21), 1703–1708.

Lantz, P. M., Lynch, J. W., House, J. S., Lepkowski, J. M., Mero, R. P., Musick, M. A., & Williams, D. R. (2001). Socioeconomic disparities in health change in a longitudinal study of US adults: the role of health-risk behaviors. *Social Science & Medicine*, *53*(1), 29–40.

Lindahl, M. (2005). Estimating the effect of income on health and mortality using lottery prizes as an exogenous source of variation in income. *Journal of Human Resources*, *40*(1), 144–168.

Mackenbach, J. P. (2010). New trends in health inequalities research: now it's personal. *Lancet*, *376*(9744), 854–855.

Mackenbach, J. P. (2011). What would happen to health inequalities if smoking were eliminated? *British Medical Journal*, *342*, d3460.

Mackenbach, J. P. (2012). The persistence of health inequalities in modern welfare states: the explanation of a paradox. *Social Science & Medicine*, *75*(4), 761–769.

Mackenbach, J. P., Kulhánová, I., Menvielle, G., Bopp, M., Borrell, C., Costa, G., et al. (2014). Trends in inequalities in premature mortality: a study of 3.2 million deaths in 13 European countries. *Journal of Epidemiology and Community Health*, jech-2014-204319.

McFadden, E., Luben, R., Wareham, N., Bingham, S., & Khaw, K.-T. (2008). Occupational social class, risk factors and cardiovascular disease incidence in men and women: a prospective study in the European Prospective Investigation of Cancer and Nutrition in Norfolk (EPIC-Norfolk) cohort. *European Journal of Epidemiology*, *23*(7), 449–458.

Morris, J. N., & Titmuss, R. (1944). Health and social change: recent history of rheumatic heart disease. *Medical Officer*, *69–71*, 77–79, 85–87.

Morris, J., Donkin, A., Wonderling, D., Wilkinson, P., & Dowler, E. (2000). A minimum income for healthy living. *Journal of Epidemiology & Community Health*, *54*(12), 885–889.

Mulder, B., de Bruin, M., Schreurs, H., van Ameijden, E., & van Woerkum, C. (2011). Stressors and resources mediate the association of socioeconomic position with health behaviours. *BMC Public Health*, *11*(1), 798. doi:10.1186/1471-2458-11-798

Oliver, A., Healey, A., & Grand, J. L. (2002). Addressing health inequalities. *The Lancet*, *360*(9332), 565–567. doi:https://doi.org/10.1016/S0140-6736(02)09713-1

Östlin, P., Schrecker, T., Sadana, R., Bonnefoy, J., Gilson, L., Hertzman, C., et al. (2011). Priorities for research on equity and health: towards an equity-focused health research agenda. *PLoS Medicine*, *8*(11), e1001115.

Pampel, F. C., Mollborn, S., & Lawrence, E. M. (2014). Life course transitions in early adulthood and SES disparities in tobacco use. *Social Science Research, 43*, 45–59.

Peto, R., Darby, S., Deo, H., Silcocks, P., Whitley, E., & Doll, R. (2000). Smoking, smoking cessation, and lung cancer in the UK since 1950: combination of national statistics with two case-control studies. *British Medical Journal, 321*, 323–329.

Pluess, M., & Bartley, M. (2015). Childhood conscientiousness predicts the social gradient of smoking in adulthood: a life course analysis. *Journal of Epidemiology and Community Health, 69*(4), 330–338.

Popay, J., Whitehead, M., & Hunter, D. J. (2010). Injustice is killing people on a large scale – but what is to be done about it? (Editorial). *Journal of Public Health, 32*(2), 148–149.

Rehkopf, D. H., Berkman, L. F., Coull, B., & Krieger, N. (2008). The non-linear risk of mortality by income level in a healthy population: US National Health and Nutrition Examination Survey mortality follow-up cohort, 1988–2001. *BMC Public Health, 8*(1), 383. doi:10.1186/1471-2458-8-383

Rosengren, A., Hawken, S. H., Ounpuu, S., Sliwa, K., Zubaid, M., Almahameed, W. A., et al. (2004). Association of psychosocial risk factors with risk of acute myocardial infarction in 11 119 cases and 13 648 controls from 52 countries (the INTERHEART study): case-control study. *Lancet, 364*(9438), 953–962.

Sarlio-Lahteenkorva, S., & Lahelma, E. (1999). The association of body mass index with social and economic disadvantage in women and men. *International Journal of Epidemiology, 28*(3), 445–449.

Siegrist, J., Peter, R., Junge, A., Cremer, P., & Seidel, D. (1990). Low status control, high effort at work and ischemic heart disease: prospective evidence from blue-collar men. *Social Science and Medicine, 31*(10), 1127–1134.

Skalická, V., van Lenthe, F., Bambra, C., Krokstad, S., & Mackenbach, J. (2009). Material, psychosocial, behavioural and biomedical factors in the explanation of relative socio-economic inequalities in mortality: evidence from the HUNT study. *International Journal of Epidemiology, 38*(5), 1272–1284.

Smith, G. D., Neaton, J. D., Wentworth, D., Stamler, R., & Stamler, J. (1996). Socioeconomic differentials in mortality risk among men screened for the Multiple Risk Factor Intervention Trial: I. White men. *American Journal of Public Health, 86*(4), 486–496.

Sverke, M., Hellgren, J., & Naswall, K. (2002). No security: a meta-analysis and review of job insecurity and its consequences. *Journal of Occupational Health Psychology, 7*(3), 242–264.

Toch-Marquardt, M., Menvielle, G., Eikemo, T. A., Kulhánová, I., Kulik, M. C., Bopp, M., et al. (2014). Occupational class inequalities in all-cause and cause-specific mortality among middle-aged men in 14 European populations during the early 2000s. *PloS one, 9*(9), e108072.

Torén, K., Schiöler, L., Giang, W. K., Novak, M., Söderberg, M., & Rosengren, A. (2014). A longitudinal general population-based study of job strain and risk for coronary heart disease and stroke in Swedish men. *BMJ Open, 4*(3), e004355.

Townsend, P., Davidson, N., & Whitehead, M. (1986). The Black Report and the health divide. In *The Black Report and the Health Divide*. Harmondsworth, UK: Penguin.

van Oort, F. V. A., van Lenthe, F. J., & Mackenbach, J. P. (2005). Material, psychosocial, and behavioural factors in the explanation of educational inequalities in mortality in the Netherlands. *Journal of Epidemiology and Community Health, 59*(3), 214–220.

van Rossum, C. T. M., Shipley, M., van de Mheen, H., Grobbee, D., & Marmot, M. G. (2000). Employment grade differences in cause specific mortality. A 25 year follow up of civil servants from the first Whitehall study. *Journal of Epidemiology and Community Health, 54*, 178–184.

Wilkinson, R. G. (1996). *Unhealthy Societies: the afflictions of inequality*. London: Routledge.

Wilkinson, R., & Pickett, K. (2010). *The Spirit Level*. London: Penguin.

Woolf, S. H., & Laudan, A. (2013). Individual behaviours. In S. H. Woolf & A. Laudan (Eds.), *US Health in International Perspective: shorter lives, poorer health* (pp. 138–160). Washington, DC: US National Academies Press.

29

Poverty reduction among older people through pensions

A comparative analysis[1]

Olaf van Vliet, Koen Caminada, Kees Goudswaard and Jinxian Wang

Introduction

In the analysis of the developments in monetary poverty, older people constitute an important group within populations. Older people who quit the labor market are, by definition, vulnerable to financial poverty, and with the ageing of many Western societies this group is growing rapidly. Interestingly in this respect, earlier research has shown that poverty rates among older people have declined in many European countries over the past few decades (van Vliet et al., 2012). Poverty among older people is linked to several factors, such as gender, social class, age and marital status (Kangas & Palme, 2000; Price, 2006). Yet an important reason for the declining poverty rates over the past few decades is the expansion of pension systems and hence the increased expenditures on pension benefits. A study by the OECD (2008) concludes that the poverty reducing effect of transfers and taxes is the strongest for older people, because of the impact of pensions. Across OECD countries, the poverty reducing effect of the tax/benefit systems for people of retirement age is, on average, 1.5 times as high as for people of working age. Based on a comparative analysis across countries and over time, Been et al. (2017) concluded that high levels of public pension expenditures are associated with lower levels of income inequality and poverty in old age. Recently, Jacques et al. (2018) came to similar conclusions. Both studies examined the association between at-risk-of-poverty rates based on EU-SILC data and social expenditures data from the OECD or Eurostat with panel data regression analysis. An important advantage of this approach is that in addition to the redistributive effect of pensions, the effects of various other socio-economic developments, such as unemployment or ageing of the population, can be taken into account too.

In the current study, we do not *estimate* the redistributive effect of pensions on poverty among older people. Instead, we *measure* the poverty reduction that results from redistribution via tax/benefit systems (i.e. through pensions). We focus on the actual income redistribution for older people (65 and above), which is the difference between the market income (before income taxes and social benefits) and the disposable income (after income taxes and social benefits). For this analysis, we utilize a new dataset on fiscal redistribution and relative income poverty rates that is based on data from LIS: Cross-National Data Center in Luxembourg (Caminada & Wang, 2019).

The remainder of this chapter is organized as follows. First, we introduce and discuss the key concepts used in our analysis, being poverty incidence and the poverty reducing effect of social transfers and income taxes (i.e. lifting people out of poverty via tax/benefit systems). Then, we show the variation in old-age poverty rates across LIS countries and over the period 1985–2016. Furthermore, we employ a decomposition analysis to examine the underlying dynamics in redistribution by social transfers (mainly pensions) and income taxes.

Core concepts

Measuring poverty incidence

A *good* pension system protects people against poverty and smooths people's income over their life-cycle. To achieve these goals countries organize their pension system in different ways. Considerable effort has been made to compare pension systems across countries and to identify strengths and weaknesses of different systems. To be able to evaluate *adequacy* we need to know how much resources retirees need. A variety of standards can be chosen against which to judge adequacy (Knoef et al., 2016). A widely accepted standard in the literature is having a retirement income of 70 percent of previous earnings (Haveman et al., 2007). Another approach is to set a social standard for adequacy. In such an approach, retirement income could be considered *adequate* when it is equal to or greater than the poverty threshold.

There are three common ways of setting the poverty line: an absolute standard, a relative standard, and a subjective standard (see also Chapters 2–4). The U.S. poverty threshold is based on an absolute poverty standard, which remains fixed over time in real terms. The EU agreed upon a relative poverty line that is set as a fixed percentage of the median income in each country, which may change over time if median income changes in real terms. The subjective poverty line is based on respondents' answers to questions regarding what they consider an adequate standard of living. Following international standards, we use the relative rather than the absolute or subjective approach in measuring income poverty. This means that we define those households that have an equivalent disposable income below a certain threshold representing the level of well-being of the population in a specific country as being poor. In a number of comparative studies, the poverty threshold has been set at 50 percent of median equivalent disposable income. However, we employ the EU-agreed definition of poverty. The official EU indicator for social cohesion is the at-risk-of-poverty rate after social transfers. This rate is defined as the share of persons with an equivalized disposable income below the risk-of-poverty threshold, which is set at 60 percent of the national median equivalized disposable income.

Caminada et al. (2019a) performed a sensitivity analysis for all waves of the 49 LIS countries 1967–2016 when different poverty lines are applied. They found that all poverty lines (PL60, PL50, P40) follow more or less the same pattern. The country ranking changes only slightly when a threshold of 40 percent instead of 60 percent is applied (although there are some exceptions). As a result, in most cases empirical findings will hardly be affected by applying a 60 instead of a 40 or 50 percent poverty line.

It should be noted that there have been controversial arguments regarding the issues in the measurement of income poverty. These arguments have their own merits and shortcomings, and there has been little professional consensus among researchers with regard to the theoretical superiority of a particular way of measuring poverty. The aim of this chapter is not to review definitional issues that arise in assessing the extent of, and change in, income inequality and poverty across countries. We simply refer to a vast literature on the sensitivity of measured results to the choice of income definitions, inequality and poverty indices, appropriate equivalence scales, and other elements that may affect results in comparative research; see Caminada et al. (2019a) and all papers cited therein.

Unit of analysis

The unit of analysis is an important issue in poverty and income distribution studies. It is evident that the ultimate source of concern is the welfare of the individual. However, an individual is often not the appropriate unit of analysis. For example, children and spouses working at home do not have recorded income, but may nevertheless be enjoying a high standard of living as a result of income sharing with parents/spouses. Traditionally, studies have used household income per capita to adjust total incomes according to the number of persons in the household. In recent decades, equivalence scales have been widely used in the literature on income distribution (Figini, 1998). Equivalence scale elasticity for the LIS database is set around 0.5. This implies that where the income of a household of one person is 100, a household of two persons must have an income of 140 to have equivalent incomes. Alternatively, a one-person household must have 70 percent of the total income of a two-person household to have equivalent income. In our comparative analysis we use this equivalence scale of LIS. Caminada et al. (2019c) show that the results of such an analysis are hardly influenced by the equivalence method used.[2]

Measuring the poverty reducing effects of social transfers and income taxes

Usually, the impact of social programs on poverty and income inequality is calculated in line with the work of Musgrave et al. (1974), i.e. statutory or budget incidence analysis. A standard analysis of the redistributive effect of income taxes and social transfers is to compare pre-tax-transfer poverty or income inequality and post-tax-transfer poverty or income inequality (OECD 2008: 98). A well-known critique of this approach is that pre-transfer poverty is compared to post-transfer poverty keeping all other things constant, thus disregarding any possible behavioral changes that the situation of absence of social transfers would involve. In particular, labor supply responses could be expected. However, in our analysis of poverty and the poverty reducing effects of tax/benefit systems among older people, labor supply effects are obviously less relevant, as older people have a very low labor supply.

In order to assess the partial effects of pensions and income taxes on the overall poverty reducing effect of tax/benefit systems, we apply a sequential accounting decomposition technique followed by Jesuit and Mahler (2010 and 2017) and Kammer et al. (2012). This enables us to calculate poverty rates without a certain type of social transfer or income tax. Consequently, we can determine the effective antipoverty impact of different income sources. Likewise, the poverty reducing effects of all income components on poverty within the trajectory between market income and disposable income can be calculated using this approach.

Data

For this chapter we use data from the Luxembourg Income Study. The LIS Cross-National Data Center in Luxembourg provides the largest available income database of harmonized microdata collected from 49 countries in Europe, North America, Latin America, Africa, Asia and Australasia. Harmonized into a common framework, LIS datasets contain household- and person-level data on labor income, capital income, social security and private transfers, income taxes and social contributions, demography, employment and expenditures (LIS, 2019). The LIS database allows scholars to access the microdata, so that income inequality measures and fiscal redistribution (and the partial effect per social program) can be derived consistently from the underlying data at the individual and household levels. LIS microdata seem to be the best available data for describing how poverty and the redistributive effects of taxes and transfers vary across countries (Nolan & Marx, 2009; Smeeding & Latner, 2015). However, country-comparative and trend analyses of income distribution based on LIS gross/net datasets should be done with caution (Gornick et al., 2013; Nieuwenhuis et al., 2017). LIS provides gross income data for most countries and years while providing income data that are net of (income) taxes in others. Of the 339 LIS datasets available at the time of writing, 214 are classified as gross, 103 as net and 22 as 'mixed'; see Caminada and Wang (2019, Documentation Guide) for a specification. Since we are interested in the redistributive effects of pensions and income taxes and social contributions, this analysis only considers LIS countries for which full tax-benefit information is available (classified by LIS as 'gross').

In the empirical literature, the selection of countries and data-years varies due to the consideration of data quality. From nearly 300 variables in the dataset, we select those related to household income (all kinds of income sources), total number of persons in a household and household weight (in order to correct sample bias or non-sampling errors) to measure poverty and the redistributive effect across countries. In line with LIS conventions and the work by Mahler and Jesuit (2017) and Caminada et al. (2017 and 2019b), we have included households which report zero market income (i.e., all of their income is derived from the state) but have excluded households that report zero disposable income.

How to deal with pensions?

An important choice in this analysis is whether pensions should be earmarked as market income or as transfers and therefore pension contributions as taxes. This choice is of vital importance for the results. Most studies conclude that the redistributive effect of transfers is much more important than the redistributive effect of taxes. But Guillaud et al. (2017) show that if pensions are categorized as market income rather than transfers, tax redistribution dominates transfer redistribution in most countries. Countries differ to a large extent in public versus private provision of their pensions (OECD, 2008: 120). Public pension plans are generally seen as part of the safety net, generating large antipoverty effects. Occupational and private pensions, on the other hand, generally aim to redistribute income inter-temporally over the life-cycle. These pensions are not redistributive programs per se, although they too have a significant effect on redistribution when pre-tax-transfer inequality and post-tax-transfer inequality are measured at one moment in time, particularly among older people. The standard approach treats contributions to government pensions as a tax that finances the retirement pensions paid out in the same year, while contributions to private pensions are effectively treated as a form of private consumption. This may affect international comparisons of redistribution effects of social transfers and taxes. We deal with this bias rather pragmatically by following the LIS Household Income Variables List: occupational and private pensions are earmarked and treated as social transfers. Jesuit and Mahler (2017) also consider the pension system as a whole, because the distinction between public and private pensions is somewhat artificial.[3] For a substantial number of LIS countries it is impossible to disaggregate income from public and private schemes. The implication hereof is that the measured redistribution through pensions cannot be fully considered as interpersonal redistribution. Other transfers and benefits, such as housing transfers, for instance, are also included in the decomposition analysis; they are included in 'other transfers'.

Empirical analysis

Decomposition analysis

Because the data for a number of countries are not detailed enough for performing a decomposition analysis, the decomposition analysis is based on 25 LIS countries. Table 29.1 shows poverty rates and the antipoverty effect of social transfers and income taxes and social contributions around 2013. The numbers presented are unweighted averages of the values of 25 LIS countries, see list of countries in Table 29.1. The table indicates that the poverty rate based on market income is the lowest among the working-age population and the highest among older people. Among the working-age population, 26 percent of the population has a market income that lies below the risk-of-poverty threshold of 60 percent of the national median income. Among older people, 76 percent of the population has a market income that is lower than the poverty threshold. This difference in poverty rates reflects the fact that many older people are retired from paid work. The poverty rate based on disposable income is also lower for the working-age population than for older people, but the difference is much smaller; 17 percent for the working-age population versus 21 percent for older people. The reason why this difference in poverty rates is smaller is that the tax/benefit system has lifted many more people out of poverty in the case of older people than in the case of the working-age population. In the case of older people, 55 percent of the population has been lifted out of poverty via social transfers and income taxes. For the working-age population, income taxes and social benefits have lifted 9 percent of that population out of poverty. In contrast, for children the difference between the poverty rates based on market and disposable income amounts is 8 percent and for the total population this is 16 percent.

Table 29.1 Poverty (alleviation) and poverty reducing effects of social programs in 25 LIS countries around 2013

	Total population		*Working-age population*		*Children*		*Older people*	
(a) Poverty market income	35.0		25.5		30.4		76.3	
(b) Poverty disposable income	19.1		16.8		22.7		21.4	
Poverty reduction (a – b)	15.9		8.7		7.7		54.9	
		Share		Share		Share		Share
Old-age/disability/survivor transfers	13.1	82%	6.1	70%	2.3	30%	55.7	101%
Other transfers	5.9	37%	5.3	61%	8.9	116%	2.2	4%
Income taxes and social security contributions	–3.1	–19%	–2.7	–31%	–3.5	–45%	–3.1	–6%
Residual	0.0	0%	0.0	0%	–0.1	–1%	0.1	0%

Notes:

When we take the mean of the decomposition results across countries, the sum of all partial antipoverty effects amounts to (a little) over 100 percent due to missing observations. We rescaled the antipoverty effects of each social program by applying an adjustment factor, which is defined as the overall poverty reduction (=100%) divided by sum of all partial antipoverty effects of all programs (over 100%), in order to correct for an over-estimated effect.

LIS 25: Australia, Austria, Brazil, Czech Republic, Denmark, Estonia, Finland, Germany, Greece, Guatemala, Iceland, Ireland, Israel, Luxembourg, the Netherlands, Norway, Panama, Peru, Slovakia, South Africa, Spain, Switzerland, the United Kingdom and the United States.

Source: Database Caminada & Wang (2019) based on LIS, and own calculations.

The lower part of the table displays the results of the decomposition analysis. The overall poverty reducing effect of income taxes and social transfers presented in the upper part of the table is decomposed in order to determine the effective antipoverty impact of different income sources. The first income category that we use, consists of old-age, disability and survivor transfers. Further disentanglement of these three types of transfers is problematic in the LIS data, but for the group of older people we can reasonably assume that this category consists mainly of old-age transfers, being pensions. The results of the decomposition analysis show that in the case of the older people, the overall poverty reducing effect of tax/benefits systems can be almost completely attributed to old-age transfers. In other words, pension schemes are responsible for lifting roughly 55 per cent of the older population out of poverty.[4] Since we are mainly interested in the older population in this chapter, we do not go into detail about the social transfers which are mainly aimed at the working-age population, such as family, unemployment and education transfers. Instead, we group them together into 'other transfers' as the second income source. Indeed, the table shows that for the older population only two percentage points of the poverty reduction via tax/benefits systems can be attributed to these other transfers. This equals 4 percent of the overall poverty reduction via tax/benefits systems. Third, we present the distributional effect of income taxes and social security contributions. Since income taxes and social contributions reduce the disposable income, they may draw incomes below the poverty threshold, which is indicated by the negative sign. So for older people, income taxes and social security contributions contribute to an increase of the poverty rate based on disposable income with three percentage points on (unweighted) average.

Cross-country variation

Figure 29.1 shows the cross-country variation in poverty rates and in poverty reduction by tax/benefits systems among older people for 32 countries around 2012.[5] The figure indicates that the poverty rates based on market income vary substantially across the countries. The highest poverty rate can be found in the Netherlands where 91 percent of the older people fall below the poverty threshold, followed by Sweden (89 percent), Finland (88 percent), Germany (87 percent) and the Czech Republic (87 percent). The countries with the lowest poverty rates based on market income are Guatemala (34 percent), Taiwan (45 percent), the Dominican Republic (46 percent) and Peru (53 percent). Subsequently, the figure also shows substantial variation in poverty rates based on disposable income. The countries with the highest poverty rates are South Korea (56 percent), Australia (50 percent) and Peru (42 percent) whereas the countries with the lowest poverty rates are the Netherlands (7 percent), Brazil (8 percent) and Luxembourg (8 percent).

Interestingly, the countries with the highest poverty rates based on market income are not the countries with the highest poverty rates on disposable income. The reason for this is that there is substantial variation in the magnitude of poverty reduction (i.e. lifting older people out of poverty) via tax/benefits systems across countries, which is graphically indicated by the grey bars in the figure. The most notable example is the Netherlands, as this is the country with the highest poverty rate based on market income, the lowest poverty rate based on disposable income and the largest poverty alleviation. Here, 84 percent of the older people are lifted above the poverty line via social transfers. Also in Luxembourg, Czech Republic, Poland and Germany, the share of older people with a disposable income below the poverty threshold is more than 70 percentage points lower as a result of the tax/benefit systems. The countries with the smallest antipoverty impact of social transfers are Guatemala, the Dominican Republic and South Korea. In these three countries, the difference between poverty rates before and after redistribution is smaller than 10 percentage points. It should be noted that these countries are

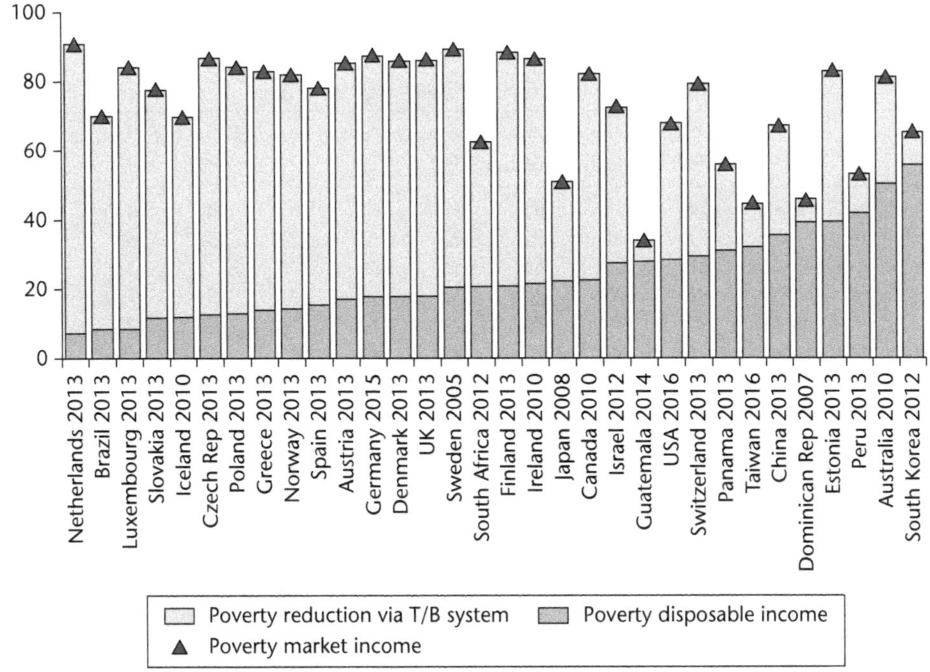

Figure 29.1 Relative poverty rates (PL 60) among older people in LIS countries around 2012.

Source: Database Caminada & Wang (2019) based on LIS, and own calculations.

among those with the lowest poverty rates before redistribution. Yet, with the small magnitude of redistribution by income taxes and benefits, these countries end up in the group of countries with the higher poverty rates based on disposable income.

Developments over time

Subsequently, we examine the developments in old-age poverty and poverty reduction through pensions between 1985 and 2013 in Table 29.2a. In Table 29.2b, we present the same concepts but for the working-age population. The selection of countries for which at least three waves are available (around 1985, around 1997 and around 2013) limits the analysis to a sample of 14 LIS countries. Between 1985 and 2013, poverty rates among older people based on market income declined in only four countries, namely Denmark, Sweden, Switzerland and the U.S. In all other countries, the poverty rates among older people increased, with modest increases in the majority of the countries. In contrast, the poverty rates based on disposable income declined in almost all countries between 1985 and 2013. They only increased in Australia and Taiwan. A remarkable trend can be observed in Sweden, where the poverty rate declined from 21 to 8 percent and then increased to 21 percent again, which is probably related to the Swedish pension reform that was adopted in 1998.[6]

The antipoverty effect of tax/benefit systems (i.e. pensions) increased in all countries but the U.S., where the antipoverty effect slightly decreased from 40 to 39 percent. In a number of countries the poverty rates based on disposable income sharply declined as a result of strong increases in redistribution. For example, in Denmark the poverty rate dropped from 56 to 18 percent and the reduction of poverty via the tax/benefit system increased from 31 to 68 percent.

Table 29.2a Poverty rates and poverty alleviation, older people, 14 LIS countries, 1985–2013

	Poverty market income (PL60)			*Poverty disposable income (PL60)*			*Poverty alleviation*		
	Around 1985	*Around 1997*	*Around 2013*	*Around 1985*	*Around 1997*	*Around 2013*	*Around 1985*	*Around 1997*	*Around 2013*
Australia (85-95-10)	78	79	81	49	44	50	30	35	31
Canada (87-97-10)	77	81	82	25	17	22	52	63	60
Denmark (87-95-13)	88	89	86	56	35	18	31	54	68
Finland (87-95-13)	86	90	88	32	18	21	54	72	67
Germany (84-98-15)	87	89	87	23	16	18	65	73	70
Ireland (87-96-10)	76	*81*	86	25	*42*	22	50	*40*	65
Israel (86-97-12)	73	76	73	32	35	27	41	40	45
Netherlands (83-99-13)	90	94	91	14	15	7	77	79	84
Norway (86-95-13)	79	86	82	39	29	14	40	57	67
Sweden (87-95-05)	92	93	89	21	8	21	71	86	69
Switzerland (82-00-13)	83	83	79	37	28	29	46	55	50
Taiwan (86-97-16)	26	44	45	24	33	32	2	11	13
UK (86-99-13)	86	87	86	24	34	18	62	53	68
US (86-97-16)	70	74	68	31	30	28	40	44	39
Mean-14	78	82	80	31	28	23	47	54	57

Table 29.2b Poverty rates and poverty alleviation, working-age population, 1985–2013

	Poverty market income (PL60)			*Poverty disposable income (PL60)*			*Poverty alleviation*		
	Around 1985	*Around 1997*	*Around 2013*	*Around 1985*	*Around 1997*	*Around 2013*	*Around 1985*	*Around 1997*	*Around 2013*
Australia (85-95-10)	20	23	23	14	16	15	6	7	8
Canada (87-97-10)	20	24	28	15	17	19	6	8	9
Denmark (87-95-13)	19	22	23	11	8	12	8	14	12
Finland (87-95-13)	19	29	25	8	9	13	11	20	11
Germany (84-98-15)	18	20	23	11	10	16	7	10	7
Ireland (87-96-10)	33	*32*	39	22	*17*	15	11	*15*	24
Israel (86-97-12)	25	26	29	15	18	21	9	8	7
Netherlands (83-99-13)	25	19	22	9	10	13	16	9	9
Norway (86-95-13)	12	19	23	8	10	14	4	9	9
Sweden (87-95-05)	20	29	23	11	12	10	10	17	14
Switzerland (82-00-13)	10	12	12	10	10	11	1	2	1
Taiwan (86-97-16)	10	12	12	9	12	12	0	0	1
UK (86-99-13)	25	26	28	14	16	15	12	10	13
US (86-97-16)	22	22	25	19	19	21	3	3	4
Mean-14	20	22	24	13	13	15	7	9	9

Notes: Ireland 1996: income data net of income taxes (marked italic). Sweden is included although latest data year available is 2005.

Source: Database Caminada & Wang (2019) based on LIS, and own calculations.

Also Norway witnessed substantial declines in poverty rates as a result of an increased antipoverty effect of social transfers. In other countries, the increased antipoverty effect of tax/benefit systems was used to offset (to some extent) the increased poverty rates based on market income. In Ireland, for instance, the poverty rate based on market income rose from 76 to 86 percent over the period 1985–2013, whereas the poverty rate based on disposable income declined from 25 to 22 percent. In Taiwan, the increase in poverty based on market income from 26 to 45 percent was translated into a relatively modest increase in poverty based on disposable income from 24 to 32 as a result of the increased antipoverty effect of the tax/benefit system.

Interestingly, the trends in poverty rates and the share of older people lifted out of poverty seem to follow a different path from the trends in poverty and antipoverty effects of tax/benefit systems among the working-age population The most notable difference between the two groups is that the old-age poverty rate based on disposable income declined in most countries whereas for the working-age population it increased in most countries. The averages of the country groups display similar trends. A remarkable case in this respect is the Netherlands. As a result of increased redistribution, the old-age poverty rate based on disposable income declined between 1983 and 2013, whereas in the working-age population the poverty rate increased as a result of smaller antipoverty effects of the tax/benefit system. Interestingly, in 2013 the poverty rate based on disposable income is even lower among older people (7 percent) than among the working-age population (13 percent). Yet it should be noted that the Netherlands is an exception in this respect, as in the other countries with such opposite trends between older people and the working-age population the poverty rate remains higher among older people. Finally, Norway is an interesting case. Here the opposite trends of old-age and working-age poverty after transfers converged to a similar poverty rate of 14 percent in 2013. However, the underlying dynamics differ significantly. In the case of older people, there was a relatively modest increase in the poverty rate based on market income and a substantial increase in the antipoverty effect of the tax/benefit system. In contrast, in the case of the working-age population there was a relatively large increase in the poverty rate based on market income and a relatively small increase in the share of people lifted out of poverty via the tax/benefit system.

Analysis of the results: the role of pensions

In response to the pressure stemming from the ageing of populations, pension reforms have been implemented in many Western countries over past years. More structural long-term reforms of the pension systems entail changes from the defined benefit to the defined contribution system (Barr & Diamond, 2009). In more recent years, many countries have opted for changes in the parameters of their pension systems. In particular, the retirement age has been changed in a number of countries.[7] Many countries have implemented automatic links between pension benefits and life expectancy. Other changes that have been implemented entail increases in employee contributions, changes in the tax incentives related to pensions, measures to increase the coverage of pensions, for instance by using auto-enrollment, or changes of the indexation rules (OECD, 2017; Bridgen, 2018). Obviously, these institutional changes will affect the level of pension benefits and that might explain the varying incidence of old-age poverty and the varying extent of the share of older people lifted out of poverty via pensions as presented above.

First of all, the level at which the first layer of (public) pension benefits are set will be an important factor that might explain the variation in old-age poverty. In OECD countries this first layer consists of basic pensions, minimum pensions or social assistance; in some countries a combination of these programs can be seen. OECD data allow us to roughly compare, for a number of countries, old-age poverty with the benefit levels of these safety net schemes. The OECD (2017) provides these public benefit levels as a percentage of average economy-wide earnings (see Table 29.3, left panel). Several countries combine relatively high minimum level pension benefits with relatively high poverty alleviation and relatively low poverty rates: Luxembourg, Netherlands, Denmark, Norway, Sweden, Finland, Slovakia and Austria. The US, Japan and South Korea combine relatively low minimum benefit levels with relatively low poverty alleviation and relatively high poverty rates. Germany combines low minimum benefits with low poverty and high poverty alleviation. This implies that the second (or third) layer of the pension system is relatively important in this country. Australia on the other hand, combines relatively high minimum benefits with relatively low poverty alleviation. For some other countries, including Switzerland, the UK, Israel and Iceland, we do not find a clear relationship between the level of minimum benefits and poverty rates and poverty alleviation.

Table 29.3 Minimum pension benefits and net pension replacement rates

	Minimum pension benefits as a % of average earnings in a country, 2016			*Net pension replacement rates for low, average and high earners (% of individual earnings)*		
	Basic	*Minimum*	*Social assistance*	*Low*	*Average*	*High*
Australia	27.6	–	–	95.0	42.6	45.4
Austria	–	–	27.8	92.2	91.8	90.9
Brazil				92.4	76.4	76.4
Canada	13.5	–	19.2	62.2	53.4	38.5
China				104.4	83.0	77.0
Czech Republic	8.9	11.7	12.4	88.3	60.0	48.7
Denmark	17.6	–	18.6	110.3	80.2	76.2
Estonia	14.7	–	14.7	73.7	57.4	51.1
Finland	17.4	–	21.0	66.9	65.0	65.1
Germany	–	–	20.1	54.7	50.5	49.8
Greece	23.0	–	–	60.7	53.7	54.1
Iceland	5.7	–	17.9	85.5	75.7	77.8
Ireland	34.1	–	32.4	70.0	42.3	32.4
Israel	12.9	–	23.5	100.4	75.1	54.9
Japan	15.3	–	19.0			
Luxembourg	9.8	36.7	28.8	98.3	88.4	83.6
Netherlands	26.3	–	–	105.1	100.6	100.2
Norway	32.5	–	–	64.8	48.8	41.3
Poland	–	22.2	15.2	37.2	38.6	37.9
South Africa				32.1	17.1	11.9
South Korea	–	–	5.5			
Slovak Republic	–	40.7	19.8	85.0	83.8	83.5
Spain	–	33.3	19.3	79.3	81.8	81.7
Sweden	22.3	–	–	62.4	54.9	67.6
Switzerland	-	16.5	22.6	57.4	44.9	31.5
UK	22.2	–	–	52.1	29.0	20.7
US	-	–	16.7	59.9	49.1	42.4

Note: Dashes indicate that a country does not have such a pension scheme; empty cells indicate that information is not available.

Source: OECD (2017), pp. 89 and 109.

Another comparison can be made between redistribution and old-age poverty, on the one hand, and replacement rates of pension benefits on the other. The replacement rate is defined as pension entitlement as a percentage of gross pre-retirement earnings. Replacement rates can be calculated in gross or in net terms. For the disposable income of older people, net replacement rates will matter more than gross rates. The OECD has calculated net replacement rates from public and private (mandatory) pension schemes for different levels of earnings: low, average and high (see Table 29.3, right panel).[8] It appears that most of the countries that show low old-age poverty rates and high poverty alleviation have relatively high replacement rates for low-income earners. In Denmark, the Netherlands, Luxembourg, Austria, Czech Republic, Denmark, Slovak Republic and Brazil these low-income earner replacement rates lie above 85 percent. Australia and Israel remarkably combine relatively high replacement rates for low-income earners with relatively high old-age poverty rates and relatively small poverty alleviation. The targeting of pension benefits does not seem to be optimal in these countries. On the other hand, some countries, including Germany, Sweden, Norway and the UK combine relatively low replacement rates for low-income earners with relatively low poverty and relatively large poverty alleviation. For these countries, replacement rates for low-income earners are not a good indicator of the effectiveness of pensions to reduce poverty.[9] A few countries, including the Netherlands, Luxembourg, Austria, Denmark and Slovak Republic also have high replacement rates for average- and high-income earners. These countries have relatively universal and generous pension schemes, that also succeed in keeping most of the older people out of poverty.

Conclusion

Given the ageing of the populations in many Western countries, older people constitute an important group in the analysis of poverty. In this chapter, we examined the poverty incidence among older people across LIS countries, relying on data from the Luxembourg Income Study. The data show that poverty rates are substantially reduced via tax/benefit systems (mainly by pensions); on average 56 percent of older people are lifted out of poverty. These results are in line with the results of studies which are based on regression models (Been et al., 2017; Jacques et al., 2018). Furthermore, the data show that old-age poverty rates and the redistribution through pensions vary substantially across countries. A closer look at minimum pension benefits and at pension replacement rates for different earnings levels provides insight into the varying incidence of old-age poverty and the varying magnitude of redistribution through pensions.

Finally, we examined the developments in the old-age poverty incidence over time. In almost all countries, the poverty rates based on disposable income declined substantially between 1985 and 2013. The reason for this substantial reduction in old-age poverty is the increase of the share of older people lifted out of poverty via tax/benefit systems, mainly through pensions. Interestingly, the trend in the poverty rates of the working-age population differs from that of older people; in most countries of our sample, the poverty incidence increased for the working-age population. However, it should be noted that in most Western countries, poverty rates for older people are still at a higher level than for the working-age population.

Notes

1 This study is part of the research program *Reform of Social Legislation* of Leiden University. Financial support from *Instituut Gak* is gratefully acknowledged.
2 Caminada et al. (2019c) applied three widely used equivalence scales methods: from LIS (this study), OECD modified, and OECD original. Pearson correlation of levels of income inequality and fiscal

redistribution via tax-benefit systems across 31 countries for the three equivalence scales methods show values of .99 and over (not shown), indicating that the equivalence scale method used hardly matters.

3 For a more extensive discussion about the distinction between public and private pensions in empirical research, see Been et al. (2017).

4 More precisely: 55.7 percent of the older population is lifted out of poverty by pensions. Taking into account other transfers and income taxes and social security contributions, the calculation is as follows: 55.7 + 2.2 − 3.1 = 54.9.

5 The seven additional countries (compared to the 25 countries included in Table 29.1) are: Sweden, Japan, Canada, Taiwan, China, Dominican Republic and South Korea.

6 Sweden transformed its public pension system to a notional defined-contribution plan; that is a defined-contribution plan financed on a pay-as-you-go basis.

7 Interestingly, in the Czech Republic and Poland the retirement age was reduced, which will directly lead to lower replacement rates (OECD, 2017).

8 It should be mentioned that these calculations are made for 'standard' workers, on the basis of various assumptions. For an analysis of replacement rates of actual workers in the Netherlands, using extensive microdata see Knoef et al. (2016).

9 For a more general discussion about the limitations of the use of replacement rates of pension benefits, see Chybalski and Marcinkiewicz (2016).

References

Barr, N., & Diamond, P. (2009) Reforming pensions: principles, analytical errors, and policy directions. *International Social Security Review* 62(2): 5–29.

Been, J., Caminada, K., Goudswaard, K., & van Vliet, O. (2017) Public/private pension mix, income inequality, and poverty among the elderly in Europe: an empirical analysis using new and revised OECD data. *Social Policy & Administration* 51(7): 1079–1100.

Bridgen, P. (2018) The retrenchment of public pension provision in the liberal world of welfare during the age of austerity – and its unexpected reversal, 1980–2017. *Social Policy & Administration*, doi.org/10.1111/spol.12444.

Caminada, K., & Wang, J. (2019) Leiden LIS Budget Incidence Fiscal Redistribution Dataset on Relative Income Poverty Rates for 49 LIS countries, 1967–2016. Leiden University.

Caminada, K., Wang, J., Goudswaard, K., & Wang, C. (2017) Income inequality and fiscal redistribution in 47 LIS-countries (1967–2014). *LIS Working Paper Series* no. 724, Luxembourg.

Caminada. K., Wang, J., Goudswaard, K., & Wang, C. (2019a) Relative income poverty rates and poverty alleviation via tax/benefit systems in 49 LIS-countries, 1967–2016. *LIS Working Paper Series* no. 761, Luxembourg.

Caminada, K., Goudswaard, K., Wang, C., & Wang, J. (2019b) Has the redistributive effect of social transfers and taxes changed over time across countries? *International Social Security Review* 72(1): 3–31. http://dx.doi.org/10.1111/issr.12193.

Caminada, K., Goudswaard, K., Wang, C., & Wang, J. (2019c) Income inequality and fiscal redistribution in 31 countries after the crisis. *Comparative Economic Studies* 61(1): 119–148.

Chybalski, F., & Marcinkiewicz, E. (2016) The replacement rate: an imperfect indicator of pension adequacy in cross-country analyses. *Social Indicators Research* 126(1): 99–117.

Figini, P. (1998) inequality measures, equivalence scales and adjustment for household size and composition. *LIS Working Paper Series* no. 185, Luxembourg.

Gornick, J.C., Ragnarsdóttir, B.H., & Kostecki, S. (2013) LIS, Cross-National Data Center in Luxembourg: an overview. *LIS Technical Working Paper Series* no. 5, Luxembourg.

Guillaud, E., Olckers, M., & Zemmour, M. (2017) Four levers of redistribution: the impact of tax and transfer systems on inequality reduction. *LIS Working Paper Series* No. 695, Luxembourg.

Haveman, R., Holden, K., Romanov, A., & Wolfe, B. (2007) Assessing the maintenance of savings sufficiency over the first decade of retirement. *International Tax and Public Finance* 14(4): 481–502.

Jacques, P., Leroux, M., & Stevanovic, D. (2018) Poverty among the elderly: the role of public pension systems. Working Paper 18–07. Chaire de recherché Industrielle Alliance sur les enjeux économiques des changements démographiques.

Jesuit, D.K., & Mahler, V.A. (2010) Comparing government redistribution across countries: the problem of second-order effects. *LIS Working Paper Series* no. 546, Luxembourg.

Jesuit, D.K., & Mahler, V.A. (2017) Fiscal redistribution in comparative perspective: recent evidence from the Luxembourg Income Study (LIS) datacenter. *LIS Working Paper Series* no. 717, Luxembourg.

Kammer, A., Niehues, J., & Peichl, A. (2012) Welfare regimes and welfare state outcomes in Europe. *Journal of European Social Policy* 22(5): 455–471.

Kangas, O., & Palme, J. (2000) Does social policy matter? Poverty cycles in OECD countries. *International Journal of Health Services* 30(2): 335–352.

Knoef, M.G., Been, J., Alessie, R., Caminada, C.L.J., Goudswaard, K.P., & Kalwij, A. (2016) Measuring retirement savings adequacy: developing a multi-pillar approach in the Netherlands. *Journal of Pension Economics and Finance* 15(1): 55–89.

LIS Cross-National Data Center in Luxembourg (2019) *Luxembourg Income Study (LIS) Database*, www.lisdatacenter.org/ (accessed between December 2017 and December 2018, through the secured remote-execution system from the LIS database, for 49 countries). Luxembourg: LIS.

Musgrave, R.A., Case, K.E., & Leonard, H.B. (1974) The distribution of fiscal burdens and benefits. *Public Finance Quarterly* 2(July): 259–311.

Nieuwenhuis, R., Munzi, T., & Gornick, J.C. (2017) Comparative research with net and gross income data: an evaluation of two netting down procedures for the LIS Database. *Review of Income and Wealth* 63(3): 564–573.

Nolan, B., & Marx, I. (2009) Economic Inequality, Poverty, and Social Exclusion. In: W. Salverda, B. Nolan & T.M. Smeeding (eds.), *The Oxford Handbook of Economic Inequality*, New York: Oxford University Press: 315–341.

OECD (2008) *Growing Unequal? Income Distribution and Poverty in OECD Countries*. Paris.

OECD (2017) *Pensions at a Glance 2017: OECD and G20 Indicators*. Paris.

Price, D. (2006) The poverty of older people in the UK. *Journal of Social Work Practice* 20(3): 251–266.

Smeeding T., & Latner, J. (2015) PovcalNet, WDI and 'All the Ginis': a critical review. *The Journal of Economic Inequality* 13(4): 603–628.

van Vliet, O., Been, J., Caminada, K., & Goudswaard, K. (2012) Pension reform and income inequality among the elderly in 15 European countries. *International Journal of Social Welfare* 21, 4(s1): S8–S21.

30

Behavioural public policy and poverty

Katherine Curchin

Introduction

This chapter examines attempts by policy makers to incorporate insights generated by the behavioural sciences into policy aimed at alleviating poverty. These attempts are part of a larger push to use behavioural insights to transform public policy and international development in fields as diverse as energy consumption, organ donation, recycling, healthy eating, and taxation compliance (Shafir 2013; OECD 2017; Oliver 2013a). Changing the behaviour of people living in poverty is often a focus of policy, but this chapter focuses only on the movement linked to behavioural economics and related fields which has emerged in the last two decades.

This chapter begins by explaining the core concepts of 'behavioural economics' and 'libertarian paternalism'. It then describes how behavioural economics came to be influential among policymakers. Special attention is paid to two particular aspects of behavioural economics – the concept of 'nudge' and the idea of developing and implementing programmes through randomised controlled trials. The chapter then describes the research into the psychological effects of poverty. Though this field is still in its infancy, a range of ways that behavioural knowledge of scarcity might be applied to policy and programmes are canvassed, including interventions aimed at influencing household saving and borrowing, productivity and investment in human capital through responsive parenting and post-compulsory schooling. Behavioural insights also have implications for the design of labour regulations and welfare state transfers. Attention then turns to critiques directed at behavioural public policy, including concerns about paternalism and what critics see as a misguided focus on individual-level causes of poverty at the expense of structural causes.

Behavioural economics and nudge

The branch of economics called behavioural economics has been central to the rise of behavioural public policy. Behavioural economics incorporates into economics findings from psychology about how people make judgements and decisions. It is concerned with the ways that the decisions of real people depart from the rationality assumed by neoclassical economics. The work of Amos Tversky and Daniel Kahneman (Tversky and Kahneman

1974; Kahneman and Tversky 1979) was particularly influential to the establishment of the field of behavioural economics.

Behavioural economics has shown that due to cognitive biases, people make systematic errors when making many decisions, including decisions about how to spend and invest their money. Because these errors are systematic rather than random they do not cancel each other out across the population. Part of the reason people make suboptimal decisions is that they do not always have all the relevant information. But more than that, people process that information and form judgements in ways that are not always rational, at least in a narrowly defined utility-maximising sense.

Unlike *homo economicus*, humans are unable to accurately calculate the net utility produced by all available options (Thaler and Sunstein 2008, 6–8). Instead they tend to make decisions based on 'heuristics', in other words, rules of thumb. Just as internet connections have limited capacity to carry data (bandwidth), human brains can only take in and process a limited amount of information at any given time. Behavioural scientists have drawn attention to two different modes of thinking – a fast, automatic mode that relies on mental associations, and a deliberative mode which is slower and more effortful (Kahneman 2011). People rely greatly on the automatic mode to cope with the volumes of decisions they must make in daily life.

Making rational decisions requires understanding probability, yet behavioural science shows that people generally have a poor grasp of probability. Even people possessing a postgraduate education in statistics have faulty intuitions about probability (Kahneman 2011). People also make errors because they have limited attention. They focus on the more attention-grabbing features of a product for example, at the expense of other features that are important but less obvious. People are loss averse, which means that they are more affected by losses than gains, and they are reluctant to part with what they already have in exchange for something of equal value (Laibson 1997). This leads them to stick with what they know (the default) rather than risk trying new things. People are very impatient in the short-run, but very patient in the long-run. This means they are inconsistent in how they discount the future, and makes them vulnerable to actions that are gratifying in the present but have long-term costs. They also have limited willpower, so sometimes make choices they know are not in their best interests, for example by spending money they intended to save. Finally, people are social creatures and greatly influenced by the people around them. Social norms, role models, group identities, peer pressure and perceptions of fairness have all been shown empirically to have a large effect on behaviour.

The development of these insights in the laboratory and in the field has filtered into policy discussion. In the early years of the twenty-first century several behavioural economists proposed that the presumption against paternalism should be overturned on the grounds of empirical evidence that people often make choices that are contrary to their own welfare (Camerer et al. 2003). Because people make systematic errors in their reasoning, paternalistic intervention could help them better achieve their intentions. Behaviour economist Richard Thaler and legal scholar Cass Sunstein proposed that paternalism need not be coercive (Thaler and Sunstein 2008). Behavioural science has demonstrated that, because of the biases mentioned above, minor details such as the order in which options are presented and the language in which options are described (framing) can substantially affect which options are more likely to be chosen. In some situations, changing the decision-making context can have a greater impact than improving incentives. People can respond to cues from their immediate environment in ways that are beneath their conscious awareness.

Thaler and Sunstein suggested that by tweaking the way choices are presented governments can 'nudge' citizens toward the option which is in their best interest. For example, by setting one option as the default, the proportion of people choosing that option could be greatly increased. Careful attention to the order options appear in and the way they are framed (in their parlance, the 'choice architecture') could also affect what people choose. They argued that by employing nudges governments could reduce the need to rely on forms of stronger regulation which deny people freedom to choose. For example, consumer protection could be improved by requiring companies to disclose information about their products and prices in a form that will be easy for consumers to understand and use. They held that the opportunity to choose was valuable in itself. They coined the intentionally oxymoronic term 'libertarian paternalism' for their new philosophy of regulation, which they promoted as a new Third Way, capable of appealing to progressives (who seek to prevent harm) and libertarians (who want to preserve choice) (Thaler and Sunstein 2008, 252–253).

Nudge has gained popularity as a low cost method of improving the effectiveness of existing programmes. The prestige of economics no doubt helped attract policy makers' interest in this new approach to thinking about policy tools (John 2018). In 2010 the Cameron government in the United Kingdom was persuaded to set a specialist unit (the Behavioural Insights Team (BIT)) within the Cabinet Office whose job was to promote behavioural economics within the civil service. The way had been paved by earlier work by the strategy unit of the UK Cabinet Office into possible applications of behavioural science to policy (Halpern et al. 2004). The term 'behavioural insights' was coined to encompass not just findings from behavioural economics but also from other behavioural sciences, many of which predate behavioural economics and have been influencing specialised policy areas in less high profile ways for decades (John 2018). They created accessible summaries of behavioural findings and worked with civil servants to create demonstration projects which they evaluated using randomised control trials (RCTs).

In RCTs, experimental subjects are randomly separated into a treatment group which receives the intervention and a control group that does not, and the outcomes for the two groups are compared in order to discover the impact of the intervention. Under ideal conditions, RCTs are a relatively straightforward and intuitive way of demonstrating whether an intervention works and they allow policy makers to gauge its cost effectiveness. While many of the psychological concepts inspiring these interventions were developed through laboratory experiments in which the research subjects are often college students, field experiments have become a popular way of testing whether interventions work on the actual targets of interventions in natural settings (Glennerster and Takavarasha 2013). Although RCTs have a long history in social policy, their use is more established in the field of medicine (Leigh 2018). The demonstration projects of the BIT typically involved small tweaks to existing government programmes for which outcome data was already being collected and this made it easier to run an RCT.

BITs demonstrated that compliance rates could be cheaply improved by reducing the cognitive difficulty in complying with government's expectations, for example by redesigning forms to make them easier to fill in. The money that BIT generated for the government by improving the effectiveness of tax collection far outweighed the cost of running the BIT. This persuaded other governments to copy this approach and BITs were established in many other countries (John 2018). The practice of evaluating innovations using RCTs became a hallmark of these teams. By 2014 there were 51 countries whose central governments were implementing behaviourally informed policy (Whitehead et al. 2014).

Behavioural policy has been spread globally by international organisations such as the European Commission, by development agencies and charities, and through the corporate social responsibility activities of multinational corporations (John 2018; Whitehead et al. 2014; Mayne et al. 2018). A major milestone in the spread of these ideas was their endorsement in *The World Development Report 2015: Mind, Behavior and Society* produced by the World Bank (World Bank 2015). Developed with input from leading behavioural scientists, this report urges development practitioners to apply behavioural insights in interventions addressing poverty, early childhood education, household finance, productivity, health, and climate change and to measure the effectiveness of interventions using RCTs (World Bank 2015). It should, however, be noted that in some less economically developed countries the incorporation of insights from behavioural sciences into programmes in fields such as HIV prevention predates the coining of the term nudge in the West (Whitehead et al. 2014).

Although much attention has been given to nudge, it is important to recognise that the influence of behavioural insights on policy is potentially much broader. BITs have not done away with traditional tools of government such as prohibitions, the provision of information, or the use of incentives (John 2018). Rather they have aimed to improve the effectives of these tools, often by improving the way government communicates. For example, incentives can be made more influential if they are more salient and more immediate. Scholars have also argued that behavioural sciences can offer grounds for coercive regulation to, for example, prevent manipulation of consumers by unscrupulous firms (Oliver 2013b). As we will see below, behavioural insights are being used to argue in favour of important features of the welfare state.

The psychological effects of poverty

Up to this point this chapter has described the emergence of behavioural public policy in general. I now want to turn to its application to policy aimed at alleviating poverty. Of particular relevance to anti-poverty interventions is an emerging body of research showing that the experience of economic scarcity and financial insecurity can result in suboptimal decision making (Mullainathan and Shafir 2013).

Trying to survive with an inadequate income is stressful and tiring. The working hours of those experiencing poverty may fluctuate and their income may be volatile. Unlike people with greater financial resources, people who live from pay packet to pay packet have no slack in their budgets. This means that all their spending decisions involve trade-offs. Unlike better-off people, they cannot afford to give in to temptation or make mistakes and they are very vulnerable to sudden changes in their income or unexpected expenses. Having no financial slack is expensive: people with inadequate incomes to pay their bills are often forced to pay reconnection fees or late fees or resort to high-interest loans such as payday lenders. Researchers have argued that the mental effort devoted to making financial decisions leaves people on low income cognitively taxed (Mullainathan and Shafir 2013). Attention, will power and fluid intelligence are all limited resources that poverty depletes. People on low incomes often live in noisy, crowded spaces and this makes it harder to get the sleep and relaxation needed to replenish cognitive resources (Gandy et al. 2016).

The mind fixates involuntarily on immediate unfulfilled needs. Mullainathan and Shafir (2013) have argued that this is true not just of money but other needs such as time, food, and social interaction. This can cause people experiencing deprivation to discount the future severely, focusing on getting by day-to-day rather than on preparing for the future. Less urgent problems, though potentially serious and worthy of attention, fall outside of their mental tunnel. The intense focus created by scarcity is, in some ways, adaptive because it helps people solve their immediate problems (Sheehy-Skeffington and Rea 2017). But it makes more difficult the actions that enable people to exit from poverty – including studying, looking for work, improving productivity, saving money and paying off debt. Researchers have shown that the cognitive effects of scarcity can be induced in well-off college students in experiments designed to make them feel scarcity (Mullainathan and Shafir 2013).

Researchers have also shown that socioeconomic status affects people's sense that they have power over what happens in their lives. People who perceive themselves to be low status have lower self-efficacy and, in experiments, artificially making people feel lower status induces lower self-efficacy (Sheehy-Skeffington 2015). Together these findings explain why people living in disadvantaged communities are often observed to make counterproductive choices that trap them in poverty. Researchers hope that identifying the root of problematic behaviour in the cognitive features humans share might promote compassion for people living in adverse circumstances (Mullainathan and Shafir 2013).

Using behavioural insights to alleviate poverty

Various applications of behavioural insights to policy aimed at alleviating poverty have been proposed and developed. These concern household saving and borrowing, job seeking, productivity, working conditions, families' investment in education and parenting, social programmes and welfare state transfers.

Helping people accumulate savings has been an important focus of behavioural policy. The behavioural research on scarcity makes clear that having some money in savings – perhaps the equivalent of a month's wages – serves as a cushion, helping people on low and erratic incomes deal with unforeseen expenses (and reducing some of the negative effects of scarcity on cognitive load). Yet various psychological biases such as discounting the future makes saving difficult. Friction costs – such as the time taken to travel to a bank – and procrastination may also lead people to delay saving.

Behavioural researchers identify a lack of access to financial services such as savings accounts as an explanation for why people on low incomes do not save more (Bertrand, Mullainathan, and Shafir 2006). Various programmes have therefore been created to encourage people to save by making it easier for them to open bank accounts, by sending them text messages to prompt them to put money in their account, or by enabling money to be automatically diverted into a savings account every payday. It should be noted that these interventions are classic nudge-style approaches. They do not rely on incentives or coercion, and individuals are able to opt-out (thereby preserving choice).

In addition, matched savings schemes have been created which give people a direct financial incentive to put money away regularly (Gandy et al. 2016). Standard economic approaches can be used alongside behavioural interventions. One proposed way to help people to save is to increase the friction costs involved in making discretionary purchases. Such approaches have been referred to as a 'sludge', whereby small barriers are put in people's way, making the less desirable behaviour slightly more difficult. The BIT has been working on creating an app that will enable people to make it harder for them to access their money at times they know they are vulnerable to temptation (Money Advice Service, Behavioural Insights Team, and Ipsos MORI 2018).

Behavioural researchers have identified demands and expectations of friends and family as an important reason for low rates of savings in some communities (Dupas and Robinson 2013). They have interpreted longstanding practices which may at first glance seem irrational – such as sinking money into illiquid assets – as ways people attempt to avoid these demands. Controversially, they have suggested innovative ways of helping people keep money away from others in their social circle. However, this comes at the risk of destroying customary economic practices which may provide an important safety net in poor communities (World Bank 2015, 90).

Consumer debt is another important focus of behavioural policy. Behavioural research has shown how easy it is for people on inadequate incomes to find themselves mired in debt. Debt can easily become a trap as people focus on the short-term and neglect the future. Unjustified optimism leads people to borrow more than they can comfortably repay. Research shows that people also often irrationally use expensive forms of credit for short-term loans when cheaper options are available. This is explained by the friction costs involved in seeking out the cheaper options (payday loans, for example, may be available at more convenient times and locations than loans from credit unions) and the difficulty of processing the relevant financial information. These problems are exacerbated by the desire of banks and other for-profit providers of financial services to exploit prospective customers' psychological weaknesses. Providers of credit often deliberately communicate their terms in manipulative ways (Bertrand, Mullainathan, and Shafir 2006; Akerlof and Shiller 2015). For example, banks will offer credit cards with initial teaser rates, knowing that many customers will focus erroneously on these initial low interest rates and fail to think about the much higher rates they will have to pay in the longer term.

Research into borrowing behaviour has been used to make arguments for tougher regulation for credit cards and payday loans. Regulation can take the form of banning unsolicited credit card offers, or proscribing the way in which the cost of the loan (interest and fees) are presented to customers. Research in the US has shown that it is easier for consumers to mentally process information about the cost of credit when it is presented in dollar terms, rather than in terms of the annual interest rate. Insights into the manipulation of cognitive biases by for-profit lenders has also been used to justify policies which make more affordable forms of credit available to people on low incomes. Policies may be designed to give not-for-profit credit unions an advantage over for-profit financial institutions (Bubb and Pildes 2014, 1662–1663), or governments and social welfare organisations might offer unsecured low-interest loans themselves.

Behavioural insights have also been applied to ways of increasing income. For example, the BIT in the UK developed and trialled a series of strategies for use in employment centres to encourage unemployed people to put more effort into looking for work. The thought behind this is that job seekers are vulnerable to procrastination and demoralisation – looking for work is arduous and the pay-off is uncertain and delayed. Behavioural researchers have also suggested that some people might also be making poor choices about which jobs to accept, leading them to quit soon after starting, and return quickly to unemployment. They propose ways to influence people to make better choices among job offers (Gandy et al. 2016). Development interventions aimed at increasing the earned income of the self-employed in the global South have made use of behavioural insights (World Bank 2015). For example interventions have been designed to encourage small-scale farmers to invest more of their money in buying fertiliser to increase their crop yield (Banerjee and Duflo 2011).

Behavioural researchers have suggested that employers can improve the productivity of low skill workers by improving pay and conditions (Meuris and Leana 2015). At a national level, the psychology of scarcity provides impetus for reversing the erosion of legislated protections for workers. Enabling workers to have more secure and certain hours is likely to relieve some of the cognitive burden of low paid workers. Similarly, there is speculation that providing accessible, affordable, high quality childcare would greatly reduce the cognitive load of working parents. Not just workers but employers would benefit from the increased attention span and fluid intelligence that these policies could plausibly produce (Meuris and Leana 2015).

Behaviourally informed policies have aimed to increase families' investment in education for their children. Much work in the US context focuses on how to encourage youth from low socioeconomic families and neighbourhoods to apply to college, and in particular to apply to more selective colleges (whose graduates on average earn more). The complexity of college application processes – especially when each college must be applied for separately – has been identified as a significant barrier to college attendance, particularly for those who may lack the confidence, agency, or social networks that their more advantaged peers take for granted. Cheap interventions such as sending high school graduates prompts by text message have proven effective in increasing their likelihood of applying for college. In developing countries the focus has been on how to encourage parents to allow their children to delay entry into the workforce and undertake more years of primary or secondary schooling. The immediate benefits of the child's earning is difficult to forgo for the sake of their greater future earning capacity, especially when the family has few other earners.

Education is not the only form of human capital development that has attracted the attention of behavioural scientists. Good parenting is also understood as a way of investing in children's future earning capacity. Responsive parenting, which supports the brain development of small children and helps get them ready for school, can be difficult for parents who are stressed and exhausted by trying to make ends meet. Behavioural insights have been applied to encouraging parents to read to their children, spend more time talking with them, and use less harsh forms of discipline.

Behaviour science also has some practical recommendations for how providers might optimise the design of programmes targeted to low-income families in order to reduce the cognitive tax they impose (Gandy et al. 2016). Governments have responded to the scarcity research by making some application forms – such as application for free school lunches and student aid for college – simpler to navigate and easier to complete (Sunstein 2016, 720–721). Another suggestion is that service providers should work together to integrate their application processes so that clients do not need to fill in multiple forms with the same information and submit the same documentation multiple times. Eligibility for one service can be a passport into eligibility for other programmes that serve the same clients. Correspondence with clients can be improved to make it easier to understand and respond to. Organisations can also use interpersonal influences on behaviour such as social norms, peer support and role models as a way of increasing the effectiveness of their programmes. Programmes can send clients timely reminders by text message to help them stay motivated and follow through on their intentions. It is also recommended that programmes and training courses meant for people on low incomes have routes to re-engagement in case crises or lack of willpower cause participants to temporarily disengage (Daminger et al. 2015).

Advocates for behavioural policy have identified a number of implications for income support policy. The first is that there are likely to be wide ranging positive consequences from making income support for poor households, especially families with children, more generous. Even one-off transfers of cash can be psychologically transformative especially if they reduce stress by enabling people to pay off loans or to put some money aside as a buffer against future financial shocks. In the US and UK researchers have argued that welfare payments should be made easier to access (Gandy et al. 2016). Take-up rates for payments vary enormously and are affected by stigma, and burdensome application processes (Bertrand, Mullainathan, and Shafir 2004).

Interestingly, the research on the cognitive impact of scarcity has led some people to argue for unconditional cash transfers to low-income families (Daminger et al. 2015, 32–33). The strings attached to payments are often intended to encourage behaviour that facilitates exiting poverty but may be having a perverse impact because complying and demonstrating compliance with conditions imposes a cognitive tax (Curchin 2017; Daminger et al. 2015). This is significant given the international trend toward greater behaviour conditionality in income support systems. Behavioural science suggests that burdensome requirements, which were designed to ensure payments and services go only to the people who most need them, might perversely be an insurmountable barrier to those very people (Daminger et al. 2015). Behavioural science also gives ground for thinking that some other aspects of welfare reform are misguided. For example, maximum lifetime duration limits on welfare receipt are likely to fall outside the tunnel of people who are struggling to make ends meet in the present, and therefore unlikely to influence welfare recipients' present behaviour. Policies such as Universal Credit in the UK which make many people's government payment rates fluctuate monthly in hard to predict ways seem likely to increase the cognitive burden on people living in or near poverty.

Behavioural science also gives us powerful reasons to try to reduce the stigma of poverty and the shame associated with relying on income support. The research on scarcity shows that behaviours that are often interpreted as the result of personal character flaws are likely to be the predictable consequences of struggling to survive on an inadequate income. Behavioural science has shown that people (including those involved in the provision of welfare services) are irrationally prejudiced against poor people and erroneously attribute blame to them (Gandy et al. 2016). The stress of dealing with the stigma of poverty leads to poorer cognitive performance and, therefore, worse decision making. Together these findings suggest that demonising people on low incomes is unfair as well as counterproductive if the goal is reducing poverty (Mounk 2017, 154–156). Behavioural experts have suggested that using intentional language instead of language which 'others' people experiencing poverty is important (Daminger et al. 2015, 42).

Criticisms

Behavioural public policy has been controversial. There is concern that insofar as behavioural policy involves steering people toward better choices, it requires decision makers to make paternalistic judgements about what is in someone else's best interest. Sometimes such interests are well known (for example, seeing their children engaged in and complete education) whereas at other times it is unclear where a person's true interest might lie (for example, saving for the future as opposed to consumption in the present). There is a real danger that programme designers will fail to take seriously, or even be unaware of, the differences between their own values and those of the people affected by their interventions, especially when the latter have different cultural backgrounds and life experiences. This danger is exacerbated because behavioural economics has many ways of explaining participant disengagement from programmes; programme designers might be slow to attribute lacklustre take-up of a programme to lack of relevance to participants' needs and values. Though advocates of nudges are optimistic that governments will use nudges benevolently, there is scope for them to be used to advance policy objectives that people subject to them would not endorse. For this reason there have been calls for greater transparency and public deliberation about the legitimate uses for nudges (Jones, Pykett, and Whitehead 2013, 46). Critics have argued that even though nudges preserve the opportunity to choose, they show little respect for autonomy because they involve manipulating people (Horton 2009).

Behavioural public policy has been criticised for narrowly focusing on the individual level rather than structural causes of poverty (Klein 2017). Nudges in particular appear to have little effect on the power imbalance between the people living in poverty and others – this is one of the reasons for their appeal to policy makers. Nudges, by definition, do not improve the array of options available. Critics argue that a lack of good options is a far more significant problem for people living in poverty than their suboptimal selection from among bad options. Focusing attention on deficient decision making amounts to blaming people for their poverty. While some advocates of nudges believe that the cumulative effect of small tweaks to programmes will eventually lead to transformative change (Halpern 2015; John 2018), critics of nudges see incremental changes as deflecting attention from the more ambitious changes that are urgently needed to address poverty.

Though, in theory, behavioural insights could be used by policy makers across the ideological spectrum (John 2018), there are concerns that, in practice, behavioural interventions are often used in the service of a neoliberal agenda (McMahon 2015). The anti-regulation rhetoric in *Nudge* was embraced by politicians in favour of small government (Horton 2009). The World Development Report 2015 has been criticised for assuming that what people in low-income countries really want is neoliberal economic development (Klein 2017). Critics of behaviourally informed policy contend that its goal is to influence people to behave as if they were the rational utility maximisers of neoclassical economics (Berndt 2015). Where behavioural economics have identified markets that are not serving participants well, policy makers have pursued interventions to try to make market participation more beneficial (or less harmful), rather than seeking to replace them with nonmarket arrangements (Bubb and Pildes 2014). The commitment to allocation through markets is defended by libertarian paternalists on the ground that opportunities to make choices are inherently valuable. The prioritisation of the opportunity to choose within a market place potentially comes at a cost to well-being when nudges are less effective than stronger forms of regulation (Horton 2009).

Conclusion

Policy makers have been attracted to behavioural economics by the rigour enabled by using experiments to establish causation. Yet the study of poverty through the lens of behavioural economics is new and there are still questions about how robust the more dramatic findings will prove as scientists attempt to replicate each other's findings (Sanders, Snijders, and Hallworth 2018, 156–157). Behavioural economics and related disciplines can generate some intriguing explanations for why programmes that aim to alleviate poverty do not always work as anticipated. They hold out the promise of enabling anti-poverty programmes to improve their cost effectiveness through relatively simple changes. This message has proven appealing to governments in high-income countries and among donors of development assistance to the global South. In practice, behaviourally informed policy has been associated with a small government agenda. But there are now scholars drawing on behavioural science to argue for a stronger welfare state on the grounds that more stable work, secure income and generous services will help alleviate the cognitive burden of poverty and enable people to plan better futures for themselves (Curchin 2017). Whether the behavioural turn will make a significant impact on poverty is contested. Opinions are divided as to whether an individual-level analysis of behaviour is helpful, and whether it can be integrated with a societal level of analysis or merely serves to deflect attention from the structural causes of poverty.

References

Akerlof, George A., and Robert J. Shiller. 2015. *Phishing for Phools: the economics of manipulation and deception*. Princeton, NJ: Princeton University Press.

Banerjee, Abhijit V., and Esther Duflo. 2011. *Poor Economics: a radical rethinking of the way to fight global poverty*. New York: Public Affairs.

Berndt, C. 2015. "Behavioural economics, experimentalism and the marketization of development." *Economics and Society* 4 (4): 567–591.

Bertrand, Marianne, Sendhil Mullainathan, and Eldar Shafir. 2004. "A behavioral-economics view of poverty." *The American Economic Review* 94 (2): 419–423.

Bertrand, Marianne, Sendhil Mullainathan, and Eldar Shafir. 2006. "Behavioral economics and marketing in aid of decision making among the poor." *Journal of Public Policy and Marketing* 25 (1): 8–23.

Bubb, Ryan, and Richard H. Pildes. 2014. "How behavioral economics trims its sails and why." *Harvard Law Review* 127 (6): 1593–1678.

Camerer, Colin, Samuel Issacharoff, George Loewenstein, Ted O'Donoghue, and Matthew Rabin. 2003. "Regulation for conservatives: behavioral economics and the case for 'asymmetric paternalism'." *University of Pennsylvania Law Review* 1151 (3): 1211–1254.

Curchin, Katherine. 2017. "Using behavioural insights to argue for a stronger social safety net: beyond libertarian paternalism." *Journal of Social Policy* 46 (2): 231–249.

Daminger, Allison, Jonathan Hayes, Anthony Barrows, and Josh Wright. 2015. *Poverty Interrupted: applying behavioral science to the context of chronic scarcity*. New York: ideas42.

Dupas, Pascaline, and Jonathan Robinson. 2013. "Why don't the poor save more? Evidence from health savings experiments." *American Economic Review* 103 (4): 1138–1171.

Gandy, Kizzy, Katy King, Pippa Streeter Hurle, Chloe Bustin, and Kate Glazebrook. 2016. *Poverty and decision making: how behavioural science can improve opportunity in the UK*. London: Behavioural Insights Team.

Glennerster, Rachel, and Kudzai Takavarasha. 2013. *Running Randomized Evaluations: a practical guide*. Princeton. NJ: Princeton University Press.

Halpern, David. 2015. "Radical incrementalism." *Evaluation* 21 (2): 143–149.

Halpern, David, Clive Bates, Geoff Mulgan, Stephen Aldridge, Greg Beales, and Adam Heathfield. 2004. *Personal Responsibility and Changing Behaviour: the state of knowledge and its implications for public policy*. London: Cabinet Office.

Horton, Tim. 2009. "The darker side of nudging." *Political Quarterly* 80 (2): 295–298.

John, Peter. 2018. *How Far to Nudge? Assessing behavioural public policy*. Cheltenham: Edward Edgar.

Jones, Rhys, Jessica Pykett, and Mark Whitehead. 2013. *Changing Behaviours: on the rise of the psychological state*. Cheltenham: Edward Elgar.

Kahneman, Daniel. 2011. *Thinking, Fast and Slow*. London: Penguin.

Kahneman, Daniel, and Amos Tversky. 1979. "Prospect theory: an analysis of decision under risk." *Econometrica* 47 (2): 263–292.

Klein, Elise. 2017. "The World Bank on mind, behaviour and society." *Development and Change* 48 (3): 481–501.

Laibson, David. 1997. "Golden eggs and hyperbolic discounting." *Quarterly Journal of Economics* 112: 443–477.

Leigh, Andrew. 2018. *Randomistas: how radical researchers changed our world*. Carlton: La Trobe University Press.

Mayne, Ruth, Melanie Kesmaecker-Wissing, Jola Miziniak, and Lucy Knight. 2018. Influencing Behaviours and Practices to Tackle Poverty and Injustice. In *Oxfam Discussion Papers*.

McMahon. 2015. "Behavioral economics as neoliberalism: producing and governing *homo economicus*." *Contemporary Political Theory* 14 (2): 137–158.

Meuris, Jirs, and Carrie R. Leana. 2015. "The high cost of low wages: economic scarcity effects in organizations." *Research in Organizational Behavior* 35: 143–158.

Money Advice Service, Behavioural Insights Team, and Ipsos MORI. 2018. "A behavioural approach to managing money: Ideas and results from the Financial Capability Lab."

Mounk, Yascha. 2017. *The Age of Responsibility*. Cambridge, MA: Harvard University Press.

Mullainathan, Sendhil, and Eldar Shafir. 2013. *Scarcity*. New York: Times Books.

OECD. 2017. *Behavioural Insights and Public Policy: lessons from around the world*. Paris: OECD Publishing.

Oliver, Adam, ed. 2013a. *Behavioural Public Policy*. Cambridge: Cambridge University Press.

Oliver, Adam. 2013b. "From nudging to budging: using behavioural economics to inform public sector policy." *Journal of Social Policy* 42 (4): 685–700.

Sanders, Michael, Veerle Snijders, and Michael Hallworth. 2018. "Behavioural science and policy: where are we now and where are we going?" *Behavioural Public Policy* 2 (2): 144–167.

Shafir, Eldar, ed. 2013. *Behavioral Foundations of Public Policy*. Princeton, NJ: Princeton University Press.

Sheehy-Skeffington, Jennifer. 2015. "Behavioural insights in the age of austerity: how research on the psychology of poverty can help us to stay focused on society." *Angle Journal* 13.

Sheehy-Skeffington, Jennifer, and Jessica Rea. 2017. *How Poverty Affects People's Decision-Making Processes*. York: Joseph Rowntree Foundation.

Sunstein, Cass R. 2016. "The Council of Psychological Advisers." *Annual Review of Psychology* 67: 713–737.

Thaler, Richard H., and Cass R. Sunstein. 2008. *Nudge*. New Haven, CT: Yale University Press.

Tversky, Amos, and Daniel Kahneman. 1974. "Judgment under uncertainty: heuristics and biases." *Science* 185: 1124–1131.

Whitehead, Mark, Rhys Jones, Rachel Howell, Rachel Lilley, and Jessica Pykett. 2014. *Nudging All Over the World: assessing the global impact of the behavioural sciences on public policy*. Swindon and Edinburgh: ESRC Report, Economic and Social Research Council.

World Bank. 2015. *World Development Report 2015: Mind society and behaviour*. Washington, DC: World Bank.

31
Poverty and family

Mary Daly

While we have a strong sense of poverty as a micro-level phenomenon, not a lot of thought has been given to the significance of poverty from a family-related perspective. This is so for several reasons. For one, the household is the dominant collective unit of analysis in poverty research. This, essentially a measurement convenience, leads to a functional and relatively simplistic understanding of how people who live together share income and resources. Our theorisations of family in poverty research are equally rudimentary. There are, of course, studies that seek to understand families in poverty. These tend to focus on revealing the conditions and exigencies of everyday living, exploring empirically how family-related considerations play out in situations of resource constraint (e.g., Daly and Kelly 2015; Hill et al. 2016). Such studies are helpful in revealing the exigencies, practices and mindsets associated with collective sharing (or not) of resources. This kind of work feeds into the considerations developed in this chapter which seeks to open up discussions about aspects of family living and 'being a family' that might pattern both (re)distribution and resource generation and influence how poverty might be affected by familial factors. But we seek to go beyond existing work – which, to the extent that it incorporates family, tends to see it in structural or organisational terms and to construct poverty as little more than a status for those who share a household (given that everyone living in a household which falls below the poverty line is said to be poor). Instead we view family as a complex entity with cultural, relational and structural elements that are relevant to poverty as a phenomenon and experience. The basic argument of the chapter is that variation in the risk, likelihood and experience of poverty is likely to be affected by family-based processes, relationships and structures by virtue of the way that these affect the generation of, access to and distribution of resources. The chapter draws on a range of empirical and theoretical literatures to deepen insights about this complex relationship. It should be noted that our aim is to offer a set of theoretical considerations – backed by evidence where it is available – rather than to test these out empirically. In essence, the chapter offers a set of ideas and a corrective to some of the assumptions underlying existing practice.

For the purposes of analysis, family is conceived as an organisational structure and set of relationships. The former is the more familiar view of the family, emphasising the structure and composition of the family. But family is also a set of relational practices and the fulcrum of certain societal-level norms, values and expectations (such as family being a unit of solidarity and sharing, for example). We do not therefore operate with a prescribed or strictly locational view of family; rather 'intra-familial' as used here refers to family as extending across the family household and beyond the nuclear family to include also extended family. The chapter proceeds as follows. In the first section we look at the prevailing definitions and conventions around poverty measurement. This is followed by a discussion of the family-related factors and the way they operate to affect the generation, access and use of resources (and hence poverty). A short overview section completes the chapter.

Definitional and conceptual considerations

The most widespread ways of conceiving of poverty are either in terms of an absolute amount of income (such as a dollar a day) or a relative cut-off or threshold of average income (see also Chapters 2 and 3). When it comes to measuring poverty, the most common way of doing so in the European countries is in terms of an income cut-off of 50% or 60% of median household equivalised disposable income. In this work households are conventionally taken as the unit of analysis, with individuals classified as poor or non-poor depending on the poverty status of the households in which they live (all members therefore have the same poverty status). Household-based studies have several merits but only if the counterfactual is measuring poverty on an individual basis. Household-level conceptualisation attempts to address issues of sharing and collective modes of living, resource accrual and usage. This work takes account of the relative economies of scale associated with households of different sizes and types. It adjusts for the pooling of income between and within units by relying on equivalence scales that weight for household size and composition. Different equivalence scales and assumptions about sharing are used. A wide range of equivalence scales exist (Buhmann et al. 1998). Among the high-income countries, the most widely used are either the OECD equivalence scale (which assigns a value of 1 to the first household member, of 0.7 to each additional adult and of 0.5 to each child) or the OECD-modified scale that Eurostat adopted in the late 1990s (which assigns a value of 1 to the household head, of 0.5 to each additional adult member, and of 0.3 to each child) (OECD 2013). While these might appear like rather small differences, the results for the estimation of poverty are quite consequential (Davies and Joshi 1994; World Bank 2018).

A problem with the use of equivalence scales though (and relying on collective units more generally) is that, apart from not being derived on the basis of known practice, the adjustment scales assume full pooling and equal sharing among adults and between adults and children. Hence, they assume away the internal processes that may be so consequential for individual and collective resource availability and use and generalise the finding of roughly equivalent levels of (household) poverty for women and men (as well as assuming away variations in child poverty rates). There is information available to cast doubt on the crucial assumption around perfect income sharing. Research on the (then) EU 27 member states – using a special module of the 2010 EU Survey on Income and Living Conditions – found that some 30% of households do not fully pool their income, with 22% partially pooling and 7% not pooling (Ponthieux 2013: 17). A further weakness is that the household is generally treated as passive in the sense that it is a site or setting in which assumed uncontested behaviours around resource accrual and allocation occur. A relatively simplified view of the household is prosecuted also by the reduction of the household to matters of size and composition (mainly understood in terms of differentiating between child and adult by an age cut-off in the weighting for household size). All of this has been subjected to criticism – not least by those studying the gender dimensions of poverty who highlight the likelihood that the assumption of equal sharing underestimates or misconstrues poverty among women and children (Chant 2010; Ponthieux 2013; World Bank 2018).

Looking at the field as a whole it is hard to conclude other than that existing research conventions misclassify and misunderstand how household practices are implicated in (individual and collective) risk of poverty.

Even more, there is also a strong argument to move beyond the household if we are better to understand the genesis, experience and changing extent and nature of poverty. This is because most people live in families rather than households, and families are quite different entities to households. The claim is not that everybody lives as part of a family or even to assert a privileged space for a particular type of 'the family'. There is no doubt that forms of family life are both variable and changing, that for some people a family-based life does not give greater resource access as compared with living alone, and that considerable numbers of people live what could be called 'a non-family-based life'. But the majority of people do have families and if we conceive of family as typically consisting of people who are either related to each other or emotionally and normatively bound together there is a specificity to family that renders it significant in a context of poverty and low income and as potentially different to the situation of people living together as members of a household. In particular, in all societies family is a normative as well as a legal construct, imbued with explicit and implicit obligations around wellbeing and protection from need or harm.

For poverty (or indeed broader resource exchange purposes) then, it is important to go beyond a view of family as a structure or living arrangement and recognise those who consider each other family as normatively positioned in key ways. Sociological work underlines families as complex and multi-layered (e.g., Smart 2007). Incorporating this kind of insight highlights a second relevant level or element of family beyond that of structure or composition: that of culture conceived in terms of practices, norms and values. Following Small et al. (2010), culture refers to people's values, the frames through which they interpret and understand their situation and their repertoires or strategies of action and meaning. From the perspective of the exercise being undertaken here, an interest in culture in the context of poverty or low income directs attention to the ways in which people's familial considerations influence their reasoning, judgements and decisions about the acquisition, management and disbursal of resources. Who 'owns' what? Who 'deserves' what? Instead of claiming that culture causes poverty, culture is of interest because it: (a) allows access to people's subjectivity which is crucial to understanding their personal and familial circumstances and (b) reveals how people's understanding of their situation and their cultural priorities affect their use of resources and their views of how resources are to be shared in a familial context (Lamont and Small 2010). Culture, of course, extends much more widely than family. There are two points to be emphasised in regard to the significance of culture in the context of the relationship between family and poverty: first the accrual and use of resources as a micro-level set of activities is likely to be influenced by beliefs and attitudes associated with familial ties and relationships; second, evidence suggests that poor and low-income sectors of the population make greater recourse to family support than other sectors (Daly and Kelly 2015).

But there is another dimension that has to be added into considerations of family also. This focuses on family-based relationships and draws attention to the exigencies, tasks, interactions and relationships associated with the maintenance and governance of family life. A key insight here is that income sharing and other matters in a context of family are not a given but have to be negotiated and constantly worked out. This perspective on family as an arena of negotiation and performance has been the wellspring of considerable work and new thinking in sociological and feminist studies for several decades now. The idea of 'family practices' as developed in the work of David Morgan (1996, 2011) has been elemental. This directs attention to examining the ways that family members organise their lives and the manner in which they 'do' (i.e., enact and live out) family life, family roles and family relationships. Morgan suggests that this approach is preferable to one which treats of 'the' family, which in his view reifies family. Instead, agency and openness as regards the conduct of family life are emphasised. While this work tends to distance itself from the idea of 'the family', it highlights close relationships, the relational character of family phenomena and the ways in which relationships are lived and seen, instead of taking institutions or cultural systems as fixed or given (Ribbens McCarthy 2012; Castrén and Ketokivi 2015).

These perspectives underline three important points. First, they direct attention to the need to take account of how family life and family relationships are lived, managed and organised and how they might be potentially pivotal in a context of poverty and low income. Second, they point to the need to understand the dynamic interaction between structure and relationships/culture within a familial context. "Poverties are caused by the interaction of micro-structures and micro processes" (Walker and Collins 2004: 212). Third, they direct attention to processes of consumption as well as income and other resource generation. A key challenge, therefore, is to theorise intra-familial processes and relationships together with structural factors. How might we do this?

Analysing intra-familial processes[1]

For this purpose, it is necessary to separate out resource generation, resource access and resource disbursal/consumption and to identify the role of family in each. Obviously, this is a 'theoretical' separation and in the quotidian practice of family life these processes and decisions are heavily intertwined.

Family as affecting resource generation

There are different elements involved here, some of which relate to all forms of collective as against solo living and some which differentiate family as against household.

First, living with others tends to reduce one's risk of poverty and low income because of the economies of scale associated with sharing fixed and other costs among more than one person. If X number of people use the same living space, the costs of maintenance are less than if the space is utilised by only one person. This is one of the reasons why family breakdown is so threatening to income level (and also a reason why so many young people remain in or move back to the parental home). Roberts (2004, cited in Handler and Hasenfeld 2007: 287) calculated for the US that if a couple with one child separates into one two-person unit and one single-person unit they would need an extra 40 per cent on top of their original income to avoid poverty. The act of establishing two households from one involves a set of additional costs. While some of this is passive, there are likely to be more active aspects in the sense of active sharing of costs in a familial setting. Hence, while economies of scale pertain potentially to any type of collective living unit, the way they are managed undoubtedly differs among families and between families and other types of living arrangement.

Second, the poverty-relevant contribution of the family also resides in the activities or tasks that it engages in. When viewed as an economic unit, the family is a major producer of goods for consumption (e.g., meals, laundry, personal care). A somewhat different perspective sees this as 'care' or support. Finch (1989), for example, identified five types of care-giving or mutual support that can be exchanged among family members: economic, accommodation, personal (hands on), practical and child care, and emotional and moral support. In a low-income setting where ill-health and disability tend to be widespread, such care and support can make a huge difference to the risk of poverty, as well as how it is experienced (Hill et al. 2016). The point here is not to set up families as necessarily settings or sources of care and support, or to claim that caring-related behaviour is limited to a familial or kinship setting but, rather, that care-giving and receiving are constitutive of family life in profound ways and affect resource availability and use, either positively or negatively. This kind of contribution is to all intents and purposes unmeasured and unrecognised, however; household or family production (loosely 'the work that goes on within the household or family') is typically excluded from the formal measures of economic activity in the national accounts. Some efforts have been made to value the activities involved, though, many of them by feminist scholars.[2] When the Office for National Statistics in the UK calculated estimates on an experimental basis in 2002, the results suggested that the value added to the economy by UK households in 2000 was some £695 billion (equivalent to 78% of GDP at the time as defined by the national accounts excluding household production) (Allin 2007: 50). Ringen has concluded that half of the economy in Britain is a family economy. "Society sits on a capital of family enterprise" (Ringen 2007: 159). And of course some members of the family benefit from the unpaid work of others – a key theme in gender-inequality literature (e.g., Bennett and Daly 2014).

Family as affecting resource access

First, one may gain a share of someone else's income and/or other material resources. The most obvious assumed beneficiaries here are children or those adults who have few or no resources of their own. But potentially any family member can gain resources as a beneficiary of having access to the income and resources of another family member or of the family as a whole. This 'benefit' can operate also with regard to family membership more broadly, in that we know from research that co-location is not essential for short- and long-term family-based exchanges (Heath and Calvert 2013; Daly and Kelly 2015) and that vibrant kinship networks can be a significant source of financial and other forms of support (Valentine 2008). Information from the European Quality of Life Survey (first carried out in 2003 and repeated every four years since) reveals that over 70% of people in the EU countries listed a family member as their first choice if they needed €1,000 to deal with an emergency (Saraceno et al. 2012). Family members were also a source of many other types of 'support', including material labour (as in child-minding or running errands, for example) and also emotional support (as in discussing and sharing problems, for example). This was not necessarily a co-resident family member, emphasising that 'extended' or 'non-resident' are not necessarily boundaries for familial closeness or solidarity (ibid.). Of course, there is an obverse side here also in that people may lose income and/or other material resources by virtue of having to share in a family setting. The existing research is unable to allow us to determine the overall scale of this but we can hypothesise that poverty risk is either heightened, lessened or averted by virtue of collective living and familial engagements.

There is a further level to resource gain or loss from a collective living perspective. This extends beyond sharing: familial considerations and exigencies may actually expand or limit one's income-gaining capacities/opportunities. Status and role within a family context are to the fore here. Some instances where familial exigencies act to limit earning capacity are obvious – where people have caring-related or other familial obligations and for this reason may be unable to engage in (sufficient) income-earning activity. For example, mothers' labour market participation is in most countries considerably lower than the rates for women as a whole and women subdivide into different subgroups in this regard (mainly related to family situation, including age of children cross-cut or intersecting with educational level and socio-economic status) (Bettio et al. 2013). But family responsibilities may also lead people to secure higher income – the ideal hard-working, male breadwinning husband and father, for example, is conceived in this mould. While of course it is a gendered depiction, the underlying point is that family-related exigencies and considerations exert an effect on people's capacity to earn, or secure in other ways, income and resources.

A third way in which family may affect access to financial resources is through the possibility that one's income changes because the state (and/or in some cases employers) grants income by virtue of one's family-related situation. Mothers and fathers are recognised beneficiary categories for cash benefits in most of the high-income welfare states, for example, just as childhood, motherhood and fatherhood are recognised as conditions for state intervention and support. Think of child cash supports and child-related tax allowances, as well as how family status is used to determine entitlement to a host of social services. These are not only very consequential for poverty avoidance but they are also based on exigencies that are typically (but not exclusively) related to family.

Access to resources within a family or other collective setting is not guaranteed, however. Any theory of the relationship between poverty and family needs to problematise also the principles and exigencies that govern the (re)distribution of resources within families. In this regard, cultural and relational factors loom large. This brings us to the (re)distribution of resources within a family setting.

Family as affecting the (re)distribution of resources

This too has to be seen as multi-dimensional and specific. As Curtis (1986: 169) has put it: "no matter how rewards are distributed in a society (or according to what principle), people can organise themselves (e.g., in families) to redistribute them, often according to a different set of principles". This takes us beyond monetary factors and underlines the reality that there is no necessary relationship between the amount of income available to one or a number of individuals within a family and how this and other resources are distributed (and hence the poverty situation or risk in practice). Let us tease out the different levels/processes involved.

Some work has already considered this, although there is variation in the extent to which cultural and relational factors are actively theorised in existing work. There are two main existing theorisations of intra-household/family distributive processes. These, following Kulic and Dotti Sani (2015), can be usefully thought of as unitary models and the relative resources and bargaining theory. The unitary model is associated especially with the work of Gary Becker (1981) (and the so-called 'new household economics') and Talcott Parsons (Parsons and Bales 1955); the relative resource and bargaining theory has been developed in work of mixed disciplinary heritage, but with a feminist orientation as a strong thread.

In his most relevant work, Becker posed the question: how might we assume that households function regarding resource use? Becker's model of collective decision making in a household or family setting foregrounded altruism which led him to view the household/family as led by a benevolent leader capable of both representing and taking into account the tastes and preferences of members of his unit in such a way that ensured an efficient distribution of resources. Becker's utility maximising theory took little or no cognisance of the significance of different forms of income pooling, the existence of cooperative or non-cooperative models of decision making in families, or how decision making might be non-rational or non-utilitarian. The field has been taken forward especially by work that highlights household bargaining and the conditions under which income is pooled in families (e.g., McElroy 1990). However, these rest on rationalistic and economistic foundations and assume cooperation within the family.

Within and beyond economics, sociological and feminist analyses have sought to build in the presence of inequality and relations of power within families and to move beyond economic-oriented principles and especially utility maximisation and efficiency. Families are conceived as hierarchical units in which men tend to dominate women who in turn tend to have less power and authority (and adults dominate children, albeit to a lesser extent). Unequal control over income and other resources follows from this, with patriarchy as a concept widely employed in this work (Barnard 1981; Hartmann 1981; Sokoloff 1980). Feminist work has especially highlighted the weaknesses of a preference approach, the influence of norms, culture and institutions within and without the family, and the implications for how we should conceive of families and redistribution. Contra Becker and the new household economics approach, we have to be open to the possibility that families are both diverse and stratified internally and that neither individual nor collective dimensions are straightforward, not least because they are embedded in relationships. What this means above all is recognising that decision making is complex and that varying principles and practices of distribution may operate in a family setting at any one time (Bennett and Daly 2014).

What are such principles? Research on families, and that on families in situations of poverty and low income in particular, helps significantly here. It indicates that there are at least three principles or systems for redistributing resources in families: need, place in or relation to the power hierarchy, and emotional/relational grounds.

To the extent that 'sharing' of resources within families has been examined empirically, it has been the subject of research which asks people about how they conceive, budget and spend their income (e.g., Pahl 1989; Zelizer 1997). The evidence suggests that need and exigency are the over-arching considerations in money management in low-income situations. These manifest in careful planning of expenditure around perceived need, with a prioritising of the most essential spending on rent/mortgage, utilities and food (the latter two somewhat more flexible than the first). Work by Walker and Collins (2004), among others, indicates that a low income means that families have little choice but to plan budgets meticulously: setting priorities, storing money for later, making lists even before wages or benefits are collected, tallying up the bill as they shop, and shopping frequently to avoid supplies at home being used up prematurely (Daly and Kelly 2015). It is women who typically take on such activities. It is important to point out, though, that 'need' is not necessarily fixed and that it is not necessarily interpreted to relate to material matters (Daly 2018).

There is evidence to suggest also that other factors sit alongside need as a guiding principle in the distribution of income/resources in a familial context (Bennett et al. 2012). Authority and power are important considerations here. In the hands of economists the outcomes depend on bargaining, whereas in the service of more feminist and sociologically informed accounts bargaining is not the originating concept in that it rests on power and authority. For example, Blood and Wolfe (1960) developed the resource theory of power to underline and explain how individuals' comparative resource levels determine decision making in relationships. Pahl (1989) saw this reflected in the systems of money management that people have in place. Her research on money management among married couples identified four different systems, varying in terms of which partner had control and whether and to what extent the income was pooled or kept separate. Taking an overview of the findings of a range of this and subsequent research which has sought to develop the field of intra-household distribution further, Bennett (2013: 588) sums up by saying that the intra-household distribution of resources might be influenced by a combination of different factors including employment, marital status, ideologies of breadwinning and domesticity and gendered perceptions of consumption as individual or collective (inter alia). Feminist scholars have also posited the notion of the 'other economy' (Donath 2000) which, among other things, functions by gift and reciprocity rather than by economic 'exchange'. The underlying effect of taking these perspectives into account is to destabilise the notion that processes internal to households and families can be viewed solely in instrumental and economic terms.

But much of this literature still works with the household rather than the family as its conceptual unit and so leaves us with the question of how a familial dimension and context are implicated in the disbursal of resources. This is where family-based cultural and relational dimensions come in – they must be theorised as at least cutting across if not superseding a rational and/or a power-based approach. There is evidence of this happening in low-income settings, especially in work from the UK. One of the most widely reported occurrences is of parents (and especially mothers) often compromising their own needs to ensure children do not go without (see, for example, Kempson 1996; McIntyre et al. 2003; McKendrick et al. 2003). The principle of 'children first' – which may require considerable altruism from parents – seems to be quite widely validated (Kochuyt 2004). Synthesising findings from a subset of studies that focused on diet, nutrition and health in poor families, Attree's systematic review (2005) found that low-income mothers felt obliged to purchase foods that were similar to what children from more advantaged households ate so that their children would fit in with their more affluent peers. The concept of children's 'belonging' has been used in this context (Raine 2005). But there are other family dimensions also – research has found that everyday financial activities of spending, saving and borrowing are family practices in the sense that they are bound up with the relational and emotional experiences and negotiations of family life and they involve a set of interpersonal and intergenerational gendered practices (Hall 2016). This is just one set of examples of relational factors at play. There are others, some of which may relate not to the welfare of any one individual or age group but to collective family considerations as a whole – what Bourdieu (1984: 22) has called the 'constant maintenance work' whereby the feelings, dispositions and commitments necessary for the integration of the unit as a whole are engendered in each individual family member. The reputation of the family or the avoidance of shame might be other factors influencing how resources are disbursed in a situation of low income (Walker 2014).

Overall, then, the likelihood of poverty – for individuals and the family unit as a whole – is signally influenced by the principles, processes and practices governing the exchange of resources within families and these processes should not be seen as guided by economic rationality alone but, rather, also by relationships of affect and power and concerns grounded in relational and cultural considerations.

Conclusions

In a context where poverty is undertheorised and where the relationship between collective units and individual poverty is little understood, the chapter's main aim has been to elucidate and explore how poverty is (or can be) associated with the family. The approach developed aims to help open up the 'black box' of the family. It suggests that the relevance of the family for theorising poverty lies not only in patterns associated with its economic and compositional structure but also in how cultural and relational factors are implicated in relevant processes and commitments regarding resources and their (re)distribution. Hence, patterns of resource accrual and use in a familial context can be anticipated to be shaped by relationships and bonds that derive from and are maintained by interpersonal and kinship ties and felt responsibilities in these regards rather than rubrics of utility and/or personal preference. In short, family processes change both the resources available and the way these are used.

The family as a structure and set of economic and social relations and activities has many dimensions that are relevant to poverty but the primary ones are in terms of how it affects the generation of resources, access and distribution or utilisation. Among the structural factors identified are the size of the family, the age distribution of family members, the number of earners and how family-related exigencies affect the adults' income-earning capacity. Cultural and relational factors – in the form of norms and values and felt exigencies arising from relational and emotional considerations – also act to affect resource use. To understand this it is helpful to differentiate between the household as a primarily economic unit and the family as a social and affective as well as economic entity. This understanding opens the possibility of non-economic principles of resource use operating in a family context and heightens the significance of people's (family) situated agency for poverty as a potential or actual outcome.

The line of thinking developed here does not view poverty as originating in the family but recognises that family may play a causal role, especially in relation to particular constraints and/or practices regarding resource levels and the use of resources, and the significance of caring-related responsibilities associated with family. Second, the family is not viewed as a self-contained unit; each of the three dimensions reflects and refracts societal influences. We have viewed exchange as occurring primarily within the residential family unit but of course there are also family-based exchanges among non-residential kin.

By way of conclusion, the set of theoretical points underlying this chapter and the framework it has developed might be emphasised. To be properly understood, poverty needs to be conceptualised (also) from a family or collective perspective, because the incidence, experience and meaning of poverty rely crucially on resources generated in and through family and other collective arrangements. This is true at both micro and macro levels. In situations of low income, it is difficult to avoid poverty independently of others with whom one is close. That said, resources are not necessarily forthcoming – rather they are embedded in relational and familial considerations and relevant history and negotiations. Second, while much poverty research assumes a utilitarian perspective on resource use, this chapter underlines that resource use within families is likely to be governed by both non-economic and economic principles of exchange.

Notes

1 This section draws from Daly (2011) and (2018).
2 This work has typically proceeded along a number of lines but has especially converged around time use surveys, the imputation of a monetary value to time spent on unpaid work and the creation of so-called 'satellite accounts' to shadow the national accounts.

References

Allin, Paul (2007) 'Measuring Societal Wellbeing', *Economic and Labour Market Review*, 1(10), 46–52.

Attree, Pamela (2005) 'Parenting Support in the Context of Poverty: A Meta Synthesis of the Qualitative Evidence', *Health and Social Care in the Community*, 13(4), 330–37.

Barnard, Jessie (1981) 'The Good Provider Role: Its Rise and Fall', *American Psychologist*, 36, 1–12.

Becker, Gary S. (1981) *A Treatise on the Family*, Cambridge, MA: Harvard University Press.

Bennett, Fran (2013) 'Researching Within-household Distribution: Overview, Developments, Debates and Methodological Challenges', *Journal of Marriage and Family*, 75(3), 582–97.

Bennett, Fran and Mary Daly (2014) *Poverty through a Gender Lens: Evidence and Policy Review on Gender and Poverty*, Oxford: Department of Social Policy and Intervention.

Bennett, Fran, Jerome De Henau, Susan Himmelweit and Sirin Sung (2012) 'Financial Togetherness and Autonomy within Couples', pp. 97–122 in J. Scott, S. Dex and A.C. Plagnol (eds) *Gendered Lives: Gender Inequalities in Production and Reproduction*. Cheltenham, UK: Edward Elgar.

Bettio, Francisca, Janneke Plantenga and Mark Smith (eds) (2013) *Gender and the European Labour Market*, London: Routledge.

Blood, Robert O. and Donald M. Wolfe (1960) *Husbands and Wives: The Dynamics of Married Living*, New York: Free Press.

Bourdieu, Pierre (1984) *Distinction* (R. Nice, Trans.), Cambridge: Cambridge University Press.
Buhmann, Brigitte, Lee Rainwater, Guenther Schmaus and Timothy M. Smeeding (1998) 'Equivalence Scales, Well-being, Inequality and Poverty: Sensitivity across Ten Countries Using the Luxembourg Income Study (LIS) Database', *Review of Income and Wealth*, 13(2), 115–42.
Castrén, Anna-Maija and Kaisa Ketokivi (2015) 'Studying the Complex Dynamics of Family Relationships: A Figurational Approach', *Sociological Research Online*, 20(1), 1–14.
Chant, Sylvia (ed.) (2010) *The International Handbook of Gender and Poverty: Concepts, Research, Policy*. Cheltenham, UK: Edward Elgar.
Curtis, Richard F. (1986) 'Household and Family in Theory on Inequality', *American Sociological Review*, 51, 168–83.
Daly, Mary (2011) *Welfare*. Cambridge: Polity Press.
Daly, Mary (2018) 'Money-related Meanings and Practices in Low-income and Poor Families', *Sociology*, 51(2), 450–65.
Daly, Mary and Grace Kelly (2015) *Families and Poverty: Everyday Life on a Low Income*, Bristol: Policy Press.
Davies, Howard and Heather Joshi (1994) 'Sex, Sharing and the Distribution of Income', *Journal of Social Policy*, 23, 301–40.
Donath, Sue (2000) 'The "Other Economy": A Suggestion for a Distinctively Feminist Economics', *Feminist Economics*, 6(1), 115–23.
Finch, Janet (1989) *Family Obligations and Social Change*, Cambridge: Polity Press.
Hall, Sarah Marie (2016) 'Everyday Family Experiences of the Financial Crisis: Getting by in the Recent Economic Recession', *Journal of Economic Geography*, 16, 305–30.
Handler, Joel F. and Yeheskel Hasenfeld (2007) *Blame Welfare, Ignore Poverty and Inequality*. New York: Cambridge University Press.
Hartmann, Heidi (1981) 'The Family as the Locus of Gender, Class and Political Struggle: The Example of Housework', *Signs*, 6, 366–94.
Heath, Sue and Emma Calvert (2013) 'Gifts, Loans and Intergenerational Support for Young Adults', *Sociology*, 47, 1120–135.
Hill, Katherine, Abigail Davis, Donald Hirsch and Lydia Marshall (2016) *Falling Short: The Experience of Families Living below the Minimum Income Standard*, York: Joseph Rowntree Foundation.
Kempson, Elaine (1996) *Life on a Low Income*, York: Joseph Rowntree Foundation.
Kochuyt, Thierry (2004) 'Giving Away One's Poverty: On the Consumption of Scarce Resources within the Family', *The Sociological Review*, 52(2), 141–61.
Kulic, Nevena and Giulia Dotti Sani (2015) *Intra-household Sharing of Financial Resources: A Non-technical Review of the Research Field and its Historical Development*, MPRA Paper 68420, Munich: Munich Personal RePEc Archive.
Lamont, Michèle and Mario L. Small (2010) *Cultural Diversity and Anti-poverty Policy*. ISSJ, UNESCO, Oxford: Blackwell.
McElroy, Marjorie B. (1990) 'The Empirical Content of Nash-bargained Household Behavior', *Journal of Human Resources*, 25(4), 559–83.
McIntyre Lynn, Suzanne Officer and Lynne M. Robinson (2003) 'Feeling Poor: The Felt Experience of Low-Income Lone Mothers', *Affilia-Journal of Women and Social Work*, 18(3), 316–31.
McKendrick John H., Sarah Cunningham-Burley and Kathryn Backett-Milburn (2003) *Life in Low Income Families in Scotland: Research Report*. Edinburgh: Scottish Executive Social Research.
Morgan, David H. J. (1996) *Family Connections: An Introduction to Family Studies*. Cambridge: Polity Press.
Morgan, David H. J. (2011) *Rethinking Family Practices*. Basingstoke: Palgrave Macmillan.
OECD (2013) *OECD Framework for Statistics on the Distribution of Household Income, Consumption and Wealth*. Paris: OECD.
Pahl, Jan (1989) *Money and Marriage*, Houndmills, UK: Macmillan Education.
Parsons, Talcott and Robert E. Bales (1955) *Family Socialization and Interaction Process*. Glencoe, IL: Free Press.
Ponthieux, Sophie (2013) 'Income Pooling and Equal Sharing within the Household: What Can We Learn from the 2010 EU-SILC Module?' *Eurostat Population and Social Conditions: Methodologies and Working Papers*. Luxembourg: European Commission.
Raine, Kim D. (2005) 'Determinants of Healthy Eating in Canada: An Overview and Synthesis', *Canadian Journal of Public Health*, 96 Supplement 3, S8–S14.
Ribbens McCarthy, Jane (2012) 'The Powerful Relational Language of "Family": Togetherness, Belonging and Personhood', *The Sociological Review*, 60(1), 68–90.

Ringen, Stein (2007) *What Democracy is For: On Freedom and Moral Government*, Princeton, NJ: Princeton University Press.

Saraceno, Chiara, Manuela Olagnero and Paola Torrioni (2012) *First European Quality of Life Survey: Families, Work and Social Networks*, Dublin: Eurofound.

Small, Mario L., David J. Harding and Michèle Lamont (2010) 'Reconsidering Culture and Poverty', *The Annals of the American Academy of Political and Social Science*, 629(1), 6–27.

Smart, Carol (2007) *Personal Life*, Cambridge: Polity Press.

Sokoloff, Natalie J. (1980) *Between Money and Love: The Dialectics of Women's Home and Market*, New York: Praeger.

Valentine, Gill (2008) 'The Ties that Bind: Towards Geographies of Intimacy', *Geography Compass* 2(6), 2097–2110.

Walker, Robert (2014) *The Shame of Poverty*, Oxford: Oxford University Press.

Walker, Robert and Claire Collins (2004) 'Families of the Poor', pp. 193–217 in J. Scott, J. J. Treas and M. Richards (eds) *The Blackwell Companion to the Sociology of Families*, Oxford: Blackwell. Studies Institute (PSI), London.

World Bank (2018) *Poverty and Shared Prosperity 2018: Piecing Together the Poverty Puzzle*, Washington, DC: World Bank.

Zelizer, Viviana (1997) *The Social Meaning of Money: Pin Money, Paychecks, Poor Relief, and Other Currencies*. Princeton, NJ: Princeton University Press.

Part IV

The way forward

What will influence poverty in the years to come?

32

Poverty

It is still here

Bent Greve

Introduction

Poverty has been analysed and discussed for centuries. Despite this, there are still, depending on whether we look into absolute or relative poverty, many people living in poverty and there is still a strong debate around the globe related to the degree of poverty and its impact on societies' development. The goal of eradicating poverty still seems to be far away, despite considerable progress being made over the last 20–25 years. This chapter does not, however, focus on the development or the lack thereof in some countries, albeit it aims to briefly present in the next section the situation and how it has evolved. Instead, the chapter discusses and presents options and possibilities as to how under a range of different circumstances although poverty cannot be eradicated completely, the number of people living in poverty could be reduced, given that there are examples and cases of policies and activities that have been able to reduce the number of people living in poverty.

The development in poverty in brief

The following brief depiction of the development presents only a few pieces of data related to absolute and relative poverty. This is in order not to neglect issues of deprivation (see Chapter 3) and multidimensionality (Alkire et al. 2016; Alkire and Santos 2014; see also Chapter 4). The use of multidimensionality in the EU relates to relative income poverty, material deprivation and household joblessness (Whelan, Nolan, and Maître 2014). Naturally, there is a bias in using income in understanding poverty, as one might want to look more into opportunities, as has been central in the capability approach (Hick 2012). The reason is that, for example, people with disabilities might need a higher income in order to have the same standard of living as others.

Since the beginning of this century, there has been a decline in absolute poverty, as measured by the US$1.90 per day poverty line, from 25.8% of the world's population in 2002 to 10.9% in 2013. Still in sub-Saharan Africa the figure in 2013 was 43.7%, whereas Central Asia at 10% is below the world average.[1] So, the picture of the development in absolute poverty is a positive one, even though it has not been reduced to low levels, such as the low level of 0.3% in Europe, in all parts of the world.

In Europe, despite low levels of absolute poverty, in several countries since the millennium there has been an increase in the relative poverty rate (here 60% of median income) also as a consequence of the financial crisis. As a result, for example, two-thirds of those in the EU at risk of poverty in 2017 were not able to meet unforeseen expenditures, whereas for those above the poverty line it is close to one in four.[2] Thus, living in poverty increases the risk of having an unstable economic position and stronger vulnerability to changes in life-circumstances. High relative poverty rates can also be found in developing countries, and in countries such as the US, Israel and Turkey based on 50% of median income.[3]

Besides these changes in poverty there have been increasing levels of inequality in many countries (OECD 2015; Piketty 2014; Atkinson 2015), which can also have a negative impact on social cohesion of societies.

So, on the one hand, there has been positive development with regard to the overall absolute level of poverty, whereas the relative level of poverty has deteriorated, also causing the possible risk of less cohesive societies. This might help in explaining the rise of populism and nationalism (Greve 2019b).

The development has varied across countries, between rich and poor, but also within countries there might be variations in different geographical locations. Policies, and sometimes the lack thereof, have also varied. The development in itself does not further explain the reason why the development has been as it has. This partly reflects developments in the market, but it is also a policy choice. Policies aimed at reducing poverty are the focus of the next section.

Policies aimed at reducing poverty

A first and generally possible way is to try to prevent poverty from arising (see Chapter 6). Naturally, the policies that might have an impact on preventing poverty, such as education and labour market intervention, can overlap policies aimed at reducing poverty once it has developed (see also Chapters 21–31 for several examples, as well as the chapters covering individual countries or continents).

Generally, it is known that the generosity of the welfare states influences the level of poverty (Saltkjel and Malmberg-Heimonen 2017), and this is also witnessed by several chapters in this book. Thus, developing welfare state policies, especially income transfers to those having a low level of income or no income, could be an important issue in order to reduce poverty, and material deprivation and inequality as well. Naturally, welfare states were not developed overnight, and there are thus historical reasons for differences, but also different ideas about what the welfare state should engage in, which also helps in explaining the varieties of welfare states around the globe (for essays dealing with this, see Greve 2019a). A focus on social investment in people, such as human capital development, including policies to reduce poverty is possible if there is the willingness to develop more comprehensive welfare states and an ability to finance this investment.

Cash transfers do not only work in rich countries, but they also have an impact in low- and middle-income countries (Bastagli et al., n.d.; see also Chapters 13, 16 and 17).

Looking into more specific elements in more mature welfare states, such as those in Europe, it is seemingly the case that increasing child benefits and social assistance is the most cost-effective policy (Leventi, Sutherland, and Valentinova Tasseva 2017). Transfer of resources is not only between rich and poor, but also between generations, which might influence poverty over the life cycle (see Chapter 5), but might also be influenced by what is happening within the families (see Chapter 31).

When we know that growing up in jobless households increases the risk of living in poverty, as "there are long scars to experiencing a jobless household" (Macmillan et al. 2018, 353), then this indicates that a focus on how to avoid child poverty could be an important issue, even if it is not the same in all welfare states (see also Chapter 8). This can include a variety of instruments from different kinds of family benefits to help in getting an education, and labour market policy with a focus on a high level of poverty. Some historical data (2001–2007) point to the fact that at least in Europe it has been difficult to achieve the aims of both providing more jobs and reducing poverty (Taylor-Gooby, Gumy, and Otto 2015), which also points to the fact that employment protection does help in alleviating poverty.

However, the importance of getting a job is diluted if this job is a working-poor job, which implies that there is further need for policies that can help in if not eliminating, then at least reducing, the number of jobs with the risk of being working poor (see also Chapter 19), which was still around 10% globally in 2017 and more than 33% in sub-Saharan Africa.[4]

A change in pension systems toward a higher reliance on private pensions might cause more poverty among elderly people (Been et al. 2016), thus the specific balance between state and private social security can influence the level of poverty (see also Chapters 20 and 29). Therefore, for people in old age, the balance between state and market can also have an impact on the number of people living in poverty or at risk of poverty.

In developed countries having a job is, as mentioned, very important in order to avoid living in poverty, this is even more so for lone parents, as they live in poverty to a greater degree than others. This has the further implication that children will grow up in poverty. As many studies have shown, this is a major problem for their future development (see, for example, Lesner 2018). Thus, looking into the family composition might also have an impact, although also here more generous welfare transfers reduce child poverty (Chzhen and Bradshaw 2012). The distribution of resources in families might also influence who is living in poverty (see Chapter 31).

Whether or not one should target social transfers as a way of reducing poverty has been discussed for a long time. One argument is that targeting also implies fewer resources for the poor (Korpi and Palme 1998) and risks a Matthew effect – e.g. more will be given to those who already have. However, this does not seem to be the case, at least for all benefits, and as something that might be applied across the board (Marx, Salanauskaite, and Verbist 2013). At the same time, it might be argued that the universal more encompassing welfare states with a higher level of spending, and often with less stringent targeting, fare better in relation to reducing poverty (Jacques and Noël 2018).

Can we end poverty as we know it today?

The short answer is, yes it should be possible; however, at the same time, this will depend on the political willingness across and within countries to do so. This is exemplified by the many suggestions throughout the book and also as depicted in the previous section. Thus the end of poverty is also a question of ideologies and beliefs in the possible causes of poverty (see also Chapters 9 and 27).

Across countries, there is still a need to transfer money from richer to poorer people, including in a life-course perspective, in order to help in reducing poverty. Transfers from richer to poorer countries can also have an impact. Both types of initiatives can be done in a variety of ways, but it should be possible.

Within countries, transfers are also dependent on national policies and the ability to get support for policies helping those living in poverty to move away from this position.

Overall, the central answer is first to try to prevent poverty, but if the outcome of market forces is that people still end up living in poverty, then a battery of policies might help in reducing or alleviating it. This includes education, the creation of jobs and social transfers to the most vulnerable.

This also points to the fact that the options and possibilities to do so will be highly reliant on the ability to finance these initiatives. In the more mature welfare states, this is about not only the willingness to pay, but also the ensuring of stable ways of financing spending. In less developed welfare states and less rich societies, it can be a question of, at least to some extent, the transfer of resources from richer to poorer countries.

Notes

1 United Nations (2018), Progress towards the Sustainable Development Goals, E/2018/64.
2 Eurostat, accessed 24 November 2018.
3 https://data.oecd.org/inequality/poverty-rate.htm, accessed 12 February 2019.
4 United Nations (2018), Progress towards the Sustainable Development Goals, E/2018/64.

References

Alkire, Sabina, and Maria Emma Santos. 2014. "Measuring Acute Poverty in the Developing World: Robustness and Scope of the Multidimensional Poverty Index." *World Development*. https://doi.org/10.1016/j.worlddev.2014.01.026.

Alkire, S., C. Jindra, G. Robles, and A. Vaz. 2016. "Multidimensional Poverty Index 2016: Brief Methodological Note and Results." *Global MPI 2016*. https://doi.org/10.1016/j.amc.2006.04.049.

Atkinson, Tony. 2015. "What Can Be Done about Inequality?" *Juncture*. https://doi.org/10.1111/j.2050-5876.2015.00834.x.

Bastagli, Francesca, Jessica Hagen-Zanker, Luke Harman, Valentina Barca, Georgina Sturge, and Tanja Schmidt. n.d. "The Impact of Cash Transfers: A Review of the Evidence from Low- and Middle-Income Countries." *Journal of Social Policy*. Cambridge University Press, 1–26. https://doi.org/DOI: 10.1017/S0047279418000715.

Been, Jim, Koen Caminada, Kees Goudswaard, and Olaf Vliet. 2016. "Public/Private Pension Mix, Income Inequality and Poverty among the Elderly in Europe: An Empirical Analysis Using New and Revised OECD Data." *Social Policy & Administration 51* (7). John Wiley & Sons, Ltd (10.1111): 1079–1100. https://doi.org/10.1111/spol.12282.

Chzhen, Yekaterina, and Jonathan Bradshaw. 2012. "Lone Parents, Poverty and Policy in the European Union." *Journal of European Social Policy*. https://doi.org/10.1177/0958928712456578.

Greve, B. 2019a. *The Routledge Handbook of the Welfare State*. Edited by B. Greve. 2nd ed. Oxon: Routledge.

——. 2019b. *Welfare Populism and Welfare Chauvinism*. Bristol: Policy Press.

Hick, Rod. 2012. "The Capability Approach: Insights for a New Poverty Focus." *Journal of Social Policy*. https://doi.org/10.1017/S0047279411000845.

Jacques, Olivier, and Alain Noël. 2018. "The Case for Welfare State Universalism, or the Lasting Relevance of the Paradox of Redistribution." *Journal of European Social Policy*. https://doi.org/10.1177/0958928717700564.

Korpi, W., and J. Palme. 1998. "The Paradox of Redistribution and Strategies of Equality: Welfare State Institutions, Inequality and Poverty in the Western Countries." 174. LIS Working Paper Series. Luxembourg.

Lesner, Rune V. 2018. "The Long-Term Effect of Childhood Poverty." *Journal of Population Economics 31* (3): 969–1004. https://doi.org/10.1007/s00148-017-0674-8.

Leventi, Chrysa, Holly Sutherland, and Iva Valentinova Tasseva. 2017. "Improving Poverty Reduction in Europe: What Works (Best) Where?" *EUROMOD Working Paper Series*. https://doi.org/10.1177/0958928718792130.

Macmillan, L., P. Gregg, J. Jerrim, and N. Shure. 2018. "Children in Jobless Households across Europe: Evidence on the Association with Medium- and Long-Term Outcomes." *Journal of Poverty and Social Justice 26* (3): 335–58.

Marx, I., L. Salanauskaite, and G. Verbist. 2013. "The Paradox of Redistribution Revisited: And That It May Rest in Peace?" IZA DP No. 7414. Bonn.

OECD. 2015. *In It Together: Why Less Inequality Benefits All*. Paris: OECD Publishing.

Piketty, T. 2014. *Capital in the Twenty-First Century*. London: Harvard University Press.

Saltkjel, Therese, and Ira Malmberg-Heimonen. 2017. "Welfare Generosity in Europe: A Multi-Level Study of Material Deprivation and Income Poverty among Disadvantaged Groups." *Social Policy and Administration*. https://doi.org/10.1111/spol.12217.

Taylor-Gooby, Peter, Julia M. Gumy, and Adeline Otto. 2015. "Can 'New Welfare' Address Poverty through More and Better Jobs?" *Journal of Social Policy*. https://doi.org/10.1017/S0047279414000403.

Whelan, Christopher T., Brian Nolan, and Bertrand Maître. 2014. "Multidimensional Poverty Measurement in Europe: An Application of the Adjusted Headcount Approach." *Journal of European Social Policy*. https://doi.org/10.1177/0958928713517914.

Index

Page numbers in **bold** refer to tables; those in *italics* refer to figures.

www.ingramcontent.com/pod-product-compliance
Lightning Source LLC
LaVergne TN
LVHW080122011026
849160LV00013B/1155
9780367726706